D0435112

SECRET CHANNEL
TO BERLIN

SECRET CHANNEL
TO BERLIN

The Masson-Schellenberg Connection and
Swiss Intelligence in World War II

PIERRE TH. BRAUNSCHWEIG

Translated by
Karl Vonlanthen
With additional translations for the 2004 edition by
Frances Stirnemann-Lewis

CASEMATE
Philadelphia

Published by
CASEMATE

© 2004 Pierre Th. Braunschweig

ISBN 1-932033-39-4

First published under the title *Geheimer Draht nach Berlin.*
Permission to publish in English has been generously granted by
Verlag Neue Zürcher Zeitung of Zürich, Switzerland.

Library of Congress Cataloging-in-Publication Data
Braunschweig, Pierre Th.
[*Geheimer Draht nach Berlin.* English]
Secret channel to Berlin : the Masson-Schellenberg connection and Swiss intelligence in
World War II / by Pierre Th. Braunschweig ; translated by Karl Vonlanthen ; with
additional translations for the 2004 edition by Frances Stirnemann-Lewis.
p.   cm.
"Thoroughly revised and updated with newly available documents by the author"—T.p. verso.
Includes bibliographical references and index.
ISBN 0-932033-39-4 (alk. paper)
1. World War, 1939-1945-Secret Service-Germany.
2. News agencies-Switzerland-History-20th century.
I. Title.
D810.S7B6613   2004
940.54'8743-dc22   2003064308

Manufactured in the United States of America

To my parents
Alfred and Fanny Braunschweig
with gratitude

CONTENTS

ON THE COVER:

Top *(in color, from left to right)*: Colonel-Brigadier Roger Masson (head of Swiss Intelligence); SS General Walter Schellenberg (head of German SS Foreign Intelligence); Paul Meyer-Schwertenbach (instigator of the Masson-Schellenberg connection).

Bottom *(black and white, from left to right)*: General Henri Guisan (Commander-in-Chief, Swiss Armed Forces); Colonel Henry Guisan Jr. (son of the General); Irene Schellenberg (wife of General Schellenberg); SS General Walter Schellenberg; Alfred Ernst (Intelligence officer critical of the connection); Max Waibel (Intelligence officer critical of the connection); Hans Hausamann (head of Intelligence service Bureau Ha, critical of the connection); Allen W. Dulles (OSS station chief in Bern, critical of the connection)

All photos are from the author's private archives.
Cover design by the author.

Foreword

By Joseph P. Hayes

PIERRE TH. BRAUNSCHWEIG has written a superb book, a significant addition to the world of important works on Intelligence. As a lifelong student and practitioner of Intelligence I found myself both engrossed and challenged by the extraordinary human story Braunschweig tells as well as by the powerful analytical insights he derives from the tale. This is a book which should be read and studied by anyone seriously interested in Intelligence in all of its domains: strategic warning; tactical maneuver; denial and deception; perception management; covert action; the complex interplay between Intelligence and policy; the relationship between diplomacy, Intelligence, and law enforcement.

The book is impressively relevant to many of the most significant issues in Intelligence today. In the United States, we are redefining the roles and responsibilities of our national security and law enforcement communities as we develop a new strategic paradigm to address the menacing new challenges posed by an increasingly fragmented and dispersed set of adversaries. The seriousness of purpose and true patriotism displayed by the Swiss in developing their own national security strategy during World War II contain lessons of enormous importance and timeliness for us today.

Much of the literature on Intelligence is rooted in anecdote and, however entertaining or occasionally useful, such accounts rarely rise above the level of interesting war stories. On the other hand, much of the more academic work on Intelligence, while more rigorous and conceptually helpful, typically suffers from a lack of immediacy. This is particularly true for the serious Intelligence professional or student of the profession who seeks to understand the mission of Intelligence in all of its operational, substantive, and political complexity. Case studies often manage to bridge these two extremes and have provided some of the most valuable work done in the field.

Pierre Th. Braunschweig has produced a work of rigorous scholarship, with all of the supporting structure such scholarship demands, while at the same time telling a lively, immensely readable, fast-moving story. In these pages he describes an episode in the annals of Intelligence operations that must stand as one of the most consequential contributions made by an Intelligence service to its national society. The story of the role played by members of the Swiss military Intelligence agency is far more than an interesting footnote to the broad story of World War II. The stakes were high—national survival.

Once Nazi Germany had reached the height of its power during World War II, there was no nation as vulnerable to a sudden surprise attack as Switzerland. By 1942 it stood alone as the sole remaining democracy in continental Europe, completely surrounded by the Axis powers. That it had not suffered invasion like a dozen other countries during the preceding years was due to several factors, including the determination of Switzerland's army and people to resist, their natural ally of the Alps, and highly developed Swiss diplomatic skills honed over centuries. Another significant factor was that the Axis' primary enemies—Britain, the Soviet Union, and finally the United States—could only undertake major operations on the periphery of Europe and thus Switzerland's central locale, once vital in intra-European wars, temporarily became less important once the war went global.

But in 1943, the imminent liquidation of the Axis armies in North Africa, combined with Russian victories on the Eurasian steppe, meant that the war would soon be falling back on Europe. Germany would need secure transit routes across the Alpine mountain belt to its south, even as the Swiss government firmly denied access to its passes, roads, and tunnels for any movement of foreign troops or military matériel. Despite a great disparity in power, the unwillingness of the Swiss to cede their sovereignty remained as irrevocable as the strategic imperatives perceived in Berlin. And in this realm of uncertainty that separated German intentions from Swiss resolve stood the Intelligence service, to ascertain whether an attack was indeed forthcoming.

In accounts written in the years since the war, Switzerland has been described as a beehive of foreign Intelligence activity during this period, yet little has been said about the vast effort undertaken by Switzerland's own military Intelligence agency, headed during the war years by Colonel Roger Masson. In this book, Pierre Th. Braunschweig unveils the scope of that effort while examining many of the fascinating personalities who played major roles. His penetrating analysis of universal Intelligence problems—"signals" versus "noise," and the general uncertainty principle that pertains to all Intelligence work—is superbly supported by the case of Switzerland in World War II, a country that braced for invasion on several occasions, even while recognizing that Nazi methods were often characterized by an attack when least expected.

The core of this book is Braunschweig's newly researched account of the relationship between Swiss Intelligence chief Masson and the head of German SS Foreign Intelligence, Walter Schellenberg. The notorious Schellenberg visited Switzerland several times during the war, and at one point Masson arranged for him to confer with the commander-in-chief of the Swiss Army, General Henri Guisan. This occurred at a time when the Germans knew the Allies were about to pursue Churchill's theory of the "soft underbelly of Europe," and that invasions of the southern flank of the continent were imminent. These meetings with Schellenberg were unknown to the Swiss public during the war, and caused an outcry when they were revealed afterward. Within the Swiss Army and Intelligence service they were controversial from the start, the primary accusation being that Masson, by relying largely on personal instincts, might have been fooled by his opposite number. Here the author does a masterful job of examining all sides of the controversy.

In the world of Intelligence, one can seldom choose bedfellows, and Pollyannas are not welcome. In the duel of wits between Schellenberg and Masson, it has heretofore been intriguing to speculate who may have been playing whom, or whether, as Masson firmly believed, he had arrived at a unity of purpose with an important contact in the Third Reich, who thence became instrumental in sparing Switzerland from invasion in 1943. In these pages we have the clearest elucidation to date of the facts surrounding the affair, and in Braunschweig's own conclusions, the most authoritative view.

As the United States has recently been reminded, a failure of Intelligence can have catastrophic results. Purely defensive operations will usually fail to succeed in uncovering the true intentions of an enemy. Probing into an enemy's camp, by whatever means, is more difficult to achieve, and at times unsavory, yet can provide the most vital knowledge. This is the context in which we must view the Masson-Schellenberg connection, which, though much derided by the Swiss public after the war, must be viewed primarily through the gray area which is the province of any responsible Intelligence chief.

If any country has held a tenuous geostrategic position, it was Switzerland in World War II. Though from our current vantage point the course of the war is now clear and the Swiss did not suffer an invasion, Braunschweig, through his thorough examination of Swiss Intelligence operations, informs us in real time how dangerous the future then seemed. The first ingredient of a successful military offensive is surprise, and the role of Intelligence, though necessarily played out beneath the notice of the public, can be as significant to the outcome as the ensuing clashes of armies. It is part of the lesson of this valuable study in history that a nation's Intelligence can never be too strong, so long as it is supported by an equal measure of patriotism.

The book is also a cautionary tale on the seemingly inevitable but still vexing issues of the bureaucratic relationships and conflicts which inevitably arise between Intelligence officers, diplomatic colleagues, and (where applicable) parliamentary oversight.

A note to the reader: read the endnotes. The endnotes almost comprise a companion volume to the main story. Pierre Th. Braunschweig has documented his arguments scrupulously and, in doing so, has presented a compelling account of life in Switzerland during World War II. He has also presented fascinating essays on such issues as the origins and early experiences of Interpol.

As with many important stories which are told well, this is a book which can be read on many levels and for many purposes. On the level of narrative, the book is a riveting account of complex and fascinating people engaged in Intelligence operations of extraordinary daring, carrying out and then acting upon assessments of a rival's motivation and strategy in the context of a global war. As an insight into the nature of strategic thinking in Intelligence, the book brings into sharp focus the fundamental need for an Intelligence organization, a government, and a society to understand with the utmost clarity its needs, strengths, and vulnerabilities, and how these are perceived by its adversaries.

JOSEPH P. HAYES *retired from active duty with the Central Intelligence Agency in December 2000 following a 35-year career in Intelligence work. At the time of his retirement, Hayes was the first appointee to the Richard Helms Chair for Espionage at the CIA. Hayes served seven tours of duty abroad during his career and held a number of senior positions in the CIA in Washington. He managed major national and international programs and was honored with a number of awards including the Distinguished Career Intelligence Medal, the Director's Award, the National Intelligence Distinguished Service Medal, the Intelligence Medal of Merit, the Donovan Award and many others. Dr. Hayes was the founding Director of the CIA Center for the Study of Intelligence.*

Preface

JOHN MCCONE, WHO SUCCEEDED Allen Dulles as head of the CIA in 1961, stated, "Every war of this century, including World War II, has started because of inadequate intelligence."[1] Two English historians, Christopher Andrew and David Dilks, in their book dealing with the influence of intelligence services on governments, argue along the same line. Their slim 1984 publication carries the fitting title *The Missing Dimension,*[2] a term that the well-known British diplomat Sir Alexander Cadogan had coined in his diary. During World War II, Sir Alexander had been in charge of the secret service at the Foreign Office. When reading the major works on 20th-century diplomacy, he noticed that hardly any author took into account the role of the secret service, whose contribution is indispensable for any government to function. Sir Alexander wrote in his diary that the world of the secret service was the "missing dimension" in the history of diplomacy that helped elucidate the past.

Sir Alexander's statement holds true not only for the history of diplomacy. Andrew and Dilks point out in their book that in most cases the secret service is also a missing dimension in works dealing with political and military history. In his classic work on intelligence written almost seventy years ago, Richard Wilmer Rowan rightly remarked, "Spies and Speculators for thirty-three centuries have exerted more influence on history than on historians."[3] There are several reasons for this. First of all, historians generally tend to concentrate on existing evidence and neglect the subjects on which they do not find any documents. (*Quod non est in actis, non est in mundo!*) The "secret service" or "intelligence service"—this author prefers to use the second term[4]—has basically become a missing dimension because it is not easy to get hold of hard sources.[5]

The lack of interest on the part of historians contrasts with the vivid interest that the general public shows in everything that has to do with secret service or intelligence work. Tabloids and fiction writers discovered this market niche a long time ago, producing an ever-proliferating amount of spy literature. Unfortunately, though, these efforts have often been inspired by lively imagi-

xvi   SECRET CHANNEL TO BERLIN

nations, thereby blurring more facts than they illuminate. On the other hand, it is precisely because intelligence matters have been dealt with so trivially that until recently historians considered it beneath their dignity to make them an object of focus. However, historians writing about World War II, above all, had to realize that neglecting the intelligence aspect could result in misinterpretations. When it became known in the mid-1970s that the Allies had been able to read nearly all important Axis codes during the war and therefore found out in advance what moves the enemy was planning, more and more historians recognized that an assessment of the events also had to take into account the intelligence aspect. For example, how could the decisive Battle of Midway be understood without knowing about the Americans' success at reading the Japanese naval codes? Or how can Britain's success at intercepting German-Italian supply convoys to North Africa be assessed without recognizing that British cryptographers had cracked Germany's supposedly foolproof Enigma device?

Professor F. H. Hinsley, the official historiographer of the British Intelligence Service during World War II, speculated that the Allies' supremacy on the intelligence level shortened the war by a full three years. It is of course difficult to prove such statements. Moreover, it should be kept in mind that the intelligence service does not always exercise such a great influence. Even persons who are directly involved often disagree on its significance in specific instances. In many cases, intelligence findings are misunderstood, or not considered by governments or military leaderships in the decision-making process. Also, in some instances the findings of intelligence are simply wrong. However, this merely proves the point made by John McCone that every war in the 20th century started because of inadequate intelligence.[6] By referring once again to the opening quote in this preface, this author would simply like to indicate that in order to understand the entire historical picture, it is crucial to also touch upon the missing dimension of the secret service.

There is another reason why historians should not leave the intelligence domain to journalists and publicists. In many areas, and especially in the areas of intelligence and espionage, authors have no qualms using questionable material, and reviewers take an uncritical approach in reviewing their books. William R. Harris, who in the late 1960s compiled and annotated a bibliography on intelligence-related subjects, commented that "the process is deleterious to scholarship."[7] Because it is characteristic of this topic that reliable source material is not as easily available as for other subjects, authors writing on intelligence are perhaps more prone to making mistakes at the risk of unintentionally spreading false information. In his 1980 publication *Wilderness of Mirrors*,[8] David Martin, a former editor at *Newsweek* and the son of a CIA analyst who has valuable insider connections, remarks that it is alarming how much false information and how many mistakes and wrong conclusions are printed in books, and thus have been raised to the level of historic "truths" because they were constantly repeated and quoted in other books.

If historians show no enthusiasm for taking intelligence and espionage seriously enough to deal with them on a scholarly level, we should not be surprised to see that myths, half-truths, and rumors circulate in public. Historians are facing a challenging and—due to the difficulty of finding source material—time-consuming task, but it is an important one if they do not want to continue neglecting an entire dimension of the forces that have an impact on history.

The main focus of this study on aspects of Switzerland's military intelligence during World War II is the connection between the Swiss Army Command and the Reich Security Central Office in Berlin, one of the most amazing and delicate contacts of that time, whose protagonists were Colonel-Brigadier Roger Masson and SS Brigadier General Walter Schellenberg. In the process we will analyze three basic questions:

1. How did this connection come about?
2. What purpose did it serve?
3. What were the results of the Masson-Schellenberg connection?

In order to answer these questions, this author was able to draw on an abundant number of documents that had previously been inaccessible. The source material that he found at several archives in the United States was particularly interesting. But the research for this study is based above all on unpublished documents at the Swiss Federal Archives and other archives in Switzerland and abroad. Even if for obvious reasons intelligence is a field where facts are kept secret and are not well documented, it is nevertheless possible through patience and meticulous research to overcome a large number of the difficulties that inhere in this subject and to clarify a surprisingly large number of issues.

Among the files that are analyzed for the first time in this study, the unpublished works of Captain Paul Meyer, alias Wolf Schwertenbach, and the papers of Wilhelm Lützelschwab, a state attorney and head of the Political Police in Basel at the time, were particularly copious. In addition, this study refers to files of the Swiss Federal Department of Military Affairs and military and civilian courts; documents from General Henri Guisan's Personal Staff; the papers of Allen W. Dulles, the head of the United States Intelligence Service in Bern at the time; as well as numerous other documents that were made available to this author by archives, involved persons, and witnesses.[9]

The serious conflicts that existed between Swiss Intelligence and the Swiss Federal Department of Foreign Affairs, as well as within the intelligence service, are documented extensively for the first time in this study. Based on newly available source documents, the alert of March 1943, in which Switzerland braced for an invasion, is seen in a surprising new light. Colonel-Brigadier Masson's secret channel to Berlin was unusual, and the circumstances surrounding the connection were curious; nevertheless, one should keep in mind that this was just one among a large number of contacts that Switzerland's Intelligence Service maintained during the war years. Therefore this study gives a detailed account of the structure, responsibilities, and working methods of the service, thereby putting the Masson-Schellenberg connection, which will be examined very closely, in a larger context. (In the text to follow, some words or phrases have been italicized by this author to give them more emphasis, even within quotations. Whenever the emphasis appears in the original source, it has been specifically called out.)

When this study was first published (in German) toward the end of the Cold War, it had a tremendous impact, quickly reaching the top spot on the non-fiction bestseller list, and has been reprinted several times. It also became mandatory reading for several parliamentary investigating committees, which both houses of the Swiss Parliament set up after the fall of the Berlin Wall to resolve issues surrounding activities of Swiss Military Intelligence during the Cold War.

At the end of a guest lecture at the University of California at Berkeley, a gentleman approached me and introduced himself as the novelist Paul Erdman. He had, based on this book's first edition, written a captivating half-fictional thriller, *The Swiss Account,* which also quickly turned into a bestseller.

This shows that serious scholarly research and writing can have an impact on both politics and the world of fiction, helping the latter to become more realistic—which certainly is not to its detriment.

I have used the opportunity of the publication of the American edition of *Secret Channel to Berlin* to update the manuscript by adding newly available source material. While there was no need to correct the story told in this book, the new material has enabled me to shed more light, and focus more closely, on several aspects discussed hereafter.

Pierre Th. Braunschweig
New York, Fall 2004

Acknowledgments

THIS BOOK COULD NEVER have been written without the contribution of a great number of people, all of whom it would be impossible to thank in this limited space. The names mentioned here are just the tip of the iceberg, so to speak, and I should like all of those who are not named individually to rest assured of my lasting gratitude for their time and their assistance in giving me access to sources or providing me with hints and documents which made it possible to undertake this study.

I would like to thank Dr. Hans Senn, Lieutenant General and a former Chief of the General Staff of the Swiss Army, for kindly helping me to obtain permission to consult some classified or other inaccessible reference material. I am particularly grateful to Professor Dr. Christoph Graf, the director of the Swiss Federal Archives, for drawing my attention to the papers of Captain Meyer, thereby having a substantial influence on determining the topic of my research. He was instrumental in getting several depositories—above all, Mrs. Patrizia Verena Frey-Schwertenbach and the family of the late Basel State Attorney Wilhelm Lützelschwab—to agree to my evaluating a large number of highly interesting unpublished private documents. I would also very much like to thank Professor Dr. Hans Rudolf Kurz, a distinguished and prolific military historian from Bern, for generously giving me access to his extensive personal archives and offering me advice and providing me with useful information on many different issues. I am indebted to the Military Attorney General, Brigadier Raphael Barras, for exceptionally giving me permission to consult the files of the military courts, thereby allowing me to elaborate on a number of key issues.

I am obliged to Major General Ernst Wetter, a former Chief Instructor for Switzerland's Air Force and Antiaircraft Defense, for supplying me with a number of valuable complementary documents and information; moreover, he kindly made available to me the pre-publication manuscript of his book on the 1944 emergency landing of a secret German nightfighter aircraft at Dübendorf airfield. I also received very interesting firsthand information from Major General Peter L. Burckhardt, who started working as a military attaché at the Swiss Legation in Berlin in 1943 and personally had to deal with all the protagonists featured in this study. Lieutenant Colonel Erwin Tschudi of the General Staff corps spontaneously supplied me with information and extensive private reference material, mainly the files from his legal battles with Hans Hausamann, the founder of the intelligence agency *Bureau Ha*. In his capacity as Chief Cartographer, Mr. Tschudi had been working both with Masson's Intelligence Service and temporarily with the Commander-in-Chief's Personal Staff and had been involved in, and concerned by, the contacts to Berlin. On several occasions, his material shed light on the complex relations among the staff of Army Intelligence as well as the relations between the staff and outsiders. Throughout the drafting of this study, Mr. Adrian Florian of Switzerland's Attorney General's Office was willing to offer me valuable information; even though my questions certainly increased his workload, he never made me feel that he did not have time to answer them. With a sense of humor typical of the people from Basel, he obligingly and patiently explained to me the multifaceted context that I needed to know in order to be able to find and interpret clues contained in the reference material.

I would like to extend my thanks to Professor Dr. Klaus Urner for allowing me to use the Archives of Contemporary History at the Swiss Federal Institute of Technology in Zürich that he directs and, in particular, for organizing interesting colloquia with individuals who either witnessed or actively took part in the events of wartime duty; by creating numerous opportunities for establishing valuable new contacts, Professor Urner has had an inspiring influence on contemporary historians. I am also grateful to Mr. Werner Rings for repeatedly offering me complementary information and making available reference material from his private archives. His many interviews (transcripts of which are now available at the Archives for Contemporary History) are a unique reference source for scholars. Thanks are due to Colonel Rudolf J. Ritter, a former vice director of the Intelligence Directorate at Switzerland's General Staff corps, for spontaneously supplying me with files that complemented my own reference material and for carefully checking through part of my manuscript.

During my various research trips to the National Archives in Washington, DC, I received valuable advice and information from Mr. John Taylor, the archivist in charge of OSS documents. With Mr. Taylor's assistance, I was able to find the documents from among the wealth of files of the Office of Strategic Services that were relevant for my study. Miss Sally Marks of the Diplomatic Branch at the National Archives facilitated my research in the files of the U.S.

State Department. I would also like to thank Mrs. Nancy Bressler, curator of the Public Affairs Papers at Princeton University's Manuscript Library, and her colleague, Mrs. Jean Holliday, who made available to me the private papers of Allen Dulles and General Philip Strong, and made my work at the archives on Olden Street very enjoyable. I am obliged to the Dulles family, particularly Mrs. Clover Dulles Jebsen, for allowing me to evaluate her father's unpublished papers. Special thanks go to Mrs. Annemarie Willi, an associate of the military attaché at the Embassy of Switzerland in Washington, DC, who selflessly and generously assisted me during all my research trips in the United States.

I would very much like to thank Dr. Daniel Bourgeois, Eduard Tschabold, Hans Kohler, Hans Walther, Robert Rösch, and André Wälti of the Swiss Federal Archives in Bern for facilitating my work throughout the years with their friendliness, expertise, and helpfulness.

Very special thanks go to Swiss International Air Lines' personnel service and work schedule coordinators, who were understanding and obliging in meeting my special requests concerning flight schedules and destinations that were dictated by my research; due to their excellent planning, my scholarly activities could be combined in a fortunate manner with my other obligations as a Swissair crew member.

I would like to thank Dr. Peter Keckeis of the *Neue Zürcher Zeitung* book publishing company for his unfaltering involvement over the years when this manuscript was created. His inspiring enthusiasm was a constant motivation, and I am most recently grateful to Verlag NZZ for generously granting permission for this book to be published in the United States.

My special thanks go to Ambassador Faith Whittlesey who, along with Georg Gyssler, has encouraged the translation of classic Swiss history titles into English. Her benevolent understanding of the author's wishes has been deeply appreciated, and I hope that the result will prove her right in trusting his concept. Partial funding by Presence Switzerland (PRS), the Sophie and Karl Binding Foundation of Basel, Switzerland, and the Arbeitskreis Gelebte Geschichte of Bern, Switzerland, is gratefully acknowledged.

Any author is blessed to have a good translator at hand. In this case I could count on two very able minds: Karl Vonlanthen, who carefully translated the German language edition along with much of my new material, and Frances Stirnemann-Lewis, who worked hard on the manuscript revisions. Their patience and diligence in understanding my exact intentions and their interest in Switzerland's military history during World War II resulted in many refinements in the manuscript of the American edition of my book.

I would also like to thank John Gardner and Dr. Donald Hilty for their editing of the initial English-language draft and especially Kelly Waering for his meticulous technical editing and for checking proofs at all stages of the manuscript's preparation before printing.

My most heartfelt thanks go to my brother, Dr. Jean Braunschweig, who has encouraged and generously supported my research over the years. His understanding and confidence that all the efforts that were put into this study would not be in vain were a constant reassurance to me.

1

The "Masson Affair"

Masson's Interview

ON SEPTEMBER 11, 1945, representatives of the United States, Great Britain, the Soviet Union, France, and China began a series of meetings in London to hammer out a peace accord for Germany after its unconditional surrender. In Switzerland, these important diplomatic negotiations made the front pages of that country's traditionally well-informed and foreign policy-oriented newspapers. At one point, however, the news from London was pushed into the background as a result of more pressing domestic news relating to the war. Federal politicians were assessing the experience of the Swiss military as it had coped with the world war that had raged at the country's doorstep. The Swiss Army officially went off duty on August 20—and now that the threat was over, it had become time to deal with some lingering issues that could not be resolved during the war.

During the second week of parliament's 1945 fall session, the National Council, Switzerland's House of Representatives, discussed the Military Department's annual report for the year 1944. More than 30 members of parliament from all parties spoke during the floor debate. The Bern-based *Bund* newspaper commented that "after six years of war, during which some great achievements but also quite a few psychological mistakes had been made,"[1] the

1

numerous speeches served to "bring tensions that had built up over time into the open and surmount them."[2]

This easing of tensions did not have a lasting effect, however, as the Military Department was back in the headlines at the end of the second week of the session, when news reached the members of parliament "through the noon edition of their newspapers about an interview that was presented as sensational, which it was indeed."[3] On September 28, 1945, the London-based Exchange news agency carried an article titled "The Threat Switzerland Was Facing in 1943" that created a storm of indignation in the Swiss press. The article read:

> London, Sept. 28 (Exchange)—The special correspondent of the *Daily Telegraph* in Paris reports that he had an interview with Robert [*sic*] Masson, whom he calls the Head of 'Swiss Counterintelligence.' Masson told the correspondent that in March 1943, the Germans had intended to attack Switzerland and annex it after finishing their campaign. He explained that Hitler had personally ordered that preparations be made for this "military and political campaign" and had a total of 30 special divisions deployed near the [Swiss] border.
>
> Masson said that surprisingly the plan was abandoned after Walter Schellenberg, Himmler's right-hand man and head of German Intelligence, had been able to convince Hitler during a General Staff meeting on March 19, 1943 that Switzerland was more useful as a neutral country than as an occupied country because it would better cover Germany's southern flank. According to Masson, in the heated debate during that meeting, Schellenberg gave his word of honor that the Allies would face fierce resistance if they tried to infringe Switzerland's neutrality; he said there was no doubt that the Swiss Army would take up its arms if Allied armies launched an attack on the Swiss Confederation. Masson explained that Hitler finally calmed down and heeded Schellenberg's advice.
>
> Masson assured the correspondent that Schellenberg was no fanatic Nazi and had serious doubts as early as 1943 whether Germany would win the war. Masson insisted that in certain respects Schellenberg had sided with Swiss Intelligence and cooperated with it to save the lives of several well-known French prisoners of war. In addition, Schellenberg supposedly stood up for de Gaulle's niece, Geneviève de Gaulle, and had [General Henri] Giraud's family freed in April 1945.

Masson told the correspondent that at the same time that Schellenberg negotiated with the Swedish peace mediator Count Bernadotte in Northern Germany, Schellenberg's 1st adjutant Hans Wilhelm Egger [sic] traveled to Vienna to prevent the local SS there from carrying out Hitler's orders. He explained that after Germany's capitulation, Schellenberg had to return from Sweden to the Reich, from where he was transferred to London.[4]

The following day, *Der Bund* reported that the Swiss who had granted the interview was *Roger* Masson, "a colonel-brigadier who was Assistant Chief of Staff during wartime duty and Chief of Intelligence and Security. Hence, the information comes from someone who is in a position to know the facts."[5] The newspaper initially did not comment on the explosive content of the agency report but contented itself with expressing its annoyance about the Federal Council's[6] delay in informing the public in Switzerland about the threats the country had had to face during the years of the war. It said that because of this delay the public had to find out indirectly, through a foreign agency report, what a dangerous situation Switzerland had escaped, adding, "Once again the thorough Swiss have been put behind by busy foreign publicists."[7]

The reactions were vehement all the way from conservative newspapers such as the *Neue Zürcher Zeitung* to the leftist press such as *Vorwärts*.[8] However, the Swiss press was less indignant about the fact that it had "been cheated by a foreigner out of publishing this important information first"[9] than about the fact that it was Colonel-Brigadier Masson—of all people—who had granted the spectacular interview. According to historian Georg Kreis, Masson had been ascribed "a not at all insignificant part"[10] in imposing a strict censorship on the press during the war,[11] explaining, "Even though press policy was not part of the tasks of [Masson's] section per se, one of its duties consisted of procuring information about foreign countries and forwarding it to interested offices. As a consequence, the P.R.S. (Press and Radio Section)[12] continuously received articles published by the German press or reports by the military attaché in Berlin or by Swiss who had informed Intelligence about their impressions upon returning home."[13] Concerning the Swiss press, Masson "fervently advocated remaining ideologically neutral and [at the same time] tirelessly supported the blood guilt theory"[14]; moreover, he was in favor of introducing pre-print censorship.[15] Masson's interview consequently had to be considered as particularly objectionable.[16]

In a first reaction, the Federal Council described Masson's action "as tactless, to say the least."[17] The same day, it asked the military administration to look into the circumstances of the interview.[18] The investigation inevitably uncovered details about the explosive relations between the Swiss and German

Intelligence Services. However, Masson denied the accusation that he had disclosed secret information in the interview. He argued that in summer 1945, several months earlier, a book had been published in Zürich and Lausanne[19] in which Swedish diplomat Count Folke Bernadotte reported Schellenberg as claiming that he had entered into contact with Swiss friends in order to prevent plans by Joachim von Ribbentrop and Martin Bormann to attack Switzerland from being carried out after they had been approved by Hitler. Masson's conversation with the foreign journalist, which resulted in the "interview," had actually revolved around the subject of Bernadotte's book.[20]

In an extensive letter to Chief of the Swiss General Staff Louis de Montmollin, Colonel-Brigadier Masson explained how the contact with the journalist had come about and what they had discussed during their conversation.[21] That letter is interesting not because of the extended publicity that the matter received at the time but because it is quite revealing about the character of the Chief of Intelligence. To a certain extent, Masson's meeting with the American journalist Paul Ghali was a repetition of the circumstances surrounding his connection with SS Brigadier General Schellenberg that had come close to having disastrous consequences for him a few years earlier. He incontestably acted out of good intentions, once again trying to correct the wrong image that he thought foreign countries had of Switzerland; however, he forgot that even if he was most certainly qualified to do so through his position in the military, most likely he acted without having a political mandate.

Paul Ghali, a Paris correspondent for the *Chicago Daily News* whom Masson described as "a former comrade," used to live in Bern for several years, where the two men had met.[22] On September 21, 1945, they ran into each other[23] in Bern when Ghali was back in Switzerland for a short visit. Masson explained to Montmollin:

> Since I considered that what he had to say was always interesting, I once again spoke with him about several issues dealing with the recent conflict and the current international situation. . . . At a certain point during the conversation—I think that we were talking about the impression Americans who are on leave here have of our country— Ghali said to me that it was regrettable that the United States did not know more about Switzerland, in particular about its delicate situation during the war, and that it might be desirable to publish something on that subject. . . . When he mentioned Schellenberg again, Ghali told me that in France one knew that it was due to this irregular connection that we had been able to get some French, American, and English citizens freed. I told him no secret when I replied that I had indeed had

the opportunity to meet with [Schellenberg] on three or four occasions exclusively in the interest of my country . . . and indirectly even in the interest of the Allies (repatriation of prisoners, etc.).

At the American's repeated request, under the condition that the text would not be disseminated in Europe, Masson agreed to submit to the *Chicago Daily News* a note for the press on that issue. Ghali accepted Masson's condition. Masson continued his explanation by stating, "As a precaution, I asked him to draft a text that he should submit to me for approval. But Ghali had to leave for Geneva, and the following day he was in Paris." As Masson had no opportunity to look over the article, he began to have doubts, explaining, "The 'conversation' I had with [Ghali] could be interpreted in a wrong way. I telegraphed to him in Paris on 27 September, asking him to put off publishing his text." However, there is written evidence that the message was returned to the sender, stating, "address unknown." The following day, Masson was shocked to find out that the *Exchange* news agency had distributed to newspapers in Switzerland excerpts of Ghali's uncorrected article from the United States. Masson immediately called Gaston Bridel, the Editor-in-Chief of the *Tribune de Genève* and President of the Swiss Press Association, to ask him to intervene with the agency to hold back the article. However, it was too late to do so.

The mutilated text that the London-based *Daily Telegraph* and the *Exchange* news agency published of the original U.S. article[24] was clearly aimed at "creating a stir," as Masson put it. In his letter to Chief of the General Staff Montmollin, Masson protested that the agency report misstated the facts, explaining:

> I never said that Schellenberg was Himmler's "right-hand man." He was one of his many aides. . . . I said that Schellenberg was a friend of our country and that in my opinion, in March 1943 he had done everything he could to make clear to the OKW [German Armed Forces High Command] that it could have confidence in our willingness to defend ourselves against anyone. At that time, one of [Germany's] main arguments for planning to take preventive action against us was the fact that "it did not trust our attitude" and believed that we would forsake our neutrality in favor of the Allies as soon as the opportunity presented itself.

Concerning the contacts that Swiss Intelligence had entertained with the SS Brigadier General and that the public found out about through the "interview," Masson solemnly declared, "It is not true that Schellenberg had certain connections with Switzerland's Intelligence Service. He had a certain amount of contact only with me, in most cases through Eggen." This statement will be shown to be inaccurate in the course of this study, as Roger Masson was not at all Schellenberg's only contact person; moreover, the "certain connections" should not be downplayed. The controversy that erupted during the war and flared up once again after the war regarding the opportunism of the connection between Masson and Schellenberg was precisely due to the fact that the contacts had gone much further than Masson admitted.

By making his corrective statement to Montmollin, Masson did not manage to stop the course of events; in fact, he no longer had any control over them, as his "interview" became a topic of discussion for the Federal Council and parliament.

Interventions in Parliament

The "revelations by Masson"[25] that had been published during the weekend of September 28-29 were brought up at the weekly Federal Council meeting the following Monday. The federal government felt under pressure to take action. During the National Council's session of June 1945, Urs Dietschi, a Radical Democrat from Solothurn, and 19 co-signatories had submitted a petition to the Cabinet asking it to inform parliament as soon as possible about the political and military threats that Switzerland had encountered during the war.[26] Since then, the departments involved had been trying to process the large amount of material, "compare the files of the Justice and Police Department with those of the Department of Foreign Affairs and the Military Department, and write one complete report as a synopsis of the department reports."[27] The Federal Council had intended to inform parliament in December 1945. It tried to appease the increasingly impatient general public by explaining that gathering, selecting, and compiling the files was creating "quite some difficulties."[28] Following the meeting at which the Federal Council discussed Masson's "interview," the *Neue Zürcher Zeitung* reported that the Department of Foreign Affairs was not yet able to provide the required information. Moreover, it explained that on the military level "the greatest difficulty with writing about the actual threats [consisted] of assessing the source material. Even during the war, the decision-makers often disagreed on how to interpret the information that Intelligence had procured."[29]

Due to Masson's "interview" and the reactions that it triggered in the entire country, the Federal Council could no longer wait for the General's report on war-time duty to be published as originally planned; instead, the Cabinet decided to inform parliament and the public during the ongoing fall session on the dangers that Switzerland had encountered during World War II. In fact, it was about time to do so. The *Neue Zürcher Zeitung* for example openly accused the Federal Council of lacking "any sense for the people's emotional needs,"[30] adding:

> The information was unnecessarily sparse during the war, and since 8 May, the people have been told to wait and be patient when they should have received extensive information about what really happened during those dark years. The Federal Palace correspondent still hears the words with which he has been hushed out of government offices on innumerable occasions, "You better not say anything about that in your newspaper." Very frequently something had to be said after all, but quite often by then the "right moment" was already over. It inevitably took a very unpleasant outside initiative to shed some light onto the great dark spot after the fact, and inevitably this initiative focused around a personality who had been *particularly obstinate* about keeping information from the public to which it was entitled.[31]

"Masson's bombshell"[32] aroused the curiosity not only of journalists but also of members of parliament. On October 1, 1945, Eugen Dietschi, a Radical Democrat from Basel, and Walther Bringolf, a Social Democrat from Schaffhausen, asked the Federal Council to inform parliament about the "strange revelations by Colonel-Brigadier Masson."[33] Both interpellations were signed by numerous other National Councillors.

Dietschi asked to receive general information about the military threats, whereas Bringolf asked some specific questions:

1. What information is the Federal Council going to give parliament and the Swiss . . . concerning German plans for an attack on Switzerland in March 1943?
2. Is it true that Mr. Masson entertained personal contacts with German SS leaders and even with Himmler's right-hand man, as he declared?
3. Based on the information that is available to the Federal Council, are the plans for an attack on Switzerland that Colonel [Brigadier] Masson mentioned not simply an attempt to clear SS leader Schellenberg and other SS heads?[34]

It was not easy to give an overview of the dangers that Switzerland had encountered during the war, and it was even more difficult to answer Bringolf's specific questions.

During the following few days, several people tried to influence the Federal Council on how it should answer the Representatives' questions. Considering the partly conflicting arguments that were presented, the Head of the Military Department, who had to present the government's reply to the National Council, was not in an enviable position.

Wilhelm Lützelschwab, who had been State Attorney in Basel-Stadt until 1944 and Head of Basel's Political Police between April 1941 and November 1943, was one of the first persons who addressed Federal Councillor Kobelt. The way in which he wrote his letter may be surprising; however, later on in this study it will be shown that the Head of the Military Department had known Lützelschwab for a long time to be a reliable informant in intelligence matters. Lützelschwab asked Kobelt "to make very clear that Colonel-Brigadier Masson's connection with Himmler's representatives had been condemned from the very beginning by officials of our Intelligence Service, and that from February 1943 on, Masson's subordinates had repeatedly told the concerned authorities that this connection was inadmissible and dangerous."[35] He argued that the public should not be made to believe that because of Masson's behavior the officers, noncommissioned officers, and soldiers on the Intelligence Service who were not part of the group surrounding Masson, Meyer, and Holzach were unreliable. He stated, "[The officials of the Intelligence Service] who, in spite of the risk that they ran, did not refrain from sounding the alarm and protesting when Mr. Masson began his dangerous game have a right to be defended in public by the head of our army."[36] He explained that it was not the fact that Colonel-Brigadier Masson had reported about Hitler's plans for an attack that worried the citizens but the fact "that our Chief of Intelligence had been in close contact with people around Himmler and had been their close friend, as clearly indicated in the interview. [The citizens] would have to be much more worried if they knew about some of the *rather dubious circumstances* of the whole affair."[37]

On the same day, the Swiss Army's Commander-in-Chief during wartime duty, General Henri Guisan, addressed a letter to Kobelt that sharply contrasted with Lützelschwab's view. Desperate after being heavily attacked, Masson had appealed to his former superior, Guisan, for assistance, stating:

[Since Federal Councillors von Steiger[38] and Kobelt] are not well inclined toward me at all, there is a risk that I will be abandoned by them when they answer the parliamentarians' interpellations. . . . The journalists who dislike me for some reason that I ignore (by the way, please let me remind you that you shared my concerns in this respect in 1940, 1941, 1942) have raised this affair to the level of a "mystery," allowing the wildest and most serious allegations to be voiced, which really beats everything. Due to your great authority and immense popularity, General, you are the only one who can shield me from, and *defend me* against, all this slander![39]

Masson asked the General to make clear once and for all "that [he] did not sell the fortress of Sargans to have the Giraud family freed!!"[40] General Guisan reacted immediately. In his written intervention with Federal Councillor Kobelt, he regretted that Masson had acted rashly by giving the "interview," because to a certain extent that meant that Swiss Intelligence endorsed the publications by Sweden's Count Bernadotte. Guisan argued, however, that "one should not blame Masson for every sin nor hold the connection with Eggen and Schellenberg against him. On the contrary, this connection was probably very useful for our country in spring 1943 . . . at the moment when *Case Switzerland* was discussed at the German Armed Forces High Command."[41] In addition, the General defended his subordinate against potential criticism that he had acted on his own authority, explaining, "Masson always kept me informed about his connection with Eggen and Schellenberg, up until the time that it became a political issue when the Justice and Police Department intervened because it considered Eggen a suspicious individual. As far as I know, however, Eggen has been completely cleared in the special investigation that was carried out against him."[42]

Federal Councillor Kobelt was sure to have the attention of the Representatives and the general public when he entered the floor of the National Council to comment on the "Masson Case" and the various dangers that the country had encountered between 1939 and 1945. The arguments with which the three Representatives backed up their interpellations had already revealed some surprising details about the matter and showed that the two Radical Democratic Dietschi cousins and the well-known Social Democrat from Schaffhausen were fairly well informed about what had been going on "in the sealed-off, top secret districts over the past few years."[43]

National Councillor Dietschi from Basel expressly acknowledged that "our Intelligence Service supplied very good information" and admitted that "the officials of the Intelligence Service [could] not be over-scrupulous in their work." Dietschi explained why he intervened with the government by referring to the Colonel Affair during World War I,[44] in connection with which the

Chief of the General Staff at the time, Sprecher von Bernegg, had told the military courts about the special situation of the Intelligence Service. Dietschi stated, "This is . . . not about shedding light onto all—clean and dirty—channels now that the danger is over. Nevertheless, it must be said that even Army Intelligence is subject to certain boundaries, which have to be respected whenever the interests of our state might be at stake. Colonel-Brigadier Masson was really rash by laying his cards on the table before an international public. That way he offered them a glimpse of a *chemical laboratory in which it appears that a lot of poisonous substances were concocted.*"[45]

In his interpellation, Dietschi described Schellenberg as "the more or less famous General of the Police who has been mentioned many times" and who was perfectly identified through the fact that he used to be one of Himmler's closest staff members. Dietschi explained:

> Two major German intelligence organizations were at work, the one of the German Armed Forces headed by Admiral Canaris and the one of the SS headed by SS Brigadier General Schellenberg. It appears that the relations between our Intelligence Service and the latter organization were particularly close. Through Colonel-Brigadier Masson, both General Schellenberg and his right-hand man, SS Major General [*sic*][46] Eggen, enjoyed special relations and privileges. It is highly interesting that especially the very dubious Major General Eggen was able to develop a very questionable activity and continued showing up in Switzerland through Colonel Masson's mediation even though he was not allowed to enter our country.

Walther Bringolf had known Masson since 1937. When they met for the first time, Masson had "just started in his new job. He was in a completely empty office, had absolutely no equipment available and probably did not have much experience either, let alone any staff, as no one had been assigned to him yet."[47] Masson seemed to him to be a person of integrity; however, he also thought the new Chief of Intelligence lacked experience in the political field and a flair for politics. Bringolf explained, "His aversion to unionists and Social Democrats was based more or less on traditions; he was from the canton of Vaud, and that is the only way I can fathom that he ended up entering into relations with German National Socialists. It was understandable that he did so in order to obtain information."[48]

In his interpellation, Bringolf explained that he had found out about Masson's contacts with SS officials as early as 1943, stating:

The interview . . . reminded me of a short intervention that I allowed myself to make during a meeting of the National Council Foreign Affairs Committee.[49] I asked the Head of the Department of Foreign Affairs whether it was true that Switzerland's Chief of Intelligence, Colonel-Brigadier Masson, had met with high-ranking SS leaders on Swiss soil and whether it was true that as a consequence of this meeting, an exchange of opinions or perhaps something even more far-reaching had developed. I was forced to ask these questions on the committee because I could not believe this information when I first heard it a short time earlier. The Head of the Department of Foreign Affairs, Federal Councillor Pilet-Golaz, confirmed that the meeting had taken place.[50]

Foreign Minister Pilet-Golaz was interested to know who had told Bringolf about the meeting. However, Bringolf did not reveal the name of his informant during the committee meeting nor later in his memoirs. As it turned out, the informant was Wilhelm Lützelschwab.[51] Bringolf shared his informant's opinion about Masson's and Meyer's connection with Schellenberg and Eggen. In parliament he explained, "My impression about the meeting was the same in spring 1943 as it is now. However, in view of the situation which our country was facing back then, I considered it to be my duty not to make a big deal out of the meeting and everything surrounding it but to keep the information to myself. I did not even talk about it confidentially to my fellow Representatives during any internal meeting of the social-democratic Representatives." Bringolf did not question Masson's honest intentions but expressed serious reservations about whether the same held true for his German counterparts, asking, "What could be the reason for Schellenberg . . . to try to get to Switzerland with his adjutant Eggen in order to establish contact with our Chief of Intelligence?" To Bringolf, the answer was obvious. He stated:

> It takes no rocket scientist, nor do we need to ask Hitler's astrologer or his successors all over our country, in order to know that in early 1943, Schellenberg and his entourage already considered the war to be lost, so they mainly attempted to get some re-insurance in Switzerland for their future. I am perfectly willing to accept that *Colonel Masson was too naïve* to realize that. [Laughter.] It is very regrettable that other important gentlemen did not realize it either. I cannot help but think that Masson was taken in [by the Germans] in this matter.

Bringolf did not realize that the hypothesis of the "re-insurance" was not necessarily an argument that could be held against Masson's connection with Schellenberg, as the German officer could have been inclined to actually render valuable services to Switzerland as some kind of "insurance premium." In Bringolf's opinion, it was implausible for Schellenberg to be "destined, through his relations with Mr. Masson, to give his word of honor that Switzerland [would] remain neutral on the military level" if his ulterior motive was to provide for the time after the war. This objection could be refuted in part by arguing that Schellenberg had an obvious personal interest in keeping the country where he might need to seek refuge from being drawn into the war. In that case, his disloyal behavior would have been directed against the Third Reich, not against Switzerland.

In the upcoming chapters, we will examine the documents that are available today to see whether Bringolf's negative assessment was correct or if "the German SS, Schellenberg, and his adjutant Eggen [actually deserve] to be credited" with preventing an attack on Switzerland in March 1943, as Masson and General Guisan believed.[52] Nevertheless, even if Bringolf was right, that would be no reason to disavow Masson's contacts with Schellenberg—at least not until it can be demonstrated that Schellenberg caused harm to Switzerland through his connection with Masson. Bringolf looked at the issue from a different angle, however, suspecting more serious and damaging consequences from these contacts than the results of excessive trustfulness. He argued:

> One knows very well what to expect from an SS general and an SS chief, a person who approved of, covered, or carried out all crimes that were ordered and committed in the past years by Hitler, Himmler, and National Socialism! Do you think that such people come to Switzerland, enter the country by passing through Wolfsberg Castle in the canton of Thurgau,[53] hold negotiations with a country's Chief of Intelligence, and make concessions without wanting anything in return?

Bringolf was at least as concerned about the domestic political aspect as he was about possible German demands, explaining, "If certain circles in our country have a foible for people like Schellenberg . . . there is a 'risk' that one might tend to treat other people of a similar sort who have similar political convictions the same way. Moreover, from this attitude one might be tempted to draw conclusions about the way in which we purged our country from the leading Nazis who constituted the 5th column here." For that reason (once again showing that he had detailed information about who participated in the Masson-Schellenberg connection), Bringolf asked the Federal Council:

> It has to be elucidated what role Meyer from Wolfsberg Castle played, what the dinner was all about that took place at a certain location.[54] It has to be elucidated what Colonel-Brigadier Masson was doing in Waldshut in 1943.[55] It has to be elucidated what kind of protection Schellenberg's adjutant Eggen enjoyed here in Switzerland. In early May 1945, Eggen was still on German soil, fleeing from the advancing Allies. He came to Switzerland; he was not imprisoned in Lenzburg, Bellechasse, Bern, or anywhere else where political criminals or anti-National Socialist refugees were put away in the last years if they had committed some minor offense or perhaps no offense at all. Strangely enough, Mr. Eggen enjoyed special treatment in Switzerland. And it is even more strange that Mr. Eggen was deported from Switzerland last Monday, two days after Colonel-Brigadier Masson's interview had been published.

In his detailed reply to the three interpellations, Federal Councillor Kobelt focused on the military threats that Switzerland had encountered between 1939 and 1945, mentioning Colonel-Brigadier Masson only in passing. This was in line with the circumstances and with parliament's expectations.[56]

Kobelt willingly "recognized Colonel-Brigadier Masson's merits in connection with expanding and directing Swiss Army Intelligence"[57] and attempted to create the necessary understanding for the peculiarities and inherent laws of the Intelligence Service. "One must not forget," he stated, "that working for Army Intelligence is a very delicate and perilous job. If you have to get onto slippery ground while doing your duty as a soldier, you risk slipping.[58] . . . An intelligence officer is comparable to a horseback rider who treads on a frozen lake without realizing it until the ice suddenly breaks beneath his feet. Those who stand on solid ground must not make judgments about people who have to take that perilous road in the country's interest."

Kobelt did "not a priori take exception to" Masson's entering into contact with Schellenberg, explaining, "In his function as an official, Masson maintained relations also with high-ranking personalities of the other warring parties."[59] Moreover, he argued that Schellenberg's position on Himmler's staff was "similar to Masson's position in Switzerland's Intelligence Service." Nevertheless, Kobelt did not hide the fact that the Federal Council had decidedly *opposed* Masson's connection with Schellenberg, and he described Masson's own assessment of the connection and of its achievements as "highly subjective."

Even if Kobelt did not state his reservations directly, one can read between the lines that both the Head of the Military Department and his colleague, Federal Councillor von Steiger, objected to Masson's getting *personally* involved in the connection. Kobelt asserted, "The Federal Council warned [Colonel-Brigadier Masson] several times about this connection, and in particular the Head of the Federal Justice and Police Department [von Steiger] and myself pointed out on several occasions that the relations between Switzerland's Chief of Intelligence and SS General Schellenberg were unacceptable."

During the war, Masson had been subject to two investigations in connection with his contacts with SS personalities. The first investigation was started in the second half of 1943, after Masson "had allowed Eggen to enter Switzerland despite the expressed immigration ban by the Federal Justice and Police Department."[60] Federal President von Steiger pushed the General to carry out a second investigation in May 1945, which was once again triggered by Eggen entering Switzerland in spite of the Justice and Police Department's opposition.[61] Von Steiger loudly denounced the fact that Masson had "abused his Intelligence Service and his position in the military as the Chief of Intelligence to free internees or prisoners from Germany, especially General Giraud and his family."[62] He argued that under civilian law this would be described as abuse of power, adding, "People smuggling illegal aliens into the country are punished. Colonel-Brigadier Masson did the same thing; he abused his position in the military to accomplish tasks that do not fall under his responsibility."[63]

Kobelt alluded to these two earlier investigations, stressing that "Masson had in fact made some mistakes, but there could be no doubt about his sincerity and his willingness only to serve the country." Nevertheless, Kobelt took the new Masson case seriously and did not consider it merely as a "storm in a teacup,"[64] stating, "I do not simply want to brush the matter aside. The Federal Council considers that the case has to be thoroughly investigated. By the way, the investigation has already been initiated." He explained that Colonel-Brigadier Masson would of course be held accountable for his actions. Kobelt concluded his remarks by indicating that parliament would be kept up to date about the results of the investigation, adding, "By the way, Masson no longer acts as an Assistant Chief of Staff. He has also resigned from his post as Chief of Intelligence and is on a leave of absence at his own request."[65]

For the time being, Kobelt's intervention in parliament satisfied the need for information. In its weekly review of parliament's session, the *Neue Zürcher Zeitung* commented that during his one-hour address Kobelt provided enough information for the three National Councillors who had raised the issue, the parliament, and the public to be pleased.[66]

The Investigation by Supreme Court Justice Couchepin

Federal Councillor Kobelt asked Supreme Court Justice Louis Couchepin to carry out an administrative investigation of Masson. In addition to examining how Masson's indiscretion in the "interview" should be viewed, Couchepin was to look into the relations between Colonel-Brigadier Masson and SS General Schellenberg, as the Military Department had received important new documents on that matter.

On October 2, 1945, Major Max Waibel[67] of the General Staff had submitted to the Military Department and the Military Attorney General photocopies of the deposition that Schellenberg had made during his interrogation by the Allies. This deposition shed a strange light on the fact that in his conversation with Paul Ghali, Masson had spoken very favorably of the German Chief of Intelligence. Schellenberg stated to the English: "I knew Colonel Masson personally; I do not think I am wrong in thinking that there was a certain mutual sympathy on both sides, which had gradually developed through our political discussions."[68] Schellenberg explained that he had originally intended to establish a regular exchange of information with Masson but said that Masson did not accept that idea. However, Schellenberg claimed:

> [Masson] certainly wanted to give me more and more important help in the political field, for at that time I was already considering preparations toward bringing the war to an end. Masson and his colleague, Dr. Meyer, were the contacts with whose help I hoped to bridge the gap either to the British or American military attaché. . . . I was always consciously aiming at representing the contact with Masson as an important *political* contact, and at doing all I could to fill Masson with a sense of his own importance.

These statements did not exactly match the image that Masson had drawn of Schellenberg. The things that Schellenberg stated about the go-betweens on both sides in retrospect also made the Masson-Schellenberg connection appear more risky than Masson had made it look. As the SS officer described:

> Eggen, through whom I had obtained all these Swiss connections, enjoyed Dr. Meyer's confidence. . . . Eggen was in a position to learn much from Meyer in the course of conversation. He used the knowledge so obtained as if it were his own for the purpose of talks with a certain Swiss intelligence officer named Holzach. . . . Eggen's actual sources of information were therefore in the main Holzach and Meyer,

and Eggen's playing off one against the other of these two undoubtedly played an important part.

Eggen then checked the information that he had obtained from Meyer and Holzach by presenting bits and pieces of it to Masson, "and from the latter's reaction, whether it was evasive, reserved, or if he avoided the subject, [Eggen] was able to make a further revision of his own information." During the interrogation, Schellenberg admitted that he had used Colonel-Brigadier Masson's name whenever he wanted his reports to carry more weight, explaining:

> Masson's cover-name in these political reports was "Senner I," I called Meyer "Senner II," and later on, Holzach "Senner III.". . . According to the importance I attached to the contents of the report (always taking my own political views into consideration),[69] it developed into my handing in military information, which Eggen periodically furnished, to the higher authorities under Masson's name, in order to make a greater impression. I had to be very careful in my account not to portray Masson in a false light, for he had always refused to allow himself to be known as cooperating with me in military matters.

Even if one has to take into account that in October 1945 Schellenberg's first objective was to save his own skin and that therefore his statements to the British have to be viewed with caution, they confirmed that the Federal Council's reservations about the connection had been justified.

Another reason for Switzerland's authorities to be interested in shedding light on Masson's incriminating contacts with Schellenberg was the fact that a special committee of the American Office of Strategic Services (OSS) had uncovered a gigantic banknote and passport counterfeiting operation[70] that had been planned and carried out by Branch VI of the Reich Security Central Office.[71] The extent of the operation could have caused serious damage to the entire international financial world for several years.[72] Schellenberg had been in charge of Branch VI since 1941[73] and consequently seemed to be a prime suspect in the counterfeiting operation. There was reason to fear "that this [could] ultimately rub off on Schellenberg's Swiss friends."[74] Federal Councillor Kobelt therefore asked Supreme Court Justice Couchepin to focus his investigation on the following issues:

1. When and how were the contacts between Colonel-Brigadier Masson and Schellenberg initiated and maintained?

2. Was this a connection built up and maintained on behalf of Army Intelligence, or did it serve other purposes?

3. What information was received through this connection, were there any services attached to it in return, and, if so, what were these services?

4. What were Colonel-Brigadier Masson's relations in this matter with Captains Holzach and Meyer and his collaborators on the Army Staff?

5. What were the Commander-in-Chief's and the Chief of the General Staff's positions regarding the connection between Colonel-Brigadier Masson and Schellenberg? When and how did they find out about it, did they approve or disapprove of it?

6. What was the attitude of the federal government and its members regarding the Masson-Schellenberg connection, when and how were they informed about it, did they approve of it or object to it?

7. How should the connection between Colonel-Brigadier Masson and Schellenberg be assessed on the military and political levels?

8. Was Colonel-Brigadier Masson's connection with Schellenberg legal, objectionable, or illegal?[75]

Supreme Court Justice Couchepin was expedient. As early as November 30, 1945, he submitted a draft report and on January 28, 1946, the final investigation report. Colonel-Brigadier Masson had the opportunity to view the voluminous report for eight days.[76] After the members of the Federal Council had been able to analyze it as well, on March 8, 1946, the Military Department published an "official statement to the press on the matter of Colonel-Brigadier Masson"[77]—a 12-page synopsis of Couchepin's report and the numerous documents that were attached to it, stating the facts and assessing them. In agreement with Supreme Court Justice Couchepin, the Military Department concluded:

Colonel-Brigadier Masson began and maintained his connection with SS General Schellenberg in agreement with, and with the approval of, his superiors in the military. Even if one may argue about whether this connection was admissible and useful, it should be acknowledged that Masson acted out of the good intention to serve the country. The investigation has also revealed that he did not provide any information to foreign countries that was damaging to Switzerland; instead, he made efforts to remove difficulties in the relations between the two countries. It has also been established that he did not seek to derive any advantages for himself through the connection, nor did he personally benefit from it. His honorableness remains untouched. He has been reprimanded by the Head of the Federal Justice and Police Department and rebuked by his superior in the military for overstepping his authority when crossing the border without authorization; that aspect of the matter is therefore closed. However, he has to be sanctioned for granting the interview, which was incompatible with his duties as an official. According to Supreme Court Justice Couchepin's request, he is issued a rebuke.

Hence, Colonel-Brigadier Masson was basically rehabilitated. The official communiqué ended by stating: "Some individual errors that were made in good faith have to be seen in the context of the overall achievements in order to be assessed correctly. As Chief of Intelligence, before the war Masson created an organization that had to pass the acid test during wartime duty, and it did."

The press release also explained that there was no evidence that the other participants in the Masson-Schellenberg connection had committed espionage on behalf of Germany.[78] The Military Department concluded that in the cases of both Meyer-Schwertenbach and Holzach, "who as intelligence officers were under Masson's direct supervision . . . we were unable to uncover any evidence that, in connection with Schellenberg's statements,[79] is sufficient for convicting them." Moreover, an investigation into whether the German intermediary Eggen used his stays in Switzerland for spying activities did not yield "any conclusive evidence."

On the other hand, the Federal Council's "official statement" did not hide the fact that the connection constituted a *substantial risk* because Schellenberg "misused his relations with Masson and maintained them especially in order to be able to use Masson as a tool for his own political goals," as indicated by Schellenberg's deposition. It explained that Masson had "absolutely overstepped his authority as the Army's Chief of Intelligence [if he asserted] that the main purpose of his relations with Schellenberg was to remove [the Germans'] mistrust of our neutral attitude." The official communiqué ended by stating, "We herewith consider this matter as closed." From a *legal* perspective, that was the case; however, many questions had remained unanswered. In fact, the press release admitted that it had not been possible "to fully clarify the existing contradictions nor establish all the facts."

The investigation took place more than 40 years before this study was undertaken, and Schellenberg, Masson, and Meyer-Schwertenbach are no longer alive. Even the last legal battle in connection with the matter ended in the early 1970s[80]—in short, the Masson-Schellenberg connection is now history. This author has undertaken a new study on the subject not in order to rekindle the unpleasant controversy that surrounded the connection but in order to examine newly available source material that offers a unique glimpse of the way in which the connection was established and the way in which it worked. In addition to numerous other references, this source material includes the writings by Captain Meyer-Schwertenbach, who established the connection, and by State Attorney Lützelschwab, who attempted to put an end to it.

2

The Tasks and Characteristics of an Intelligence Service

BECAUSE MASSON'S CONNECTION with Heinrich Himmler's staff was so unusual and the circumstances surrounding it were so strange, it is easy to forget
that this was just one of many contacts that Swiss Intelligence maintained during the war. In order to be able to appropriately assess the role and significance
of the Masson-Schellenberg connection, it must be viewed in the context of
intelligence as a whole.

It is essential for every political and military leadership to have reliable
updates on the situation in other states and on other governments' intentions.
Accurate information is the basis for any action, any assessment of the situation, and any decision by the authorities in charge. To put it in Kurz's words,
"A leadership that has no information available is blind; it gropes and is incapable of taking action on its own initiative."[1] It risks being *taken by surprise*.
During domestic and foreign political crises, procuring intelligence is therefore
a basic requirement for any national leadership. Intelligence consequently ful-
fills an important task, even though it is only a tool.[2] Walter Laqueur poig-
nantly remarks, "Intelligence is an essential service, but only a service. It is an

important element in the decision-making process, but only one element; its usefulness depends entirely on how it is used and guided."[3]

On the military level, an assessment of the situation is based on a careful evaluation of easily accessible, *open* sources of information,[4] and on information procured *secretly*, through what is commonly called *espionage*.[5] After the war, Colonel-Brigadier Masson wrote an essay on the basic principles of military intelligence;[6] this author would like to present some of the fundamental ideas that he developed therein.

During times of war, military intelligence[7] has to find out primarily about the morale and the material strength of potential enemies—as well as of potential allies.[8] Since wars, once confined to field armies, had evolved into total warfare in the twentieth century, in addition to strictly military intelligence, information on economic, financial, scientific, political, and personnel matters (just to name a few) has also become relevant. However, the main objective is to obtain detailed information about an opponent's operational capabilities, to find out about "its strategic arrangements, the concentration of its forces, the position and distribution of its tank force, . . . the fighting power and status of its air force, its main reserves and their potential mobility, and the morale of its army and population."[9]

Masson continued, "The main task of Intelligence in every army is to preclude the risk of a strategic or tactical surprise."[10] It was not until the mid-1960s that the phenomenon of "surprise" began to receive attention in the field of intelligence on both a practical and a theoretical level, even though unexpected, sudden action by the military was not at all a new trend. It has of course been possible at all times to surprise the opponent on the battlefield by developing new tactics, using uncommon strategies, deceiving him, or making the troops extraordinarily disciplined.[11] However, up until the 19th century, it was hardly possible to use these means to create a *strategic* surprise. It is telling that even Clausewitz did not pay much attention to this aspect. To him, a strategic surprise was interesting in theory but did not have any practical value.[12] Around the mid-19th century, that perception began to change. When the era of locomotion commenced and the means of communication started improving—generally speaking, when the technological and industrial revolution began—it became possible to deploy large numbers of troops over long distances within a very short period of time. Before then, mobilizing and deploying troops had been time-consuming, and an opponent's offensive intentions could be discovered in time to call up one's own troops and prepare for the expected attack.[13] New command instruments, such as the general staff, and new methods for solving problems systematically that emerged in the course of the industrial revolution as a result of progress in scientific thinking offered governments a wider range of possibilities to stage strategic surprises.[14] Prussia was the first power to take advantage of these new possibilities for conducting wars, successfully using them in the confrontations with Austria in 1866 and France in 1870–1871. However, in the 20th century, there were so many discoveries and new developments that the quality of the strategic surprise changed. Toward the end of World War I, the use of tracked vehicles and tanks made it easier to move troops across difficult terrain. By using aircraft, a third dimension was added, making it possible to surmount all natural barriers in the terrain in every direction within a very short time. Through the air force, the chances of making a strategic surprise a success became virtually one hundred percent.[15] In the 20th century in general, the *technological surprise* became one of the most terrifying, or at least one of the most amazing, ways of catching the opponent unawares, as demonstrated by the first massive use of poison gas in the Great War and the use of radar in World War II.[16]

It was Roberta Wohlstetter, with her brilliant 1962 study on Pearl Harbor,[17] who aroused scholars' and theoreticians' interest in the phenomenon of strategic surprise, and consequently also in the factors that can cause Intelligence to fail in its strategic task of warning against such surprises. More recent works[18] were written primarily in the second half of the 1970s and the early 1980s, triggered by Israel's experience in the 1973 Yom Kippur War on one hand and Western fears of the increasing military potential of the Soviet Union on the other.[19]

Roberta Wohlstetter examines why the Japanese were able to strategically surprise the United States on December 7, 1941, at Pearl Harbor. As it turned out, U.S. Intelligence in Washington had received enough information about Japan's diplomatic and military intentions to take precautions against the disaster. In order to explain why the U.S. naval base became subject to the surprise attack in spite of the existence of that information, Wohlstetter uses two terms from communications theory that have since become common knowledge because they are so graphic. She puts the huge amount of information with which intelligence specialists are confronted when assessing a situation into two categories, *signals* and *noise*. She defines a *signal* as "a clue or a sign or a piece of evidence that tells about a particular danger or a particular enemy move or intention."[20] These signals are generally confusingly complex and are associated with other—competing or contradictory—signals providing information that has nothing to do with the actual danger. Roberta Wohlstetter calls these competing and contradictory signals *noise*.[21]

Separating the signals from the noise is "an extremely delicate and difficult task."[22] Wohlstetter argues that "honest, dedicated, and intelligent men"[23] were in charge of Pearl Harbor, and yet the Japanese successfully surprised the

Americans because of the "conditions of human perception and . . . uncertainties so basic that they are not likely to be eliminated, though they might be reduced."[24] The relevant signals cannot always be heard clearly.[25] Moreover, people focus on events that they consider to be likely to happen. Hence, if one says that a signal has been received, that does not mean that it has actually been *understood*, i.e. that the recipient considers it as a clue or a request to take certain action, nor does it mean that the sender and the recipient consider it as a clue for the same danger.[26] Wohlstetter explains that one of the major lessons of Pearl Harbor consists of the fact that "intelligence will always have to deal with shifting signals"; the signals will never supply all the evidence, and the conclusions that are drawn from them "will always be hazardous."[27]

Critics later pointed out that Wohlstetter's distinction between *signals* and *noise* was incomplete because it did not take into consideration the notion of *deception*.[28] Indeed, according to Wohlstetter's definition, *noise* includes a whole range of information that flows through a large variety of channels[29] and, because it is so abundant, covers up the meaningful pieces of information that in retrospect are recognized as clear warning signals. The "noise" or "interference" coming from all the other, irrelevant information renders the interpretation of relevant signals ambiguous and unclear—or even worse, the really meaningful information may be so distorted by the background of noise that it actually seems to speak *against* an attack.[30]

Wohlstetter's concept of *noise* is based on the assumption that the interfering and misleading signals are created haphazardly. However, that is true only as long as interfering signals are not sent out deliberately in order to *deceive* foreign intelligence. One critic remarks that there is no reason to assume that what Wohlstetter describes as *noise* is the result of a *haphazard* process. On the contrary, everything suggests that the opposite is true.[31] Barton Whaley[32] points out that in cases where an opponent is expected to use ploys, the main difficulty consists less of sorting out the important signals from the surrounding noise than of recognizing whether the intercepted signals are *true* signals or *inverted/distorted* signals. When the deception is intentional, it becomes particularly difficult to identify it as such because its initiator undoubtedly undertakes every effort for inverted signals not to be completely covered up by the noise as defined by Wohlstetter.[33]

In this study, Wohlstetter's easy-to-remember distinction will be used only in a figurative sense; *noise* means any signal that is suitable to cover up the real warning signals, regardless of whether it is sent out deliberately or not. However, one has to admit that distinguishing between these two terms may be useful on a theoretical level, but in reality noise is rarely pure noise and signals are rarely clear-cut signals. In most cases, the information procured by intelligence is a combination of the two and can therefore not be categorized as absolutely reliable nor as entirely unreliable.[34] Hence, one has to be prepared to receive intentionally (*inverted*) or unintentionally misleading (*distorted*) signals.

An incident that occurred in May 1944 offers a good example of the difficulty in distinguishing between the different categories of signals. Policymakers in Switzerland were worried at that time because of information that had been received from the Swiss legation in Budapest. The legation had been informed directly by the French military attaché in Budapest, Hallier, that a pre-emptive German attack on Switzerland was imminent and would be staged according to the same scenario as the occupation of Hungary. In addition, the Swiss legation pointed out that the wicked Reich plenipotentiary for Hungary, Veesenmayer, had made some similar statements as well; however, these statements did not go beyond the aggressive, unfriendly remarks that other militant SS people had been making all along about Switzerland. Swiss Intelligence also received other information from Berlin that confirmed, complemented, or modified the information from Hungary, which it had received through the Department of Foreign Affairs.

In order to examine the various reports carefully, Swiss Intelligence could not limit itself to looking at the factual information but also had to consider how reliable the reports were and take into account their special nature. And most of all, as a matter of principle it had to put the information in the context of the overall situation, in view of all other information that had been gathered. Only by looking at all these aspects was Intelligence able to determine whether the information from Hungary was important in the overall picture, whether it was actually necessary to make a new assessment of the situation, or whether the information was in no way connected to the general context so that it did not deserve to receive any special attention.

Army Intelligence concluded that, just like a lot of other information, the messages from Budapest and Berlin were inverted signals that were supposed to trigger a reaction from Switzerland. As the Allies were advancing in Italy and about to launch their invasion of France, Germany had to have an interest in getting Switzerland to boost its defensive potential to the highest possible level. The German Armed Forces High Command feared that the Allies might use Swiss territory to bypass the German front in case their operations did not advance as fast as expected, or land troops and materials there in order to make an assault on southern Germany at the beginning of the invasion. Hence, the Allies would have had to interpret a massive mobilization by the Swiss army as a warning that they should not consider integrating Swiss territory into their operations.[35]

Chief of the General Staff Huber writes on June 1, 1944, to General Guisan about German troops massing near the Swiss border, but after meeting with Chief of Intelligence Masson and the head of the Allied section, Cuénoud, he recommends not calling up any additional troops for the time being. (BAr E 27/9911, vol. 1)

Mit einer feindlichen Überfalls geht uns die Pferde-Kol mit Aufmarsch nach O/= Befehl N° 15.

Die Durchführung dieser Maßnahme ist durch die bis jetzt vorhandenen Nachrichten nicht gerechtfertigt. Halbe Maßnahmen, wie etwa die Jg Tfn,

1. Aufgebot von Tfn nach den Dienstlichkeits-Tabellen vom 30.12.43, Benachrichtigung

2. Marsche ins Volk u würden abstellbar auf die angebotenen Tfn werden, dann wahrscheinlich Monate lang, im Dienst gehalten werden müssen.

Die einzige Vorkehr, die allfällig schon jetzt angeordnet werden könnte, wäre Bereitstellung der Einsatz-Reserve. Ich Armee an der Bahnt eingängen in erhöhter oder Alarm Bereitschaft; Aufhebung der Beurlaubungen u Ergänzung der Pferde u Motorfzge auf Sollbestand. Ich kann entsprechende Weisungen an die P.K. vorbereiten, damit sie gegebenenfalls sofort verschickt werden können. Die An-Bildg der Einsatz-Reserve würde durch diese Maßnahme stark beeinträchtigt.

Die gestern besprochene Erhöhung der Beweglichkeit der Einsatzreserve ist ohne Aufgebot u Requisitionsfzge P.T.T.Kol ez nicht möglich.

1 Beilage: ---

In view of this example, it is understandable that, on numerous occasions in World War II, Intelligence and the military or political authorities that it supplied with information had a sufficient number of alarming hints available but were unable to prevent a strategic surprise from being staged. Operation *Weserübung*, which began on April 9, 1940, was one instance where Germany was able to carry out a *blitzkrieg* against Denmark and Norway even though a number of signals had been received announcing the upcoming invasion. The *blitzkrieg* strategy requires a large number of troops to be concentrated at the decisive location, be very mobile, and create the effect of a surprise. On April 3, Britain's Military Intelligence warned the chiefs of staff that the latest reports indicated that Germany was going to invade Scandinavia. However, one day later, on April 4, it toned down its warnings, explaining that the indications for a German invasion were not strong enough. As on many previous occasions, there were plenty of signals, but none of them unambiguously confirmed the original warning.[36] In addition, British Intelligence had organizational short-comings, as the warnings that it intercepted were forwarded to different branches without being compared to one another. Hence, significant links between different messages were overlooked. As long as most of them were ambiguous, they seemed to confirm one's own prejudices.[37]

Possibly an even more impressive case where the complex interaction of signals, noise, and deception came into play was *Germany's attack on the Soviet Union* just over a year later, in summer 1941, which left Stalin shocked by Hitler's strategic surprise. The main difficulty for Soviet Intelligence lay in the fact that the information as a whole, which consisted of *signals* (which were later confirmed), noise, and inverted signals through which the Germans intentionally misled the Soviets, did not allow it to draw a clear picture of Hitler's intentions.[38] The surprise attack was successful not at all because Stalin's Intelligence service had received too little information—in fact, it even knew the exact date of the attack—but because the reports could be interpreted in different ways. It was difficult not only to distinguish the signals from the noise but also to identify the cunning disinformation that the Germans disseminated. Stalin based his interpretation of the numerous warnings that he had received on suppositions and preconceived ideas that appeared to make sense but turned out to be wrong.[39] In connection with Pearl Harbor, Thomas Schelling states that human beings have a general tendency "to confuse the unfamiliar with the improbable. The contingency we have not considered seriously looks strange; what looks strange is thought improbable; what is improbable need not be considered seriously."[40]

History has shown that it is difficult even for a well-functioning intelligence service to recognize a strategic surprise in time and thereby kill its effect.[41] Intelligence always has to work with information that is fragmented and messages that partly contradict each other, do not make perfect sense, or can be interpreted in different ways, particularly when the information concerns the intentions, capabilities, and plans of operation of a potential aggressor.[42] Wohlstetter explains:

> Afterward, when we know the actual physical links between the signals and the event, it seems almost impossible that we could have ignored the now-obvious connection. We forget how matters looked at the time the signal appeared in the midst of thousands of competing indications, the signal itself compatible not only with a single catastrophe, but also with many other possible outcomes. . . . The point is that the puzzle is never complete.[43]

This inevitable uncertainty can cause the political or military authorities to consider the warnings by Intelligence as inconclusive. Moreover, both the intelligence service (the body that should serve as the strategic warning instrument) and the government system (the body that has to *take action* based on the warning) are bureaucratic organizations with many branches and divisions. While such a structure allows the individual branches and divisions to specialize on certain issues, it also causes tasks to be split up into a number of smaller tasks. In fact, intelligence is divided into *procurement* and *evaluation*, a separation that is to a certain degree artificial, and into sections specializing in specific countries. This separation of tasks is all the more cumbersome as the communication between the different branches and divisions is generally not frictionless. In connection with the Japanese attack on Pearl Harbor, Wohlstetter notes that collecting intelligence is closely linked to evaluating it,[44] explaining:

> A sensitive collector knows what sounds to select out of a background of noise, and the presentation of the significant sounds is in itself a major first step in evaluation. For perception is an activity. Data are not given; they are taken. Moreover, the job of lifting signals out of a confusion of noise is an activity that is very much aided by hypotheses and by a background of knowledge much wider than the technical information.[45]

As mentioned, in the 1970s and 1980s, a large number of publications looked into the reasons that may cause Intelligence and decision-makers to make mistakes in finding clues for crises. Some of these reasons have been described in the examples above. In summary, one may say that those who evaluate intelligence have to rely on hypotheses in order to determine what signals are relevant; these hypotheses can be incorrect, however, because they are based on wishful thinking, preconceived ideas, or a tendency to always expect the worst. Intelligence may misinterpret an opponent's intentions because it believes that he acts as rationally as it does or because it has a wrong perception of how the opponent views the situation.[46]

The risk of *being taken by surprise* can be reduced by finding out the possible sources of error, but it cannot be eliminated.[47] Nevertheless, states have a number of possible means to avoid falling victim to a strategic surprise. Klaus Knorr explains that in addition to being prepared on the military level and being skillful on the foreign political level by not overly provoking another state,[48] a state has to see to it that the consequences of a strategic surprise are limited if it does happen.[49] In her authoritative study, Roberta Wohlstetter draws the same conclusion, stating:

> We cannot *count on* strategic warning. We *might* get it, and we might be able to take useful preparatory actions that would be impossible without it. . . . However, since we cannot rely on strategic warning, our defenses, if we are to have confidence in them, must be designed to function without it. If we accept the fact that the signal picture for impending attacks is almost sure to be ambiguous, we shall prearrange actions that are right and feasible in response to ambiguous signals. . . . It is only human to want some unique and unequivocal signal, to want a guarantee from intelligence, an unambiguous substitute for a formal declaration of war.[50]

Taking defensive precautions definitely simplifies the task of Intelligence and decision-makers. Uncertainty is a factor that has to be part of the planning process.[51] At the same time, that puts the role of intelligence in perspective. Intelligence is certainly a precondition for making reasonable policies or strategies, but it cannot replace them. Laqueur comments: "In the absence of an effective foreign policy even the most accurate and reliable intelligence will be of no avail."[52]

It is not very comforting to know that there is no perfect way of guaranteeing that Intelligence will issue a timely warning against a strategic or tactical surprise attack.[53] The risk is of course smaller for states that have a standing army, which can be alerted right away. Switzerland's Chief of Intelligence Masson added: "At the beginning of [World War II], the two main opponents were able to rely on heavily fortified lines, the Maginot Line and the Siegfried Line, which created a strong cordon making it virtually impossible to carry out any reconnaissance activities in the opponent's camp. Under these circumstances, even if intelligence is inadequate, it is difficult to stage a complete surprise because the troops are permanently in a state of readiness."[54]

As a result of the 1938 Troop Ordinance, on the eve of the war Switzerland for the first time had actual border troops. However, they had to be mobilized first; for political and economic reasons, this could be done only when there was a real threat. Masson explained, "Due to the militia system—our army is sometimes called an 'army staying at home'—it was primarily Intelligence's task to be vigilant."[55] Under the system of the militia army, good intelligence is actually imperative; being taken by surprise can be the end of a militia army that has to assemble first.[56]

In early September 1939, after the outbreak of the war in Poland, Swiss Intelligence had to realize that it had great difficulties following in detail the strategic course of the war on the various battlefields,[57] even though it had made contact with the informants, established the "connections,"[58] and set up the intelligence network in the country.[59] As Masson explained, this entailed additional risks insofar as the Commander-in-Chief depended on information that was as complete as possible "in order to set up and structure the defense, allocate troops to focal areas, and ultimately make the far-reaching decision about the number of troops that should be kept under arms or sent off duty in order to provide the industry and agriculture with the workforce that they required to keep the economy running."[60]

The difficulties that Switzerland had procuring intelligence were due mainly to new developments in war technology. During World War I, Swiss Intelligence could basically focus on the areas near the front.[61] Masson explained:

> Back then, Intelligence worked primarily with agents who operated in the border areas where foreign troops were expected to be assembled. . . . Furthermore, one was able to expect that any deployment of foreign troops for an operation against Switzerland would be revealed through several clear indications: the noise of horse-drawn vehicles, clouds of dust from the line of supply carts on unpaved roads, long columns of infantry, preparations in the assembly area, and preparations for crossing rivers and lakes along the Swiss border. Hence, there was *enough time* to get the defense in place.[62]

The situation was completely different in World War II. Masson remarked:

Beginning in 1939, airplanes and motorized troops, the main driving forces of the strategic surprise, made it much more difficult to procure information. One had to travel very far to get to the foreign troops in order to get to know their structure and organization and draw up the battle order; in addition, Intelligence had to pay attention to a large number of potential areas of operation in order to be able to follow on a large scale the camouflaged movements of combat troops and transport units.[63]

This reconnaissance across thousands of kilometers was important because "it mattered to [Swiss Intelligence] whether the mountain divisions of the German Armed Forces, whose exact number and structure [it] knew, were still in Finland or the Caucasus or whether they had been redeployed to areas near Switzerland for a new mission; that issue became particularly relevant in early 1943."[64]

A great number of different means were used during World War II to procure intelligence; one could not be picky, using virtually every possibility that offered any prospects of success, i.e. useful information.[65] One of Swiss Intelligence's major sources, which supplied particularly useful information about operational movements of German troops, was located as high as the Führer's headquarters. Through this source Masson found out about pending movements of major units long before they were actually deployed to a new area. Prior to the offensive of May 1940, before Hitler left Berlin, a connection that Max Waibel had established reported to Switzerland's Army Command that the Führer's headquarters were going to be transferred to Ziegenberg in western Germany.[66] Information such as this was subsequently verified by agents.[67]

Procurement is only the first, albeit decisive, step undertaken by Intelligence.[68] During the subsequent *evaluation* process, it has to make sure that the individual pieces of information that frequently contradict each other are put together in order to create a whole picture. Masson expected his staff in the evaluation section to keep cool, show understanding for the actual capabilities of potential aggressors, and be able to make sober assessments, especially because they had to try to see through their opponents' ploys and misinformation.[69] The intelligence services of all states had to realize that they could accomplish this task only in part, since none of them were protected against failing to identify false information.[70]

The Structure of Swiss Army Intelligence

Before the 1939 Mobilization

FROM THE 1920S ONWARD, section 5 of the General Staff unit, the Intelligence Service, was headed by pro-French officers[1] who had graduated from the *Ecole supérieure de Guerre* in Paris. In 1925, Gustave Combe was succeeded by Charles Dubois, and Lieutenant Colonel Roger Masson was put in charge of the section in 1936.[2] At that time, the staff of Army Intelligence consisted only of the head and his secretary. The intelligence organization that had been set up during World War I had been virtually dissolved because of personnel problems and because people lacked understanding, disliked the idea of having a permanent Intelligence Service in the country,[3] naïvely believed that peacetime sources of information would continue to be available during times of crises, and had unrealistic expectations about the collective security system of the League of Nations.[4] Between 1937 and 1938, Masson tried to rebuild his section. As a consequence, some officers were detailed and a few experts were assigned to Army Intelligence. From humble beginnings,[5] in early 1938 the staff increased to three; in summer 1938 to four; in fall 1938 to five; and in the course of 1939 to seven. When the army was mobilized in September 1939, the staff consisted of 10 people. During the war, the section expanded up to a maximum of 120 staff, and then by June 20, 1945, it was downsized to 66, and by August 20, 1945, the day the troops officially went off duty, to a staff of 40.[6]

Masson's main problem was the lack of means that he had available; in fact, they were not sufficient to make Army Intelligence effective. In a 1967 interview, Major Hans Hausamann, the head of *Bureau Ha*, hardly exaggerated when he stated that the funding had been just about sufficient "to pay the subscriptions to the various newspapers and cover some other expenses."[7] Hence, the excellent performance of Masson's Intelligence Service during the war was all the more remarkable.

Between 1930 and 1937, the terms of reference for the Intelligence Section did not change, consisting of the usual tasks of military intelligence. They included:

- gathering information on foreign armies and war preparations in the border areas around Switzerland (construction of roads, fortifications, and other infrastructure that could be used by the military);
- procuring information on the activities on battlefields abroad;
- organizing Army Intelligence and liaising with the army;
- communicating with customs authorities;
- the cipher service (decoding foreign codes and developing new codes for its own use);
- organizing the transmission of intelligence by pigeon carriers;
- handling military police matters;
- evaluating articles in the press;
- communicating with Swiss representations abroad and foreign military attachés in Bern.[8]

The annual budget initially amounted to 10,000 francs. In May 1934, at the request of the Chief of the General Staff,[9] Colonel Heinrich Roost, Federal Councillor Rudolf Minger raised it to 30,000 francs.[10] As tensions were rising on the international level, Section 5 began to be viewed as important. In early March 1938, Minger increased the budget to an annual 50,000 francs[11] after Colonel-Corps-Commander Jakob Labhart, Roost's successor, had made clear to him that the old budget was "not sufficient to meet the basic requirements of the very limited information service."[12] Nevertheless, Intelligence continued to eke out a bare existence.

The difficult conditions under which Army Intelligence had to work were no secret to the public. Between January and March 1938, the weekly *Nation* published a series of articles entitled "The Characteristics of Army Intelligence."[13] Its author was Jürgen Luternau, alias Hermann Hagenbuch,[14] a former *Neue Zürcher Zeitung* military correspondent who had triggered a scandal three and a half years earlier by writing the so-called "Letters by a member of the General Staff,"[15] which had the effect of ruining the military careers of Lieutenant General Ulrich Wille and Divisional Commander Eugen Bircher. In his articles in the *Nation* newspaper, Hagenbuch focused primarily on the military attachés that Switzerland sent to foreign countries, but he also pointed a finger at the inadequacies of Army Intelligence, writing:

> Well, let us see who serves at [Intelligence] headquarters. One single General Staff officer, who is allowed to use the services of a cartographer from the Military Department for drawing jobs and has to rely on one single secretary for everything else. In addition to doing his regular work, this officer also has to teach courses to the General Staff; he accompanies foreign guests to maneuvers and generally serves as master of ceremonies for the army. He is absorbed by too many tasks; he even has to do all the coding and decoding. He is frequently away from Bern, and when the secretary is out sick at the same time, there is no one left to give out any information. . . . Those who know what Intelligence is, i.e. an entire organization that tries to find out about the strength and intentions of armies of potential opponents, and those who know what personal and material means are required for such an organization to function will not be very surprised to hear that near Switzerland's southern border, a large number of [Italy's] Alpine units may be transferred from Lake Garda to the Aosta valley without Bern finding out about it for eight weeks.[16]

As far as the General Staff unit was concerned, by describing these unsatisfactory conditions Hagenbuch was fighting a battle that was already won. In early 1938, the situation at Switzerland's doorstep turned increasingly tense, making the shortcomings of Section 5 impossible to bear. On February 8, 1938, Labhart consequently issued new service regulations[17] that redefined and extended the terms of reference of Army Intelligence for the first time since 1930. However, it appears that these updated regulations did not meet the actual requirements. Two weeks later, on February 22, 1938, shortly before Austria's *Anschluss* to the German Reich, the Chief of the General Staff issued extensive, detailed *instructions for rebuilding Army Intelligence.*[18] The Intelligence Service thereby received the following terms of reference:

1. communicate with the top customs authorities, the Department of Foreign Affairs, and the Attorney General's office;
2. communicate with foreign representations and their military attachés;[19]
3. communicate with the "Patriotic Federation";[20]
4. supervise Switzerland's military attachés abroad;[21]
5. reconnoiter the areas bordering on Switzerland;[22]
6. take precautions against a surprise attack. For that purpose, in an area located 30-100 kilometers from the Swiss border, in cooperation with the Department of Foreign Affairs, Intelligence was to create a network of Swiss informants who were to report any movement of troops. The network was to focus mainly on southern Germany, but informants were to be recruited in Italy and France as well.
7. carry out the actual Secret Service, communicate with agents,[23] etc.
8. organize Army Intelligence and liaise with the army;
9. handle military police matters;
10. manage the cipher office;
11. manage the press office.

For all these tasks, in 1938 Intelligence had a budget of only 50,000 francs. For the press service alone it spent 20,000 francs, and only 3,000 were allocated for agents.[24]

Through Labhart's "instructions," Masson basically received authorization to set up a *strategic* Intelligence Service, even though that term was not yet used. In a discussion, William J. Donovan, the founder and head of the United States Office of Strategic Services (OSS), defined strategic intelligence as "the ascertainment to the greatest possible degree of the total capabilities of every other nation and their intentions toward us."[25] Considering the limited possibilities of a small, neutral state, Allen Dulles' definition may apply better to Switzerland's case; he stated, "It is all the information that the policy makers require in order to direct a proper policy with respect to those countries that threaten our security."[26]

The need for strategic intelligence arose mainly from the Third Reich's surprising victories. Soon after Hitler's rise to power, it became apparent that the National Socialists skillfully used economic, political, and psychological means to pursue their military objectives; they were able to hide their real intentions from foreign nations by consciously blurring the distinction between peace and war.[27] Shortly after the end of World War II, George Pettee, one of the guiding American intellectual forces of strategic intelligence, wrote, "Everything that men do in peace was put at the service of war, and the date when military war began or ended became an arbitrary point in a combined process of broader and longer dimensions."[28]

The National Socialists' strategy of conducting wars through non-military means was successful. In 1936, they succeeded at having the Rhineland remilitarized in a surprising move, and during the time that German weapons and combat methods were being tested in the Spanish Civil War, Hitler annexed Austria. Czechoslovakia soon suffered the same fate. In all these instances, the Germans used a new combined strategy of which the actual means of combat were only one element, serving mainly to back up the impact of the economic and psychological weapons that Hitler used to achieve his political goals.[29]

Masson deserves to be credited for recognizing these connections at a fairly early stage. He concluded that Swiss Intelligence could no longer deal exclusively with purely military matters such as the composition and state of armament of foreign armies, etc., but had to keep an eye on *all means that an opponent could use against Switzerland.* The fact that Masson's strategic Intelligence Service subsequently clashed with the Department of Foreign Affairs, which tried to keep Army Intelligence away from politics, considering them to be its own domain, was due mostly to organizational shortcomings and flaws of character; it did not mean that Masson's concept was fundamentally wrong.

Austria's Anschluss just three weeks after Labhart had issued his instructions drastically demonstrated that there was a large gap between concept and reality; Swiss Intelligence did not even have the personnel available to put Masson's ideas into practice. Hagenbuch wrote: "It may be said in public what Switzerland's Intelligence is *not* at the present time. That is the only way to make it what it is supposed to be and especially what its current head would like it to be. . . . If our former neighbor [Austria] had not suffered such a sad fate, one could say that luckily this lesson came just in time."[30]

Colonel-Corps-Commander Labhart was quick to react. On March 29, 1938, he submitted requests to Federal Councillor Minger, who headed the Military Department, to hire additional personnel for the General Staff unit, explaining:

> During the most recent events in Austria it became obvious that Section 5 (Intelligence) is seriously understaffed. During that critical time, the head of the section had to be at his office practically 24 hours a day just to receive messages and take care of the most necessary business. It was not possible to immediately evaluate the information in detail. Considering the importance of intelligence especially during times of tension, it is perfectly justified to create an organization that

Swiss Army Intelligence, status of early 1939

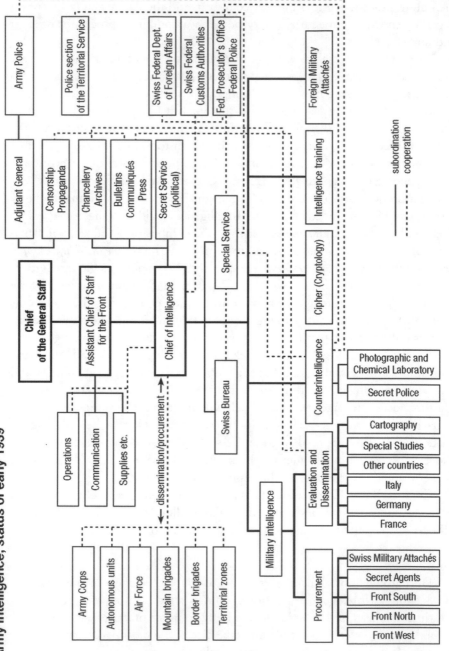

subordination
cooperation

Army Police

Police section
of the Territorial Service

Swiss Federal Dept.
of Foreign Affairs

Swiss Federal
Customs Authorities

Fed. Prosecutor's Office
Federal Police

Foreign Military
Attachés

Adjutant General

Censorship
Propaganda

Chancellery
Archives

Bulletins
Communiqués
Press

Secret Service
(political)

Special Service

Intelligence training

Chief
of the General Staff

Assistant Chief of Staff
for the Front

Chief of Intelligence

Cipher (Cryptology)

Swiss Bureau

Counterintelligence

Photographic and
Chemical Laboratory

Secret Police

Operations

Communication

Supplies etc.

dissemination/procurement

Evaluation and
Dissemination

Cartography

Special Studies

Other countries

Italy

Germany

France

Military intelligence

Army Corps

Autonomous units

Air Force

Mountain brigades

Border brigades

Territorial zones

Procurement

Swiss Military Attachés

Secret Agents

Front South

Front North

Front West

has the necessary number of staff to keep up with the events. At least the skeleton of Army Intelligence has to be in place already during times of peace. The Intelligence Service needs a minimum of seven General Staff officers; it would be totally wrong to believe that other General Staff officers could immediately start working effectively if the army is mobilized in the event of a war. Moreover, it is extremely important for Intelligence to be reliable and well informed in the event that the authorities need to have documentation available in order to make decisions during times of tension. However, at the present time Intelligence does not have nearly enough staff to accomplish this task. In order to procure, study, and evaluate information, the head of the section needs at least a deputy,[31] another officer,[32] and an additional secretary.[33]

Other sections of the General Staff unit were also understaffed, but not in the same dramatic manner as the Intelligence Service.[34] As a short-term solution, officers were temporarily detailed to the General Staff unit and a number of instructors were asked to serve as deputy heads of section for two years. Several of Masson's aides who will be presented in the upcoming chapters joined Army Intelligence in that manner.

In retrospect, it appears that the instructions of February 1938 provided the most significant impetus for expanding Army Intelligence. Once Masson and his staff had succeeded in obtaining satisfactory results during the Munich crisis of fall 1938 and when the remainder of Czechoslovakia was crushed,[35] policymakers were willing to accept that a well-functioning Intelligence Service was useful. However, there was a price tag attached to this expansion. In mid-April 1939, Labhart asked Minger to increase the budget to a level that was *five times* higher than the 1938 budget, quoting as a reason the "increasingly complex political situation [that made it indispensable] to substantially expand our Intelligence and Information Service."[36] Labhart explained that there were plans to create three field offices at the northern, western, and southern front, which required a budget of 50,000 francs each. Another 50,000 francs were to be allocated for sending additional informants and agents to foreign countries.[37]

The Head of the Military Department agreed to the budget increase[38] and asked the Department of Finance for approval. In a detailed letter to Federal Councillor Wetter, Minger explained how useful Intelligence was, stating:

For the last several months, the National Defense Committee and the Federal Military Department have been discussing whether we should deploy troops to guard our country's borders. You certainly know that no troops were called up last year even though the public disagreed with us on that issue; in retrospect, this decision was justified through the subsequent events of September 1938. The Swiss were consequently spared from all the hassle and inconvenience caused by calling up troops. And during the [German] operation against Czechoslovakia in early March of this year we did not need to take any additional steps either. . . . All international events have been discussed in detail among the National Defense Committee; the General Staff unit's *information bulletins*, with which you are familiar, serve as a *valuable basis* for these discussions. In all these quite *threatening* situations, both the members of the National Defense Committee and I have been *extremely glad to be able to base our decisions on reliable information from abroad*. It is interesting to note that during the recent discussions about whether additional measures were required to guard our borders, several *commanders of border brigades*, who would be the first ones to have to withstand an enemy attack and who are primarily responsible for guarding the border, remarked that for the time being it was not necessary to call up additional troops, arguing that due to *our effective Intelligence we were well safeguarded against surprises*. In this connection, it may be said that an Intelligence Service *that works fast and is reliable is the best guarantee that the army will be ready in time*. If we had to rely on last-minute information that cannot be verified, it would currently be irresponsible not to better guard our borders, as they are not protected well enough against a coup.[39]

Minger argued that "a reliable Intelligence Service [was] the main requirement" for the NDC and the Military Department to make their decisions and that it was therefore indispensable to expand it, adding:

Until now, the Intelligence Service of the General Staff unit has been able to work only with very limited means. The more the tensions rise and the better the powers hide their intentions, the more difficult it becomes for Intelligence to be able to receive and transmit reliable information. Hence, we plan to *substantially expand Intelligence because we consider such an organization to be rather useful*. The events of September 1938 and early March 1939 have shown that through its reliable information, this organization helps us keep expenditures low for mobilizing troops and keeping them on duty; these savings are far more substantial than the financial means that Intelligence requires for its own operations. When considering whether the budget should be increased, we must not be influenced by *the ugly word "espionage"*; instead, we must remember that we want to enable ourselves to provide the country with as much security as possible. According to the calculations by the General Staff unit, Intelligence should henceforth have a budget of *250,000 francs* available.[40]

Minger asked his colleague on the Federal Council to "favorably examine the urgent requirements of our Intelligence Service," which Wetter did the same day, giving his approval to the budget hike in an annotation on Minger's letter.[41]

During World War II

As soon as the first news arrived of the conclusion of the German-Russian non-aggression pact on August 22, 1939, Swiss Army Intelligence was put on call and started working around the clock. The staff was mobilized "as planned; no frictions occurred. The additional staff that joined the organization took on their duties without creating any interruptions to the service."[42]

After the entire army was called up on September 1, 1939, Intelligence and Operations initially made up one section in the Front Subgroup (Ia) of the Army Staff. In connection with operations order No. 12b (later renumbered No. 13),[43] on February 21, 1941, Commander-in-Chief General Henri Guisan asked the Army Staff to be partly reorganized. As part of that reorganization process, Intelligence was expanded to the *Intelligence and Security Section* and was henceforth supervised directly by the Chief of the General Staff.[44] The expansion concerned primarily security matters; the former Police Section was transferred from the Territorial Service, and the Military Police Section from the Adjutant General's Office to Masson's Intelligence Service. The new section's quarterly report stated, "Now the tasks of safeguarding the country from strategic and domestic political surprises are combined and are under the direct supervision of the Chief of the General Staff."[45] One year later, the new section became the independent *Group Id*,[46] and effective March 1, 1942, Masson was promoted to Assistant Chief of Staff, receiving the rank of colonel-brigadier,[47] a fact that was accompanied by some grumbling behind the scenes. General Guisan justified his move by arguing that Intelligence had become increasingly important.[48]

The squabbles that were triggered by Masson's promotion to colonel brigadier were characteristic of the atmosphere in which he had to work as head of Army Intelligence. By promoting him, General Guisan basically wanted to

Intelligence and Security Service (as of March 25, 1941)

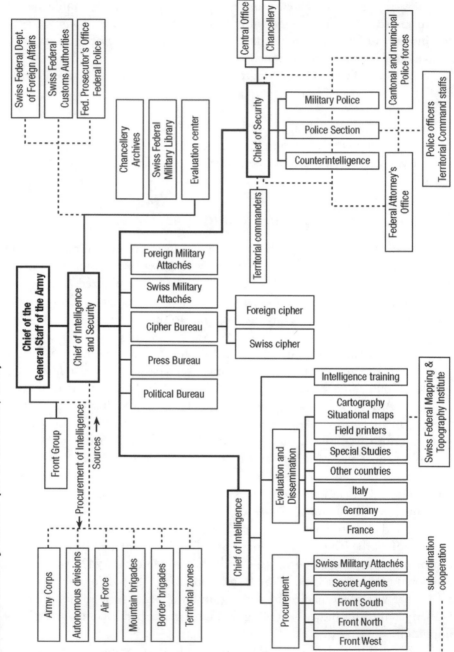

acknowledge Masson's good performance, and had just been looking for a plausible opportunity to do so.[49] Federal Councillor Kobelt was not delighted about the move,[50] nor was his colleague Pilet-Golaz, who was annoyed to find out about it in a *Neue Zürcher Zeitung*[51] article.[52] Masson ran into serious trouble due to this short item of news, which was broadcast on the radio and published in daily newspapers, citing the Army Staff as a source.[53] The Chief of the General Staff criticized that this was not a promotion but simply the bestowing of a title on Masson that was associated with the position of an Assistant Chief of Staff. He even considered the communiqué as a violation of the military penal code, arguing that Masson had misused the right of the Chief of Intelligence to issue press releases "because this [did] not concern an official but a personal matter."[54] Moreover, Colonel Huber disapproved of the communiqué because Masson had thereby publicly announced how his unit was organized, even though it was an internal army matter and Masson himself had repeatedly complained about an increase in foreign espionage.

Federal Councillor Kobelt expressed his disapproval in a letter to the Commander-in-Chief, using arguments that had to do with Masson's status as a government employee, adding, "Let me also tell you that during today's Federal Council meeting several people voiced their surprise and displeasure."[55] General Guisan tried to downplay the move, arguing that the Army Staff was not being restructured but one of its heads was "simply given a new title."[56] However, this explanation did not put an end to the differences; Kobelt, General Guisan, and Labhart, who had also been called upon in this matter by the Head of the Military Department, continued exchanging letters on the subject until May 19, 1942.[57] It is obvious that this incident did not help improve Masson's relations with Federal Councillors Kobelt and Pilet-Golaz.

One and a half years later, Army Intelligence again underwent a change in organization. Effective January 1, 1944, Group Id was expanded to include the Territorial Service and the Mobilization Section, and it was renamed Group Ib.[58] Past experience had shown that Security needed to work closely with the Territorial Section; moreover, the Territorial Service and the Mobilization Section were tied together insofar as the officials of the Mobilization Section were usually assigned to the Territorial Service once the troops had been mobilized.[59] As a consequence, Colonel-Brigadier Masson henceforth headed a very diverse group[60] and was in charge of more than 300,000 men.[61]

Internal Structure of Army Intelligence

After looking at the position of Intelligence within the army, it is equally useful to examine the internal structure of the Intelligence Service. Due to the small number of staff that served on Army Intelligence before the war, several positions had to be combined into one. Nevertheless, three "special bureaus"[62] focusing on Switzerland's neighboring countries each had one officer in charge. Hence, at the beginning of the war, the French Bureau, the Italian Bureau, and the German Bureau were in charge of *procuring intelligence.* In 1940, a bureau was added for "Other Countries" and another bureau for political matters and issues relating to censorship.[63]

At the beginning of 1940, Intelligence was organized into working groups. As chief of the "Military Intelligence (Procurement and Dissemination)" group, Lieutenant Colonel Max Schafroth was to coordinate the work of the German, French, Italian, and "Other Countries" Bureaus.[64] In May 1940, Bureau 5 ("Political Bureau and the Press"), which had been headed by Bernard Barbey, was subdivided into two bureaus that were to report directly to Masson. Arnold Schwengeler was put in charge of the Political Bureau, while Hans Rudolf Schmid headed the Press Bureau. Barbey was detailed to General Guisan's Personal Staff on June 11, 1940.[65]

The new position of *Chief of Military Intelligence* did not exist for a very long time. At a first glance, it may have made sense to create the position, but upon close examination it did not meet the organization's needs. The fact that it was done away with may have had to do with Schafroth, but above all it was superfluous because it created "an unnecessary step between the Chief of Intelligence [Masson] and the Bureaus, which had to be in permanent close contact with him in the interest of the matter."[66] It was eventually realized that there was no need to coordinate the work among the different Bureaus because their areas of activities overlapped only in a few exceptional instances. Major Alfred Ernst commented, "Whenever that is the case, for example between the French and German Bureaus after the Germans occupied part of France, so far we have always been able to come to an understanding among comrades and find a solution that is acceptable to everyone."[67] In addition to being unnecessary, reality also showed that the new structure was not applicable; it would have required the Chief of Military Intelligence, who was to brief Masson, to be "as well-informed about the German Army and the political situation in every country as the heads of bureau. However, that [was] impossible."[68] As a consequence, the heads of bureaus had to be called into the briefings after all, which resulted in bothersome delays. Hence, the position was canceled in late fall 1940, and the bureau heads once again reported directly to Masson.[69]

In August 1942, new developments in the international strategic situation resulted in a permanent restructuring of Swiss Intelligence. Masson argued, "Battlefields are no longer contained within a small geographic area as they were between 1939 and 1941, when only two opponents were facing each other

Structure of Group I b (as of January 1, 1944)

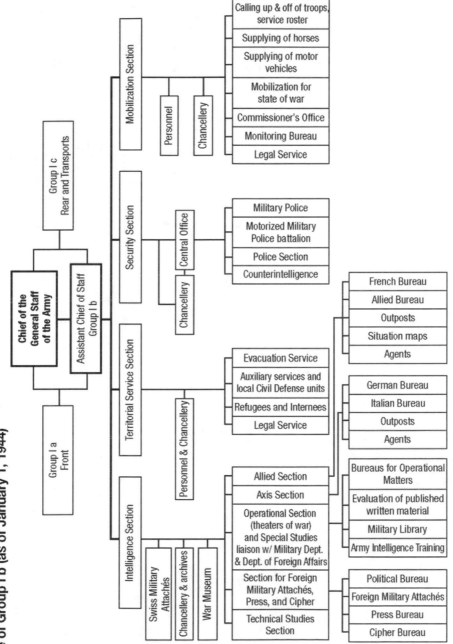

Personnel structure at Army Intelligence and Security, early 1941

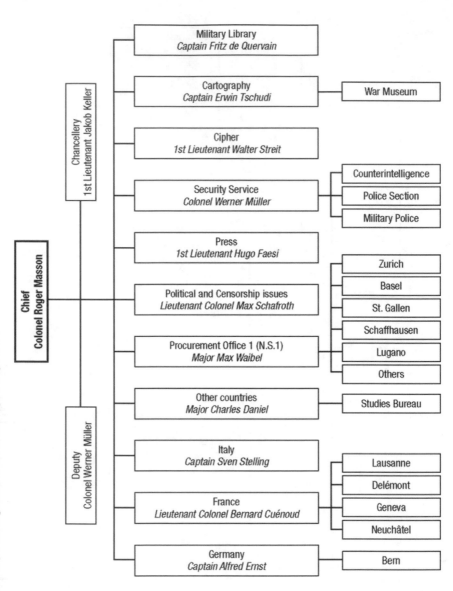

Chief
Colonel Roger Masson

Chancellery
1st Lieutenant Jakob Keller

Deputy
Colonel Werner Müller

Military Library
Captain Fritz de Quervain

Cartography
Captain Erwin Tschudi

War Museum

Cipher
1st Lieutenant Walter Streit

Security Service
Colonel Werner Müller

Counterintelligence

Police Section

Military Police

Press
1st Lieutenant Hugo Faesi

Political and Censorship issues
Lieutenant Colonel Max Schafroth

Zurich

Basel

St. Gallen

Schaffhausen

Procurement Office 1 (N.S.1)
Major Max Waibel

Lugano

Others

Other countries
Major Charles Daniel

Studies Bureau

Italy
Captain Sven Stelling

Lausanne

Delémont

France
Lieutenant Colonel Bernard Cuénoud

Geneva

Neuchâtel

Germany
Captain Alfred Ernst

Bern

(Germany vs. Poland, Germany vs. France, Italy vs. Greece, etc.)."[70] Instead, he explained, "troops are now part of one of two belligerent groups, the Axis Powers and the Allies."[71] Masson speculated that the creation of a second front in Western Europe might soon result in a battle of France, in which Germany, Italy, and other allies of the Axis would face the armed forces of the Anglo-Saxon Allies.

Due to this new development, Masson ordered the creation of an *Axis Section* and an *Allied Section*.[72] Major Alfred Ernst of the General Staff, the head of the German Bureau, was put in charge of the Axis Section, which included the German and Italian Bureaus and also dealt with the Axis' allies in Europe and with Japan. The internal structure of the Bureaus was not affected by this reorganization, with the exception of the Bureau for Other Countries, which was dissolved. Lieutenant Colonel Bernard Cuénoud of the General Staff became head of the Allied Section while remaining in charge of the French Bureau.

The terms of reference for the individual Bureaus were only slightly modified when Army Intelligence was restructured. The French Bureau continued to have to inform the German Bureau (following the restructuring of the Allied Section) about the arrangement of the German occupation forces in France, Belgium, and Holland. Major Charles Daniel of the General Staff, the head of the *Studies Bureau*[73] who became Chief of Intelligence after the war, continued to be in charge of following the events in the different war zones and identifying the lessons that could be interesting for the Swiss Army. According to his terms of reference, he had "to be constantly able to provide the Chief of Intelligence with the elements on which the latter [based] his assessment of the overall situation."[74] Hence, Daniel had to keep a close eye on the *battlefields*, whereas the Axis and Allied Sections analyzed the *composition of foreign military forces*, their locations and fighting strength, their war economies, etc.

Masson offered his staff as much leeway as possible, explaining, "I did not give my Bureaus *any written instructions* on how they should work."[75] He made do with occasional meetings with his top aides, adding, "Due to the large size of our Service, and due to the decentralization that was imperative in view of the experienced officers [who worked for Army Intelligence], such as Colonel Cuénoud and Major Waibel, it did not make sense for the person who headed the whole organization to interfere with the procurement process in the domains that were run primarily by agents. The Chief of Intelligence should not know the agents; that is one major principle of running any i[ntelligence] s[ervice]."[76]

Meetings with his staff were not held very frequently. At the end of 1940, Chief of Security Werner Müller informed the top aides that, in the future, meetings would be held once or twice a week and would deal with administrative issues as well as with fundamental technical matters relating to Intelligence. Alfred Ernst asked that "at these meetings there should be a discussion of the situation during which the heads of the different Bureaus should be given the opportunity to express their views and the chief should give them *guidelines* for their future activities."[77] Ernst's request was submitted to Masson for examination, but it appears that the meetings were not held as planned because in early 1942 Masson once again expressed the need to meet with his closest aides more frequently, stating:

> As I would like to discuss with my top aides some issues concerning our Service, I have decided to establish regular meetings. The frequency of these meetings will depend on whether there are any pending issues and how urgently decisions have to be made. These meetings should allow the invited officers to express themselves freely about problems that they consider useful discussing in the framework of our activities. A fruitful exchange of ideas on the way in which our Service as a whole and our Bureaus operate and on their effectiveness should allow us to better coordinate our efforts and provide the staff not only with a sense of moral and intellectual unity but also with the guidelines that will inspire them for their work. However, the freedom of action that I have been granting them will not be curtailed in any way.[78]

An investigating judge later explained to the Military Attorney General, "Everyone on the Intelligence Service basically worked autonomously,[79] using his own know-how and methods."[80]

In addition to the Bureaus for the various countries, Army Intelligence had a number of specialized institutions. During the months before the war broke out, some preliminary steps were taken toward setting up Counterintelligence by creating a chemical and photographic *laboratory*,[81] analyzing and organizing the *cipher service*, and establishing its structure.[82] However, the *Cipher Bureau* needed some time to become familiar with its work. Already before the war, in cooperation with some university professors, Major Cuénoud of the General Staff had managed to assemble a group of mathematicians who were interested in cryptology. During the early part of 1939, they were trained by Cuénoud and others for their future tasks, although an actual cryptology group could be set up only when the army was called up; it included mathematicians, meteorologists, and linguists.[83] According to an activity report, "Cooperation with the bodies of the Federal Department of Foreign Affairs was smooth and was characterized by mutual goodwill."[84]

The Cipher Bureau was divided into a group (called "Cipher I") establishing and checking new systems and installations for Switzerland's own use and teaching staff and troops how to use them, and a group (called "Cipher II") decoding foreign diplomatic codes, in particular the telegrams by foreign military attachés in Bern.

Even though their organization was modest, in the course of the first year the cipher specialists were able to crack two foreign codes and uncover the weaknesses of a code used by the Department of Foreign Affairs. By the end of August 1941, they had managed to crack 13 additional foreign codes, including two German ones. By the end of 1943, they were able to read another eight codes by foreign diplomatic and intelligence services. However, in 1944–1945, due to serious personnel cuts, they were no longer allowed to work on decoding new codes but had to limit themselves to evaluating codes that they already knew.[85]

At the beginning of the war, *Counterintelligence* was still in its infancy as well. Without waiting for the necessary legislation to pass, in early 1939 Masson began setting up a counterintelligence organization for the army in cooperation with Colonel Robert Jaquillard and Lieutenant Colonel Werner Müller. Suitable staff that were recruited from cantonal police departments received some basic information and training. The Attorney General's Office and the Federal Police and Justice Department formally protested against these activities. An activity report by Intelligence later ironically stated, "The differences concerning this matter had not yet been settled when the army was called up and the zeal that the civilian authorities had criticized so harshly turned out to be absolutely indispensable."[86]

In an order to the Armed Forces dated October 5, 1939, Counterintelligence was officially recognized as an institution[87] of the army, and its structure and terms of reference were established. During the course of the war, its chemical laboratory turned out to be extremely important. Its head was an excellent criminologist whose know-how and abilities made it possible to carry out several risky operations. As an example, the lab produced 35 French stamps and 10 German stamps, foreign train passes, work cards, certificates by the Commander of Greater Paris, food cards, foreign identity cards, and other documents for the French Bureau and later for the Allied Section. In addition, it was able to uncover an invisible ink used by the Germans and develop an invisible ink for Switzerland's own agents. Cuénoud commented, "The laboratory should be highly commended for its work."[88] However, British and American documents turned out to be more complex and counterfeit-proof, making it impossible to reproduce them.

The relations between Intelligence and Counterintelligence were not always unproblematic. In the final activity report of the Allied Section, Cuénoud complained, "It is very regrettable that our relations with Counterintelligence were not that good. Intelligence undeniably suffered from that. It seems that we were allowed to expect more understanding and perhaps also more efficient assistance from Counterintelligence. It was undoubtedly very skillful in its domain, but it did not always comprehend the difficulties, responsibilities, and needs of Intelligence."[89] On several occasions, Counterintelligence intervened out of its own initiative without previously consulting with the concerned intelligence officers, thereby interfering in an unfortunate and sometimes harmful manner with bodies procuring intelligence.

Shortly after the army was mobilized, a *Swiss Bureau*[90] and a *Bureau for Special Services* were added to the peacetime structure of the Intelligence Service. The Swiss Bureau was to keep abreast of the positions of Switzerland's Armed Forces,[91] and the Bureau for Special Services headed by Captain Paul Meyer-Schwertenbach handled security and secrecy issues in cooperation with Counterintelligence and the police. [92]

Due to the lack of personnel, no special body could be set up to communicate with the foreign military attachés. The Chief of Intelligence continued to maintain contact with them in person, as he had done before the war, or through an officer who handled additional tasks within Intelligence.[93] The contacts with the military attachés working in Bern soon took up a considerable amount of time. Shortly after the beginning of the war, the military attachés of Germany, France, and Italy were joined by nine additional military attachés; some of them brought along their adjutants and aides, who also had to be taken care of. Curiously, the representative of France carried the title *navy attaché*.

When the Army Staff moved to Spiez and later to Langnau, it became more difficult for intelligence officers to do their work, as they frequently had to spend a lot of time traveling to Bern and other major communication centers in order to meet with the military attachés, agents, and aides. This inconvenience was eliminated only in part through the creation of outposts that were in charge of procuring intelligence. For similar reasons, in October 1939 the Chief of Counterintelligence requested to have his group retransferred to Bern; however, that made it more difficult to communicate with Intelligence, a task that was henceforth handled mainly by Meyer-Schwertenbach's Special Services.[94]

Before the war, Army Intelligence set up a network of reliable connections for *procuring intelligence*. The most significant ones included the Federal

Department of Foreign Affairs, with which it exchanged ideas about current political problems; the national customs authorities, whose border patrols were in charge of guarding the country's borders; and the Attorney General's Office, with which it communicated on how to counter subversive political activities and espionage.[95] In his secret supplementary report on Intelligence's activities during the war, that he addressed exclusively to the Chief of the General Staff, Masson mentioned some additional connections, stating, "The contacts with the various federal and cantonal authorities, which had gained an insight into certain foreign plans and intentions or were able to shed light on certain incidents, were satisfactory in every respect; we were grateful for their cooperation. The contacts with the Swiss National Bank and the Department of Economy and its Commerce Section[96] were particularly valuable, and so were the contacts with the Federal Office of Health, with which we exchanged some information, and the Federal Office of Veterinary Science."[97]

Intelligence also collected information by *intercepting radio signals and conversations*. On August 27, 1939, Signals Company 2 was detailed from the Engineer Corps to Intelligence in order to listen in on international radio communications. Its results were considered to be "very satisfactory."[98] Once the army was mobilized, Signals Company 2 was replaced by a *monitoring detachment* of the signals unit that tapped long-wave and medium-wave telegraphs and telephones.[99] It was joined by short-wave monitoring and plotting detachments, one of which operated at the top of the Jungfrau mountain as a pilot project for very high frequencies.[100] The up to 200 daily *monitoring reports* by Signals Company 7 and later by Signals Company 20 included political and military information as well as material for the Cipher Bureau.[101] The *plotting reports* by the signals unit that were also submitted daily as of late November 1939 made it possible to locate a few pirate transmitters.

In retrospect, Masson considered the intercepted radio telegrams as

very valuable, especially during times of great tension; in many instances, the information that they included could not have been procured through any other channel. . . . By setting up interception stations at suitable locations near the border, it was sometimes[102] possible to follow radio communications all the way to the battlefield. It is worth mentioning that in winter 1940-1941 radio messages (spoken in plain language) were intercepted from the radio stations of Italian regiments and battalions in Albania and from tank-based radio stations in northern Africa. During the final phase of the war in the West and the North, the radio telegrams by reconnaissance and liaison pilots provided up-to-date and precise information on the locations of advance units and resistance centers.[103]

The monitored radio communications between England and the resistance fighters in France and Italy were particularly interesting. However, due to a lack of personnel, it was not possible to systematically monitor and evaluate them. Additional means that were used for procuring intelligence, especially informants and agents, will be discussed in upcoming chapters in connection with the activities of the Axis Section and the Allied Section.

The material that was procured through a multitude of sources was utilized in several ways.[104] The most important publication was the *information bulletin*. The procured information was processed by each bureau under the supervision of an expert officer and was included in the information bulletin by the Head of Bureaus; Masson or his deputy Werner Müller then checked the contents. Masson occasionally consulted with his staff in order to see whether certain information should really be included in the publication.[105] The information bulletin, which was printed on pink paper and was classified as secret,[106] contained a synopsis of the information that had been received on the military and military-political situation. The first issue was published on August 22, 1939, more than a week before the war started; until the end of the year, it was produced daily, with the exception of Sundays. In the first half of 1940, it was published every other day, and starting in mid-1940 twice a week. Masson insisted on keeping the concept as it was. When General Guisan asked him to include an assessment of the situation in the information bulletin once a month, he vehemently opposed the idea, arguing, "I have always made a very clear distinction between the 'information bulletin' and an 'assessment of the situation'. [The information bulletin] must contain only 'tangible' facts on the different scenes of operation. . . . The bulletin mentions *actual facts*; it does *not interpret* them nor does it speculate on future developments."[107] Masson explained that assessments of the situation had a different objective:

> They do not only give a synopsis of the overall political-military situation but also closely take into account Switzerland's position from a strategic viewpoint. The Assistant Chief of Staff for Group Ib has been drafting assessments in person (thereby expressing the intellectual aspect of his work) whenever it was of any interest to the national defense and particularly when it could have an influence on the state of preparedness of our army (increasing or reducing the number of

troops on duty, shifting the bulk of the armed forces elsewhere and consequently changing the existing lineup, etc.).[108]

In August 1939, "Reports by the Intelligence Section," which dealt with general tactical and military-political issues, also began to be published.[109] Charles Daniel from the Bureau for "Other Countries" was responsible for putting them together.[110] In June 1941, the first issue of "Lessons from the War" was published; it was written in German and French and was distributed to the commanders of all combat units.[111] Intelligence also used other channels to make its findings available to interested bodies. During wartime duty, it produced a total of 697 information bulletins, some of which included voluminous appendices, 68 "Reports by the Intelligence Section," 70 reports on "New Weapons," 14 issues of "Lessons from the War,"[112] and several overviews of uniforms of foreign armies. Moreover, it produced a large number of maps that were constantly updated to reflect the size of the area of operation, maps of specific areas, summaries of military operations that had been completed or were under way, and tables and overviews of the events over a certain period of time.[113]

The majority of the publications met with approval; the Commander-in-Chief actually commended Intelligence for them.[114] However, the content and layout of the information bulletin gave rise to continuous criticism.[115] In November 1942, following repeated criticism, including from the Federal Council and the Commander-in-Chief,[116] concerning the political information in the bulletin, Intelligence stopped publishing the special section entitled "General Political Situation" and focused exclusively on strictly military issues.[117] However, criticism was also frequently voiced concerning the reporting on military matters.

Staff members of Intelligence were particularly sensitive about misstated facts in the bulletin, and the documents that still exist on that matter are interesting in several respects. They provide an insight into the section's working procedures, exemplify with what issues it was dealing, and discuss fundamental ideas about the tasks and methods of an Intelligence Service. When Deputy Chief Werner Müller noticed that the bulletin of June 17, 1941, contained information about Germany that he described as "wrong and unverified," he told Max Waibel:

First of all, it is not true at all that 10 German divisions and 20 Romanian divisions are stationed northwest of the Black Sea. If you had verified this information with Major Daniel of the General Staff, you would have known right away that it was wrong because a few days ago one of our most reliable couriers returned from Bucharest with valuable information. . . . The lives of our own people are put at risk every day in the border area in the West in order to obtain reliable information. What use is their sacrifice if their results are not evaluated? I know where you obtained the information about the divisions in question; this source has to be considered as suspicious because the information could not be verified *before* it was issued; hence, the most basic criterion was missing for using this information. I no longer authorize you to use this source without verifying with the French Bureau the information that it provides.[118]

Müller was particularly annoyed because he had signed the bulletin before it was published without reading it and consequently had his name associated with the false information. However, unlike Masson, he blamed his subordinates for the mistake, arguing:

As I had too much to do in the morning of 17 June [1941], I could not go over the information bulletin before it was printed. However, I should not have to do that because I am allowed to assume that after doing this work for so long, the bureau heads should be able to judge how useful a piece of information is and should be aware that Intelligence's good reputation concerning the credibility of its information must not be carelessly jeopardized. General Staff officers should be expected to work together as a matter of course. Once France had disappeared from the scene of the war, it was established that the French Bureau would handle the military information in the sector between Basel and Geneva, the occupied and unoccupied part of France, and the French colonies. The French Bureau is extremely well organized for this task, and its head is very diligent, as should be expected. Even though it . . . transmits the information to the German Bureau for inclusion in the bulletin, the French Bureau is therefore fully responsible for the military information that comes from the areas mentioned above. The German Bureau handles the military information in the sectors to the north and northeast, as has been the case since the beginning of wartime duty. Regarding the areas that are occupied by Germany or are under its direct military influence, particularly in the southeast, the texts for the bulletin have to be finalized above all with Major Daniel of the General Staff (Bureau for Other Countries), as he is the officer who organizes the courier service in that area.

Likewise, for the sector to the south, i.e. Italy, texts have to be finalized with Captain Stelling.[119]

Occasionally the appendices to the information bulletins were not written with the necessary care, either because of time pressure or for some less objective reason, resulting in information being circulated that was "superficial, contradictory, or even wrong."[120] In March 1943, a particularly blatant case induced Waibel to write a sarcastic five-page letter to Colonel Müller in which he stated:

I am under the impression that Major Ernst's absence was used by certain gentlemen to have their supposed knowledge printed on paper. . . . Another appendix to the bulletin[121] was apparently written by the same circle of amateurs. It is titled "New Weapons—Germany.". . . The gossip and insinuations that it contains are more suitable for a tabloid than for official information on new weapons in an official publication by the Army Command. . . . For instance, what do they mean by the sentence, "at this range (1000 meters), each thrower should cover an area of 300 square meters"? Well, of course any piece of artillery with an 18 cm caliber will have an impact in an area of 300 square meters! 300 square meters correspond to a circle with a radius of less than 10 meters! Who is it who produces these platitudes, which show every officer that the manufacturer knows nothing about ballistics and lacks the basics of arms theory. Since when does the range have an influence on the impact of a warhead? What will the experts of the armament section think about this nonsense? In the same appendix, it is claimed that the MG 42 [machine gun] has been seen for the first time among the troops fighting in Tunis. Maybe the author saw them for the first time in a weekly news show on Tunis, but this is definitely not an "observation" that Intelligence should include in a bulletin. The MG 42 has been used for many months at the front both in the East and in Africa. Moreover, it is well known that in their weekly news shows in foreign countries, the Germans like to introduce secret weapons as novelties; hence, cinemagoers can procure intelligence for a small amount of money and without taking any risks. *Sancta simplicitas*.[122]

The criticism that was voiced about the content of the information bulletins raises the question about the quality of the *evaluation* of intelligence. The procurement apparatus of both the Axis Section and the Allied Section was continuously expanded, whereas the organization of the evaluation team remained on the same modest level throughout wartime duty even though the amount of incoming information increased constantly. This situation inevitably put a great strain on the evaluation staff; eventually they were overworked, which affected their output. In addition, they were unable to analyze or interpret the large amount of available information as thoroughly as they could have done if they had had additional staff to assist them. In his final activity report on the Axis Section, which he headed at the end of the war, Captain Rolf Eberhard dryly stated, "There was enough material available that *could* have yielded worthwhile and interesting information."[123] Nevertheless, the most essential information was processed.[124] However, from the very beginning the evaluation staff could not afford to systematically process the numerous short messages, even though that would have been the only way to pick up in time the "signals" that were hidden among the "noise." Due to the permanent pressure to "economize" on personnel and material, the evaluation staff had to focus on the plans of operation and actions that could potentially be directed against Switzerland.[125] In other words, the material that was received from the different sources mentioned earlier in this chapter had to be evaluated mainly in view of being regularly published in the pink information bulletin.

As the bulletin was published daily at first, then every other day, and then twice a week, before being published only once a week as of mid-May 1945, it was not possible to amass the incoming information up to a point in time where it could systematically be presented in a larger context. Eberhard remarked, "It was possible to report on individual issues (losses, backup troops, transport situation, and similar matters) in a larger context only during times when there was relatively little fighting."[126] However, most of the time matters were so pressing[127] that the latest development could be mentioned just in a few key words. Following this first basic processing, the material had to be filed[128] in order to be at hand whenever one of the numerous questions had to be answered that a number of authorities addressed to the individual sections of Intelligence, or in order to be used for regular synopses.

An essential aspect of the evaluation process was briefing the Chief of Intelligence whenever he had to make an *assessment of the situation* for the Commander-in-Chief or the Chief of the General Staff. During critical times, the Axis Section had to bear the bulk of the responsibility for this preparation, as the threat emanated mainly from the Germans.

The more the German Armed Forces disintegrated, the more difficult it became to undertake studies on their organization, as had been done at the beginning of the war in order to assess the Reich's operational capabilities. Eberhard stated, "The improvisations that were spreading among the German

Army made it impossible to assess the Germans' remaining capabilities purely based on military aspects."[129] In order to get a rough idea about these capabilities, other factors, such as the economy, the state of nutrition, the state of traffic routes and means of transport, as well as other aspects had to be taken into account. Eberhard commented, "[In] many instances, it was considered that making observations and reporting about these other factors went beyond Army Intelligence's responsibility."[130]

The Security Service

Any overview of the structure of Swiss Intelligence would be incomplete without also briefly analyzing the domestic Security Service; its close connection to the Intelligence Service was expressed as of 1941 in the official name "Intelligence and Security Section."

The Security Service played a role in the connection between Masson and Schellenberg insofar as some of its staff had close ties with the Intelligence Service. This chapter only gives a brief overview of the Security Service because specific issues will be discussed later in connection with Meyer-Schwertenbach's activities.

The close ties between the Security Service and the Intelligence Service were obvious above all through the fact that the head of the Security Service, Colonel Werner Müller of the General Staff,[131] was at the same time Masson's deputy in the Intelligence Service. Of all the branches that became part of the Security Service in the course of wartime duty, at the beginning of the war only Counterintelligence was integrated into the Intelligence Service, using *Groupe du Lac*[132] as a cover name. From 1939 to March 1941, the Military Police reported to the Adjutant General's Office, and the military police officers were brought together, technically under the Police Section of the Territorial Service, reporting to the Head of the Territorial Service. This separation of powers and tasks[133] soon proved to be inconvenient, particularly because "in the era of total warfare the police-related tasks of the army and the federal civilian authorities were frequently bound to overlap."[134] Hence, in March 1941 all military police bodies were brought together under the Security Service. Henceforth the Security Service consisted of Counterintelligence,[135] which was headed by Colonel Robert Jaquillard,[136] the Military Police, which was headed by Lieutenant Colonel Jakob Müller, and the Police Section, which was headed by Lieutenant Colonel Lang.

The main tasks of the Security Service[137] included:

• coordinating the work of the army's security and police bodies;

- preventing unrest inside the country;
- carrying out counterintelligence activities and preventing sabotage;
- taking steps to safeguard military secrets;
- monitoring subversive elements (Swiss and foreign nationals);
- combating subversive propaganda in the army;
- training, equipping, and organizing the Military Police.

The frictions between Intelligence and Counterintelligence will be discussed later. It is important to know, however, that differences, difficulties, clashing intentions, and disagreements also existed within the Security Service itself as well as between the Security Service and the Federal Police. While Masson tried to find a solution for improving cooperation within the Security Service, he failed to do so within the Intelligence Service, as will be seen in the next few chapters. At first one might be surprised to hear that there were conflicts within the Security Service because it seemed to have clearly defined responsibilities. At the end of September 1939, Federal Councillor Obrecht, Minger's deputy, had asked the government's authorization to create a *military counterintelligence service*,[138] explaining, "Counterintelligence shall deal exclusively with crimes that are directed against the Swiss Army. Hence, any other similar crimes that are not directed against the army shall continue to be handled entirely by the regular police authorities and the Attorney General's Office."[139] The need for a counterintelligence service arose from the experiences of World War I as well as "from the recognition that at the present time belligerent countries [considered] espionage and sabotage activities to be even more important than back then, so that it [is] absolutely necessary to have strict surveillance in this area."[140]

The way in which Obrecht formulated his request was an indication of the fact that the existing police authorities viewed the creation of Counterintelligence with skepticism, fearing that the new body would interfere with their own activities. However, that was not intended; the police of the Attorney General's Office (the Federal Police) were to monitor and counter political and economic espionage, whereas Counterintelligence was to prevent military espionage. Hence, in theory the two bodies had two different functions. In reality, however, political-economic espionage very often went hand in hand with military espionage because agents working for foreign countries frequently had complex missions involving military as well as political or economic issues. Especially during times of total warfare, the two activities could not be clearly distinguished. As long as the two counterespionage organizations did not coordinate their efforts, the measures that they took independently from each other were bound to overlap time and again. Since it was difficult to determine what kind of intelligence a spy was procuring to begin with, it was indispensable for the two bodies to work together if they wanted to avoid doing the same job twice, and thwarting, or even rendering illusory, each other's efforts.[141] An investigating magistrate later observed, "However, they . . . did *not* work together; this flaw . . . was due mainly to personal tensions and reservations."[142]

In addition to personal differences, there were objective reasons for the frictions between the two bodies, resulting from the different ways in which they worked. The *Attorney General's Office* and its police authorities focused on identifying punishable offenses, i.e. on having offenders punished according to the law or, if the offender was a foreign national, on establishing the constitutional facts based on which the Federal Council could expel him. Consequently, the Attorney General's Office proceeded cautiously and relatively slowly; even in cases where it was convinced that the law had been broken, it sometimes had to wait for a suitable moment to secure the evidence. *Counterintelligence* on the other hand was set up to *fight* other countries' military spying activities. It had to intervene whenever an activity posed a potential threat to the national defense, and it had to do so quickly. Counterintelligence had to prevent harm from being done. It was not interested in a spy being punished after the fact but in preventing him from spying.[143]

Apparently the personal differences were more serious than the objective dissimilarities. Bracher, the deputy director of the Federal Military Administration, explained to Federal President Kobelt, "One should know that before the outbreak of the war, both Colonel Jaquillard and Colonel Werner Müller were hoping to be put in charge of the Federal Police. When their hopes were shattered, both candidates began to display a bitter attitude which has been running like a thread through all relations between the Federal Police and Counterintelligence."[144] On the other hand, Bracher admitted that the Federal Police had not always acted adroitly. After the war, in connection with the security measures taken in advance of official visits by Field Marshal Montgomery, Queen Juliana, and Churchill, he was surprised "to have to notice that several commanders of cantonal and city police corps were not delighted about the interference by the Federal Police."[145] Bracher considered that this reluctance was due to the fact that the cantons were used to having authority in police-related matters, as well as to the Federal Police's inability to establish a trusting relationship with the commanders of the cantonal and city police authorities. Bracher added: "This is where Counterintelligence, which was headed by chiefs of cantonal and city police forces, came into play. Messrs. Jaquillard from the canton of Vaud, Müller from the canton of Bern, and Haudenschild from the canton of Thurgau were better than the Federal Police at working together with their colleagues from the cantons and cities. That in turn aroused the suspicion of the Federal Police."[146]

The Federal Police evidently endeavored to establish contact with Counterintelligence, but Counterintelligence was standoffish. It failed to give up its reservations even when it was indispensable for the two organizations to exchange information. Counterintelligence Inspector Gohl asserted: "At briefings we kept being told that the issues were kept separate; Counterintelligence was responsible for countering espionage activities, and the Federal Police were responsible for political matters. Hence, we generally did not inform the Federal Police about our observations and inquiries."[147]

In early 1943, Masson called a meeting to consult with the concerned bodies on how to overcome the unfortunate situation and coordinate the various activities of the Security Service. The meeting resulted in the creation of an umbrella organization called *Bureau R*. According to the terms of reference that Masson gave the new body, its purpose was to coordinate the activities of all bodies working for the Security Service in order to step up their efforts at countering espionage, sabotage, and illegal border-crossings; in particular, it was to collect the information that the various bodies and offices were gathering and forward it to the interested military and civilian bodies. Through this cooperation, a maximum of information was to be evaluated and overlapping activities and conflicts were to be avoided. Hence, in this instance, Masson tried to come up with a solution for existing problems; as will be pointed out in the upcoming chapters, he failed to do so in the case of the Intelligence Service.

The coordinating body was not able to accomplish its task as well as had been intended, which was due to the fact that the bodies of Counterintelligence continued to show a standoffish attitude. Nevertheless, it is remarkable that Masson made an attempt at creating an institution that was to systematically coordinate the activities of all bodies among the Security Service and at getting them to cooperate in the interest of the overall objective. Strangely, it appears that in the area of the Intelligence Service no effort at all was made toward finding a solution. However, this statement needs to be qualified by adding that institutions are only as good as the people who work for, and with, them. As long as there was no *willingness* to work together, a coordinating bureau or a meeting to assess the situation could do little to effect change.

4

The French Bureau—
Allied Section

A CLOSER LOOK at the Allied Section and the Axis Section[1] demonstrates how Swiss Army Intelligence operated on a day-to-day basis and what difficulties it faced in procuring intelligence. These case studies reveal some fundamental aspects of Swiss Intelligence during World War II. Moreover, they shed light on the atmosphere and the working conditions in the Intelligence Service and on the mentality of some of the staff—people who had an understanding for what was essential, were courageous and ready to make sacrifices, were fighting an uphill battle against people who were shortsighted, small-minded, fearful, cowardly, envious, put their personal interests first, or had a tendency to plot against others. This internal struggle sometimes required more energy than the actual task of finding out about the intentions of *foreign* opponents. These circumstances make it easier to understand why the Masson-Schellenberg connection acted as a catalyst within Army Intelligence.

The events surrounding the French Bureau, which was expanded to the Allied Section in mid-summer 1942, make clear how Swiss Intelligence tried to adjust to the constantly changing situation during World War II. In the case of the French Bureau, the numerous stages in setting up and expanding the procurement activities can be divided into five phases: the time of the Phony War

(September 1, 1939 to May 10, 1940); Germany's campaign in the West (May 10 to June 25, 1940); the period from the armistice to Germany's occupation of all of France (June 25, 1940 to November 11, 1942); the time from Germany's occupation of Vichy to the Allied invasion of France (November 11, 1942 to June 6, 1944); and the time from the Allied invasion to Germany's capitulation (June 6, 1944 to May 8, 1945).

The Phony War
(September 1, 1939 to May 10, 1940)

The first eight months of World War II provided Swiss Army Intelligence with a much needed opportunity to expand its structure. In his activity report after the war, Major Bernard Cuénoud of the General Staff, the head of the Allied Section, commented, "Recruitments [were] pushed to the extreme."[2] When the army was called up, a substantial weakness instantly became apparent within Army Intelligence. According to Cuénoud, "Our service lost a number of its best informants because they had to leave their home in order to join the Swiss Army. Hence, the Intelligence Service, which was based on volunteer informants, showed its first *major flaw*, which must be described as a *fundamental shortcoming*."[3] Virtually all Swiss males who lived abroad were to serve in the Swiss Army; Intelligence's best sources in France and Belgium were therefore gone from one day to the next. Cuénoud remarked, "It is not exaggerating to say that we had to start from scratch."[4]

Similar to Max Waibel from the German Bureau who activated his contacts in Berlin,[5] Cuénoud made use of contacts "with some French personalities and Swiss living abroad" whom he had met when he was detailed to the French 25th Division and 13th Army Corps.[6] These connections turned out to be valuable.

Despite the inadequate means that Intelligence had available, the information that it procured at that time can be considered as satisfactory; however, that information did not meet its needs. In particular, Intelligence was not able to verify the obtained information in a fast and reliable manner because, among other reasons, it did not have any *agents* whom it could use on a regular basis. Cuénoud explained, "[We] had to find some specialists as fast as possible, train them thoroughly, and organize a system of tours that allowed them to get to the regions that were occupied by French troops, using valid reasons, such as commercial or industrial interests."[7] Cuénoud was quite successful with this system, by which the agents followed a carefully planned route and were back in Switzerland within two or three days. This procedure was continuously refined,

Agents used by the French Bureau and the Allied Section

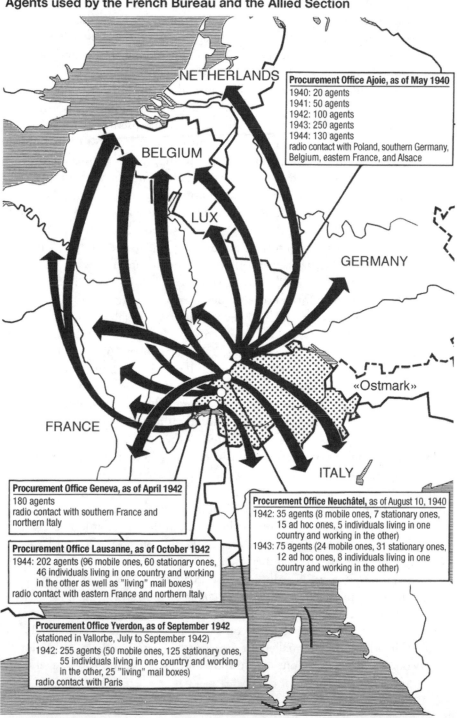

NETHERLANDS

BELGIUM

LUX

GERMANY

«Ostmark»

FRANCE

ITALY

Procurement Office Ajoie, as of May 1940
1940: 20 agents
1941: 50 agents
1942: 100 agents
1943: 250 agents
1944: 130 agents
radio contact with Poland, southern Germany,
Belgium, eastern France, and Alsace

Procurement Office Geneva, as of April 1942
180 agents
radio contact with southern France and
northern Italy

Procurement Office Lausanne, as of October 1942
1944: 202 agents (96 mobile ones, 60 stationary ones,
46 individuals living in one country and working
in the other as well as "living" mail boxes)
radio contact with eastern France and northern Italy

Procurement Office Yverdon, as of September 1942
(stationed in Vallorbe, July to September 1942)
1942: 255 agents (50 mobile ones, 125 stationary ones,
55 individuals living in one country and working
in the other, 25 "living" mail boxes)
radio contact with Paris

Procurement Office Neuchâtel, as of August 10, 1940
1942: 35 agents (8 mobile ones, 7 stationary ones,
15 ad hoc ones, 5 individuals living in one
country and working in the other)
1943: 75 agents (24 mobile ones, 31 stationary ones,
12 ad hoc ones, 8 individuals living in one
country and working in the other)

and for the first time it allowed Intelligence to cross-check the information that it had received.

In accordance with the preferred way of camouflaging the missions, during the first months of wartime duty most agents were traveling salesmen and industry or business representatives who had spontaneously and selflessly agreed to help out Swiss Intelligence. Even though many of them took great risks on the routes that the French Bureau had established for them, they did not even ask to be reimbursed for the expenses they incurred during their extended reconnaissance tours. In addition, Cuénoud used a number of itinerant agents who occasionally visited informants in France. Most of the informants were Swiss living abroad who were able to supply a lot of precise information that they had obtained from friends or family members or through their own observations. Other sources of information included customs officials and border patrols with whom Cuénoud managed to establish good relations. Contacts with employees of the French railways were also useful, as they were able to provide first-rate information on movements of troops. Moreover, French deserters and travelers were questioned when entering Switzerland; their place of origin and place of destination were recorded on so-called immigration forms.[8] However, the information recorded on the immigration forms was used only to verify information that had been procured through other means.

Together with the rest of the Army Staff, on September 5, 1939, Intelligence moved from Bern to Spiez, and on October 16, 1939, from Spiez to Langnau, where they remained until June 3, 1940. Due to the need to receive information as quickly as possible, Cuénoud had the idea of creating outposts that were closer to the country's border. The first outpost was set up in May 1940 in *Porrentruy*, and a second one was established soon thereafter in *Lausanne*. These two outposts immediately turned out to be extremely useful. The information that the French Bureau procured became much more precise right away. Additional outposts were created in *Neuchâtel*, *Yverdon*, and *Geneva*. Their staffs were paid out of the Army Staff budget. In addition to these outposts, with time several other external bureaus were created whose staff were volunteers and whose heads continued to work in their regular jobs as civilians.

After a short time, the French Bureau had nine outposts between Basel and Geneva, and in 1942 the number increased to as many as eleven;[9] they were named "N.S. 3, N.S.3a, N.S.3b, N.S.4, N.S.5," etc. "N.S." being an abbreviation for the German word *Nachrichtensammelstelle* (intelligence procurement office). Toward the end of the war, the number of outposts decreased to six; they were located in Geneva, Nyon, Lausanne, Yverdon, Neuchâtel, and Ajoie;[10] in addition, two smaller outposts were operating in Bern and Fribourg. Every outpost had a head, one or two staff, and a variable number of agents and sub-agents in foreign countries who could be used continuously, temporarily, or on a volunteer basis.[11]

The most essential *tasks of the outposts* consisted of recruiting and training urgently needed agents. There were six categories of agents: agents crossing the border on a regular basis; living mail boxes with whom messages could be left; stationary agents; itinerant agents; passive informants; and active informers.[12] They were supervised by the outposts according to the requirements of the French Bureau. In addition, the outposts also monitored the German and French border police, liaised with the Swiss customs authorities, questioned immigrants (in 1941, Cuénoud distributed about 130 forms a day to the individual outposts), and interrogated French prisoners of war who had fled from the advancing German troops, as well as civilian refugees from Alsace (they were handled primarily by the outposts in *Ajoie* and *Neuchâtel*). Cuénoud assigned a specific area to every outpost for reconnaissance activities; however, the areas intentionally overlapped, "making it possible to cross-check information practically in an automatic manner."[13]

Germany's Campaign in the West (May 10 to June 25, 1940)

Things changed once France capitulated. Until June 1940, it was relatively easy, albeit not without danger, to obtain information about events in the neighboring country to the west. Cuénoud reported, "The French are talkative and carefree, so they were happy to talk about what they knew.[14] The French border troops did not always take their job seriously; they had numerous shortcomings, of which we took advantage."[15] When the Germans arrived at the border between France and Switzerland, the French Bureau was shocked to find out that for the second time in the middle of a critical period of time, the majority of its *sources of information were gone*. When the Germans abruptly decided to virtually seal the border, the entire procurement system that had been set up during the first months of the war collapsed. Cuénoud explained, "Within a very short period of time, the border officials and the border patrols have turned blind. The trains no longer run and mail service no longer exists. The people who live in one country and work in the other no longer cross the border. The Swiss industrialists who have relations with France can no longer leave Switzerland."[16] No one at the French Bureau had expected this to happen.

A new organization had to be created in a hurry, and new ways and means had to be found to reach into occupied France in a *clandestine* manner. The Germans' draconian measures were effective, deterring most agents from going on any new mission to France. It was all the more difficult to recruit new agents, as Cuénoud preferred to use only Swiss who made themselves available out of patriotism and were willing to work for free if possible. Only a few French nationals were recruited whose pro-Swiss attitude was beyond the shadow of a doubt.

The search for new agents turned out to be a permanent, challenging task.[17] Cuénoud commented, "After a first 'outing,' many agents were impressed by the many dangers that they had encountered and declared that they would under no circumstances do this again. The Germans do not only very closely monitor our border but at numerous checkpoints also stop anyone who travels inside the country."[18] An officer traveling from Pontarlier to Vesoul via Besançon and back to Switzerland via Gray, Dijon, and Dôle was checked a total of 17 times during his trip. On six occasions, his car was taken apart. He got away each time by convincing the Germans that he was the director of a factory near Mouchard. When he clandestinely crossed the border into Switzerland at Les Verrières, he explained that it was absolutely impossible to conduct any more reconnaissance activities. It had taken him five days for a trip that he used to be able to easily complete within 24 hours.

From the Armistice to the Occupation of All of France (June 25, 1940 to November 11, 1942)

The need for additional procurement agents resulted in the creation of further outposts. By August 10, 1940, an outpost was operating in Neuchâtel, and as of July 1942, another outpost was operating in Vallorbe; it was later transferred to Yverdon. The three outposts near Switzerland's northwestern border, Porrentruy, Neuchâtel, and Vallorbe, were dealing with France, Belgium, and Holland; moreover, they received the information originating from Great Britain. The outposts in Lausanne and Geneva were focusing on the unoccupied part of France and the countries in the south.[19]

In the 1941 activity report, Cuénoud remarked, "More than ever before, today the German authorities suspect any Swiss who is staying in the occupied zone of being an agent of the [British] 'Intelligence Service'[20] and accuse him of clandestinely crossing our border in order to report to the British officials in our country what he has seen or heard."[21] Countless difficulties had to be surmounted every day, and on numerous occasions small details nearly brought the entire operation to a halt.[22] Nevertheless, during peak times the number of successful border crossings by agents reached almost 50 a week. Cuénoud added, "By December 1, 1941, one Swiss soldier alone had undertaken a total of 120 trips abroad, crossing the border clandestinely 240 times without encountering any difficulty."[23]

The French Bureau was in contact with a large number of *informants* who all agreed to supply information for free. Interesting connections existed with Paris, Le Havre, Nantes, Bordeaux, Bayonne, and most other major cities in unoccupied France.

When the French Bureau was expanded to the Allied Section in August 1942, the most important change consisted of transferring one officer from the outpost in Lausanne to Intelligence headquarters in Interlaken, where he handled issues pertaining to England and the United States.[24] However, it was almost impossible to procure information from these two countries because Swiss Army Intelligence had not established any structures there. The Allied Section could not afford to send agents across the Channel or the Atlantic. Moreover, the courier service was irregular, making it impossible to procure intelligence in a systematic manner. At least it had some stationary agents in Great Britain who transmitted their information via Cherbourg, Le Havre, and Antwerp.

From Germany's Occupation of Vichy to the Allied Invasion of France (November 11, 1942 to June 6, 1944)

When German troops occupied the "free" part of France, in response to the Allied landings in North Africa in November 1942, Switzerland became completely encircled by the Axis powers. However, the Allied Section now had more funds available for its agents and consequently obtained some "very good results."[25] Agents working for Swiss Intelligence, some of whom were equipped with micro-cameras, were able to get hold of Germany's potential evacuation plans from France and procured information based on which the Allied Section was able to draw a detailed map of all German fortifications along the Atlantic wall, among other things.[26] At the same time, Swiss Intelligence observed how underground French resistance organizations were created, and was kept informed about their planned acts of sabotage. Cuénoud explained, "Through original documents we knew well in advance what the entire set-up was for sabotaging the French railway network."[27]

These results were all the more remarkable as the conditions for procuring intelligence had probably become even worse by that time.[28] The Allied Section continued using as stationary agents some Swiss who had been living in Belgium or France for many years, but as the war progressed it used fewer and fewer Swiss as itinerant agents. According to Cuénoud, "The increasing number of difficulties that had to be surmounted showed that in France the role of itinerant agents could be accomplished only by French nationals who *thoroughly* knew their country and its ways and traditions, and who had many friends and acquaintances where they could hide at any moment; very few Swiss could do that."[29] (A difficulty of its own kind for Cuénoud's staff consisted of getting gasoline and tires for the itinerant agents' vehicles.) Recruiting new agents was dangerous. Employees of the French national railways could no longer be asked for information because they were very closely monitored by officials of the German railways. The Gestapo was omnipresent, and Cuénoud commented, "It recruits French personnel and pays them well. Denouncements have reached a level that one would not have thought possible in France; the confidence is gone. There is a much greater risk now of *hiring a double agent.*"[30] On two occasions, the Allied Section fell victim to double agents. In one instance, an outpost hired an agent who secretly worked for the Germans;[31] and he betrayed seven Swiss agents, six of whom were executed.[32] In the other instance, a female agent working as a liaison person between the outpost in Ajoie and Alsace denounced a number of other agents to the other side.

The new situation called for a different kind of agent. Cuénoud explained, "Small agents who provide a limited number of services have to be dropped. One has to find agents who are up to the task, intellectuals who are capable of evaluating the situation and analyzing problems on a larger scale."[33] On the organizational level, a change had to be made as well; isolated agents who relied on themselves had to be replaced by cells—small, independent groups of foreign-based sub-agents whose work was coordinated by a head. For security reasons, only the itinerant agent knew who the head of a cell was. For the same reason, the sub-agents were not allowed to know how the Allied Section was structured.

The increasing risks associated with crossing the border forced Cuénoud and his staff to come up with new methods for transmitting intelligence. Up until that time, carrier pigeons had been used after being smuggled across the border in baskets. However, due to the tightened screening procedures and in view of the limited value of some of the information that was procured in that manner, it was not always justified to take the risk of getting caught. Therefore, dogs were successfully used instead of birds, and even *cats* turned out to be approachable for the needs of Swiss Intelligence; many of them successfully crossed the border unharmed. The more unorthodox the methods, the more effective they were; for example, the Allied Section was successful in hiding important information inside cowbells.

While it was possible to procure interesting information about the fighting in North Africa, it continued to be difficult to set up an intelligence mechanism in England. As a rule, Swiss Intelligence had to make do with reports from

Switzerland's military attaché in London, but his messages could never be evaluated as such; they contained very general information that, if anything, only served to verify other information. This fact could not be held against the military attaché; the connection was simply not as useful as others. Moreover, as his information reached Switzerland through diplomatic channels, it was prone to disruptions. Cuénoud explained, "On the eve of the invasion, when England forbade all diplomatic communication and did not even allow coded telegrams to be sent out, the effect could be felt right away."[34] Connections with anti-British French officers and marines who tattled interesting details to agents of the Allied Section were of more immediate value. For information from the United States, the Allied Section had to rely entirely on Switzerland's military attaché in Washington, DC, plus newspapers and magazines. Cuénoud also had considerable difficulties procuring intelligence about the military situation in southern Italy; the news from the Anglo-American front there reached Intelligence headquarters on a detour via Tunis, Algiers, and Spain, frequently resulting in delays.[35]

From the Allied Invasion to Germany's Capitulation (June 6, 1944 to May 8, 1945)

Once the Allies landed in Normandy, Swiss Intelligence faced new challenges. It was difficult to pick out the signals from the background of noise and keep up with the events in the war. It was particularly difficult to verify procured information. Cuénoud commented, "This was the time of false rumors, of intentionally disseminated misinformation."[36] It was much easier to follow Germany's retreat than to stay on top of the situation in the Allied camp. The foreign agents whom the Allied Section had been using successfully were willing to work against the Germans, the enemies of their home country; however, they categorically refused to pass on information about the Allies, their liberators. Cuénoud stated, "For that reason, many agents completely refused to assist us, even though they were very devoted to us."[37]

For the third time during the war, after September 1939 and June 1940, Cuénoud considered it necessary to reorganize his intelligence network. This task was all the more demanding as the Swiss had to deal not only with an increasing mistrust on the part of the French but also with numerous new security measures and monitoring activities that the Allied troops established at Switzerland's western border. When the Allies reached the Swiss border in September 1944 they replaced the Germans' procedures, which had been seen through by then, with entirely new measures. According to Cuénoud, this was a "new war zone; there was a different password for every sector; road traffic was checked; flying patrols were used; one was not allowed to approach border checkpoints; the forbidden zone was re-established at our border into which Swiss were not allowed to enter; *ordres de mission* from the American forces or the new French Army were required in order to travel inside France; and for a long time, all trains were canceled."[38] In addition, it was almost impossible for Swiss Intelligence officers to establish reconnaissance activities on the Allied side because they were well known after having been in close contact with people in France earlier in the war. Also, as a handicap on the psychological level, after the Allied landing Swiss Intelligence had to deal with the widespread opinion in its own country that the war was practically over and therefore Switzerland was no longer under any threat. Cuénoud summarized the change of mood by stating, "The Swiss' fear of a German invasion gave way to their frequently excessive, indiscriminate sympathy for everything that had to do with the Allies."[39]

The German Bureau—
Axis Section

THE PROBLEMS THAT EXISTED in the German Bureau and the Axis Section were one of the reasons why Masson considered it necessary to establish his own connection with Walter Schellenberg. On the other hand, the Masson-Schellenberg connection was precisely what triggered a major stir within the German Bureau.

Before the war, the *German Bureau* of the Intelligence Section comprised one single General Staff officer who had to handle the entire procurement and evaluation process. At the beginning of June 1939, Alfred Ernst, a Ph.D. in law[1] who had been working for a private law firm, became its head, initially on a temporary basis. He replaced Arnold H. Schwengeler, who joined the *Bund* newspaper as an editor.[2] Ernst realized that the lack of personnel had negative consequences, stating, "Because the [international] situation kept deteriorating as of mid-July, I had to pay more attention to the movements of troops in Germany. As a consequence, I was so busy that I could not pay the necessary attention to organizing the procurement process for the event of a war."[3]

Six Sources of Information

When the war began, the German Bureau had only six sources of information available, and they did not all meet the same quality standards.[4]

1. *Bureau Ha*

This was an intelligence service set up in Teufen near St. Gallen on the initiative of Hans Hausamann, who had excellent contacts and enjoyed a special status[5] within Army Intelligence.[6] He maintained a long-lasting, trusting relationship with Masson.[7] The two officers had met when Masson became head of Section 5 of the General Staff Unit. Hausamann explained: "From that moment on, until the war broke out I was in constant close contact with Colonel-Brigadier Masson. Before the war, I saw him practically every week."[8] It is understandable that Masson was very interested in this contact because the official Intelligence Service was in its infancy at that time and Hausamann's own intelligence service met a real need.

At the end of May 1938, upon returning from an "information trip," Hausamann told Masson:

I now have several connections. In my opinion, it should now no longer be possible:
1. for Germany to decide to attack without my finding out about it in time through quasi "official channels";
2. for Germany to deploy a large number of troops to areas around Czechoslovakia without my finding out about it in time, this time through "illegal" channels.
Obviously the "legal" channels do not know that "illegal" channels now also exist, and vice versa. The legal authorities still communicate with me directly in a quasi unofficial manner, but for the illegal collaborators I have established a post office box under a cover name at the main post office in a major Swiss city where all messages are addressed according to a pre-established code. All necessary security measures have been taken—in a warlike fashion.[9]

Hausamann's best-known connection was the one with Rudolf Roessler, alias *Lucy*.[10] In addition, he had connections in a number of European capitals and headquarters from Helsinki to Madrid.[11] Hausamann explained, "To give an example, when Admiral Canaris, the head of the German Armed Forces Intelligence, traveled to Madrid in order to have a top-secret meeting with a

Swedish liaison person for the Allies, I knew about it through Madrid before Canaris returned to Berlin, and I also knew what was said [at that meeting]."[12] Hausamann had radio contact with some particularly important bodies.[13] He later explained that the cipher branch of German Intelligence, which had of course listened in on his radio communications, had never been able to decipher any of the outgoing and incoming telegrams because the code was changed constantly—the keys were actually changed daily according to a carefully prepared plan—and because radio messages were never sent or received in one piece via one frequency but were cut up and sent via two or three different frequencies.[14]

Hausamann was very productive. During the course of the war, he submitted more than 10,000 messages and reports to Swiss Army Intelligence; however, in these written pieces he often expressed his own political convictions. The Commander-in-Chief was not the only one who repeatedly criticized Hausamann's tendency to mingle facts with commentary.[15] *Bureau Ha* wrote some good reports and several excellent ones,[16] but it was not immune from transmitting false information. In 1942, Hausamann remarked to Masson: "I remember the first months of the war when I transmitted the reports of aides. You certainly also remember how many complaints were voiced back then. The complaints ceased the day I began writing my reports and messages on my own again."[17] Because of the inaccurate reports during that time, the Assistant Chief of Staff for the Front, to whom the Intelligence Service reported at the beginning of wartime duty, had actually tried to dismiss Hausamann from Army Intelligence. At the end of September 1939, he wrote to Masson: "Due to the constant false information that the so-called Bureau Hausamann keeps sending us, and in view of the self-important and agitated behavior of Captain Hausamann (poster on his front door), I order you to close the Bureau in Teufen and dismiss Captain Hausamann from his post. He could perhaps be transferred to the reserves. Please let me know by what date these measures can be carried out. The deadline is October 5, 1939."[18] However, Masson did not want to do without this source of information.[19]

There were repeated frictions between Hausamann and other members of Army Intelligence that were due to objective reasons as well as to differences of character. Based on the written evidence, one gains the impression that Hausamann felt hampered by regulations and hierarchical structures that were over-emphasized for reasons of prestige.[20] Moreover, as a self-confident free entrepreneur,[21] Hausamann was bound to clash with the officials at the Intelligence Service who were small-minded and arrogant. An incident that occurred in May 1940 exemplifies the tensions that existed: Hausamann was summoned to Procurement Office 1 of Army Intelligence by telephone; there

Schafroth told him in a heated tone that Intelligence had found out that the reports by *Bureau Ha* were being sent to other bodies as well. Hausamann claimed to be entitled to this privilege, as he had made sure that he was able to have direct access to the Federal Council and General Guisan at any time. The other members of Army Intelligence, including Masson, who ended up having to authorize Hausamann to maintain these direct contacts, were deeply annoyed by this special treatment. However, Hausamann insisted on his privilege, pointing out that even though he put his own private intelligence service at the disposal of Army Intelligence, he continued to be his own boss. It appeared that Schafroth had not known that.[22]

In addition to such heated discussions, which were due to a lack of finesse and to strained working relations, there were also "factual differences of opinion and clashing views about certain issues in connection with the number of German troops in certain areas."[23] Moreover, some disputes were rooted in Hausamann's tendency to exaggerate about his secret sources. One of his "casual connections to England, which [he said] he [had been] able to establish because [he] was trusted to be absolutely discreet, set up and maintained with great difficulty on behalf of" Masson, and with which he claimed to be in permanent contact via telegraph, turned out to be a subscription to the Zurich-based *Exchange Telegraph* press agency.[24] In May 1940, Max Waibel sharply criticized Hausamann's predisposition, arguing:

> From the perspective of someone procuring intelligence in a serious manner, it is objectionable for *Pilatus*[25] to combine miscellaneous messages from sources of heterogeneous quality into one report and mystify them. Moreover, one should not weave subjective opinions into a report, as does Hausamann. The Intelligence Service needs factual, objective information mentioning from what milieu the sources originate. That is the only way to verify and evaluate the information from such reports and documents. First Lieutenant Meyer[-Schwertenbach] told me that French Intelligence refused to accept one of Hausamann's important sources even though France is at war; it appears strange that we do not only accept these reports but also pay a lot of money for them.[26] Also, yesterday we found out that unfortunately another one of Hausamann's important sources, "at Ribbentrop's office," is an agent who supplies other places with the same information.[27]

Hausamann was an extraordinary personality who had incontestable merits;[28] but as a man with a distinctive character,[29] he obviously also had some rough edges. Hans Rudolf Fuhrer rightly describes him as someone who was "very contested at times."[30] In late fall 1942, the Commander of the 7th Division told Masson about his impressions of Hausamann, stating:

> Based also on earlier observations, I consider Hausamann as an over-excited, agitated person who has a pathological need for recognition; he could actually become dangerous if he [continues to] work for Army Intelligence. By the way, this head of a secret intelligence bureau showed his need for recognition by putting a large poster on his front door in Teufen on which it said, "Bureau Capt. Hausamann, Army Staff." Hausamann is not a bad person, but in my opinion he is very dangerous precisely because he is over-excited and self-important.[31]

Toward the end of his life, Masson made a similar statement, complaining, "I am troubled by his over-excitement and his lack of moderation and composure."[32] A remark by Chief of the General Staff Huber expressed the ambivalent attitude that many members of Army Intelligence had about Hausamann. He stated: "I personally do not like Captain Hausamann; his need for recognition and tendency to act pompously do not befit the head of an intelligence section, who should keep a low profile toward the outside world. However, he holds most of the reins that go to Germany, and he is undeniably[33] a patriot."[34]

2. Switzerland's Military Attaché in Berlin

Even if Swiss Army Intelligence considered him as a source, in 1944 Masson explained to the Chief of the General Staff that the military attaché's reports had to be viewed from a certain perspective:

> Our attaché is in a position to procure objective information only in exceptional cases. That is not his task anyway. On the contrary, he has to report the official view of events. For Intelligence, part of the evaluation process consists of comparing [this view] with reality, which does not necessarily match the official German view. It is also very interesting to see what the intentions are behind the information that our military attaché receives, especially when the information does not necessarily correspond with reality.[35]

In the fall of 1939, however, the military attaché who had been sent to Berlin was not even able to provide the little information that he was expected to supply. Due to the attaché's apparent inability to make assessments of military matters,[36] Waibel wrote a harsh letter to Masson in which he demanded,

"Since I am entrusted with procuring intelligence from Germany for Army Intelligence, I feel obligated to ask you to *immediately recall* Colonel von Werdt from his post as military attaché."[37] (Von Werdt was eventually recalled, in 1943.)

3. Officers Detailed to Germany

Captain Waibel of the General Staff, who was a student at the War Academy in Berlin before the war broke out, supplied the most valuable reports among the Swiss officers living in Germany.[38]

4. *Private Persons* Returning from Germany

Before the war, people arriving in Switzerland were not systematically registered, and neither were they interrogated as a matter of course. As Alfred Ernst observed, "Everything depended on coincidental personal relations."[39]

5. Individual *Diplomats*

The inevitably overlapping activities of the diplomatic service and Army Intelligence would soon lead to unending disputes. As we will show later in this chapter, the friction grew worse in 1940 when Federal Councillor Pilet-Golaz succeeded Giuseppe Motta as Head of the Department of Foreign Affairs. Pilet-Golaz's ambivalent attitude toward Army Intelligence hardly encouraged diplomats to lend a helping hand to the needs of Masson's Intelligence Service.

6. Border Patrols[40]

In the areas along the border, Alfred Ernst had a source available that had been providing information for many years: the border patrols. Official relations between Army Intelligence and the country's top customs authorities had been established on January 22, 1923, during a visit by Colonel-Divisional-Commander Emil Sonderegger, who was Chief of the General Staff Unit at the time, with the Director of the Federal Customs Authorities, Arnold Gassmann.[41] On June 21, 1923, based on suggestions by Chief of Intelligence Gustave Combe, the customs authorities issued instructions to the heads of the border patrols to reorganize and resume intelligence activities on behalf of the military.[42] The heads of the border patrols had been informed about Major Combe's suggestions as early as March 1923 at a briefing in Bern,[43] and they approved of them. At the end of April 1923, Combe was pleased to note, "For about two months now, we have been receiving some very interesting information, which shows that the higher-ranking members of the border patrols[44] are very well suited for procuring military intelligence and that we can expect some good results from their end."[45]

In the instructions of June 1923, the heads of the border patrols were told to report "any incident or observation in the border areas of the neighboring countries that could be of any interest to Switzerland's national defense." Observations about troops were considered to be particularly important; the General Staff Unit classified them as "high priority," so they had to be addressed directly to Section 5 as quickly as possible. For other matters, however, the General Staff Unit did not communicate directly with the customs officials cooperating with Army Intelligence; the contact was maintained via the federal customs authorities, which forwarded the border patrols' information to Major Combe.[46]

The development of the increasingly worrisome general situation in Europe at the end of the 1930s provided an opportunity not only for Army Intelligence but also for Customs Intelligence to accustom itself to its work. After the crisis concerning the Sudetenland, and a few weeks following the crushing of the remainder of Czechoslovakia, the inspector of the federal customs authorities was pleased to report "that our intelligence service worked well, especially in customs districts I to III (German border)."[47] He added that from the other border areas "a great amount of good and useful information"[48] had been received as well. In early April 1939, based on "the recent experience as well as the experience from the critical days of September 1938,"[49] the federal customs authorities established sub-offices that continuously gathered the information that the border patrols in the field were transmitting by telephone and forwarded it to the federal customs authorities twice a day. Any communication with the General Staff Unit and Section 5 regarding information that was of interest to the military continued to be handled exclusively by the federal customs authorities.

During the entire war, the border patrols and Army Intelligence worked well together. The border patrols' understanding of the requirements of Army Intelligence and their willingness to provide assistance created a trusting relationship that bore satisfactory results.[50]

Alfred Ernst was aware that these six sources of intelligence were far from meeting the needs of the German Bureau. He found a highly qualified, like-minded person named Max Waibel who systematically established and expanded the procurement of intelligence. Waibel returned from Berlin on September 2, 1939, and was assigned to Army Intelligence. In mid-September, he was transferred to the German Bureau as Ernst's closest aide.[51] Waibel had met Ernst only in connection with his activity in Berlin, yet they soon became friends. Their trusting relationship "not only survived the storms of wartime duty but lasted until [Waibel's death]. Without the integrity and strong personality of Captain Ernst, many successful operations would not have been possible."[52] Initially the two officers worked together without dividing up their tasks. However, Ernst commented, "with time we realized that it was inevitable to clearly separate procurement and evaluation of intelligence."[53] Waibel consequently took care of *reorganizing the procurement process*,[54] and Ernst focused on *evaluating* the procured *intelligence*.[55]

Procurement Office 1

Gerold Walser, who worked for the *Pfalz* sub-office of the German Bureau, recalls that Max Waibel was a "sensitive, gentle person; he was a brilliant speaker when he was among a small group of people, yet he was modest and friendly. I never heard him yell, nor did I ever see him behave arrogantly.[56] Toward the troops he was scholarly and reserved. He was not a popular troop commander."[57] However, organizing the procurement of intelligence required a different set of qualities. According to Ernst:

[Waibel] knew how to encourage his subordinates to be proactive and make them understand that they were all working together on the same task. There was nothing he hated more than pedantry, harassment, and stiffness. . . . Waibel had a clear and simple way of thinking. He was able to distinguish between what was important and what was trivial. He was a real boss also insofar as he was able to get the most out of his staff. He was extremely decisive; he never wavered in critical situations. Whenever he was convinced that something was right, he stood by his decision even when he had to overcome resistance and difficulties.[58]

Waibel soon realized "that for setting up the procurement process for [the] German Bureau, it did not make sense to operate from the Intelligence Section at the Army Command. Hence, on November 15, 1939, [he] moved [his] office to Lucerne."[59] The Army Command was stationed in Langnau in the Emme Valley, far away from the main communication channels, which made it difficult to maintain contacts. In addition, as a matter of principle, "members of Army Intelligence who could easily be identified as such had to stay away from connections (agents, etc.) that could have compromised the Army

Command. That way the Army Command would not have been incriminated if something had gone wrong."[60] In retrospect, Captain Eberhard, who headed the Axis Section by the end of wartime duty, admitted, "It may have been exaggerated to take this precaution; there were no serious complaints about any activity by the Axis Section nor its procurement bodies."[61] Waibel had only modest means available[62] to set up an organization on the shores of Lake Lucerne, for which he used the easily identifiable cover name "Rigi." Its official name was *Nachrichtensammelstelle 1 (N.S.1)*,[63] *Ter Kdo 8*. However, it did not have anything to do with territorial command 8; this extensive organization was used to camouflage the activities of *N.S.1*, a strategy that proved to be successful. *N.S.1* had its headquarters at the Schweizerhof hotel in Lucerne.

Procurement Office 1 had the straightforward yet comprehensive task of collecting intelligence on Germany and above all on the German Armed Forces, their structure, intentions, and activities. At a later time, its task was extended, as it had to procure intelligence on the entire area that was held by the Axis powers and on their armed forces. In order to accomplish this task, Waibel's office mainly used informants and agents in foreign countries, evaluated information received from the border, questioned Swiss citizens returning from abroad, interrogated deserters and internees, and studied the German press and German weekly film shows. Waibel initially focused on *interviewing* the Swiss returning from Germany[64] and *processing the information by Bureau Ha* before forwarding it to the Intelligence Section.[65]

Because Swiss citizens were arriving from every part of the Third Reich, the interviews made it possible to cover a large geographic area. Waibel explained, "We frequently received very interesting and precise information from faraway places in the Reich where we could not place any agents, such as East Prussia, Silesia, etc."[66] The material that was received daily from Bureau Ha was compared with, and verified against, other sources of information as far as possible. This could be done for some of the information concerning the positions of troops. *Rigi* also carefully read the German press. German newspapers and magazines yielded valuable information precisely because they were monitored by the Reich Propaganda Ministry. There were times when N.S.1 regularly checked 30–40 German periodicals. In addition to information on German culture and the German economy, experienced readers also found interesting news on the German Armed Forces. For an extended period of time, Lucerne systematically evaluated the published death notices of members of the German Armed Forces. Ernst von Schenck,[67] a staff member at the *Pfalz* sub-office, successfully skimmed the German press for hidden hints about Germany's plans on the domestic and foreign political levels. Unfortunately, Procurement Office 1 was less successful at systematically monitoring and evaluating German radio programs and Allied propaganda shows that were addressed to the German Armed Forces.

The procurement bodies of the German Bureau also evaluated *photographs and films* in detail, a source of information that carried no risks with it and provided an unexpectedly large amount of useful material, especially after Germany's invasion of Russia in summer 1941. Even though the battlefields in the east were very far away, it was possible to collect reliable information on the arrangement of the German Army and smaller units in their areas of deployment. By systematically analyzing photographs in the press and clips from weekly shows, the German Bureau obtained conclusive evidence about the structure, organization, and operations of parts of the German Armed Forces. By fall 1941, every film that was distributed in Switzerland was examined; and individual shots were enlarged, copied, and combined into photo albums that served to document the equipment, tactics, and technology of foreign armies.[68]

The "very surprising and important findings"[69] that resulted from this evaluation of photographs and films by the German Bureau caused Army Intelligence to create a special *Bureau for Technical Studies*, which was integrated into the German Bureau and was headed by Captain Paul Schaufelberger.[70] It was put in charge of collecting and evaluating information, particularly through pictures, on weapons and equipment used by the belligerent armies. To Masson, some of the *official* German films yielded "such interesting and up-to-date information" that he commented, in a secret report to the Chief of the General Staff: "The possibilities that this source of information offered were one of the surprises of this war. It seems that up until the end, neither [warring] party realized how much explosive information [their films] contained. The films of both [the Axis powers and the Allies] were real treasure troves all the way until the armistice was concluded in the West."[71]

The fact that no agent structure existed in Germany at the beginning of the war initially made it "tremendously difficult"[72] for N.S.1 to accomplish its task. Waibel reported, "In an effort to register all travelers crossing the border with Germany[73] and record their stories and observations, *immigration forms were created* that served to collect information on military, political, and economic issues."[74] On these forms, the travelers[75] indicated their itineraries, which allowed Army Intelligence to narrow down the interview process to persons arriving from interesting areas. A carbon copy of the form was sent to the Attorney General's Office right away,[76] and the original was submitted to Army Intelligence. The responsible Head of Bureau[77] then forwarded it to the outpost that was to conduct an interview with the traveler. The form was presented to the traveler at the beginning of the interview and sent back to the Bureau

Hof.Gz.Rgt.55 pale [Spez.-D.Nr. 123] 22.3.40 1.

E i n v e r n a h m e von:

En circulation
aux ofs   Intellektueller

Der Einvernommene reiste am 21.3.40 1410 von Stettin ab. Route:
Berlin-Würzburg-Erfurt-Stuttgart-Singen. Ankunft in Schaffhausen
22.3.40 1300.

Dem Einvernommenen ist, acht Tage vor seiner Abreise, folgender
Fall passiert: Als er auf der Amtsstelle das deutsche Visum bekam,
wurde er erst einem Polizei-Of., dann einem Gestapo-Beamten vorgeführt.
Als diese zwei Unterredungen beendet waren, bat ihn ein Mayor der
Wehrmacht, der auf dieser Amtsstelle als Nachrichten-Of., in Uniform
tätig ist, in ein Zimmer. Der Mayor, in der Meinung, er sei Deutscher,
führte mit ihm nun folgendes Gespräch: " Wenn Sie nun nach der Schweiz kommen,
sehen Sie genau zu, was die Franzosen, Engländer und Belgier in der
Schweiz treiben." Der Einvernommene: " Ich halte aber die schweizerische
Neutralität sehr hoch und möchte mir dadurch kein Gewissen machen
müssen." Der Mayor: " Deswegen müssen Sie ja keinen Spionagedienst
treiben, wenn Sie nur die Augen offen halten. Wir haben in der
Schweiz genug Leute, die zum Rechten sehen." Als der Mayor dann
erfuhr, dass der Einvernommene Schweizer ist, war er sehr verlegen
und nahm ihm das Versprechen ab, dass er die Angelegenheit so schnell
als möglich vergessen wolle. //

Auf der Reise ab Stuttgart fuhren 18 Infanteristen mit, die in
Tuttlingen den Zug verliessen. - Stettin selbst hat verschiedene
Kasernen, wo Flak und Scheinwerfertrp. ausgebildet werden.

Die Stimmung bezüglich des Krieges ist sehr zuversichtlich. Gegenüber
der Schweiz hört man momentan nichts schlechtes.

Die Ernährung der Bevölkerung ist besonders qualitativ minderwer-
tig.

Einvernommen durch: Kpl. felix

Travelers returning to Switzerland were valuable sources of information for Army Intelligence. This traveler, who is described as an "intellectual," reported an incident that had occurred in Stettin; thinking that the traveler was German, an Intelligence officer of the Wehrmacht asked him to keep his eyes open during his trip to Switzerland. When the officer found out that the potential informant was Swiss, he felt embarrassed and asked him "to forget about the matter as quickly as possible." The traveler also reported that 18 infantrymen got on the train in Stuttgart and got off in Tuttlingen. (BAr E 27/10113)

together with the interview report. When it was deemed unnecessary to question the traveler a second time, the Bureau destroyed the form.

The other Bureaus took over this simple, plausible procurement method; however, the procedure gave rise to some serious disputes, and it took some time for the immigration forms to be used consistently at all border checkpoints because not all involved bodies seemed to realize right away how important this source of information was. The Swiss Federal Railways refused to offer the officials free train tickets on the southern stretch of the Gotthard route; Army Intelligence consequently had to purchase monthly passes for them.[78] It was not until mid-1942 that Intelligence reported that the procedure was being "routinely applied without much trouble in cooperation with the Police Section and cantonal police authorities." Nevertheless, it added, "Our diplomats and overly fearful Swiss living abroad are regularly up in arms about Swiss immigrants being questioned."[79] Army Intelligence countered these complaints by pointing out that Germans were authorized to leave their home country for Switzerland only after receiving orders from German Intelligence. It said that German Intelligence actually went as far as using threats to force Swiss living in Germany who asked for a German emigration visa in order to temporarily return home, to spy for the *Abwehr*.[80]

As soon as a dense network of agents and informants was set up, the interviews with travelers became less important. Due to the decreasing number of travelers and the lower percentage of people arriving at the Swiss border who were interviewed (at first the rate dropped to 10 percent of immigrants, toward the end of the war to as little as 5 percent),[81] "luckily the constant complaints by [Swiss] representatives abroad to the Department of Foreign Affairs ceased."[82]

Foreign military personnel who arrived in Switzerland were questioned by a group of specially trained officers at N.S.1. However, the pilots of both warring parties who entered Swiss territory because of emergency landings were not very talkative. Army Intelligence reported: "The task was rendered far more difficult because the German pilots were disciplined and kept silent. Nevertheless, the results were satisfactory."[83] At the end of 1942, Group Id chivalrously acknowledged that Allied soldiers had the same attitude, stating: "We would like to commend the members of the English Armed Forces, especially its air force pilots, for their exemplary, *unforthcoming* attitude during interrogations. With a few exceptions, they refuse to answer questions even about trivial issues."[84]

On certain occasions, especially when larger units entered the country at the time the Fascists were ousted in Italy, during the battle at the threshold of Burgundy and in Alsace, and during the advance of the French 1st Army in southern Germany, Swiss Intelligence undertook large-scale efforts to question soldiers; virtually the entire staff of the outposts was involved in these operations. These efforts usually paid off, as the information supplied by the internees made it possible to verify a large number of the agency reports and messages by informants as well as to update and obtain additional details about the composition of the German Army and Air Force. In retrospect, Waibel considered the results to be "extremely satisfactory."[85] Intelligence also collected valuable information through the documents and papers that deserters and internees carried with them. The identification cards and papers of members of the German Armed Forces were invaluable for Switzerland's agents; they were particularly useful for a connection of the *Pfalz* sub-office that was operating in southern Germany.

In Switzerland, the interrogation of deserters and internees was equivalent to the interrogation of prisoners of war in the belligerent countries. *Rigi* quickly realized how much meaningful information it could gather through that channel and deliberately expanded its activities in that area. The results were especially good when the interrogations were conducted over an extended period of time and the interrogated persons were able to take their time thinking about what they knew. Waibel explained that "with a few exceptions, [they] were eager to supply information."[86] In order to create favorable conditions on the psychological level, at Waibel's initiative a special camp called "Felsberg" was set up for internees in Lucerne. In summer 1940, interned pilots were sent there. Waibel later extended the camp and transferred it to Dietschiberg. Some internees spent a few days at the camp, others several weeks. Officers and other persons whom N.S.1 expected to provide very valuable information because they had been in high-ranking positions in Germany were lodged in guarded rooms in the west wing of the Schweizerhof hotel.[87]

Over the course of time, Waibel became aware that 80 percent of the quality of any interrogation depended on the quality of the interviewer, and only 20 percent depended on the interrogated person.[88]

Outposts of Procurement Office 1

Even though, initially, many parties strictly opposed the immigration forms,[89] Procurement Office 1 soon received more than 300 forms a day for processing. However, the existing setup did not allow N.S.1 to interview the most important immigrants while their observations were still fresh in mind. In an effort to solve that problem, Waibel came up with the idea of decentralizing the interviewing process. In close cooperation with several cantonal Political Police departments, he started creating a number of sub-offices.[90] It soon turned out that sub-offices were also interesting for economic reasons; Waibel observed, "The more restrictions there are on gasoline consumption, the more difficult it becomes to travel, making it clear that regional offices are necessary."[91]

The first outpost that was created was the *Pfalz* sub-office in Basel; it turned into the largest sub-office of Army Intelligence and was headed by Captain Emil Häberli, the Chief of the Political Section of the Basel Police Department.[92] Its main tasks consisted of interviewing immigrants, establishing, and making use of, contacts with persons who had connections abroad (which was not very difficult in that border city), procuring intelligence through agents, utilizing its relations with the police for the military, and providing technical assistance to other offices of Army Intelligence by using Häberli's position on the police force.[93]

The internal structure of the *Pfalz* outpost was changed on several occasions; by fall 1942, the number of interviews and interrogations began to drop, whereas the activities involving agents were on the rise. There were several reasons for the decrease in the number of interviews: first of all, Swiss citizens had difficulties obtaining a visa to travel abroad; second, travelers inside Germany were generally allowed to use only the main railroads; and third, because secrecy was enforced more rigorously, travelers in the Third Reich found out "hardly anything anymore about military matters."[94] In order to make up for the lack of information collected from travelers, the operations involving agents had to be expanded and intensified.[95] In fact, by that time agents were practically the only means through which information could be procured from southern Germany. A number of successful channels went through the Pfalz sub-office, including four major long-term connections: "Viking," "L,"[96] and two connections to southern Germany.[97] Häberli never revealed all the links of a connection to his staff, explaining, "For security reasons, our work was organized according to the principle that there should be only one contact person per agent."[98]

Like other Intelligence offices, Pfalz realized that only permanent staff who had been trained could work effectively.[99] Their capabilities were more important than their rank in the military. The procurement outpost in Basel was very successful with a highly heterogeneous team, which included one banker, one senior judge, two homemakers, one industrialist, two journalists, one museum curator, three lawyers, one female singer, one state attorney, one student, and one typesetter.[100] The staff at Pfalz felt like a team not because they belonged to the same military unit but because they all vehemently opposed National Socialism "in one way or another, depending on their connections with Germany."[101] Moreover, one of the former staff members recalls, "Häberli did not make his presence felt as head of office. He observed his staff very closely, but apart from that he did not get involved in everyone's day-to-day activities. Once he accepted a staff member, that staff member had a lot of leeway, and Häberli backed his or her actions as a matter of principle."[102]

Other outposts were created based on the example of the Pfalz sub-office. In *Schaffhausen*, the *Salm* outpost was established. Its head, Captain Strauss, continued working as an engineer while directing the sub-office, and he "successfully set up and organized the entire intelligence network in the canton of Schaffhausen."[103] The outpost was located in suite no. 23 of the *Bahnhof* hotel in Schaffhausen. Together with the Speer outpost, it was in charge of getting the agents of one of the connections of the Pfalz sub-office into and out of southern Germany. In addition, *Salm* established its own connection, "Philipp," with the German Legation in Bern.[104]

Pfalz and Salm also gathered valuable information from people living in one country and working in another. Moreover, they worked closely with the border patrols and the command post of the city of Basel and border regiment 53, respectively. During times of increased activities in the border area, very good results were obtained by observing road traffic and railroad traffic from specific observation points in Switzerland. At particularly important places, railroad traffic was monitored continuously during the day by taking photographs. These photos yielded interesting information, complementing, or sometimes actually contradicting, eyewitness accounts from military personnel. Shortly after the beginning of the war, Waibel realized that the monitors at the border did not supply very systematic reports and provided imprecise and unreliable information concerning troops because they lacked training.[105] Hence, he had the idea of systematically photographing German military trains with Leica zoom lenses in order to get a clear picture of the movements along the Rhine and the Wutach River. After a relatively short period of time, Waibel was pleased to report, "Considering their possibilities, the border patrols have been doing *a very good job.*"[106]

In Zürich, Army Intelligence established the *Uto* outpost. In 1943, Captain Meyer-Schwertenbach was assigned to this sub-office; he "was exclusively in charge of communicating with the [Zürich] city police and was working directly with Colonel-Brigadier Masson."[107]

In St. Gallen, the *Speer* outpost worked with approximately 30-35 agents, most of whom were German railway and customs officials. Other agents included German business people, persons crossing the border several times a month, and business people living in the Rhine Valley south of Lake Constance. The agents transmitted their information to main agents, who in turn passed the information on to communication offices in St. Margrethen and Buchs. The communication offices wrote daily reports to the outpost in St. Gallen for processing, except for important information, which they communicated by telephone. The intelligence activities of the *Speer* outpost covered the regions of Allgäu, Vorarlberg, and Tyrol, including the garrisons of Bregenz, Landeck, Innsbruck, Feldkirch, Lindau, and Kempten. In addition, *Speer* monitored railroad traffic across the Arlberg and the Brenner mountains.

Speer was headed by Konrad Lienert, the commander of the St. Gallen cantonal police. Overall, this was a satisfactory solution, even though after three years of experience Lienert was self-critical, remarking, "We are not perfectly pleased with our intelligence service because we have to rely on too many coincidences and have great difficulties procuring the information we absolutely need. Time after time we notice that intelligence activities failed to be organized during times of peace; this handicap is hard to overcome now."[108]

By working with the political departments of the St. Gallen cantonal and city police, the passport offices in St. Margrethen and Buchs, police stations in the Rhine Valley, and border patrols, *Speer* was able to create a dense intelligence network and interview immigrants and refugees within a short period of time. The four staff members who took turns manning the outpost in teams of two were Corporals Rusch and Hedinger, Private 1st Class Kunz, and Auxiliary Service Member Keller. Lienert described his staff as "reliable and industrious."[109] Indeed, they were industrious, as can be seen from the amount of work they did. From September 1942 to December 1943, *Speer* interviewed 323 Swiss returning from abroad, interrogated 77 deserters and 30 civilian and military refugees, and received, processed, and forwarded 249 reports by agents, as well as an incalculable number of messages concerning positions of foreign units, police reports, and other documents.[110]

In early January 1941, the *Nell* sub-office started operating in *Lugano* under its original cover name "Baro."[111] Its head was Captain Guido Bustelli, a Ph.D. in law who showed a lot of initiative. In May 1941, he succeeded in stationing an agent in Milan who continuously reported on the military, economic, political, and social situation in Italy. The observer worked very well, but for personal reasons[112] he was forced to return to Switzerland as early as August 1941. The head of the Italian Bureau remarked, "Hence, we lost our best agent in Italy, [adding] since we have no network of informants in Italy, we have to get the most out of the accounts by travelers returning from Italy, newspapers, agency communiqués, tapped telephone conversations, intercepted radio communications, and censored letters and telegrams."[113] The lack of a network of agents in Italy was all the more noticeable as the outpost in Lugano was able to procure only a very limited amount of military-related information through other means, and, with a few exceptions, that information was rather imprecise.[114] Moreover, with the exception of the immediate border area, it was almost impossible to verify the information.[115] Intelligence activities in Italy were limited to contacts with Swiss living there. In the course of the war, Bustelli managed to set up a network of close to 300 informants who directly or indirectly cooperated with *Nell*.[116]

By the end of wartime duty, the German Bureau/Axis Section had set up the following additional outposts:

- The *Hörnli* sub-office in Frauenfeld, which was headed by Lieutenant Colonel Haudenschild, the chief of the Thurgau cantonal police;
- The *Bernina* sub-office in Samaden, canton of Grisons, headed by Sergeant Gartmann;
- The *Simplon* sub-office in Brig, canton of Valais, headed by Captain Bammatter.

The outposts in Brig, Lugano, and Samaden did not report to the same bureau throughout the war. They used their own means for procuring intelligence, sending agents to Italy, observing the border area with binoculars, and evaluating the local press.

Hence, in the course of the first months of wartime duty, a far-reaching intelligence network was created, "frequently in spite of a lot of red tape and resistance by certain people."[117] It collected military and political information from the Axis powers, supplying Alfred Ernst with valuable clues for assessing the events of the war.

Informants and Agents

The most productive way of procuring intelligence was through *informants* and *agents*. Eberhard reflected: "Relations with informants in Germany were particularly valuable. Some of them were in key positions. It was not possible to buy or bribe these informants because people in Germany who had a certain status refused to take bribes; moreover, we did not have the means for paying bribes."[118] Swiss Intelligence was lucky to find people who were willing to cooperate with it for ideological reasons.[119] Eberhard explained, "In particular, we recruited some senior officers from the former Austrian armed forces who remained Austrian after being incorporated into the German Army and had obligations toward Switzerland."[120] In view of the increasingly short supply of consumer goods in Germany, small favors were more important than money. By the end of the war, people who could not have been tempted at all by money were ready to render considerable services in exchange for some coffee or tobacco. However, Eberhard remarked, "In some cases, the responsible Swiss customs authorities lacked understanding."[121]

From the point of view of intelligence, the quality of any information that is received randomly is inferior to information that has been specifically requested, even if its content may be of some importance. Evaluating random information is subject to far more discretionary powers than evaluating messages answering specific questions. The interviews with civilians arriving from abroad revealed a lot of interesting details. However, since this information was unpredictable and could not be scheduled to arrive at any particular time, it could only serve to confirm facts that were already known. (Nevertheless, this information was obviously quite useful because, as a matter of principle, any intelligence service has to try to confirm or invalidate information by collecting additional information.)[122]

Information that is procured *on a regular basis* about specific geographic areas or specific subject matters is the most reliable and most profitable information for the evaluation bodies. The only way to obtain such information is by using *agents*. Hence, agents are indispensable for any intelligence service. In a report in which he talked about the experiences of the Allied Section, Cuénoud remarked, "There are many sources of information, but *with the exception of the service provided by agents*, only few offer a regular and steady output."[123] In his final report on the activities of the Allied Section during wartime duty, Cuénoud pointed out, "Contrary to what a layperson might believe, we owe more than 75 percent of the reports that we obtained to our agents who had been recruited, trained, and briefed under very difficult conditions and in delicate situations."[124]

According to one activity report, it was due to agents that Swiss Intelligence was able "to register and report in time the different stages of the German Reich's military and political preparations for its campaign against the Soviet Union. Our reports were merely confirmed when the war started. At the same time, it was possible to obtain unambiguous information about the movements [of troops] near our borders. This information was the basis for the Army Command's decision to drastically reduce the number of troops on duty."[125]

The fact that Swiss Intelligence had to pay attention to the war against the Soviet Union was due to the long-distance motorized and airborne operations that became possible in the course of World War II. As a consequence, it had to extend the area that it monitored beyond the 100- or 200-kilometer-wide corridor along the country's border that had been considered sufficiently large at the beginning of the war. Masson observed, "Even small, seemingly insignificant details had to be reported in order to be able to register any indication of military operations being prepared against our country far away from the usual area of deployment, or to recognize in time that the direction of a military operation had changed."[126] The procurement of intelligence from distant places was intensified above all in 1941 as German operations spread through the Mediterranean and European Russia.

In retrospect, one can say that the performance by agents met expectations and was generally satisfactory.[127] Masson added: "[We] were pleased to note that the attitude of the authorities, in particular the Department of Foreign Affairs, did justice to the valuable work that was done by the agents. They willingly and persistently intervened on behalf of members of Army Intelligence who had been imprisoned or even been sentenced to death.[128] In most cases, the interventions were successful."[129] Nevertheless, Swiss Army Intelligence lost a total of 48 agents who were verified as killed in the line of duty—31 of them were sentenced to death and executed, 11 died while in prison, and 6 died as a result of accidents.[130]

Seven of the 48 killed agents were Swiss. During the course of the war, Cuénoud gained the impression that Swiss citizens were generally unfit to work as agents abroad, saying, "It seems to me that Swiss personnel have only a few of the qualities that are required to be a first-rate agent."[131] He expected agents to be "active, wily, alert, daring, cunning, and at the same time honest,"[132] a profile that was obviously not easy to fill. Cuénoud knew what he was talking about; during World War II, the Allied Section, which he headed, used a total of more than 1,500 agents.

In spite of the evident risks that were associated with using informants and agents abroad, at the end of wartime duty, Waibel had to acknowledge, "This activity is *indispensable* for intelligence; it cannot be replaced by anything else."[133] As illustrated by two incidents that occurred in 1940 and that are described below, Procurement Office 1 repeatedly received very valuable information *exclusively* through agents and informants. Their information turned out to be accurate even though it contradicted the information obtained through Swiss military attachés and other sources that always had a substantial influence on the official opinion.

In mid-March 1940, *Rigi* was informed through one of its channels that Germany's first operation in the West would be directed against Norway and Denmark, not against France, and that the operation would be launched in the first half of April. This information contradicted all other reports, making even the Army Command very skeptical about its reliability. As we now know, the information was accurate.

Shortly afterward, on May 1, 1940, Procurement Office 1 was told by the same excellent connection that Germany would launch its campaign in the

West "within the coming two weeks"[134] and that the attack would be so concentrated and fierce that Germany would subjugate Western Europe within two months. The connection reported that *this attack would not affect Switzerland*; instead, the bulk of the operation would be conducted on the right wing. Waibel explained, "Due to a special code system, our informant was in constant contact with us over an extended period of time. On the so-called 'critical day of May 14,' [1940] he assured us that no operation whatsoever was planned against Switzerland."[135]

Rigi received the same reassuring information through one of Waibel's other informants in Italy who was in close contact with an important Italian personality and sent daily reports to Lucerne. In addition, on the critical day of May 14, when the Swiss Army fully expected to be attacked, another informant of Procurement Office 1 went on a secret reconnaissance mission in the area of Constance, Donaueschingen, Villingen, Tuttlingen, Sigmaringen, and St. Margrethen; he reported that he had noticed no military activities whatsoever in that area, beyond the normal operations at the level of the garrisons. There were no transports, nor did anyone make preparations for taking any military action.

These pieces of information by first-rate informants contrasted sharply with the general opinion about the situation, and above all they contradicted the numerous German and Allied inverted signals that had been leaked into Switzerland through various channels. Waibel commented, "Hence, toward mid-May [1940], strangely, in Worb[136] archives were being burnt, whereas the command post of N.S.1 in Lucerne considered the situation as *absolutely calm*."[137]

Throughout the remainder of the war, agents continued providing Swiss Intelligence with important information that could not have been procured in any other fashion. Between the fall of 1944 and early 1945, due to its agents, N.S.1 knew for certain that no sizable combat units were stationed in the Black Forest nor in any other area in southern Germany. This information clearly contradicted other reports received by Army Intelligence according to which Germany was withdrawing major units to a hedgehog position in southern Germany. Based on the reports by his agents, Waibel tirelessly pointed out that *southern Germany was manned by a strikingly low number of troops.*

Overall, Waibel commented about his sources of information: "We had a relatively large number of good connections all the way to the Führer's headquarters and the Reich War Ministry. Some of them were actually outstanding. However, this does not mean that we found out *everything* that happened there; nevertheless, we [received] *a lot of* very valuable information in time."[138]

As the Third Reich began to collapse, it became more difficult to recruit and keep suitable agents. In the second half of 1944, the Axis Section of Swiss Army Intelligence had to realize "that sooner or later several of the people whom [it] used were looking for backing among Allied intelligence organizations."[139] In a number of cases, after initially working for Swiss Intelligence, agents started supplying their information to additional bodies. Rolf Eberhard considered that this was bound to happen under the prevailing circumstances: "Considering the limited means that Swiss Intelligence had available—even if these means were substantially greater than before the war,[140] they were far smaller than those of foreign intelligence services—it was inevitable that really useful agents could be made to work for us only if their own interests ran parallel to ours."[141]

At times Counterintelligence and the Federal Police showed little understanding of those circumstances when investigating the cases of agents in whom Swiss Intelligence had a lively interest.[142] On several occasions, the Axis Section gained the impression that it was Army Intelligence, not the agent under investigation, that was accused of playing a double game and acting with ill intent.[143] Rolf Eberhard, the head of the Axis Section, noted:

> [A] statement that Army Intelligence made in its final report on the First World War has to be reiterated [in the final report on World War II]: "It was virtually impossible to protect our agents from the clutches of Swiss police authorities (cantonal and federal police), which had to be considered as a serious impediment. Some of our agents were continually bothered when they crossed the border or were accused of playing a double game by failing to supply their results exclusively to our own procurement bodies."[144]

Similar to the Allied Section, albeit for different reasons, from summer 1944 onward it became increasingly difficult above all for Procurement Office 1 and *Bureau Ha* to procure intelligence from the Axis powers. In early 1945, the head of the Axis Section remarked, "Contrary to what one might have expected, the fact that life in Germany is becoming more and more disorganized has not contributed to making it easier to procure intelligence; in fact, it has become more difficult to do so."[145] Connections were continuously interrupted and networks were destroyed through the damage caused by Allied bombing and the subsequent movements of the population. When Germany mobilized its entire adult male population, informants and agents were called up who had previously been believed ineligible for service. Moreover, it became almost impossible to travel inside Germany. Also, due to the continuous depre-

ARMÉE SUISSE   SCHWEIZERISCHE ARMEE   ESERCITO SVIZZERO

LE COMMANDANT EN CHEF   DER OBERBEFEHLSHABER   IL COMANDANTE IN CAPO
DE L'ARMÉE   DER ARMEE   DELL'ESERCITO

No. 16046

1/Vo/sch   A.H.Q., 7.12.44

G e h e i m .

An den Chef des Gst. der Armee.

      Der Verlauf der Kriegsoperationen an unserer
Nordwestgrenze und ihr vorläufiger Abschluss mit der Er-
reichung des Rheins durch die Alliierten hat eine Vermin-
derung unserer kriegsmobilisierten Truppen gestattet.

      Diese Reduktion kann jedoch nur verantwortet
werden, wenn wir über die Lage im Grenzraum genügend und
rechtzeitig orientiert sind, da mit einer Wiederaufnahme
der Operationen gerechnet werden muss.

      Während die Informationen über Bestände und Be-
wegungen auf alliierter Seite in den vergangenen Monaten
ausgiebig waren und ihre Genauigkeit durch die Entwicklung
der Operationen bestätigt wurde, gestatten die uns zur
Verfügung stehenden Unterlagen über Truppenbewegungen und
Bestände an unserer Nordgrenze, insbesondere im Schwarz-
wald, eine zufriedenstellende Beurteilung der Lage nicht.

      Ich ersuche Sie deshalb, unseren Nachrichtendienst
zu veranlassen, diesem Gebiete erhöhte Aufmerksamkeit zu
schenken. Es wäre auch von grosser Wichtigkeit, sich da-
rüber Rechenschaft zu geben, ob der noch anscheinend starke
deutsche Brückenkopf im Raume von Kembs und nördlich davon
als Ausgangsstellung einer Offensivhandlung bewertet werden
kann, welche, wenn auch nur von taktischer Bedeutung, dennoch
zu einer Gefährdung unseres Hoheitsgebietes führen müsste.

                            Der General:

From summer 1944 on, it became more difficult to procure intelligence from the Axis powers. In December 1944, in a letter to the Chief of the General Staff, General Guisan asked Army Intelligence to pay closer attention to the area north of the Swiss border in order to verify whether an offensive could be launched from there against Switzerland. He argued that he could take responsibility for reducing the number of troops that were kept on duty only if he had "a sufficient amount of up-to-date information on the situation in the border areas because operations might resume." (BAr E 27/9914)

ciation of currencies, Swiss Intelligence was not able to achieve anything any-more with money; it had to pay in kind or grant privileges such as residence permits. However, in this realm, difficulties had to be surmounted in dealing with the responsible Swiss authorities, who frequently failed to show the neces-sary understanding for Army Intelligence's concerns.[146]

In addition to the problems mentioned above, there was constant internal turmoil that could have been avoided. For both Procurement Office 1 and the outposts, Waibel considered a major difficulty the fact "that no trained person-nel were available when the army was mobilized, nor were any trained person-nel assigned to us in the course of wartime duty."[147] The same was true for the French Bureau. Waibel, Cuénoud, and the heads of the sub-offices whom they had appointed had to rely entirely on themselves for recruiting and training their personnel. Due to the fact that Waibel had some extraordinarily capable personalities available as heads of sub-offices, a number of mishaps could be prevented. As heads of Cantonal Political Intelligence sections, four command-ers of outposts had the necessary experience and expertise for accomplishing their task in the military. In retrospect, Waibel remarked, "The only *positive* aspect about this procedure [was] the fact that only very familiar people were recruited for the structure of N.S.1; for that reason . . . we all became close friends."[148] The friendships among the staff survived numerous, frequently inevitable frictions and lasted beyond the five and a half years of wartime duty. However, the improvised recruitment procedure worked to the *disadvantage* of the staff members, who usually served on a unit and were detailed to the Army Staff only on a temporary basis or for the duration of wartime duty; their chances of making a career in the military were limited,[149] and their troop com-manders often created insurmountable difficulties for them. Hence, to a certain extent, motivated and capable staff members who had been willing to work for Army Intelligence in the country's interest (and who frequently agreed to serve longer than the troops) were "punished" because their useful activity was not considered as valuable as that of the troops.[150]

Couriers and Consular Agents

The German Bureau could not have worked effectively without Procurement Office 1 and its outposts.[151] Waibel noted: "Obviously [our activ-ities] focused mainly on the *Third Reich's intentions toward Switzerland*. Our main task during wartime duty consisted of recognizing in time Germany's preparations for a war against our country and studying the [Nazi] party's and the Wehrmacht's combat methods in order to be able to prepare our own defense accordingly."[152]

Based on the example of the outposts of Procurement Office 1, in the winter of 1940–1941, a sub-office called *Mutz* was established in Bern. For matters of expediency, it reported directly to the Head of the German Bureau.[153]

The German Bureau deliberately did not strictly separate the procurement process from the evaluation process. Ernst explained, "The Head of the German Bureau occasionally has to conduct interviews and establish connections, otherwise he turns into a scholar and loses touch with the work in the field."[154] Ernst interviewed acquaintances,[155] foreign military attachés, Swiss diplomats, and employees of the federal administration. The German Bureau gathered a large amount of valuable material on Germany when it interrogated the Polish and French officers who arrived as internees in Switzerland on June 17, 1940.[156] In one of its reports it commented, "We were pleased to see that in spite of their huge infrastructure the French were generally not better informed than we were."[157]

Like the German Bureau, N.S.1 did not focus exclusively on one activity. As a procurement organization, it reported to the German Bureau (as of 1942 to the Axis Section), which received its information and defined the requirements for Intelligence (i.e., it issued orders concerning the procurement of intelligence). However, N.S.1 sometimes also evaluated intelligence. The Chief of Staff of *Rigi* explained, "In principle, as far as possible every staff member made use of the sources of information that were available to him."[158] Hence, it is understandable that, in addition to taking care of the evaluation process, Alfred Ernst also actively procured intelligence. His main activity in that area consisted of organizing and managing the *courier service*. Before the war, he had set up *teams* that collected valuable information in Germany by going on pre-established *tours*. Once the war had begun, however, the system of the tours had to be given up because it was no longer possible to travel around without having a valid reason. Instead, the German Bureau started sending officers as diplomatic couriers to Germany.[159] Of course, these couriers not only liaised with the staff at Swiss consulates and the military attachés, but also had orders to observe movements and concentrations of troops and develop impressions about the political situation in Germany. Ernst explained:

> The couriers initially traveled by car. Some went all the way to the Rhineland, the North Sea, and Hungary. Above all, however, they permanently and systematically monitored the important operational area of southern Germany. They returned from their trips with very good results. As long as they could travel by car, we hardly missed any major movement of troops in southern Germany. The main advantage of the courier service is that it allows us to have questionable information ver-

ified on the spot by trained, absolutely reliable individuals. The courier service cannot be replaced by any other means.[160]

The Swiss Legation was extremely annoyed by Army Intelligence's courier service. In October 1939, Max Waibel returned to Berlin for two weeks "in order to secure some important connections."[161] He was worried when he got back to Switzerland, stating, "Based on the experience that I had in Berlin with our legation,[162] Swiss Intelligence could not expect any support from that end; in fact, it had to fear that it might be drawn into a *war on two fronts*."[163]

The number of difficulties increased in January 1940, when Federal Councillor Marcel Pilet-Golaz was put in charge of the Department of Foreign Affairs. After the collapse of France, Envoy Frölicher considered that it was useless for Swiss couriers to continue monitoring Germany.[164] Hence, when Germany banned the use of cars, Army Intelligence could not expect any support from Switzerland's top representative in Berlin. From that moment on, the couriers had to travel by train. The German Bureau reported: "Understandably the results were no longer satisfactory. Nevertheless, a few skillful couriers managed to look around in some important areas. However, since then the Black Forest, which is particularly interesting for us,[165] has been almost completely sealed off from us."[166]

As Waibel had predicted, Frölicher and his staff not only failed to support Army Intelligence but also put obstacles in its way whenever they could. Among other things, the Envoy forbade the consuls to travel on behalf of Swiss Intelligence, "even though they had agreed to do so, and even though the trips were absolutely necessary."[167] At that time, the Swiss living in Berlin used a pun to describe their Envoy's attitude, stating, "*Wenn Frölicher nicht ein trauriger Schweizer wäre, wären die Schweizer fröhlicher*" (If Frölicher were not such a pathetic Swiss, the Swiss would be more cheerful). When the Head of the German Bureau complained about the Department of Foreign Affairs' lack of support in military matters, Karl Stucki,[168] a close aide of Pilet-Golaz, dismissed the criticism, replying, "Apparently you do not yet understand that we have to learn to think differently. Times have changed, and we have to *adapt* accordingly."[169]

The criticism about lack of understanding on the part of the Department of Foreign Affairs continued throughout the war. In late fall 1941, during an assessment of the situation, the Head of the German Bureau had to admit to Masson:

If Germany lines up troops against us, possibly by camouflaging the operation, I cannot guarantee that we will be able to recognize the maneuver in time. Major Waibel of the General Staff did his utmost to set up an illegal network of agents. However, the numerous difficulties that the Germans as well as our own authorities (above all the Department of Foreign Affairs) create for us make it very hard for us to get a clear picture [of Germany's preparations]; in fact, we *are not sure at all whether we will be able to recognize a threat in time.*[170]

In addition to the couriers, Alfred Ernst had some Swiss officers in Germany who were stationed in Munich, Stuttgart,[171] and Mannheim as *consular agents* and who supplied very good information.[172] Moreover, in spite of the difficulties that Frölicher created for them, a few consuls were willing to support Swiss Intelligence on their own initiative.[173] Another task of the German Bureau consisted of communicating with Switzerland's military attaché in Berlin. Like the military observers at the consulates,[174] the military attaché did not have any orders to spy on Germany; in fact, he had been explicitly forbidden to undertake any spying activities. Ernst stated about the tasks of the military attachés:

> Our military attachés have been assigned to the legations as official observers. We only expect them to forward to us the information that is accessible to them. They should not expose themselves. However, one has to realize that in belligerent countries *any* information that has to do with the military, military-political matters, or the defense economy is considered as secret. If one abided strictly by the laws of the respective country, the military attaché would have to be recalled from Germany. Leaving him in Berlin is justified only in view of the information that he occasionally receives through personal contacts in spite of all the bans that are in place.[175]

The performance of the military attaché in Berlin, which was poor at the beginning of the war, improved slightly in March 1940 after he had established "closer contact"[176] with the German Bureau; nevertheless, it remained below the expectations that Army Intelligence had for the person occupying that post. Cooperation with the German Bureau was hampered because of Colonel von Werdt's lack of expertise as well as due to differences of opinion. In fall 1940, Ernst described the difficult situation by stating: "In accordance with the Minister, [the military attaché] believes that Switzerland now has to humble itself [before Germany] and adjust [to the New Europe];[177] however, we are more and more convinced that the only way to keep from perishing is by remaining firm and proud. We wonder if Swiss who basically have such an un-Swiss attitude actually defend our interests in Germany."[178]

Conflicts between Army Intelligence and the Department of Foreign Affairs

In early 1943, relations with the Swiss military representative in Berlin improved when Colonel von Werdt was finally replaced by Major Peter Burckhardt, a capable future divisional commander. Army Intelligence's differences with the Department of Foreign Affairs, however, developed into a lasting conflict. The controversies, some of which were fierce, transpired in extensive exchanges of letters between Foreign Minister Pilet-Golaz, Chief of Intelligence Masson, General Guisan, and Defense Minister Kobelt. Luckily for scholars, a number of these documents survived, making it possible to identify the different opinions and views. They clearly show how difficult it was for Masson to put his concept of *strategic* intelligence into practice.

The conflict erupted in early August 1940 in a meeting that Foreign Minister Pilet-Golaz held with General Guisan and Federal Councillor Minger during which he accused Army Intelligence "of *interfering in foreign policy issues*."[179] In his reply,[180] Masson fundamentally contradicted Pilet-Golaz, arguing that it was "impossible to clearly distinguish between specific military matters and political matters," because they were two aspects of the same issue. He added: "When we have certain political information, it is up to us to regularly inform our Foreign Minister about it through his service. For that reason, we have never failed to maintain contact with the Department of Foreign Affairs. By the way, the Department of Foreign Affairs for its part has been sharing its own information with us." Masson considered this routine of exchanging information between Foreign Affairs and Army Intelligence a necessity, explaining: "We consider that it is simply our job to procure and utilize, through our network of specialized agents, information—including on political matters—that is normally not accessible to our ministers abroad and then transmit it to the concerned Department. That is what we have been doing. *An intelligence service cannot limit its investigations to strictly military information.*"

Pilet-Golaz supported his accusations with specific examples, but Masson was able to refute them with convincing arguments. The complaints that Pilet-Golaz voiced show in what style the conflict was carried out; at the same time they make clear that the Foreign Minister quite deliberately obstructed the work of Army Intelligence.

One of the accusations that kept surfacing concerned the *case of Dr. Monfrini.* According to Pilet-Golaz, Masson came up with the idea of sending

Q.G.A., 19.5.44.

No. ....

EIDGENÖSSISCHES
MILITÄRDEPARTEMENT
🕂 ➝ 9. AUG. 1944 🕂

Personnel.

Par exprès   481.10

Au Chef du Département militaire fédéral,

Monsieur le Conseiller fédéral Kobelt,

B E R N E.

Monsieur le Conseiller fédéral,

       J'ai l'honneur de porter à votre connaissance les faits suivants, dont j'estime nécessaire que vous soyez informé :

       Me trouvant invité à Lausanne, dimanche dernier, au repas qui précédait la représentation officielle de la "Colonne de Feu" en même temps que M. le Conseiller fédéral Pilet-Golaz, celui-ci, après m'avoir entraîné à part, m'entreprit, d'un ton très vif, sur le compte du Col.brig. Masson, et me dit, en substance, ce qui suit :

       ".... Ce n'est pas la question des avions qui m'intéresse, mais ce qui a précédé, c'est-à-dire les agissements antérieurs du Chef du Service de renseignements.... J'ai un dossier.... Cela ne peut plus durer.... J'exposerai le cas à la prochaine séance du Conseil fédéral : Masson doit s'en aller d'ici au 31 mai. Si ce n'est pas lui qui s'en va, ce sera moi !"

       Je fis remarquer au Chef du Département politique qu'une telle décision ne pouvait être prise ex-abrupto, qu'un chef du service de renseignements - en admettant qu'il doive être changé - ne se remplace pas d'un jour à l'autre.

       Monsieur le Conseiller fédéral Pilet-Golaz s'attaqua ensuite au Major Burckhardt, notre attaché militaire à Berlin, réclamant également son départ. Je lui fis valoir que j'étais

.2

[handwritten notes in left margin and bottom]

à voir
9. 8. 44 R

Am 23. 5.44 mündl. im AHQ mir
mündl. erled. Ein Begehen des H. BR Pilet
dem Masson u. Burckhard erneut wurde ...
...bei Behandl der Angelegenheit im BR nicht ...
Angelegenheit kann als erledigt betrachtet ...

très satisfait des services de cet officier, qui n'avait démé-
rité en aucune façon, ni outrepassé ses compétences, puisqu'il
avait agi par ordre et, d'ailleurs, pris soin d'informer son
Ministre. A quoi M. Pilet-Golaz me répondit, sur le même ton
emporté : "Le Ministre partira, lui aussi, s'il le faut".

Si je tiens à relever ce que ces paroles avaient de
déplacé, c'est que je ne puis accepter ni l'ingérence qu'elles
représentent dans les compétences du Commandant en Chef, ni
le ton sur lequel elles étaient dites. Elles constituent un
nouvel indice de certaine "animosité" manifestée par le Chef
du Département politique, que je vous avais déjà signalée,
sous point IV de ma lettre personnelle du 15.1.44.

Ceci dit, je suis, naturellement, tout prêt à m'en-
tretenir avec vous du cas du Col.brig. Masson, afin d'envisager
la meilleure solution qui devrait être adoptée à son égard.
Son état de santé me préoccupe d'ailleurs, depuis quelque temps,
et j'ai prescrit de le faire passer maintenant à la "visite
sanitaire périodique".

Nous pourrions, si vous le vouliez bien, nous rencontrer un jour de la semaine prochaine à mon P.C., où nous
examinerions par la même occasion diverses autres questions
en suspens.

Je vous prie d'agréer. Monsieur le Conseiller fédéral,
l'assurance de ma haute considération.

Le Général :

[signature]

P.S. Cette lettre vous est transmise en deux exemplaires,
dont l'un, à titre personnel, à l'adresse de M. le
Président de la Confédération.

There was a constant conflict between Swiss Foreign Minister Pilet-Golaz and Swiss Army Intelligence. In 1944, in connection with the emergency landing of a secret German aircraft at the airfield in Dübendorf, canton of Zürich, Pilet-Golaz demanded that General Guisan remove Chief of Intelligence Masson and Military Attaché Burckhardt from their posts. The Commander-in-Chief wrote to the Head of the Military Department that he disapproved of Pilet's getting involved in internal army matters. Federal Councillor Kobelt annotated Guisan's letter by stating in handwriting: "[Matter] resolved verbally at AHQ with General, 23/5/44. At the Cabinet meeting dealing with the matter, Federal Councillor Pilet did not ask that Masson or Burckhardt be replaced. Matter can be considered as resolved." (BAr E 27/9539)

Dr. Monfrini, of whom he had heard through Marcel Regamey, a lawyer in Lausanne, and who supposedly entertained friendly relations with Mussolini, on a mission to the Duce "in order to tell him that the Swiss Army was very worried about the international situation and to ask him to protect [Switzerland] or intervene on our behalf in one way or another." It was true that during a private conversation Regamey had told Masson about the possibility of a connection between Monfrini and Mussolini;[181] however, Masson made clear to Regamey right away "that it was the Department of Foreign Affairs that handled such missions; it could be informed about Mr. Monfrini's presence in Lausanne and do with this information whatever it might find useful."[182] Masson had never met Monfrini, nor had he ever entrusted him with any mission. However, Monfrini had already been in contact with the Federal President about a possible mission to Rome.[183] Once Masson had explained that any mission of that kind fell under the responsibility of the Department of Foreign Affairs, Monfrini once again addressed Pilet-Golaz. In the meantime, however, Pilet-Golaz had changed his mind. Regamey stated, "The Federal President considered that the situation was much less serious than the military believed, that it was not necessary to travel to Rome, and that *the army should mind its own business instead of infringing on the civilian authorities.*"[184] Regamey commented to Masson, " I was surprised and troubled by [Pilet-Golaz'] judgment. The public knows that the Head of the Department of Foreign Affairs is tired of seeing that the Commander of the Armed Forces is so popular; however, the top official should keep from expressing this human feeling through an unfounded observation."[185]

Masson was able to refute in a similar manner the three other accusations voiced by Pilet-Golaz against Army Intelligence, or he was able to show that in the interest of the country, Army Intelligence *had* to act the way it did.

The *Ketterer case* concerned a consular agent working for the German Bureau. Lieutenant Colonel James *Ketterer* was one of three officers who had been detailed from Army Intelligence to the Department of Foreign Affairs; he was assigned to the Swiss Consulate in Stuttgart as an "expert on economic affairs" and had orders to collect military information concerning southern Germany and transmit it to Army Intelligence. For that purpose, he contacted Swiss citizens whom the Consul or his secretary had rated as reliable, asking them to procure information pertaining to the military.[186] However, Ketterer was betrayed to German Counterintelligence by a double agent.[187] On January 13, 1940, the Gestapo arrested him as he was crossing the German-Swiss border in Singen.[188] Since it could not prove anything against Ketterer, it had to set him free after four days.[189]

Masson emphasized that this mishap did not speak against the principle of using consular agents. He added that Pilet-Golaz had no reason to have a negative attitude toward officers who were detailed to his Department because "the issue of the consular agents (officers) was handled in agreement with the Federal Department of Foreign Affairs; hence, in this domain, we should not be accused of interfering in political matters."[190]

In the *Ritter case*, Pilet-Golaz raked up an allegation that he had made earlier, accusing Army Intelligence of unilaterally ordering Swiss Consul Ritter in Munich to travel to Procurement Office 1 in Lucerne. Masson referred to a letter that the Chief of the General Staff had written to Pilet-Golaz at the time, which stated, "Indeed Mr. Ritter and Army Intelligence have agreed that in the event of any danger, Mr. Ritter would travel from Munich to Switzerland, which would allow him to observe certain concentrations of troops that might interest our Intelligence Service."[191] Huber had pointed out, "Ritter, who is friends with Captain Waibel, declared that he would work for us as a volunteer."[192] For Army Intelligence, this was the only way to receive up-to-date information. It was agreed that this scheme should be used only in exceptional cases.

During the critical days of May 1940, a large number of German troops were concentrated in the Black Forest, at Switzerland's doorstep, making the Swiss fear the worst. In this tense situation, "as the border between Switzerland and Germany was sealed for [its] other investigating bodies,"[193] Army Intelligence considered that it was indispensable to use the services of Consul Ritter. Chief of the General Staff Huber and Masson acknowledged that consuls reported exclusively to the Department of Foreign Affairs and the Army Staff was not authorized to issue orders to them; nevertheless, they stressed that it was "important for some consuls to be authorized, if necessary, to procure information for us that no one else could supply in time."[194] During the time around May 10, 1940, when Germany attacked France and the Low Countries, Consul Ritter was the only person who could provide Army Intelligence with precise information on the important strategic area between Munich and Lake Constance.[195]

Even though Army Intelligence made clear that it had called on Consul Ritter's services in the country's interest, in retrospect one has to ask oneself if for tactical reasons it would not have been better for Masson or Waibel to communicate with Consul Ritter via the Department of Foreign Affairs. On the other hand, previous experiences[196] probably made Masson fear that Pilet-Golaz would not authorize Ritter to go on a mission for Army Intelligence.[197] Army Intelligence, which depended on the Consul's assistance, was therefore facing the question whether it could afford to deprive itself of its valuable source by communicating through official channels.

In October 1941, the dispute between the Department of Foreign Affairs and Army Intelligence flared up again in reaction to a letter by Minister Paul Ruegger to the Head of the Department of Foreign Affairs, in which the Swiss Envoy in Rome reported that there were rumors about Swiss Intelligence being active in Italy.[198] Ruegger explained that the Swiss Legation in Rome was suspected "of *spying*, particularly on the movements of troops in Italy. The information [was said to be] communicated to Bern, some of which [was supposedly] transmitted to the *British* authorities."[199] Once again, however, upon close examination the criticism turned out to be unfounded.[200] Pilet-Golaz addressed two letters to Kobelt,[201] who in turn asked General Guisan[202] and Masson[203] to comment on the matter.

In order to gather material for his report to the Commander-in-Chief, Masson held a briefing in Interlaken with Müller, Schafroth, Cuénoud, Waibel, Ernst, Daniel, and Hausamann. The minutes[204] that Alfred Ernst kept of the briefing reflect the mood among the top Intelligence officials. Masson opened the meeting by declaring, "In this report, our view will be expressed in unambiguous language." Then he read the complaint by the Head of the Department of Foreign Affairs to Federal Councillor Kobelt and General Guisan and pointed out that he considered the complaint as completely unfounded, and was ready "to fight for the needs of the Intelligence Service, [adding] unfortunately the Department of Foreign Affairs does not show any understanding at all toward Army Intelligence even though we tried everything to improve relations. Of course the behavior of the Department of Foreign Affairs must not prevent us from accomplishing our task in the army's interest."

The participants at the briefing remarked that *Swiss Intelligence did not have any structure in Rome* and that its courier did not make any reconnaissance apart from traveling on his assigned route. Schafroth was the only participant who used two informants in and around Rome, but they were not connected to the Legation; on exceptional occasions, they met with the courier. The minutes stated, "The *totally unjustified accusation* that we communicate with the *English Intelligence Service* may be due to the fact that Minister Paravicini, Colonel v[on] W[attenwyl's][205] brother-in-law, had good relations with England and is suspected by the Italian Legation in Bern [of spying on behalf of England]."[206] Several heads of bureau strongly defended the concept of the reinforced consulates that Pilet-Golaz criticized, arguing, "We cannot do without this source of information. These officers do not spy; they merely observe what everyone is allowed to observe. They have not set up any organization."[207] Cuénoud, Waibel, and Ernst pointed out:

> All neighboring states [of Switzerland] maintain an extensive intelligence service at their consulates here. The German Consulates have actual "military attachés." All other states also have a courier service; unlike our service, they do not only use professional couriers but constantly change their personnel in order to allow as many informants as possible to get to know Switzerland. This courier service primarily serves spying purposes. *Hence, Federal Councillor Pilet's attack is absolutely unjustified.*[208]

All participants at the briefing agreed that without couriers or outposts at the consulates Intelligence would miss out on some major events. They explained:

> The legations promise to supply us with reports. However, in most cases, the most interesting information from the consulates is withheld [from us]. There is no cooperation with our representatives abroad, nor can it be established now. That would have had to be done during times of peace, but back then the Department of Foreign Affairs was against cooperating with us. The only legal means for procuring intelligence is through our own bodies at the legations and consulates.[209]

The extensive report[210] that Masson wrote after the briefing with his top aides is a key document because the Chief of Intelligence did not simply refute Pilet's accusations but used the opportunity to explain why it was necessary for the Department of Foreign Affairs and Army Intelligence to work closely together. He argued that the main task of every intelligence service was to supply the Army Command with the basic information that it required to make decisions, adding, "[This] is a fierce, relentless battle against the risk of a *strategic surprise.*" Masson explained that this task was all the more difficult because nowadays armed conflicts erupted without preliminary diplomatic skirmishing (exchange of notes or ultimatums) and that "any country—whether it [was] neutral or not—[could] be in a state of war from one day to another without war being declared on it with more or less ceremony."

Masson also argued that the Army Command had to constantly take into account the requirements of the national economy (industry and agriculture); the Federal Council had urged the Commander-in-Chief "to agree that the bulk of our major units go off duty" as soon as the general situation permitted.

Masson said that consequently it was the task of Army Intelligence to warn the Commander-in-Chief in time "in order for him to take, as quickly as possible, the steps that serve to get the army prepared again to go to combat and face the decisive test with united forces." Masson remarked that in theory the concentration of [German] troops that Swiss Intelligence had noticed near Switzerland's border would justify keeping a large part of the Swiss Army under arms, as "any military situation [had] to be assessed based on the immediate *capabilities* of a presumed opponent, not its *intentions*, which [could] be kept secret until the last moment." He said that the Swiss Army had been mobilized from September 1939 to June 1940 because war operations were being conducted close to Switzerland's borders, making a threat *possible*. The Chief of Intelligence argued that by the fall of 1941, the situation had changed insofar as the *strategic* threat of a southward move by the German or French Army to bypass the enemy's defense line was gone as a result of the German-French armistice, adding, "Today there is a danger above all on the *political* level.[211] It would manifest itself as an armed conflict only at a later time." He explained that therefore it was Army Intelligence's duty to *be in regular contact with the Department of Foreign Affairs* "in order to exchange political and military information and verify information that [came] from different sources."

Masson pointed out that before the beginning of the war the Department of Foreign Affairs had in principle agreed to establish regular contacts with Army Intelligence, and that "these contacts [had] always yielded positive results." He added that both Federal Councillor Motta and his successor Pilet-Golaz had always had "a clear vision of the needs of [the] two services." He explained that the contacts, which were maintained through a liaison officer who communicated with the responsible officials at the Department of Foreign Affairs, had soon resulted in a certain "interpenetration of common interests," which was almost bound to manifest itself in a "more active cooperation" because in reality it was often difficult "to make a clear distinction between strictly military issues and political issues."

Masson stated that since 1940 the borders between Switzerland and the Axis powers had become increasingly impermeable for political, military, and economic reasons; in order to ensure that it could continue to procure information in foreign countries, Army Intelligence had suggested that the Department of Foreign Affairs send consular agents and couriers to Swiss representations abroad. He pointed out that the Department of Foreign Affairs had gladly accepted that idea and approved the creation of the new posts without delay because that was a *legal* means for procuring intelligence, which all foreign representations used in Switzerland. Masson formally declared, "Army

Intelligence did not take any initiative without the approval, and even the active cooperation, of the Department of Foreign Affairs."

In fact, *consulates and legations* had been cooperating with Army Intelligence for many years. As early as the beginning of 1923, in agreement with the Military Department and the Department of Foreign Affairs, the General Staff Unit had sent the Swiss legations and consulates instructions from the Intelligence Section titled "Matters That Interest the General Staff at Any Time." In 1937, the envoys and consuls were reminded of that document. Because Switzerland did not have any military attachés yet at that time, the General Staff Unit gathered information on foreign armies through the legations and consulates. Hence, the two institutions had been working together for almost two decades. Commonly, an aide of the Envoy or Consul was in charge of evaluating the foreign military literature (magazines, publications) and regularly transmitting to the Intelligence Section the information that was worth knowing. Masson commented, "This procedure was so free from suspicion from foreign governments that in some countries the Attaché who was in charge of the issues that were of interest to us was sometimes actually considered as a *military* attaché and was often invited to the army's exercises."[212] That was true above all for Max Grässli in Berlin and Louis H. Micheli in Rome.

Masson explained that Army Intelligence had not changed that traditional procedure. At legations that did not have an actual military attaché, the Envoy continued to supply the Intelligence Service with specific information via the Department of Foreign Affairs. Moreover, he made it clear that Army Intelligence did not misuse legations and consulates for spying activities, adding that even the Intelligence staff at the consulates had orders to keep their hands off espionage. He asserted that Swiss Intelligence was not in contact with any foreign intelligence service.

Masson also stated that the system of the immigration forms and the interrogations could not spoil Switzerland's relations with its neighboring states; instead, he claimed, "The fact is that these relations have been compromised by the attitude of some of the *Swiss press*." He said that, like the Swiss populace, the press did not always abide by the strict neutrality policy that the Federal Council tried to uphold; however, Pilet-Golaz should not make Army Intelligence responsible for that fact. Masson continued:

> I am surprised and pained by the apparent hostility that the Head of the Department of Foreign Affairs shows toward Army Intelligence and that he has just expressed once again (following some other interventions that I know about, particularly on the subject of the *Fonjallaz affair)*[213] through his serious accusations. . . . For over two years, our

service has been the only body among the Army Staff that operated day and night as *in a state of war*. In this constant struggle that entails serious responsibilities for us, we have the right to ask others to help us accomplish our task. In particular, we have the right to demand that we not constantly be suspected of machinations with which we have nothing to do.

The bitterness that is inherent in these words, as well as Masson's sharp tone throughout the document, reflect the sentiment among the staff at Army Intelligence. They felt that Pilet-Golaz was treating them all the more unfairly, as he backed up his allegations with evidence that Masson and his officers considered farfetched, making them believe that the Foreign Minister acted out of maliciousness.[214] The Commander-in-Chief, General Guisan, fully supported Intelligence's arguments.[215]

Pilet-Golaz for his part also had the feeling that he was misunderstood; he had wanted to express some fundamental criticism. In his reply to Masson's report, he tried to use a conciliatory tone. His reaction is all the more interesting as it shows why Pilet-Golaz acted in such an awkward and contradictory fashion, as Army Intelligence believed. In theory he assured Intelligence of his full understanding for its important work, but in practice he kept sabotaging its initiatives and creating obstacles for Masson.

Pilet-Golaz asserted that he had no grudge against the Chief of Intelligence but instead held him in high esteem,[216] stating:

> Is he not in the field artillery? I had the honor of being a field artillerist myself;[217] so many of them have become top-ranking officers in the army. I know and appreciate his strict idea of the service; I know that he wants to be useful to the country, and I know with how much zeal he pursues that objective. I am also aware how difficult and delicate his task is; very few officers are willing to take on such a task. It has never been my intention to criticize his activity. If possible, I very much prefer to help him through my advice, experience, and observations.[218]

Pilet-Golaz also explained that he fully understood the needs of Army Intelligence, stating, "I am really *not hostile at all toward the Intelligence Service* per se; the constant cooperation that exists between my Department and the Intelligence Service proves that fact. I personally wanted to intensify this cooperation by suggesting that Colonel Masson come to see me from time to time to go over a few matters." However, Pilet-Golaz was uncompromising con-

General Guisan, in the front passenger seat, and the head of the Special Service, Captain Paul Meyer, aka Wolf Schwertenbach (dressed in civilian clothes), who established the secret channel to Berlin. Army Intelligence viewed Meyer with suspicion because he had direct access to the Commander-in-Chief. Also pictured are Major Armand von Ernst, left, and Major Mario Marguth, two members of the General's Personal Staff. (Photo filed at BAr J.I.121 1985/100, vol. 1)

Until his retirement from the government, Rudolf Minger, second from right, the head of the Military Department, tried to mediate between Federal Councillor Pilet-Golaz, center, and General Guisan, far right, two natives of the canton of Vaud. Guisan would have liked Claude Du Pasquier, second from left, who was informed about the secret negotiations with the French Army ("*La Charité*"), to succeed Minger on the Federal Council, but Karl Kobelt was elected instead. Also pictured is Pierre de Muralt, far left. (Photo from Zürich Central Library, FP 6534)

Maneuver exercises headed by Lieutenant Colonel Ernst Koller in the area between Hitzkirch and Baldegg, canton of Lucerne. Pictured are, from left to right, Germany's military attaché in Switzerland, Lieutenant Colonel von Ilsemann; Henri Guisan, commander of Switzerland's 1st Army Corps; Lieutenant Colonel Masson, who accompanied the foreign military attachés; and the French military attaché in Switzerland, Colonel de la Forest-Divonne. Once the war had started, the Army Command avoided inviting attachés from the Allied countries and from the Axis powers to the same maneuvers. Taking care of the foreign military attachés was one of the tasks of the Chief of Intelligence. When the war started, 3 military attachés were stationed in Bern; a year later, the number increased to 12, and by the end of the war, 15 nations were represented in Switzerland by 19 military and air force attachés and 23 aides. (Photo from the author's private archives)

Bernard Barbey, left, sitting in front of Gümligen castle together with General Guisan in December 1939. Barbey, chief of Guisan's Personal Staff, warned Masson against getting involved in political talks with the Germans. His trust in the Chief of Intelligence waned because of the connection with Schellenberg. (Photo from the author's private archives)

Heinrich Himmler, center, provokes Swiss border guards at the French–Swiss border at Les Verrières, canton of Neuchâtel, in July 1940 just after the fall of France. To his left (also wearing glasses) stands the commander of the 6th Mountain Division, Major General Ferdinand Schörner (who was later promoted to command of an army). To Himmler's right stands Lieutenant General Wilhelm Weiss, also editor-in-chief of the *Völkischer Beobachter*. (BAr E 27/9945)

Roger Masson, top left, Chief of the Swiss Army's Intelligence and Security Service; Werner Müller, top right, Head of the Security Service and Masson's deputy; Robert Jaquillard, bottom left, Head of Counterintelligence; and Ernst Mörgeli, bottom right, who was arrested by the Gestapo in 1942. Through the connection with Schellenberg, Masson managed to have Mörgeli released from the Welzheim concentration camp. (Photos from the author's private archives)

Alfred Ernst, left, Head of the German Bureau, and Max Waibel, right, Head of Procurement Office 1, two outstanding personalities of Swiss Intelligence, pictured in front of the Dufour Barracks in Thun in 1940. Both of them served detention sentences there because they had been involved in the "Officers' Conspiracy" that followed the fall of France. They used the time they were detained to rethink the concept of how news was gathered and analyzed. Waibel noted ironically on the back of the photo, "Dear Colonel [Masson], this is a picture of two of your sinful aides standing at the edge of the territory which they currently have authority over, the courtyard of the barracks in Thun." (Photo from the author's private archives)

Staff members of Swiss Intelligence during World War II: from left to right, Georges Knopf, bookkeeper at the Intelligence and Security Service; Erwin Tschudi, head of Cartography; Paul Schaufelberger, head of the Technical Studies Bureau; and Alfred Alder, head of the Cipher Bureau. (Photo from the author's private archives)

Left: During the mid-1930s, Hans Hausamann created a private intelligence organization called *Bureau Ha.* In 1933 he had initially sympathized with the Third Reich but soon began fearlessly raising an admonitory finger against its machinations. There was no doubt about his patriotic feelings, but some staff members at Army Intelligence suffered from what Colonel-Corps-Commander Hans Frick called his "over-excited, agitated" manner and his "pathological need for recognition." Hausamann was one of the most fervent opponents of the Masson-Schellenberg connection. (Photo from the author's private archives)

Right: Rolf Eberhard, a Protestant minister, was in charge of Army Intelligence's *Axis Section* following Alfred Ernst's resignation. He is pictured at his office at the *Jungfrau* hotel in Interlaken, the headquarters of Swiss Army Intelligence. (Photo from the author's private archives)

Top (from left): Emil Häberli, head of Intelligence sub-office *Pfalz* in Basel. In his civilian career as State Attorney he had successfully been investigating the Gestapo kidnapping of a German journalist in Basel and was therefore, from 1938 onward, on the Gestapo's most-wanted list. *Middle*: Bernhard Mayr von Baldegg was Max Waibel's Deputy Head of Procurement Office *N.S.1* in Lucerne. Due to his professional contacts with Rudolf Roessler he fell victim to scandal-ridden infighting between Intelligence and Counter-intelligence. *Right*: Federal Councillor Eduard von Steiger headed the Department of Justice and Police and had numerous jurisdictional disputes with Masson. He criticized the Chief of Intelligence for freeing prisoners from Nazi concentration camps, describing Masson's actions as "inadmissible acts of encroachment." The head of the Political Police of Basel called von Steiger an "unprincipled old fox." *Bottom*: Roessler, alias *Lucy*, was one of the most important sources for *Bureau Ha* but also worked for the Soviet spy ring of Alexander Rado in Geneva. Roessler's connections and secret channels later inspired numerous authors to wild speculations about his activities. (Photos from the author's private archives)

The owner of Wolfsberg Castle, Paul Meyer (aka Wolf Schwertenbach), sitting at his desk. The lawyer and writer of detective stories set up the secret channel to the Reich Security Central Office in Berlin. (Photo from the author's private archives)

General Guisan, left, and Federal Councillor Pilet-Golaz. Markus Feldmann, a future Federal Councillor, described Pilet's ambiguous attitude toward the needs of Army Intelligence as "*piletiful*." (Photo from the Federal Archives, Bern)

Colonel-Brigadier Masson, left, speaks with Chief of the General Staff Jakob Huber in the yard of Gümligen castle in 1942. That year, Masson wrote to Huber, "You have always shown a lot of understanding as my superior. Let me therefore tell you frankly that I am discouraged; I have decided to give up my military career. . . . The 'shadow fights' that one has to carry out with people from the General's entourage who drag us through the mud without revealing their names go against my open and straightforward character. I will not accept being accused of meeting with 'dubious persons' or having relations with them." (BAr E 27/9528)

General Henri Guisan, left, and his son Henry. Guisan Jr.'s business contacts were at the root of the Masson-Schellenberg connection. (Photo from the author's private archives)

Irene and Walter Schellenberg in 1940. Masson was impressed by the young, elegant general. The photo on the right, showing Schellenberg together with SS Major Otto Skorzeny in Friedenthal, suggests that Schellenberg was not always a charming gentleman. Schellenberg had several of his agents shot after they had successfully carried out their reconnaissance missions. (Photos from Walter Schellenberg, *Aufzeichnungen: Die Memoiren des letzten Geheimdienstchefs unter Hitler*, ed. Gita Petersen [Wiesbaden/Munich, 1979])

Top: Schellenberg's Foreign Intelligence Service, office VI of the Reich Security Central Office, at the former Jewish retirement home at Berkaerstrasse 32, at the corner of Hohenzollerndamm, Berlin. (Photo from Berlin Document Center)
Bottom: Max Waibel established Procurement Office 1 (N.S.1) at the *Schweizerhof* hotel in Lucerne to collect intelligence on the Axis powers. (Photo by Lüönd)

cerning the actual subject of the debate. He once again accused Army Intelligence of *interfering in foreign and domestic policy issues*, leaving no doubt that he would not give in on that matter. He stated: "It is true that I reacted resolutely when certain Intelligence officers tried to interfere in the country's foreign and domestic policy. The army must stay out of [these issues]; it is not, nor can it be, its role to get involved in them." Pilet emphasized that as long as he was Federal Councillor, he would fight against this tendency with all his energy "and with utmost perseverance." He claimed that the Officers' Alliance (a secret society of young officers committed to national resistance) was an example where Intelligence had interfered in politics, explaining, "Last year, some *elements* of the group in Lucerne (N.S.1, if I am not mistaken) came up with the idea of staging some sort of *conspiracy*.[219] At that time, I demanded that these elements (Waibel, Ernst, Hausamann, etc.) be removed from the [General Staff]. It seems that this was done temporarily but that this decision has been revoked since then. I do not understand why this happened, nor will I accept it." Pilet-Golaz pointed out:

> The Intelligence Service has to try to put the [Army] Command in a position to assess the *military* situation abroad so that we will be able to determine our own situation, as the military situation has an influence on ours. This is an important, difficult, and delicate task. In order to be accomplished in the highest interest of the country, it has to be fulfilled without seriously harming the country's other general (political, economic, financial, personal) interests. [Of course there has to be close cooperation between Army Intelligence and the Department of Foreign Affairs] because it is solely the government's responsibility to safeguard the "other general interests" toward foreign countries. That is why the *Department of Foreign Affairs* has an obligation to *intervene* when it notices that the Intelligence Service *oversteps* the boundaries of its own activities, uses objectionable methods, or employs unsuitable agents.[220] By acting that way, it does not show any hostility toward the Intelligence Service nor its chief; on the contrary, it makes sure that the cooperation bears a maximum of results.

In Pilet's opinion, however, the two cooperating partners were not equal. He set clear limits for Army Intelligence, as an instrument of the Army Command, and it was not allowed to jeopardize the Federal Council's superior interests. Pilet-Golaz continued:

You know that I am the first one to understand the need for a good intelligence service. Nevertheless, there are certain ways of doing things, and there are limits. Of course the army has to be alerted in time. However, that is the responsibility not only of the Commander-in-Chief, whose only task it is to command [the army], but also of the Federal Council, the supreme authority that is responsible for the destiny of the country as a whole. Assessing the international situation and deciding on the various measures that this situation requires is actually one of its essential tasks. You know from your own experience how imbued [the Federal Council] is with this vital duty. You also know that preparing and reinforcing the national defense cannot be its only concern. For Switzerland, the war is not a goal in itself; it is the ultimate means for safeguarding [the country's] independence.

Pilet-Golaz considered that the Federal Council had to see to it that this ultimate means did not need to be used and that the country could *continue to live*, adding, "When you are aware of the political and economic difficulties that we are going through, that word takes on its full meaning."

Masson did not agree with Pilet's view on the limited tasks that should concern Army Intelligence. He ordered his deputy Werner Müller, the Chief of Security, "to produce, item by item, the materials that [were] required to answer Pilet-Golaz' letter and *refute* [the arguments that he presented]."
In his reply to Masson,[221] Müller concluded:

I do not agree with Federal Councillor Pilet-Golaz' opinion about the range of tasks of our Intelligence Service. . . . Obviously we do not attempt to find out what our diplomats do and do not do abroad. Just to give an *example*, however, we were told, without our soliciting the information, that the former Swiss Consul in Prague regularly received a Gestapo agent who—trusting that a representative of a Swiss Consulate knew whom he invited—subsequently went and told the relevant German authorities the things that had been discussed at the Swiss Consul General's about the Swiss and the Germans. I considered it as our duty to inform the Department of Foreign Affairs about that. . . . Moreover, I do not agree with Federal Councillor Pilet-Golaz' opinion about our Intelligence Service. Even if the diplomatic service actually collected the amount of relevant political information and information on the war economy that was needed to obtain a reliable picture of the situation, we could *not*, and would not be allowed to, *limit ourselves to doing purely military reconnaissance.* We know about the state of affairs in the diplomatic service; it is sufficient to recall that the Swiss diplomatic representative accredited in a neighboring state was on vacation (!) at the time that the country ordered its armed forces to mobilize for war and the diplomatic corps of all other states were working day and night. The information according to which Italy was about to collapse *definitely* did not come from Army Intelligence.

Müller stated that one should always keep in mind "that it [was] *impossible* for a country's diplomatic service to procure all the information that an army command [required] in order to make arrangements ahead of time. *Only the Secret Service* [was] able to collect that much information." He explained that it was no coincidence that "all states in the world, even those states whose diplomatic service [was] known for its excellent work, [had] a worldwide secret service that [had] vast means available." He pointed out that no secret service limited itself to procuring purely military information, adding, "Because the secret services of these countries are unimpeded, they pull their tightly-knit nets through *all* ponds, whereas diplomats are able to catch a piece of information here and there if at all *because they are tied down.*"

Müller also explained that the memoirs of numerous statesmen showed that Switzerland was not the only country where the Diplomatic Service and the Secret Service inevitably had overlapping activities[222] "because both Services [had] to work independently from each other." He added, "It is the authorities' job to combine the results of the work done by the two Services and evaluate them, and at the same time prevent serious conflicts from being created. That would be the perfect art of politics. . . . The Head of the Department of Foreign Affairs has to mediate in the same way as the Chief of Intelligence does between the Bureaus of his section, which work independently from each other." Müller did not hide the fact that it was unpleasant "to have to waste time dismissing unjustified attacks instead of cooperating in a reasonable manner with the Department of Foreign Affairs."

Even though Müller identified the sore point, in this author's opinion he drew the wrong conclusion from his observations. The heart of the matter was indeed "to combine the results of the work done by the two Services," but this should have been done at a lower level than the one suggested by Müller. As the dividing-line between military intelligence and political-diplomatic intelligence was blurred, the two Services (not the Chief of Intelligence and the Head of the Department) should have sat together in order to regularly *coordinate* the objectives concerning the procurement activities. In fact, Masson had the experience that even a few regular contacts with the Foreign Service of the Department of

Foreign Affairs had a beneficial effect on the two parties by creating a better mutual understanding, resulting in an "interpenetration of common interests." Regular *conferences* among representatives of the two departments, if necessary with the involvement of other parties such as the Justice and Police Department, the Commerce Section of the Department of Economy, and the General Attorney's Office, could have helped smooth out differences, find common positions, and encourage each other.[223] In retrospect, it appears difficult to believe that during the entire period of wartime duty no provisions were made to create such a coordinating body. However, the involved parties were blinded to this need through the rivalries that existed between the Department of Foreign Affairs and Army Intelligence as well as through the fact that intelligence activities did not carry the same weight for the two departments. Moreover, the tendency of wanting to be better informed than the other party did not help to bring things into the open. It is known that Pilet-Golaz was absolutely convinced that due to his numerous official contacts his Intelligence Service was far better than Army Intelligence.[224] This attitude explains why he frequently used an arrogant tone in the dispute with Army Intelligence.

One and a half years following the major falling-out between Army Intelligence and the Department of Foreign Affairs it became obvious once again that, even though Pilet-Golaz expressed some understanding of the requirements of Army Intelligence, he failed to back up this understanding with actions.[225] In May 1943, the army once again asked the government to establish so-called reinforced consulates in Munich, Stuttgart, and Milan.[226] General Guisan wrote to Federal Councillor Kobelt: "The staff that we would send there would in fact be in a position not only to estimate the number of troops and the quantity of material but also interpret the meaning of any deployment [of troops] and advise our agents in what direction they should pursue their investigation after supplying their information. As you know, these three staff members should be assimilated with the consular staff in the three big cities." Guisan therefore asked Kobelt: "[Please try] to remove the prejudices that the Federal Department of Foreign Affairs still seems to have concerning this idea and thereby contribute, in the highest interest, to *establishing normal cooperation* in this area between the Government and the Army Command. I am very grateful to you for skillfully pleading the army's cause in the matter of the couriers; due to your intervention, they can now be interrogated exclusively by Major Daniel, which is the right thing to do."[227]

The liaison officer with the Department of Foreign Affairs considered "that it was not very desirable to communicate in writing about this delicate matter. The Head of the Federal Department of Foreign Affairs feared that some written records might be found about these things and compromise his diplomatic service."[228] Kobelt nevertheless chose to present General Guisan's request to Pilet-Golaz in writing, stating:

> Major Daniel has explained to me several times that it is necessary to be able to continue having at our disposal the channels that have been operating in a reliable manner so far. I know that in a few instances these channels did not meet your approval because occasionally some clumsy mistakes were made. However, now that Major Daniel, an officer who is guaranteed to be loyal and willing to also take into account your Department's interests, is in charge of arranging the channels on behalf of the Army Command, I consider that the former situation should be *re-established*. Therefore please allow me [to request] that you make arrangements for *suitable people to be re-appointed to Munich, Stuttgart, and Milan*. Major Daniel assured me that these people would in no way enter in contact with any agents but would receive verbal orders directly from the Army Command. The more difficult our situation becomes and the more impenetrable the cordon is at the border, the *more necessary* it is *to reuse this service, which used to work well*. Please allow me to express my expectation that you will approve this urgent request.[229]

However, Pilet-Golaz failed to show any understanding for the request; several weeks went by before he gave Kobelt an evasive answer. He remarked that he had already told Liaison Officer Daniel that it was "*difficult* to re-establish the—*highly uncommon*—information network that had been put in place in fall 1939, at a time when the Department of Foreign Affairs did not have any leadership," adding:

> I explained to [Major Daniel] how much damage had been done, which he loyally admitted because he is an intelligent and understanding officer. I pointed out [to him] the precautions and conditions under which the army's [task] might be somewhat facilitated without taking the serious risks that were taken back then and that unfortunately turned out to be very real. For the most part, he personally agreed with my suggestions, for others he had to refer the matter [to the Army Command]. It was agreed that he would come back to see me once the army had examined [my suggestions].[230]

Hence, Pilet-Golaz put the issue off. Three months later, in September 1943, Kobelt inquired about the latest developments in the matter, writing:

> I know that, after the Army Command had made some guarantees, an agreement was made and you merely wanted to clearly define the involved persons' position and terms of reference in a memorandum addressed to them before the project was to be definitely implemented. However, I have noticed with some concern that nothing has happened for two months in this important matter. Since you also recognize how important military information is, and since unpredictable events may occur any time, I believe that the Army Staff's plans must no longer be put off.[231]

However, Pilet-Golaz maintained his silence. In order to finally speed up the process, Masson addressed the Chief of the General Staff, who in turn asked the Commander-in-Chief to intervene with Kobelt once again, stating: "This problem has to be resolved quickly, in particular concerning northern Italy, where our regular means of investigation are limited. The current events there are of paramount importance to us."[232] General Guisan agreed, "urgently and insistently" pointing out to Kobelt "how important it [was] to find a positive solution as quickly as possible at a time when the events in Italy [contained] such frightening unknown factors for us."[233] As a consequence, the Head of the Military Department once again wrote to Pilet-Golaz, stating:

> I feel obliged to come back to my various letters concerning the Swiss consulates abroad. . . . In view of the current development it is possible that sooner or later the existing connections will be interrupted so that we will run the risk of no longer being informed in time about events abroad. I do not want to go into more detail in this letter because the whole issue has been explained to you several times both verbally and in writing, allowing me to assume that there were no more objections to implementing the project. I would therefore like to ask you to inform me about your outstanding approval or to at least bring up the issue verbally in the Federal Council.[234]

Pilet-Golaz still did not react. In mid-November 1943, the Commander-in-Chief asked Bernard Barbey, the Chief of his Personal Staff, to have the issue of the consular agents resolved. Barbey spoke with Bracher, who drafted a note on their conversation to the attention of Kobelt in which he stated: "[Barbey explained that] above all in Italy, our Intelligence Service [was] facing almost insurmountable difficulties as long as the planned measures could not be applied to make its work easier. Maybe the issue could be brought up at today's Federal Council meeting."[235] Kobelt did raise the issue in the Cabinet meeting, but Pilet-Golaz showed no sympathy for the plan. After the meeting, the Head of the Military Department remarked underneath Bracher's note, "F[ederal] C[ouncilor] Pilet explains that it is currently *impossible* to resolve the issue of the consular agents, as suggested by the Commander-in-Chief."[236] In a letter to General Guisan, Kobelt added, "The Head of the Department of Foreign Affairs agreed that he would consider the Army Command's proposals if any post became vacant."[237] Otherwise, Pilet-Gilaz seemed determined to preside over the status quo, at the expense of the desires of Army Intelligence.

Lack of Coordination

In retrospect, some of the difficulties were due to shortcomings in the structure of Army Intelligence itself. It would therefore be unfair and biased to hold the Department of Foreign Affairs responsible for all the difficulties that the German Bureau and Procurement Office 1 were facing. Relations with the Justice and Police Department were not exactly smooth either.[238]

If an intelligence service is supposed to work efficiently, it depends on official bodies to *cooperate* with it, *support* it, and *accept* it.[239] In his final activity report for N.S.1 during wartime duty, Waibel did not hide the fact that this was not always the case, observing:

> [In fall 1939,] when everyone in the country was aware of the serious-ness of the situation, it was easy to cooperate with any military and civilian authority. Over the years, however, some unpleasant differ-ences emerged, and on several occasions Army Intelligence had to defend itself against a large number of attacks. Especially the Federal Police and Counterintelligence lacked understanding, forcing us to cover up our agent service and our communication with informants in Switzerland the same way we had to cover them up in foreign coun-tries. The measures serving to cover our agents from the Federal Police and Counterintelligence took a lot of effort, time, and work. Nevertheless, fortunately on both bodies there were a few personalities who were exceptions to the rule, showing the necessary understanding for us.[240]

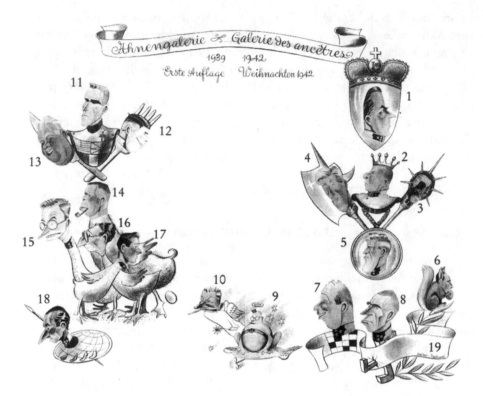

1 Roger Masson	11 Bernard Cuénoud
2 Werner Müller	12 Pierre Pélissier
3 Jakob Keller	13 Hans Joho
4 Georges Knopf	14 Hans-Rudolf Schmid
5 Paul Meyer	15 Hugo Faesi
6 Charles Daniel	16 Jakob Tobler
7 Alfred Alder	17 Marcel Diday (?)
8 Alfred Ernst	18 Erwin Tschudi
9 Edi Siegrist	19 Alfred Seiler
10 Auguste Delay	

Army Intelligence was hampered by a lack of coordination, causing very capable staff members to isolate themselves instead of working together, to be overly secretive, and to consider each other as rivals. This "gallery of ancestral portraits" was drawn by Erwin Tschudi. (BAr E 27/9544)

The sharp criticism of the Federal Police and Counterintelligence was undoubt-edly due to the unpleasant error of judgment that had been made in the case of *Mayr von Baldegg*.[241]

Army Intelligence worked closely, and generally well, with cantonal police authorities.[242] Relations were ideal in cantons where the head of the Political Police was at the same time in charge of an Army Intelligence's outpost, such as in St. Gallen and temporarily in Basel and Zurich. N.S.1 was "sometimes on excellent terms, and sometimes on less good terms" with the customs adminis-tration; however, Waibel acknowledged that frictions were not due to a lack of goodwill but were almost inevitable because of what Army Intelligence consid-ered too narrow an interpretation of rules and regulations. He added, "Gradually we were able to establish satisfactory relations with the border brigades and border police; at times we worked very well together."[243] According to Waibel, among the federal police authorities dealing with foreign nationals, Robert Jezler[244] showed "a great deal of understanding" for N.S.1's requests and needs.[245]

Coordination problems existed within Army Intelligence as well. Waibel considered that the various internal difficulties among Group Ib in the course of wartime duty were due to a lack of leadership by the Chief of Intelligence, explaining:

Maybe the real reason [for the difficulties] was the fact that every sec-tion of the Intelligence Service had to be as independent as possible in order to be able to carry out its work. All of us highly appreciated this great amount of freedom, but on the other hand we would have liked to have *close coordination* to counterbalance this freedom. The issue of how to lead the Intelligence Service might be one of the toughest chal-lenges for any top military command because, as indicated, the initia-tive and eagerness of the subordinate bodies to take on their own responsibilities put a limit to the coordination efforts.[246]

Because he had the impression that *Army Intelligence lacked coordination*, as early as the end of 1942, in his annual report under the subheading "Experiences and Suggestions," Alfred Ernst felt obliged to repeat "a very old request that [he] had expressed a long time ago," stating: "It seems to me that the whole work in Group Id[247] suffers from a lack of contact between the Chief and his staff as well as among the staff. The frequent personal incidents and fric-tions are due to this lack of contact, which has been the case since about June 1940."[248] Ernst therefore suggested that Masson hold meetings at least twice a week during which the staff could bring up any issue relating to Army

Intelligence as a whole, adding, "This would be the only way to give everyone the opportunity to express their views and make sure that the Chief's decisions and opinions are the result of the input and views of all officers who bear part of the responsibility."[249] Instead, Masson led Army Intelligence on a case-by-case basis by making most decisions following more or less coincidental meetings with individual staff members; in most cases, the expert in charge actually did not know anything about the decision and did not get any chance to defend his opinion. This leadership style was bound to create unclear situations, result in agreements and discussions that were held behind other people's backs, and create a breeding ground for plots[250] and disputes that seriously hampered the team spirit among Army Intelligence.[251] As early as 1942, Alfred Ernst assessed that "confidence [had] been seriously shaken"; he explained that open meetings with all concerned persons, as well as decisions by the Chief that were made with full knowledge of the facts and pointed the way ahead for everyone working for the Intelligence Service, were required in order to create "a spirit of friendship and cooperation in the service of a common cause; today this spirit does not exist at all."[252]

The fact that the different activities were not better coordinated also had a direct effect on the work of the individual bodies of Army Intelligence. Both the procurement bodies and the evaluation bodies were at a disadvantage because most of the time Army Intelligence lacked a common, binding starting position. This starting position could have been established at internal briefings during which all information that the different sections had collected and interpreted could be processed. This lack of a common starting position occasionally resulted in conflicting views on the way in which an operation was progressing, the expected duration of the war, and even the way the war would end. The readers of the Army Intelligence bulletins were sometimes confused when, due to a lack of internal discussions, several conflicting, apparently contradictory, views were expressed in one and the same update.

Even though cooperation was facilitated through personal ties, for example between Alfred Ernst and Max Waibel, it is obvious that the tasks, authority, and responsibilities were not clearly defined nor differentiated, resulting in overlapping activities and rivalries that proved to be burdensome. In 1945, an investigating magistrate qualified the structure of Army Intelligence as "rather loose and somewhat unclear," adding: "It is often not quite clear who issues orders, i.e. who reports to whom, and the responsibilities have been changed many times. Hence, some officers are not absolutely sure who their direct superior or subordinate is. What is more, in some instances not even Chief M[asson] is able to provide satisfactory answers."[253] On the other hand, due to this flexible structure the staff of Army Intelligence had the necessary freedom of action. In order to be able to take unconventional action, one accepted the inevitable flaws that are inherent in any improvised structure.[254] The independent investigating magistrate who had the opportunity, during a hearing of evidence, to get a glimpse of Army Intelligence's activities admitted that the staff successfully made use of this freedom of action, saying: "Since I am not an expert, I cannot assess the activities [of the Intelligence Service]; however, I must say that I am amazed by the amount of work that has been done and the results that have been achieved. My investigation has reinforced my impression that [the staff of] this service has been very hard-working and committed, but also clever, astute, resourceful, and nimble-minded."[255]

American readers who are surprised to read about this unpleasant and quite detrimental squabbling among the Swiss intelligence agencies and the Department of Foreign Affairs and other Federal bodies may be interested to learn that the United States Office of Strategic Services encountered similar experiences throughout the war.[256]

Five months before the Japanese attack on Pearl Harbor precipitated America's entry into World War II, President Roosevelt had created an Office of the Coordinator of Information (COI), soon to become the OSS, and put at its helm William J. Donovan, who had been known since his youth as "Wild Bill." General Donovan had the "power to visualize an oak when he saw an acorn," in the words of the OSS Psychological Staff. Under the General's leadership, the OSS quickly grew and expanded—and aroused the resentment of other official bodies. From the moment that the COI was created, a host of predatory government agencies "forgot their internecine animosities and joined in an attempt to strangle this unwanted newcomer at birth."[257] The Federal Bureau of Investigation under J. Edgar Hoover viewed this newcomer to the clandestine world with a particularly suspicious eye. Although OSS relations with the FBI seemed to improve as the war progressed, Hoover remained hyper-vigilant about suspected encroachments.

As was the case in Switzerland, the OSS also had running bouts with the Department of State. The COI had just acquired a few temporary rooms in the State Department Annex in its very early days when Secretary of State Cordell Hull's assistants started worrying about competition from the new agency. When COI requested access to some State files, Foreign Service officers nervously jibed that Donovan was "a man who could tell you the time if you loaned him your watch."[258] Officials at the State Department had every reason to feel concerned, as the improvised but brilliant achievements of Donovan's officers sharply contrasted with the tradition-bound, sluggish actions of the Diplomatic Service. The disappointment Masson, Waibel, and Ernst experienced regarding the Swiss Foreign Service was shared in a similar manner by OSS members dealing with Foggy Bottom, finding the State Department hopelessly hamstrung by bureaucratic inertia and a "spirit of smug self-satisfaction."[259] In August 1941, the alarmed State Department signed an uneasy pact with COI, assigning some vague responsibility for intelligence collection and overseas propaganda to Donovan's group—a concession accepted by Undersecretary of State Sumner Welles. However, not all officials at State were happy with the agreement. In late 1941, Assistant Secretary of State Brickingridge Long wrote in his diary: "One of the most important things to be controlled is Donovan." Four months later, in April 1942, he added that Donovan "has been a thorn in the side of a number of the regular agencies of the government for some time—including the Department of State—and more particularly recently in Welles'."[260]

A second dispute involved the use of American diplomatic facilities by the OSS. The American Ambassador to Vichy, Admiral William Leahy, tried to impose restrictions on the espionage operations of OSS agents attached to the American consulates in southern France. "General Donovan accused me of interfering in his work," recalls Leahy. "I told him the diplomatic service was *my* business."[261] In all the neutral countries of Europe—Sweden, Spain, and Portugal in addition to Switzerland—the assignment of OSS officers to the American embassies under diplomatic cover met with strong resistance from the professional diplomats.[262] The State Department also objected to issuing passports to OSS officers. Mrs. Ruth Shipley, who ran the State Department's passport division as her own personal empire, insisted that Donovan's agents travel abroad with their passports clearly marked with "OSS." It took considerable discussion at high levels to convince the State Department that Mrs. Shipley's whims were seriously impeding espionage operations. Later in the war she struck back by interminably delaying, on "security" grounds, the passports of Japanese-Americans bound for OSS posts in the Far East.

In early 1941, before the formation of COI, lan Fleming (the future creator of "James Bond"), then a ranking officer in British Naval Intelligence, suggested to Donovan that he should select as intelligence officers men who had "absolute discretion, sobriety, devotion to duty, languages, and wide experience." Their age, Fleming added, should be "about 40 to 50."[263] Donovan rejected Fleming's advice. Instead, he promised President Franklin Roosevelt an international secret service staffed by young officers who were "calculatingly reckless," with "disciplined daring" and "trained for aggressive action."[264] Those were the qualities with which the OSS men in Bern, Rome, Beijing, Bangkok, Paris, and Algiers were imbued. Their devotion and energy, fantasy and daring, had much in common with that of their Swiss counterparts. In Masson's Intelligence Service, of course, nobody knew about the problems it shared with the OSS at the time, yet the American experiences put the Swiss incidents in perspective.

6

The Initiator of the Connection

PAUL MEYER, AKA WOLF SCHWERTENBACH, was a lawyer, a writer of detective stories, and a member of the Intelligence Service on the Swiss Army Staff. The names that he used were as diverse as his careers. As a civilian he went by the name *Meyer* (spelled with a "y"), as a writer he assumed the pen name *Wolf Schwertenbach,*[1] and at hotels and restaurants he used to sign in as *Dr. Ritzburg.*[2] Moreover, when he was on missions for the Security Service, he occasionally identified himself as *Police Officer Hans Kunz, from Grafenried.*[3] In documents and reference works he is usually referred to as *Meyer-Schwertenbach.* He should not be mixed up with the other "Meyer" working for Army Intelligence, Johann Conrad Meyer, a *Neue Zürcher Zeitung* correspondent and economic advisor who was better known under his cover names *Sx.* and *Q.N.* and who was one of Swiss Intelligence's most reliable informants.[4] For some time both Paul Meyer and Johann Conrad Meyer were members of the *Uto* sub-office, although in different positions. Another staff member of Army Intelligence with a similar name was Bernhard Mayr von Baldegg from Lucerne; like Paul Meyer, he was a lawyer and held the rank of captain. He was Max Waibel's deputy at Procurement Office 1.

Civilian Career

Captain Meyer was born on August 4, 1894 in Dübendorf, in the canton of Zürich, to a well-to-do family; his legal name was Paul Eduard *Meier*. After graduating from high school in his home town of Zürich, he began studying architecture at the Federal Institute of Technology in Zürich. Two years later he transferred to the University of Zürich, where he began studying law, graduating in 1920 with a Ph.D. Then he started working for the Zürich district court as an intern preparing for the bar. In 1923 he joined a law firm. In 1924 he married his first wife, with whom he had a daughter. Through that marriage, which ultimately ended in divorce, Meyer was brought into close contact with financial and industrial circles in Zürich. About 10 years later, he resigned from the law firm and began focusing on economic issues.[5]

In the 1920s he developed a passion for writing fiction that he pursued until his death. In the 1930s, under his pen-name *Wolf Schwertenbach,* he published a series of adventure and detective stories.[6] His best-known works were first published or reviewed in the literary supplement of the *Neue Zürcher Zeitung.*[7] In 1932 he became a member of the Swiss Authors' Association. His interest in criminology was aroused while beginning his career as a lawyer in Zürich due to several murders that occurred and were very difficult to solve. In a scholarly study, which he signed as "Dr. Paul E. Meyer, Ph.D. in law," he demanded that an existing police dispute over respective areas of authority be settled and that a special homicide committee be created. This study brought Meyer-Schwertenbach into contact with leading personalities among the police who dealt with combating crime.

Schwertenbach had a keen sense of observation, which turned out to be a great asset both as a writer and as an intelligence officer during the war. In retrospect, Major Hans Rudolf Schmid,[8] the head of the press office at army headquarters, characterized him as a man with a good memory and "an absolutely unbelievable ability to distinguish and unravel things, making him an expert and a master in deciphering coded messages. He was capable of solving the most complicated riddles and brain-teasers and developed a habit of being curious, looking beyond the obvious and studying people in detail."[9]

Even though Schwertenbach accomplished his most significant and, at the same time, most dangerous and daring feat in his capacity as intelligence officer *Captain Meyer,* on several occasions his civilian occupation worked to the advantage of his military career, since he retained good personal relationships with city and cantonal police authorities as a consequence of his earlier dealings in criminology issues. Besides, the fact that he was familiar with methods and issues pertaining to police investigations made it easier for him to accomplish

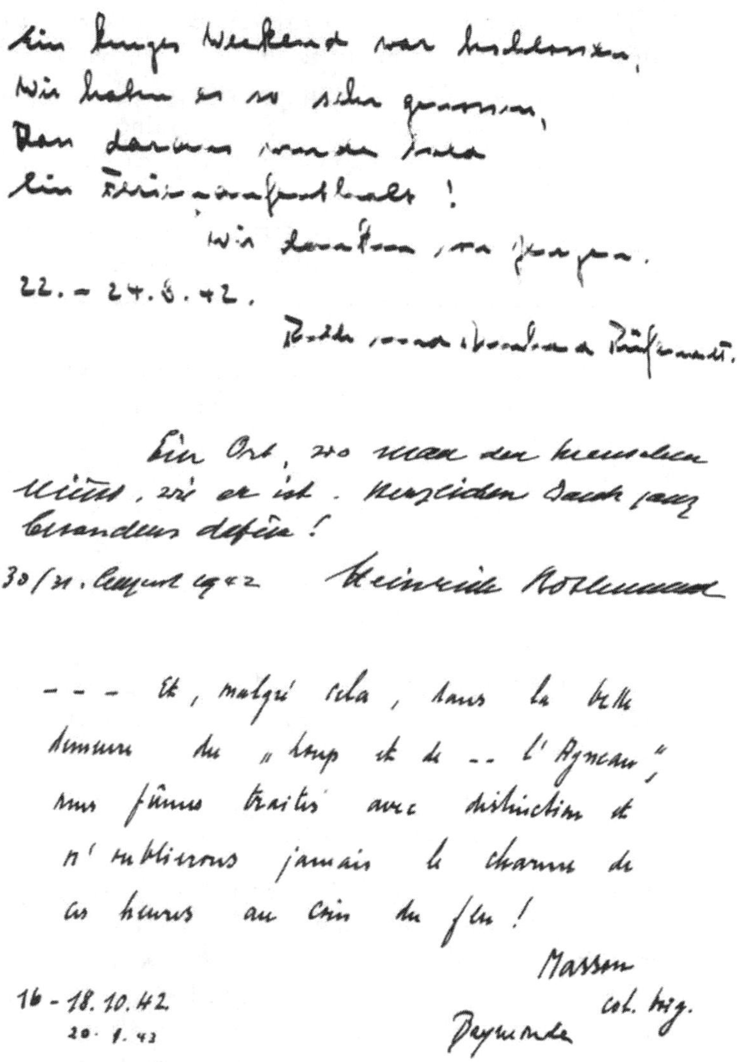
Ein kurzes Weekend war beschieden,
Wir haben es so sehr genossen,
Dann darum wurde heute
ein Ferienaufenthalt [illegible]!
Wir danken, wir [illegible].
22.–24.8.42.
Bertha und Bernhard Rüfenacht.

Ein Ort, wo man den Menschen nimmt, wie er ist. Herzlichen Dank ganz besonders dafür!
30/31. August 1942 Heinrich Rothmund

--- Et, malgré cela, dans la belle demeure du „Loup et de .. l'Agneau", nous fûmes traités avec distinction et n'oublierons jamais le charme de ces heures au coin du feu!
Masson
col. brig.
16 - 18.10.42.
20. 1. 43
Reymonde

Captain Meyer-Schwertenbach used his privately owned Wolfsberg Castle as a site for establishing and maintaining relations between Swiss Army Intelligence and the German SS. General Guisan as well as the German Chief of SS Intelligence, Schellenberg, were invited there on several occasions. According to the copy of this page from the guest book, within three months Meyer-Schwertenbach also received the deputy head of the Security Service, Bernhard Rüfenacht, the head of the Federal Police Section at the Justice and Police Department, Heinrich Rothmund, and Switzerland's Chief of Intelligence, Colonel Brigadier Masson. (Document from author's private archives.)

his various tasks for the Security Service of the Army Staff. The years of wartime duty demonstrated that, due to his ability to judge human nature, Meyer-Schwertenbach was one of the men on the Intelligence and Security Service "who were not afraid to do their duty and—like real fighting soldiers—were imbued with a dash of audacity in order to take risks and get through daring feats unharmed."[10]

Following two years of preliminary negotiations, on March 23, 1938 Meyer-Schwertenbach purchased Wolfsberg Castle near Ermatingen, canton of Thurgau.[11] During the war, the castle served as a stage for fostering the contacts between the chief of Swiss Military Intelligence, Roger Masson, and the head of SS Foreign Intelligence, Walter Schellenberg, as Meyer put his estate at their disposal as a discreet yet stylish meeting place and transit point.[12] After 1945, a number of rumors surfaced concerning the purchase of the estate, resulting in several investigations. Hans Hausamann, the head of *Bureau Ha*, for example, allegedly told high-ranking officers that he suspected Meyer-Schwertenbach had been able to purchase the castle after the war with *funds from spying activities*.[13] However, it should be pointed out that Meyer purchased the estate about a year and a half *before* the war broke out and half a decade before he met Schellenberg.[14]

In 1941, Captain Meyer married his second wife.[15] During the secret meetings, "*la Schlossherrin*" (the mistress of the castle), which was the title that General Guisan used to refer to her, acted as hostess and secretary.[16]

Military Career

Shortly after the outbreak of the war, Meyer's civilian jobs as a lawyer and author of detective stories, which had brought him into close contact with police authorities, helped him to be transferred from the troops to the Army Staff. On August 29, 1939, 1st Lieutenant Paul Meyer had gone on duty as a member of a reserve fusilier company that was part of the border troops.[17] Just five weeks later, he was detailed to the Intelligence Section of the Army Staff at army headquarters.[18] On November 7, 1939, he began working for the Security Service,[19] where his direct superior was Werner Müller,[20] Masson's deputy on Army Intelligence. As the head of the Special Service,[21] Meyer-Schwertenbach dealt with issues relating to the domestic Security Service. However, his terms of reference[22] indicate that he had to work closely with Military Intelligence, as his tasks included:

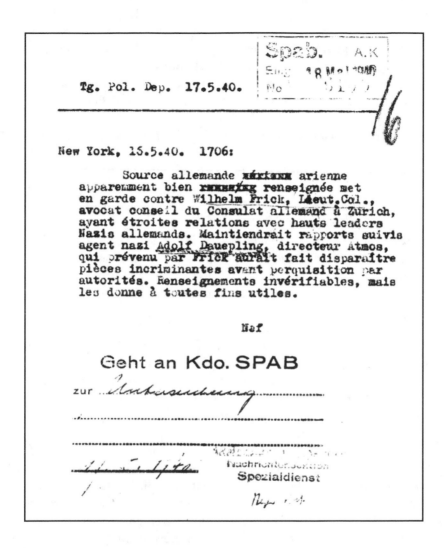

A typical case for Meyer-Schwertenbach's Special Service: a telegram by the Swiss Consulate General in New York to the Department of Foreign Affairs. Lieutenant Colonel Wilhelm Frick, who is mentioned in the document, was a lawyer, a former leader of the "Swiss Federal Front," a legal counsel for the German Consulate General in Zürich, and president and board member of *Atmos AG* in Zürich. He appointed "Nazi agent" Adolf Däumling as head of *Atmos AG*, giving him full signing powers. From 1936 to 1938, Däumling had been the leader of the local NSDAP group in Zürich. In 1940, when he escaped to Germany, he was replaced at *Atmos AG* by Erwin Lemberger, a German spy. In August 1942, Lemberger was arrested on charges of political and military espionage on behalf of Germany. (BAr E 27/10395)

1. *evaluating and forwarding the special reports* by the procurement offices to the subordinate sections, counter-intelligence,[23] the police section, army police, attorney general's office, etc.;
2. *monitoring*, in part by means of an independent organization, *the domestic political situation*[24] (pro-German revival movements,[25] political activities by officers,[26] etc.;
3. *verifying, evaluating, and distributing the transcripts of tapped telephone conversations*;
4. *writing a bulletin containing the results of the tapped telephone conversations*;
5. *carrying out special orders* (contacts with foreign agents aimed at procuring intelligence);[27]
6. *checking*, before they were printed, whether *the annual reports* of the cantonal military departments contained any information that had to be kept secret;
7. performing chancellery duties for the Security Service dealing with personnel issues.

On August 23, 1941, in a letter to Chief of the General Staff Huber, General Guisan appointed Meyer-Schwertenbach as his unofficial intelligence officer.[28] From that moment on, he entrusted him with delicate special missions and gradually put him in charge of his personal security.[29] On January 20, 1943, Meyer was named *head of intelligence at the branch office in Zürich*, as a result of which he left the Security Service.[30] At the same time, for objective organizational reasons the Special Service was abolished,[31] as it had become redundant following the expansion of and redistribution of a number of tasks to the Security Service. Under the restructuring plan, Masson had ordered Major Max Maurer to act as a liaison officer with the Attorney General's office, for which Maurer had already been working as a commissioner in his civilian career.[32] In an official letter to his superior Masson on January 16, 1943, Werner Müller argued:

It is therefore useless to have another liaison officer. Moreover, I prefer to deal with Major Maurer in person concerning the issues that are of interest to us. . . . Whenever I am unavailable, my deputy at the [Security Service] is in charge. The contacts with the cantonal and municipal police authorities have definitely become the business of the [Security Service] as a whole (headquarters, army police, counter-intelligence, police section. In special cases I go through the federal police),

and the coordination activities increasingly require my own involvement.[33]

Also, by then the Security Service was able to communicate with
Switzerland's major police authorities directly by telex. In addition, Werner
Müller had started personally verifying the transcripts of the tapped telephone
conversations "in order to make clear who was responsible."[34]

On the same day, in a personal letter to Masson, Werner Müller mentioned
the real reasons why Meyer had left the Security Service, explaining, "[In the
official letter, I] took into account the purely official, objective reasons in order
to allow [Meyer-Schwertenbach] to leave [the Security Service] in a correct
manner by giving him a clear explanation. However, I also no longer trust
Captain Meyer."[35] The Head of the Security Service had met with Meyer, hoping to overcome a certain feeling of uneasiness that he had about him; instead,
he realized:

> [The meeting provided reliable evidence] that Captain Meyer had been
> *plotting* against me and Colonel Jaquillard [the head of
> Counterintelligence], that his role in the matter concerning the tapped
> telephone conversations had been anything but impeccable, that you
> cannot rely on him to keep things secret, and that through certain con-
> nections he has gained some *detrimental influence* (all the way to the
> top), resulting in mistrust and uneasiness. That is all the more unpleas-
> ant as Captain Meyer is responsible for hardly anything in which he
> thinks he has to get involved.[36]

Colonel Müller concluded his letter by stating with determination, "*I no
longer want this man to be part of the Security Service,*[37] however, due to his character he is not capable of serving in any other branch."[38]

In fall 1942, in connection with the affair concerning the tapped telephone
conversations, it had become obvious that Meyer-Schwertenbach had direct
access to the Commander-in-Chief, a fact that was viewed with suspicion by
Colonel Werner Müller and others. As head of the Special Service, Meyer used
to receive the transcripts of tapped telephone conversations. On November 7,
1942, he was indignant, telling General Guisan about "the fact that for more
than one year, the private telephone conversations of all officers on the Army
Staff had been monitored on orders of Counterintelligence."[39] Without giving
away the name of his informant, General Guisan ordered Barbey to get Masson
"to immediately suspend, until further notice, all telephone monitoring activities that have been established in Interlaken."[40] The Commander-in-Chief did

not want this matter to be trifled with because one year earlier he had personally been the victim of abusive tapping activities. The head of the Security Service had confidentially informed him "that as former head of the Communications and Railway Department, *Pilet-Golaz* [had] *ordered that the Commander-in-Chief's telephone conversations be monitored!*" [41]

At the end of November 1942, Chief of the General Staff Huber called Masson, Werner Müller, who was Masson's deputy and head of the Security Service, the Military Attorney General, whom the Commander-in-Chief had asked to investigate whether the tapping activities were legal, and Chief of Counterintelligence Robert Jaquillard into a meeting to discuss the matter of the "tapped telephone conversations" at army headquarters. At the meeting, Huber explained, "[The Commander-in-Chief has] received complaints from an unidentified source about telephone conversations of officers being tapped by bodies of counterintelligence, which means that the concerned officers are suspected of espionage."[42] The meeting brought things into the open. It was concluded that in this instance *no abuse* had been committed. The monitoring activities were carried out on the basis of a security ordinance of September 22, 1939 and instructions of October 5, 1939 by the Chief of the General Staff regarding counterintelligence activities in the army. However, the meeting revealed that no one was well informed about the issue. The participants were surprised to hear that technically it was not possible to have the sworn tapping agents[43] listen in only on the telephone conversations of a selected number of people. Consequently, *all telephones* had to be monitored, whether used by civilians or members of the military. It was therefore not feasible to monitor only suspects, as Masson had assumed. Jaquillard explained that in addition to counterintelligence, the federal Attorney General's office and the Federal Department of Economic Affairs[44] had also ordered telephones to be tapped. Chief of the General Staff Huber concluded:

> Counterintelligence and the head of the Security Service are not to blame in this matter. If anyone is to blame, it is me and Colonel-Brigadier Masson, who approved the telephone tapping activities in Interlaken in early 1941. It is justified to blame us for our bad memory because we had simply forgotten about the events of early 1941. To be honest, though, the major part of the blame has to be attributed to Colonel-Brigadier Masson because as the direct superior he is responsible for supervising counterintelligence; he should be better informed about its activities than I am. However, what is *unpleasant* about the matter is the fact that there are *anonymous cowards* among the officers

of the Army Staff who fail to try to settle disagreements with their superiors in a straightforward, soldierly manner by asking for a meeting or lodging a complaint, as stipulated in clause 48, paragraph 4 of the [service regulations]. Instead, they *clandestinely bring their information to the attention of the Commander-in-Chief and are taken seriously by him.* . . . One has to wonder how many of these cowards there are on the Army Staff and what their names are. The fact that the informant has not been identified leaves a serious feeling of mistrust.[45]

In spite of the devastating criticism that the head of the Security Service had voiced about Meyer-Schwertenbach, Masson did not want to do without him. He agreed to remove him from the Security Service, but in his capacity as Assistant Chief of Staff Id, he informed Meyer's new superior, Max Waibel, "As of today, Captain Meyer, who has been head of the Special Service (Security Service) until now, will be at your disposal to take over the command of your sub-office in Zürich. . . . I reserve the right to put this officer in charge of some special missions, for which I will deal directly with him."[46] By *special missions,* Masson had his connection with SS Brigadier General Schellenberg in mind. Based on these instructions, Meyer-Schwertenbach henceforth reported directly to Procurement Office 1[47] and was assigned to the *Uto outpost* as a liaison officer with the Zürich cantonal and city police, particularly their intelligence services. In secret terms of reference[48] dated July 16, 1943, Waibel, the head of N.S.1, defined Meyer's tasks, which he was to accomplish at Waibel's instructions by using his own connections. His tasks included:

1. Establishing and utilizing sources of information among banks, industry, and commercial circles in Zürich and Eastern Switzerland as well as other sources that could be interviewed about foreign military, economic, and political matters.

Meyer-Schwertenbach was to convince people from these target groups to report their observations, or help, through their own contacts, establish new connections. These new sources of information were to be interviewed and questioned, and they were to be convinced to continue working with Army Intelligence.

2. In close cooperation with the intelligence sections at the Zürich cantonal and city police,[49] all potential informants were to be approached who were in custody (arrested civilians, deserters, illegal immigrants, etc.).

N.S.1 was interested only in information on military, economic, and foreign policy matters. Matters related to domestic policy and the police fell to the responsibility of the respective police authorities, i.e. the intelligence services of the canton and city of Zürich, the federal police, and, if necessary, Counterintelligence. Meyer was to foster relations with the cantonal and city police in order for their offices, archives, and means of communication to be available to Army Intelligence for gathering information and undertaking investigations.

As an outpost of N.S.1, the *Uto sub-office*, to which Meyer-Schwertenbach was assigned, was procuring intelligence exclusively from the Axis countries. Nevertheless, as of summer 1943, Meyer also made attempts "to come into direct contact with the British Intelligence Service in order to establish a connection that was similar to the one [with Schellenberg]."[50] In October 1943, he was successful, and as of November 1943 he regularly sent Masson numbered messages that he had received from the new connection. From the written evidence that is available today, it is not clear whether in this instance Meyer acted on his own initiative. However, it does not seem to be erroneous to assume that he had two main reasons for being interested in approaching the British Intelligence Service: he personally wanted to establish a connection with the Allies that was as unusual as the one with Schellenberg; and he may have received more or less clear hints from Eggen or Schellenberg that they were interested in entering into contact with the Allies. The following year, when Meyer-Schwertenbach began to have personal contact with Allen Dulles, the initiative had definitely been taken by both the Allies and the Swiss. On the Swiss side, Masson primarily tried to transmit Schellenberg's wish to enter into contact with the Americans.

The Zürich city police let the *Uto* sub-office use two adjacent rooms at the *Amtshaus III*, one of the city's administrative buildings, as its offices. *Uto's* task was to question persons about foreign military, political, and economic issues. N.S.1 communicated the potential informants' addresses to the sub-office by sending it the so-called immigration forms.[51] Whenever possible, the potential informants were interviewed at their home or workplace. All reports and correspondence had to be submitted to N.S.1. On Waibel's orders, the *Uto* sub-office and Meyer-Schwertenbach were allowed to communicate directly with the army command "only if they had to carry out orders that had been issued personally by the head of Group Id or his deputy."[52] The head of the sub-office, Eugen Gyr, was in charge of military and administrative matters; Meyer-Schwertenbach primarily carried out special missions in addition to liaising between N.S.1 and the police authorities of the canton and city of Zürich.[53] If necessary, the sub-office was allowed to request additional army personnel for temporary or long-term assignments. Nevertheless, *Uto's* administrative expenses were minimal; it had 100 francs available per month for its operating costs[54] and ten times that amount for the actual interviews,[55] which was the same amount that was allocated to the *Pfalz* sub-office in Basel.[56]

In winter 1943, Meyer-Schwertenbach felt obliged to ask to be relieved of his duty as liaison officer at *Uto* effective at the beginning of 1944. On December 17, 1943, Masson decided, "At your own request, I am temporarily relieving you of your duty at our sub-office in Zürich, effective Dec. 31, 1943. . . . I would like to thank you for the services you have rendered since the army was mobilized. You are leaving under perfectly honorable conditions, at your own request. Granting your request is possible because you have been serving as a volunteer."[57] However, Meyer was to continue working for the Intelligence Service. Masson added, "I would like to ask you to remain at my own disposal for the *special mission* with which I will continue to entrust you."[58]

Masson's expression, "under perfectly honorable conditions," may make readers wonder about the real reason why Meyer quit his job at the sub-office in Zürich. Meyer's unpublished papers indicate that there were serious frictions between him and his direct superior Max Waibel at N.S.1 that apparently began when Waibel appointed Captain Gyr as head of *Uto* instead of Meyer.[59] Meyer commented, "W[aibel] obviously did not call me or send me a letter, nor did he make any request or issue instructions to me, so I had to interpret [Gyr's appointment] as an act of animosity. However, I did not yet see things clearly."[60]

In September 1943, a Swiss informant told Meyer that "Waibel was gathering material in order to shed light on [his] activities with the Germans, [his] finan[cial] gains, etc., and that the Commander-in-Chief had been informed[61] and had been asked to receive Waibel in order to be briefed on the issue."[62] A short time later, German circles[63] confirmed that Waibel had asked a German agent to collect material on Meyer's activities. Hence, it became clear to Meyer why Waibel had been "tight-lipped"[64] toward him, adding, "I complained to Masson, who confirmed to me that the Commander-in-Chief even intended to receive W[aibel][65] in order to see the file on my 'business activities'; [Masson said that] he would speak with W[aibel] and assured me that if I could produce evidence that Waibel was also gathering material in G[ermany] on [Masson], he would be fired."[66] Meyer refused to take up Masson's offer, telling him that Waibel was a comrade in the military with whom he had not had any other unpleasant experience.[67] On the other hand, however, he refused to give Waibel any information on his activities.[68]

Meyer-Schwertenbach was disgruntled about Waibel's attitude and was convinced that he was the target of a plot. Actually, he was. Lützelschwab's comment on the Masson affair[69] indicated that some people within Army Intelligence had serious reservations about Meyer's activities on behalf of the Masson-Schellenberg connection. When discussing the alert of March 1943 later in this volume, we will examine whether Max Waibel had valid reasons to be so reticent about Meyer-Schwertenbach. Waibel was annoyed about Meyer's private business activities because they helped maintain Masson's risky contact with Schellenberg. However, Meyer would have been astounded to find out that, by making a comment that was meant to be positive, he was actually the one who had pointed out to Waibel that there were some questionable aspects about the channel to the Reich Security Central Office.[70]

As mentioned, Waibel was not the only staff member of Army Intelligence who was suspicious about Meyer-Schwertenbach.[71] The fact that he was transferred from army headquarters in Interlaken to Zürich could indeed be viewed as an attempt to demote[72] him by placing him in a less delicate position.[73] Meyer did not fail to notice this, stating:

> First they tried to make me stumble because of my private legal activities (received large sums of money—set the tax authorities on me because I allegedly made profits as a result of the war); then they removed me from headquarters in I[nterlaken] because I saw too many things. . . . In Zürich they continued snooping around me, and when they could not hold anything against me, [they] turned into sticklers for the rules, [asking me] why I did not obey the military orders issued by my superior in the army.[74]

The last remark referred to Meyer's refusal to abide by the terms that Waibel had dictated to him for his job in Zürich.

The situation was unpleasant for both parties. Knowing that Waibel disapproved of the connection with Schellenberg, *Captain Meyer* kept hiding behind *special missions* about which he did not have to report to his superior at N.S.1.[75] *Major Waibel*, who suspected that Meyer was involved in some dubious business activities and feared that his own connection, Viking, was in jeopardy, tried to have Meyer investigated by the military administration and removed from the army. Waibel was only partly successful; even though at the end of 1943 Meyer quit his post at the sub-office of N.S.1 in Zürich,[76] he continued to be in a position of trust with Masson, keeping up, via Eggen, the connection with Schellenberg.[77] From then on he reported directly to Masson, which was what he had wanted for a long time.[78] In 1943, Meyer had been on duty three days a week; after that, he served only sporadically, i.e. nine days in January 1944, eight days in February 1944, and 71 more days during the remainder of 1944; according to Group Ib of the army command, from January to April 1945 he served another 41 days.[79]

7

Early Stages of the Masson-Schellenberg Connection

Meyer Establishes Contact with Eggen

THE HISTORY OF THE controversial connection between Masson and Schellenberg goes back to the fall of 1941. The connection essentially became possible because Captain Paul Meyer was friends with Lieutenant Colonel Henry Guisan, the Commander-in-Chief's son. Guisan Jr. was a member of the Army Staff.[1] Based on his notes, the circumstances under which Meyer met Schellenberg's aide and courier Eggen were different from the ones described by historian Hans Rudolf Fuhrer, who used the reference material that was available to him at the time.[2] Following is a short account of what happened.

Henry Guisan Jr. was a shareholder and member of the board of directors at a company that did business with the *Warenvertriebs G.m.b.H.* in Berlin, which was owned by Hans Wilhelm Eggen. Because Meyer was not only Guisan's friend but also his legal advisor, the Commander-in-Chief's son introduced him to Eggen. These are the facts that are established on the basis of the available reference material. However, once an attempt is undertaken to look into the circumstances under which the connection was set up, matters become complex and confusing. Fuhrer rightfully states, "The early history in itself is already very contradictory."[3] Indeed, in many instances the written evidence tells two conflicting stories. Some parts of the history of the connection resemble pieces of a puzzle that do not perfectly fit together; some pieces may be missing, but it is not always clear which ones. As a result, this author asserts that his attempt at reconstructing the facts offers only a plausible overview of the connection as he has been able to reconstruct from the written records.

At the end of October 1940,[4] Eggen arrived in Switzerland to purchase a large quantity[5] of submachine guns on behalf of the Reich Ministry of Economic Affairs.[6] This event, in connection with which Eggen was mentioned for the first time, is interesting not only because of its consequences, but also because it already shows that due to his winsome manner, the German managed to circumvent bureaucratic procedures in an elegant fashion. After the fact the involved Swiss authorities felt cheated, yet it remained unclear whether Eggen had intentionally pulled the wool over their eyes.

In February 1940, the Government of Finland had indicated that it was interested in purchasing the Swiss submachine guns in question. Even though Switzerland's Army Command approved the sale, it did not go through, apparently because of the political situation at the time.[7] The Swiss Army for its part was interested in purchasing about 275 submachine guns of the same type. They would have needed 200,000 pieces of ammunition for the guns. The problem was that the ammunition was neither being manufactured in Switzerland, nor was it available in Germany in early 1940. It was not until August 1940 that the *Deutsche Waffen- und Munitionsfabrik A.G.* had that quantity in stock for sale to Switzerland. On November 6, 1940, despite the fact that Chief of the General Staff Huber consequently requested funds from the Commander-in-Chief to purchase the submachine guns from the manufacturer in Neuhausen, canton of Schaffhausen, and the ammunition from Germany, the purchase did not materialize. The following day, the head of service for Ammunitions at the Ordnance Section called the head of the Ordnance Section, Col. Alfred Muntwyler, to tell him that a representative of the German Reich Ministry of Economic Affairs named Eggen and a representative of the Luchsinger company in Zürich had come to see him. Chief of the General Staff Huber explained: "They declared that for some reason or other they were interested in the submachine guns in question. The two men supposedly made a good impression, and the Ordnance Section considers that it is advisable to allow the submachine guns to be sold, not least because the required ammunition, which we have to purchase in Germany, would not be released for sale if we created difficulties."[8]

Apparently Eggen was in a great hurry to conclude the deal. Immediately after seeing the head of service at Ammunitions, he succeeded in arranging a meeting with Colonel Muntwyler at the train station in Thun.[9] At that meeting, acting as the representative of the German Reich Ministry of Economic Affairs, Eggen confirmed that Germany set great store on purchasing the guns. In exchange, he presented a document promising that Germany would supply Switzerland with gasoline.[10] Colonel Muntwyler explained to Eggen that in order to wrap up the deal the military attaché at the German Legation in Bern had to officially confirm that Germany was in need of the material, and that "in any event, the Swiss Army wanted to keep 25 of these arms for test purposes."[11] Eggen and his business partner from Zürich accepted these conditions and traveled to Bern to see Military Attaché von Ilsemann. Meanwhile, Muntwyler asked the Intelligence Section "whether currently there was any interest in doing the German Government or the German Military Attaché a favor. The Intelligence Section gave an affirmative answer."[12]

As early as the same afternoon, Ilsemann called the head of the Ordnance Section to supply the requested confirmation.[13] The head of Materials and Technology at the Ordnance Section informed Chief of the General Staff Huber about Ilsemann's telephone call, and Huber approved the arms sale, later explaining to Minister Jean Hotz, "I did so mainly because the guns were useless to us without the ammunition and it was highly questionable whether the ammunition could be imported."[14] On that same day, November 7, 1940, Ilsemann was informed over the telephone about Huber's approval. The following morning, the Army Command confirmed in writing that it approved the sale of 250 submachine guns, whereupon the deal was concluded,[15] and it was agreed that in return Germany would supply 200,000 liters of gasoline. Until the present day the exact circumstances of the transaction have been contested[16] because it is one person's word against another's.[17] In the context of this study, only the consequences of the deal, which ended up falling through, are significant; because the gasoline in question was not delivered,[18] "[Switzerland's] Department of Economic Affairs supposedly asked the Department of Foreign Affairs to prevent E[ggen] from entering Switzerland in the future."[19]

It is not possible to establish when exactly Meyer-Schwertenbach found out about this matter. In the note for the file dated November 14, 1941 concerning his first contact with Eggen, Meyer was vague, stating that "weeks ago"[20] his friend Henry Guisan had told him about Eggen and the trouble he had entering Switzerland, adding that "Eggen supposedly had *good connections with Himmler* and was certainly *interesting for our intelligence service.*"[21] Meyer consulted with his superiors, Colonel Werner Müller and Colonel[22] Masson. With their approval, he established contact with Eggen.[23] However, that was not very easy because apparently the Swiss authorities had serious reservations about this particular German re-entering Switzerland. Meyer made inquiries with several governing bodies, explaining:

> I had that[24] verified and was informed by Berlin that E. would like to come to Switzerland to justify himself [because] it was not his fault that the deal in question[25] had fallen through. It was Switzerland that had refused to accept leaded gasoline. He was also said to be able to provide Switzerland with orders that would create jobs. Through an informant, I tried in vain to make the Department of Economic Affairs[26] change its mind. I subsequently noticed that the German Legation backed [Major] von Steiger [of the Ordnance Section],[27] as Ilsemann[28] and E[ggen] are opponents because [Eggen] is a member of the SS.[29]

With Masson's approval, the head of the Special Service subsequently called on the Swiss Federal Police Section[30] about Eggen "and asked them to authorize him to enter the country as *there was an interest in his being available*[31] *in Switzerland*."[32] Meyer managed to get a three-day single-entry visa for Eggen. The trip must have meant a lot to Eggen as well. Meyer remarked, "He arrived right away by plane, and one of my informants received him in Dübendorf. "[33]

On October 30, 1941, at the Schweizerhof hotel in Bern, Meyer-Schwertenbach and Eggen met for the first time; the Swiss introduced himself as *Dr. Ritzburg.*[34] Guisan Jr. introduced Eggen to him by remarking that he was "a capable man for the connection with well-known personalities in Berlin."[35] It will be shown below in this chapter that, by making that statement, Guisan not only had intelligence matters in mind but also had high hopes as a businessman. Eggen soon talked about business as well. Meyer noted: "[Eggen] thanked me because he had heard that he owed it to me that he was allowed to travel to Switzerland. He told me that the [German] Army needed *wooden barracks* and that he had flown to Switzerland to purchase them because his ministry was responsible for the troops' well-being and safety."[36] According to Meyer: "[The first] meeting was friendly and lasted about 45 minutes. I accompanied him to the train station, and he asked me to see to it that he could come back one more time. He said that he wanted to go to see the Department of Economic Affairs with me in order to set the record[37] straight."[38]

The wooden barracks deal that Eggen brought up and that Meyer had probably already heard about through Guisan Jr. played a *key role* in Meyer's meeting with Eggen, and therefore also in establishing the Masson-Schellenberg connection. The barracks deal had several aspects; it was a private business transaction that had implications for the Swiss economy as a whole, as well as for the intelligence services of two countries. In the framework of this study, the intelligence aspect is obviously particularly interesting. In the next section it will be demonstrated that the influence of Swiss Intelligence actually facilitated the establishment of business relations in which Guisan Jr. was interested as a private individual.[39] However, since Guisan's German partner Eggen was indeed a promising contact for Swiss Intelligence, it is questionable whether this instance should be considered as a case of *abuse of the intelligence service for personal purposes*; the contact with Eggen was business that could be profitable to both sides.

Opponents of the connection with Schellenberg later accused Meyer of misusing his position as an army official for his own business purposes. In early 1943, Colonel Werner Müller used Meyer-Schwertenbach's business relations with Eggen as a pretext to remove him from the Security Service. Müller explained to the Chief of Intelligence: "[The fact] that Captain Meyer is the lawyer of a foreign national who occupies an important position should be taken into special consideration in connection with the Intelligence and Security Service. I know that Captain Meyer received substantial payments for his services and that—regardless whether this is done intentionally or not—to a certain extent *civilian and military activities* have been *combined*."[40] He acknowledged that Meyer had the right to work as a lawyer because "an officer with his social status [could] not live from a soldier's pay."[41] Nevertheless, the head of the Security Service feared that Meyer's business relations could result in "extremely delicate concomitants," arguing:

> Even if these relations are absolutely honorable—I have no reason to believe that they are not—as a matter of principle contacts with an officer holding a major position are not allowed. For domestic political reasons such contacts are dangerous merely because they exist. I insist on pointing out these circumstances because it is of importance to me to prevent a scandal from being created one day that would have serious consequences for the army.[42]

Hence, the head of the Security Service suggested to Masson that "for special official reasons" he indefinitely put Meyer-Schwertenbach on stand-by.

In fact, the owner of Wolfsberg Castle benefited from his contact with Eggen as a private individual. However, considering the identity of the Germans who were involved in the connection, it could be argued that Meyer had realized that contact with them could only be established and consolidated through interesting business proposals.[43] Meyer's relatively small income from the connection and his rather substantial expenses incurred through his involvement in it[44] speak in favor of this argument.

The Barracks Deal

At the end of 1940, in response to Swiss offers, the German Armed Forces High Command (OKW) attempted to purchase wooden barracks in Switzerland.[45] When negotiations with the Swiss Wood Syndicate (SHS)[46] broke down in 1941, the *Waffen-SS* took over.[47] As a member of the SS procurement office,[48] Hans Wilhelm Eggen, a major in both the regular SS and the Waffen (armed) SS,[49] was put in charge of the transaction. He did business through the *Warenvertriebs G.m.b.H.* in Berlin, a firm that had apparently been created by the SS.[50] According to Eggen, the company's "main activity was to carry out international compensation deals, especially with Denmark, Switzerland, Slovakia, Sweden, [and] Spain."[51] Eggen was the company's manager. In order to make progress with the purchase of the barracks, his deputy, Max Baumann, "initiated contact with [Hermann] Weidenmann, a German living in Zürich who had a bad reputation,"[52] who in turn contacted Rudolf Haenger and his son Rudolf Walter Haenger, two businessmen whom he knew in Basel.[53] Haenger and his son subsequently founded a shareholding company in Lausanne called *Extroc S.A.* They were both named to the new company's board of directors, along with an industrialist from Lausanne[54] and a "higher-ranking officer,"[55] *Lieutenant Colonel Henry Guisan*, the son of the Swiss Army's Commander-in-Chief.

The available reference documents reveal a lot of details about Guisan Jr.'s relations with the Extroc S.A.[56] The company, which was incorporated on August 29, 1941, purchased, sold, imported, and exchanged a large variety of goods.[57] It primarily arranged for the delivery of goods that did not go through Switzerland at all. According to a report by the Basel-Stadt police department, in terms of exports the company arranged the sale of Swiss-made wooden barracks to Germany and Italy as well as the sale of paintings.[58] The report also stated: "In reality the company is directed by Mr. Haenger and his son. The company's entire business transactions are carried out by these two gentle-

men."[59] Lieutenant Colonel Guisan, whom the two businessmen had first contacted in June 1941, initially hesitated to join Extroc's board of directors.[60]
However, after making some inquiries and informing his friend Meyer-
Schwertenbach,[61] Guisan agreed to do business with Haenger and his son
under the condition that Director Ernest-Otto Knecht was also named to the
board.[62] The two businessmen from Basel agreed, so on August 27, 1941,
Extroc S.A. was founded.[63] Was Lieutenant Colonel Guisan supposed to have
served as a bulwark against potential claims by the tax authorities looking into
excess profits from war-related sales?[64] After the war, Director Knecht made no
secret of the role that had been assigned to Guisan, stating, "*Through his father's
position*, he had *access everywhere*. Even though we considered him mostly as a
'piece of ornament,'[65] a few times we actually had to use his services."[66]
Furthermore, Knecht commented: "Fortunately Guisan *Sr.* was commander-
in-chief, not his son. The son has a bad reputation. We had no good experience
with him.[67] Nevertheless, at certain times he rendered us some good services.[68]
Some deals became possible through his father."[69] During the same conversation,
Knecht described Guisan Jr.'s two business partners from Basel as "*dangerous
black marketeers with innocent manners.*"[70]

Soon after the company had been founded, it became known that everything had been arranged for the barracks deal. In retrospect, the Commander-
in-Chief's son admitted, "From that moment on, I was in a delicate situation."[71] In addition, it turned out that Haenger and his son were not in a position to hold the negotiations for the barracks transaction, so Guisan Jr. "personally intervened in order to get the Swiss Wood Syndicate to act as a substitute for Extroc S.A."[72] Guisan henceforth took an active part as a mediator on
the Swiss side and enlisted the head of the Special Service as his legal advisor.[73]
As a legal advisor, Meyer-Schwertenbach had to advise and represent the group
of Swiss brokers. He saw to it that "Eggen could directly address the official
Swiss authorities."[74] The relations that Meyer arranged[75] worked out; at the
end of November 1941, the Swiss Wood Syndicate and Eggen, the representative of the *Warenvertriebs G.m.b.H.*, held first talks in Bern. In January 1942,
with the approval of the Commerce Section of the Swiss Federal Department
of Economic Affairs, the SHS management traveled to Berlin, where the negotiations continued under the direction of the Swiss legation.[76] On January 22,
1942, they ended with an agreement[77] on the delivery of 2,000 barracks buildings.[78] A first partial delivery[79] of 500 wooden barracks[80] was made in early
spring 1942.[81] In supplementary agreements dated April 15 and August 6,
1942, the two parties agreed on the delivery of another 500 barracks, which
were shipped in fall 1942.[82] According to the SHS President, "At the end of
1942, new negotiations were held that resulted in an agreement on 1,000 bar-

racks,[83] but it was not executed because several compensations and services had not been rendered in return."[84] However, in fall 1943, new talks were successful, culminating on October 7, 1943 in an agreement[85] on the delivery of 70 wooden apartment buildings,[86] which were shipped in January-February 1944.[87] Later several rounds of new negotiations were held, but they did not result in any agreement.

Once the barracks deal between the Swiss Wood Syndicate and the *Warenvertriebs G.m.b.H.* had been sealed, Meyer changed sides, becoming the German party's purchasing commissioner. He later explained to a military court, "In that position, I had to see to it that the barracks, which had generally been manufactured by craftsmen, were delivered as stipulated in the contract."[88] Hence, Meyer continued to play the role of an intermediary in this "barracks deal," which generated a turnover of about 12 million francs within a few years. What appears more problematic about the deal than the financial aspect,[89] however, is the fact that Meyer switched to the German side. He consequently became Eggen's contractor and therefore practically a purchasing commissioner for the *Waffen-SS*,[90] while at the same time holding a delicate position in Switzerland's Army Command as a captain in the Intelligence and Security Service. But was that not precisely the kind of constellation that opened up highly interesting new avenues?

After the war, during the investigation that a military court opened (but later abandoned) against him, Meyer explained why he started working for the German side, stating, "I did not seek to play the part I played in the barracks deal. However, I allowed myself to become involved because it gave me an *opportunity to establish contact with competent German authorities.*"[91] He argued that the business actually did not have anything to do with his position in the military, conceding, however, "I welcomed the business from the perspective of my official duty," explaining that it allowed him to establish the connection between Masson and Schellenberg. He added, "So first there was the *business*; it was not until *afterward* that the *connection* was established for Army Intelligence. It was not the other way round. Hence, I definitely did not misuse my official position as an intelligence officer to do private business."[92] The investigating judge naturally asked Meyer whether he believed that it was admissible for a [Swiss] intelligence officer to represent German interests and Meyer replied, "I was absolutely frank about that. In my request for a leave of absence to the Chief of the General Staff, I wrote that I was the representative of a German firm and therefore had to travel to Berlin."[93] Several letters by the Wood Section of the War Industry and Labor Office[94] and the Swiss Wood Syndicate[95] prove that Switzerland's national economy did benefit from Meyer's contacts with Germany. Meyer stated, "In fact, I primarily defended *Swiss* inter-

No. ....
In der Antwort vermerken — A indiquer dans la réponse
77T.   Da indicare nella risposta

A.H.Q., 22.12.42.

An das Kommando S p a b

An die Schweiz. Bundesanwaltschaft für sich und z.H. der N.D.
in den Kantonen.

Es wird uns gemeldet, dass schon seit einigen Wochen die
besten Agenten, über welche man deutscherseits verfüge, in der
Schweiz im Einsatz seien. Diese reisen fast ausnahmlos in sog.
Wirtschaftsangelegenheiten, als Wirtschaftsleute getarnt und
halten sich zur Hauptsache in Zürich, Bern und Basel auf. Was
von diesen Assen des deutschen Nachrichtendienstes bearbeitet
werde, seien nur grosse Dinge. Des öftern fahren diese Herren,
um nicht aufzufallen, über Genf nach Lyon weiter, oder aber, sie
reisen über Genf in die Schweiz ein. So sollen drei solche Herren
in der Nacht zum 4. Dezember in Bern genächtigt haben. Zur glei-
chen Zeit seien zwei als Kunsthändler reisende Herren in Bern
tätig gewesen.

Oberstlt. i.Gst. Trachsel.

Business contacts were frequently used as a starting point or cover-up for intelligence activities. In this letter to Counterintelligence, the Attorney General's office, and the cantonal intelligence services, Switzerland's Army Command warns about some of Germany's top agents covering up their missions as business trips. (BAr E 27/10113)

ests even though I had been appointed as official representative of the [German] *Warenvertriebs G.m.b.H.*"[96] The letters by the Wood Section and the SHS support his point of view.

Meyer therefore did business with a German company in an effort to establish contacts for Swiss Intelligence, as has been mentioned. Minutes kept by the Swiss Attorney General's office clearly indicate that the same was true for the *German* side. In 1946, it questioned the former head of the economic section at Office VI of the Reich Security Central Office, Hans Martin Zeidler.[97] His task had been "to provide the individual country bureaus with economic assistance for carrying out their intelligence activities,"[98] i.e. to procure the necessary foreign currencies for Schellenberg's espionage and sabotage activities. Zeidler said, "Concerning Switzerland, I primarily had to see to the economic needs of *Amtschef* Schellenberg's intelligence connection."[99] Consequently, Zeidler had received "detailed information about a barracks deal that the 'Warenvertriebs G.m.b.H.' was carrying out for the Economic and Administrative Office of the *Waffen-SS,* [explaining] because Office VI had only a small amount of foreign currencies available for its intelligence activities in Switzerland, *Head of Office Schellenberg intended to support his special intelligence connections with that barracks deal.*"[100] Thus, for the Germans the business relations also served to cover up planned intelligence activities. The barracks deal not only provided Schellenberg with promising new contacts but also gave him the opportunity to keep sending his intermediary Eggen to Switzerland for a plausible reason. (However, if Schellenberg also had *financial* goals, i.e. if he tried to obtain foreign currencies, he did not succeed with the barracks deal—because the price of the barracks had already been approved by the Reich Ministry of Economic Affairs, no additional funds could be funneled into his intelligence service.) The fact that the Germans also tried to use the barracks deal for their own intelligence activities was practically inevitable and does not speak against the deal in itself.

In retrospect, one should also point out that *every successful intelligence service abides by its own rules*. It is active in a gray area in which questionable means may sometimes be used in order to achieve an objective. Making a judgment about these means becomes a matter of discretion. In the case under study, if the barracks deal was considered a means *to establish a connection with Himmler's entourage for intelligence purposes*, it can be viewed positively. On the other hand, a risk was associated with the deal that could not be underestimated; in a letter to Federal Councillor Kobelt, State Attorney Lützelschwab voiced serious reservations concerning Colonel Guisan's involvement in the business, stating:

The business relations of people such as the Haengers—from the notes on their [tapped] telephone conversations one gains a really pitiful impression about their business ethics[101]—with the son of the Commander-in-Chief of our army who is a high-ranking officer as well, can have very serious consequences for the General's prestige and therefore also for Switzerland. These consequences can be all the more serious as Messrs. Haenger have close ties with several . . . major personalities abroad, especially in Germany. It is not impossible at all that *one day*, maybe at a time that is very unsuitable for us, *a foreign country could provoke a crisis surrounding the Commander-in-Chief by defaming Guisan Jr.*[102]

Meyer-Schwertenbach did not know how Lützelschwab found out about the wooden barracks deal. He would have been surprised to hear that he of all people had unintentionally created an influential opponent for himself. The incident by which Meyer-Schwertenbach revealed his contact with Eggen sheds light on the degree of his commitment to the Masson-Schellenberg connection; moreover, it indicates that Meyer's initial latent mistrust against Eggen, which was certainly justified, was soon lulled by the good impression that he had of the German. In addition, the incident demonstrates that any intelligence service has to expect a secret connection to be uncovered at any time for the most unexpected reasons; in this case, the triggering event was actually a rumor that turned out to be inaccurate.

On November 17, 1942, an informant from Basel working in the wood industry whom he personally knew and trusted—possibly Dr. (honoris causa) Gustav Bohny—informed Lützelschwab:

I have been told that tonight somebody named Dr. Meyer, a German living in Basel, is allegedly having a secret meeting with several German and Swiss gentlemen at the *Schweizerhof* hotel in Zürich. Among the Germans, only one name has been mentioned to me, Egg, Ecken, or something similar. I have not been able to find out who the Swiss are, but they seem to be influential personalities. The talks, which will be held by using harmless negotiations about wood deliveries as a cover-up, seem to have the anything-but-modest objective of reshaping Switzerland's foreign political position. These talks and the commitments made therein are supposed to put the Federal Council in a predicament, forcing it to give up its "unyielding" position toward the efforts of the Axis; the army will allegedly have to demobilize and

the "pro-English" General Guisan will have to be replaced as commander-in-chief. Above all, however, supposedly the activities of the
official and unofficial agents of the Allies will have to stop.

The informant told the Basel State Attorney that he had received the information through an indiscretion within the wood industry, but he qualified his
statement by remarking, "I obviously do not know if this is actually true.
However, I consider the matter to be very important, so I feel obliged to report
it to the Political Police." Lützelschwab also considered the information "not to
be very credible, at least not the way in which it [was] presented." He wanted
to verify it before forwarding it to the federal authorities and the army command. Nevertheless, the fact that a "Dr. Meyer from Basel" was implicated in
the matter made Lützelschwab suspicious; he believed that this man could only
be *Dr. Otto Eberhard Majer*, an attaché at the German Consulate in Basel who
was considered to be a Gestapo agent and was seriously suspected of espionage.
The Political Police knew Majer "through numerous incidents"; he seemed perfectly capable of taking part in negotiations such as the ones described by the
informant.

Since Lützelschwab's officers knew Majer well but the police in Zürich
probably did not know him at all, and since it appeared that no time should be
wasted, Lützelschwab chose not to involve the Zürich police in the verification
process; instead, he sent one of his own men to the *Schweizerhof* in Zürich to
make inquiries. In particular, the officer from Basel was supposed to find out
with whom Dr. Majer was meeting and who the man named Egg or Ecken was.
Of course the officer did not find Dr. Majer there; however, he was able to track
down a German named *Eggen*, but he considered that the young salesman
"could hardly be considered [able to take part] in such negotiations."

On November 18, 1942, Lützelschwab's informant confirmed the information that he had supplied the previous day, adding that "what he had found
out since [the previous day] by verifying things on his own reinforced him in
his belief that this was a *rather fishy matter*." Moreover, he said that he had
found out that Eggen was supposed to travel to Bern that day. Lützelschwab
asked two of his officers to make inquiries at the *Schweizerhof* hotel in Bern,
where they were indeed able to trace Eggen. However, they were not able to
determine why the German had been to the capital because he had already
returned to Zürich. Hence, Lützelschwab decided to halt the inquiries for the
time being.

*This might have been the end of the matter if Captain Meyer had not person-
ally intervened.* On November 21, 1942, first someone named Sergeant Bleiker
of the Zürich city police[103] called up the Political Police Section in Basel to ask

if "Mr. Max Hauser," who had stayed at the *Schweizerhof* in Zürich on November 17, was one of their officers. Basel said that he was and explained what the purpose of his mission had been and why the inquiries had been made without involving the Zürich police. Half an hour later, Lützelschwab received a telephone call from "Captain Meier of the Special Service at the Security Service," whom he did not know. Meyer wanted Lützelschwab to tell him whom Hauser had kept under surveillance in Zürich. When Lützelschwab replied that he could not give him any information over the telephone, Meyer-Schwertenbach used Colonel Müller of the General Staff as a reference and remarked that with this surveillance activity the Political Police had *poached on Army Intelligence's preserve*. Basel's state attorney once again asked Captain Meier "to put his request in writing, which he [accepted] only after making several attempts at getting [Lützelschwab] to talk."[104] Lützelschwab concluded the note for the file on this strange conversation by remarking, "The way in which 'Capt. Meier' insisted, and based on his obvious excitement, this seems to be a case where things are *shrouded in mystery*. Let us wait and see if a written request will be submitted."[105]

The written request was actually submitted the same day by telex.[106] However, it was characteristic that it was unsigned; instead, it included the abbreviation "ahq-sd." By then Lützelschwab had become alert; instead of sending a telex back, he decided to send his reply in a letter addressed directly to the head of Army Security.[107] In addition, since Meyer-Schwertenbach's excitement had made him wonder, he checked with the Zürich city police to determine the identity of the individual who had shown such an interest in the surveillance activity by the officer from Basel.[108] At that occasion, Lützelschwab was told that on orders of a military court, *Eggen* had been *under surveillance* for a long time. Furthermore, the Zürich city police informed the head of the Basel Political Police, "And then we received orders from someone named Captain Meier of the Special Service, who claimed that he had a feeling that he was kept under surveillance; he said that someone had told him about it." Lützelschwab, who did not know anything about the Masson-Schellenberg connection, considered that Meyer's intervention was unauthorized and presumptuous because he tried to use his position in the military to obtain information as Eggen's legal advisor, i.e. as a private individual, not as a staff member of Army Intelligence. However, the officer at the Zürich city police informed Lützelschwab that "certain military authorities" knew about these contacts and had an interest in them.

Nevertheless, Meyer's superior, Colonel Müller, considered Meyer's telex improper. In a telephone conversation that he transcribed, he told Lützelschwab, "I would like to state that I am extremely indignant about the fact that [Captain Meyer] allowed himself to send this [telex]. . . . This is an unacceptable interference in someone else's authority."[109] He said that even though he did not believe that Meyer had become involved in talks that were as serious as the informant from the wood industry had reported, he and Masson would like to ask the Basel State Attorney to further look into the matter. He added, "As I said before, personally I do not like the whole connection."[110] Later during the conversation, Müller explained, "Obviously these serious allegations have to be looked into. Perhaps some discretion is required in order to avoid a mishap, because as far as I can tell [Eggen] once really did us a great favor; I used to get together with him frequently, but for certain reasons I stopped having any contact with him."[111]

As a result of Meyer-Schwertenbach's intervention, the Basel State Attorney became aware of the relations that evolved into the Masson-Schellenberg connection.[112] The more details Lützelschwab learned about these contacts during the following months, the more convinced he became that they bore uncontrollable risks for Switzerland and the more relentlessly he tried to put an end to them. One of his efforts consisted of repeatedly and insistently urging Federal Councillor Kobelt, and later also General Guisan, to remedy the situation.

The Federal Council shared Lützelschwab's fears about a possible *crisis surrounding the Commander-in-Chief* and viewed the matter a lot more critically than Guisan Jr. and Meyer-Schwertenbach.[113] For that reason,[114] serious[115] doubt was cast on Guisan's promotion to the rank of colonel for some time. In a draft letter to the Commander-in-Chief, Federal Councillor Kobelt explained that inquiries had revealed that Lieutenant Colonel Guisan had business relations with German authorities concerning the delivery of wooden barracks to the SS, adding, "Even though we have some understanding for bilateral business relations, which may absolutely be in the country's interest, we doubt whether Lieutenant Colonel Guisan's business relations in question can currently[116] be accepted without reservation."[117] What made Guisan's role questionable was the fact that he was the Commander-in-Chief's son.[118] As head of the Special Service, Captain Meyer had also laid himself open to attack. However, Kobelt's reservations did not apply to him, or they did so to a much smaller extent because Meyer might very well have been interested in the contacts with the SS *as a private citizen*. If Meyer's enterprise fell through,[119] key personalities such as the Commander-in-Chief and Masson, as well as Army Intelligence, would not be affected.

In summary, due to Guisan Jr.'s business relations with Eggen, Meyer-Schwertenbach had the opportunity to establish a contact that was quite promising for Swiss intelligence. All the same, the significance that the business venture with the SS had in establishing the Masson-Schellenberg connection is not evidence that the barracks deal itself was an unusual undertaking. Documents at the National Archives in Washington, DC, demonstrate that the *United States* armed forces, which were involved in invading Europe in 1944, were also interested in purchasing wooden barracks in Switzerland. In the files of the U.S. State Department, this author came across classified documents concerning negotiations that took place in December 1944 with a U.S. military delegation in Bern.[120] Close examination of the material revealed that some of the Swiss intermediaries had already had a hand in bringing the deal with the *Waffen-SS* to a close.[121] The talks with the U.S. delegation were successful as well. On December 30, 1944, Counselor J.K. Huddle at the United States legation in Bern cabled to Washington, DC, "Contract for 500 army barracks . . . signed today calling for delivery within 48 days of signature."[122]

After this excursion into the world of the wood processing industry, let us return to Meyer-Schwertenbach's first encounter with Eggen on October 30, 1941.[123] Meyer, alias Dr. Ritzburg, who had apparently received a good impression during this first contact,[124] "managed to have the Swiss legation in Berlin issue short-term visas [to Eggen] without having to ask for [Bern's] go-ahead."[125] As agreed, "through Mr. W.,"[126] Meyer informed Eggen about the arrangement. "Mr. W." was Hermann *Weidenmann*, a German living in Zürich who was the director of the *A.G. für Metallverwertung*. As seen earlier in this chapter, he was also the contact person between the *Warenvertriebs G.m.b.H.* in Berlin and the two businessmen Rudolf and Rudolf Walter Haenger in Basel. Moreover, Weidenmann paid for the submachine guns that Eggen had purchased at the time.[127] Police files clearly show that Weidenmann did not enjoy a good reputation as a businessman,[128] nor was he very trustworthy in political matters.[129] After December 1, 1941, Meyer wrote in his diary that "utmost care should be used" in dealing with "W.,"[130] a remark next to which he put three exclamation marks that may have referred to Weidenmann. In any event, Weidenmann's connection to Berlin worked because about two weeks after the first meeting between "Dr. Ritzburg" and Eggen, Meyer was informed that the SS officer had returned to Dübendorf by plane.[131] Eggen first traveled to Geneva,[132] and on his way back to Zürich, on November 14, 1941, he met with Meyer for the second time in Bern.

The Business Contact Turns into a
Connection for Army Intelligence

In the previous section, in an effort to *describe the milieu* that ultimately generated the Masson-Schellenberg connection, this author tried to "clear up the rather muddled and confusing circumstances"[133] surrounding the early history of the connection. It remains to be clarified who Eggen was. During the second meeting with him in mid-November 1941, Meyer-Schwertenbach received some detailed information about his background.

Meyer invited Eggen for a weekend[134] to Wolfsberg Castle. The host noted in his diary, "That weekend was a gradual ice-breaker. It was not until Sunday night that I was able to talk about everything that might interest us [at Army Intelligence]."[135] In connection with his activities in Berlin, Eggen also talked about his relations with the Operations Department of the SS Central Office, the Procurement Office, and the Reich Security Central Office, especially Office VI, which was in charge of foreign intelligence.[136] That was how Meyer learned more about his guest.

Hans Wilhelm Eggen was born on June 5, 1912. He was the son of a well-to-do district court Councillor. After an apprenticeship in agriculture—he was expected to take over his father's farm in East Frisia later on—he went back to high school and then studied law at the Universities of Tübingen and Berlin. He also took some classes in technical sciences.[137] After graduating he worked at the *Vereinigte Textilwerke Berlin* before becoming the manager of the *Warenvertriebs G.m.b.H.* It did not take the bright and ambitious young man long to notice which way the wind was blowing. As early as April 20, 1933, Eggen became a member of the Nazi Party, and in early May of the same year he joined the SS.[138] At the beginning of the war, he served as an officer in Cavalry Regiment 9. Because he was a member of the SS, on April 20, 1940 he was transferred to the *Waffen SS* and assigned to Office IX of the Operations Department of the SS Central Office, which was headed by Lieutenant General Juettner, the future deputy commander of the *Ersatzheer* (Replacement Army). Eggen was put in charge of the *Foreign Countries and Currencies* division. One of his duties consisted of acting as liaison officer between the Operations Department of the SS Central Office and the Reich Ministry of Economic Affairs.

At the initiative of Reinhard Heydrich,[139] the Reich Ministry of Economic Affairs and the Reich Security Central Office (RSHA) had signed an agreement according to which "funds [were] made available to the Operations Department of the SS Central Office only in cooperation with the RSHA."[140]

The agreement aimed to allow the RSHA to utilize the Waffen SS's foreign business ventures. Eggen later explained:

> Through his activity, the head of the SS procurement office at the Operations Department of the SS Central Office was supposed . . . to be informed about the economic situation, the management of raw materials, and the [state] of the labor market in the countries for which he had requested funds to liquidate a planned purchase.[141] Subsequently this information was supposed to be passed on to the economic section of Office VI at the RSHA.[142]

As a consequence, Eggen had to submit every request by his division as well as requests for passports and visas to Office VI of the RSHA. Hence, he came in *close contact with Walter Schellenberg*, who headed Office VI, foreign intelligence, as of summer 1941. Even though Schellenberg, who was only two years older than Eggen, frequently used Eggen for the connection with Masson, Eggen made sure that he did not become Schellenberg's direct subordinate, in order to maintain some independence. It seems that he did so successfully. At Nuremberg, he explained that in many cases Schellenberg had had "a feeling of uncertainty" about him, adding, "It was clear that I reported to Juettner. I was not Schellenberg's subordinate."[143]

It did not take Captain Meyer long to realize that the contact with Eggen was *a tremendous opportunity for Swiss Intelligence*. Meyer wrote a very detailed account of the extensive conversations that he had with Eggen during the weekend at his estate. This account is all the more interesting as Eggen supposedly did not yet know what position his host held in the military—the head of the Special Service at Army Intelligence and Security continued to pretend that he was *Dr. Ritzburg*, a legal advisor to the Swiss Wood Syndicate who was merely trying to bring the barracks transaction with Germany to a close.[144] However, the recorded conversations indicate that Eggen had already seen through Meyer's camouflage; at the very least he had to suspect that his host had contacts with Swiss Intelligence. This author found evidence for that supposition at the National Archives in Washington, DC. In 1948, in the course of being interrogated by the United States investigating judge in Nuremberg, Eggen stated, "[Captain Meyer] was not presented to me as Captain Meyer but as Dr. Ritzburg. However, it was clear to me that he worked for Swiss Counterintelligence. I did not know that when we first met, but I found out shortly afterwards. . . . Through several conversations, after a short time I realized that he worked for the Swiss secret service."[145] Apparently both Meyer and

Structure of the SS offices and the Reich Security Central Office

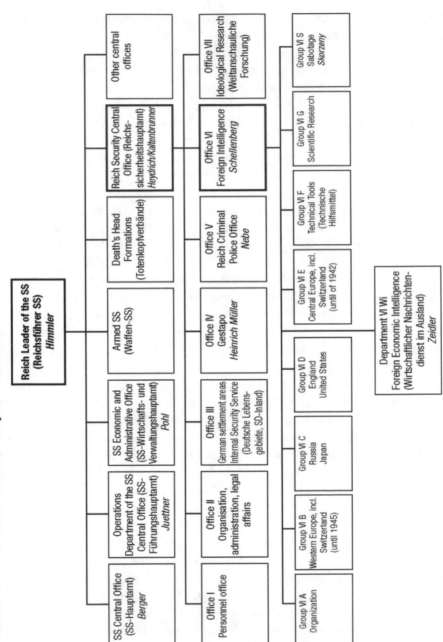

Eggen were testing the waters. In the following paragraphs, only a few key passages will be quoted from Meyer's account of the conversations.

For obvious reasons the two men talked about Russia because the battle of Moscow was then in full progress and because the Swiss wooden barracks were supposed to be sent to the German front in the East.[146] Meyer noted:

> Concerning Russia, [Eggen] admitted that G[erman] I[ntelligence] had failed because it had counted on Russia collapsing from the inside. He said that he had to praise Swiss Intelligence because before the war and at the beginning of the war it had been better informed than [German Intelligence] about the East; for a long time, [German Intelligence] obtained its information via Switzerland. He said that very often the same had been true . . . concerning *Belgium* and *Holland*, adding that in general Germany had a lot of respect for Swiss Intelligence.[147] He explained that for the time being Switzerland was not very interesting for [Germany], but that would change once *America entered the war* and the English and Americans had to go and get their information [on] Germany [and] France via the Swiss border. He said that the [British] Intelligence Service was receiving its best information from the Americans, adding that Lisbon, where England and America were in direct contact, was currently the most interesting place for spies. He advised us to be on our guard because the English and Americans had started increasing the number of personnel in Switzerland in order to be able to deploy them via the Swiss border; [Switzerland] should be careful in this respect.[148]

Regarding *Italy*, Eggen confirmed to Meyer that "the economic situation was becoming untenable and that Germany expected Italy to collapse; hence, [the SS] was continually increasing its staff there; they were all dressed in civilian clothes because officers wearing a uniform were not welcome." He argued that if Hitler was to carry out his *Alarich* plan,[149] by which he was to occupy Italy,[150] Switzerland would also be affected. He explained, "In this case, a request will have to be made to Switzerland that is similar to the one we made to Sweden *in order to be able to use our [Swiss] railroad [via] the Gotthard*." Captain Meyer, alias Dr. Ritzburg, replied that "Switzerland was not Sweden and that because of our neutrality we [could] not grant that request." The owner of Wolfsberg Castle reported Eggen as being "very surprised and startled" by his reply and advised him to "use your channels to report this to the German Armed Forces right away. Do it right away." Eggen claimed that a war would not pay off for Switzerland "because in two days we would be in the *Reduit*." Their conversation continued as follows:[151]

> Meyer: Maybe, but by then the bridges would be blown up!
> Eggen: Are you sure?
> Meyer: Yes, absolutely sure because we have changed and redone many things since finding out that your people . . . were interested in them "out of sheer curiosity."
> Eggen: Well, in that case it is OK.

That was a surprising reply when one considers that it came from a major of the regular SS and the *Waffen SS*. However, the entire conversation leaves a strange impression, as evidenced by the following excerpts from Meyer's notes. The head of the Special Service pointed out to Eggen that Switzerland was on its guard, so that the Germans living in Switzerland would not achieve anything. Eggen agreed:

> Eggen: We know that you prepared all traffic routes [for demolition], so we will need 1,000 men; I don't think I would be able to get them into the country unnoticed.
> Meyer: Not even 9 men, because within 36 hours the airport destroyers were behind bars.[152]

Meyer reported Eggen as being very amused by this reply, admitting, "Yes, we know, your service is well organized. In our service, on the other hand, many things are too organized, but that is not surprising when you consider the size [of our country] and the added protectorates." Eggen suggested that Meyer get a firsthand impression about the situation in Germany, stating, "Why don't you come to see me in Berlin; I will show you the organization. Or if you want to go to the front in the East for two or three days, I will be happy to take you there." Eggen was apparently interested in keeping up the contact with "Dr. Ritzburg." When Meyer gave an evasive answer, Eggen proposed to his host, "If you agree, I will give you the number to a *direct telephone line in Berlin* through which we can be in contact with each other at any time . . . without anyone eavesdropping." It had to be clear to both parties that Eggen did not make this statement as a client interested in purchasing wooden barracks.[153] If it was not yet clear at that point in time, it definitely was when the German openly wanted to know "how long technical secrets could be safeguarded." The conversation went as follows:

Eggen: Let me ask you a question. If you mention the right thing, I will not deny its existence. What do you know about Germany's new means of combat?

Meyer: You mean gas?

Eggen: No.

Meyer: But why do you produce such tremendous amounts of it?

Eggen: Because the old supplies would not have been sufficient for this long front.

Meyer: So you want to start using it after all.

Eggen: No, never. Because . . . we are perfectly consistent with everything we do, we make provisions for that as well. Well, I see that our service has kept its lips tight. (He is pleased.)

Meyer: You don't want to give me any hint?

Eggen: How could I if the whole organization has been keeping its lips tight.

At this point Meyer dropped his cover as "Dr. Ritzburg" and acknowledged that he was Captain of Intelligence Dr. Meyer-Schwertenbach. The two men then talked about Colonel Gustav Däniker[154] and General Guisan. Eggen asked his host "if the Commander-in-Chief had really had ties to Gamelin?"[155] Meyer said "No." Eggen subsequently commented, "Among ourselves we do not talk much about [Guisan][156] because he is not an influential figure nor very impressive. The Army Command is considered the weakest spot in [the Swiss] army."[157] Eggen "recommended that we take a firmer stand toward Germany; that was the only attitude that would impress [Germany]. . . . He said that Germany was impressed by England's absolute refusal to make any compromises; through this attitude it gained Germany's respect even as an opponent." Then Eggen once again emphasized that "it was necessary for the future of, and the relations between, the two countries to establish a *very direct contact* between Switzerland and Germany." He said that was the reason why he had given his host the number to a direct telephone line.[158]

One of the two officers had taken the bait. Or had both of them taken it? In any event, the contact was established. The next step was to make it useful for Masson.

Meyer Puts Eggen in Contact with Masson

It seems unusual that the Chief of Swiss Army Intelligence would have become personally involved in the contact that Captain Meyer established with Eggen. However, there is written evidence that a combination of basic considerations and relevant political issues prompted Masson to decide to meet the German of whom Meyer-Schwertenbach had received a very encouraging impression.[159]

In the era of strategic surprise attack, it is not sufficient to gather information on the composition of foreign military forces; an intelligence service has to also be informed about a potential opponent's *intentions*. Based on this concept, as early as before the war Masson had started setting up a *network of personal informants* that went in every direction and had offshoots in France, Italy, and Germany.[160] The connection with Italy was maintained by the director of a prestigious boarding school in central Switzerland[161] who was a close friend of Max Waibel's.[162] Masson hoped that this personal network would complement the professional Intelligence Service. At the end of the war he explained to the Military Attorney General, "[My private network] tried to *record some 'imponderables' of the war* rather than get specific information on the static arrangement of foreign troops near Switzerland's borders."[163]

An intelligence service procures information about the capabilities or intentions of potential opponents. Michael Handel states:

> It is far simpler to obtain information about *capabilities* than about *intentions*. *Capabilities* can be material or non-material. Material capabilities, that is, weapons, their performance specifications, and quantities, are not easy to conceal. Non-material capabilities such as the quality of organization, morale, and military doctrine are more difficult to evaluate in a precise way, although considerable knowledge about them can be obtained. A pitfall to be avoided at all costs is concentrating on the measurable and quantifiable while neglecting the less precise, non-material ones.[164]

Political and military *intentions*, on the other hand, are much easier to conceal. A state's strategy is determined by a small number of individuals, or sometimes by a single individual, as was sometimes the case with Hitler. Intentions may change at the last minute, and decisions may be revoked. It is almost impossible for an intelligence service to find out about these intentions and decisions if it does not have direct access to the political-military leadership. Nevertheless, by analyzing their earlier memoranda and speeches, or by evaluating the information contained in orders that have been leaked to the outside world, an intelligence service might discover that even the most taciturn leaders sometimes unintentionally give away their intentions.[165]

By means of his personal network, Masson tried to get hold of some of this inside information. His object was not only to obtain precise information about the other party's intentions but also to understand how the other party reacted to Switzerland's intentions and how they assessed Switzerland's capacities,[166] so as to be able to work toward correcting that image if necessary.

Even though an opponent's intentions have to be recorded and evaluated with the same care as its strength, experts generally believe that less attention should be paid to its intentions than to its real capabilities—simply because intentions are subject to more imponderables and are more likely to be drastically modified than, for example, the equipment of a tank division. Interestingly, Michael Handel actually considers that the opposite is true, supporting his case with arguments that are in line with the objective that Masson had regarding his personal network. Handel thinks that an opponent can decide to launch an attack even if it has relatively little striking power; it may underestimate the targeted victim's strength and determination (as was the case for the Germans in their 1941 invasion of the Soviet Union and for Argentina in its 1982 invasion of the British Falkland Islands), or it may believe that it will make up for its inferiority by staging a surprise attack.[167] Moreover, Handel argues:

> War and surprise attack are determined not by the existence of capabilities *per se*, but by the political intention to use them: The mere possession of superior, equal, or inferior strength is therefore less important. . . . Since it is, of course, much easier to obtain information on *capabilities* than *intentions*, the temptation to concentrate on that which is simpler to identify or measure must be consciously resisted.[168]

Masson was not the only one who had the idea of creating a personal network that was to complement the procurement activities of the official intelligence service. Admiral Canaris, the head of the *Abwehr*, the German Army's Foreign and Counterintelligence Service, also established a private set of connections. Oscar Reile commented:

> Evaluating every important piece of information that was received by his office and having a lively exchange of opinions with his staff yielded good results. Nevertheless, these activities by themselves would not have sufficed to make Canaris a master in assessing the situation and making forecasts. The Admiral had additional sources available, as he had time to create a network of informants all across Europe. In many instances, through this network he gained the insight that allowed him to make an assessment of the situation. However, this was not a network of informants as defined in the world of the secret service; they

were influential personalities in numerous European countries with whom Canaris managed to establish friendly official relations and continued exchanging ideas.[169]

This German equivalent of Masson's personal network bore valuable results in several respects. Reile explained: "As a matter of principle, the Admiral did not only look at things from the German perspective. Before giving his opinion about important issues, he tried to find out how important personalities in other countries, especially in countries that were interested in the matter, viewed the respective issues."[170]

Masson apparently used a pragmatic approach in setting up his private network. He selected his informants randomly[171] rather than according to a pre-established plan. Masson explained, "One of these contacts was established *by chance* with Mr. Eggen and later with General Schellenberg."[172]At that point, none of the persons involved suspected that that was the beginning of the connection with the head of German SS Foreign Intelligence. Nevertheless, the military-strategic and political situation that presented itself to Switzerland's Chief of Intelligence at the time he came into contact with Eggen must also be kept in mind. Masson stated, "At the end of 1941, after defeating France (in 1940), laying its hands on the Balkans (Yugoslavia, Greece, etc.), Germany *was omnipotent*, and in spite of the campaign in Russia, which began on June 22, 1941 and was still progressing well for the Axis armies at the time, it had numerous *strategic reserve troops* left."[173]

In view of this situation, Masson was all the more concerned about Switzerland's troubled relations with its superior, unpredictable neighbor to the north. In fall 1941, Germany launched one of its press campaigns against Switzerland, accusing it of a *lack of neutrality*. In addition, based on questionnaires that had been found with arrested agents, Masson knew that the German Armed Forces High Command had considerable doubts about Switzerland's determination to defend itself against *any* aggressor. (Similar, albeit less serious, frictions also existed with the other Axis power, Italy.) Masson added, "In late 1941 and early 1942, the tensions between the two countries had reached a climax, and (according to our informants) numerous Germans in France openly declared, 'It will be Switzerland's turn soon.'"[174]

As a consequence, Masson tried several times to have the Department of Foreign Affairs publish an official rebuttal in the event that the controlled German press should make unjustified reproaches to Switzerland. He stated, however, that "the [Department of Foreign Affairs] considered that it was not worth denying the lies that were spread about us."[175] Masson did not delude himself about the fact that Germany might attack Switzerland for purely strategic reasons and that the attitude of neither the Swiss press (which generally countered the attacks, even though it was subject to censorship) nor the population could change anything about that. Nevertheless, there was also a risk that *Germany might launch a preventive attack on Switzerland because it did not trust Switzerland's neutrality.* Masson considered that it was his duty "to correct the wrong impression that one had of us in Germany"[176] and thereby contribute to reducing the tensions between the two countries. Switzerland's Chief of Intelligence argued, "I may say that our failure to react (which I would call [a failure] to enact an 'offensive policy') on the level of the government did not help to ease the situation between Germany and Switzerland."[177]

Meyer-Schwertenbach, who knew about his superior's ideas,[178] described Eggen as "an interesting man who was informed about a lot of things (which later turned out to be true)"[179] and suggested that it might be useful for Masson to take a close look at the German. Masson agreed and asked Meyer to organize a meeting with Eggen. Hence, Masson met Eggen as early as eight days after the first weekend that Eggen had spent at Wolfsberg Castle.[180] Meyer, still alias Dr. Ritzburg, had invited his German guest back to his estate, and on the evening of November 24, 1941, he took him to Bern, where Masson was waiting for them at the bar of the *Schweizerhof* hotel.[181] As usual on such occasions, Masson was wearing civilian clothes and used a cover name. He pretended to be a journalist who was interested in press-related matters, particularly the war between the German and Swiss press.[182] The conversation was informal and dealt with general topics, such as the death of a top German pilot, and Italy, France, and Greece. "Dr. Ritzburg" viewed this first contact between Masson and Eggen rather enthusiastically, characterizing it as "cordial."[183] Masson also had a good first impression about the German, stating, "I found Eggen interesting, intellectually nimble; he was well informed about the general situation between Germany and Switzerland and showed some sympathy toward Switzerland, where he said he wanted to establish residence after the war."[184] Masson consequently decided to meet Eggen again during the latter's next trip to Switzerland. He considered Eggen to be suitable to correct Germany's wrong impression about Switzerland[185]—especially because he seemed to have access to key authorities; Masson argued, "Eggen regularly saw certain leaders in Berlin, even at the German Armed Forces High Command."[186]

In early December 1941, Masson had the opportunity to strengthen the promising contact with Eggen. On that occasion, Switzerland's Chief of Intelligence and Security once again pretended to be a press representative, which was quite credible when he addressed the issue of the attacks by the German press against Switzerland. He showed Eggen a copy of one of Franz

Burri's information bulletins in which the head of the International Press Agency (IPA) seriously denigrated the Commander-in-Chief of the Swiss Army.[187]

In 1938, the Federal Council had banned the IPA. Burri, a native of the Entlebuch region in canton Lucerne, subsequently transferred the agency headquarters to Vienna, and in 1940 to Budapest, where he continued to engage in subversive activities.[188] The IPA's relentless smear campaign and unscrupulous attacks were particularly dangerous because they were spread above all in foreign countries where they created a completely distorted image of Switzerland.[189] Right-wing extremist Burri, who was later stripped of his Swiss citizenship and in 1948 was sentenced to twenty years in prison,[190] "considered his publications as a means to break the Swiss' determination to put up resistance and to offer a pretext to the German Reich to put Switzerland under pressure in order to establish a Nazi government there."[191]

Masson asked Eggen[192] to use his influence to get the IPA to cease publication of its defamatory bulletins,[193] which the German promised to do. Eggen later explained:

> Upon returning to Berlin, I contacted Maj[or] Gen[eral Gottlob] Berger, the head of the SS main office to explain to him[194] that *the entire Swiss Army was indignant* about the series of articles and that these articles would accomplish the opposite of what [Berger] wanted them to accomplish, i.e. strengthen Swiss Germans' [sympathy for the] German Wehrmacht. B[erger] listened to my arguments because during the meeting I explained to him that this type of propaganda would make him lose face as general and head of the Expansion [and Confiscation] Office[195] and that he would recruit only bad elements instead of upright individuals among the German-speaking Swiss. B[erger] thereupon ordered the bulletin to cease publication.[196]

However, Eggen later admitted to the Swiss Attorney General's office that his initiative was only temporarily successful, as the IPA bulletins began being published again several months later.[197] Eggen subsequently addressed the issue with Schellenberg, and with his assistance it was allegedly possible to "get the newspaper to cease publication once and for all."[198] It was not until then that Eggen was officially told who the supposed press representative was with whom he had met twice and what position the owner of Wolfsberg Castle held in Army Intelligence. Eggen had to have suspected, if not known, these facts for quite a while.[199]

An entry in Barbey's diary indicates that Masson had decided early on, i.e. no later than following his second meeting with Eggen, to include the German in his personal network. On December 12, 1941, the Chief of the General's Personal Staff noted, "Masson talks to me about contacts that he has established, through his aide Captain Meyer from Ermatingen, with *a German from Himmler's entourage who supposedly has access to the Führer*."[200] However, Barbey made a more sober assessment than Masson of the information that he had received from Eggen until then, stating, "there is nothing miraculous . . . about the predictions that this personality made a few months ago."[201] Also, when Masson told Barbey that Himmler had apparently expressed the wish to meet Switzerland's Chief of Intelligence, Barbey advised him "to keep the secret of this 'connection' for himself, no matter what happened, [adding] I did not need to tell him that; Masson entirely agrees with me. By the way, he *refused to have a direct line set up between Berlin and Ermatingen*, and rightly so."[202]

Barbey's last statement is particularly revealing, showing the strange status that the contact with Eggen had in Masson's opinion. On the one hand, Masson was obviously so proud of his new channel that he gave up his principles, telling an outsider about it; on the other hand, however, Barbey's note demonstrates that in spite of the favorable impression that he had gained about Eggen, Masson was clever, keeping a certain distance from his new acquaintance.[203]

8

Extending the Connection: Masson Establishes Contact with Schellenberg

EGGEN'S FREQUENT TRAVELS to Switzerland gave Masson the opportunity to intensify the exchange of ideas with the German SS officer. During one of their meetings in early 1942, when Masson made a specific request,[1] Eggen made him understand that the matter was beyond his authority. Masson consequently asked the German, "Is there nobody who is understanding and human enough in Hitler's entourage who I could have an open and straightforward discussion with like *between soldiers*?"[2] Eggen spontaneously mentioned *Walter Schellenberg*, explaining that more than once he had shown a benevolent attitude toward Switzerland, was cultivated and well educated, and would be an interesting person to talk to. Masson later commented: "I had no further information about Schellenberg but decided to suggest to him that we meet somewhere in Switzerland, *on strictly private terms.*[3] In my opinion, this contact was going to be one of the international relations that any chief of intelligence has to maintain as part of his official duties."[4]

Eggen informed Schellenberg about Masson's invitation, but Schellenberg was not at all interested in traveling to Switzerland.[5] He had Eggen tell Masson that he had no time to go on vacation, that he was busy because his country was at war, and that if Masson wanted to ask him something he should travel to Berlin to do so.[6] He even proposed to take Masson on a tour by plane to Germany's eastern front.[7] However, for neutrality reasons, at the time[8] Masson did not consider it appropriate to accept Schellenberg's proposition. After months of going back and forth, the two men finally made a compromise, agreeing to meet, on September 8, 1942, in the German town of Waldshut near the Swiss border. Meyer-Schwertenbach had once again acted as a mediator.

Preliminary: Meyer Meets Schellenberg

In retrospect, one is tempted to think that the Germans masterminded the get-together. However, the history of the encounter between the two chiefs of intelligence began as a pure coincidence, an unexpected meeting between Schellenberg and Meyer-Schwertenbach. In July 1942, Masson's deputy, Colonel Werner Müller of the General Staff, was supposed to travel to Berlin to join delegates from other neutral countries for the annual meeting of the *International Criminal Police Commission* (in German: Internationale Kriminalpolizeiliche Kommission, or IKPK).[9] Müller in his civilian career was head of the Security Police and Criminal Investigation Department in the city of Bern, and was the Federal Council's representative at IKPK meetings.[10] Müller was even a member of its administrative board.[11] In that function, he had met Reinhard Heydrich before the war.[12]

At the annual meetings in Paris (in 1931), Rome (1932), Vienna (1934), Copenhagen (1935), Belgrade (1936), and London (1937), developments in Germany had not been foreseen. This explains why the 1934 decision to set up the IKPK headquarters in Vienna was not reversed. At the 1938 annual meeting in Bucharest, the atmosphere was tense. Shortly before that meeting, Hitler had forced Austria into the Reich, and the delegates intended to transfer the IKPK Secretariat to a neutral country. However, it was apparently already too late because, according to one scholar, "Heydrich had an arrogant and demanding attitude."[13] SS Oberführer Steinhäusel became the IKPK's chief executive, and, when he died of tuberculosis in 1940, the head of the Reich Security Central Office named himself IKPK president and decided then and there to move the headquarters to Berlin. That meant that a criminal was in charge of the predecessor of *Interpol,* which was supposed to combat international crime.[14] As of 1940, de facto, the IKPK was integrated into the Reich Criminal Police Headquarters and was no longer functional. In 1942, the Commission's headquarters were located at Berlin-Wannsee, and Heydrich singlehandedly headed its "international" bureau.[15]

Eggen,

Kontrolle der Einreisenden — Contrôle des voyageurs — Controllo viaggiatori

Name und Vorname / Nom et prénom / Cognome e nome	*Eggen Hans-Wilhelm*	Geburtsdatum / Date de naissance / Data di nascita	*5. 6. 1912*
Sta...angehörigkeit / N...alité / Nazionalità	*Deutsch*	Beruf / Profession / Professione *Kaufmann*	Paß Nr. / No du passeport / No del passaporto *II 4955/41.*
Ein. ..evisum erteilt vom schweiz. Konsulat in / Visa suisse octroyé par le Consulat de / Visto d'entrata rilasciato dal Consolato di Svizzera a		*Berlin 1220 Ref 30113.*	
Wohnort und Adresse im Ausland / Adresse à l'étranger / Domicilio all'estero (indirizzo)	*Berlin Dahlmannstr. 33*		
Kommt von / Vient de / Provenienza	*Berlin*	Dauer des Aufenthaltes in der Schweiz / Durée du séjour en Suisse / Durata del soggiorno in Svizzera *4.5 Tage*	
Genaue Adresse in der Schweiz (bei wem, Hotel, Pension) / Adresse exacte en Suisse (chez qui, hôtel, pension) / Indirizzo esatto in Isvizzera (presso chi, albergo, pensione)		*Zürich Schweizerhof*	
Adresse der Personen und Firmen, die ev. besucht werden / Nom des personnes ou des maisons qui seront visitées / Nome ed indirizzo delle ditte e persone che saranno visitate		*A. G. für Metallverwertung*	
Zweck der Reise / Motif du voyage / Scopo del viaggio	*Geschäftl. Besprechungen*	Referenzen (nur bei Ausländern) / Références (pour les étrangers) / Referenze (per gli stranieri) BAr 40	
Gr. Übergang / Poste de / Valico di		Datumstempel / Date d'entrée / Data (timbro)	Unterschrift des Reisenden / Signature du voyageur / Firma del viaggiatore
		SCHWEIZ E -7. APR. 42. ZÜRICH-FLUGPLATZ	*Eggen*

Like most other travelers, SS Major Eggen had to fill out the "immigration form" created by Swiss Army Intelligence whenever he arrived in Switzerland. On most occasions, including on April 7, 1942, he indicated that the purpose of his trip was "business talks" with the Swiss Wood Syndicate, or *AG für Metallverwertung*. (BAr E 27/10631)

Under these circumstances, Colonel Müller refused to accept Germany's invitation to the 1942 annual meeting, apparently fearing that the regime might use his presence for its own ends. Masson could not force Müller to attend the meeting,[16] but he did not want to miss this opportunity to explore contacts for the intelligence service. As a way out of the dilemma, the two men turned to the head of the Special Service. Masson later explained: "[So] we asked our devoted Captain Meyer from our Security Service to take care of this mission because in the area of intelligence, *nothing could be neglected in order to secure as many contacts as possible, no matter what kind of contacts they were.* In this specific case, the subsequent events proved us to be right."[17]

Masson informed Chief of the General Staff Huber about Meyer's planned mission; Huber agreed to it and granted Captain Meyer a leave of absence from July 6 to 11, 1942.[18] In a meeting with the Chief of Intelligence and the Head of the Security Service, Meyer-Schwertenbach was given four specific tasks for his mission to Berlin:[19] first, to establish contact with key people on Himmler's staff; second, to familiarize those officials with Switzerland's situation and correct certain impressions that the SS had of the country; third, to use his influence to have Ernst Mörgeli, who had been held in custody for four months on suspicion of espionage on behalf of England, released from prison; and fourth, to address a number of police-related bilateral issues because for several months Heinrich Rothmund, the head of the Swiss Federal Police Section, had been waiting in vain to obtain a visa to travel to Germany.

At Schellenberg's invitation, Captain Meyer traveled to Berlin as a *private citizen.*[20] Schellenberg sent his intermediary Eggen to Dübendorf to pick up his guest.[21] Were they trying to impress Meyer-Schwertenbach by showing him how powerful the SS was in the Reich? In any event, Meyer noticed[22] that his trip went smoothly even though he did not yet have a visa for Germany. In Berlin, an SS car picked him up, and on July 8, 1942 Schellenberg received him at the SS guest house on Wannsee.[23] Masson later reported:

> During a private conversation, of course Schellenberg brought up the affair of *La Charité*[24] (documents that the Wehrmacht had found, during its offensive in France, in Gamelin's train, which was stopped at the small train station there. As you know, these documents contained evidence of a preliminary military agreement between France and Switzerland concerning the joint defense of the sector between Basel, Gempen, and Olten in the event of a German threat). Meyer told Schellenberg that it might be useful for him to meet [me] because our comrade [Meyer] knew how anxious I was to reduce the importance that the Germans attached to this affair.[25]

Meyer-Schwertenbach wrote detailed notes about his talks in Berlin[26] that give quite a clear picture of the attitudes and intentions of the people who were involved. From the Swiss perspective, Masson could say that through Meyer he accomplished his goal of establishing contact with an SS authority that had some influence on the *Secret State Police* (Gestapo), which gave him access to people who held the reins of power. He had been unable to establish such contacts through the German Ministry of Foreign Affairs, the Military Attachés, or the Wehrmacht's Foreign Intelligence and Counterintelligence *Abwehr* (Admiral Canaris). But didn't Masson and Meyer venture too far out, and did that not unintentionally make them pieces on Germany's chessboard?

Unlike Colonel-Brigadier Masson and Captain Meyer, Albert Müller, the head of the foreign news desk at the *Neue Zürcher Zeitung*[27] who had found out about these contacts[28] through Editor-in-Chief Willy Bretscher, considered direct relations between two armies that bypassed the countries' political leadership as a dangerous example of the Third Reich's successful *extended strategy*.[29] In an extensive memorandum that he submitted to the Federal Council,[30] Müller presented the technique "that Germany [was using] toward a state that it [wanted] to subjugate,"[31] explaining:

> Germany avoids using diplomatic channels, circumventing them. It closes down the normal channels that are used in bilateral relations and visibly despises the time-consuming and elaborate methods of official authorities and responsible bodies with which obstacles and delays have to be expected. Instead, Germany stresses the advantages of taking shortcuts via influential bodies as well as the advantages of "direct contacts." Germany is willing to show its partner how efficient its preferred method is by paying the acting "influential bodies" or other instruments that are part of the "direct contacts" an advance premium in the form of favors or services that cannot be obtained from the competent authorities nor by following standard procedures.[32]

Furthermore, the *NZZ* editor pointed out that the extended strategy was clever because it could be adapted so as to take the circumstances of each country into account. "Under the current circumstances," he added, "one has to assume that the German mediators will try even harder to . . . show their honest intentions and well-meaningness when they initiate a direct contact."[33] Moreover, Müller wrote that it had to be expected that with this method, Germany did not intend to achieve its objective straight away but only take a first major step in that direction. He warned, "With this method of direct contacts with individual bodies, at a suitable moment in time [Germany] might simply want to cause a crisis of confidence and a rift among the partner's authorities, which would create favorable conditions for taking action. In any case, Germany would 'swiftly strike' to take advantage of the favorable conditions even if it had not planned to create them."[34]

Meyer-Schwertenbach's notes about his talks at the SS guest house on Wannsee read like an unintentional case study in support of Albert Müller's theory of the *extended strategy* that Germany had honed to a specialty. Meyer wrote: "The meeting could be characterized as a *private, friendly* exchange of ideas. It was agreed that the meeting should be kept secret even though it was unofficial; its only purpose was to put Germany and Switzerland on friendlier terms. These meetings [were] expected to give both states the opportunity to present their requests, concerns . . . and to correct false information through the *most direct*, unofficial channel."[35] Meyer described the "contacts," which *deliberately avoided the existing diplomatic channels between the two countries*, as

> all the more important as [he] was able to find out that the German Legations in the few remaining neutral states were desert islands; their voice [was] not heard among the leading circles around H[immler] and H[itler]. From the outset, one [was] skeptical [about] everything that [arrived] in Germany through diplomatic channels because the leading figures at the German Legation (Köcher, Ilsemann) [were] considered people of a long-gone past.[36]

When the Germans pointed their finger at "several items in [Switzerland's] *catalogue of misdeeds*"[37] and mentioned, in spite of the censorship that was in place, the unmistakably critical attitude of the Swiss press toward the Third Reich, the owner of Wolfsberg Castle fearlessly replied that in Switzerland there was too much talk about Switzerland waiting to be integrated into the Reich as a province, adding, "To us, Germany [is] the bad guy!"[38] He explained that if the Germans were interested at all in improving bilateral relations with Switzerland, they should recall Councilor *von Bibra* from Bern "because he was the most hated man in Switzerland and stood in the way of a better understanding between the two states."[39] Concerning the press, Meyer argued, "By curtailing the freedom of the press in Switzerland, you would knock down a pillar of democracy and put an end to our state system."[40] When the issue of Switzerland's independence was addressed, Meyer was told:

> *Switzerland* [is] currently *not a burning issue* for the Führer. He [does] not have time to deal with internal [*sic*] matters because he [is] fully

absorbed in military issues. It should be possible to keep Switzerland independent; contacts such as the one we [are] having today, which [are] far from the diplomatic realm and [are] based exclusively on good faith and human trust, [can] accomplish this. In order to further cultivate these contacts, [we will] issue you a *permanent visa*."[41]

As instructed, Meyer-Schwertenbach brought up the issue of Ernst Mörgeli's release from prison. He noted, "I ask the gentlemen"—two unidentified SS officers took part in the meeting together with Schellenberg—"to render me this service out of friendship; after the [service concerning] the IPA,[42] this will be the second pillar that we can build [our relations] on. They promise that they will do something about it and ask me to write a short report, which I put together the following morning."[43] However, Masson ended up having to personally intervene with Schellenberg to get Ernst Mörgeli out of prison.

The meeting at Wannsee convinced Meyer "that in the event of a German victory, it [would] be *military authorities with a politically clean record*, not *civilian authorities* such as the Legation or the Federal Palace, that [had] to contribute to making relations bearable."[44] It is therefore not surprising that Meyer wrote:

> During the friendly meeting, we mutually made a commitment [to report on it] only to the direct superior; we will not tell the civilian authorities anything about it in order to avoid creating unnecessary difficulties and misunderstandings. [We will] also keep the granting of my visa *secret* in order for me not to be drawn into the battle between the forces. Everything that [has been] said [is] unofficial; this is a strictly personal conversation that should contribute to improving relations between Switzerland and Germany in view of keeping Switzerland autonomous.[45] I promise [that I will keep everything secret] and pass this promise on as a commitment.[46]

The following day, on July 9, 1942, Meyer-Schwertenbach returned to Switzerland to report to his superior about what he considered a successful mission. In his opinion, Swiss Intelligence had managed to establish a personal, trusting contact with key German authorities. The head of the Special Service concluded, "I traveled to Germany without a passport, and after my meeting I received a permanent visa and a residence permit; meanwhile, [Heinrich Rothmund] the head of the Swiss Federal Police Section has been waiting in vain to obtain a visa, even though I am at least as patriotic as he is. This is striking evidence [of] *who* is in power in Germany."[47]

The Meeting in Waldshut

Reasons for the Meeting

The Germans apparently also viewed Meyer's visit to Berlin as a success and considered that the ties could be strengthened. As little as seven weeks later, on August 27, 1942, Schellenberg sent his intermediary, Eggen, to Zürich, supposedly only with instructions "to smooth the great tensions that existed between Germany and Switzerland in police-related matters."[48] For that purpose, the SS said that it would make it possible for Heinrich Rothmund, the head of the Swiss Federal Police Section, to travel to Berlin provided that Masson and Meyer guaranteed that the German Legation would not find out about it.[49] However, now Schellenberg was primarily interested in establishing contact with Switzerland's Chief of Intelligence. Fuhrer comments:

> Schellenberg tried to create his own sources of information as far as possible because his 'official' connections with Switzerland did not live up to his expectations. The fact that he trusted himself more than anyone else might have played a role in that matter. These personal contacts with Switzerland could be called Schellenberg's *special channels*. The Swiss Desk at the Reich Security Central Office was not let in on these connections.[50]

Like Masson, Schellenberg established his special connections as a complement or an independent corrective to the work done by the country desks.[51]

On August 27, 1942, when he met with Masson and Meyer at the *Baur-au-Lac* hotel in Zürich, Eggen prepared the ground for a face-to-face meeting between Schellenberg and Masson by remarking that Germany used to think that Masson was hand-in-glove with the British Intelligence Service, but that today he was considered a *person who could be trusted*. He said that Masson mostly had to thank Meyer for that change of opinion. Eggen urged Masson to meet Schellenberg very soon. Meyer noted: "[Eggen said that Masson] had to confirm to Schellenberg the things that [Eggen] and I had told Schellenberg."[52] Eggen explained that "if Masson spoke with Schellenberg, he would become their right-hand man with whom they would raise any issue or problem between Switzerland and Germany; [he said that] that was not possible through official channels because things were being stalled there."[53] The German intermediary added that Himmler kept being told "that the little organ [called] Switzerland was sick, so it had to be removed from the European belly. [He claimed] that Germany did not know anyone in Switzerland who it could solve general problems with in a friendly, trusting manner; *Masson therefore had the chance to save Switzerland.*"[54]

Meyer-Schwertenbach agreed with Eggen, who then addressed the military-political situation. A few days earlier, the German 6th Army had crossed the Don River, and Wehrmacht units had started advancing through the northern outskirts of Stalingrad. Eggen was confident, asserting that "currently Germany could no longer lose the war.[55] [He said] that this winter they would be in a better position [than the previous one], that the meat and flour rations would be increased shortly, that in Ukraine they had a huge sunflower crop to produce oil, and that after the battle of the Caucasus, Europe would be economically [restructured]."[56]

By 3 a.m., when the two Swiss said goodbye to Eggen, Masson had been won over. He told Meyer that he felt compelled to agree to the meeting and asked him to make preparations for it.[57] Meyer consulted with Captain Peter Burckhardt of the General Staff, choosing the German town of Laufenburg near the Swiss border as the venue for the meeting.[58]

Masson seemed to be perfectly aware of the fact that he was about to become involved in a delicate undertaking. He decided to take the risk mostly for the same reasons that had inspired him to meet Eggen.[59] There is evidence for that argument both through Masson's own explanations and a second-hand account by Barbey, who wrote an extended note on the matter in his diary. Masson went to see Barbey on September 3, 1942 "to tell [him] about the project that [took] up all his time and [fascinated] him." Barbey wrote:

> He offers to go to Germany shortly to meet a personality who has significant influence in Himmler's and even Hitler's entourage, a young, fine, very well educated general whose task he says makes him the *Masson of the SS*, so to speak. This man is supposedly open to receiving a real 'Swiss message' and is able to make that message heard, not among Ribbentrop's entourage, which is very hostile toward our country, nor among the Wehrmacht, but among the entourage of the SS that is gradually gaining control.[60]

According to Barbey, Masson's "Swiss message" consisted of two parts: first, he wanted to convince the Germans that Switzerland was determined to defend itself against any aggressor; and second, he intended to persuade them to stop their intensive intelligence activities against Switzerland.[61] Barbey continued:

"Masson elaborates on the issue. I gradually understand that in the absence of his direct superior, the Chief of the General Staff, who is on vacation, he wants to have the Commander-in-Chief's approval. This is a delicate matter."[62] The Chief of General Guisan's Personal Staff immediately understood how problematic Masson's plan was, stating:

> I tell Masson that at first glance, there are two aspects to this matter: the aspect of "*intelligence*," i.e. we might be able to test the ground concerning the arrangements that the SS has made, which is undoubtedly valuable information; and the "*negotiation*" aspect, into which he risks being entangled. Instead of "entangled," I feel like saying "outplayed." I do not need to say it; Masson understands my hint. He sees himself as someone who uses the opportunity to advocate Switzerland's cause and to have it advocated in key positions there.[63]

Barbey did not hide the fact that he felt uneasy when he heard Masson talk about his plan. He advised him to keep the meeting secret, adding, "Then I leave him, uncertain."[64] A short time later, he noticed that Masson approached the Commander-in-Chief "to briefly inform him about his plan. The General does not voice any objection."[65]

It is difficult to determine whether in the fall of 1942 it was more important for Masson to tackle the long-term objective of correcting "the wrong impression that Germany had of [Switzerland]"[66] or to resolve specific issues. In either case, the prospect of success seemed to be best if he entered into personal contact with Schellenberg. He explained:

> I originally had Admiral Canaris in mind, the chief of the German Army's Foreign and Counterintelligence Service; I knew that he was sympathetic toward Switzerland and that there was constant friction between him and the Nazi party.[67] My most urgent request was to save my Swiss officer who was in prison in Stuttgart.[68] Canaris was unlikely to be able to help me with that because my young staff member [Mörgeli] was being held in the clutches of the Gestapo, that is, Canaris' political opponents. He would not have been useful to me concerning the other issues either because they lay outside his sphere of influence. It was therefore important to me to choose my means according to the objective that was to be achieved. In spite of the respect that I had for Canaris, I felt that it was more useful to approach Schellenberg.[69]

For the same reason Masson ruled out two other options, even though they would have involved fewer risks; he could have presented his requests to the German military attaché in Bern, General von Ilsemann, particularly because, as many as 20 years after the end of the war, Masson praised "his perfectly correct professional attitude"[70]; or he could have gone through the Swiss military attaché in Berlin, who had the advantage of being at the place where decisions were made. Masson actually gave these two options some thought but rejected them by arguing that both of them carried with them "the dualism and conflict between authority and competence. . . . By going through the military attachés, you actually reached the army, which was fighting at the front, not within the omnipotent party inside the country. Schellenberg, who had a status within Intelligence that was similar to mine but above all carried some weight in international political matters, had valuable contacts with the Gestapo."[71]

Masson's main reason for approaching Schellenberg was probably the strained relationship between Swiss Army Intelligence and Switzerland's Department of Foreign Affairs. Shortly after Mörgeli had been arrested, Alfred Ernst, the head of the German Bureau, was outraged, informing Masson that the Intelligence Service could not expect any assistance or understanding from the Swiss Government. In that matter, he wrote:

> Captain [Max] Maurer[72] has just informed me that a German consular agent who was guilty of espionage and was supposed to be arrested in order to be exchanged with Dr. Mörgeli had to be returned to Germany.[73] He said that the Department of Foreign Affairs had considered that it was better not to provoke the Germans, that we were weak and they were strong, so we should not do anything that could upset them. . . . I would like to ask you to vehemently protest against one of our most valuable officers being abandoned because of the Department of Foreign Affairs' cowardice and inexplicable softness toward every German demand. Captain Maurer confirmed that it would have been easy to exchange our officer with the German agent. . . . I will under no circumstances abandon Dr. Mörgeli; I am going to move heaven and earth to help him if nothing is done for him.[74]

Ernst Mörgeli had been "extremely carefully selected"[75] to replace James Ketterer, who had been expelled from Germany,[76] at the Swiss Consulate in Stuttgart. The Head of the German Bureau was acquainted with the young second lieutenant, having served in the same unit with him during their initiation course in the army. Ernst explained: "I knew that he had an impeccable reputation both in the military and in his life as a civilian and was generally viewed as a skillful, reliable officer and jurist. As it turned out, our expectations were entirely fulfilled."[77]

Before being sent to Stuttgart, Mörgeli was briefed extensively about the Ketterer case. Ernst told him that he had to expect "the Germans to be suspicious of him because they would probably consider him as Dr. Ketterer's successor. Because of this, [Ernst] *explicitly forbade*[78] him from setting up any structure for procuring intelligence or from doing anything that the Germans could use as evidence for their accusations."[79] In order to avoid taking any unnecessary risks, Mörgeli was not allowed to carry any documents whenever he crossed the border. He was only allowed to verbally communicate his information to a diplomatic courier, who was to pass the information on to Ernst orally. The Head of the German Bureau commented: "I do not have any reason to believe that Dr. Mörgeli failed to abide by these instructions. On the contrary, during the entire time that we worked together I had the impression that he was an extremely cautious, levelheaded officer who never showed the slightest sign of any weakness."[80]

On March 17, 1942, Mörgeli left the consulate to pick up a courier at the main train station in Stuttgart. In the street he was stopped and arrested by two officials wearing civilian clothes.[81] Mörgeli later stated, "The Gestapo did not declare that I was put under arrest, they only made a gesture and said, 'Follow us!'."[82] No one told him why he was to follow them. For three months, he remained incarcerated at a prison on Münzenstrasse in the heart of Stuttgart and was subsequently transferred to the Welzheim concentration camp.[83] Even though he was subjected to very long interrogations, Mörgeli was never told why the Gestapo had arrested him. A fellow Swiss who had also been arrested incriminated him by stating that "through the mediation of another Swiss national, [he had] gathered information in Stuttgart that could be significant only to Allied intelligence. Hence, Dr. Mörgeli was sure to work for Germany's enemies."[84]

The unfounded accusation corroborated the suspicion that the Germans had set a trap for Mörgeli in order to produce the evidence that they had been trying to find for a long time, i.e. that Swiss Intelligence was cooperating with the British Intelligence Service. It appears that Mörgeli had been in contact with a Swiss living in Stuttgart. Ernst recalled: "Without my soliciting it and without informing me in advance, he once gave me the design of an airplane cooling system that he said he had received from a Swiss. I told him that I did not want to receive any such material from him and explained to him that he put himself in danger by accepting it; I told him that it was not impossible that the Germans were trying to set a trap for him."[85] As Ernst suspected, it is

19.4.1942

Herrn Oberstbrigadier Masson

Herr Oberstbrigadier,   × Zwei Teil

Soeben teilt mir Hptm.Maurer mit,dass auf Befehl des politischen Departementes ein der Spionage schuldiger deutscher Konsulatsbeamter,der festgenommen werden sollte,um später gegen Dr.Mörgeli ausgetauscht zu werden,nach Deutschland entlassen werden musste.Das politische Departement habe die Meinung vertreten,es sei besser,die Deutschen nicht zu reizen.Wir seien schwach und sie seien stark.Also müssten wir vorsichtig sein und nichts tun,was sie ärgern könnte.

Da es mir als Chef des Dr.Mörgeli nicht gleichgültig ist,dass er infolge solcher Fehler des politischen Departements auf unbestimmte Zeit in Haft bleiben muss,gestatte ich mir,Ihre Aufmerksamkeit auf diesen Vorfall zu lenken.Es ist--darin musste mir Hptm.Maurer recht geben--ein Skandal und ein schwerer Fehler,wie das politische Departement gehandelt hat.Jeder,der die Deutschen nur ein wenig kennt,weiss,dass sie sich durch Unterwürfigkeit nicht im geringsten imponieren lassen.Ihnen gegenüber hilft nur eine entschlossene Haltung und der Mut zu Repressalien.

Ich bitte Sie,mit allem Nachdruck dagegen zu protestieren,dass durch die Feigheit des politischen Departements und seine ▓▓▓▓▓▓▓▓ unbegreifliche Nachgiebigkeit gegenüber allen deutschen Begehren einer unserer wertvollsten Offiziere,der wie mir Hptm.Maurer bestätigte,leicht hätte ausgetauscht werden können,im Stiche gelassen wird.

Ich bin gewohnt,mich für meine Untergebenen einzusetzen und daher nicht gesonnen,solche Fehler,wie sie das politische Departement in dieser Sache begeht,stillschweigend hinzunehmen.Ich denke nicht daran,Dr.Mörgeli im Stiche zu lassen und werde,wenn nichts für ihn getan wird,meinerseits alle Hebel in Bewegung setzen,um ihm zu helfen.

Nächste Woche kommt Dr.Frölicher nach Bern.Da anzunehmen ist,dass er, wie gewohnt,nicht das schweizerischen,sondern den deutschen Standpunkt vertreten wird,wird es gut sein,wenn Sie das politische Departement mit allem Nachdruck darauf hinweisen,dass gegen Dr.Mörgeli vorläufig nur Behauptungen der Deutschen vorliegen,die vermutlich der Wahrheit nicht entsprechen.Wir müssen sonst befürchten,dass das politische Departement sich ebenfalls den deutschen Standpunkt zu eigen macht und behauptet, Dr.Mörgeli sei an seiner Verhaftung selber schuld.Wir müssten ▓▓▓▓▓ ihn also seinem Schicksal überlassen.

Major · Gst. Ernst

Au colonel E.M.G. Müller

          Je vous transmets, à toutes fins utiles, la présente lettre du major Ernst, dont le contenu a déjà fait l'objet d'un entretien avec vous. Comme convenu, je vous prie de suivre cette affaire et de tout mettre en oeuvre pour obtenir dès que possible la libération du Dr. Mörgeli. Le lt.colonel Schafroth ou le major Daniel sont à votre disposition pour traiter avec le Département politique fédéral.

                              COMMANDEMENT DE L'ARMÉE
                                   Groupe I d
                              Le sous-chef d'état-major: *Masson*

7.5.42.

Letter from Alfred Ernst to Chief of Intelligence Masson, asking the latter to put pressure on the Department of Foreign Affairs to have Ernst Mörgeli, who had been arrested by the Gestapo, released from prison (BAr E 27/9528).

absolutely possible that the Germans were using the Swiss who incriminated Mörgeli as an agent provocateur in order to create the link between him and Mörgeli that they were looking for.[86] However, even by using that ploy, Mörgeli could not be accused of espionage because he had not instructed his fellow citizen to obtain a copy of the design; he had simply accepted it.[87]

It is also possible that the Gestapo considered the "evidence" against Mörgeli unreliable, as had been the case in the Ketterer case; or perhaps it had pursued another objective[88] by arresting Mörgeli. In any event, the case was never tried. Mörgeli was kept under arrest for more than nine months without ever being told why. In order to intimidate him, the Germans threatened to *execute* him and hinted that he "might simply disappear one day."[89]

The lack of cooperation[90] between the Swiss Federal Department of Foreign Affairs and Army Intelligence manifested itself in the Mörgeli case as well as in other matters.[91] In fall 1942, the German Bureau was presented with the fact that all its outposts at the Swiss consulates in Germany (Mannheim, Stuttgart, Munich, Vienna) had been closed. In the Bureau's 1942 annual report, Ernst observed: "Hence, an important means for verifying information is gone; it will be difficult to replace it. In view of the political authorities' resistance, it will be impossible to resume the same or similar surveillance activities in the major German centers."[92] It was not hard at all to realize that this handicap would have troublesome consequences for the quality of the procured intelligence. Ernst stated: "We should not fool ourselves into believing that the intelligence service will be able to recognize a sudden threat in time. In 1940 that had been possible to some extent, but currently the procurement bodies are so badly impeded [by the Department of Foreign Affairs] that we can no longer accept any responsibility for noticing in time the preparations for an attack."[93]

This was probably the main reason for Masson to meet Schellenberg in Germany. It is questionable whether Masson realized that by doing so he was abandoning the realm of *intelligence* in favor of a *political plea*, as Barbey had feared. Twenty years later, in an interview with Major Hugo Faesi, Masson claimed that his requests had not had "anything political about them at all."[94] Moreover, he argued that he had preferred to be personally in charge of the "German dossier,"[95] stating, "If there had been any mishap, which is something an intelligence service has to expect at any time, my superior, the Commander-in-Chief, could have disapproved of my action [even though] I had kept him up to date on my plan."[96] Also, Masson considered that it was rather academic to accuse him of becoming involved in politics, arguing, "Did I really become involved in something that was none of my business? Is a man who happens to walk past a burning house and has the possibility of extinguishing the fire guilty of 'becoming involved in something that is none of his business' just because he is not part of the fire brigade?"[97] If the Department of Foreign Affairs was not capable of improving bilateral relations, and if Masson believed that he had the opportunity to accomplish that objective with his own means, was it not his *duty* to accept the risk of meeting Schellenberg in Waldshut?

Fuhrer speculates that *Masson* also had a *purely personal interest* in contacting a high-ranking SS personality. Ever since the Germans marched into Czechoslovakia in 1938–1939, Masson had supposedly been concerned that they might discover a document that he had written in 1937 for the Czech Chief of the General Staff, General Krejcí, regarding the German Army. In September 1936,[98] the Czech Chief of the General Staff had paid an official visit to Switzerland; in exchange, he invited Lieutenant General Labhart[99] and Switzerland's Chief of Intelligence at the time, Charles Dubois, to the large-scale maneuvers that the Czech Army was to hold in Bohemia in August-September 1937.[100] After returning from these maneuvers, Labhart ordered Masson to write a study for General Krejcí on the German Army and its new strategy. Masson hoped that Schellenberg would be of assistance to him if the Germans discovered that document.[101]

Fuhrer was not the first scholar to mention Masson's concern about the 1937 document as a possible motive for trying to enter into contact with Schellenberg; Bonjour had also referred to the 1937 study in connection with the meeting in Waldshut.[102] However, this author considers that viewing this issue as an affair as serious as the affair of *La Charité* is too far-fetched. What *was* incontestably a factor prompting Masson to enter into contact with Schellenberg was the discovery by the Germans of a number of files concerning the Swiss Army at La Charité-sur-Loire and Dijon, France.[103] Masson himself kept insisting that his efforts to confirm Switzerland as a credible neutral state to the Germans stemmed from their discovery of the files documenting the 1939–1940 secret cooperation talks between Switzerland and France.[104] The discovery of these files had also become a matter of deep concern to General Guisan, who as commander of the 1st Corps prior to the war had been the principal Swiss figure involved in coordinating plans with the French. However, from the material that has been available to this author, it is not possible to determine with absolute certainty whether it was "most likely"[105] General Guisan in person who encouraged Masson to contact Schellenberg. Concerning the meeting in Waldshut, Barbey's diary notes indicate that Masson responded to Schellenberg's initiative mainly on his own accord.[106]

The Course of the Meeting

On September 8, 1942, Masson encountered more difficulties leaving Switzerland than entering Germany. The Head of the Swiss border brigades had instructed the border guards to let Masson and Meyer-Schwertenbach, who were both traveling in civilian clothes[107] without carrying any identification,[108] cross the border into Germany without checking them.[109] However, the army's border troops had not been informed about the upcoming crossing, and sure enough a sergeant of the territorial service created some difficulties for the unidentified travelers.[110] The incident, which could have put an abrupt end to the endeavor, shows how amateurishly the event was planned; at the same time, it is an impressive example of the vigilance of the Swiss Army. This high degree of alertness had caused Göring's earlier *Wartegau* commando operation to fail,[111] and it could be achieved only because every single soldier was absolutely committed to doing his best in his post.

On the German side of the Rhine, another unpleasant surprise was awaiting Colonel-Brigadier Masson and Captain Meyer: their German counterparts were not there. The long period of uncertainty during the wait at the Reich border checkpoint gave Masson the opportunity to think at length about the risk he was taking by not carrying any identification papers. It turned out that, on his way from Berlin to the Swiss border, Schellenberg had been involved in a car accident.[112] After the war, Masson admitted that he had been in great danger; luckily for him, Schellenberg survived the accident. Masson commented, "Otherwise I would undoubtedly not have escaped the Gestapo, who would have arrested me at the customs office where I was stuck after crossing the Rhine without any ID, wearing civilian clothes."[113] It is not difficult to imagine that in that event the German border police officer would have stopped exercising restraint; in fact, he would have been sure to be rewarded for arresting a foreign chief of intelligence. Moreover, one would have had to expect Goebbel's ministry to exploit the incident for propaganda purposes, using it as evidence of Switzerland's non-neutral conduct.

It was Eggen who finally showed up at the German border checkpoint, having driven there ahead of Schellenberg. "In order to gain time,"[114] the three men went to meet Schellenberg at the restaurant at the Waldshut train station. (The account by the French journalists Accoce and Quet[115] contains several pieces of false information; N.S.1[116] had *not* given Masson photographs of Schellenberg to allow him to recognize his German counterpart; that was unnecessary because Meyer had already met him in Berlin. In addition, neither Waibel's procurement office nor anyone else in Lucerne was informed about the secret meeting.)[117]

The SS Chief of Intelligence, who was only 32 years old, was polite but cool when he received the Swiss Chief of Intelligence. Masson later remarked, "Psychologically he had an advantage over us because he was the party that did not have anything to ask for."[118] Schellenberg asked Masson right away why he had asked for the unusual meeting.[119] Masson later explained, "I truthfully replied that I wanted to speak with him as soldier to soldier, that I regretted that there were unbelievable tensions between our two countries but that these tensions were due in large part to the arrogant attitude of the German press."[120] Schellenberg countered with "the traditional small verse about [Switzerland's] lack of neutrality"[121] and by accusing Swiss Intelligence of being financed by the United States. Masson later explained, "On one hand we were stupefied by this revelation; on the other hand we were pleased to hear that we appeared to be richer than we actually were. We were decidedly off to a bad start."[122] Schellenberg supported his claim by showing Masson the copy of a telegram dated late April 1940, in which the U.S. military attaché in Bern[123] had reported to Washington, DC, "Special conference with Masson. He confirms that 25 German divisions are stationed at Switzerland's border. He considers that they are standing by for an attack."[124] In reality, Masson had not confirmed anything to the U.S. official. Even though he knew how many troops were stationed in southern Germany, for neutrality reasons he could not tell the American any details. Masson explained, "In order not to 'lose face' (since the Black Forest is close to Switzerland, I could not possibly be unaware of what was going on there), I used a commonplace, telling the excellent comrade, 'it must be crowded there.'"[125] How had the Germans gotten hold of the telegram that compromised Masson? Masson speculated, "Without any doubt [through] the famous wastepaper basket and the photographer of the 5th column."[126] According to Accoce, the U.S. military attaché had handed his telegram to a courier at the legation who was a German agent.[127]

After what Masson called "this sweet-and-sour preamble, during which Schellenberg did not fail to point out to me that *I was in the top portion of Germany's list of wanted persons*,"[128] the conversation took a turn for the better. Masson later stated: "[Schellenberg] told me that he had studied law, that he loved his country and had a lot of sympathy for Switzerland; he knew its institutions well and admired the balance that we had achieved between the different ethnic groups that live in our country. He also told me that Switzerland had friends in Germany on whom it could count."[129] Masson immediately took up that point, asking Schellenberg "whether he was willing to give [him] a token of his sympathy by setting [his] officer in Stuttgart free."[130] The SS officer promised to do that and made him understand "that he did not agree with the regime's exaggerations, that Hitler's entourage was bad, and that [Schellenberg] had several enemies in the Führer's entourage precisely because he had broader and more humanitarian ideas. He declared that he was ready to help [Masson] as long as he did not have to compromise his sense of duty as a German officer."[131] Masson showed full understanding for Schellenberg's concern; he for his part hoped "that an honest discussion between two officers who [were] equally attached to their respective countries could result in some kind of mutual trust that could be beneficial for the good relations that *neutral* Switzerland wished to entertain with all belligerent parties."[132]

Once the two parties had found a common ground, Masson was able to present his requests one by one. Schellenberg was understanding, kind, and approachable. In addition to having Mörgeli set free, he promised to put an end to the IPA's slander campaign, obtain a visa for Heinrich Rothmund, and see to it that the Swiss living in Germany finally received authorization to leave the country in order to meet their obligation to serve in the Swiss Army. Masson concluded, "Generally speaking, I considered that Schellenberg was likely to 'put the record straight' at the German Armed Forces High Command concerning Switzerland's determination to fight against anyone who infringed its territory."[133] Masson felt that his assessment was all the more justified as he did *not* view Schellenberg as a *fanatic National Socialist*, explaining: "Without his spelling things out, it was my understanding that Schellenberg wanted to find a solution to bring the war to an end; however, during that first meeting with a foreigner, he did not dare go too far with his criticism. From 1942 on, *Schellenberg 'felt' that the war would end badly for the Germans;* he suffered from that but did not yet know what to do about it."[134]

After taking a "walk in the woods," near the restaurant at the Waldshut train station the four men ate some canned food that Eggen had brought with him from Berlin. Schellenberg talked about the front in the East; Masson quickly realized that the SS officer's *knowledge about strategic matters was very limited.*[135] When Schellenberg asked Masson what he thought about the situation there, Masson was frank, telling him that he considered Germany unlikely to win, arguing that the 6th Army, commanded by General Paulus, was bound to capitulate.[136]

Toward 8 p.m., Masson and Meyer said goodbye to Schellenberg and Eggen after agreeing that they should meet again. Masson added, "We were both convinced that through this *channel* we could work toward alleviating the rather critical situation that existed between Germany and Switzerland at the time."[137] Nevertheless, from the very beginning Masson made clear to Schellenberg, "We agreed—I insist on this issue—that this was not about exchanging information because 'two soothsayers are bound to laugh when they

Personal-Bericht

des **Walter Schellenberg**　　　　　　　　(Dienststellung und Einheit)　　　　　　**SS-Oberscharführer,**
　　　(Vor- und Zuname)　　　　　　　　　　　　　　　　　　　　　　　　　　　　　(Dienstgrad)

Mitglied-Nr. der Partei: **3.504.508**　　　　　　　SS-Ausweis Nr. **124.817**

Seit wann in der Dienststellung:　　　　　　Beförderungsdatum zum letzten Dienstgrad: **13.9.36**

Geburtstag, Geburtsort (Kreis):　**16.1.1910 zu Saarbrücken**

Beruf: 1. erlernter: **Jurist**　　　　　　　　2. jetziger: **Angestellter**

Wohnort: **Berlin SW 68**　　　　　　Straße: **Wilhelmstr. 102**

Verheiratet? **nein** Mädchenname der Frau: **------**　　　Kinder? **---**　Konfession: **gottgl.**

Wirtschaftliche Verhältnisse:　**geordnet**

Vorstrafen:　**keine**

Verletzungen, Verfolgungen und Strafen im Kampfe für die Bewegung:

Beurteilung:

I. Rassisches Gesamtbild:　**Rein nordisch.**

II. 1. Charakter: **Offener, einwandfreier, lauterer Charakter; er ist SD-Mann.**

　　2. Wille: **Fest, zäh, besitzt Energie.**

　　3. Gesunder Menschenverstand: **Sehr scharf denkend.**

　　Wissen und Bildung: **Assessorexamen: gut; überdurchschnittliche Allgemein-bildung.**

　　Auffassungsvermögen: **Erfasst überraschend schnell das Kernproblem.**

　　Nationalsozialistische Weltanschauung: **Durchaus gefestigt.**

III. Auftreten und Benehmen in und außer Dienst: **Soldatisches Auftreten in und ausser Dienst.**
　　(Besondere Neigungen, Schwächen und Fehler)

The first page of Schellenberg's personnel file, which was established on March 27, 1937. He is described as someone who is "very sharp . . . extraordinarily knowledgeable, is surprisingly quick at grasping the key issue, very definitely believes in the National Socialist ideology, has a soldierly manner both in his official capacity and outside of it." (Berlin Document Center)

look in each other's eyes.' Moreover, it would be silly to bombard each other with newspaper clippings."[138]

The meeting left a deep impression on Masson. Three weeks later, he told Barbey that the fine, cultivated Schellenberg was *"a man with whom [he] immediately was on the same wavelength."*[139] In his diary, Meyer-Schwertenbach expressed both his relief that everything had gone well and Masson's satisfaction, stating:

> [We] drive to Liestal, from there [we take the] train to Bern; *Schweizerhof* hotel. Masson expresses his heartfelt thanks. He says that he is very satisfied, that he will never forget what I have done for him.[140] He openly talks about the risk—loss of pension, being suspended—and about the fact that Barbey had called him once again to ask him whether he . . . was still planning to go. [Masson replied that] he did not revoke any decisions.[141]

Through this meeting, the Masson-Schellenberg connection was established. In the following few years it was used intensively and fostered. During the war, Masson and Schellenberg met on three other occasions in Switzerland: in October 1942 at Captain Meyer's Wolfsberg Castle, in March 1943 in Bern, Zürich, and at Wolfsberg Castle, and in October 1943 again at Wolfsberg Castle. Between these meetings, the contact was maintained during Eggen's frequent travels; on most occasions, Meyer-Schwertenbach acted as a liaison person between Masson and Schellenberg's emissary.

Results

The main result of the meeting in Waldhut was that *Masson began trusting Schellenberg*. In his diary, Bernard Barbey, who went to see Masson in Interlaken three weeks after the meeting, recounted: "[Masson] is pleased, very pleased. He did not 'compromise' anything, nor 'give' anything; on the contrary, he considers that we have gained a lot from this meeting with Schellenberg, 'a man who is trusted by the Führer,' who has access to him whenever he wants."[142]

Barbey had an ambiguous impression when he left Masson. That same evening, he made an assessment of the meeting that strikes even today's readers as being clear, precise, and subtle. Barbey viewed as *positive* the possibility "to 'speak' with someone from the Führer's entourage,"[143] allowing Switzerland to emphasize, before key German authorities, its absolute determination to defend itself. He argued that Masson could also benefit from the contact with

Schellenberg, stating, "He can gain a—right or wrong—'impression' of Germany's arrangements against us; at least it will be an impression."[144] However, in Barbey's opinion, in addition to these positive, albeit questionable, results, the Masson-Schellenberg connection had some serious *negative* aspects. He explained: "Schellenberg did not [meet Masson] without wanting anything in return. His not making any formal request so far does not mean anything for the future."[145] Masson later argued that Schellenberg had agreed to "selflessly" assist him because he had made Schellenberg feel that he trusted him and held him in high esteem,[146] adding, "That is an invaluable asset that you cannot quantify in terms of 'services rendered in return for other services'."[147] Barbey analyzed the situation in a more sober, and probably more realistic, fashion, writing in his diary: "No matter what affection he may have for Masson and Switzerland, Schellenberg is above all German and first of all a man of the Party. His educated mind does not change anything about that."[148] Moreover, based on Masson's account, Barbey felt that by meeting Schellenberg Masson had been tempted to leave the realm of intelligence per se and become involved in negotiations, as he had feared from the beginning.[149] However, the Assistant Chief of Staff Id did not have any mandate, nor the necessary slyness, to conduct negotiations with an SS official.

It was too early to weigh the advantages and disadvantages of the channel to the Reich Security Central Office. Nevertheless, Barbey's concluding remarks indicate that he did not quite share Masson's enthusiasm. He wrote, "Above all Masson must avoid being incited to go to Germany. Maybe Waldshut was a stroke of genius; if not, it may have simply provided a useful contact. [Going to] the headquarters in the East or to Berlin would be dangerous."[150]

Paradoxically, the first tangible result achieved by the connection reinforced the reservations about it. On December 24, 1942, when Eggen finally[151] accompanied Ernst Mörgeli back to Switzerland,[152] the Swiss officer's liberation did not only spark feelings of relief. Alfred Ernst, the Head of the German Bureau who had repeatedly intervened with Masson to push for Mörgeli's release from prison, was thankful but added:

> Nevertheless, the whole matter makes me feel somewhat uneasy because I fear that the personalities with whom you have been in contact did not do us this favor without sooner or later achieving a certain objective. . . . Hence, even though I am thankful, please do not be mad at me for urgently *warning* you now more than ever *not to trust your German partners*, or else we may one day have to pay a high price[153] for the favor they did us in the case of Dr. Mörgeli.[154]

Could Masson actually have paid a high price without realizing it? Was the "evidence" that the Germans tried to find, through Mörgeli's arrest, of the alleged cooperation between Swiss Intelligence and the British Secret Intelligence Service merely a pretext for achieving a different objective? Considering the consequences that the Mörgeli case ended up having for the Masson-Schellenberg connection,[155] it is not impossible that Masson's aide at the Swiss Consulate in Stuttgart was a pawn on Schellenberg's chessboard, so to speak. It is not outlandish to think that the incident had been carefully staged for the purpose of the connection. Eggen had met Mörgeli *before* Mörgeli was arrested. Masson's aide in Stuttgart recalled, "I had briefly met Eggen; I think it was a chance encounter during a meeting with members of our intelligence service."[156] This author agrees with Mörgeli, who believed that, based on this short encounter with Eggen, he could have been singled out for the unpleasant part that he had to play. The difficulties that Eggen and Schellenberg said they had in freeing Mörgeli from the clutches of the Gestapo could have been put forward merely in order to strengthen Masson's confidence in the *secret channel to Berlin* and make him grateful to his German partners once they had succeeded at having the prisoner released. This interpretation of Schellenberg's possible motive is speculative; nevertheless, it helps to demonstrate that Masson's connection to the Reich Security Central Office was a delicate matter and that ultimately it is highly difficult to assess.

9

General Guisan's Involvement
in the Connection

In fall 1945, at the general assembly of the Officers' Society of Canton Vaud, General Guisan defended his former Chief of Intelligence against the severe attacks from the press, to which he had been subject because of his secret channel to Berlin. The General stated:

> I knew about the connection with Schellenberg. Colonel-Brigadier Masson informed me about this connection[1] as well as connections that were maintained with the Allies. However, the Commander-in-Chief should not deal with the connections of his Intelligence Service; the chief of that service is solely responsible for them. The Commander-in-Chief must not know about these connections, nor must he know the people who maintain them. Nevertheless, Masson considered that in view of its significance, it was advisable to inform me about the connection with Schellenberg.[2]

The General added that he had replied to the Chief of Intelligence, "Masson, you know what I think about your service. You work on your own account, and so far I have been perfectly pleased with the work of the

Intelligence Service."[3] However, the Commander-in-Chief was being less than revealing to his audience in Canton Vaud. At that time General Guisan *hid* the fact that on two occasions he, too, had met Schellenberg *in person*.

Guisan's Meetings with Schellenberg in Biglen and Arosa

In retrospect, it is surprising how quickly the Masson-Schellenberg connection was further extended. How is it explicable that six months after the meeting in Waldshut even the Commander-in-Chief of the Swiss Army could be persuaded to become involved in it? In the official communiqué on the Masson case, the answer was short; the single sentence read, "In early 1943, Masson considered that it was appropriate to establish a personal contact also between Schellenberg and General Guisan, especially because since 1940 the German Armed Forces High Command had apparently been pointing out again and again that it had found material in France that incriminated Switzerland and was justified in casting a doubt on our absolute determination to remain neutral."[4]

The upcoming sections will show whether this explanation stands up to closer scrutiny. After the meeting in Biglen, Barbey, who had not been consulted by Masson nor by General Guisan ahead of time, asked himself, "Was it Masson who had suggested a meeting between Guisan and Schellenberg, or was it the Germans?"[5] Georg Kreis argues, "The fact that in March 1943 a meeting took place between Schellenberg and Guisan cannot be explained by the fact that the Swiss or the Germans wanted to address the issue of 'La Charité'."[6] In 1970 Bonjour commented that it was indeed not easy "to separate the wheat, i.e., the historical truth, from the chaff, i.e., the sensational news and subjective interpretations."[7]

Reasons for the Meetings

The existing reference material clearly indicates that Barbey was right to raise the question on whose initiative the meeting in Biglen had been organized. As was the case with the meeting in Waldshut, the *Germans* were first to suggest an encounter with Switzerland's Commander-in-Chief. Meyer-Schwertenbach noted in his diary, "[On December 25, 1942,] Eggen informs me that in February [1943] Schellenberg is planning to spend eight days in a chalet; during that time, *together with Masson and the Commander-in-Chief, he wants to secure the general situation in favor of Switzerland*."[8]

The military and political situation to which Eggen referred in his statement had drastically changed since Masson's trip to Laufenburg and Waldshut.[9]

Four months prior to the meeting in Biglen, in the early morning hours of November 8, 1942, 84,000 American and 23,000 English troops had landed in North Africa under Eisenhower's supreme command, launching Operation Torch at Casablanca, Oran, and Algiers. The Allied invasion came as a complete surprise to the German leadership.[10] In reaction to that move, on November 11, 1942 Hitler occupied the zone in southern France that had previously been "free."[11] Operation Torch was a great organizational, technical, and tactical achievement accomplished by "transporting by sea and over great distances a large military force with an enormous amount of equipment without being noticed by the enemy, and [landing] simultaneously at several locations that were far apart from each other";[12] in addition, as early as the day of the invasion, Barbey remarked, "What is striking is that the landing in Africa will *change the course of events.*"[13] Less than a week later, in his "Chronicle of World Events" on Swiss national public radio, historian J.R. von Salis rightly speculated that the Allies had launched the invasion to make Africa a deployment area for additional operations.[14] At the end of November 1942, Churchill declared on the radio, "Africa is no halting-place: it is not a seat but a springboard. We shall use Africa only to come to closer grips. . . . Our operations in French North Africa should enable us to bring the weight of the war home to the Italian Fascist State, in a manner not hitherto dreamed of by its guilty leaders."[15] Once the Axis powers lost control of Africa, the Mediterranean was sure to follow, thereby opening the southern flank for the Allied attack on the *European fortress.* On the Eastern front, the situation also changed to Hitler's disadvantage; the Germans were only weeks away from capitulating at Stalingrad.

In view of that situation, Switzerland's *Reduit*, the hedgehog position in the Alps into which the bulk of the Swiss Army had withdrawn following Germany's invasion of France, became extremely important on the strategic level for the OKW's plans. In the event that Germany considered the creation of a consolidated "European fortress," Switzerland was going to play a key strategic role.[16] Hence, a coup on Switzerland's mountain passes and railroads across the Alps was worth considering for Hitler. Masson later stated that these routes "would obviously have been the only possible links between the partners of the Axis in case the other routes had been cut."[17] In view of the expected Allied invasion of Sicily, and because the Brenner mountain pass in Austria was subject to constant British bombing raids, Switzerland's Gotthard and Simplon railroads[18] gained importance as supply lines for the German troops in northern Italy.

In an assessment of the situation that he submitted to the Federal Council on January 6, 1943, General Guisan raised the issue of Switzerland's key strategic position by asking, "Is this new idea [of turning Europe into a fortress that is defended on every front] compatible with *respecting Switzerland's neutrality?*"[19] Guisan argued that Switzerland, which was not under the control of the Axis powers, risked being occupied in a sudden preventive move, especially if the Germans feared that the Allies could use the country for staging military operations.[20]

To a certain extent Guisan's argument was confirmed by Eggen. During a meeting[21] at the office of Albert Wiesendanger,[22] the inspector of the Zürich city police, the SS officer from Berlin reported that "Schellenberg had been at the Führer's headquarters to ask permission to travel to Switzerland, as indicated earlier on. Hitler reportedly said that his trip was unnecessary, that the Swiss had lied to him and cheated him for three years, and that he was not going to make any commitments to those people who continually took without giving anything in return. *He said that he knew what he would have to do with Switzerland if Italy was drawn into the events.*"[23] Hence, based on the strategic situation of winter 1942–1943, the explanation that Eggen gave why Schellenberg wanted to meet Guisan seems credible. He claimed that for Schellenberg it was a matter of prestige to receive confirmation from Switzerland's top military authority what he had been saying all along in Berlin, i.e., that Switzerland would remain neutral, defending itself also against the Allies.[24]

What motives did Masson and General Guisan for their part have to meet the head of foreign intelligence of the Reich Security Central Office? They were both aware that the fact that the war was about to reach its final turning-point did not mean that Germany no longer posed any threat to Switzerland. The Commander-in-Chief later explained that relentless attacks by the controlled German press testified to Germany's "very clear determination to create a state of mind that would have been favorable for invading Switzerland."[25] Hence, Guisan and Masson were mainly concerned about convincing Hitler that Switzerland was *credible* as a neutral state, a fact that Swiss intelligence had never tired of pointing out. At the end of January 1943, Alfred Ernst, the head of the Axis Section, sent Masson a special report by *Rigi*,[26] stating, "The number of [German] troops that are stationed in the border area would hardly be sufficient to dare launching an attack. However, the number of troops stationed there is irrelevant. . . . It is not enough for us to be prepared; *the Germans also have to believe that we are prepared.* In this context, it would be very valuable to reiterate the order of April 18, 1940."[27] Ernst argued: "[I know] from well-informed sources that influential German circles do not really take seriously [Switzerland's] determination to fight. Let us see to it, through military measures and an appropriate statement by the Commander-in-Chief and the government, that this opinion changes."[28]

Based on this concern about making it known that Switzerland was serious about honoring its commitments as a neutral state, it is obvious that the affair of *La Charité* played a part in General Guisan's decision to meet Schellenberg in Biglen and Arosa. Masson remarked: "The documents of *La Charité* . . . are evidence of a *unilateral* act on our part, which is therefore against our principle of neutrality." He emphasized that this was "the main issue around which [his] whole argument in the Schellenberg affair [was] centered."[29] In a draft letter to Federal President Chaudet, Masson later explained that in Germany's opinion the 1940 discovery of the files at *La Charité* had *compromised* Switzerland's *neutrality*, which prompted him to take action. He stated:

> I therefore took it upon myself to try to *re-create an atmosphere of confidence between the Germans and us*. Of course I was not naïve to believe that my modest efforts could prevent the OKW from occupying Switzerland if (in 1943!) it had a vital strategic interest in doing so. Nevertheless, it was interesting to instill into the Germans the *certainty* that we would defend our country under any circumstances against *anyone* attacking it. This objective could be reached only through personal relations. *This is why I was in contact with Schellenberg.*[30]

In a letter to Meyer-Schwertenbach, Masson expressed that idea in even terser terms, writing, "It was [the meeting in] Biglen that allowed Guisan, with his declaration, to blot out the uneasiness following *La Charité*."[31]

Even though the discovery of the files at *La Charité* was not expressly mentioned during the talks between General Guisan and Schellenberg, this author considers that it would be wrong to conclude that the affair did not play any role in bringing about the meetings. Masson's own statements, which he made after the fact,[32] are not the only evidence to support that argument; on January 27, 1943, Captain Meyer informed the Commander-in-Chief in private about Schellenberg's travel plans. He wrote in his diary:

> I explain to [General Guisan] that Schellenberg is willing, with the approval of his superiors Himmler and Hitler, to come to Switzerland for discussions with him. I tell him that I believe that if [the Germans] hear from the General in person that Switzerland is firmly and unshakably determined to defend its borders *against anyone*, we will be able to do so on our own in the event that Italy becomes involved in conflicts. He is willing to make such a declaration to General Schellenberg if that

is to any avail. I can continue the *unofficial negotiations* along that line.[33]

General Guisan used the same argument to justify his entering into contact with Schellenberg, stating, "I considered that I should not miss any opportunity to further persuade our neighbors to the north, who were apparently not very convinced of our determination, that our army intended to accomplish its task under any circumstances, fighting against anyone infringing our neutrality."[34]

The Course of the Meetings

Once General Guisan had told Meyer, on January 27, 1943, that in principle he was willing to meet Schellenberg,[35] in February 1943 Masson, Eggen, Meyer, and Wiesendanger met several times to plan the details of the encounter.[36] The border checkpoint at the main customs office in Kreuzlingen was instructed to let Schellenberg's car cross the border without verifying the passengers' identity.[37] The German visitors arrived in Switzerland in the early afternoon of March 2, 1943. Captain Meyer and Police Inspector Wiesendanger were waiting for them at the border and accompanied them to Wolfsberg Castle, where Sergeant Detective Bleiker mounted Swiss license plates on the Germans' car.[38]

Meyer-Schwertenbach used the opportunity to speak extensively with Schellenberg. In his notes, he wrote, "Schelli[39] and I establish the agenda; [first] the Commander-in-Chief should make a declaration about Switzerland's absolute determination to defend itself and its intention to remain perfectly neutral, then there should be a declaration from the other side that [Germany] would respect [Switzerland's] sovereignty; *later the army should be partly demobilized in order to make people available for agriculture and the industry,*[40] which is also to Germany's advantage."[41,42]

Captain Meyer did not realize that there was an inherent contradiction between the army's "absolute determination to defend itself" and the demobilization of troops. Apart from the fact that a Swiss intelligence officer had no business negotiating the strength of the Swiss Army with an SS officer, Meyer also dangerously misjudged reality by making the Swiss Army's state of readiness fit in with a German declaration of intent; after all, the past few years had shown only too well what such declarations were worth. However, Meyer did not look at the matter from that angle, being imbued with the idea that as *a military person with a clean political record* [43] he had the chance of creating a solid basis for a trusting relationship between the two countries.[44] He consid-

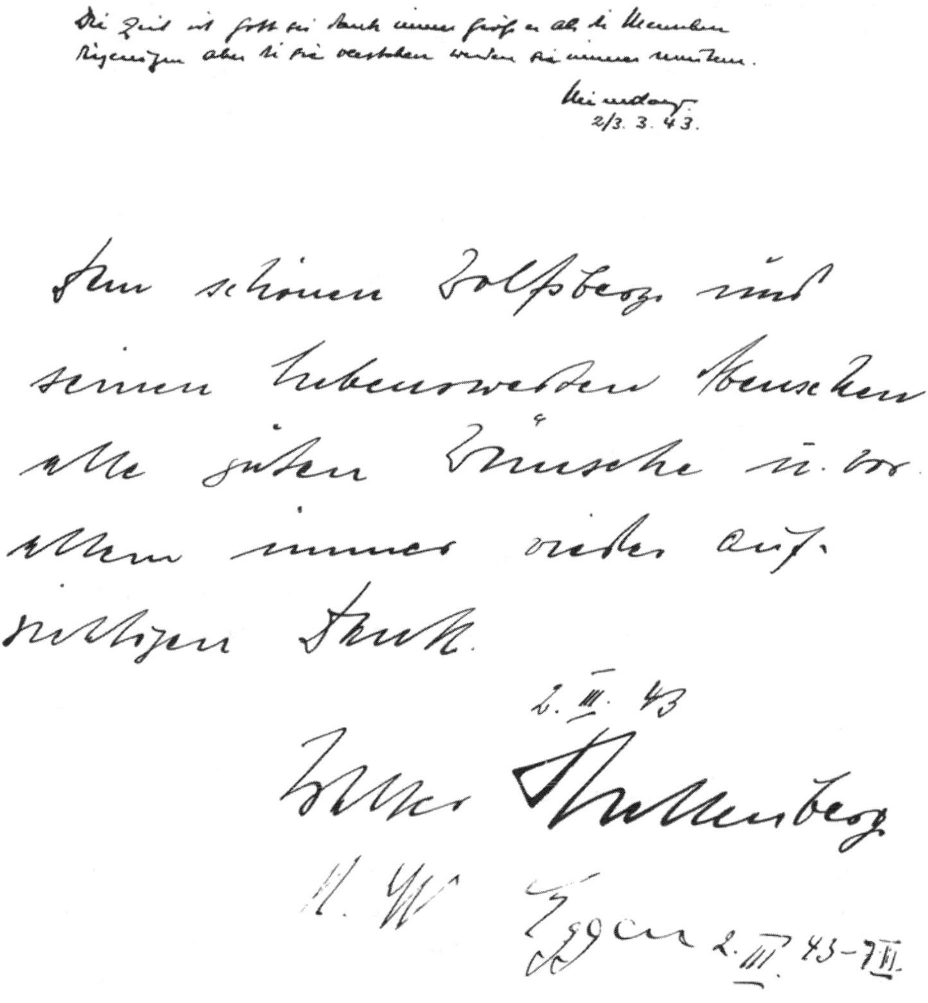

[handwritten note, partially legible, dated 2/3. 3. 43.]

[handwritten dedication in German, signed]

2. III. 43

Walter Schellenberg

Eggen 2. III. 43 – 7 III.

Schellenberg's first stop on his way to the meeting with General Guisan was Wolfsberg Castle. Together with Zürich's Police Inspector Wiesendanger, who escorted the SS colonel to the meeting, and SS Major Eggen he signed Captain Meyer-Schwertenbach's guest book. (Document from the author's private archives)

ered that Schellenberg and Eggen were suitable partners for accomplishing that objective. Whenever someone voiced reservations about his conviction, he failed to understand that the concerns were based on prudent, cautious thinking; he shrugged his critics off, trying hard[45] to dispel their mistrust. A letter by Heinrich Rothmund, the head of the Federal Police Section, to Federal Councillor von Steiger, provides conclusive evidence for that fact. Over a year after the meeting in Biglen, Rothmund explained to his superior:

> Captain Meyer [came to see me and] *kept insisting*[46] . . . that Mr. Eggen had a particularly good attitude toward Switzerland and had been trying, through his very good relations, to eradicate prejudices against our country all the way to the top authorities. In order to make the matter easily digestible for me, Captain Meyer insistently declared that one knew that *all Swiss officials were following the same mandatory course* without showing any consideration for the *new situation*, and that *none of them had the courage to break free and lead the way on the new path to which the Intelligence Service had opened the door*.[47]

Hence, Barbey's fears that Army Intelligence might become involved in political talks[48] had come true; what was not least dangerous about the situation was the fact that Meyer was apparently unaware of the consequences that such discussions carried.

The following day, on March 3, 1943, Masson picked up the delegation in Zürich. Through the army's Security Service, Meyer-Schwertenbach had reserved a suite at the Bellevue Palace Hotel in Bern for the second night of the Germans' visit to Switzerland.[49] They did not have to show any identification to check in. In the evening they were scheduled to meet General Guisan. "In order to keep the meeting private and short,"[50] Masson had suggested that the Commander-in-Chief meet with the German SS officer for a cocktail in the small reception room at the *Schweizerhof* hotel in Bern, where Masson often met with foreign military attachés.[51] However, General Guisan wanted to become more closely acquainted with Schellenberg and asked Masson to organize a dinner at a country inn somewhere near Bern. Hence, the *Bären* inn in *Biglen* was chosen as the venue for the meeting of March 3, 1943.[52]

Masson and the Commander-in-Chief drove separately to the meeting, while Meyer-Schwertenbach, Wiesendanger, and several police officers from Zürich accompanied Schellenberg and Eggen, driving to Biglen in two cars.[53]

At the *Bären*, six people sat down at a table that was decorated in the colors of the Swiss flag.[54] Masson recounted about the evening:

> The dinner, to which we had also invited Eggen, Meyer, and the head of the Zürich police, who had become Schellenberg's guardian angel and was definitely constantly concerned about his safety in our peaceful country, was imbued with an atmosphere of *frank cordiality*. Schellenberg . . . who was sitting to Guisan's right . . . listened to [General Guisan] reminiscing about his time as a farmer in the canton of Vaud, interspersed with spicy anecdotes from his native area. Then our Commander-in-Chief buttonholed him with the culture of wine-growing. . . . And all that with perfectly simple good-heartedness! Schellenberg came to life again. In this pleasant, relaxed atmosphere far away from the bombardments of which his country was the target he seemed happy, and for the first time we noticed that he laughed like a child. One would have thought that he had completely forgotten why he was there. Without a doubt General Guisan had won him over merely through the radiance of his presence.[55]

After dinner, General Guisan, Masson, and Schellenberg retired to a small table in the corner of the room that was separated from the rest of the inn by a sliding-door, where "one could tackle the serious matters."[56] Schellenberg explained to the Commander-in-Chief and Masson "that in the framework of [their] *trusting relations* he continuously tried to *ward off any danger of Hitler aggressing Switzerland.*"[57] Schellenberg made the Swiss officers understand that he was not sure whether in view of the Swiss Army's good defensive potential and determination to defend itself, as well as in view of the fact that Switzerland would destroy the Gotthard and Simplon railroads, the OKW would be able to allocate the material means that were required to carry out its bold plan of occupying the country. It was even less likely because one was prepared for the creation of a second, and probably even a third, front in France and because *Germany's reserves* were *limited.*[58] He said that several generals at the Führer's headquarters had been warning against attacking Switzerland, but due to the Führer's erratic, unpredictable character one constantly had to fear the worst. Schellenberg subsequently addressed the key issue that weighed upon the relations between the two countries: Germany's doubts about Switzerland's neutrality. The SS spymaster explained to General Guisan that if it was possible to officially convince Hitler that Switzerland would defend itself against any aggressor, including the Allies—that is, that Switzerland would put up resistance against the Allies if they tried to turn the Siegfried Line from the south by advancing through Switzerland—the Führer might be made to give up what Masson called his "absurd plan." However, Schellenberg qualified his statement by adding that his own reputation in Berlin had declined and that his contacts in Switzerland were viewed with mistrust; Masson explained, "Schellenberg pointed out to us that in Berlin . . . his declarations about our unyielding willingness [to defend ourselves] were considered as a distorted image of his mind."[59] He claimed that at a recent banquet Hitler had called him *the German general who had been indoctrinated by the Swiss.*

After preparing the ground with those explanations, Schellenberg came out with his request, asking General Guisan, in his capacity as commander-in-chief of the Swiss Army, to issue and personally sign a declaration[60] stating that Switzerland would defend itself against any attack, no matter where it originated. He argued that the declaration would allow him to prove to Berlin that his reports were not merely the result of his imagination.

Schellenberg's request did not come as a surprise to the Commander-in-Chief, even though he had not expected him to ask for a *written* statement. His reaction was decisive and Masson commented, "At that moment, Guisan's authority was astonishing. He was no longer the friendly guest at the dinner table telling [Schellenberg] stories from Vaud, but the chief who spoke very firmly without losing his composure. Without reacting, Schellenberg heard a few truths that were said with the tact that is owed to a guest but that General Guisan undoubtedly hoped [Schellenberg] would not keep to himself."[61] Not without putting some cards on the table that Schellenberg did not previously know, the Commander-in-Chief made it clear to the German visitor, for the attention of his superiors, that *a campaign in Switzerland would not be an easy stroll for the German military.*[62] Masson also deliberately added some details concerning the Swiss Army's defensive capabilities and determination to fight. Schellenberg seemed to be particularly impressed by the number of sites that had been prepared for demolition.[63] Masson gained the undeniable impression that Guisan's assurance had convinced the SS officer that the Swiss Army would defend itself also against the Allies. He commented, "Schellenberg ended up being more convinced about it than I was!"[64]

An incident that occurred following the conversation had far-reaching consequences even though it began as a very harmless event. The manager of the *Bären* brought the guest book to the illustrious visitors' table, presenting it to General Guisan for signature. The book showed that numerous ambassadors, ministers, diplomats, and other prominent figures had been at the inn in Biglen, a fact that Masson had not known. The participants at the secret meeting all signed the guest book. As a criminologist, Captain Meyer, who signed last, suddenly realized that the guest book had become a compromising document. Hence, later, when the guests said goodbye to each other, he cut out the page with his pocket knife and hid it in his jacket.[65] A short time later, when the manager of the inn wanted to check with whom the Commander-in-Chief had been dining, he noticed that the page was missing.[66] As he was outraged about that impertinence, he immediately called a military police officer who happened to be staying at the *Bären*. The military police officer informed his superior because he feared that the Germans might misuse the General's signature for their own purposes. The superior in turn informed his superior. As a result, soon thereafter the entire government and diplomatic corps knew that General Guisan had held a secret meeting with a German officer. When the manager of the inn sent the damaged guest book to Interlaken, asking the General to sign it again, army headquarters also found out about the encounter.

The following afternoon, Schellenberg and Eggen traveled to Arosa, discreetly escorted by the police. In that mountain resort, the Germans once again met with General Guisan, who had traveled there to make an appearance at the Swiss Skiing Championships. Schellenberg organized a cocktail party in his honor. In the course of a conversation in a relaxed atmosphere, Guisan produced a letter with the handwritten declaration for which Schellenberg had asked him in Biglen. The declaration read:

The balance [of power] in Europe requires Switzerland to be neutral toward all sides and in every respect. The great statesman and Reich Chancellor Bismarck also recognized and declared that its location and its historical mission called it to be the custodian of the mountain passes across the Alps. Switzerland has always fulfilled this task with all its energy and means. Switzerland considers that accomplishing this task, which every Swiss acknowledges, is not only an honor but a matter of course. We are aware that our country's sovereignty depends on whether this conviction is abandoned or slackens. Therefore all Swiss and the entire army are perfectly willing to sacrifice everything in order to defend their independence and honor. Whoever invades our country is our enemy. He will face a highly powerful, united army and a people imbued with *one and the same* determination. At that moment Switzerland will be steadfast and fight with *one* determination. The topography of our country enables us above all to defend our Alpine front. This statement will remain unshakeable and unchangeable, no matter what happens. There is no room for any doubt about that, neither today nor tomorrow.[67]

The text of the declaration was almost identical[68] to an excerpt from an interview that the Commander-in-Chief had granted Ms. Ljungström of the conservative *Svenska Dagbladet* one month earlier[69] during a ski competition between Switzerland and Sweden.[70]

If the second meeting between Schellenberg and General Guisan was meant to be kept secret, the venue and the event had once again not been very carefully chosen.[71] During that time, a corps commander, division commander, and a brigade commander of the Swiss Army were staying at the same hotel, the Excelsior.

Masson did not travel to Arosa but joined the rest of the party in the evening in Zürich after their return from the meeting with Guisan. From Zürich they traveled to Wolfsberg Castle, where they spent the weekend. The Swiss and German chiefs of intelligence met in private for two hours, whereupon Schellenberg told the party about his encounters with Hitler.[72] Once the two Germans had retired to their rooms, Masson informed the host and the police inspector about his conversation with Schellenberg. Captain Meyer noted in his diary: "[Masson says that] the Germans do not know nearly as much about Russia as we do; in fact, they hardly know anything. Only 35% of the Siberian Army has been used this winter, not 80% [as German intelligence erroneously believes]. He says that sooner or later Germany will be lost, [but] they do not want to admit it to themselves, even though Schelli is very intelligent and deep inside is no optimist."[73]

On Sunday, March 7, 1943, Masson, Wiesendanger, and Meyer accompanied the Germans to the border, where Masson saw to it that they could leave the country once again without being checked. The Swiss were apparently pleased that everything had gone well. Meyer noted in his diary, "Masson thanks me for everything I have done on behalf of our country and asks me to take a few days off."[74]

Through Barbey's testimony,[75] it is known that General Guisan considered his personal contact with Schellenberg a success. The Chief of SS Intelligence apparently also had a *positive* impression following the talks in Biglen and Arosa; in any case, when he was back in Berlin he reported to Ribbentrop that Switzerland was determined to defend its neutrality against *anyone* by taking up its arms if necessary. In an interesting "Note to the attention of the Führer," on June 22, 1943 the Reich Foreign Minister suggested to Hitler how Germany should reply to General Guisan's declaration, writing:

So far no new contact has taken place between *Standartenführer*[76] Schellenberg and the Commander-in-Chief of the Swiss Army,

Guisan, in the matter of the meeting that Schellenberg held in early March of this year with Guisan, in the course of which the Swiss General assured us that Switzerland would defend the mountain passes in the Alps at its southern border against any enemy and under any circumstances. According to my suggestion that the Führer had approved the previous month, in April [1943] I authorized Mr. Schellenberg to make the following verbal statement to General Guisan: "Berlin has taken note of the General's information. It welcomes Switzerland's decision to defend its neutrality at all cost. However, Berlin considers that Switzerland's intention to defend its mountain passes in the Alps against an attack from the south is not a reality because the Axis powers are determined to chase the English and Americans out of the Mediterranean area as soon as possible." Colonel Schellenberg has just informed me that he is about to enter in contact with Guisan again but that, considering the way things stand now, the sentence at the end of the declaration is perhaps not exactly accurate anymore.[77] I therefore suggest that Schellenberg meet with General Guisan again and make the following modified statement: "Berlin has taken note of the General's information. It welcomes Switzerland's decision to defend its neutrality at all cost. However, Berlin considers that Switzerland's intention to defend its mountain passes across the Alps against an attack from the south is not a reality because the Axis powers are determined to prevent the English and Americans from landing on the European mainland." Moreover, I suggest that Schellenberg establish even closer contact with Guisan than originally planned in order to try to find out more about the intentions of Switzerland's military.[78]

The Chief of General Guisan's Personal Staff did not share Guisan's, Schellenberg's, and Masson's opinion that the meeting in Biglen had been a success. Barbey was surprised that the Commander-in-Chief talked about the meetings with the SS officer in a matter-of-course fashion, concluding the entry in his diary by remarking:

To be honest, I would be totally relieved if I was certain that this path will not be further pursued and that nothing about this encounter will leak out that could be distorted or exploited inside the country and abroad. I have to admit, though, that if I had been with him at the moment when he made his decision and if he had honored me with the question what I thought about it, I would have advised him *not* to receive Schellenberg. That would have been my gut reaction and also my reaction after giving the matter some serious thought.[79]

From today's perspective, knowing who the involved individuals were, this author tends to share Barbey's reservations. Thirty years after the fact, Alfred Ernst wrote the most extensive piece of criticism on that matter, stating:

> In my opinion, Masson definitely should not have arranged for the General to meet with Schellenberg. There was no compelling reason for the Commander-in-Chief of the [Swiss] Army to meet with a figure as dubious as Schellenberg in order to confirm that we were determined to remain absolutely neutral. *Our official declarations were clear enough.* Ultimately the General's assertions in Biglen *weakened our point of view.* Someone who has emphatically expressed his intention in public will only arouse doubts by repeating that intention in secret talks with a dubious intermediary. *The Commander-in-Chief was not supposed to have anything to do with a key member of the SS security service.*[80]

The Federal Council Intervenes

The General Is Reprimanded

On March 11, 1943, Major Hans Bracher, who was secretary of the National Defense Committee before the war and liaison officer between the Head of the Military Department and the Commander-in-Chief during wartime duty, told Federal Councillor Kobelt about the unusual meeting in Biglen.[81] On that occasion, the Head of the Military Department heard about Masson's friendly relations with SS officer Schellenberg for the first time. Guisan for his part informed Federal Councillor Kobelt during a meeting at army headquarters the following day, distinctly trying to downplay the matter. Kobelt noted in his diary: "[General Guisan said] that he had recently been in Biglen, where he met a German personality who gave him interesting information on the situation in Germany and Italy. He said that the situation was considered to be very serious, particularly in Italy. He was told that Germany did not understand why Switzerland had such an unfriendly attitude toward Germany."[82] The General explained to Kobelt "that he was very glad to be able to explain to the German personality that Switzerland would always remain neutral and defend itself against any aggressor. He said that it was very important for the German personality to spread that message abroad."[83] When the

Federal Councillor inquired about the foreign personality, asking the General whether the meeting had been planned, Guisan claimed that "he did not know the German's name"[84] and had been told about him "by a trustworthy Swiss personality who was close to him"[85] but whose name he was not allowed to reveal to Kobelt. When Kobelt wanted to know more about the German personality, Guisan added that he was a private individual who was ranked general but that he was not a general in the military. When Kobelt suspected that he consequently had to be a party general, Guisan replied that "he did not think so,"[86] and then he once again emphasized how useful the meeting had been.

Without revealing that Major Bracher had already supplied him with detailed information, for the time being Kobelt contented himself with stating that "the Commander-in-Chief of the Armed Forces should take care not to enter into relations with foreigners [in order to] procure intelligence on his own, arguing that he had his organizations to do that."[87] In addition to pointing out how dangerous such meetings were, Kobelt asked Guisan to bear in mind "that if the German in question was a private individual, such a discussion would not have the expected effect; if he was an official, it was none of the General's business to get mixed up with him."[88]

The incident kept bothering Kobelt; when he found out that *Masson* had arranged the meeting,[89] he contacted him and informed General Guisan about it.[90] The Commander-in-Chief subsequently wrote to Masson, "It is *stupid* how much importance is attached to this affair. I would like to ask you to make Kob[elt] understand that this is a *private*[91] matter *that concerns only you and me.*"[92] However, Federal Councillor Kobelt disagreed with him. At the end of March 1943, he informed the General that he was forced to bring the matter up at a Federal Council meeting, adding, "I will gladly acknowledge that both Colonel-Brigadier Masson's actions and your willingness to meet [the German general] in Biglen and Arosa were based on an effort to serve the country."[93]

Guisan had no interest in having the matter discussed by the federal government. In a skillful tactical move, the night before the next scheduled Cabinet meeting he called up Federal President Enrico Celio to ask him whether he could stop by "to have a little chat" with him, as Celio later put it.[94] "I was a bit surprised,"[95] the Federal Councillor from the canton of Ticino recalled, because he was not used to the Commander-in-Chief making such a request. He continued, "The General came to see me and talked about this and that, of things that were of interest to Switzerland; it was very interesting to me."[96] At a certain point in time during the conversation, "in passing, the way it is done with matters of *little importance*, he said to me, 'this morning I had a meeting with, a visit by, a German general, a certain Mr. Schellenberg. We talked about some quite interesting things, some of which concerned Germany, and some of which concerned Switzerland.' I did not consider this matter as important, and the conversation followed its course."[97] About half an hour later, the General said goodbye to the Federal President and his wife, who had taken part in the conversation.

The following morning, on April 5, 1943, the Federal Council held its meeting. Before the agenda could be addressed, Foreign Minister Pilet-Golaz asked to speak. He was upset, telling his colleagues on the Cabinet that General Guisan had supposedly received Schellenberg in Switzerland without consulting the federal government in advance and without informing it about the meeting. He argued that if that was true, it was *unpermittable*. Celio immediately replied, "It is true, but General Guisan told me about it."[98] The Federal President failed to say that Guisan had told him about it only *after* the meeting with the SS officer.[99] Pilet-Golaz, who was highly respected among the Cabinet, was annoyed, remaining silent during the subsequent thorough discussion of the matter by his fellow Cabinet members.

Following an extended discussion, the federal government decided to inform the Commander-in-Chief in writing about its opinion on the matter.[100] The Federal Council had no doubt that Guisan's intentions had been good but did not hide the fact that such meetings were *inadmissible*. Kobelt explained:

> The Federal Council does not understand that the Commander-in-Chief of the Armed Forces enters into relations with high-ranking officials of a belligerent state and makes declarations *without first informing the Federal Council* about that intention nor giving it the opportunity to voice its opinion on the matter. The Federal Council also has serious concerns about the extraordinary circumstances of the talks in Biglen and Arosa as well as the unusual police escort, even more so because the meeting did not go unnoticed by the public.[101]

He argued that the fact alone that Guisan had met with high-ranking German officials could cause the Allies to become mistrustful if they found out about it.[102] The Axis powers on the other hand could be led to believe that the Commander-in-Chief of the Armed Forces held similar talks with Allied officials and might erroneously conclude "that it [was] the General, not the Federal Council, that [decided] about Switzerland's stance in any war situation."[103] Concerning the written declaration that General Guisan had handed to Schellenberg in Arosa, the federal government acknowledged that it was in line with the view that the Federal Council had repeatedly voiced in public; nevertheless, it pointed out that the Federal Council alone was authorized to make *declarations* to official foreign personalities *regarding the country's policies*,[104] and that based on the instructions to the army command the Federal Council alone decided about deploying the armed forces.

In his reply, General Guisan reiterated why he had met with Schellenberg, adding that in his opinion the importance of the meeting had been blown out of proportion. He stated:

> [The meeting] had only one goal, that of *reestablishing confidence*, and I dare to hope that this goal has been accomplished. The [statements that I made] can hardly be viewed as a "declaration regarding the country's policies" because they merely served to confirm what the Federal Council and the Commander-in-Chief have been saying over and over again: our determination to defend ourselves against anyone who infringes our neutrality, no matter where he comes from. This cannot be said often enough these days, and I acted according to the meaning of the mission with which I have been entrusted.[105]

Guisan wrote that he hoped that the matter was now closed.[106] However, that was far from being the case; two months later, National Councillor Bringolf brought up the issue on the National Council Foreign Affairs Committee,[107] and another four months later the *Biglen* affair resurfaced once again, this time presented in a new light. The strange circumstances surrounding the new version of the story have not been entirely cleared up.

At the end of October 1943, Hans Hausamann, the head of *Bureau Ha*, attended a reception in Zürich during which Allen W. Dulles took him aside to tell him in a slightly embarrassed tone:

> "You certainly know that some gentlemen from [your Intelligence Service] are in close contact with some German gentlemen . . ." (he held back the rest of the sentence, making an unambiguous gesture). "We have been informed by a first-rate source in Germany (Berlin) that around last March a dinner was held at a country inn outside Bern that was attended by General Guisan, Colonel-Brigadier Masson, one or two other Swiss gentlemen . . . and two quite high-ranking German SS officers named Schellenberg and Eggen. . . . However, *Schellenberg . . . apparently had a bad impression after all when he returned to Berlin*; at least he *wrote a very critical report*. The report was so critical that the Ministry of Foreign Affairs in Berlin took it up."[108]

Dulles told Hausamann that the German Ministry of Foreign Affairs had informed the German Envoy in Bern, Otto Carl Köcher, about the content of Schellenberg's report[109] and asked him whether his assessment of the situation in Switzerland had also changed. Hausamann quoted Dulles as saying that "Minister Köcher replied[110] that . . . in his opinion the doubts expressed by Schellenberg were not at all justified. Köcher said that he '*knew the history of Switzerland but did not know of any case when the Swiss failed to keep a word that they had given.*'"[111] Dulles added that the Allies absolutely trusted General Guisan, that they knew that he was a man of integrity. However, he said that they felt highly concerned because certain aides of the Commander-in-Chief were known to entertain close relations with German officers and National Socialists. He argued that the Allies did not understand what mysterious talks high-ranking Swiss officers could hold with the Germans and were surprised that the Federal Council, which was bound to have been informed about these matters, permitted such negotiations.[112]

Why did the chief of United States Intelligence in Switzerland[113] give that information to the head of *Bureau Ha*? Between November 1942 and July 1945[114] Allen Welsh Dulles, who was later, in 1953, appointed director of the CIA by President Eisenhower,[115] was stationed in Bern as delegate[116] of the U.S. Office of Strategic Services.[117] From his office at Herrengasse 23,[118] located just a few blocks from the Federal Palace, he set up an extensive,[119] highly successful, reputable Intelligence Service.[120]

Once the *Journal de Genève* had announced his arrival in Switzerland, introducing him as "the personal representative of President Roosevelt,"[121] with a "special duty" assignment, it did not take Dulles long to have easy access to Swiss authorities. Masson's deputy opined, "His reports to President Roosevelt[122] are probably considered as important as those by the Envoy."[123]

Interestingly it took the Germans a long time to realize the real nature of the OSS mission[124] that had brought Dulles to Bern. In spite of some unambiguous hints by the Swiss press, which initially worried Dulles because publicity and espionage generally do not go together,[125] Berlin believed that the former Wall Street lawyer was conducting economic warfare against Germany or was making preparations for the postwar economy.[126] This blatant misjudgment, which obviously facilitated Dulles' task of establishing his networks, has to be seen against the background of the National Socialists' contempt of, and disregard for, the United States; while they had perhaps *too much* respect for the British Intelligence Service—Schellenberg for example dreamed of creating an

OSS
Form 69 (Revised)

OFFICE OF STRATEGIC SERVICES
OFFICIAL DISPATCH

DATE   March 29, 1944

FROM
    BERN, SWITZERLAND

	PRIORITY
	ROUTINE

TO
    OFFICE OF STRATEGIC SERVICES

From

	DEFERRED
	IN 6259

DISTRIBUTION

(FOR ACTION)	(FOR INFORMATION)
DIRECTOR	SECRETARIAT, MAGRUDER, SHEPARDSON

U. S. GOVERNMENT PRINTING OFFICE   16—37893-1

RECEIVED IN CODE OR CIPHER

#2630-31. CASTLE* To 154 and 109. In reference to your #1382.

I fully understand your attitude, and am governing my actions along those lines. Recently I talked with General G. and made known to him that the situation in general was causing me some concern. He said that he would begin an investigation on his own. I think that his reason for requesting a talk with me was to try to gain some indication of whether or not it is probable that France will be invaded in the near future. It is evident that he fears the threat to Switzerland present in the fact that the Nazis may wish to use Swiss railroads to transport Nazi forces into safety in the event of a retreat of the Germans from the South in case the attack is carried on simultaneously in the North and South. We have assigned General G. our 839.

*Indicator inserted by Washington Message Center.

TOR: 3/29/44   5:50 PM

Allen W. Dulles, the head of the OSS in Bern, was in regular contact with General Guisan. (National Archives, Washington, DC, RG 226, Entry 134, Box 307, Folder 2)

exact German equivalent of it[127]—they viewed the Americans as decadent, infested with Negro thinking, or, to say the least, insignificant.

As early as 1920, the United States Military Attaché in Bern had reported to Washington, "Switzerland is the *whispering gallery of Europe*; and although unquestionably much of the political information to be gained is second-hand and in the nature of political international gossip, it has, if properly evaluated, great value as corroborative data."[128] During World War II, Switzerland once again turned out to be a highly interesting observation post for the United States. Moreover, at the end of World War I, Colonel Godson had stated, "In a milieu like Berne much is always floating in the air. The attitude of the Swiss is friendly and I get many a good turn done me quietly."[129] This statement applied to the time of World War II as well. Even though the Swiss authorities took great care to treat both warring parties in the same manner,[130] the Americans benefited from the favorable attitude with which the majority of the population viewed them.[131]

Dulles quickly established personal contact with both General Guisan[132] and Masson; with Switzerland's Chief of Intelligence he later even developed ties of friendship. Nevertheless, Masson's relationship with Dulles was not the same as his one with Schellenberg; at the end of the war he explained, "My Allied connections were also valuable but in a way that was different from the one with Schellenberg. . . . Because the *threat* posed by *the Germans* was permanent between 1939 and 1945, I maintained that connection without interruption. The other contacts, particularly with the Allies, were cherished in accordance with the very unstable circumstances on that side and according to the country's short-term interests."[133] Józef Garlinski described the contacts between Masson and Dulles as "of an official rather than a working nature."[134] That approach was consistent with Masson's way of dealing with Schellenberg. At their first meeting in Waldshut, he made it very clear to the German that he was against exchanging information on a regular basis.[135] In a classified report concerning his contacts with Switzerland's general staff, the United States Military Attaché in Bern, Colonel Banwell R. Legge, explained why Switzerland's Chief of Intelligence was so cautious, stating:

> Some months ago I attempted to transmit certain general information on Germany to the A[ssistant] C[hief] of S[taff], G-2, Swiss Army [Masson]. In conversation with one of his assistants I gave him a typed sheet without identifying remarks, which he accepted for his chief. The paper came back to me by the assistant the next morning with G-2's [Masson's] apologies for not being able to accept. The story of "l'Affaire des deux Colonels"[136] was then rehashed to me.[137]

A short time later, when Legge met Switzerland's Chief of Intelligence in person, Masson told him that "General Guisan had frequently stressed to the General Staff the necessity for a strictly neutral attitude toward the Attachés. . . . Swiss General Staff officers have frequently expressed opinions freely to me and have frequently given information of value. However, I am convinced that any effort to obtain periodic information . . . would prejudice my standing with the Swiss Army and would meet with refusal."[138]

The principle of showing a strictly neutral attitude applied to military attachés as well as to representatives of foreign Intelligence Services. The contacts *per se* were maintained on a lower level; Dulles for instance fostered relations with the head of Bureau Ha, with whom he met up to once a week at the home of *Emil Oprecht*, a publisher in Zürich. The regular contacts developed into a friendship that lasted until Dulles' death.[139] The two men quickly started actively exchanging information,[140] which was in both parties' interest.[141] Both Hausamann and Dulles made great efforts to be discreet, as is usual in that line of work. Even when he had received information through his connection with *Rudolf Roessler,* alias *Lucy,* Hausamann did not disclose to Dulles what an excellent source he had available. In return, Dulles supplied his Swiss contact with information on plans by the United States that could be of interest to Switzerland.[142]

The fact that in October 1943 Dulles informed Hausamann that Schellenberg had reported negatively about his meeting in Biglen when he was back in Berlin was part of the cooperation between the two men that was built on mutual respect and trust. In order not to give away his informant[143] and to avoid being ordered to testify as a soldier,[144] Hausamann went through Basel's State Attorney Lützelschwab,[145] who in turn informed Federal Councillor Kobelt about the matter without mentioning Hausamann's or Dulles' name.[146] In his report to Kobelt, Lützelschwab remarked: "I do not consider the whole issue as trivial at all. On the contrary, I believe that it is about time to take drastic steps so as to finally put an end to *the army's detrimental amateurish involvement in politics.*"[147]

Kobelt agreed with Lützelschwab and forwarded his report to Masson, but without mentioning the name of his informant. Masson never found out who was behind the report.[148] He commented, however, "I found it unpleasant that people could believe for one moment that this was a scam by Schellenberg and that I was unusually naïve. In order to *verify* the Allied report, I believed that the best thing to do was to find out whether Minister Köcher had actually received the document in question from the Ministry of Foreign Affairs in order to double-check the information contained therein."[149] On December 16, 1943, Masson consequently told Germany's Military Attaché von Ilsemann about the Allied supposition. Von Ilsemann promised to ask Envoy Köcher whether he had received instructions from Berlin to comment on the alleged statements by Schellenberg. Masson explained, "In the afternoon, von Ilsemann answered in the *negative*, so I had proof that part of the story had been invented." [150]

Masson did not let the matter rest after receiving von Ilsemann's reply, sending his aide Captain Paul Holzach, an intrepid courier for Swiss Intelligence, to Berlin to see Schellenberg. Masson argued, "In order not to use trickery anymore, it seemed useful to me to inform Schellenberg about what certain Allies and Swiss thought about his 'honorability'."[151] Schellenberg did not take long to react. In a handwritten letter to Masson's attention that Holzach brought back with him from Germany, the SS officer categorically denied the rumors, stating:

Dear friend!
Mr. Holzach just came to see me . . . to tell me such unbelievable things that I am almost at a complete loss for words while writing this letter. I need not repeat the rumors; you know what they are all about, concerning *our connection and friendship and my attitude toward your country*. Please note that as a man of honor I will not comment on these events, but I will look into the matter and find out who is playing underhanded games with us! Please show this letter to General [Guisan] as well; I would like to tell him in person what I think about these matters. Maybe that can be arranged soon! I will ask Eggen[152] to coordinate everything with you before Christmas![153]

Considering the rivalries that existed between the Intelligence services of the Wehrmacht and the SS and their relentless struggle to increase their influence, it does not seem erroneous to *assume* that in his letter Schellenberg told the truth and the information that had reached Dulles might have been part of a plot by the German *Abwehr* (Armed Forces Intelligence and Counterintelligence) against Foreign Intelligence at the Reich Security Central Office—unless Dulles single-handedly made up the story[154] or had become the victim of a ploy. In any case, this author did not come across any evidence in German or American archives of Schellenberg making a negative assessment of his meetings with General Guisan.[155] Regardless of whether Schellenberg was truthful or not, the incident shows that the Allies were fairly well informed about the Masson-Schellenberg connection and eyed it suspiciously.

Masson Is Banned from Traveling Abroad

The Federal Council reacted to the meeting in Biglen not only by repri-
manding the Commander-in-Chief but also by taking a measure that directly
affected the Masson-Schellenberg connection. In mid-April 1943,[156] Eggen
presented Switzerland's Chief of Intelligence with an official invitation to travel
to Berlin.[157] Schellenberg planned to introduce Masson to Heinrich Himmler,
hoping that the visit would consolidate his contested position among the
German leadership. Masson accepted the invitation, provided that he could
find a plausible reason to travel to the German capital. As it happened, he did
find a reason in the form of an unfounded rumor that German and Italian
Intelligence had spread, according to which a British aircraft had been allowed
to perform three secret nighttime landings at the Belpmoos airfield outside
Bern in order to pick up some Polish and French citizens as well as a number
of documents.[158] Eggen reported that Hitler and Mussolini had talked in detail
about that matter during their meeting at the Brenner Pass.[159] Even though
Masson had been able to convince Schellenberg's emissary that due to technical reasons secret landings could not be performed at that airfield, the rumor
could not be silenced.[160]

Masson asked the Commander-in-Chief's permission to personally settle
the matter concerning the alleged secret landings by traveling to Berlin. Guisan
told him that this was a *political* matter that did not concern the army and
therefore wanted Masson to obtain the Federal Council's approval before granting his request.[161] Hence, Masson broached the issue with Kobelt, who referred
him to Pilet-Golaz. Masson did not tell the Foreign Minister right away why he
had gone to see him but started talking about his secret channel to Berlin. After
Masson had left his office, Pilet-Golaz recalled, "He supplies me with detailed
information, so first I believe that he comes to see me because of the rumors
that have been circulating and because of the past."[162] On that occasion, the
Head of the Department of Foreign Affairs heard about Eggen—he had no idea
that he would meet him soon thereafter—and the meeting in Waldshut for the
first time; he wrote:

> [Masson] has been put in contact with Schellenberg by Eggen, a Nazi
> who often comes to Switzerland to place orders for the army.
> Schellenberg, who is Eggen's chief, supposedly has the rank of a gener-
> al. Himmler is said to be his superior, and he is supposedly in charge
> of the politico-military section of the party, the equivalent of Canaris
> outside the party. Every week or so he is said to go to the Führer's head-

quarters. Last year Eggen suggested to [Masson] that he meet Schellenberg. The meeting took place near Waldshut. Masson was dressed in civilian clothes. He crossed the border, then went for a walk with Schellenberg. They had a chat somewhere in the woods. The contact was established within a short period of time, and according to Masson, *they hit it off with each other* right away.[163]

In his conversation with the Foreign Minister, which lasted well over an hour, Masson was vague about his subsequent encounters with Schellenberg. Pilet-Golaz merely noted that Masson had met with Schellenberg on two other occasions since Waldshut—first "near Lake Constance, I think during a weekend at a friend's house,"[164] and then again "in January or February 1943." It appears that the Federal Councillor did not realize that the Chief of Intelligence was referring to the meetings in Biglen and Arosa; Masson understandably did not have any interest in reminding the magistrate that these were the meetings that had created a stir at a Cabinet meeting a few weeks earlier.[165] Masson may have mentioned the former contacts only in passing because he wanted to get to the point and present his request. He showed Pilet a letter from Schellenberg dated May 19, 1943, in which the SS officer invited him to Berlin and alluded to the alleged secret British landings at the Belpmoos airfield.[166] Pilet remarked, "Masson supposedly has to go to Berlin to look into that matter and discuss it."[167] Colonel-Brigadier Masson did not hide the fact that the Head of the Military Department had reacted "rather coolly" to the idea, prompting him to see the Head of the Department of Foreign Affairs.

Pilet-Golaz did not give Masson an answer to his request then and there, telling him instead that he wished to consult with Kobelt first and see how his other colleagues on the Federal Council felt about the issue. However, he indicated that the matter seemed to be "very risky," adding, "The inconveniences caused by a potential fuss might outweigh the advantages gained through the trip. . . . As a private individual, and as a former machine gunner,[168] I did not hide from Masson that if an indiscretion was committed and if he was not fully covered in public, he would expose himself to a campaign that would cost him his job."[169] According to Pilet, "[Masson] replies that he likes to follow the game through and that he does not have any political ambitions for the time after the war. He is well aware that certain circles, such as Bringolf and Oprecht,[170] would not hesitate to give him a hard time."[171] After making that remark, which once again revealed how courageous and audacious he was, Masson said goodbye to Pilet. The meeting had lasted well over an hour.

As early as the following morning, on June 25, 1943, the Federal Council discussed Masson's travel plans at its regular meeting. After Kobelt and Pilet had presented the matter to their colleagues,[172] the Cabinet decided not to author-ize the Chief of Intelligence to travel abroad.[173] The federal government's deci-sion was based in part on an argument that the Foreign Minister had present-ed.[174] He later stated, "There was no room for any hesitation. What would the Allies have thought if they had found out about it? *The Biglen affair was enough.*"[175]

Apparently Masson and Meyer-Schwertenbach had ventured too far for-ward with the Germans. In any case, Masson was not willing to accept the Federal Council's negative response.[176] One week after the Cabinet meeting, when Charles Daniel, the liaison officer between Army Intelligence and the Department of Foreign Affairs, was invited to one of the regular meetings with Pilet-Golaz, Masson decided to personally attend the meeting in his stead in order to once again bring up the invitation to Berlin. Pilet showed some under-standing for Masson's arguments and agreed to receive Eggen at his private res-idence if necessary.[177] He consequently ordered minister Karl Stucki to hold a preliminary meeting with the German.

Stucki wrote an interesting note for the file about that meeting, to the attention of the Foreign Minister, which clearly shows how much importance Masson attached to reversing the Federal Council's decision. Seconded by Meyer, the Chief of Intelligence struck a pessimistic note, pointing out the neg-ative consequences that declining the invitation could have. Eggen, whom Stucki described as "a relatively young, nice, calm, and level-headed man,"[178] gave several reasons why Masson should travel to Berlin. Stucki reported, "In passing, Mr. E[ggen] indicated that it might be interesting for Colonel Masson to see what the concentration camps were really like and to see for himself that the damage caused by the English bombings in Berlin was not as serious as the English propaganda made it sound."[179] Eggen considered that those were two plausible reasons *for the Swiss.* He explained that the *Germans* had another objective in inviting Masson to Berlin. After returning from Biglen and Arosa, Schellenberg had not taken Masson's reservations seriously enough, telling everyone "that his friend Masson would go to see him in Berlin. The group that was hostile toward Sch[ellenberg], and also toward Switzerland, i.e. the Foreign Minister and his entourage, was said to be incredulous of that and did not hide its doubts. If Colonel M[asson] 'fail[ed]' to keep his word,' he [would] make General Sch[ellenberg] lose face and thereby personally contribute to the tri-umph of Switzerland's enemies."[180] Minister Stucki tried in vain to explain to Eggen that the foreign travel restrictions imposed through Switzerland's neu-trality policy also applied to high-ranking officials and officers. Stucki com-mented, "I do not delude myself into believing that I convinced the person to whom I was talking; he immediately brought up Lieutenant General *Wille* and

Colonel *Bircher* as counter-examples."[181] Interestingly, Eggen argued, "The Germans [will] be particularly sensitive to the fact that the veto comes from Switzerland's top civilian authorities rather than the army command."[182] Several days later, Pilet-Golaz, whom Stucki had briefed right away by telephone about the results of the meeting, remarked to Kobelt, "[Since Masson's first meeting with Schellenberg in Waldshut,] the whole matter has taken shape and has become more intricate."[183]

Switzerland's top diplomat ultimately agreed to personally explain the Federal Council's point of view to Eggen. On July 14, 1943, he received the German emissary in the presence of Minister Stucki.[184] Pilet-Golaz later noted:

> I explained to [Eggen] that traveling to Berlin was out of the question for our Chief of Intelligence, that such a trip would be against our usual caution, our very strict traditions, and our neutrality. Eggen replied that he did not understand our position because the army approved of the trip. That was exactly what I had feared and what made this matter particularly unpleasant because the roles were reversed; it was the Department of Foreign Affairs, which is normally in charge of maintaining correct relations with foreign countries, if possible, that had to display a totally negative attitude. So it was the government that opposed the plan. Eggen argued that that would leave an even worse impression in Berlin.[185] That attitude would be interpreted as distinctly unfriendly. I retorted that since our neutrality was at stake, that was a political issue that fell under the sole responsibility of the political authorities and that they were the only competent body to deal with that issue.[186]

When Eggen realized that Pilet-Golaz would not give in, he came up with a compromise, suggesting that Masson meet Schellenberg in Stuttgart instead of Berlin and that the meeting be staged in a very discreet manner. However, the Federal Councillor remained firm, explaining, "I refused that idea as categorically as the first one. Of course I did so in a polite manner.[187] By the way, I must say that Eggen also had a correct attitude during the conversation; no matter how much he insisted and no matter what a bleak picture he painted of the consequences should we refuse [to let Masson travel to Germany]."[188]

The encounter between Pilet-Golaz and Eggen was not the end of the matter. The Federal Council considered that it was necessary to prevent Masson from coming up with any other travel plans. It asked the Commander-in-Chief to see to it that in the future no high-ranking officer made any preparations whatsoever for traveling abroad without *previously* informing the government

3.8.43.

No. ....

In der Antwort vermerken — A indiquer dans la réponse
Da indicare nella risposta

Confidentielle/personnelle

     Au Chef de l'état-major de l'armée

       J'ai l'honneur de vous faire connaître que, conformément aux in-
structions du major Lauener, médecin de l'état-major de l'armée, je me trou-
ve, depuis le 31.7.43. en traitement médical à St.Moritz (Hôtel Kurhaus, tf.
no.710).

       La fin de mon congé régulier (Gryon) ayant coincidé avec les récents
événements d'Italie, j'ai tenu à différer de quelques jours mon départ pour
St.Moritz et c'est la raison pour laquelle je ne suis arrivé ici qu'à la fin
de la semaine dernière.

       Il m'importait en effet de chercher à préciser la situation de la Suis-
se dans le cadre des nouveaux événements et notamment de connaître, dans la me-
sure du possible, la réaction allemande en fonction de l'évolution politico-
militaire italienne. L'attitude de l'Allemagne et les intentions immédiates de
ses dirigeants doivent retenir notre attention et justifier notre vigilance, bien
plus que la nouvelle orientation de l'Italie.

       J'ai en conséquence fait prendre, la semaine dernière, à Berlin, les con-
tacts que vous savez. Il en est résulté les informations que vous voudrez bien
trouver résumées dans la notice confidentielle ci-jointe.

       Je maintiens d'ici ce contact personnel et ne manquerai pas de vous te-
nir au courant des nouvelles informations qui pourraient me parvenir.

       Le colonel EMG.Müller, dans l'aptitude duquel j'ai toute confiance, assu-
rant la direction du service de renseignements pendant mon absence, je vous prie
de ne pas considérer les présentes lignes que comme un témoignage personnel
de l'intérêt que je ne cesse de porter aux événements actuels. Elles ne constituent pas une appréciation de la situation générale, Mais je n'ai pas pu m'em-
pêcher d'exploiter, en cette période critique, une de mes sources personnelles les
plus importantes et de vous transmettre, à toutes fins utiles, le résultat de mes
investigations.

1 notice confidentielle/personnelle

Copie: au Général
        au colonel EMG.Müller

COMMANDEMENT DE L'ARMÉE
Groupe I d
Le sous-chef d'état-major:

Masson

In a letter to Chief of the General Staff Huber dated early August 1943, Masson
described his secret channel to Berlin as "one of [his] most important personal sources."
(BAr E 27/9911, vol. 2)

about it and obtaining its permission.[189] The Cabinet argued that such trips always had *political* implications, so the only way to "prevent such unpleasant incidents from happening"[190] in the future was for the Commander-in-Chief to expressly forbid his officers to travel abroad. Nevertheless, the Federal Council offered Masson a way out that helped him save face by adding, "Of course this does not include purely private business trips undertaken by anyone who is not a commissioned officer."[191] Masson and the Commander-in-Chief consequently asked Captain Meyer to accept the invitation to Berlin in Masson's place.[192]

On July 28, 1943, Captain Meyer flew to Berlin for the second time[193] on orders of Swiss Army Intelligence.[194] Schellenberg was thankful for that gesture, telling his Swiss guest that he had asked him to come to Berlin because Masson's last-minute refusal had put him in an uncomfortable position. He said that his opponents claimed that Masson was *insincere*, playing games with him, and that the only way to deal with Switzerland was by whipping it rather than by being nice to it. Schellenberg recounted that Kaltenbrunner, the chief of the Reich Security Central Office, had asked him to report on Switzerland the following night. He said that he would use the opportunity to once again point out that Switzerland was determined to remain absolutely neutral and defend itself and that its Commander-in-Chief had promised to do so. He explained that he would tell Kaltenbrunner that Masson had not been able to come because due to the *events in Italy*[195] he was indispensable for the time being.[196]

Meyer-Schwertenbach's talks in Berlin did indeed focus on the events in Italy. The optimistic impression that he gained on that occasion is reflected in an extended report entitled "The Events in Italy and Switzerland's Situation" that Masson wrote based on Meyer's information.[197] In that report, Masson wrote:

> In the course of this new assessment of the situation, the OKW did not fail to attach utmost importance to the attitude of the *Swiss* concerning their armed neutrality. . . . Through a top authority, we may assert that the OKW finally seems to be *convinced that we are determined to defend ourselves* (it had not been convinced before) and that at this point in time a preventive attack against Switzerland would be a political and strategic mistake. Hence, it appears that according to those who are in power in Germany or are able to influence the Führer's decisions, the *suspicion* about our "lack of neutrality" that weighed upon us and constrained us for many years has been *diverted once and for all.*[198]

Masson and Meyer believed that they owed this change of opinion among the German Armed Forces High Command to their connection with Schellenberg. Was that really the case? The fact that the majority of the other officers at Swiss Army Intelligence did *not* share their chief's opinion was due in large part to events that had occurred in March 1943, shortly after the meeting in Biglen. Because the circumstances surrounding them are ambiguous, these events have come to be seen as a test case for the channel to the Reich Security Central Office. In this author's opinion, a final assessment of the connection can only be made after taking a close look at these events.

10

Test Case for the Connection: The Alert of March 1943

TWO WEEKS FOLLOWING THE MEETINGS in Biglen and Arosa, on March 18, 1943, the *Viking* connection reported that *Case Switzerland* had become a pressing matter and a German offensive had to be expected before April 6. That warning was the beginning of one of the toughest trials for the Swiss during the entire war. However, whether Switzerland was actually in particular danger at the time was a bone of contention until recently because the only reference material that had been available to scholars were the documents of Swiss Intelligence; no written evidence had been found at any of the following archives: the Military Archives in Freiburg (Germany), the German Federal Archives in Koblenz, the Political Archives of the German Foreign Ministry in Bonn[1]—nor at the National Archives in Washington, DC.

This lack of available reference material has resulted in a lot of speculation about the veracity of the alert of March 1943; some people argue that it was merely a *bluff*,[2] some claim that Swiss Army Intelligence was fooled by cunning German intelligence,[3] and others believe that it was part of a deliberate war of nerves. As early as a few weeks after the critical days of March 1943, it was suggested that the alert was staged out of *economic* considerations, the rumors being "spread intentionally in order to make [Switzerland] comply"[4] with

German demands and advance stalled negotiations on a new bilateral trade agreement.[5] The alarming news could also have been spread in an attempt to incite Switzerland to reinforce its defensive efforts in order to prevent the Germans from launching a preventive attack or discourage the Allies from seizing the strategically interesting terrain in an assault. Or perhaps the informants of the *Viking* connection sounded the alarm because they attached too much significance to, or misinterpreted, bits and pieces of information that they had picked up while eavesdropping at the Führer's headquarters, interpreting them as discussions about specific plans.[6]

The alert of March 1943 is a perfect textbook example of the difficulties that an intelligence service faces. On various occasions during the winter of 1942-1943, Swiss Intelligence believed that it heard *signals* through the *noise* in the background, without being able to establish whether they were *true* or *inverted* signals.[7] The fact that even today, more than half a century later, it is not possible to specifically assign the individual reports, hints, pieces of information, impressions, rumors, and suppositions to one or the other category shows how difficult it was back then to clearly identify the intercepted signals. Nevertheless, due to newly available source material it is now possible to shed enough light onto the alert of March 1943 and the role that the Masson-Schellenberg connection played in that context to determine whether Switzerland was under any actual threat.

Warnings Received by Swiss Intelligence

Even those who have argued away the crisis of March 1943 by describing it as a *false alarm* have had to admit that in view of the military-political situation of the winter of 1942-1943, the alarming reports could not be downplayed as fantasy but appeared to be completely plausible.[8]

A first "very serious warning"[9] reached Swiss Intelligence as early as *December 3, 1942*. The secret report was written "by one of [its] best informants on matters concerning Germany"[10] who had on several previous occasions allayed the Swiss' fears when many others sounded the alarm bell. He reported that since occupying Vichy France, the German leadership had become less and less reluctant to attack Switzerland, arguing that its change of mind was due to Germany's critical supply situation. By using forced laborers from Switzerland it expected to be able to free up an additional 80,000 to 100,000 Germans for the armed forces. The report stated, "As little as five or six months ago, such a modest figure was irrelevant to the German OKW or the Authorized General Representative for the Allocation of Labor."[11] In addition, the report pointed out that the military preconditions for a strategic surprise attack on Switzerland were considered favorable and objects that had been prepared for demolition did not act as a strong deterrent to the key German authorities nor the Armed Forces High Command. It said that after experiencing the scorched earth strategy of the retreating Russian troops in the East, "where due to perfect technical preparations hardly any tool or machine from Russian factories fell into German hands undamaged,"[12] Germany was used to dealing with a high level of destruction; moreover, the Germans did not think that Switzerland was capable of preparing the same number of objects for demolition as Russia, and they expected to be able to prevent the Swiss from blowing up these objects.

Even though Swiss Intelligence took the secret report seriously, it hesitated to sound the alarm right away because no similar reports had been received from the Swiss lines in the Allied camp. The Allies were bound to find out about any decision that the German leadership might make concerning Switzerland. The report argued, "If the Allies receive any such information, it will not remain hidden from our observers who are placed there. So we will hear it from that side as well, and quickly so."[13] The report concluded, "Once the same warning comes from that [Allied] sector as well, it will be *time* for us *to call up the entire army.*"[14]

As little as three days later, on *December 6, 1942,* Waibel's Procurement Office N.S.1 in Lucerne received another worrisome report, part of which appeared to confirm the first alarm. It was written by agent *Sx,* whose real name was Johann Conrad Meyer.[15] The independent economic advisor from Zürich and former economic affairs correspondent for the *Neue Zürcher Zeitung* in Berlin had already been working for Swiss Intelligence before the war and had valuable connections to several top military authorities in Germany. His most important source was a colonel at the OKW who was in charge of supplying food to the offensive armies. That officer had supplied *Sx* with the data concerning the interventions against Czechoslovakia and the attacks against Poland, Norway, Holland, and Belgium. Swiss Intelligence consequently attached considerable importance to J.C. Meyer's reports. On December 6, 1942, *Sx* reported to Lucerne:

By March 1943, supposedly a new army with 2 million men will be set up to create a so-called southern army; it is to be used to defend the southern front, i.e. occupy all of France and Italy. In this context, the informant reports that *the mood concerning Switzerland has substantially worsened,* and party circles are apparently talking about also occupying Switzerland on that occasion, i.e. in spring 1943. The informant considers that Switzerland should absolutely take unambiguous defensive measures in order to make the German general staff realize right away that an operation against Switzerland would involve too heavy losses. If that is done, the informant believes that the operation against Switzerland is unlikely to be carried out. However, Switzerland must ignore Germany's proposal to occupy only the southern border in case Italy secedes; instead, it must be strong also at the northern border.[16]

On *December 17, 1942*, a new warning was issued, this time by Waibel's *Viking* connection. An informant who was placed in a high position at the Wehrmacht told Emil Häberli, the head of the *Pfalz* sub-office in Basel: "At the present time there is apparently no immediate danger for Switzerland. However, please note that I said, 'at the present time' and 'apparently,' because it is the Führer who makes the decisions on his own, and he is unpredictable."[17] He said that depending on his mood it was perfectly possible for Hitler to spontaneously decide to solve the *problem of Switzerland*, adding that obviously deployment plans had been prepared and the German Army Command was likely to know all the details about Switzerland's defensive capabilities. The informant told Häberli:

> I assure you that you cannot imagine what goes on in your country in the area of German espionage. . . . Keep a close watch over your Gotthard because the setup that is supposed to allow [Germany] to conquer the Gotthard railroad without having it destroyed is much larger and better than you can imagine. You will have *trouble recognizing the German deployment against Switzerland in time;* the assault on Switzerland will be staged *like a coup* because the army command is aware that the *Reduit* will be impregnable for several months or more if its defense is organized. You will have to expect the attack to be launched from a distant standby area with the latest tank force and air force technology, including a large number of airborne troops.[18]

As early as the following day, in a new special report Waibel was able to provide additional information on that issue. A German general who had allegedly taken part in the discussions told one of *Viking's* contact persons about two conferences that had supposedly been held in late November at the Führer's headquarters under Hitler's chairmanship.[19] In view of the fact that this information had been supplied by an excellent source, it was taken very seriously, even more so because in the meantime N.S.1 had received similar reports from other connections. One of the two conferences had supposedly been attended by the leading commanders of the German army police, the SS, the Security Service of the SS, and the Gestapo,[20] and the other meeting by the Führer's top aides and advisors. General Dietl and Himmler were reported to have taken part in both meetings.

The German general told Waibel's informant that if Germany had to pull its southern front back to the ridge of the Alps, a pro-Allied Switzerland would become unbearable from an operational and strategic point of view, explaining, "It would be irresponsible to leave one-third of the Alpine front in the hands of the Swiss, who are unreliable for the Axis. [Germany] thinks very highly of the Swiss Army's fighting strength; the Swiss mountain troops are estimated to be 45% more powerful than the *current* German Alpine divisions. . . . About *one million men* will be used for a surprise attack. That way it can be ensured that the entire country will be occupied swiftly."[21] The informant explained that this attack would be preceded by a nighttime occupation of the hills and plains located at the foot of Switzerland's mountains; for this operation 100,000 para-troopers and airborne troops and 1,000 transport aircraft were considered to be sufficient. He added:

> [Germany] will refrain from deploying any troops toward Switzerland [ahead of the operation] in order not to incite Switzerland under any circumstances to call up its army. The offensive columns that are on standby in staggered positions will begin their operation simultane-ously with the airborne troops, advancing at maximum speed (it is said that the speed will be about 60 to 70 km/h)[22] from the German hin-terland. One considers that the troops that are stationed in the *Reduit* will be insufficient to defend these areas.[23]

He argued that if this surprise push were successful, preventing Switzerland from mobilizing the entire army and increasing the number of troops in the *Reduit*, Germany was sure to be victorious. General Dietl was said to have been selected as commander of the army group that was to carry out the operation.

At that time the figures of one million men and 100,000 airborne troops that were supposedly slated for a campaign against Switzerland should have made *Rigi* suspicious. Klaus Urner rightly describes these figures as part of a "grotesque tall story."[24] Even though the fate of the 6th Army near Stalingrad clearly showed how poor Germany's human and material reserves were, Waibel considered the report to be credible. He did so not only because the report had been transmitted via the *Viking* connection, which had always turned out to be well informed and reliable until then, but also because Lucerne received a num-ber of other signals that appeared to confirm these warnings. Moreover, in Waibel's and his collaborators' opinion the fact that German General *Eduard Dietl* was mentioned in the report added credibility to the warning. At that time Dietl was viewed as the foremost German specialist in mountain warfare and far beyond Germany was the acclaimed "hero of Narvik." However, after doing some research Hans Rudolf Kurz has been able to establish that "most likely Dietl did not receive any specific order to conduct an operation against Switzerland. Such an order could not have been issued without involving the operations branch [of the OKW], which had no knowledge of any plans of that kind."[25] Hence, the rumors concerning the German general may be considered as cunning propaganda "because no one else would have personified a threat better than Dietl. His case is a perfect argument for describing the information as German propaganda serving as a *warning tool*."[26]

In the meantime, Swiss Intelligence found out that the German high command had seriously discussed *Case Switzerland* as early as November 8, 1942.[27] Hitler allegedly intended to occupy Switzerland at the same time as the unoccupied zone of France, arguing that as a result of the Allied landings in northern Africa, integrating Switzerland into the European defensive front had become indispensable. He was said to speculate that due to the expected effect of surprise it should be possible to occupy Switzerland before the Swiss Army could demolish the production facilities that were important to Germany. The generals were said to agree with Hitler's arguments but had to advise him against attacking Switzerland because the required number of troops could not be made ready within two or three days.[28]

While the previous warnings had given at least some cause to question whether in winter 1942–1943 Germany actually made plans to intervene in Switzerland, the warning concerning November 8 makes it perfectly clear that this was an inverted signal. On November 7, 1942, the war journal of the German Armed Forces High Command states, "Due to the Führer's absence, during the following days no proposals were made concerning the state of affairs; instead, under Colonel von Buttlar the Armed Forces High Command only assessed the situation."[29] Hitler, who was allegedly discussing Switzerland's occupation at his headquarters, had actually left the *Wolfsschanze* headquarters in East Prussia[30] the day before at 1:40 p.m. Together with his immediate entourage, including Field Marshal Keitel and General Jodl, he drove via Berlin to Munich, where as usual on the evening of November 8 he addressed the *Alte Kämpfer* at the *Bürgerbräukeller*.[31] The news about the Allied landing in French-owned northern Africa reached Hitler during the night of November 7-8, 1942 at a train station in Thuringia, where his train had stopped.[32] The fact that Hitler originally called Italian Foreign Minister Ciano[33] and French Foreign Minister Laval to a meeting in Munich in order to decide on a military alliance with Vichy France[34] instead of marching into France's unoccupied zone demonstrates that even at that moment in time the German dictator did not consider launching an operation against Switzerland. The High Command's war journal clearly shows that the German leadership was not very well informed about the events that took place between November 8 and 11, 1942 in Morocco and Algeria. Its surprise and perplexity are reflected in the words of General Warlimont,[35] Jodl's deputy at the German Armed Forces High Command, who wrote:

> In view of the situation in the war, during those days the state of affairs among the German high command could hardly be described as anything less than grotesque. Hitler was somewhere in Munich, waiting for the conference to be held with the Italians and French. His special train was stationed on one of the main tracks at the train station there, albeit it was closed off from the public transport area; his entire "entourage" had taken off, except for the Chief of the Armed Forces High Command, his adjutant, and now also his deputy, who were working hard under difficult conditions. For the time being the field team was left behind in East Prussia because Hitler apparently no longer knew where he should stay next. The chief of the army's general staff, Hitler's advisor for the Eastern front, was also in East Prussia; in Munich he was not even represented by a liaison officer. The whole atmosphere was characterized by a feeling of concern and uncertainty.[36]

At that time Swiss Intelligence did not know about these internal circumstances among the German leadership. Nevertheless, as early as January 1, 1943, just a few weeks after reporting about a possible German military threat, Johann Conrad Meyer, alias *Sx*, toned down his warning, explaining that one of his most reliable sources had told him "that a threat against Switzerland and Spain was out of the question."[37] However, the fact that N.S.1, the Procurement Office in Lucerne, simultaneously intercepted several inverted signals that appeared to complement and confirm the warnings resulted in its interpreting them as *true* signals. As a consequence, Waibel desperately tried to obtain additional information on the plan for the attack against Switzerland that was supposedly in the making.

On *January 16, 1943*, Waibel believed that he was in a position to confirm special reports no. 42 and 43 of December 17 and 18, 1942; moreover, by making inquiries through a second channel, he had found out additional details about the supposed threat. He was told that in the event that the Germans could not keep their positions in southern and central Italy after the expected Allied invasion, forcing them to pull back their defense line to the area between

Livorno, Ancona, Rimini, and La Spezia, the attack would be launched by an army group that was standing by. The German Army High Command was said to assume that based on its conviction and tactical (nowadays one would say "operational") mission, the Swiss Army was "an advance guard of the attacking Anglo-Saxon armies."[38] According to Waibel, the German invasion of Switzerland, which had been planned by General Dietl,[39] the commander-in-chief of the 20th Mountain Army in Lapland, was to be carried out in two stages; first, paratroopers and airborne troops were to attack the plains and the foothills of the Alps outside the *Reduit* while the major cities in these areas were to be subjected to heavy bombing raids. No sooner than one hour after being informed that the airborne attack had been successful, the tank columns were to launch their offensive. Dietl's plan expressly called for the tank army to assemble *outside* so-called deployment areas in order not to provide Swiss Intelligence with any opportunity whatsoever to warn the army command, thereby preventing the Swiss Army from mobilizing its entire forces. The advance tank units were to be deployed at night from as many as 500 kilometers away in order to clear the terrain that the airborne troops had conquered and break any leftover resistance centers. The tank units were to be joined by major motorized SS intervention troops that had orders to eliminate resistance among the population and the army. This operation was described as "*casting the shroud over the territory located at the foot of Switzerland's Reduit.*"[40] Waibel was able to find out that Dietl then planned to break the *Reduit* apart in order to prevent the Swiss mountain troops from coordinating their arrangements concerning supplies and reserve troops. According to Waibel's report, key SS people, including Himmler, as well as Bohle[41] and Counselor von Bibra agreed with Dietl to go ahead with the invasion, whereas economic leaders, top officials, and the generals apparently tried to use their influence to keep the plan from being carried out. Interestingly, the report mentioned that the Führer's headquarters seriously wondered whether the losses that Germany had suffered since mid-November 1942[42] had not reached a level that no longer allowed it to attack Switzerland.[43] This last argument was absolutely plausible and was actually taken into account by the Swiss; however, the fact that Bohle and von Bibra were mentioned shows that the report of mid-January 1943 once again blended truth and fiction. It is known today that there was no way that Hitler and his closest collaborators at his headquarters could be interested in Bohle's opinion on an issue such as this. Even though before the war Bohle had earned his patron Rudolf Hess' and Hitler's sympathy and was viewed benevolently by Himmler, who bestowed the honorary rank of SS lieutenant general on him, by the time Hess flew to England on May 10, 1941, for several reasons he had completely faded into the background. The opinion of Bohle's subordinates, who included von Bibra, the national NSDAP leader in Switzerland, mattered even less to the Führer's headquarters.[44] Swiss Intelligence was not well enough informed about who had influence and power among the German leadership to be able to identify improbabilities such as the ones contained in special report no. 44.

Ten days after that worrisome warning, which appeared to be all the more credible as it included a rather large number of details, on *January 26, 1943, Rigi* reported that Great Headquarters had been set up in Freising.[45] The Swiss informant added that this was part of the Führer's headquarters, whose tasks included coordinating the operations of the special SS units that were standing by for the event of an attack on Switzerland. He said that the Wehrmacht systematically stirred up hatred against Switzerland and that so far it had done so successfully. The report also pointed out how much influence von Bibra had, pressing for action in the near future and claiming that he had seen signs of Switzerland increasing the state of readiness of its military. By January 29, 1943, General Guisan considered the different pieces of information serious enough to forward special reports 42 to 45 to Federal Councillor Kobelt and Federal President Celio.[46]

It is usually difficult to measure how much impact an intelligence service has. In this specific case, however, a document exists that demonstrates that the warnings by *Viking* and other connections affected the federal government's assessment of the situation. On February 12, 1943, Federal Councillor Kobelt spoke to the Advisory Board for Press-Related Matters[47] on the military-political situation and its possible repercussions on Switzerland.

The Head of the Military Department stated that one could see that the Intelligence Service had been doing a very good job; nevertheless, he said that it could not guarantee anything, especially because nowadays an invasion was bound to be launched in the form of an assault. He added, "Even if [Germany] has worked out plans for an invasion of our country, and even if it intends to attack us, we believe that at the present time it does not have the capability to carry out such an undertaking."[48] He predicted that in the very near future the threat might diminish rather than increase. This was a reference to the situation on the Eastern front,[49] where the Russian counter-offensive had not yet come to a standstill, for the time being preventing Germany from freeing up reserves to resolve other issues such as Switzerland. Kobelt argued, "Based on these considerations, in the coming weeks the risk of a military intervention against our country is expected to be small; however, during the spring and summer that risk could increase substantially, raising the possibility of a military threat from one side or another."[50] He said that therefore it was necessary to modify the existing rotation schedule, due to the expected reduced risk from abroad. In

February and March the number of serving troops should be lowered in order to be able to call up more troops between April and June 1943, when the threat was expected to increase. Kobelt concluded, "I declare that there is no cause for concern, but there are reasons to be very vigilant."[51] A few days later, during an assessment of the situation from the perspective of Army Intelligence, Masson reached the same conclusion, but he added that it was essential to show, "through deeds,"[52] Switzerland's determination to defend itself. The meeting in Biglen demonstrated that by deeds Masson did not only mean keeping troops on duty but also verbally convincing the potential aggressor of that determination.

The following day, on February 17, 1943, Johann Conrad Meyer joined Kobelt and Masson in their interpretation, briefly reporting to *Rigi* that another one of his reliable informants saw "no threat for Switzerland."[53] One month later, however, on the afternoon of Thursday, *March 18, 1943,* the warnings of December 1942 and January 1943 seemed to come true. Waibel's informant *Viking* received an urgent warning through his German liaison person at the staff of the German Armed Forces High Command stating: "*A German operation is imminent against Switzerland and is very likely to be carried out before April 6, 1943.*"[54] Max Waibel immediately called Masson at army headquarters and sent him a copy of the message, adding that the warning was to be taken very seriously because *Viking* had been one of the best, most reliable, and experienced informants so far. He explained: "In May 1940, based on his connection he denied that there was any danger for Switzerland because he had not received the agreed warning from his liaison person. *This time around, the warning has been issued in an urgent manner.* He advises us to put the military on alert in order to make the prospects of success of a surprise intervention look slim for the German OKW."[55]

The message by *Viking* did not cause any state of panic.[56] Based on reliable intelligence material and his own studies, Masson had a clear idea of the way in which an invasion would be staged. By the following day, *March 19, 1943,* he had worked out a detailed "potential scenario for a German attack on Switzerland."[57] In that study, he recalled that in an effort to prevent the Swiss Army from mobilizing in time and dragging them into a tedious and costly war in the mountains for several months, the Germans would launch the invasion in a sudden move without a large number of troops being visible beforehand. Masson expected the invasion to be carried out in two stages. First, an assault group would try to prevent the Swiss Army from deploying its troops to the *Reduit* and suppress the slightest inclination to put up resistance by taking strong action against soldiers and civilians. The night before the surprise attack, rapid Army and *Waffen SS* units, followed by special police and security service

INCOMING MESSAGE

MESSAGE CENTER COPY
CCWD

RC 30
filed 29/1920Z
dm

Jan 29
2108Z

G-2 report on rumors of German invasion of Switzerland

From: Bern
To: Milid

No. 450 January 29, 1943

Following 60$:303 has been aware some for
Special General Staff studying new plan invasion
of Switzerland under direction Diete recently
in Munich latter reports have stated event invasion of Italy by Allies Germany could not have
large part mountainous frontier held by a nation
which was only advance guard of Allies.

Plans based on surprise air invasion before
Swiss could concentrate in National Redoubt
parachute and air landings troops neutralizes
troops concentration, Deny roads and destroys
critical points. Motorized and mechanized ground
invading forces in order to retain surprise makes
last march considerable distance from frontier.

1:25000 scale map of Redoubt prepared by
Germans have been obtained by 303 agent.

Situation German Army precludes this as
present danger but Swiss alert to possibility.

Legge

ACTION: G-2

INFORMATION: OPD
CG AAF

CM-IN-14129 (30 Jan 43) 1210Z emsi

Distribution	
BS	STRONG
	KRONER
BRATTON	MA
SIT	FL
TIB	CIG
SW	SSB
AIR	FIN
NA	TRNG
FE	POW
GA	PERS
AIC	CC
PUBL	
COLL	
PWB	

CONFIDENTIAL

The rumors about an imminent German invasion of Switzerland were no secret to
Banwell R. Legge, the U.S. military attaché in Bern. However, in early 1943 he considered an attack to be very unlikely. (National Archives, Washington, DC, RG 319)

units, would land near the Swiss frontier and cross the border with the mission to eliminate any personalities that were known to be driving forces of the spirit of resistance. Masson rightly[58] claimed that lists had already been prepared with the names of people who were to be arrested. He said that the surprise attack would be carried out primarily by SS units that knew Switzerland well and had received special training for that kind of operation. Second, in order to capitalize on the successful first stage, a number of mountain divisions that were motorized in an improvised manner would invade the *Reduit.*

In the afternoon of that day, Friday, *March 19, 1943,* at 17:25 hours, a new warning was issued, stating: "*Viking* reports that there is a serious threat. The Führer's headquarters is intensely discussing the urgent issue. No decision has been made yet, but the button may be pushed at any moment. Do not trust negotiations if there are any. An attack may be launched in the midst of negotiations; in fact, experience has shown that this is exactly when it will be launched."[59]

On Saturday, *March 20, 1943,* at 8:30 a.m. *Viking* once again sounded the alarm, reporting[60] that Dietl's Army Group, including the paratrooper and airborne units, had assembled in Bavaria and been placed on a heightened state of alert; all units were to be ready for deployment within six hours. The report said that the opinions among the German Armed Forces High Command diverged concerning the development in northern Africa; in particular von Manstein[61] was said not to expect the Allied troops to immediately cross over to Sicily nor Sardinia/Corsica. Nevertheless, the situation was considered to be serious, and all troops that were slated for deployment in Italy were told to go on stand-by. In that connection, Dietl and Himmler allegedly urged the OKW not to wait and see whether Italy could be successfully defended; instead, *the operations against Switzerland should be launched within four weeks* regardless of the Italian issue. The war economy experts at the OKW were said to oppose rushing things. The report explained that it was Counselor von Bibra who kept pestering Dietl and Himmler to tackle the case of Switzerland right away.

The report by *Viking* was complemented by two additional pieces of information. One of them stated, "It is important to know that an expert on gas has been detailed to Dietl's staff. At Himmler's and von Bibra's suggestion, during the surprise attack on Switzerland, in special areas one intends to *use gas.*" The other piece of news was not less worrisome, stating, "Two days ago von Bibra set up a *special task force* whose mission it is to kill General Guisan shortly before the attack is carried out."[62]

At 16:00 hours, General Guisan received Chief of the General Staff Huber, Colonel-Brigadier Masson, and the head of the operational section, Colonel Gonard of the general staff, to discuss the situation.[63] Based on the various reports by *Viking*, the Chief of Intelligence gave an overview of the situation, explaining that Rommel was about to give up Tunisia and that Italy was undecided. He added:

> German troops are concentrated in Austria and Bavaria. Are they slated for Italy, which would be normal, or are they to occupy a new sector of the European fortress? Dietl's general staff is still working in Munich. What means does it have available? The land forces have been identified with certainty; they include the equivalent of two to three tank divisions and probably several mountain divisions. As for the air force, about a third of the German air force is said to be tied up at the front in Russia. Hence, the threat—if there is a threat—does not seem to be disproportionate to our means, provided that we are not taken by surprise.[64]

Masson pointed out that according to *Viking* the state of uncertainty should be over by April 5. Chief of the General Staff Huber and Colonel Gonard suggested a few additional security measures, with which the Commander-in-Chief agreed.

It took the army command only a short time to establish what measures should be taken.[65] The scheduled operational exercise was postponed indefinitely; the staffs of the army units were to keep a minimum number of heads of service on duty in order to be able to issue instructions for mobilizing the armed forces any time; and the leaves that used to be granted on weekends were to be spread across the entire week so as to have only one out of every seven serving soldiers[66] on temporary leave on any given day. In addition, General Guisan requested that the Head of the Military Department ask the Federal Council's authorization to carry out mobilization exercises with the border troops. During the following critical weekends, the border brigades were to be called up for three or four days each on a rotational basis. At the same time, in an effort to offer the federal government some preliminary information, the Commander-in-Chief told Kobelt that he planned to take three preliminary steps before calling up the border troops or the field army. In a first stage, 60,000 men, including some air force and anti-aircraft troops, some artillery companies at fortresses, and all factory garrisons would be called up in order to protect the armed forces should they have to be mobilized; also, they were to guard airstrips, railroads, and objects that were prepared for demolition. In a second stage, the entire staffs of the army units, border brigades, and territorial commands, totaling 35,000 men, would be called up and transferred to their war command posts. In a third stage, the 35,000 troops stationed in the zone lying outside the *Reduit* would be evacuated.[67]

In spite of the alarm from *Viking*, everyone at the Commander-in-Chief's small office remained calm and composed. Barbey asked himself, "What is the reason for this composure? Certainly not the confidence instilled by the Schellenberg connection (except for Masson perhaps), but the confidence that we have in the 'Viking' connection. Rightly so or not."[68]

It appeared that the army command was right to be confident. On the afternoon of Monday, March 22, 1943, *Viking* was relieved to report:

> The decision at the *Führer's* headquarters has been made. *Switzerland will not be attacked for the time being.* However, in early April—probably not before April 4, 1943—another country will be attacked, most likely Turkey. Due to special circumstances, the name of that country could not yet be determined, but we will know in a few days which one it is. In view of the [limited] German reserves, our informant considers a simultaneous operation against Switzerland to be impossible *as long as Switzerland is ready and makes an attack appear unlikely to be successful.*[69]

Masson informed the Commander-in-Chief that "Plan Switzerland" had been called off and the alert of March 1943 was over, adding, "I am sure that our activities (which have been going on for more than a year) have played a crucial role in this matter."[70] Was that really the case? The available reference material contrasts sharply with Masson's conviction. The OKW's war journal does not contain any indication of a planned invasion of Switzerland. Moreover, Germany's lack of reserve troops—a fact of which its top commander was absolutely aware—was an argument against occupying its neighbor to the south. In early July 1943, shortly before launching Operation *Citadel*,[71] concerning the situation of winter 1942-1943 Hitler was reported as remarking, "[The Allies] would be able to land in Italy and advance across the Brenner without meeting any resistance because due to Russia's breakthrough at Stalingrad Germany *did not have one single man available* to face them. This was bound to result in [Germany] losing the war within a short period of time."[72]

Also, through his research Hans Rudolf Kurz has provided convincing evidence that *in early 1943 the German leadership did not have any intention whatsoever of attacking Switzerland.* General[73] von Butlar, who had been the German Army's first general staff officer and the head of the army operations branch at the OKW staff from January 1, 1942 to November 1944, told H.R. Kurz[74] that

he had never heard about any operation being planned against Switzerland. He
stated:

> My branch processed all operational instructions that were issued at
> the time and undertook the operational studies that concerned the so-
> called "OKW theaters of war."[75] These were the theaters of war where
> combat operations were handled directly by the OKW, i.e., virtually all
> theaters of war except the East. More specifically, they included
> Finland, Norway, Denmark, Holland, Belgium, France, Italy, North
> Africa, and the Balkans; of course the OKW initially dealt with the last
> three theaters only in the framework of the frontiers that had been
> established in the war alliance with Italy.[76]

Hence, von Butlar's operations branch dealt with every theater of the war
bordering on Switzerland; he concluded:

> It is therefore impossible that the authorities drafted any operations
> against Switzerland without my being informed. During the time that
> I was a member of the OKW staff, my branch and I *definitely did not*
> *prepare nor draft any study, nor plan of operations that dealt with*
> *Switzerland in any manner whatsoever.* Moreover, neither Hitler nor
> General Jodl ever—at least not in my presence—mentioned wanting
> to intervene militarily in Switzerland. Once during the Allied landing
> in northern Africa, in connection with the occupation of the remain-
> der of France, there was one brief discussion on how the police and
> customs authorities should monitor the stretch of the Swiss border that
> borders on southern France. However, no operational or tactical issues
> were discussed, only administrative and safety issues on the level of the
> Wehrmacht quartermaster.[77] From a military point of view, during the
> time that I was in charge [of the operations branch,] in my opinion
> there was no objective or event that would have justified a military
> intervention against Switzerland and would have had any prospect of
> success. In addition, when I was a member of the armed forces high
> command staff the means that were required for a *quick* success, which
> would have been indispensable in our situation, were never available.
> In support of what I just said, I would like to mention that studies and
> drafts for an operation against Switzerland that had been prepared
> before I joined the OKW staff were not even presented to me when I
> took over [the operations branch], nor was I informed about them at
> any later point in time. Even if the issue of a military confrontation

with Switzerland had been mentioned in passing, I would have been informed right away about the documents that had previously been prepared. However, it was not until after the war that I found out through books that during the first stage of the war this issue had once been examined, albeit only in a rough outline.[78] Of course I believe that it is possible that economic circles exercised some pressure by threatening to use military means, but that was definitely a *pure bluff* that was not based on any actual preparations by military authorities. A different assessment should perhaps be made of Schellenberg's report and Boehme's plan.[79] In these instances, it is absolutely possible that some bodies outside the Wehrmacht theoretically dealt with an intervention against Switzerland. It is also possible that these bodies presented proposals to Hitler on that issue. However, if such proposals were presented to him, Hitler definitely rejected them or did not think that it was necessary to have the Wehrmacht command verify whether they were feasible. I did not know about the plans of operations for an attack on Switzerland that Hitler, Ribbentrop, and Bormann had approved, nor about Boehme's plan, nor about the OKW studying the case of Switzerland as reported by Switzerland's "Viking line." If such plans existed at all, or if studies were made, they could be prepared only by totally irresponsible bodies that were not involved in the operations command.[80]

The declaration made by the author of the OKW staff's war journal, Helmuth Greiner,[81] corroborates General von Butlar's unambiguous statement. Due to the task with which he was entrusted, Greiner was bound to gain insight into all planning activities by the top German leadership. He told Hans Rudolf Kurz:

As long as I kept the war journal of the German Armed Forces High Command, i.e. from August 18, 1939 to March 17, 1943, as well as in April and May 1943, when I trained my successor at the Führer's headquarters, Hitler and his military advisors *never even considered* occupying Switzerland by force. I am in a position to affirm this with certainty because I was really informed in every detail about any of Hitler's considerations, intentions, and plans.[82] After France's capitulation, occupying Switzerland would not have made any sense anyway, and during the planning stage for the offensive in the West, Switzerland did not play any role, not even during Army Group C's preparations for the attack on Alsace-Lorraine because the main offensive focused on the north and later, in the second stage, on the center of the army. On the other hand, from the very beginning Hitler thought so highly of Switzerland's defensive power and real neutrality that during the campaign in Poland, and also later on, he at no moment in time feared, nor thought possible, that the French could march through northern Switzerland in order to bypass the Westwall to the south.[83]

Hence, there is a sufficient amount of firsthand written evidence available to be able to assert that the alert of March 1943 was not the result of any *real military threat*. Even though the worrisome reports by *Viking* were based on accurate bits and pieces of information, these bits and pieces of information had been interpreted in a wrong way and had been transmitted in a distorted manner.[84] Nevertheless, based on the international strategic situation, Swiss Intelligence did the right thing by taking seriously the warnings that had been leaked to it. It has repeatedly been argued that the Axis powers could not be expected to launch an attack because the Germans did not have enough forces left. Even if that argument was not refuted by the fact that Germany did not invade Switzerland, Swiss Intelligence was not allowed to base its judgment exclusively on that information. At the same time, one cannot help but wonder whether Swiss Intelligence did not work itself up into a state of heightened alert about something that, upon close examination and cool analysis, was less threatening than it appeared to Procurement Office 1 and Masson.

On October 2, 1945, after inquiring with his predecessor about that issue, Federal Councillor Max Petitpierre told Kobelt, "Pilet-Golaz told me that in spring 1943 our General Staff was very worried but that he did not share their concern at the time.[85] He said that Swiss Intelligence had lost its critical mind."[86] The fact that Cuénoud, the head of the Allied Section, did not think of the alert as an expression of a real threat[87] might be an indication that the staff of the Axis Section at Swiss Intelligence had begun to show signs of blind zeal, interpreting the intercepted warning signals with a certain number of preconceived ideas. However, this should not be held against them; the fact that it was the tested and tried *Viking* connection that had sounded the alarm would have induced Procurement Office 1 to take the warning seriously even if the reports had not fit as perfectly into the overall picture of the international strategic situation as they thought they did.

It seems plausible that the bluff surrounding the alert of March 1943 was an attempt to make Switzerland comply more readily with German demands concerning the stalled bilateral trade negotiations. The threat to use military means was therefore part of a war of nerves, as indicated in a report by *Sx* that N.S.1 received in mid-April 1943. On April 14, 1943, Johann Conrad Meyer

In a letter to General Guisan, Chief of the General Staff Huber described Army Intelligence's connections to Germany as "alarm bells." Hausamann, Ernst, and Waibel feared that, through his involvement with Schellenberg, Masson would single-handedly deprive Swiss Intelligence of these alarm bells. (BAr E 5795/327)

was told by an intermediary who was in contact with one of his two main sources on military matters:

> Switzerland is under absolutely no immediate threat. Bendlerstrasse (the OKW) explained that after Ribbentrop's last stay in Italy, in connection with the trade negotiations, Wilhelmstrasse (the Ministry of Foreign Affairs) suddenly expressed the wish to "put ants in the pants of the Swiss." This was done by staging exercises and organizing fake assemblies of troops—sappers and airborne troops—along Lake Constance. There was nothing else to it, nor are there any plans for the future. In the meantime these troops have moved east. Bendlerstrasse says that "even if there were any serious intentions, materially speaking it would remain impossible to attack Switzerland." The informant says that we should go to sleep without worrying because he will find out as soon as there are any intentions concerning Switzerland.[88]

After the war, General von Ilsemann confirmed, "The issue of coercive measures was raised also whenever difficulties arose during trade negotiations between Germany and Switzerland."[89]

Masson ignored these circumstances surrounding the alert of March 1943; in fact, there was no way for him to know about them. He was nevertheless very relieved to see that the warnings did not materialize. Barbey, who saw Masson the day after *Viking* reported that the alert was over, wrote in his diary, "met Masson, who was radiant—more than that, he was moved. He received a *message from Eggen* informing him that *Schellenberg* had said that we should be 'pleased with him.' According to his connection, the threat is gone; Switzerland is no longer 'in the hot seat.'"[90] What convinced Masson to think so? By trying to find the answer to this question, one is confronted with one of the strangest chapters in the history of Swiss Intelligence during those years.

Bringing the Masson-Schellenberg Connection into Play

Considering how competently Masson usually analyzed potential threats to Switzerland, remaining perfectly levelheaded, it is all the more difficult to understand how he handled the alert of March 1943.

On the evening of Friday, March 19, 1943, a few hours after Waibel had reported that the Führer's headquarters was discussing *Case Switzerland*, the Chief of Intelligence called Captain Meyer-Schwertenbach at Wolfsberg Castle to tell him about *Viking's* bad news. He asked him to contact Eggen about the issue the following morning.[91] Meyer noted in his diary, "sleepless night. Call Dr. Wiesendanger to ask him if he has received similar news[92]—he says no. Tell Masson about that."[93]

On Saturday, March 20, Meyer traveled to Zürich. Together with Police Inspector Wiesendanger he went to see Weidenmann,[94] through whom he was able to reach the *Warenvertriebs GmbH* in Berlin at 7:00 p.m. Zürich's Police Inspector took shorthand notes of the telephone conversation. After exchanging greetings, Eggen explained that he was planning to travel to Switzerland within a few days. Then Meyer told him:

After the board meeting with Dr. Berg[95] here [in Switzerland] that had the purpose of putting the firm back on its feet, German shareholders have told us that [in Germany] there is no interest in restoring it to profitability, and that the firm is therefore in jeopardy. Do you know anything about the mood among the German shareholders? And if the reports are true, do you think that there is any means to prevent that from happening? My managers would like to know what you think about that! What do you think about a second board meeting in Berlin? What does Dr. Berg say about his efforts? Please get back to me soon so I can reassure the Swiss shareholders.[96]

Because the telephone line risked being tapped, Captain Meyer used a mutually agreed code[97] to speak with Eggen. In plain language, his message read:

After Guisan's meetings with Schellenberg in Biglen and Arosa, which served to restore the situation in Switzerland's favor, informants among Germany's leadership have told us that Berlin is not interested in keeping Switzerland independent—which means that Switzerland is in danger. Do you know what the German leadership thinks about that? And if the reports are true, do you think that there is any means to prevent that decision from being made? Colonel-Brigadier Masson would like to know what you think about that. What do you think about a meeting between Masson and Schellenberg in Berlin? What does Schellenberg say about his efforts in favor of Switzerland? Please get back to me soon so I can reassure Swiss Army headquarters.

Eggen reassured Meyer, replying, "I have heard only good things so far, there are *no reservations whatsoever nor is there any reason to worry*. Here everything is merry. Regards to everyone."[98] Meyer-Schwertenbach immediately informed Masson about his conversation with Eggen.

In the morning of Monday, March 22, 1943, Weidenmann called Meyer at Wolfsberg castle to ask him to call Berlin in the afternoon. At 3 p.m., two hours before *Rigi* reported that the alert was over, Meyer once again spoke with Eggen over the telephone. The German explained that everything was normal and that he was scheduled to arrive in Basel the following day. Meyer again informed Interlaken about that. At 11 p.m., Masson called Meyer at the Schweizerhof hotel in Zürich, asking him to urgently call him back the following morning from a public telephone.[99] The following morning, Masson told Meyer about *Viking* sounding the all-clear, stating, "The decision has been made, but not against us—*I suppose*[100] *that this is due to Dr. Berg's intervention. Could you verify that with E[ggen]* in order to allow me to report that information to my chief [General Guisan]."[101]

With that order in mind, Meyer drove to Basel to pick up Eggen at the train station. He noted in his diary that during a casual conversation he told his guest from Berlin, "We were informed about the [planned] incursion into Switzerland; . . . yesterday it was decided [to call it off].—*[Eggen] is visibly dis-*

Top photograph: secret meeting at Wolfsberg Castle. From left to right, SS Major Eggen, SS Colonel Walter Schellenberg, Police Inspector Albert Wiesendanger, and the hostess, Patrizia Verena Meyer-Schwertenbach. (Photo from the author's private archives)
Bottom photograph: SS Major Eggen (pictured together with Captain Meyer-Schwertenbach's wife) was Schellenberg's intermediary and was frequently invited to Wolfsberg Castle. Eggen was also received by Federal Councillors Stampfli and Pilet-Golaz. (Photo from the author's private archives)

Left: Heinrich Rothmund, Head of the Police Section at the Swiss Federal Justice and Police Department. Due to the Masson-Schellenberg connection, after waiting for a long time, in 1942 Rothmund finally received a visa for an official trip to Berlin, where SS Colonel Schellenberg invited him to a hunting party at Wannsee.

Right: Wilhelm Lützelschwab, State Attorney and head of the Cantonal Political Police in Basel-Stadt, asserted, "I did not plot against Masson, Meyer, Eggen, etc. but tried to curb their influence." In order to do that, he was in contact with Federal Councillor Kobelt and the Commander-in-Chief, explaining, "I very openly told General Guisan that in spite of all his virtues, Colonel Masson was the wrong man in the wrong place." (Statement as a witness before the Zürich district court, 2 May 1947. Both photos courtesy of Basel University Library)

On April 20, 1941, in Bern, the soccer match between Germany and Switzerland ended in a 2-1 victory for the Swiss team. Nazi propaganda minister Joseph Goebbels was furious that the "little porcupine" (as the Nazis liked to call the Swiss) was triumphant, especially since it took place, of all days, on Hitler's 52nd birthday. Masson had to organize the maintenance of order with the Military Police (in civvies). To the left of General Guisan sat Federal Councillor Karl Kobelt, who had at his left side Minister Otto Carl Köcher, the Envoy of the Third Reich. Between Guisan and Kobelt on a seat higher up sat Masson. (Photo from the author's private archives)

From November 1940 onward, every Friday evening Jean Rudolf von Salis delivered his weekly situation report "Weltchronik" on Swiss national public radio. Professor von Salis' assessment of what was going on in the various theaters of war soon became famous, all the more so because it was rebroadcast over short-wave radio and was followed closely overseas, as well. The instigator of this highly popular radio series was Federal Councillor Pilet-Golaz. Interestingly, von Salis maintained no contact with Swiss Intelligence but managed to keep himself informed through open sources. (Photos from the author's private archives)

Allen Dulles' *Special Passport No. 19102*. *Top photograph*: In this diplomatic passport, Dulles' position is defined as "Assistant to the Envoy Extraordinary and Minister Plenipotentiary of the United States of America at Bern, Switzerland." Once the *Journal de Genève* had announced his arrival in Switzerland, introducing him rather incorrectly as "the personal representative of President Roosevelt," with a "special duty" assignment, it did not take Dulles long to have easy access to Swiss authorities. Masson's deputy observed, "His reports to President Roosevelt are probably considered as important as those by the Envoy." *Bottom photograph*: The passport bears a visa for Switzerland and the entry stamp of the Swiss border control at the Eaux-Vives train station in Geneva, dated November 8, 1942. Dulles was the last American to arrive via that railway route, as immediately afterward the Germans closed the French–Swiss border when they occupied Vichy France. A few hours earlier on that same day, Allied forces had begun Operation Torch, the landings in North Africa. (Photo courtesy of Princeton University Library, Allen W. Dulles Papers, Box 122.)

In November 1942, Allen W. Dulles, the future CIA director, set up a successful intelligence service in Switzerland's capital, Bern, on behalf of the U.S. Office of Strategic Services. (Photo from Princeton University Library, Allen W. Dulles Papers, Box 272)

Top photograph: Allen Dulles at Herrengasse 23, Bern. *Bottom photographs*: Allen Dulles' identity card as an official of the Office of Strategic Services (front and back). It was signed by General William J. Donovan, head of the OSS. (Photos courtesy of Princeton University Library, Allen W. Dulles Papers, Box 122.)

Mary Bancroft (1903–1997) in Bern, 1943. Married to a Swiss, Mary Bancroft was Allen
Dulles' OSS research assistant and mistress. A student of Carl Gustav Jung, Mary Bancroft
became a lifelong friend of Clover Dulles'; their love for the same man was more a bond
than an obstacle. (Photo from Mary Bancroft Papers MC 454, Schlesinger Library,
Radcliffe College)

Allen Dulles in front of Emil and Emmi Oprecht's house in Zürich, where he met Hans Hausamann of *Bureau Ha* once a week during the war. Dulles and Hausamann became good friends and regularly exchanged intelligence of mutual interest. The photo was taken a few years after the war, in 1953, when Dulles visited Switzerland again. At that time, he was already Director of the Central Intelligence Agency. (Photo from the author's private archives)

Swiss soldiers awaiting railway transportation at the start of their customary weekend leave. When early in 1943 Waibel's Viking connection led the Swiss Intelligence Service to assume that Case Switzerland was under discussion at the Führer's headquarters and that a German invasion appeared to be possibly imminent, General Guisan remained cool-headed but decided, "The time has come to prove to foreign countries as well as our own country, through actions, that we adapt our preparations to the latest situation and to any contingency." Among many other measures undertaken, the customary weekend military leaves were cancelled in favor of one- or two-day passes spread throughout the week, so as to have only one out of seven serving soldiers on temporary leave on any given day. (Photo from the author's private archives)

Top photograph: On 28 April, 1944, a German Messerschmitt Me-110 nightfighter aircraft, which was equipped with new top-secret nocturnal plotting instruments and a modern shooting mechanism, was forced to make an emergency landing at the Swiss airfield in Dübendorf. The Führer's headquarters feared that the Swiss would let the British Intelligence Service get a close look at it—which the Germans wished to prevent at all costs. Once again, the secret channel Schellenberg maintained with the Swiss Intelligence Service came into play.

Bottom photograph: After hectic negotiations behind Pilet-Golaz' back, the Swiss agreed to blow up the nightfighter and in exchange got 12 Messerschmitt Me-109 for half a million Swiss francs apiece. Eggen later boasted of his role in this affair when establishing his contact with Dulles' OSS. (Photos from the author's private archives)

General Staff members from three countries talking together in March 1945 in Ascona, canton of Ticino: Swiss Intelligence officer Max Waibel, left, U.S. General Lemnitzer, center, and Britain's General Airey, right, review a meeting with SS General Wolff. Masson bitterly complained about public opinion using different standards for him and Waibel; he said that, due to the contact with SS General Wolff, Waibel was celebrated as a hero, whereas he was harshly criticized because of his own relations with SS General Schellenberg. (Photo courtesy of Princeton University Library, Allen W. Dulles Papers, Box 210)

October 20. 1945

Major Max Waibel
Dorenbach 642
Luzern.

Dear Major Waibel,

Before leaving Switzerland, I want to express to you
the pleasure it has been to me to have known you. You had
a clear appreciation of the realities involved in the great
struggle which has just ended, and a discerning judgement of
passing events.

Your outstanding part in the "Sunrise" operation is now
a matter of public record, and I need hardly tell you how invaluable your assistance was in bringing this important matter
to a successful conclusion. I realise that in this operation
you were always working with a view to the vital interests of
your own country. The part you played in helping to bring about
the early surrender of the German armies in Italy not only
saved many Allied lives and spared North Italy from further
vandalism, but it was also a very real contribution to the
welfare of Switzerland, where I have spent so many crowded
years, both in this and the last world war.

With kindest regards to Mrs. Waibel and yourself, and
hoping to see you again soon,

                              very sincerely yours

                              Allen W. Dulles

Allen Dulles later observed, "Misunderstandings were minimized by the fact that one set of
Swiss intelligence officers worked chiefly with the Germans, and another with the Allies.
Colonel Roger Masson, of the Swiss General Staff, had contact with Walter Schellenberg,
the head of Himmler's Intelligence Service, and Max Waibel and his close associates
consulted with us." In December 1942, Masson was strongly admonished by Chief of the
General Staff Jakob Huber not to "neglect" the Allies. Nonetheless, Dulles himself toward
the end of the war was interested in establishing contact with Schellenberg and Eggen, too.
(Photo from the author's private archives)

In Schaffhausen. Allen Dulles, left, and Laughlin Currie, center, the head of a U.S. economic and trade delegation, meet with the mayor of Schaffhausen, National Councillor Walther Bringolf, right, on February 22, 1945. Bringolf and Dulles had first met in 1943 at the home of Emil and Emmie Oprecht. (Photo courtesy of Ringier Documentation Center)

August 20, 1945, at the square in front of the Federal Palace in Bern, the salute to the flag that marked the end of wartime duty in Switzerland. On the rostrum, from left to right, Federal Councillors Enrico Celio, Karl Kobelt, and Eduard von Steiger, and General Guisan. In one way or another all of them were involved with the Masson-Schellenberg connection during the war. (Photo by Hans Steiner)

On October 4, 1945, Federal Councillor Kobelt reported to Switzerland's House of Representatives on the "Masson Affair." Here he is pictured showing a map drawn by the Germans of Switzerland's railroads. (Photo by Karl Lüönd)

mayed about our being informed; late that evening he admits that [the operation] was scheduled to be carried out on March 25, 1943."[102] That is what the owner of Wolfsberg Castle reported about Eggen's reaction. However, there is reason to wonder whether in this instance Meyer-Schwertenbach's account should be taken at face value. Because it is known today that at that time *Germany had no plans for an invasion of Switzerland,* there is every reason to argue that Meyer misinterpreted Eggen's reaction.

When he told Eggen about Swiss Intelligence being informed about Germany's intention to attack Switzerland, Meyer probably did see a reaction in Eggen's face, but instead of being *dismayed* the German was *astonished.* Eggen had not expected such a revelation, and he tried to think how he should react to it. As it turned out, that revelation unexpectedly made it easier for him to accomplish the mission that had brought him to Switzerland. He probably hesitated because he tried to see how far he could venture forward, but Meyer misinterpreted that moment of hesitation. In an effort to present his superior Masson with the requested confirmation to General Guisan's attention, Meyer unintentionally supplied the SS major with the information that he needed to convincingly play the role that the Swiss had intended for him. Meyer, who had turned rash as a result of the called-off alert, told Eggen that a connection of Swiss Intelligence had warned them about the upcoming invasion but had been able to say only that the operation would take place no later than April 6. Eggen consequently had enough information available to "admit" to Meyer, who was all ears, that the attack had been scheduled for March 25, 1943.

Then Eggen started spinning yarns. He claimed that Switzerland's fate had been hanging by a single thread, but luckily Schellenberg arrived at the Führer's headquarters in time to defend Switzerland's interests. Eggen reported that Schellenberg initially had a tough time, and after Hitler's return he called Eggen to tell him that he believed that everything was lost. It was only due to Himmler's and Ribbentrop's support that he was able to reverse the decision to invade Switzerland.

Captain Meyer was deeply impressed by Eggen's account and immediately called Masson at army headquarters to tell him about it. The Chief of Intelligence wanted to personally consult Eggen on the matter. Meyer and Eggen traveled to Zürich, where Zürich's Police Inspector Wiesendanger was expecting them. At 9 p.m., Meyer left the German in Wiesendanger's company and went to pick up Masson at the train station. He gave his superior a detailed account of what Eggen had told him. Meyer's notes indicate that he and Masson were both in high spirits because they considered that "their connection" had obviously saved Switzerland from an invasion. He wrote:

I congratulate [Masson] on what he [has] done for Switzerland, telling him that the country could never be thankful enough to him. He slaps me on the shoulder and proudly says, "I am not the only one to whom the credit goes for this, Meyer. I know who else is owed the same amount of credit." I tell him that in the last few decades no other Swiss has done as much for his home country as he has. I tell him that Dr. Wiesendanger considers that Masson should receive an honorary doctorate for that—and Peter [i.e. Eggen] and Schelli should be made honorary citizens of Switzerland.[103]

Meyer informed Masson that Eggen had mentioned in passing that Schellenberg would appreciate Masson's sending him a short thank-you note,[104] adding that at the same time he should accept Schellenberg's invitation to travel to Berlin within the next two weeks, where Masson was said to be scheduled to meet Reichsführer of the SS Himmler.[105] Meyer said that the purpose of Masson's visit was "to feel Switzerland out concerning *the sacrifices that it might be willing to make if the Führer publicly acknowledged its neutrality* because now [they had] to continue [their] efforts in order to get things straightened out between the two states, both on a *political* and *economic* level."[106] Masson commented to Meyer that now they were facing the most difficult part of their task, thereby indicating that he was perfectly willing to go on a mission to Berlin.

When Meyer and Masson arrived at Wiesendanger's office, Eggen repeated to the Assistant Chief of Staff what he had told Meyer. Masson thanked the German for his efforts, then called General Guisan to tell him that he had received confirmation of the information about the called-off invasion, explaining, "The disaster would have hit us the day after tomorrow."[107] Meanwhile, Captain Meyer the writer had drafted Masson's letter to Schellenberg.[108] The Chief of Intelligence agreed with the draft and typed the letter from dictation. By that time Eggen and Wiesendanger had left for the Schweizerhof hotel. Later that night the four of them celebrated the connection's successful intervention[109] before discussing the steps that should be taken ahead of Masson's visit with the Reichsführer SS. They deliberated whether it was better to inform the Federal Council or the Commander-in-Chief. Meyer recounted, "We decide in favor of the second option because if the Federal Council does not authorize Masson to travel, the Führer risks becoming furious; Eggen confirms that indeed that is what will happen, adding that that shows that in a democracy it is impossible to negotiate anything in a legally binding manner with one single individual."[110]

The three Swiss among the party did not realize that their German guest was celebrating a different kind of success. To Eggen, the festive mood of the three Swiss confederates proved that Schellenberg had a reliable secret channel available to Switzerland's army command. While Masson and Meyer interpreted the outcome of the alert of March 1943 as convincing evidence of the value of *their* connection to the Reich Security Central Office, German reference material shows that Berlin viewed the line with Masson and Meyer so positively—probably *too* positively—that it believed that there was no need for any other line. A letter that SS Lieutenant General Gottlob Berger,[111] the head of the SS Central Office, wrote a few weeks later to Himmler is an interesting piece of evidence for that fact. Shortly after *Viking* had sounded the all-clear, a retired high-ranking Swiss officer took a private trip to Germany to visit relatives. Franz Riedweg,[112] who dealt with issues pertaining to Switzerland at the SS Central Office, suggested that the officer "use the opportunity to tell some people the truth about the perspective of a neutral and well-inclined country."[113] For that purpose, he organized a luncheon at his office at Grunewald[114] to which he also invited his chief Berger and Permanent Secretary Stuckart. Berger reported to his superior Himmler about that meeting:

> In my opinion, [the retired Swiss officer] is no longer a candidate for a leading political position because he will never make the break from a Swiss Confederate to a National Socialist, no matter how small the break is. This is what I told SS Major Dr. Riedweg in a matter-of-fact and clear manner, and I gave him strict orders to maintain the contact on a personal and friendly level, if possible in an even more cordial manner, but without talking about any political issues. Dr. Riedweg does not know that *we have another promising connection to Switzerland*. I will keep an even closer eye on how Switzerland is dealt with.[115]

Reactions among Swiss Intelligence

Masson and Meyer were absolutely convinced that due to their secret channel to Berlin they had saved Switzerland from a German invasion.[116] However, it did not take long for their enthusiasm to be dampened by everyday reality. On April 8, 1943, when Captain Meyer told his superior, "Peter has informed us that he will arrive next Tuesday [April 13] to transmit the invitation to Berlin,"[117] Masson explained to his intermediary, "This is where the most difficult phase begins of our efforts to build up relations."[118] He said that Kobelt had informed the Federal Council about the meeting in Biglen and reprimanded the Commander-in-Chief. Meyer added, "Moreover, he explains that some officers of his service have threatened to resign if he does not give up the friendly relations with the SS people Eggen and Schellenberg."[119] Masson argued that these circumstances would make it more difficult for him to travel to Berlin, and he would imperatively have to inform the federal government about the trip. Captain Meyer suggested to him:

> If that is the case, next week [you] will have to go and see the Cabinet in the Commander-in-Chief's company to explain the situation, show-ing them the invitation. That will allow [you] to counter every accusa-tion and refuse to accept any responsibility [for] the consequences that the country will suffer if the invitation is not accepted. I envy [you] for being able to defend yourself before the entire Cabinet because [you] have a clear conscience and on 25 March you *saved the country through our relations*. [You are] *no Quisling* because [you] consider Germany's situation as hopeless; everything is just a matter of gaining time.[120]

Masson did not tell his staff member that by making some thoughtless remarks at army headquarters a week earlier Meyer-Schwertenbach had con-tributed in large part to making the connection to the Reich Security Central Office highly contested. In addition to the Federal Council, the opponents of the connection now also included Chief of Security Werner Müller, the head of N.S.1, Major Waibel, and the head of the Axis Section, Major Ernst.

On March 30, 1943, Captain Meyer had gone to see Colonel Werner Müller at army headquarters in Interlaken. In a letter to Masson, the Chief of Security explained:

> [Meyer] was dressed in civilian clothes, paying me a visit from old loy-alty, as he put it. Among other things, he told me about his interven-tion in Berlin in connection with the "Viking" message that you know about. . . . I had an interest in letting the man talk even though I was about to lose my mind. Several things have become clear to me. . . . In connection with the "Viking" matter I have the definite impression that Captain Meyer more or less thinks of himself as the savior of our country, and that he very deliberately plays the role of someone who is supposedly in a position to check if our Intelligence Service works properly and to evaluate its performance.[121]

The Deputy Chief of Intelligence made an absolutely correct assessment of Meyer's state of mind. That same evening, Meyer told other officers at army headquarters that he had no intention of letting anyone transfer him to the *Uto* sub-office; instead, he said that after the successful intervention by "his" connection he definitely expected to be acceptable again in Interlaken.[122]

The day before, when running into Waibel at army headquarters, it was the same enthusiastic state of mind that had caused Meyer-Schwertenbach to tell the head of N.S.1 in Lucerne about the latest accomplishment of the Masson-Schellenberg connection. Waibel later recalled that Meyer had approached him to "congratulate [him] on [his] good intelligence service because the reports by 'Viking' had been correct, as he had been able to verify himself in Berlin." Waibel commented:

> First I did not trust my ears, then I thought that Meyer's explanation about his mission to Berlin was a bad joke. When I realized what had happened, I addressed a serious written warning and complaint to Deputy Chief of Intelligence [Werner Müller]. I pointed out that there was no further need to prove that *Schellenberg* was *not sincere toward Switzerland and consequently not toward Masson either* because Schellenberg had not sent us any warning. It was not until after the fact, upon Meyer's inquiry, that he claimed that due to his intervention with Himmler the plan to occupy Switzerland had been dropped. Of course anyone could say that.[123]

Masson rejected the criticism that Schellenberg had *been insincere* toward him by failing to warn the Swiss; he argued that that had not been the purpose of the connection, stating:

> At no point in time did I expect Schellenberg to supply me with military information, and I most certainly did not expect him *to inform me ahead of time if there was a threat to Switzerland*. On the contrary, we had discussed with Schellenberg about the possible strategic need for Germany to attack Switzerland. For that event, I basically kept telling Schellenberg, *"You will face 500,000 men who are very determined to defend themselves to the last."* I tried to make us look even stronger than we were.[124]

He said that Schellenberg for his part had made him clearly understand that

> . . . if those among Hitler's entourage who were in favor of "liquidating" Switzerland gained the upper hand, he would be reduced to car-

rying out official orders, so I should not expect him to inform me ahead of time of that attack. *In March 1943, I was therefore not at all surprised to have been informed by my "Viking" connection rather than Schellenberg* about the meeting at the Führer's and the threat that was materializing against us. *The goal of the connection with Schellenberg was* to have someone high up who should prevent the Führer from "playing the madman" to our detriment by giving in to his impulses.[125]

What should one think of these arguments? Schellenberg could hardly be accused (the way he was by Waibel) of playing Masson false by failing to warn him in March 1943; there had been no meeting at the Führer's headquarters concerning *Case Switzerland,* as has been shown. However, Waibel did not know that Schellenberg was indeed *insincere* toward Masson and Switzerland by taking credit for saving Switzerland at a meeting at the Führer's headquarters that did not take place. This shows that the circumstances were more complex than the involved persons realized at the time. Waibel and Masson were both partly wrong with their assessments. However, Waibel reached the right conclusion even though the information that he used to support his case was inaccurate,[126] whereas Masson, who was right not to expect any warning from Schellenberg, showed gratitude toward Schellenberg that was unwarranted. All the same, even this last statement should be put in perspective because after his meetings with General Guisan in Biglen and Arosa, Schellenberg did indeed write a report to Ribbentrop's attention that was *favorable* toward Switzerland.[127] Hence, to a certain extent Schellenberg was justified in taking credit for standing up for Switzerland's interests as an independent state—even if he did not do so in the way that he tried to make Masson believe.

In a broad sense, due to his secret channel to the Reich Security Central Office, Masson did have "someone high up who should prevent the Führer from 'playing the madman' to our detriment by giving in to his impulses." However, Switzerland's Chief of Intelligence obviously failed to realize that he had to pay a very high price for having that channel available. Was the price actually too high? Waibel definitely thought so, arguing:

> Himmler might very well be capable of having a personal direct line to Switzerland's army command in order to properly *pull the wool over its eyes* practically with his own hands, and unfortunately he has done so successfully, [adding] based on the issues raised by Switzerland's army command that Eggen and Schellenberg transmit to him, Himmler draws conclusions about the things that Swiss Intelligence knows, the same way that we are able to draw conclusions about Germany's infor-

mation and intentions from the issues that double agents report to us.[128]

Waibel considered that by asking Meyer to verify with Eggen whether the reports by *Viking* were true, Masson had made an *inexcusable mistake with far-reaching consequences*. He explained:

We have obediently told the Reichsführer SS in person that we have been informed about the talks in the immediate entourage of the Führer's headquarters. Now the Reichsführer will do whatever is necessary to prevent our informa[nt] of the "Viking" connection from doing that again. If the informa[nt] is discovered, the lives of several of our close collaborators are lost—through our own fault. That is something for which I cannot take responsibility. What is more, we have uncovered our best alarm bell, once again through our own fault.[129]

Waibel noticed that several of his informants had turned suspicious, fearing that the Masson-Schellenberg connection would be their doom. He stated: "One of our informants who works at the German security service recently expressed serious reservations about SS General Schellenberg's strange trip and the fact that this dangerous man could travel around Switzerland as he pleased and was even received by top officers.[130] This means that German circles also know about Schellenberg's mission."[131]

As it turned out, Waibel's warnings and reservations were absolutely justified. Shortly after Captain Meyer had called Eggen[132] to verify *Viking's* information, one of the key individuals in the connection was arrested on suspicion of high treason and was interrogated for five weeks. Waibel commented, "The only reason why the 'Viking' connection escaped the clutches of Himmler/Schellenberg was the fact that the 'Viking' connection was one of our best-kept secrets. Only two other people in Switzerland besides me knew the names of our brave and spirited 'Viking' people."[133] Moreover, it was extremely important for German Intelligence to know what Swiss Intelligence had been able to find out about Germany. The enraged Waibel consequently described the fact that such information had been given away to an SS leader—the Chief of Foreign Intelligence at the Reich Security Central Office, of all people—as an act of *high treason by negligence*.[134] However, objectively speaking, one must add that there is no evidence that there was a *causal* relationship between Masson verifying *Viking's* information and the *Viking* agent being arrested; the two events may simply have *coincided*. Once the suspect was released, the *Viking* line successfully resumed its activities in favor of Swiss Intelligence. The fact that the suspect was set free could actually be an indication that Germany did *not* think that he had any ties with Swiss Intelligence; otherwise, it would be hard to understand why the Germans spared him from the gruesome torturing techniques that the Gestapo used to apply with a degree of unscrupulousness typical of totalitarian systems trying to extort information from individuals. Nevertheless, this reservation does not change anything about the fact that Masson took a *great risk* by showing such unbelievably excessive trustfulness toward his German partners. It was not until much later that it must have dawned upon Switzerland's Chief of Intelligence what a *faux pas* he had made. Twenty years after the fact, he asked Meyer-Schwertenbach, "What exactly did you tell Eggen or Sch[ellenberg] during the famous telephone conversation that is held against us? I refuse to believe that we asked Schellenberg 'if the situation was serious' and if Switzerland was in danger. *After all, we are not that stupid.*"[135]

Max Waibel considered Masson's action unacceptable, prompting him to threaten to resign from Army Intelligence if the direct connection to the Reich Security Central Office was not immediately interrupted. He remarked, "I believe that it is *a threat to our country*. I may not be able to avert this threat; however, I do not want to trivialize it either by remaining on the staff of Group Id, nor do I want to terribly disappoint those who work with me because they trust me and therefore also trust the intelligence service."[136] The only reason that made Waibel stay with Army Intelligence was the fact that no one else could have stepped in to continue the important job of procuring intelligence from the Axis countries.[137]

For his part, Alfred Ernst, the head of the German Bureau, could not be made to take back his letter of resignation. Two days after the supposed day on which the "disaster" was to hit the country, on March 27, 1943, he wrote to the Chief of Intelligence:

> I am deeply concerned about your telling me that you checked with your German informants whether Switzerland was in danger. I am convinced that people like SS Leader Schellenberg and Eggen *have no honest intentions toward us but are playing a dangerous game with you that is bound to have fateful consequences*. . . . I am ready to resign if the SS leaders, who I think are capable of doing only bad things, continue to exercise any influence on Switzerland's Intelligence Service. I feel obligated to tell you frankly that I will do my utmost to fight against this influence that is fateful to our country, and I am ready to bear the consequences of my conviction.[138]

Masson threatened to sue Ernst before the Military Attorney General if he did not take back his insinuation that Masson had opened up Swiss Intelligence to SS influence. Also, he shrugged off Ernst's serious reservations by remarking, "Your judgment of Schellenberg and Eggen . . . is primarily the result of your negative reaction to everything that comes from Germany."[139] Masson argued that, after seven years of heading Army Intelligence, he knew "all the difficulties that its operations entail[ed]."[140] Moreover, he said that he had not checked with his German informants whether Switzerland was in danger, as Ernst claimed. He stated:

> It is not true that after receiving "Viking's" warning my first reaction was to ask Berlin "whether Switzerland was in danger."[141] *I am not so naïve as to believe that at the last moment even loyal informants would commit such a harmful act to their country.* In reality I notified Capt[ain] Meyer that he should be receiving news from the north these days, and I basically informed him about what we had been told through another special channel. I do not know what exactly this officer said. Besides, he corresponded with a comrade[142] whom he knows well.[143]

When Alfred Ernst realized that the Chief of Intelligence would not change his mind, he asked the Chief of the General Staff for a transfer from Group Id to the Section of Operations, arguing that his "views on fundamental issues differ[ed]"[144] from Masson's. Lieutenant General Huber granted his request.[145] Hausamann and the commander of the *Pfalz* sub-office, Emil Häberli, also considered resigning because of Masson's secret channel to the Reich Security Central Office.[146] However, like Waibel they ended up staying on their posts because they believed that by quitting the damage would be even greater.

Result

Based on the strategic situation of winter 1942–1943 it appeared plausible for German circles to talk about Switzerland and its possible reaction to an Allied invasion. Swiss Intelligence had perfectly good reason not to make light of the warnings that had been leaked to it in March 1943. However, based on the reference material that is available today, it is safe to conclude that the "March alarm" of 1943 was a product of Swiss Military Intelligence's imagination and that in an effort to consolidate the connection with Masson and strengthen the confidence that Switzerland's Chief of Intelligence had in the channel, after the fact Schellenberg and Eggen skillfully managed to take credit for saving Switzerland by making Meyer and Masson believe that they had used their influence among the German leadership to avert the threat of an invasion by the Wehrmacht.

After the war, the two SS officers actually admitted, although indirectly, to pulling the wool over the Swiss' eyes. In addition to the fact that in March 1943 the agenda at the Führer's headquarters was dictated by the events of the war in Africa, the Mediterranean, and at the front in the East, making the topic of Switzerland simply *irrelevant*, Schellenberg would not have had the opportunity to defend Switzerland's interests in what he described as a dramatic meeting at the Führer's headquarters. In spring 1945, Schellenberg told Swedish Count Folke Bernadotte, "Of course I have not seen Hitler for two or three years."[147] In fact Schellenberg had not seen the Führer since 1942.[148] Eggen made a statement that was just as revealing. In 1948[149] he told the U.S. investigating magistrate in Nuremberg, "Acting on Canaris' instructions, Gisevius was the first person[150] who informed Switzerland's General Staff that an attack on Switzerland might be planned. That was after the famous meeting at Wilhelmstrasse [at the Ministry of Foreign Affairs][151] during which the idea of an invasion of Switzerland had been *carefully considered*. I was the second person who arrived in Switzerland; *Schellenberg had asked me to tell the Swiss, 'It was Schellenberg who was able to avert things from you at the last moment.'*"[152] Masson and Meyer-Schwertenbach unintentionally facilitated Eggen's task by virtually urging Schellenberg's intermediary to admit something of which he was supposed to convince the Swiss.

One could argue that Swiss Intelligence's erroneous reports of March 1943 about Switzerland being in great danger had no very serious consequences because they resulted in Switzerland being even more alert and increasing its defensive precautions; hence, the alert of March 1943 contributed, although unintentionally and for no objective reason, to rendering the national defense even more effective. From that point of view, a false alarm was certainly better than a missed alarm. However, for Swiss Intelligence the false alert of March 1943 did have serious consequences, acting as a catalyst of the conflicts that had been smoldering for a long time.

When the staff members of Group Id heard through the grapevine that Masson had used his secret channel to Schellenberg in a highly rash manner, the malaise within Army Intelligence deepened, resulting in an éclat at the Axis Section in the short run and creating a lasting rift among the Intelligence and Security Service in the long run. Instead of showing the necessary mutual understanding and working together, staff members began eyeing each other with mistrust and suspicion. A staff member of the *Pfalz* sub-office recalls, "In 1943-1944 the Schellenberg affair served as an example of the fact that the

German leaders could not be trusted and that *our procurement lines had to be sealed off also from Chief Masson.*"[153] From that moment on, the staff at Army Intelligence were split into two irreconcilable camps, resulting in rivalries, intrigues, and lawsuits that dragged on for several decades after the end of wartime duty. From that point of view, the Masson-Schellenberg connection had disastrous, disintegrative consequences.[154]

11

Assessment of the Connection

IN LATE DECEMBER 1945, a Swiss military investigating magistrate remarked to the Military Attorney General:

> As it turned out, soon an *ugly conflict* erupted . . . among the intelligence officers over the *value* of the Masson-Schellenberg connection. Now that the public also knows about the connection through the polemics in the newspapers, that conflict must make an unpleasant and painfully embarrassing impression on outsiders. Both the defendants and their opponents take credit for making a major contribution to defending the country's interests. It will probably take historians to show some of the things in the correct light.[1]

When making a final assessment of the channel to the Reich Security Central Office, one has to keep in mind that it had some unusual characteristics.

What Did the Masson-Schellenberg Connection Accomplish?

Services Rendered to Switzerland by Schellenberg

On two occasions, in June 1945 and May 1948, Masson made a list of the "services rendered to Switzerland and the Allies by Schellenberg."[2] Five of these services have been mentioned in the course of this study: first, his bringing the *IPA's smear campaign* against General Guisan to an end; second, procuring a *visa* for Heinrich Rothmund, the head of the Swiss Federal Police Section; third, having Swiss Consular Agent *Ernst Mörgeli* freed from custody in Germany; fourth, having German Counselor *von Bibra* removed from his post in Switzerland ("he had to pack his bags and leave for Madrid"[3]); and fifth, in March 1943 *preventing a German attack* against Switzerland, which Masson considered to be Schellenberg's most important service.

The only one of these five services with which Schellenberg can definitely be credited is Mörgeli's liberation. According to a report by Werner Rings, the German Ministry of Foreign Affairs was not interested in Burri's IPA pamphlets,[4] and it is contested to what extent Schellenberg should be credited with having Bibra replaced at the German Legation in Bern.[5] While his supposed intervention in connection with the alert of March 1943 has been uncovered as a *bluff*, the example of Heinrich Rothmund's visa shows how discriminating one must be in judging Schellenberg's role. According to Gisevius, it was German Foreign and Counterintelligence rather than Eggen and Schellenberg that obtained the visa.[6] However, based on the available written evidence it is likely that Masson's channel to the Reich Security Central Office played a part in procuring the travel document. After the war, Meyer-Schwertenbach testified before the Zürich district court that Rothmund had told him that he had been trying in vain to obtain a visa to travel to Berlin. Meyer explained, "I suggested that he arrange a meeting with Eggen at the Federal Palace. He replied that receiving a member of the SS at the Federal Palace was out of the question; the only possibility was for me to invite him and Eggen to Wolfsberg. Once Federal Councillor von Steiger had given the go-ahead, I invited Eggen and Dr. Rothmund to Wolfsberg."[7] About a week later, Eggen told Meyer over the telephone from Berlin that Rothmund[8] would receive the visa.[9] A short time later, the Head of the Swiss Federal Police Section did travel to Germany, where Eggen and Schellenberg hosted him for an extended period of time and took him on hunting parties. However, in November 1943 Rothmund, who felt hurt,[10] told Meyer that "he doubted the connection was that important"[11] because he had not accomplished anything in Berlin.[12] In late fall 1945, Eggen conceded that Schellenberg had intentionally prevented Rothmund from succeeding. Because he "considered that [Rothmund's contacts] overlapped with, and harmed, his own connection via M[asson] to Switz[erland's] General Staff, he saw to it that Dr. Rothmund was received in a very friendly manner by all departments but had to return to Switzerland without obtaining any results."[13] Hence, it is rather pointless to ask whether Rothmund really received his visa due to the Masson-Schellenberg connection.

Another "service" with which Masson credited Schellenberg and Eggen was their intervention in the *incident at Dübendorf*. In the spring of 1944, a German Messerschmitt Me-110 nightfighter aircraft, which was equipped with new top-secret nocturnal plotting instruments and a modern shooting mechanism, had been forced to make an emergency landing at the Swiss airfield in Dübendorf. The Führer's headquarters feared that the aircraft might be made accessible to the British, a contingency it wanted to prevent under all circumstances. Schellenberg and Eggen were brought into the negotiations because they had good relations with Switzerland's Army Command.[14] Behind Pilet-Golaz' back, the two sides agreed on a compromise. Switzerland was willing to blow up the nightfighter; in exchange, for half a million Swiss francs apiece, it took delivery of 12 Messerschmitt Me-109 fighters that it had ordered on an earlier occasion without ever having received.[15] It is possible, although not established, that Schellenberg prevented the Germans from bombarding Dübendorf because Otto Skorzeny had been ordered to make plans for destroying the airfield where the secret aircraft was grounded.[16]

Masson also credited Schellenberg with freeing a Swiss from prison in Fresnes in 1943, England's Major Dodge and U.S. General Vaneman[17] from the Oranienburg concentration camp at the end of 1944, as well as the family of French General Henri Giraud[18] and Geneviève de Gaulle, the French General's niece, in 1945. Moreover, in spring 1945,[19] in cooperation with Carl J. Burckhardt of the International Committee of the Red Cross, the SS officer was said to have rescued Allied POWs and deportees in Germany, including 6,000 French women from the Ravensbrück concentration camp, as well as French politicians Edouard Herriot, the chairman of the Chamber of Deputies, Paul Reynaud,[20] and Léon Blum.[21] Also, Schellenberg reportedly helped delegates of Switzerland's Department of Economic Affairs[22] and other Swiss obtain visas[23] that were impossible or difficult to obtain through regular channels.[24]

This list clearly shows that with the exception of the liberation of Masson's aide Mörgeli, these services did not belong in the realm of *military intelligence* but of *political* discussions and negotiations. However, according to Masson the intelligence service should "not only listen passively; instead, if possible it should try, through its liaison persons, to discreetly influence events."[25]

Services Rendered in Return by Masson

Regardless of whether Masson was authorized and qualified to engage in political discussions and negotiations, one cannot help but ask what services he had to render Schellenberg in return. There are different opinions on that issue. In October 1945, at Masson's request, Captain Meyer confirmed, "The procurement of intelligence through the line with Eggen and Schellenberg did not entail *any official services in return*, [adding] we did not have anything to bring to bear, nor could we bring anything to bear, but the human values of comradeship and gratitude because through their efforts both [Eggen and Schellenberg] proved to be real friends of Switzerland."[26]

Colonel-Brigadier Masson made a similar statement, writing, "One may rightfully ask why a foreigner rendered us such services even though we did *not give anything*."[27] He supplied the answer himself, arguing that what had really mattered were the personal relations. He explained, "It is by looking in each other's eyes, by feeling someone else's loyal patriotism vibrate, by sticking together and accomplishing things that are important to you that you serve your country best."[28] He claimed that if he had paid Eggen and Schellenberg in cash or something similar for their services, Switzerland's authorities would not have raised any objection; however, one tended to forget "that on the level of trust and friendship, or simply respect, nothing [could] be paid with material gains, and that the only reward that [was] important to an officer [was] the moral satisfaction of having accomplished his duty under circumstances that are often difficult."[29] Of course, reality is hardly ever that idyllic. Many years later, Masson actually conceded that Schellenberg may have had other reasons than pure friendship and affection for Switzerland for being responsive to his requests. When Major Hugo Faesi wanted to know what had been Schellenberg's real motivations, Switzerland's former Chief of Intelligence replied that he was not surprised by that question, adding:

> The answer is easy. My first meeting with him took place in September 1942, shortly before the defeat at Stalingrad. Schellenberg belonged to the group of understanding men who wanted to lead Germany out of the war even if Germany had to pay a high price for that. After [the meeting in] Waldshut, did Schellenberg secretly consider the possibility of paving the way, through his contacts with us, for talks with the Allies? It was customary for such talks to be held in neutral countries.[30]

Did Masson forget that on several occasions he had personally tried to establish contact between Schellenberg and Dulles?[31] In early February 1945, Allen Dulles informed Washington about one of these attempts, writing, "Colonel Masson, head of Swiss S[ecret] I[ntelligence] who, as previously reported, has had close contact with his German opposite number Schellenberg, advised that *Schellenberg's envoy [Eggen] was here and hinted he wanted to see me.*"[32] Apparently Eggen had been able to convince Masson that Germany's dogged resistance in the West and rapid retreat on the Eastern front were part of a plan according to which the German Armed Forces intentionally opened up Germany to the Russians in order to force the Allies to give up their demand for unconditional surrender. However, Dulles categorically refused to see Eggen, telegraphing to General Donovan, "Believing that this might be a trap to cause trouble between Russians and ourselves particularly at this junction, I expressed *NO interest in seeing envoy.*"[33] Dulles concealed from Masson that he had actually first established contact with Eggen by introducing Eggen to a member of the OSS in Zürich as early on as the middle of January—a meeting which had even been arranged with the help of Meyer-Schwertenbach. Yet, the Swiss had insisted that the secret should not be divulged to Masson: "In parting Wolf [Captain Meyer] reminded me that everything was between us and *notably that he is not at present telling Masson that he introduced Ecken [sic].*"[34]

Nevertheless, Masson did not give in. In early April 1945, Dulles reported to headquarters in Washington and the outposts in London, Paris, and Caserta:

> Masson, head of Swiss Intelligence, again inquired whether I had any interest in making contact with Schellenberg of German SD [Security Service of the SS]. I replied our interest was unconditional surrender of German forces and that any contact with Schellenberg seemed quite futile. Schellenberg's idea was apparently time worn one of opening west front but holding east front. I told Masson west front was already opened up without Schellenberg's help.[35]

What Were Schellenberg's Objectives?

No matter how many reservations one may have concerning the ambivalent character of Hans-Bernd Gisevius, a *Sonderführer* (special leader) of the German *Abwehr*,[36] his judgment about Walter Schellenberg cannot simply be argued away as an expression of his personal animosity toward the SS officer. In June 1945, he told Colonel Otto Müller:

OSS
Form 69 (Revised)

OFFICE OF STRATEGIC SERVICES

OFFICIAL DISPATCH

DATE 5 APRIL 1945

FROM BERN, SWITZERLAND   1945 APR 6   11   56

	PRIORITY
	ROUTINE

TO

	DEFERRED

OFFICE OF STRATEGIC SERVICES

IN 9477

DISTRIBUTION

(FOR ACTION)	(FOR INFORMATION)
SI	DIRECTOR, SECRETARIAT, BIGELOW, MAGRUDER, FIELD SECTION, X-2

U. S. GOVERNMENT PRINTING OFFICE   16—37103-1

RECEIVED IN CODE OR CIPHER

SECRET

#8137- BERN-WASHINGTON
#9247- BERN-LONDON
#8527- BERN-PARIS
#6297- BERN-CASERTA   FROM 110

MASON, HEAD OF SWISS INTELLIGENCE, AGAIN INQUIRED WHETHER
I HAD ANY INTEREST IN MAKING CONTACT WITH SHELLENBERG OF GERMAN SD.
I REPLIED OUR INTEREST WAS UNCONDITIONAL SURRENDER OF GERMAN FORCES
AND THAT ANY CONTACT WITH SHELLENBERG SEEMED QUITE FUTILE. SHELLEN-
BERG'S IDEA WAS APPARENTLY TIME WORN ONE OF OPENING WEST FRONT BUT
HOLDING EAST FRONT. I TOLD MASSON WEST FRONT WAS ALREADY OPENED
UP WITHOUT SHELLENBERG'S HELP.

MASSON HAD INFORMATION THAT KESSELRING HAS ALREADY ABANDONED
HIS COMMAND AS HOPELESS AND GHALI OF CHICAGO DAILY NEWS HAS
INFORMATION FROM SWISS INTELLIGENCE SOURCE OF INTERCEPTED MESSAGE
FROM FHQ TO GERMAN GENERALS ON WEST FRONT TO ACT ON THEIR OWN
RESPONSIBILITY AS THEY MIGHT NOT BE ABLE RECEIVE ORDERS FROM HQ FOR
SEVERAL DAYS. QUERY: MAYBE, THEY ARE MOVING TO THE REDUIT?

DECLASSIFIED
Authority NND 857134
JT   11/4/86

OFFICE OF STRATEGIC SERVICES
OFFICIAL DISPATCH

REF. NO.

FROM BERN   TO DIRECTOR, OFFICE OF STRATEGIC SERVICES

RECEIVED

SHELLENBERG IS OBVIOUSLY ATTEMPTING TO BUY IMMUNITY AS HE HAS
JUST DELIVERED GEN. GIRAUD'S FAMILY TO MASSON WHO REPATRIATED THEM
TO FRANCE, AND IS APPARENTLY PREPARED TO RELEASE FURTHER WOMEN AND
CHILDREN.

TOR: 0148 6 APRIL 1945

Masson repeatedly tried to put Schellenberg into contact with Allen Dulles. (National Archives, Washington, DC, RG 226, Entry 134, Box 162)

As far as I can tell, *Schellenberg was the most dangerous man in the SS.* As others, he was dangerous because he tried to make a decent and reasonable impression.[37] He was definitely smart.[38] He was extremely skilled in negotiating with foreign countries whenever shady machinations were involved. He was *totally insincere.* The trust that certain Swiss authorities had in him was definitely unjustified. He pretended to be nice toward Switzerland *because it was interesting to him from the perspective of intelligence and because of financial considerations, as the SS was short of foreign currencies.* Moreover, insiders are convinced that Schellenberg intentionally blew up the matter with the aircraft[39] in order to set himself up as the savior of Switzerland.[40]

Gisevius had never met Eggen nor laid eyes on him; nevertheless, he knew, "from 1942 on, during his stays in Switzerland [Eggen] was very interested in my activities. Several sources reported Eggen as inquiring about me. I was being spied on.[41] . . . On other occasions Eggen has also been described as a shady character, for example in connection with the aircraft deal where Schellenberg secured foreign currencies for himself behind the back of the OKW War Economy Staff."[42]

As a close aide of Admiral Canaris and General Oster, Gisevius was an opponent of SS Chief of Intelligence Schellenberg and held him in abomination. Nevertheless, his assessment receives added credibility when comparing it with the independent appraisal of the future head of the Swiss Army's Operational Section and future Major General Peter Burckhardt. In his capacity as military attaché in Berlin, from 1943 on he had met several times with Eggen and had been able to closely follow Schellenberg's activities. As a witness before Supreme Court Justice Couchepin, he conceded, "According to the German officers with whom I had the opportunity to speak in connection with [Schellenberg's] nomination as head of Intelligence and Counterintelligence [in 1944], *on a personal level Schellenberg* has to be considered as *a man of integrity.* He did not seem to have an eye to his own advantage, nor did he lead a dissolute private life."[43] However, Burckhardt believed that this positive trait of Schellenberg's character should not be given too much importance nor be interpreted in a wrong manner. He explained:

Schellenberg appears to be very intelligent and bright.[44] I consider him a convinced National Socialist[45] who is ready to do whatever it takes to achieve his goals. I think that Schellenberg was far more accessible than most other SS leaders . . . when it came to extraditing prisoners because he realized that Germany's situation was becoming more and more difficult, so he tried to keep his country's relations with foreign countries from deteriorating unnecessarily. In my opinion, *his humanity was based less on feelings than on clever calculation and a weighing of pros and cons.*[46]

The Swiss Army's investigating magistrate, Colonel Otto Müller, consequently viewed as "questionable merits" the things with which Masson credited his connection to Schellenberg. Moreover, he was afraid that in return Masson unintentionally had to render two services that were open to objection: first, through his direct contact with Switzerland's Chief of Intelligence, as well as through the intensive correspondence and verbal communication that his intermediary Eggen entertained with Masson and Meyer, Schellenberg was able to satisfy the needs of his own intelligence service "without Masson, who was enthralled by Schellenberg, necessarily realizing it"[47]; and second, Masson made it possible for Eggen to move around the entire country as he pleased, a privilege of which Eggen made ample use. Otto Müller concluded, "Hence, Masson offered Schellenberg a major opportunity by leaving Switzerland to Eggen for his perusal."[48]

It remains to be examined what role Schellenberg and Eggen attributed to the connection with Masson. Both SS officers made statements on that issue that may be considered as fairly credible and show that Masson did not fully realize the implications his secret channel had in the view of the Reich Security Central Office.

In the report he wrote at the time he was held in custody by the Allies in Italy, Eggen mentioned that Schellenberg had two *intentions* in fostering the contacts with Masson and Meyer, explaining:

> As far as I know, Schellenberg, in cooperation with Heydrich and later with Himmler and Kaltenbrunner, used the connection with Switzerland's General Staff and the head of the Swiss Secret Service in an effort to integrate Admiral Canaris' office (OKW Foreign and Counterintelligence) into Office VI of the Reich Security Central Office and replace Canaris. . . . Since he did not yet know Bernadotte, through this Swiss connection [Schellenberg also hoped] to be able to hold peace negotiations with the Allies, thereby appearing as a serious rival of the Ministry of Foreign Affairs, i.e. Ribbentrop; he wanted to replace Ribbentrop with a man who was suitable to the Reichsführer SS [Himmler] should the occasion arise. (I refer to the disputes between von Ribbentrop, Himmler, and Heydrich.)[49]

In November 1946, when he was interrogated for the second time by the Americans,[50] Schellenberg partly confirmed what Masson and Eggen had suspected, stating that he had tried to get to know Masson in order to open up a channel to Germany's western enemies. At the same time, he said that in 1943 in Stockholm he made efforts to also establish contact with the Russians,[51] claiming, however, that he did not really intend to enter into a dialogue with them.[52] Instead, he wanted to use the material that he hoped to obtain through the Russian contacts for his connection with Masson in an effort to strengthen his position with the Allies. Schellenberg explained that to a certain extent Masson and Meyer supported his efforts when they realized that he was using German intelligence to lead his country out of its difficult situation. Schellenberg pointed out that his relations with Masson and Meyer were *important on a psychological level*, explaining that he had felt a need to convince Hitler of the great importance of his Swiss connections in order to forestall the planned invasion of Switzerland. He claimed that he consequently credited *Senner I* and *Senner II* with certain trivial[53] information, using Masson's and Meyer's names to play a subtle psychological game in which he tried to stress the value and reliability of his connections. He said that only those who were perfectly familiar with the situation at the time could understand his strategy.[54] Schellenberg added in handwriting, "The connection in question was the result of my efforts to sort out or maintain the relations between Germany and Switzerland. . . . I had designated it primarily as a really trustworthy line that I planned to use for *political* talks."[55]

As he was Swiss, in the long term Masson had to have a vital interest in seeing the Third Reich fall. Therefore, he evidently had *political* objectives that ran counter to Schellenberg's own interests. All the same, to a certain extent, Masson's medium-term goal of easing the tensions between Germany and Switzerland by trying to make Schellenberg's relations with Himmler and Hitler useful for Switzerland ran parallel to Schellenberg's intentions.

Alfred Ernst, Hans Hausamann, and Max Waibel considered Masson's idea an illusion and opposed the connection all the more vehemently as they witnessed how Switzerland's Chief of Intelligence fully trusted his secret channel to Berlin. However, the research undertaken by Hans Rudolf Fuhrer permits us to conclude that Masson's idea was not as far-fetched as his opponents believed it to be. As head of Office VI at the Reich Security Central Office, Schellenberg realized right away that *Switzerland had a potential value for foreign intelligence.* He knew what opportunities the country offered for the procurement of information. Hence, he appeared to accept the fact that Switzerland was a neutral country; every staff member of Office VI who was questioned in Switzerland on that issue agreed that in dealing with other offices in the Reich Schellenberg had always "very decidedly pleaded in favor of *keeping Switzerland indepen-dent.*"[56] At Nuremberg, SS Major Klaus Hügel, one of Schellenberg's aides, explained that by leaving Switzerland unharmed, the neutral country was to serve as a basis for the activities of Office VI *against* the Allies as well as for entering in contact *with* the Allies.[57] For that reason, Fuhrer thinks that it is possible that Schellenberg supported the order that Admiral Canaris had issued in late 1942 or early 1943, due to similar considerations, forbidding OKW Foreign Intelligence from conducting any spying activities against Switzerland in the future. The SS officer therefore issued the same ban to his offices, as the neutral country had become increasingly important for Germany as a center for intelligence activities and a hub for foreign currency transactions.[58]

Ultimately it is irrelevant *why* Schellenberg responded to Masson's requests; what matters is the *result*—Switzerland was not drawn into the whirl of war events. However, the *risk* consisted of the fact that Masson failed to realize that Schellenberg had different motives for being obliging to him. One is therefore allowed to question Masson's statement to General Guisan, "I was the one who tried to enter in contact with Schellenberg (or someone else), and *I was the one who won the game* (if you really want to reduce the whole story to a 'game of chess') because I gave Schellenberg nothing, whereas he rendered me some major services."[59]

Overall Assessment

With his channel to Schellenberg, Colonel-Brigadier Roger Masson had two objectives in mind. On one hand, in an effort to supplement the results of Army Intelligence, he made the SS officer part of his personal network in order to obtain reliable information about Germany's intentions. It is unlikely that Masson achieved that objective; the decisive information that saved Switzerland originated from the *Viking* line[60] and other connections that *Bureau Ha* and numerous other outposts of Swiss Intelligence had established. Masson's per-sonal connection supplied practically no important information. On the other hand, Masson hoped that the contact with Schellenberg would give him an opportunity to influence the opponent's decisions in Switzerland's favor. The Masson-Schellenberg connection could therefore be described as a *preventive channel.*[61]

It is quite ironic that one of the harshest critics of Masson's secret channel to the Reich Security Central Office, Hans Hausamann, tried to achieve the same objective as Masson, except that he directed his efforts toward Allied headquarters rather than toward Berlin. On November 28, 1944, Hausamann informed Federal Councillor Kobelt that he had "a unique opportunity to establish, through an officer who [was] part of General Eisenhower's immediate entourage, a direct line with Eisenhower's personal staff," adding that this line would be all the more valuable as "the 'liaison of[ficer' was] very fond of Switzerland and [would] consequently do anything he [could] possibly do [for our country]."[62] Hausamann had the same mission in mind for his prospective informant as Masson and Meyer-Schwertenbach had for Eggen. He stated, "The only thing that the authorities would have to do is to create the conditions that would allow the officer in question *to enter Switzerland*, for example via Geneva, *whenever his presence is required*. I could not expect the officer, who travels with Eisenhower's special authorization, to cross the border into Switzerland illegally."[63] It is striking that Hausamann justified establishing a secret channel to Eisenhower's headquarters by using practically the same argument Masson had used to set up his preventive channel to Schellenberg. He argued: "Just to give you an example, if Eisenhower was told that the Rhine Valley in Switzerland would also be in danger in case reservoirs in [the neighboring Austrian region of] Vorarlberg were bombarded one day, which is something the Americans would not necessarily take into account, the connection would be worthwhile. Through the same channel, in a covert manner we could probably much more effectively get the American pilots to respect Switzerland's airspace, and so on."[64]

Federal Councillor Kobelt responded cautiously to Hausamann's idea, telling him: "You know what my position is in the matter of the relations between Masson and Eggen. Since I reject this official connection with one side, it is not easy to favor a connection with the other side, even though I have to admit that the circumstances are not necessarily comparable."[65] He said that consequently he had to leave it up to the head of *Bureau Ha* "to establish the connections that [he] deem[ed] necessary and acceptable to accomplish [his] task."[66]

It appears absurd to play the Intelligence Service's different connections off against one another, as was done after World War II. Every channel had its own merits and special significance, and they complemented each other.[67] Masson's channel to the Reich Security Central Office was not a typical line for procuring intelligence per se; hence, it could not be expected to supply the valuable information with which other lines have been credited. Instead, the connection with Eggen and Schellenberg served to convince the German leadership of Switzerland's determination to remain neutral, as that neutrality kept being questioned by Germany in connection with a few isolated incidents.[68]

General Guisan's meeting with Schellenberg in Biglen and the written declaration that he gave the German in Arosa were part of Masson's *strategy of actively informing* the Germans, (as were Masson's own assertions to Eggen and Schellenberg) that Switzerland was sufficiently prepared to prevent the Germans from achieving an easy success during an invasion. Masson wanted his line to act as a *dissuasive* element, and he partly accomplished that objective. It appears that the head of SS Foreign Intelligence actually submitted a report in Berlin that was in Switzerland's interest, backing up with General Guisan's declaration his impression that Switzerland was absolutely determined to defend its neutrality against any aggressor. On the other hand, it is known today that Masson's strategy did not *actually* contribute to keeping Germany from attacking its neighbor to the south. On the contrary, the written evidence concerning the alert of March 1943 allows the conclusion that Schellenberg did not really "intervene in Switzerland's favor" but made the story up, or at least greatly exaggerated after the fact in an attempt to obtain services in return for an intercession that he had not made.

In addition to these *questionable* achievements, the Masson-Schellenberg connection had some obvious *negative implications*, some of which were more serious than others, reflecting the special nature of the connection. There is no unmistakable proof that in March 1943 Masson actually jeopardized the *Viking* connection by verifying its information with Schellenberg. However, it is incontestable that this incident triggered, or at least exacerbated, lingering tensions and animosities within Switzerland's Intelligence Service. In that respect, Masson's private channel unintentionally had destabilizing and disintegrative consequences. This was due not least to the fact that "almost every officer of the Intelligence Service knew that Masson and Meyer entertained relations with Schellenberg because above all Mr. Masson, who was very proud of this connection, used to talk about it very openly to the Army Staff officers."[69] When he made the unusual revelations about his secret channel, Masson had to realize that other key members of Army Intelligence did not share his enthusiasm about it. At the end of war-time duty, he admitted to investigating magistrate Otto Müller:

> It is true that several of my officers, including Colonel [Werner] Müller, Major Waibel, Major Ernst, and Major Hausamann, protested against the connection with Eggen and Schellenberg. However, I did not share their reservations but considered the connection to be valuable for our country. If I am the one who is responsible for our country's Intelligence Service, I am also the one who decides which connections shall be maintained. No one has been able to give me specif-

ic indications as to my being "misused" by the Eggen-Schellenberg connection.[70]

Nevertheless, in retrospect it is surprising that Masson insisted without wavering on maintaining the contact even though his closest aides were harshly criticizing him because of it. His statement as a witness in the 1947 case of Hausamann vs. Hans Rudolf Schmid and Gottfried Kummer clearly shows that he was not troubled by this criticism. He explained:

> In order to interest my officers in the numerous problems that constantly preoccupied us on the intellectual level during the war, I made a point of discussing them with my subordinates so as to allow them to voice their opinion. In fact, the intelligence service is a special field where it is correct and logical for different ideas to be compared with each other. I personally felt that I was sufficiently in control of the situation to accept that some officers of my service might contradict me. I did not only tolerate such exchanges of ideas but actually encouraged them. That is the reason why I had the opportunity to discuss with Hausamann and other collaborators the principle of my relations with Schellenberg. Hausamann . . . did not share my view on that particular issue. I accepted his point of view even though that did not in the least make me change mine. It is known that other officers agreed with Hausamann. I did not care about that because I had accepted once and for all that I alone had to bear the great responsibility of my task.[71]

Masson was consistent in applying that principle, telling investigating magistrate Otto Müller, "I am used to covering my subordinates. However, I am not used to being covered by them. What I am trying to say is that even if Major [Alfred] Ernst had been in favor of cooperating with Eggen, I would not hold him accountable. I am solely responsible."[72]

Masson's resolution absolutely speaks for his quality as a superior officer and demonstrates how convinced he was about the merit of his connection. However, in this author's opinion it was precisely that resolution that was one of the negative aspects of the connection—even more negative than the destabilizing consequences that the connection had on an internal level at Army Intelligence. Schellenberg was given the opportunity to use the channel for "disinformation" purposes, i.e., there was a risk for the involved Swiss to be lured into a *false sense of security* by the connection.

Nazi Germany was led by an unpredictable man, increasing the chances of even subordinate figures at the Führer's Headquarters possibly exercising major influence on his decisions. Hence, objectively speaking, it was correct to think that the Masson-Schellenberg connection might serve to make Switzerland's determination to defend itself known at the place where the decisions were ultimately made. The idea was also defensible that some contact should be established with the SS, which was gaining more and more power within the Third Reich.[73] It is therefore understandable that Captain Meyer and Colonel-Brigadier Masson were proud of the line that they had managed to set up all the way to the heart of the Reich Security Central Office, and to a certain extent their pride was justified.

Masson had some qualities that helped him get as far as he did. His various assessments of the situation demonstrate that he was an expert on intelligence matters who was able to think clearly and make perspicacious analyses; Switzerland's Chief of Intelligence was not simply a sentimentalist who was guided by his feelings. Moreover, it is proven that he had quite some charisma, was persuasive and fearless, and had experience in dealing with foreign diplomats. Nevertheless, in spite of all these excellent personal and professional qualities, in the case of the channel to Schellenberg, Masson lacked the *mistrust* and *caution* that were indispensable for dealing with such a risky connection. It is part of an intelligence service's "business" to be in contact with intelligence services from other countries, but everyone who is involved in these contacts has to be constantly aware that the other side pursues its *own objectives* with as much loyalty and that views expressed through words or deeds merely *appear* to be consistent with each other.

Both Schellenberg and Eggen had a winsome manner and charisma that Masson could not resist. In his diary, Bernard Barbey, the astute observer at General Guisan's command post, expressed a deep sense of mistrust when speaking about Schellenberg and his obvious psychological influence on Switzerland's Chief of Intelligence.[74] In early March 1943, during a conversation in which Masson spoke enthusiastically about "Schelli," Barbey could not but be silent and wonder. He noted, "I look at Masson, into his bright, slightly squinting eyes . . . and I feel like asking him, 'What in the world has gotten into you?'."[75]

Eggen and Schellenberg took advantage of Masson, who was convinced that through his relations with them he was rendering Switzerland valuable services. They made use of his idealistic and downright naïve belief that his informants from the SS were acting out of the same convictions as he was. Schellenberg did Masson some favors that did not cost him much but made Masson grateful toward the SS officer. However, it was precisely the *personal ties* that made the connection dangerous. Masson should have known about Germany's method of catching its opponents by surprise; instead, he uncriti-

262   SECRET CHANNEL TO BERLIN

cally and almost blindly accepted everything that came from "Schelli" and Eggen as being true. *The SS leadership could therefore unscrupulously misuse his excessive trustfulness.* At that time it was no secret that the SS leadership was fully capable of such methods. In the event of an attack on Switzerland, this excessive trustfulness could easily have been exploited to pull the wool over the eyes of the head of Swiss Military Intelligence at the decisive moment. Optimists may argue that Masson would not have let the Germans outwit him because he trusted the warnings issued by the *Viking* connection. However, that argument becomes rather shaky when one recalls that Masson sought to substantiate *Viking's* information through Schellenberg while continuing to rave about him. Moreover, Masson's willingness, in 1943, to consider holding political talks with Himmler shows that the Germans knew how to exploit their connection with Masson in order to ask for, and obtain, services in exchange for "services" that they had not rendered at all.

There was yet another reason why it was dangerous for Masson to insist on keeping up the contact with Schellenberg. In early January 1944, Hausamann met with Allen Dulles. In a note for the file that he wrote the same day, the head of *Bureau Ha* stated:

> [Dulles] informed me that the situation concerning Brigadier General Masson had taken a serious turn for the worse. He said that everywhere in Germany people could be bribed, even the top people at the party, the Wehrmacht, and Foreign Affairs. He explained that everything could be had these days and that not everything that the Germans offered was accepted anymore. There is written evidence from Berlin that through his line (Eggen-Schellenberg-SS leadership) Masson has been supplying Berlin with information that is very damaging to the Allies.[76]

Hausamann reported Dulles as saying that the Anglo-Saxon governments were about to lodge protests about the matter. He also wrote that Dulles had told him that "Masson had approached England's and the United States' military representatives to ask them whether they had any objection to his connection with the SS. Of course they gave him an evasive answer, but behind the scenes Masson's move was described as an *unparalleled act of naïveté*."[77]

Masson later justified taking the risk of establishing the connection with Schellenberg by claiming that there was a need to strengthen Germany's confidence in Switzerland's neutrality, which had been shaken because of the files found in France concerning the cooperation talks between the Swiss and French army commands. In 1962, he admitted to his former courier Holzach,

"I was *pushed into making this contact* (or another equivalent contact) because of the lamentable affair of 'La Charité-sur-Loire,' [adding] for twenty years I have never referred to this affair, which created violent reactions in Germany because it seems obvious that no similar move had been made in cooperation with the Wehrmacht.[78] Hence, Guisan had acted *unilaterally*, thereby *seriously infringing the principle of neutrality*."[79] Several weeks later he told Meyer-Schwertenbach that *La Charité* had been his "main reason"[80] for establishing the connection that he ended up maintaining with Schellenberg. However, there is written evidence that puts Masson's argument in perspective, showing that even before the affair of *La Charité* he was using his personal network to actively dissuade potential aggressors from laying hands on Switzerland. This written evidence was revealed to outsiders as a result of a mishap that occurred at the beginning of the war within Masson's personal network and that became known as the *Fonjallaz affair*. One of Masson's informants, Arthur Fonjallaz,[81] turned out to be a *German agent* who had kept Masson's orders on file.

According to Masson, he and Colonel Fonjallaz were "comrades, actually friends."[82] The two men had met in February or March 1939 during a chance encounter on a train ride from Bern to Lausanne. He said that during their first conversation Fonjallaz had mentioned that he occasionally traveled to Germany and Italy. Masson later could not remember whether he was the one who had suggested that during his travels Fonjallaz gather information on behalf of Switzerland or whether Fonjallaz had offered his services to him. In any case, Fonjallaz carried out a number of missions for Masson in Germany and Italy, about which he reported in writing to the head of Section 5 and for which he received a compensation of about 1,000 Swiss francs. Fonjallaz did not receive any general order to procure intelligence that would have authorized him to set up a network with subagents; instead, Masson entrusted him with what he called "systematic special missions." Whenever Fonjallaz went on a private business trip to Germany, Masson asked him "to go through certain specific locations and see whether he noticed anything suspicious, such as movements of troops or fortifications."[83] In addition, Fonjallaz was to make use of his contacts in the Third Reich to answer persistent rumors according to which Switzerland would give up its neutrality and join forces with the French if necessary.

Masson wrote several letters to Fonjallaz, asking him for information pertaining to the German military. On October 25, 1939, he asked him to gather information on the number of troops that the Germans had available and how many of them were stationed in southern Germany in the area between Munich and the Swiss border; moreover, he gave him general instructions, stating: "Should you have the opportunity to meet with important or influential personalities, you would render our country a great service by denying all the false information that has been spreading about our lack of neutrality. We are more than ever determined to fight against anyone who infringes our territory."[84]

In January 1940, when Fonjallaz was arrested in Schaffhausen on charges of working as a *double agent*, the police found several of Masson's letters in his suitcase, including the one dated October 25, 1939. Fonjallaz tried in vain to talk his way out of getting arrested by claiming that he wanted to go through the documents one more time before leaving them in a baggage locker at the train station in Schaffhausen while traveling in Germany.[85]

The Fonjallaz case clearly demonstrates that as early as *before the outbreak of the war*, i.e. at a time when the affair of *La Charité* was not yet discussed, Masson meant his intelligence service to be an *instrument for actively dissuading* foreign countries from taking any military action against Switzerland rather than an organization that merely gathers information concerning these foreign countries. With this concept, which was in fact nothing less than what is now commonly called "track two diplomacy,"[86] Masson went way beyond his terms of reference as Chief of Intelligence. Track two diplomacy refers to any informal and unofficial contacts that go beyond the formal intergovernmental relations (track one). To put it in John W. McDonald's and Diane B. Bendahmane's words:

> [Track two diplomacy] is interaction between private citizens or groups of people within a country or from different countries who are outside the formal governmental power structure. These people have as their objective the *reduction or resolution of conflict*, within a country or between countries, *by lowering the anger or tension or fear that exists*, through improved communication and a better understanding of each other's point of view. *Track two diplomacy is not a substitute for track one, but rather is in support of or parallel to track one goals.*[87]

Masson's efforts at conducting track two diplomacy inevitably resulted in a lasting conflict with Switzerland's Department of Foreign Affairs because there was no superior authority that could coordinate track one and track two diplomacy and see to it that their goals did run parallel to each other. Moreover, in his analysis of the strengths and weaknesses of track two diplomacy, Landrum Bolling rightly remarks, "Amateurs can cause trouble. First among the limitations of the informal approach is the danger of amateurism."[88] Pilet-Golaz repeatedly criticized Masson because he used self-appointed informal diplomats who, to put it in Bolling's terms, "often have an imperfect understanding of

Lt.colonel R. MASSON   Q.G., 25.10.39.

                Monsieur le colonel A. F o n j a l l a z ,

                                                   C u l l y .
                                              Chalet du Rivage

Mon colonel,

            J'ai eu l'honneur de recevoir votre aimable lettre du 24.10
dont je vous remercie. Je suis notamment heureux que vous ayez bien voulu
me signaler votre prochain voyage. N'étant pas libre vendredi soir, nous ne
pourrons malheureusement pas nous rencontrer à Berne, comme vous me l'avez
proposé; ce que je regrette vivement.

            Présumant que vous ferez le voyage en train, il m'est dif-
ficile de vous charger d'une mission spéciale. Il nous intéresserait cepen-
dant d'apprendre quelle est la densité des troupes entre la frontière suisse
et Münich (si possible composition et identification) et plus généralement
d'être informé sur l'état d'esprit et matériel de la population, ainsi que
sur les divers courants politiques en Allemagne. Le bruit a récemment couru,
notamment dans le sud de ce pays, que la Suisse ouvrirait ses frontières à
une armée française et même se joindrait à cette dernière en vue d'une action
commune contre l'Allemagne. Inutile de répéter tout ce qu'il y a de faux
dans cette nouvelle; en revanche, il serait intéressant de savoir si de tels
bruits sont répandus " consciemment " par certaines autorités ou milieux
officiaux, ou s'il s'agit simplement d'un des nombreux aspects de la campagne
de propagande.

            Si vous deviez avoir l'occasion de rencontrer des personnages
importants ou influents, vous rendriez à notre pays un grand service en
démantant toutes les fausses nouvelles qui ont couru au sujet de notre manque
de neutralité. Nous sommes plus que jamais décidés à lutter contre n'importe
qui violerait notre territoire.

            Veuilles agréer, mon colonel, l'assurance de mon respectueux
dévouement.

                                              Masson

Masson considered that the task of his Intelligence Service was not only to keep an eye
on what was going on abroad but also to actively dissuade foreign countries from taking action against Switzerland. He used every opportunity to spread the word in
Germany that Switzerland was determined to "fight against anyone infringing our territory." (Document from the author's private archives)

official policies and foreign policy objectives per se. They may not really understand what their own government is doing and why."[89]

Masson interpreted Pilet-Golaz' criticism as disapproval of his idea of a *strategic intelligence service* that would not focus exclusively on purely military issues but would also deal with political, economic, psychological, and ideological issues. There is no doubt that Masson's idea was correct, but it would have been advisable to divide up the tasks between the Department of Foreign Affairs and Army Intelligence. However, Masson did not fully realize that his detrimental dispute with the Department of Foreign Affairs was due at least to the same extent to Pilet-Golaz' taking exception to Masson *actively* intervening, viewing it as *interference* in his own area of activity. Switzerland's top diplomat was all the more annoyed about that interference as he clearly recognized the dangers that it entailed. Bolling rightly asks, "To what extent is a *track two diplomat* really carrying a serious message from one government to another?"[90] In the case of the now famous John Scali,[91] matters were very clear; his role was recognized by both parties. Masson, however, did not have any official mandate to conduct track two diplomacy. Moreover, as Bolling remarks, "Informal diplomats are often vulnerable to *manipulation*, sometimes gross manipulation for *disinformation* purposes."[92]

In retrospect, one cannot but acknowledge that the Federal Council as a whole, and Federal Councillors Kobelt and Pilet-Golaz in particular, were more aware of the risks involved in track two diplomacy than Masson was. The federal government was justified in being *skeptical*, and ultimately *indignant*, about Masson actively using the intelligence service for strategic purposes, the way he did through the connection with Schellenberg. It is indeed disturbing to see that through such relations, *a chief of intelligence personally intervened in his country's foreign policy* without previously consulting with, nor obtaining the approval of, the Federal Council. In addition, Army Intelligence should have handled *humanitarian efforts* aimed at freeing POWs, especially individuals with a political background, in cooperation with the federal government rather than presenting the efforts as a *fait accompli*. However, the government, and in particular the Department of Foreign Affairs headed by Pilet-Golaz, has to accept some of the blame for *Army Intelligence's interference in political matters*. The tensions between the two bodies, which put a great strain primarily on Army Intelligence's German Bureau and later also on its Axis Section, were undoubtedly one of the main reasons why Masson became involved in relations such as the ones with the Reich Security Central Office to begin with. If Army Intelligence and the Department of Foreign Affairs had managed to build a trusting relationship by *working together*, i.e. by organizing regular *joint* meetings in cooperation with other involved bodies, Masson would have had no reason for *actively becoming involved in politics*, which ultimately forced him to leave Army Intelligence under regrettable circumstances at the end of the war. The ugly rumbling noise accompanying his departure, followed by the public debate of the *Masson affair*, made many people forget that he had not only been entertaining a risky connection of which he never fully realized the implications but had also been *in charge of building up Swiss intelligence virtually from ground zero and turning it into a large, efficient structure*. The Federal Council, particularly Foreign Minister Pilet-Golaz, have to take a major share of the responsibility for making Masson's secret channel to Berlin a stumbling block that caused the fall of Switzerland's Chief of Intelligence.

12

Epilogue

AT THE END OF THE WAR, while he was in Bregenz helping a medical service column get from Vorarlberg into Switzerland, Eggen heard that the German Army Police had orders to blow up the bridges across the Rhine at Höchst and St. Margrethen should Allied troops approach that area. During the preceding days, Eggen had evacuated numerous Swiss returnees across these bridges. He informed Switzerland's territorial command about the order to the German Army Police, whereupon Swiss sappers commanded by Major Eggen of the *Waffen SS* removed the mines with which the bridges had been charged on the German side of the border. When German Army Police moved in, Eggen and the sappers retreated onto Swiss territory.

The Swiss commander in charge of the sector to which the border area belonged informed Masson—who in his capacity as Assistant Chief of Staff Id also headed the territorial service—by telephone about Eggen saving the bridges from being demolished. Masson invited the German to Bern in order to personally thank him. However, while Germany was disintegrating, Switzerland continued to be under the rule of law. Because Eggen did not have a visa for Switzerland,[1] two police officers accompanied him to Bern, where he was locked up in the prison of the Security and Criminal Police while waiting to be expelled. Masson had no power to dispose of Eggen there; nevertheless, he frequently visited him at the prison to keep him company. May 8, 1945, came around and the guns were finally silent in Europe. Colonel Werner Müller, who was head of the Security and Criminal Police of the city of Bern in his civilian career, desperately tried to find the Chief of Intelligence at Army Headquarters in Interlaken to inform him about the armistice. Masson later recalled with gallows humor: "[Müller] did not know that his chief was at his own prison. . . . When I left that somber place, I was told that World War II was over."[2]

A short time later, the Swiss Attorney General's Office picked Eggen up from the prison to temporarily intern him at the *Gasthof zum Kreuz*, an inn in Weier near Affoltern in the Emme Valley.[3] However, before Eggen could leave the country,[4] the Army's legal authorities instituted proceedings against him. On May 26, 1945, he was once again put under arrest. Hence, the Attorney General's Office no longer had any discretionary power over him. Even though it was established that Eggen had been in contact with members of German Intelligence in Switzerland, particularly Daufeldt,[5] making him a suspect, the investigation by the military courts did not yield any incriminating evidence. Hans Hausamann repeatedly intervened with various authorities to have them extend the scope of the investigation, but on September 11, 1945, the Military Attorney General decided to abandon the proceedings. Nevertheless, Eggen was kept in custody and put at the disposal of the Attorney General's Office, which, on September 15, 1945, interned him at the district penitentiary in Zürich. On September 29, 1945, Attorney General Stämpfli ordered that Eggen be released from prison and expelled. Two days earlier, Paul Ghali's interview with Switzerland's Chief of Intelligence had triggered the Masson affair.[6] In order not to create a stir, over the telephone the Attorney General's Office ordered Major Josef Wüest of the military courts to do whatever was necessary to have Eggen expelled. Wüest contacted the U.S. Consulate in Zürich, which in turn made arrangements with U.S. authorities in Italy and subsequently informed Wüest that Eggen could be extradited to the Allies on October 1.[7] Eggen left Switzerland three days before Federal Councillor Kobelt reported on the Masson affair.

Masson also made efforts during the years following the war to assist Eggen and Schellenberg, arguing, "Even if during the war of 1939 to 1945 our tough job forced us to primarily keep our eyes wide open to a great number of events abroad, it did not prevent us from closing them whenever feelings could matter more than reason."[8] However, that attitude made him a target for harsh criticism. Whereas Hausamann, Waibel, and Otto Pünter were commended throughout the country for running Bureau Ha, setting up and maintaining the *Viking* connection, and working as secret agent *Pakbo*, respectively, in fall 1945

On peut se demander pour quelles raisons Schellenberg
donna la preuve manifeste d'un esprit et d'un coeur gé-
néreux? Si son action humanitaire n'avait commencé qu'en
1945,alors que la guerre précipitait la défaite de l'Allemagne,on pourrait le suspecter d'avoir peut-être cherché
à se ménager la bonne grâce des vainqueurs.Mais cette attitude désintéressée,je l'ai déjà constatée personnellement
en 1942,avant Stalingrad,c'est à dire à une époque où la
plupart des Allemands croyaient encore en leur victoire.
Et c'est en 1941 (alors que l'Allemagne était encore toute
puissante) que Eggen m'avait dépeint Schellenberg tel que
j'appris par la suite à le connaître.

Sur le plan politico-militaire,je savais dès 1943 que
Schellenberg cherchait une solution pour obtenir un com-
promis permettant à l'Allemagne de "sortir de la guerre".
Mais,comme je l'ai relevé plus haut,il avait des adversai-
res farouches et il est probable qu'il rencontra de séri-
eux obstacles,qui l'empêchèrent de faire percer ou admettre
ses conceptions personnelles.En particulier,j'étais au courant des tentatives faites par Schellenberg pour chercher
le contact,vers la fin de 1944,avec M.Dulles,chargé d'une
mission spéciale à Berne,par le Président des Etats-Unis.

Je n'ai plus rien su de Schellenberg,de mai 1945
jusqu'à ce jour.Je n'ai jamais eu l'occasion de faire quel-
-que chose pour lui,en reconnaissance de tous les services
qu'il nous a rendus avec un désintéressement certain.

Je suis heureux,comme officier suisse,de pouvoir lui
rendre aujourd'hui,le témoignage de la vérité concernant
son attitude à l'égard de la Suisse.

R. Masson

Sous-chef d'état-major
de l'armée suisse (1942-1945)

(Colonel brigadier R. MASSON)

*Je confirme l'exactitude
de la présente déclaration
notamment en ce qui
concerne les services rendus
à la Suisse par W. Schellenberg. —*

Le Général Guisan

Gén. Guisan

— 10 mai 1948. — ancien Chef de l'armée 1939–1945 —

At the Nuremberg war crimes tribunal Schellenberg got away with a mild prison sentence, benefiting from a detailed statement that Switzerland's former Chief of Intelligence had written in his defense. At the end of the document, General Guisan confirmed in hand-writing that "W. Schellenberg [had] rendered some services to Switzerland." (Document at the National Archives in Washington, DC, RG 238 M 897 R 114)

Masson was forced to resign as Chief of Intelligence because of his unusual connection to the Reich Security Central Office. At his own request, he was suspended from his post and tried to establish himself in private business. However, his health had suffered as a result of his straining himself during the years of wartime duty, and the unpleasant disputes in the parliament, in public, and in court were a heavy blow for him. As a consequence his new career never got off the ground; instead, after turning half-blind, in 1947 he had to go into early retirement at the age of 53.

Captain Meyer successfully returned to writing novels under his pen-name Wolf Schwertenbach. Nevertheless, he too did not get away from the connection that he had established with the SS. As late as the 1960s, he had to take Eggen to court after the latter had tried to extort a quarter of a million Swiss francs from him after being ruined in Germany by bad management. Meyer-Schwertenbach finally realized "what kind of person [Eggen] really was," admitting to Masson that the three lawsuits in which the German got him involved and all of which Eggen lost spoke for themselves.

In 1949 in Nuremberg, in the so-called *Wilhelmstrasse* trial, Schellenberg was found guilty of crimes against humanity and of belonging to a criminal organization, the SS. The six-year prison sentence passed down to him was generally viewed as *lenient*. As early as December 1950, he was released from prison for health reasons. Even though he was only forty years old, he was terminally ill and broken. In 1951 he turned to Masson for help, so Masson referred him to a doctor in Fribourg. However, Switzerland's authorities got wind of his presence and put him on the national wanted list, which Masson had no way of preventing. Italy ended up granting Schellenberg a residence permit and he moved to Pallanza on the western shore of Lago Maggiore, some 25 kilometers south of the Swiss border, where he spent the last months of his life writing his memoirs. In these memoirs, he dedicated merely a few lines to the connection with Masson, from which he had benefited at Nuremberg[9] and which had once again turned out to be useful to him after his release from prison. Is this a reflection of the *relatively small* significance that Schellenberg attached to the channel to Bern in the framework of the entire intelligence service that he headed?

Masson had a completely different perception of the channel. After the war, in his presentations and during conversations at the annual commemorative meetings with Cuénoud and his staff of the French Bureau and the Allied Section, "the discussion always revolved around [the story of his connection with Schellenberg]; he got more and more obsessed with it and kept insisting as if this was the key to the history of his Intelligence Service."[10]

On March 29, 1952, after Masson had made a presentation at Châtel-St-Denis, canton Fribourg, a priest asked to speak with him, explaining that he had just arrived from Turin to bid him farewell from Schellenberg. The priest stated: "[Schellenberg] died yesterday. I was his confessor. Based on what he confided to me under the seal of secrecy, I know all the things he did for Switzerland."[11] Was this the final move of a sly chief of intelligence, or was there perhaps more to it than that? In any case, this is how the history ended of the connection with the man whom Masson and Meyer insisted, until the end of their lives, on considering solely as a selfless friend of Switzerland.

Notes

In Switzerland there are four official languages, and it is standard practice that, even though everyone speaks and writes in their own mother tongue, they can count on being understood by their fellow countrymen who have a different mother tongue. Hence, most of the documents of Swiss origin cited hereafter were written in either German, French, or Italian. For the original wording of those citations where only an English translation is given, readers are kindly advised to refer to my book *Geheimer Draht nach Berlin*.

Regarding the military ranks used in this book, the reader should bear in mind that Swiss terminology is being used and that, for example, *Colonel-Brigadier* in Swiss military terminology in fact corresponds to the rank of *Brigadier General* in U.S. military terminology. It is a Swiss peculiarity that the title "General" is only accorded to the Commander-in-Chief of the Swiss Armed Forces, and only so in times when the whole Army has been mobilized (which to this day has only happened four times—during the crisis of 1848, 1870–1871, and two World Wars). Therefore, in Switzerland a three-star general is called a *Colonel-Corps-Commander*, a two-star general holds the title of a *Colonel-Divisional-Commander*, a one-star general equals a *Colonel-Brigadier*. Until much after World War II it was customary to use "Colonel" without specification. Even in the minutes of the Swiss Government, Masson is therefore often simply referred to as "Colonel," although the Chief of Military Intelligence held the rank of a Colonel-Brigadier. Nevertheless, Masson was correct in seeing himself as being of equal rank to General Schellenberg.

Unless stated otherwise, italics in cited documents are those of this book's author.

Preface

1. The controversies about incomplete or distorted intelligence prior to the 2003 war in Iraq may well develop into a new case in point—not only with regard to the governments launching it but also with regard to the Iraqi dictator provoking it. One could argue that Saddam Hussein's policy of hampering the work of UN weapons inspectors was based on the assumption that the United States and its Allies would ultimately refrain from using military means, which was obviously an assumption based on insufficient intelligence on the intentions of the U.S. or inadequate use of it.
2. Christopher Andrew and David Dilks, eds., *The Missing Dimension: Governments and Intelligence Communities in the Twentieth Century* (London, 1984).
3. Richard Wilmer Rowan, *The Story of the Secret Service* (Garden City, NY, 1937).
4. Because an intelligence service comprises both the *secret* (hence, mostly illegal)

collection of data—i.e. espionage—and the evaluation of *open source* material. Of course the secret service this book deals with has nothing to do with the U.S. Secret Service, whose function it is to protect the President, even though the U.S. Secret Service obviously also relies on intelligence concerning potential threats.

5. Cf. a statement by historian Adolf Gasser from Basel in 1983: "Most of the time, historians are barred from the sphere of the secret service. Its agents have made a commitment whenever possible not to put anything in writing and to keep silent to the end of their lives. Therefore, they almost always act in the dark, leaving room only for suppositions that cannot be verified whenever anyone catches a glimpse of their activities. *Hence, it is better for scholars to stay away from this entire subject.*" (Professor Gasser did not lack personal experience; during World War II, he had been in contact with Swiss Intelligence and met Rudolf Roessler, alias "Lucy," among others, in person.) Quoted in Adolf Gasser, *Ausgewählte Schriften 1933–1983* (Basel/Frankfurt a.M., 1983), 226.

6. At least so long as one can expect politicians to behave in a rational manner.

7. William R. Harris, *Intelligence and National Security: A Bibliography with Selected Annotations* (Cambridge, MA, 1968). Quoted in George C. Constantinides, *Intelligence and Espionage: An Analytical Bibliography* (Boulder, CO, 1983), 12.

8. David C. Martin, *Wilderness of Mirrors* (New York, 1980).

9. See the "Available Source Material" section and the detailed list of consulted source material at the end of this volume.

Chapter 1: The "Masson Affair"

1. *Der Bund*, 26 September 1945, no. 449 (morning edition). At that time, major newspapers were published and delivered to subscribers twice a day, the *Neue Zürcher Zeitung* even three times a day in the form of a morning edition, a midday edition, and an evening edition.

2. *Der Bund*, 26 September 1945 (morning edition).

3. Statement by National Councillor Eugen Dietschi (Basel) as recorded in National Council 1945 shorthand bulletin, 641.

4. *Der Bund*, 28 September 1945, no. 454 (evening edition). Eggen is misspelled "Egger" in the agency report.

5. *Der Bund*, 29 September 1945, no. 455.

6. Name of the Swiss government. The Federal Council consists of a team of seven members who all have the same status; parliament elects one of them to the annually rotating presidency according to the principle of seniority.

7. *Der Bund*, 29 September 1945, no. 455.

8. See the indictment by Albert Züblin at the Zürich district court concerning Hans Hausamann vs. *Die Tat*/Dr. G. Kummer, correspondent for domestic affairs, 7 July 1947. BAr J.I.121/63.

9. Hans Rudolf Kurz, *Nachrichtenzentrum Schweiz* (Frauenfeld, 1972), 122, note 88.

10. Georg Kreis, *Zensur und Selbstzensur* (Frauenfeld, 1973), 292.

11. Concerning Masson's attitude in press-related matters, see diary entries on June

15 and 21, 1940, in Bernard Barbey, *P.C. du Général* (Neuchâtel, 1948), 18, 22.

12. In a decree dated September 8, 1939, the Federal Council asked the Commander-in-Chief of the Armed Forces to monitor publications as well as information and statements transmitted especially by mail, telephone and telegraph, the press and news agencies, on the radio, and in films and photographs. The Commander-in-Chief ordered the Press and Radio Section (PRS) to carry out the monitoring activities. On February 1, 1942, the PRS was put under the supervision of the Federal Justice and Police Department. On that matter, see "Tätigkeitsbericht der Abteilung Presse und Rundfunk," *Bericht des Generalstabschefs*, 433–462, and Christoph Graf, *Zensurakten aus der Zeit des Zweiten Weltkrieges: Eine Analyse des Bestandes E 4450, Presse und Rundspruch 1939–1945* (Bern, 1979).

13. Kreis, *Zensur und Selbstzensur*, 292.

14. Kreis, *Zensur und Selbstzensur*, 292. For example, in a cover letter for a report dated March 20, 1940, Masson remarked, "I continue to believe that certain Swiss newspapers lack objectivity, which our neutrality imposes on us. With their attitude, they risk seriously compromising our relations and creating political tensions with Germany that might have incalculable consequences." (A copy of that letter is at BAr EPD 2001 [E] 1, vol. 8. Quoted in Kreis, *Zensur und Selbstzensur*, 292–293.) Masson's opinion was a determining factor in his establishing and obstinately maintaining the connection with Schellenberg through the intermediaries Meyer and Eggen. On that matter, see for example Masson's explanation to the Military Attorney General, *La ligne Masson-Schellenberg*, 14 June 1945. BAr E 5330 1982/1, vol. 205.

15. Indictment Hausamann vs. *Die Tat*. Reprinted without naming any source in Hans Rudolf Fuhrer, *Spionage gegen die Schweiz* (Frauenfeld, 1982), 78. Even though Masson enthusiastically and successfully edited the Revue militaire suisse, his relations with the press were very ambiguous. The bitter experience that he had at the end of the war certainly contributed to his stating, shortly before he died, "On trouvera sans doute un jour un remède contre le cancer; on ne guérira jamais *cette peste noire qu'est la presse.*" ("One day there will be a cure for cancer, but there will never be any cure for the press, this black plague.") Masson, personal letter, 30 December 1966, Tschudi files.

16. Most journalists knew about Masson's repressive attitude toward the press during the war (through the Press and Radio Section). The general public was upset due to the circumstances at the time, as explained by *Die Tat* in an article dated July 10, 1964, on the occasion of Masson's 70th birthday:

> [The war] had resulted in muzzling the press and strengthening the power of the state, creating mistrust, and imposing numerous constraints on the citizens. When wartime duty ended, once the authorities had provided information, once light was shed on quite a few facts that had remained mysterious before, and once the many built-up frustrations had been released, there was a strong urge to discuss things openly. The time of reckoning had come. During wartime duty, Army Intelligence was one of the most secret elements of the inscrutable powers that had contributed to shaping

the lives of the Swiss, who were used to being free and having transparency. No matter how insignificant the details that were disclosed under such circumstances, the fact that [Masson] granted the interview to a foreigner, thereby circumventing the public in Switzerland, was bound to create a stir.

17. *Der Bund*, 29 September 1945.
18. Director of the Federal Military Administration to Chief of the General Staff Louis de Montmollin, 28 September 1945. BAr E/27/10027, vol. 1.
19. Folke Bernadotte, *Das Ende* (Zürich/New York, 1945).
20. On October 11, 1945, journalist Paul Ghali wrote to Roger Masson, "I was the one who came to see you after the publication of Count Bernadotte's book in order to ask you for clarifications on the passage dealing with Schellenberg's statement on Switzerland. Under the current circumstances, it seemed interesting to me to recall the very serious threats that Switzerland had encountered and that the country survived only due to the energy and intelligence of its government and of those who took on the heavy responsibility of providing information to that government." BAr E 27/10027, vol. 1.
21. Masson to Chief of the General Staff de Montmollin, attn. Federal Councillor Kobelt, 30 September 1945. BAr E 27/10027, vol. 1.
22. Ghali had good contacts with Swiss Intelligence, as evidenced in a secret message by the Head of the OSS bureau in Bern, Allen W. Dulles, to OSS Washington, London, Paris, and Caserta on 5 April 1945, which states, "Masson had information that Kesselring has already abandoned his command as hopeless and *Ghali of Chicago Daily News has information from Swiss Intelligence source* of intercepted message from FHQ [Führer's headquarters] to German Generals on West front to act on their own responsibility as they might not be able [to] receive orders from HQ for several days." National Archives, Washington, DC, RG 226, Berne Caserta October 44–June 45, entry 134, box 162 (declassified 4 November 1986 on this author's request).
23. Masson insisted on that fact.
24. "How Himmler's Top Aide Foiled Attack on Swiss," *Chicago Daily News*, 27 September 1945.
25. *Neue Zürcher Zeitung*, 1 October 1945, no. 1474 (evening edition).
26. Interpellation by Dietschi (Solothurn) regarding Switzerland's independence and democratic attitude, 6 June 1945, in National Council 1945 shorthand bulletin, 638 f. His interpellation as well as the interpellations by Dietschi (Basel) and Bringolf were answered by Federal Councillor Kobelt on October 4, 1945.
27. Federal Councillor Kobelt to National Council, 4 October 1945, National Council 1945 shorthand bulletin, 646.
28. *Neue Zürcher Zeitung*, 1 October 1945, no. 1474 (evening edition).
29. *Neue Zürcher Zeitung*, 1 October 1945, no. 1474 (evening edition).
30. *Neue Zürcher Zeitung*, 5 October 1945, no. 1503 (Sunday edition).
31. *Neue Zürcher Zeitung*, 5 October 1945, no. 1503. The author was probably Dr. Karl Weber, the Radical Democratic Bern correspondent of the *NZZ*.
32. *Neue Zürcher Zeitung*, 5 October 1945.

33. Interpellation by Bringolf concerning activities by Colonel-Brigadier Masson, 1 October 1945, National Council 1945 shorthand bulletin, 639.
34. Interpellation Bringolf, 639.
35. Lützelschwab to Federal Councillor Kobelt, 2 October 1945. BAr E 27/10028.
36. Lützelschwab to Kobelt, 2 Oct. 1945.
37. "Wieviel mehr müsste [der Bürger] beunruhigt sein, wenn er um die zum Teil *recht schmutzigen Hintergründe* der ganzen Affäre wüsste." Lützelschwab to Kobelt, 2 Oct. 1945. BAr E 27/10028.
38. Federal Councillor Eduard von Steiger was head of the Federal Justice and Police Department. In that position, as well as during times when he substituted for the sickly Kobelt as head of the Military Department, he had several disputes with Masson during the war.
39. "Or, Vous seul, mon Général, pouvez aujourd'hui, grâce à votre grande autorité et à votre immense popularité, me servir de Bouclier et *me défendre* contre toutes ces calomnies!" Masson to General, 1 October 1945. BAr E 27/9528 (emphasis in original).
40. Masson to General, 1 October 1945. The family of French General Giraud was freed from a prison in Germany due to Masson's relations with Schellenberg (see page 249).
41. General Guisan to Federal Councillor Kobelt, 2 October 1945. BAr E 27/10027, vol. 1.
42. Guisan to Kobelt, 2 Oct. 1945.
43. *Neue Zürcher Zeitung*, 4 October 1945, no. 1490 (evening edition).
44. In what was to become known as the *Colonel Affair* of 1916, two high-ranking officers made it look as if Swiss Army Intelligence was favoring the Central Powers Germany and Austria at the expense of the Entente when exchanging information. The two suspects received only minor sentences. See Jürg Schoch, *Die Oberstenaffäre: Eine innenpolitische Krise (1915/1916)* (Bern/Frankfurt a.M., 1972), and a more recent, excellent account based on source material from Swiss and foreign archives by Hans Rapold, *Der Schweizerische Generalstab*, vol. V: *Zeit der Bewährung? Die Epoche um den Ersten Weltkrieg 1907–1924* (Basel/Frankfurt a.M., 1988), 278ff.
45. Interpellation by Dietschi (Basel), 639 (exact wording of the interpellation), 641–643 (arguments presented to support the interpellation).
46. That rank is not correct. Eggen was *never* a major general (Gruppenführer) but a major both in the Waffen SS (Major) and in the SS (Sturmbannführer).
47. Walther Bringolf in his memoirs, *Mein Leben: Weg und Umweg eines Schweizer Sozialdemokraten* (Zürich, 1965), 353. Masson on the other hand later claimed that he had met Bringolf *only after the war* in connection with the interpellation (Masson, personal letter, 22 March 1967, Tschudi files). Even though Bringolf occasionally made some inaccurate statements and misstated some facts in his memoirs, it is likely that he did meet Masson in 1937. It is understandable that the meeting left a greater impression on Bringolf than on Masson, who met numerous Swiss and foreign nationals as head of Branch 5 (Intelligence) of the General Staff unit at the time.
48. Bringolf, *Mein Leben*, 353.
49. Pilet-Golaz informed Federal President Enrico Celio and the Head of the

Military Department on this matter in a note dated 1 June 1943. BAr E 5795/334.

50. National Council 1945 shorthand bulletin, 643–46.

51. See Masson to Kobelt, 11 October 1945. BAr E 27/10027, vol. 1. Masson's disputes with the Military Department and the Justice and Police Department were triggered by Lützelschwab. At the beginning of the war, Lützelschwab served as a corporal in a border battalion. Since as a civilian he worked as a state attorney (cf. page 447), at the beginning of June 1940 he was detailed to Counterintelligence as a commissioner. After the Head of Counterintelligence had dropped him, he continued to be well informed due to his position as a civilian and on several occasions intervened directly with the Federal Council to protest against Masson's connection with Schellenberg. As he was very knowledgeable about espionage matters and had valuable relations with foreign consulates, in agreement with Chief of the General Staff Huber, in fall 1941 Lützelschwab was recruited as a member of the *Pfalz* procurement office (see page 447ff.).

52. See Chapter 10.

53. The residence of Captain Paul Meyer, a.k.a. Wolf Schwertenbach.

54. Allusion to General Guisan's meeting with Schellenberg at the "Bären" restaurant in Biglen (March 3, 1943). See Chapter 9.

55. Bringolf was wrong about the date; the meeting took place in fall 1942.

56. *Neue Zürcher Zeitung*, 4 October 1945, no. 1490 (evening edition).

57. Federal Councillor Kobelt's reply to interpellations by Dietschi (Solothurn), Dietschi (Basel), and Bringolf, 4 October 1945, National Council 1945 shorthand bulletin, 646–652.

58. Reference to an image that National Councillor Dietschi from Solothurn had used of the *Reiter auf dem Bodensee*, a well-known ballad by Gustav Schwab.

59. Among others, with Allen W. Dulles, the head of the Bern bureau of the Office of Strategic Services (OSS).

60. Bracher to Supreme Court Justice Couchepin, 23 November 1945. BAr E 27/10027, vol. 1.

61. Cf. Masson to Kobelt, 23 January 1946: ". . . the frictions with the Justice and Police Department concerning the visa for Eggen, whom I needed in order to rescue some French nationals, partly at the request of the International Committee of the Red Cross." BAr E 27/9528.

62. Federal Councillor von Steiger to Military Attorney General Eugster, 27 April 1945. BAr E 27/10024.

63. Von Steiger to Eugster, 27 April 1945.

64. Expression used by René Payot in *Journal de Genève*, 3 October 1945.

65. In a letter to Federal Councillor Kobelt dated October 2, 1945, Masson wrote: "Colonel-Corps Commander de Montmollin forwarded to you my request for a one-year leave of absence. I would like to add that this is a short-term solution and that I intend to leave the Army, in which I have served for 27 years with loyalty and devotion to the country" (BAr E 27/10027, vol. 1). Masson's request for a leave of absence came at the right time for the Military Department, as expressed in one of its letters to the Federal Finance and Customs Department dated November 14, 1945:

Ever since the General Staff was demobilized, there have been substantial difficulties in connection with employing the Chief of
Intelligence, Colonel-Brigadier Masson, in the General Staff unit.
During wartime duty, as Chief of Intelligence and Security this
federal employee was an assistant chief of staff and was ranked
colonel-brigadier. For numerous reasons it now appears impossible
to put him once again in charge of the intelligence branch at the
General Staff unit. On one hand, Colonel-Brigadier Masson does
not want to understand that he is supposed to be downgraded
from assistant chief of staff to head of branch, even though during
war-time duty the position as assistant chief of staff was considered
to be merely an assignment in the military, not a promotion as a
federal employee. On the other hand, you know that problems
have arisen that make it impossible to keep Colonel-Brigadier
Masson on in his current area of activity. (BAr E 27/9528)

66. *Neue Zürcher Zeitung*, 7 October 1945, no. 1503 (Sunday edition).
67. Waibel was one of the most outstanding figures in Switzerland's Intelligence
Service, playing a leading role (see Chapter 5). He vehemently opposed the
Masson-Schellenberg connection (see Chapter 6). Waibel's most significant
achievements were the establishment of the "Viking" channel to the Führer's
headquarters and his activity as a mediator in connection with the capitulation
of the German troops in northern Italy. After the war, he was detailed to
Washington, DC as Switzerland's military attaché; in 1954, he became the
infantry's chief instructor. In early 1971, he committed suicide under tragic circumstances.
68. Statement made by Schellenberg, 2 October 1945. BAr J.I.121/63 and E
27/10027, vol. 1. In vol. V of his *Geschichte der schweizerischen Neutralität*
(Basel/Stuttgart, 1970), 87, note 40, Edgar Bonjour refers to this statement;
however, he erroneously writes that the deposition was made in Nuremberg
instead of London.
69. Schellenberg had made Masson understand as early as 1942 that he believed
Germany was going to lose the war.
70. Cover name "Operation Bernhard," named after the head of the counterfeiting
team, SS Major Bernhard Krüger (RSHA Branch VI F 4).
71. At the end of September 1939, the central authorities of the Security Police that
were headed by Heydrich and reported to Himmler, the (Prussian) Secret State
Police Office, the Bureau of the Political Police Commander for the Länder
(other than Prussia), the Reich Criminal HQ, the Security Police Central
Office, and the Central Office of the Security and Intelligence Service of the
SS, were combined into the Reich Security Central Office (RSCO). As of 1941,
the RSCO basically consisted of seven branches that were in charge of fighting
against and suppressing all real and supposed opponents of National Socialism.
Office III (domestic intelligence), headed by Otto Ohlendorf, primarily produced reports on the mood among the population. Office IV, the former Secret
State Police Office headed by Heinrich Müller, was the central office by which
all enemies of the Nazi regime were persecuted. In department IV B 4, Adolf
Eichmann was in charge of the "final solution to the Jewish question" and

organized deportations to the elimination camps. Office V was the Reich Criminal Police HQ. Office VI, Foreign Intelligence headed by Walter Schellenberg, was in charge of espionage and sabotage activities abroad.

72. At the printing shop that was set up in blocks 18 and 19 of the Sachsenhausen concentration camp, 140 men produced 400,000 counterfeit British banknotes a month. The quality of some of the counterfeits was so outstanding that not even the counterfeiters were able to distinguish them from real bills. A total of nearly nine million Bank of England counterfeit bills worth more than £134m were produced there. The bills were circulated in neutral foreign countries via the German legations. In Switzerland, counterfeit £5 bills worth £1m were in circulation at that time. The counterfeiting operation was transferred to the Mauthausen concentration camp at the end of February 1945 and to a small concentration camp near Redl-Zipf, between Linz and Salzburg, in March 1945. Due to the Allied advance, the production was not resumed there. Himmler ordered all traces of "Operation Bernhard" to be covered up and all bills to be burned. However, according to Major George McNally of the SHAEF [Supreme Headquarters Allied Expeditionary Forces] staff in Frankfurt, the counterfeiters could not bring themselves to destroy their virtually perfect bills; instead, they sank a large number of them in Toplitz Lake, nearby, where they were found 14 years later, in July 1959.

73. In June 1941, Schellenberg became deputy head of office; on September 1, 1941, when he was promoted to the rank of lieutenant colonel, he was put in charge of the office (see Fuhrer, *Spionage*, 126, note 207). The information given in Robert Wistrich, *Wer war wer im Dritten Reich? Ein biographisches Lexikon* (Frankfurt a.M., 1987), 307, is incorrect.

74. Waibel to Kobelt in his cover letter of 6 October 1945 for the report on the counterfeiting operation. BAr E 27/10027, vol. 1.

75. Military Department to Colonel Couchepin, 17 October 1945. BAr E 27/10027, vol. 1.

76. Note for file regarding Federal Councillor Kobelt's meeting with Colonel-Brigadier Masson, 11 February 1946. BAr E 27/10027, vol. 1.

77. BAr J.I.121/63. Reprinted in *Neue Zürcher Zeitung*, 10 March 1946, no. 403 (Sunday edition).

78. There were rumors about this allegation both in public and within Army Intelligence, as expressed in a note for the file by Hans Hausamann on 2 July 1945, which stated: "The latest is that since the SS steered off its course, Dr. Meyer (Schwertenbach) has been supplying information to the Americans. The contact person on the American side is one of Dul[les'] top aides." ("Das Neueste: seitdem die SS ausser Kurs ist, liefert Dr. Meyer (Schwertenbach) den Amerikanern Nachrichten. Für die Amerikaner hält den Kontakt ein naher Mitarbeiter von Dul[les].") BAr E 27/10035. In the upcoming chapters it will be shown that Hans Hausamann was one of the harshest critics of the Masson-Schellenberg connection. Hausamann was amazingly well informed, as was the case in many other instances during the war. According to an OSS document that has just been released for research purposes, Meyer-Schwertenbach was indeed the person who set up the contact between the OSS and Eggen; however, he did so during the final stage of the war rather than after the Armistice.

On January 18, 1945, Allen W. Dulles sent a "Top Secret" report to Washington, London, and Paris, writing that one of his staff members [OSS officer Frederick R. Loofbourow] had met with Meyer-Schwertenbach and Eggen in Zürich. In the detailed memorandum about the encounter, Dulles added, "The conversation took place *with my full prior approval.*" Dulles explained why he had agreed to the OSS entering into contact with Schellenberg's emissary, writing, "I am convinced that if we are to secure 'hot' inside information we must break into SS circles and fish around until we find the party who will sell out on a big scale." However, Dulles was not sure if Schellenberg's intermediary was the right person for that role, explaining, "I do not think Ecken [*sic*] is our man as unfortunately he seems a bit too honest but we may have another try at him." OSS—Berne to Sasac and Saint, Washington, London, Paris, 18 January 1945 (Top Secret). National Archives, Washington, DC, RG 226, Entry 214, Box 7. The document was discovered by Dr. Neville Wylie, University of Nottingham, who kindly made it available to this author for a first evaluation.

79. Schellenberg stated that Meyer and Holzach had been Eggen's actual sources of information (see page 16).

80. On June 2, 1969, Captain Meyer-Schwertenbach's widow filed a lawsuit against Alphons Matt, an editor at the *Weltwoche* newspaper, accusing him of slandering Captain Meyer in his book *Zwischen allen Fronten* (Frauenfeld, 1969). The legal dispute ended on December 20, 1971 with an out-of-court settlement; the agreement read, "The defendant would regret if based on a few passages in the book, one could come to question Captain Dr. Meier-Schwertenbach's respectability." Zürich district court, 26 January 1972. BAr J.I.121/63 (in official documents, Meyer was spelled with an "i" instead of a "y").

Chapter 2: The Tasks and Characteristics of an Intelligence Service

1. Kurz, *Nachrichtenzentrum,* 9.

2. In a manuscript that he wrote approximately in 1961, Walter Allgöwer commented: "The Chief of the General Staff, Colonel-Corps-Commander Huber, summarized the major results in his . . . report. They take up only 10 out of 514 pages in the book. That shows the actual significance of espionage; it was an *important tool,* that was all." BAr J.I.161/62.

3. Walter Laqueur, *A World of Secrets: The Uses and Limits of Intelligence* (New York, 1985), 344.

4. Those sources included daily newspapers. The German Armed Forces High Command, for example, received a total of 51 copies of nine foreign newspapers, including 17 copies of the *Neue Zürcher Zeitung,* 10 copies of the *Basler National-Zeitung,* and 6 copies of the *Basler Nachrichten.* See David Kahn, *Hitler's Spies: German Military Intelligence in World War II* (New York, 1985), 160. Fuhrer (*Spionage,* 58, 98) wrongly states that the results obtained by evaluating open sources were "of little significance."

5. Hans Rudolf Kurz ("Nachrichtendienst-Spionage," *Fourier,* September 1972) defines and explains the characteristics of espionage according to the 1907 Hague Treaty on Land Warfare.

6. Roger Masson, "Unser Nachrichtendienst im Zweiten Weltkrieg," in *Die Schweiz im Zweiten Weltkrieg*, ed. Hans Rudolf Kurz (Thun, 1959).

7. In order to take into account the different needs for information (the commander of an advance guard, for instance, requires different information than the commander of a division, who in turn does not require the same information as the Commander-in-Chief or the Federal Council), Swiss Army Intelligence makes a distinction between *combat intelligence* and *strategic-operational intelligence*. This study deals with the latter category. The time factor helps to tell the two categories apart; strategic-operational intelligence has to work already during times of peace, whereas combat intelligence comes into play only during times of war, as suggested by its name. However, it is difficult to distinguish between the two categories whenever there is a modern combination of both that blurs the boundary between peace and war. (On that issue, see also Hans Rudolf Kurz, "Nachrichtendienst," *Schweizer Soldat*, no. 5 [1972].)

8. In the era of strategic surprise attacks and *blitzkrieg*, it was a matter of principle for Switzerland to prepare for the possibility of cooperating with France. Masson was critical in his comments about these preparations. Before the war, then-Colonel Guisan frequently went to see Masson to get updates on the international situation. However, he did not tell Masson anything about his cooperation plans with France. Masson later explained:

> If the future commander of our army had considered it necessary to let us in on [the cooperation plans], maybe we would respectfully have drawn his attention to the fact that any military cooperation with France was highly hypothetical, at least in 1939. We regret to put it so bluntly, but it is not our intention to write a soap opera with a happy ending. All one needs to do is refer to French military writers, including General de Gaulle, to come to the conclusion that in 1940, in spite of its beautiful military traditions, the army of our neighbor to the West, . . . whose air force and tank force were small compared to the powerful Wehrmacht, was hardly in a position to assist us by deploying some of its forces to Switzerland, no matter what the circumstances were. However, out of politeness we will not pursue this discussion. (*Tribune de Lausanne*, 16 January 1966)

The upcoming chapters will show that the judgment that Masson made a quarter of a century after the fact may have been influenced by the experience that he had through his connection with Schellenberg.

9. Masson, "Nachrichtendienst," 69.

10. Masson, "Nachrichtendienst," 70. For a distinction between *strategic* and *tactical* warning cf. Jack Davis who, with regard to the United States, suggests the following definition: "*Tactical warning* focuses on specific incidents that endanger U.S. security interests, such as military attack, terrorism, WMD developments, illicit transactions, and political crises abroad. Tactical warning analysis is usually characterized by a search for and evaluation of diagnostic information about incident, perpetrator, target, timing, and modalities. The goal is to deter and limit damage by identifying in advance *when, where,* and *how* a declared or potential adversary will forcefully strike the United States directly, mount a

challenge to U.S. forces, personnel, or interests abroad, or make a menacing weapons breakthrough. *Strategic warning* aims for analytic perception and effective communication to policy officials of important changes in the character or level of security threats that require re-evaluation of U.S. readiness to deter, avert, or limit damage—well in advance of incident-specific indicators. Thus, strategic warning is characterized by inferential evidence and general depiction of the danger. The issues addressed here are *changes in the level of likelihood* that an enemy will strike or that a development harmful to U.S. interests will take place and *changes in enemy mechanisms for inflicting damage*. The goal is to assist policy decisions on defensive preparedness and contingency planning, including preemptive actions, to manage the risks of potential threats." Good strategic warning, therefore, has the potential to enhance both tactical warning and preparedness. Jack Davis, *Strategic Warning: If Surprise Is Inevitable, What Role for Analysis?*, The Sherman Kent Center for Intelligence Analysis, Occasional Papers: Volume 2, Number 1 (January 2003), 2–3. A *strategic* surprise is more complex than a *tactical* surprise because it can "be achieved simultaneously at several levels, in *timing*, the *place* of attack, *rapidity* of movement, the use of *new technologies delivery* and *weapons systems*, the frequent appearance of new doctrines and innovative tactics to match the new technologies, as well as in the choice of the political-military goals for war itself." Michael I. Handel, "Intelligence and the Problem of Strategic Surprise," *Journal of Strategic Studies* (June 1984): 231–232 (emphasis in original).

11. Klaus Knorr and Patrick Morgan, eds., *Strategic Military Surprise: Incentives and Opportunities* (New Brunswick/London, 2nd ed. 1984), 2–3.
12. See Handel, "Problem of Strategic Surprise," 231.
13. Handel, "Problem of Strategic Surprise," 231. However, both the Falklands War and the two Gulf Wars have demonstrated that even today it can take weeks if not months to deploy a substantial number of troops and their modern weaponry across great distances.
14. Knorr and Morgan, eds., *Strategic Military Surprise*, 2–3.
15. See Michael I. Handel, "Technological Surprise in War," *Intelligence and National Security*, 2, no. 1 (January 1987).
16. See Handel, "Problem of Strategic Surprise," 232.
17. Roberta Wohlstetter, *Pearl Harbor: Warning and Decision* (Stanford, CA, 1962).
18. Overviews are given in Klaus Knorr, "Strategic Intelligence: Problems and Remedies," in *Strategic Thought in the Nuclear Age*, ed. Laurence Martin (London, 1979), and in Michael I. Handel, *The Diplomacy of Surprise* (Cambridge, MA, 1981).
19. "Analysis has been facilitated by the emergence in recent years of a better understanding of perception and misperception—individual, organizational, and governmental—as it affects state behavior, which has permitted a better appreciation of the position of the victim in cases of strategic surprise." Knorr and Morgan, eds., *Strategic Military Surprise*, 3.
20. Wohlstetter, *Pearl Harbor*, 1–2.
21. Wohlstetter, *Pearl Harbor*, 3.
22. Wohlstetter, *Pearl Harbor*, 228.

23. Wohlstetter, *Pearl Harbor*, 397.
24. Wohlstetter, *Pearl Harbor*, 397.
25. Wohlstetter, *Pearl Harbor*, 387, 397.
26. Wohlstetter, *Pearl Harbor*, 73.
27. Wohlstetter, *Pearl Harbor*, 227.
28. In this context, "deception" means the intentional, insidious dissemination of inaccurate information that aims to mislead an opponent's intelligence service.
29. These channels include, among others, reports by military attachés, international-al negotiations, open sources such as books and daily newspapers, tapped telephone conversations, and intercepted mail.
30. William Reese, "Deception within a Communications Theory Framework," in *Strategic Military Deception*, eds. Donald C. Daniel and Katherine L. Herbig (New York/Oxford, 1981), 101.
31. Reese, "Deception," 101. To give an example, Swiss Intelligence received a multitude of different signals through a large number of channels stating that, with its fearless language, Switzerland's uncompromising press made Hitler furious and could provoke him to order a punitive expedition against the rebellious little "porcupine." These signals were part of a cunning war of nerves that the Third Reich conducted against "non-neutral" Switzerland.
32. Barton Whaley, *Codeword Barbarossa* (Cambridge, MA, 1973).
33. Reese, "Deception," 112.
34. Handel, "Problem of Strategic Surprise," 235ff. The alert of March 1943 in Switzerland is a good example of the difficulty in distinguishing between reliable and unreliable information (see Chapter 10).
35. Masson, *Bericht über den Aktivdienst 1939–1945 der Abteilung für Nachrichtendienst im Armeestab* (put together by Schafroth), 21 June 1945. BAr E 27/14849. See Lieutenant Colonel Barbey, minutes of the briefing on 5 June 1944 at the Commander-in-Chief's ("Warnings from our legation in Budapest and assessment of the situation by Assistant Chief of Staff Ib concerning the current German capabilities"). At the briefing, Masson explained that Intelligence had located 25 German divisions within a range of 150–200 km from the Swiss border, but it appeared that they had not been deployed there for strategic purposes. He warned, however: *"We must keep the example of the aggression against Yugoslavia in mind;* formations that seem to have nothing to do with each other can join forces and pursue the same objective at any given moment in time. Moreover, the situation in Italy is developing in such a way that the war is getting closer to our borders, albeit slowly. Our situation appears to be at least as delicate as it was in spring 1940." BAr E 5795/147.
36. Klaus Knorr, "Strategic Surprise in Four European Wars," in *Strategic Military Surprise: Incentives and Opportunities*, eds. Klaus Knorr and Patrick Morgan, 2nd ed. (New Brunswick/London, 1984), 22.
37. Knorr, "Strategic Surprise in Four European Wars," 22.
38. Knorr, "Strategic Surprise in Four European Wars," 36.
39. Knorr, "Strategic Surprise in Four European Wars," 38.
40. Thomas C. Schelling (Center for International Affairs, Harvard University), foreword in Wohlstetter, *Pearl Harbor*, vii.
41. In his article "Lessons for Statecraft," in *Strategic Military Surprise: Incentives*

and Opportunities, eds. Knorr and Morgan, 256ff., Klaus Knorr explains very clearly why that is the case.

42. Clausewitz persuasively argued, "A large part of the information that you receive in a war is contradictory, an even larger part is wrong, and by far the largest part is subject to quite some uncertainty." Carl V. Clausewitz, *Vom Kriege*, 16th ed. (Bonn, 1952), 156.

43. Wohlstetter, *Pearl Harbor*, 225–226.

44. Swiss Intelligence had the same experience. See Chapter 5.

45. Wohlstetter, *Pearl Harbor*, 70.

46. Cf. Wohlstetter's statement:

> All decisions are made in the face of uncertainty, even those that depend simply on an understanding of natural phenomena. But decisions based on reading the intentions of others, and in particular, the intentions of an enemy, are especially difficult. These intentions are complicated and shifting, and subject to change between the time the intent is signalized and the time of the intended act. . . . At least in reading natural phenomena, we have Albert Einstein's famous assurance that God is subtle but not plain mean. The same cannot be said for the enemy. (Wohlstetter, *Pearl Harbor*, 226).

47. See Ernst, "Der Schweizerische Nachrichtendienst im Zweiten Weltkrieg," *Allgemeine Schweizerische Militärzeitschrift*, no. 12 (1972). Cf. Jack Davis, "In any case, a strong historical argument can be made that the occurrence of incident or tactical surprise can be reduced but not eliminated. Even the best of intelligence services cannot expect to penetrate every plot or otherwise anticipate every damaging incident. . . . The fluidity as well as the complexity of relationships and rationales of foreign groups and leaders hinder timely specific warnings." Jack Davis, *Strategic Warning: If Surprise Is Inevitable, What Role for Analysis?*, The Sherman Kent Center for Intelligence Analysis, Occasional Papers: Volume 2, Number 1 (January 2003), 3. In his recommendations for strengthening strategic warning, Davis stresses the "unrealistic standard of avoidance of surprise," stating, "The ultimate goal of effective warning is to maximize damage limitation, not predictive accuracy." (p. 6).

48. In this context, being obliging should not be confused with being opportunistic. A country that is fearful and willing to adapt might be a tempting target for an aggressor. Dissuasive diplomacy, on the other hand, is based on a consistently correct attitude, which makes the country's willingness to resist calculable.

49. See Knorr, "Lessons for Statecraft," 264.

50. Wohlstetter, *Pearl Harbor*, 400–401.

51. On this issue, see the astute remarks of James J. Wirtz, Columbia University, NY, in his review of the article "Intelligence and Strategic Surprises" in the September/October 1988 edition of the journal *Survival* by the International Institute for Strategic Studies, London, 478–479. He stated: "Anticipating strategic surprise attacks *during wartime* is easier than preventing failures of intelligence *at the outset of the war*. . . . It is easier to anticipate and to respond effectively to strategic surprise attacks in an intrawar environment."

52. Laqueur, *A World of Secrets*, 338.

53. Major surprises over the decades—that is, failures to warn effectively—include

Pearl Harbor (1941), Communist attacks on South Korea (1950), the Soviet invasion of Czechoslovakia (1968), the Iran revolution (1979), and Iraq's invasion of Kuwait (1990). In the case of Saddam Hussein's invasion of Kuwait the general judgment was that Iraq was unlikely to initiate warfare in the near term (stated repeatedly in the year before the assault on Kuwait), a conclusion based on the assumption that Iraq needed several years to recover from the military and economic devastation of its long war with Iran. That assumption was so widely held by analysts that it was rarely examined critically. Nor was the heavy dependence of the *no*-war conclusion on the *recovery-first* assumption explicitly recognized. (See Jack Davis, *Improving CIA Analytic Performance: Strategic Warning*. The Sherman Kent Center for Intelligence Analysis, Occasional Papers: Volume 1, Number 1 [September 2002], 2, 4.) Even though in modern military history strategic surprises have rarely failed to have an immediate impact, one should keep in mind Michael I. Handel's observation that a successful surprise attack in itself does not mean that the aggressor has all the advantages, nor is he assured of the final victory. Handel explains, "There is, in fact, no positive correlation between the initial success of a strategic surprise and the outcome of the war." (Handel, "Problem of Strategic Success," 230.) It is striking that ultimately the Germans themselves fell victim to strategic deception. They lost a war that they had all but won because they underestimated the Soviets' power of resistance and, like Napoleon over a century earlier, the rough climate and great distances in Russia. Their fateful miscalculation was the result of wrong assumptions, as they believed that Russian soldiers had inferior fighting abilities and Stalin's regime did not know how to govern the country. Preconceived ideas and a certain degree of wishful thinking contributed to these wrong assumptions. However, even more decisive was the Germans' boundless confidence in their own military skill. After the *blitzkrieg* in the West, the German leadership was convinced that no one could stop them in a land war. (See Knorr, "Strategic Surprise in Four European Wars," 39.)

54. Masson, "Nachrichtendienst," 70.
55. Masson, "Nachrichtendienst," 70.
56. On that issue, in October 1947 Hans Hausamann wrote in an unpublished manuscript entitled *Nachrichtendienst*, "The less prepared an army is to go to combat, the greater is the importance and responsibility of intelligence." BAr J.I.137 1974, vol. 11. On August 10, 1941, Masson expressed the same idea in a letter to the Chief of the General Staff in connection with a reduction of the number of men serving on the army staff, stating, "One has to be aware of the principle that the fewer troops are out in the field, the more intensely and reliably intelligence has to work." BAr E 27/9508, vol. 9.
57. Masson, "Nachrichtendienst," 70f.
58. In this study, "connection" or "channel" in the context of intelligence means a direct link with an informant who is placed in an important position. A so-called *tasking* channel is a connection that can receive orders.
59. The international crises in 1938–1939 allowed Swiss Intelligence to become accustomed to working with its network.
60. Masson, "Nachrichtendienst," 71.
61. Masson expressed the ideas that follow in the main text in a letter to the

Commander-in-Chief as early as November 22, 1943. BAr E 27/10021. When considering that the U.S. and English studies that are discussed in this chapter were written in the 1970s and 1980s, it is remarkable that Masson realized at such an early stage the consequences that technological and industrial innovations would have for intelligence.

62. Masson, "Nachrichtendienst," 71.

63. Masson, "Nachrichtendienst," 71.

64. Masson, "Nachrichtendienst," 71–72. See Chapter 10 on that issue.

65. Cf. *National-Zeitung*, 20 October 1967, which stated:

> An intelligence service cannot pick its aides. It has to rely on the best and most intelligent people, but also on dubious characters. Being successful is all that matters. On the occasion of Masson's 70th birthday, someone who was part of the team back then [probably Rolf Eberhard, who headed the Axis Section from 1943 on] stated, "Nowhere else in the army was the roster as heterogeneous as it was at the hotel in Interlaken where Intelligence was headquartered. It included notorious playboys next to clergymen, ladies with dubious reputations next to district attorneys and scholars in oriental studies, aristocrats next to revolutionaries." Success proved Masson to be right.

66. In this case, Waibel's informant was a communications officer at the Führer's headquarters. On that issue, see Waibel's "Report on Jon Kimche's *Spying for Peace*," 26 February 1963, BAr J.I. 137 1974/64, vol. 13. For quite some time it was assumed that during Germany's Western campaign, Hitler was staying at Ziegenberg. On March 28, 1945, Allen Dulles reported to the headquarters of the Office of Strategic Services in Washington, DC that he had received a report according to which "Kesselring's HQ is, or was, at *Ziegenberg*, near Bad Nauheim, where there are large underground installations dating from 1940, when they were used by Hitler as FHQ during the invasion of France." (National Archives, Washington, DC, RG 226, Entry 134, Box 162, Folder 53). However, in his book *Geheimdienste im Zweiten Weltkrieg: Nach Öffnung der alliierten Geheimarchive fortgeführt, ergänzt und erweitert von Hans Büchler*, 6th ed. (Munich, 2002), 100, Wilhelm von Schramm states: "Ziegenberg castle, west of Bad Nauheim in the Taunus hills, had indeed been expanded to serve as FHQ for the Western campaign, but Hitler never actually moved there. On May 9, 1940, he drove via Hamburg to the 'Felsennest' FHQ in Rodert near Münstereifel, which had also been completed by then. He arrived there at 5.30 a.m. on May 10, 1940." Schramm based his statement on Andreas Hillgruber, *Hitlers Strategie: Politik und Kriegführung 1940/41* (Frankfurt a.M., 1965), 671, who lists Hitler's itinerary between September 1, 1939 and December 31, 1941. Hitler had decided as early as February 22, 1940 to move to the "Felsennest" FHQ because by then it was clear that the intelligence installations at the "Adlerhorst" Ziegenberg would not be ready in time before launching the attack in the west. Franz W. Seidler, Dieter Zeiger, *Die Führerhauptquartiere* (Munich, 2000), 164–165, and Schramm, Geheimdienste, 415, note 27.

67. Approximately 30 agents working for Swiss Intelligence were executed because of their spying activities. Couchepin, report, 31. BAr E 27/10027, vol. 1.

68. On that issue, see Masson, "Lutte dans le brouillard," *Tribune de Lausanne*, 12 December 1965.

69. The example of 1940 (see endnote 70 below) shows that *misinformation* is not necessarily directed against the first victim. Germany's ploy cunningly aimed at using the deceived Swiss Army Command to induce France to arrange its armed forces in a way that was to the aggressor's advantage. Hence, the Evaluation Section of Intelligence could not automatically conclude that the *signals* that had been received from several sources were necessarily reliable merely because they appeared to confirm one another.

70. See for example Christian Vetsch, *Aufmarsch gegen die Schweiz* (Olten, 1973). In his Ph.D. thesis, Vetsch discusses how Switzerland was misled by German Army Group C under General von Leeb in connection with case "Yellow."

Chapter 3: The Structure of Swiss Army Intelligence

1. See Georg Kreis, *Auf den Spuren von La Charité* (Basel/Stuttgart, 1976), 173. This was undoubtedly in reaction to the fact that during World War I Intelligence had been biased in favor of the Central Powers (as with the Colonel Affair).

2. In a letter to the Military Department dated August 26, 1936, Chief of the General Staff Labhart wrote, "The positions of two heads of section have become vacant in the General Staff Unit due to Colonel Bandi's nomination as commander of the Dübendorf air force base and chief of the planned air force and anti-aircraft defense unit and Colonel Jordi's appointment as chief instructor of the cavalry." He explained that he had ordered the chief instructor of the infantry to have "two capable training officers who have been trained to serve on the General Staff fill the positions of the two colonels. These two officers [were] Lieutenant Colonel [Roger] Masson and Major [Gustav] Däniker." (BAr E 27/9528.) In the afternoon of September 8, 1936, the Federal Council appointed Masson as new head of Section 5. Lieutenant Colonel Dubois, the former head of the section, was put in charge of the Section of Transportation and the Rear. *Neue Zürcher Zeitung*, 9 September 1936, no. 1539.

3. The Colonel Affair may have given rise to concerns about Intelligence posing a latent threat to, or even being in violation of, Switzerland's neutrality. See Hans Rudolf Fuhrer, "Die Schweiz im Nachrichtendienst," in *Schwedische und schweizerische Neutralität im Zweiten Weltkrieg*, ed. Rudolf Bindschedler, Hans Rudolf Kurz, et al. (Basel, 1985), 405–426.

4. Fuhrer, "Schweiz im Nachrichtendienst," 405–426.

5. In his report on wartime duty (163), General Guisan stated, "For a very long time, our Intelligence was subject to narrow-minded budget restrictions, an attitude that appears to be inexplicable today."

6. Masson, *Bericht über den Aktivdienst 1939–1945 der Abteilung Nachrichtendienst im Armeestab*. BAr E 27/14849. At Masson's request, the report was put together by Colonel Schafroth.

7. Hausamann in *Schweizer Illustrierte*, 23 October 1967. (Masson had died on 19 October 1967.)

8. *Dienstordnung der Generalstabsabteilung 1930, 5. Sektion, Nachrichten.* BAr E 27/1082, vol. 1.

9. On January 10, 1922, at the request of the General Staff unit and in agreement with the Federal Department of Finance, the Military Department granted Intelligence an annual budget of 10,000 Swiss francs. The General Staff Unit kept all receipts; the expenses were entered in the quarterly financial report as a lump-sum under one single item, "expenses for intelligence," as part of the budget line "reconnaissance activities." On April 4, 1934, Roost supported his request to the Military Department by arguing, "The requirements for Intelligence, especially for a special information service, have increased considerably; the [current] budget is therefore no longer sufficient." Roost requested that the budget be *increased to an annual 30,000 francs* and expenses be entered quarterly "under a special item, 'expenses for the Information Service' (instead of 'intelligence')." BAr E 27/9507.

10. In a decree dated May 22, 1934, Minger stated that the annual 30,000 francs for the "Special Information Service" would be debited under the credit lines "reconnaissance activities" and "unit activities," adding, "[the Special Information Service] does not need to present receipts to account for the allocated funds. . . . The Chief of the General Staff is responsible for appropriately using them." BAr E 27/9507.

11. Minger, decree of 3 March 1938. BAr E 27/9507.

12. Chief of the General Staff Labhart to Head of Military Department, 8 February 1939. BAr E 27/9507.

13. *Die Nation*, 27 January–3 March 1938.

14. Police command of the canton of Zürich, criminal investigation department, 27 July 1938. Interrogation of Hermann Hagenbuch, Ph.D., lawyer. (Document in this author's possession.)

15. On October 17, 1934, the *Basler Arbeiterzeitung* published two fake letters allegedly written by General Staff officers that made serious accusations against Lieutenant General Wille (the son of the Commander-in-Chief of the Swiss Army during World War I) concerning his relations with Germany and top-ranking officials of the Third Reich. The letters claimed that Wille was conspiring with "Nazi chiefs" and was doing everything he could to become commander-in-chief. The letters were written by Hermann Hagenbuch, who claimed that Bircher had incited him to write them. The affair grew into a scandal that got parliament and the Federal Council involved. Even though Hans Hausamann, who was press officer of the Swiss Officers' Society at the time, was able to reconcile Wille with Bircher, the incident caused lasting damage to the careers of both officers (something that Hagenbuch had not intended for Bircher). On the affair, see Daniel Heller, *Eugen Bircher: Arzt, Militär und Politiker* (Zürich, 1988), 142–146.

16. Jürgen Luternau [alias Hermann Hagenbuch], *Attachés, 'Envoyés de marque' und Agenten: Vom Nachrichtenwesen der Armee* (Zürich, 1938), 18. The small publication includes the articles that Hagenbuch had written for the weekly newspaper *Die Nation* and some supplementary information. In April 1938, the brochure became available at newsstands and bookstores; during the April session of that year, every member of parliament received a copy of it. Not one

single member of parliament objected to it. However, in August 1938, half a year after the articles had been published in *Die Nation* and four months after the brochure had been published, the publication gave rise to a smear campaign directed against Hagenbuch and the chairman of the Social Democratic Party, National Councillor Hans Oprecht, for whom Hagenbuch was working as a military consultant. The *Schweizerische Mittelpresse*, which started the smear campaign, members of the Catholic-Conservative Party, members of the Front movement, and a few members of the Radical Democratic Party accused Oprecht of giving away military secrets contained in government documents, including some files by the National Council Finance Committee. Oprecht denied the allegations, arguing that he had submitted Hagenbuch's articles to Captain Bracher, the head of personnel at the Military Department, and Masson for approval and taken their suggestions into consideration before they were published.

17. Labhart, *Dienstordnung der Generalstabsabteilung* 1938, 8 February 1938. BAr E 27/1082, vol. 1.

18. BAr E 27/9467. The structure was finalized in February 1939 (see the organizational charts in this chapter). It may be considered as established that both the "instructions" and the revised terms of reference of February 8, 1938, were drafted by Labhart's aide, Masson. However, some entries in Labhart's diary indicate that the Chief of the General Staff also took an active part in setting up an effective Intelligence Service. On February 21, 1938, he noted, "I admonished Lieutenant Colonel Masson to focus on the main tasks in his section; in particular, he should *enter into contact with the border patrols and the cantonal military and police chiefs in the border cantons* as soon as possible." (BAr J.I.49 1, vol. 2.) On March 24, 1939, Labhart's intervention resulted in Masson's writing a circular to the commanders of the cantonal police authorities in which he stated:

> The tense situation on the international level forces us more than ever to take precautions. Considering the recent events [crushing of the remainder of Czechoslovakia] and how quickly they happened, there is no doubt that we are well advised to be extremely cautious. In order to *further expand our network of sources for intelligence*, we would like to ask you for your valuable cooperation. In the interest of our national defense, it is currently indispensable for your organization to establish closer relations with our section.

Masson asked the commanders to communicate to him by telephone any information that was "likely to be reliable; please avoid using intermediaries." BAr E 27/9494.

19. At the time the war broke out, only Germany, France, and Italy had military attachés in Bern. Within a year, the number increased to 12. In August 1945, 15 states were represented by 19 military attachés and air force attachés and 23 aides (Huber, *Bericht des Generalstabschefs*, 239).

20. The "Swiss National Patriotic Federation" (Schweizerischer Vaterländischer Verband, SVV) maintained its own political information and intelligence service with a large network of connections; it cooperated with official bodies from the time that it was created. Heller reports:

> SVV intelligence, which was directed by Bircher in person, sup-

plied information to military authorities, including the Chief of
the General Staff and several divisional commanders. Bircher
received a monthly compensation from the General Staff unit for
his intelligence activities. The connections of SVV intelligence
reached all the way to the United States, Poland, Russia, Romania,
Morocco, Turkey, and Greece. It received reports from top officials
of the Munich police department, an overview of the Italian
Irredenta, reports on Tyrol, and a lot of other information. (Heller,
Eugen Bircher, 108ff.)

Even today it is considered necessary for Intelligence to cooperate with private
organizations. In March 1981, during the discussion of a special parliament
committee report on the Bachmann-Schilling matter, National Councillor Felix
Auer (Radical Democrat, Baselland), remarked, "In our militia system,
Intelligence also has to work with so-called private intelligence organizations."
He said that it was not sufficient to use exclusively or primarily career officers;
instead, non-military people were needed "who are well educated and have
some expertise, are capable, show initiative, are willing to take risks, are selfless
and discreet, instill confidence, are able to reason and separate the wheat from
the chaff, have intuition, and are perfectly loyal toward the state. . . . An
English spy book states that intelligence is such a dirty business that it can be
run only by gentlemen." *Schweizer Soldat* 5 (1981).

From the mid-1970s onward, a special Intelligence Service that was later
called P-27 (P meaning "Project") was set up outside the existing official
Intelligence Service in order to procure military as well as strategically relevant
political, economic, and technical information. This special Intelligence Service
was operating parallel to the Intelligence Procurement Section of the
Intelligence and Counterintelligence Sub-Group. The official Intelligence
Service procured information that was available through public sources or could
be obtained at a low risk; the special Intelligence Service served to procure
intelligence that involved taking some risk. At the end of November 1979, it
became known that Kurt Schilling, a Swiss citizen, had been arrested after
observing maneuvers in Austria on orders of Colonel Albert Bachmann. The
incident, which the media described as a "clumsy attempt at espionage," created
a stir. As a consequence, the inventive Colonel Bachmann had to resign as head
of both the P-27 and the Special Service (which was in charge of making preparations for resistance in the event that Switzerland was to be occupied by foreign powers). About a dozen times per year, in violation of foreign laws,
Colonel Bachmann had taken the risk of sending agents on missions abroad.
On January 19, 1981, a parliamentary task force headed by future Federal
Councillor Jean-Pascal Delamuraz presented a report on the Bachmann-
Schilling matter, which was discussed in parliament two months later.

21. It was not until 1938 that Switzerland sent its first military attachés to foreign
countries; Major Richard de Blonay of the General Staff was sent to Paris,
Colonel Hans von Werdt to Berlin, and Colonel Karl von Wattenwyl of the
General Staff to Rome. During the war, additional representatives were sent to
London (in 1941), Ankara (1942), Helsinki, Stockholm, Washington, DC
(1943), and Budapest (1944). (Huber, *Bericht des Generalstabschefs*, 238–239.)

The appointment of the first three military attachés gave rise to some criticism in parliament; National Councillor Victor Emil Scherer (Radical Democrat, Basel-Stadt) pointedly remarked, "I am surprised to see who has been appointed. Of course I do not ask Mr. Smith to be sent to Berlin, Mr. Jones to be sent to Rome, and Mr. Doe to be sent to Paris. However, . . . I find it disagreeable that the tradition of the diplomatic corps is followed by sending only gentlemen with aristocratic names abroad as military attachés." BAr E 27/9750.

22. Reconnaissance focused mainly on roads, railroads, gondolas, obstacles, fortifications, and power plants. It also served to update maps. In 1938, about 5,000 francs were allocated for that activity.

23. On this point, Labhart remarked, "one has to be extremely cautious when using special agents." He did not explain what he meant by special agents.

24. Labhart, *Weisungen für den Neuaufbau des Nachrichtendienstes*, 22 February 1938. BAr E 27/9467.

25. Transcript of the TV discussion "The Hidden Art of Intelligence," New York, March 29, 1964. The show was hosted by Hanson Baldwin, editor at the *New York Times* for military issues. Princeton University Library, Public Policy Papers, Department of Rare Books and Special Collections, Allen W. Dulles Papers, Box 237.

26. Transcript of "The Hidden Art of Intelligence."

27. At the same time, it became less easy to distinguish between strategic and operational intelligence.

28. George S. Pettee, *The Future of American Secret Intelligence* (Washington, DC, 1946). Quoted from the manual *Naval Intelligence* by the U.S. Navy Intelligence School, Washington, DC, 1951. Princeton University Library, Public Policy Papers, Department of Rare Books and Special Collections, Strong Papers, Box 9.

29. Pettee, *American Secret Intelligence*.

30. Luternau alias Hagenbuch, *Attachés, 'Envoyés de marque' und Agenten*, 33. However, in its review of the publication, the *National-Zeitung* (24 May 1938, no. 238) pointed out, "The Intelligence Section of the General Staff Unit has not worked quite as naively as Luternau describes it. In order to do justice to this official body, we would like to mention precisely the example that Luternau gives in connection with Austria's Anschluss; during those critical days of March [1938], our General Staff was informed far in advance about Germany's detailed instructions for mobilizing its troops."

31. In the same letter, Labhart wrote, "Major Gonard, an officer detailed from the artillery, is slated to become deputy of Section 5." Samual Gonard, a future lieutenant general, was Chief of General Guisan's Personal Staff until Bernard Barbey replaced him in early summer 1940, at the time he was named head of the Operational Section. Between 1964 and 1969, Gonard was president of the International Committee of the Red Cross.

32. In that letter, Labhart indicated that he had Arnold H. Schwengeler in mind for that post.

33. General Staff Unit to Military Department, 29 March 1938. BAr E 27/1082, vol. 1.

34. Cf. Labhart's statement in the letter of 29 March 1938: "Due to the *extremely*

uncertain political situation, the personnel issue is particularly pressing in
Section 5."
35. In its activity report for the period up to December 31, 1939, Army
Intelligence wrote, "The events of 1938–39 (Anschluss, 1st and 2nd crisis in
Czechoslovakia, Albania) allowed the organization to get used to its job."
Nachrichtensektion, *Eingangsbericht der Nachrichtensektion im Armeestab über
Aufgaben und Tätigkeit bis zum 31.12.39*, 14 February 1940. BAr E
27/14849.
36. Labhart to Minger, 19 April 1939. BAr E 27/9507.
37. Masson put another 50,000 francs in the budget for unforeseen expenses, but
15,000 francs of that amount was allocated for representational expenses by the
three Swiss military attachés. (Labhart to Minger, 19 April 1939. BAr E
27/9507.)
38. Handwritten annotation by Minger on Labhart's letter, 22 April 1939.
39. Minger to Wetter, 1 May 1939. BAr E 27/9507.
40. Minger to Wetter, 1 May 1939.
41. Minger stated, "Due to the fact that this is a secret matter, I consider that the
only way to inform you is by telling you in person." (Minger to Wetter, 1 May
1939.)
42. Nachrichtensektion, *Eingangsbericht*, 14 February 1940. BAr E 27/14849.
43. Operations Order No. 13 dated 24 May 1941 stipulated that the four divisions
that were still stationed outside the central area be pulled back into the *Reduit*.
BAr E 27/14299.
44. *Bericht über Organisation und Tätigkeit der Gruppe Ia Front des Armeestabes
während des Aktivdienstes 1939–1945*. BAr E 27/14833. The rearrangements
that concerned Intelligence went into effect on 25 March 1941.
45. Abteilung Nachrichten- und Sicherheitsdienst, *V. Quartalsbericht (1.1.41-
31.3.41)*, 16 April 1941. BAr E 27/14849.
46. Chief of the General Staff Huber ordered, "The establishment of Group Id
must not result in any new positions being created; no new staff shall be hired.
[Moreover,] Group Id should refrain from having new stamps made for everyone. New stamps are justified only for the heads of the groups and sections. All
other existing stamps shall be modified accordingly." Chief of the General Staff
to Intelligence and Security Section, 21 February 1942. BAr E 27/9475, vol. 1.
47. Commander-in-Chief to Chief of the General Staff, 14 January 1942. BAr E
5795/327.
48. Commander-in-Chief to Kobelt, 20 February 1942. BAr E 5795/329. During
the 1941 restructuring process, Intelligence and Security were not combined
into one group because there was already a Group Id and because it was not
advisable to create a fifth group with an Assistant Chief of Staff as its head at a
time when efforts were made to reduce the number of Army Staff. However,
when the Army Staff was restructured once again, Group Id was dissolved effective January 1, 1942, and its head, Colonel Brigadier Hold, was appointed
inspector of the territorial troops.
49. That is the conclusion that can be drawn from a letter that the Commander-in-
Chief wrote to Chief of the General Staff Huber on January 14, 1942. Guisan
stated, "Following are the main arguments on which his promotion could be

based"; first, the increasing importance of Intelligence and Security; second, Masson's position toward the foreign military attachés would be improved; and third, it seemed to be "opportune to reinforce the position of our Chief of Intelligence and Security toward the Federal Council at a time that the activities of his service have come under attack, as you know. . . . It seems to me that this promotion would be nothing but fair toward Colonel Masson." BAr E 5795/327.

50. Handwritten annotation by Kobelt in a draft letter to the Commander-in-Chief dated 27 February 1942: "Mr. Secr[etary] of the Dep[artment], I do not like it when new assistant chiefs of staff are appointed just so the rank of colonel-brigadier can be bestowed on them. I would like to discuss this matter with [General Guisan]." BAr E 27/9475. The actual letter was dated 3 March 1942.

51. *Neue Zürcher Zeitung*, 2 March 1942, morning edition.

52. Pilet-Golaz to Kobelt, 2 March 1942. BAr E 27/9475, vol. 1.

53. The press release stated: "Bern, March 1. ag. The Army Staff reports: the Commander-in-Chief has appointed Colonel Masson of the General Staff as Assistant Chief of Staff in the army and has at the same time promoted him to the rank of colonel-brigadier. Army Intelligence and Security, which includes all bodies of the Military Police, continues to be headed by the new Assistant Chief of Staff." BAr E 27/9528.

54. Chief of the General Staff to Assistant Chief of Staff Id, 4 March 1942. Personal. BAr E 27/9528.

55. Kobelt to Commander-in-Chief, 3 March 1942. BAr E 27/9475, vol. 1.

56. Commander-in-Chief to Kobelt, 6 March 1942. BAr E 27/9475, vol. 1. In his letter, Guisan rejected Kobelt's arguments, stating: "When Colonel-Brigadier Corbat was promoted at the beginning of 1941, you did not object to it. Hence, I do not consider your objection to be well-founded." The Commander-in-Chief had made it clear from the beginning that promoting Masson to colonel-brigadier fell solely under his own authority. BAr E 27/9475, vol. 1.

57. The letters are at BAr E 27/9475, vol. 1.

58. Masson, *Organisation interne du groupe Ib*, 7 January 1944. BAr E 5795/327.

59. Huber, *Bericht des Generalstabschefs*, 236.

60. On the occasion of Masson's 70th birthday, on 1 July 1964, the *National-Zeitung* commented, "It was certainly a unique event in the history of the Secret Service for the Chief of Intelligence and Security to be in charge of the military service of breeding mares and mules."

61. Masson to Federal Councillor Paul Chaudet, 25 January 1962. Archives of H.R. Kurz.

62. This expression was used only in Army Intelligence's activity report covering the period up to 31 December 1939.

63. On 20 June 1945, Masson told Colonel Otto Müller, the magistrate investigating the case, "Not all officers who worked for Army Intelligence were assigned to one of these bureaus. Several officers were available directly to me; however, they did not deal with procuring intelligence." BAr E 5330 98/39, 1945.

64. Nachrichtensektion, *I. Quartalsbericht über den Aktivdienst, 1. Januar 1940–31. März 1940*, 30 April 1940. BAr E 27/14849.

65. Nachrichtensektion, *II. Quartalsbericht über den Aktivdienst, 1. April 1940–30. Juni 1940*, 11 July 1940. BAr E 27/14849.

66. Ernst to Masson, 15 October 1940. BAr J.I.140/4, vol. 2.

67. Ernst to Masson, 15 October 1940.

68. Ernst to Masson, 15 October 1940. (After the war, being unaware of the negative experience during wartime duty, army officials made new attempts to introduce comparable intermediate positions within Army Intelligence.)

69. Bureau D, *Tätigkeitsbericht 1. Sept.1940–31.Aug.1941*. BAr J.I.140/4, vol. 3.

70. Masson, *Réorganisation interne*, 5 August 1942. BAr E 27/9520.

71. Masson, *Réorganisation interne*, 5 August 1942.

72. Masson, order of 5 August 1942. BAr E 5795/327.

73. For matters of convenience, the Studies Bureau continued to be in charge of the contacts with the couriers abroad. Gruppe Id, *II. Halbjahresbericht (1.7.–31.12.42)*, 29 January 1943. BAr E 27/14849.

74. Masson, *Réorganisation interne*, 5 August 1942. In addition, in December 1942 the Commander-in-Chief designated Major Daniel as his liaison officer with Federal Councillors Pilet-Golaz and Kobelt. See Gruppe Id, *II. Halbjahresbericht (1.7.–31.12.42)*.

75. Interrogation of Masson, 20 June 1945. BAr E 5330 98/39 v.1945.

76. Masson to Colonel Otto Müller, magistrate investigating the case, 26 June 1945. BAr E 5330 1982/1, vol. 205.

77. Minutes of briefing on 30 December 1940. BAr E 27/9503.

78. Masson, *Rapports du Groupe Id*, 17 March 1942. BAr E 27/9503. The invitation went to Werner Müller, Schafroth, Daniel, Waibel, Ernst, and 1st Lieutenants Keller, Luy, and Olivet.

79. Mayr von Baldegg stated, "When we found out about something and reported it, nobody cared *how* we had obtained the information. However, we were blamed whenever something went wrong." Interrogation of Mayr von Baldegg by Colonel Otto Müller, 8 June 1945. BAr E 5330 1982/1, vol. 205.

80. Colonel Otto Müller to Military Attorney General, 8 August 1945. BAr E 5330 1982/1, vol. 205.

81. Labhart had informed Minger about plans to set up a photographic and chemical laboratory as early as 19 April 1939; he explained that this lab was "absolutely necessary" and would also work for the Attorney General's Office. The expected setup cost for the lab was about 40,000 francs. BAr E 27/9507.

82. Nachrichtensektion, *Eingangsbericht*, 14 February 1940.

83. Nachrichtensektion, *Eingangsbericht*, 14 February 1940. One of the linguists was Olivier Reverdin, a specialist in Classical Greek Language and Greek Literature. The work atmosphere among the cipher specialists was tense at times because of flaws of human nature. For instance, an ugly scene was created when a superior complained that Charles Daniel, who was in charge of the Cipher Bureau, had gone to see one of his subordinates about an issue even though that subordinate was "only" a lecturer at the university, whereas he was a professor who had tenure and was an expert in the field. Since the cipher specialists were not allowed to talk about their work outside their professional environment, their need for recognition sometimes incited them to behave awkwardly.

84. Nachrichten- und Sicherheitsdienst, *VII. Quartalsbericht (1.7.41–30.9.41)*, 3 November 1941. BAr E 27/14849.

85. Masson, *Ergänzender geheimer Bericht über den Aktivdienst 1939–45 der Abteilung Nachrichtendienst*, to the attention of the Chief of the General Staff (not intended for further distribution), no date. BAr E 27/14849.

86. Nachrichtensektion, *Eingangsbericht*, 14 February 1940. E 27/14849.

87. The common German and French abbreviations that were used in documents for Counterintelligence were "Spab" for "Spionageabwehr(dienst)" and "SCE" for Service de Contre-espionnage.

88. Cuénoud, *Section Alliés: Rapport general d'activité*, 20 August 1945. BAr E 27/14852.

89. Cuénoud, *Rapport general d'activité*.

90. *Organisation des Bureau Schweiz*, 11 October 1939. BAr E 5795/327.

91. The Swiss Bureau included liaison officers with the army unit commands and a secretariat that kept track of the positions of all units, recording them on card files.

92. The tasks of the Special Service will be described in Chapter 6 in connection with Meyer-Schwertenbach's military career.

93. Nachrichtensektion, *Eingangsbericht*, 14 February 1940. BAr E 27/14849.

94. Nachrichtensektion, *Eingangsbericht*, 14 February 1940.

95. Nachrichtensektion, *Eingangsbericht*, 14 February 1940.

96. In a letter to Jean Hotz, the director of the Commerce Section at the Federal Department of Economic Affairs, Masson explained that the military attachés occasionally provided information on talks dealing with trade policies, adding that at Hotz' request in the future he would forward to him a copy of the information on economic matters that was sent to the Chief of the General Staff. Masson to Hotz, 5 December 1941. BAr E 27/9502.

97. Masson, *Ergänzender geheimer Bericht*. BAr E 27/14849.

98. Nachrichtensektion, *Eingangsbericht*, 14 February 1940. BAr E 27/14849.

99. It was "put in charge of that task after being put together from scratch." Rudolf J. Ritter, Vice Director of the Sub-Group for Intelligence and Counterintelligence, to this author, 25 November 1988.

100. Captain Rudolf Stuber, commander of Signals Company 7, *Zusammenfassender Bericht über Ultrakurzwellen-Empfang auf dem Sphinxgipfel (Jungfraujoch)*, 20 January 1941. (Document in this author's possession.)

101. When the signals units were restructured in 1944, Signals Company 7 was renamed "Motorized Signals Company 20"; however, its equipment and tasks did not change. The bulk of the detachment was stationed in Ramisberg in the Emme Valley, where it was doing radio reconnaissance (now called "electronic reconnaissance"). The part of the detachment that was assigned to assist Counterintelligence worked at stationary plotting stations or was used as a mobile unit. When the army withdrew to the *Reduit*, Signals Company 7 relocated to Seelisberg, and it set up additional stations on the Jungfrau and San Salvatore mountains. (Information from Rudolf J. Ritter to this author, November 25, 1988. In 1989, R.J. Ritter published a historical study based on source documents entitled *Die Entwicklung des Funkwesens bei den*

Schweizerischen Verkehrstruppen von 1905 bis 1979. Colonel Ritter of the General Staff kindly made excerpts of his study available to this author before it was published.)

102. However, these were merely chance results. If the German radio communications had been consistently followed, they would undoubtedly have yielded some valuable results. In spite of repeated efforts, Procurement Office 1 was not able to obtain the requested material from the Press and Radio Section nor from the Army's Signals Service; nor was it able to at least get them to cooperate with Intelligence. See Alfred Ernst to head of the liaison section and head of telegraphing in the army, on "monitoring foreign radio shows," 10 February 1943. (Document in this author's possession.) Waibel occasionally tried to take action on his own because, in his opinion, "The daily bulletins by the Press and Radio Section did not meet the needs of Intelligence and did not yield any useful results." (Waibel, *Bericht über die Tätigkeit der N.S.1 während des Aktivdienstes 1939–45*, 20 July 1945. BAr E 27/14850.) However, the staff and material that Procurement Office 1 had available were not sufficient to yield any significant results.

103. Masson, *Ergänzender geheimer Bericht.* BAr E 27/14849.

104. Concerning the dissemination of the information, on February 24, 1942, Masson wrote to the Commander-in-Chief:

> In principle, one of the crucial activities of any Intelligence Service consists of quickly disseminating to the concerned parties the widest possible range of information that is of any interest to them. In an effort to abide by this principle, Intelligence asks about every document that it receives, "to whom could it be useful?" Then it immediately sends the original or a copy of the information to the interested authorities and services. Hence, we regularly supply information not only to the Army Command but also to various sections of the Federal Military Department and even to the Department of Justice and Police and the Department of Economic Affairs whenever it concerns them. (BAr E 27/9508, vol. 10.)

105. During the interrogation on June 20, 1945, Masson stated, "The information that we received from outside was very rarely submitted to me, i.e. only when it was very important." BAr E 5330 1982/1, vol. 205.

106. At the Commander-in-Chief's orders, the number of people who received the bulletin kept being reduced. Nevertheless, a few bulletins got into the hands of foreigners.

107. Masson to Chief of the General Staff Huber, 23 February 1945. BAr E 27/9502.

108. Masson to Huber, 23 February 1945. Masson did not hide his surprise about the fact that after four and a half years of wartime duty and after 662 issues had been published, there were still discussions about editorial matters in the bulletin.

109. These "reports" were sent to all recipients of the information bulletin who were in the military and to the Head of the Military Department. (In the beginning, all seven Federal Councillors received the information bulletin, but later it was

sent only to the Federal President, the Head of the Department of Foreign Affairs, and the Head of the Military Department.)

110. Colonel Werner Müller, *Befehl betreffend die Arbeitszuteilung, die Stellvertretung und die Kontrolle des Nachrichtenbulletins*, 10 October 1940. BAr E 27/9502.

111. Kanzlei der Abteilung Nachrichten- und Sicherheitsdienst, *Tätigkeitsbericht für die Zeit vom 1. September 1940 bis 31. August 1941*. BAr E 27/14847.

112. In a letter to Major Huber, the head of the Chief of the General Staff's office, Schafroth explained that due to the fact that the "Reports by the Intelligence Section" had not been distributed as widely among the army units as expected, in June 1941 the "Lessons from the War" began being published; they described specific tactical scenarios. BAr E 27/9508, vol. 11.

113. Masson, *Bericht über den Aktivdienst 1939–1945*.

114. In a letter to the Chief of the General Staff, General Guisan pointed out how important the "Lessons from the War" were and said that he would like them to be published more frequently. He also praised the brochure on guerilla warfare. Commander-in-Chief to Huber, 8 July 1942. BAr E 27/9502.

115. See General Guisan's comment and Masson's reply two paragraphs above.

116. In a letter to the Chief of the General Staff, General Guisan stated, "It is very obvious that the editor of the political section of bulletin no. 429—Lieutenant Colonel Schafroth if I am not mistaken—failed to do his duty as a General Staff officer who is asked to write a text of such great importance." Guisan asked Huber to see to it that Schafroth was not given any other political tasks because such "tasks require a more astute sense for politics and a great deal of tact." (Commander-in-Chief to Huber, 27 November 1942. BAr E 5795/327.) Other readers were also annoyed by the malicious anti-American comments that were made in bulletin no. 429 of November 6, 1942; Federal Councillor Kobelt wrote several letters on that subject to the Commander-in-Chief, describing the "sneering comments about [U.S.] President [Roosevelt] and his family as inappropriate." (Kobelt to Guisan, 26 November 1942. BAr E 5795/327.) Hausamann had informed the Head of the Military Department about the article in the bulletin as early as November 8, 1942, remarking:

> Verfasser ist Oberstleutnant Schafroth. Die Darlegungen (geschrieben ausgerechnet in diesen Tagen) beweisen, wie gering die Ahnung ist, welche der Mann vom Weltgeschehen hat. Was er sagt, ist materiell falsch. Er hätte es gerne so. Was schlimmer ist und weswegen ich Sie aufmerksam mache: wenn die Amerikaner Kenntnis davon bekommen, wie man mit dem amerik[anischen] Präsidenten und seiner Gattin umgeht (dass die Amerikaner es erfahren, ist in der Schweiz durchaus möglich), dann können die Schafrothschen Darlegungen, ins offizielle Bulletin aufgenommen, katastrophale Auswirkungen haben.

[Translation:]

> It was written by Lieutenant Colonel Schafroth. The statements (which he wrote at an inappropriate time) show how little this man understands about what goes on in the world. What he says is wrong. He would like things to be that way. What is worse, how-

ever—that is why I am writing to you—is that if the Americans
find out about how the Americ[an] President and his wife are
treated (in Switzerland it is perfectly possible that they will find
out), Schafroth's statements in the official bulletin can have disastrous consequences. (BAr E 5800/1, vol. 1.)
Other documents corroborate the suspicion that Masson was not very well
advised when he picked Schafroth to foster the contacts with foreign military
attachés in his absence.

117. Gruppe Id, *II. Halbjahresbericht (1.7.–31.12.42)*, 29 January 1943. BAr E 27/14849.
118. Werner Müller to Waibel, 18 June 1941. BAr E 27/9508, vol. 8.
119. Werner Müller to Waibel, 18 June 1941.
120. Waibel to Werner Müller, 15 March 1943. BAr E 5795/327.
121. Appendix 1 to information bulletin no. 461.
122. Waibel to Werner Müller, 15 March 1943. BAr E 5795/327.
123. Eberhard, *Tätigkeitsbericht der Sektion Achse*, 25 July 1945. BAr E 27/14851.
124. At the beginning of the war, however, both procurement and evaluation were inadequate. Everyone who was on the staff of the future Axis Section at that time agreed on that. The same was true for the Allied Section.
125. See Eberhard, *Tätigkeitsbericht der Sektion Achse*, 25 July 1945. BAr E 27/14851.
126. Eberhard, *Tätigkeitsbericht der Sektion Achse*, 25 July 1945.
127. On the issue of "depreciation of intelligence with time," on 25 January 1954, the Central Intelligence Agency, Office of Scientific Intelligence, Scientific Resources Division, stated:

Their practical value leaks away every day like precious wine leaking out of a defective barrel. There is no way to prevent the
inevitable day-by-day depreciation of intelligence; but with proper
planning we can deliver the intelligence paper to the consumer
when it is fresh, up-to-date and more nearly at the top of its value.
If we could *see* the value physically leaking away, we would do
more about it. . . . Thus, as to intelligence production, the correct
policy is few and *fast*.

The paper gives as reasons for the depreciation of intelligence: "1. Actual changes in the situation; 2. Possible, but unknown, change; so that the paper cannot be used with the same confidence as formerly; 3. Loss of attention and authority. Intelligence, as it grows old, quickly loses its interest and ability to attract attention, and so to influence decisions. It is of less practical value as fewer people read or heed it." (Princeton University Library, Public Policy Papers, Department of Rare Books and Special Collections, Strong Papers, Box 9.) A lack of coordination among Swiss Army Intelligence in several cases pre-vented valuable information that had been procured from reaching the interest-ed party *in time*.
128. The different procedures that were used by the German, French, Italian, and Other Countries Bureaus were standardized to a certain degree based on propo-sitions that Captain Fritz de Quervain, the head of the bureau evaluating litera-ture, had been asked to derive. See the comprehensive list of documents of

Group Id, Intelligence Section, 3 March 1943 (BAr E 27/9510), which gives an overview of the documents that were kept at the various bureaus, the bureau evaluating literature (the Swiss Federal Military Library), and the *Pilatus* and *Rigi* Procurement Offices. The documents included newspaper clippings, magazine articles, references to literature, card files, reports, copies of literary works, photographs, and illustrations.

129. Eberhard, *Tätigkeitsbericht der Sektion Achse*, 25 July 1945. BAr E 27/14851.

130. Eberhard, *Tätigkeitsbericht der Sektion Achse*, 25 July 1945. The same criticism was addressed to Masson (see Chapter 5).

131. In his civilian career, Werner Müller was head of the Security Police and Criminal Investigation Department of the City of Bern.

132. It was easy to guess what the cover name stood for; the head of Counterintelligence was the commander of the Security Police in Lausanne; hence, *Lac* referred to Lake Geneva.

133. On December 9, 1939, at a conference at the Federal Palace in Bern, the issue of *the confusingly large number of police authorities dealing with counterespionage* was raised by Emil Häberli, the commander of Army Intelligence's *Pfalz* sub-office, who took part in the conference in his capacity as state attorney of Basel. According to the minutes, he stated, "Currently there are as many as *nine* bodies in Switzerland that can, or believe to be able to, deal with counterespionage." (Minutes, 9 December 1939. BAr E 27/10098, vol. 12). The meeting served to exchange information and share experiences among the different bodies after the first 100 days of wartime duty. It was attended by representatives of the Police Section of the Territorial Service, police officers of the territorial and city command posts, staff of Counterintelligence, commanders of police departments, heads of the cantonal political sections, and the Police Service of the Attorney General's Office.

134. Huber, *Bericht des Generalstabschefs*, 269.

135. "Interfering in any way with political, economic, and financial matters or countering espionage that was directed against any state other than Switzerland was out of the question." (Huber, *Bericht des Generalstabschefs*, appendix 2 [written by Werner Müller], 476.) Counterintelligence was only in charge of military counterespionage.

136. Robert Jaquillard, born January 31, 1886, died mid-April 1951. On January 1, 1922, he became director of the Lausanne Security Police. A history of the Vaud Police Department states, "Because he was head of three of the five services that were part of the department at the time, he was considered as the eighth member of the cantonal government." On January 1, 1941, he became head of the Vaud Cantonal Police. The history of the Vaud Police Department comments, "He was quick-witted and brilliant; he was quick to understand problems, and the determination and authority with which he solved them made him a [real] 'boss'." (Police de sûreté vaudoise, Lausanne, ed., *La police de sûreté vaudoise 1877–1977. Un siècle au service du Pays* [Lausanne, 1977], 16.) After the war, Robert Jaquillard published memoirs on his activity as head of Counterintelligence to which General Guisan wrote a handwritten preface (the differences of fall 1942 between the two men—see Chapter 6 and page 436, endnote 18—had long been settled): Colonel Robert Jaquillard, *La Chasse aux*

Espions en Suisse. Choses vécues-1939–1945 (Lausanne, 1947). Jaquillard died a few months before his scheduled retirement.

137. As listed in Huber, *Bericht des Generalstabschefs*, 276ff.
138. Cf. minutes of Federal Council meeting of September 29, 1939: The Federal Council decides to create a military counterintelligence service for the army, "but it will operate only during wartime duty." (BAr E 1004.1 1, and excerpts of the minutes at E 27/10098, vol. 2.)
139. Obrecht to Federal Council, 28 September 1939. BAr E 27/10098, vol. 2.
140. Obrecht to Federal Council, 28 September 1939.
141. Senior Judge Baur of Divisional Court 8, *Schlussbericht über die vorläufige Beweisaufnahme in Sachen Anstände zwischen Bundespolizei und Spionageabwehrdienst der Armee*, 12 October 1948. BAr E 27/9471, vol. 1.
142. Baur, Schlussbericht.
143. See recording by 1st Lt. J., 27 March 1940. BAr E 27/10098, vol. 12.
144. Bracher to Kobelt, 30 September 1946. BAr E 27/9471, vol. 1.
145. Bracher to Kobelt, 30 September 1946.
146. Bracher to Kobelt, 30 September 1946.
147. Quoted in Baur, *Schlussbericht*. Hermann Renner, the examining magistrate from Frauenfeld, canton of Thurgau, and head of the Sargans Coordination Office, confirmed: "I was frequently under the impression that the gentlemen at Counterintelligence had built a wall around themselves and were extremely reluctant to provide any information at briefings. As a consequence, often one could not but suspect that their superiors had asked them to be silent or at least to use restraint." (Quoted in Baur, *Schlussbericht*. BAr E 27/9471, vol. 1.)

Chapter 4: The French Bureau—Allied Section

1. For the Axis Section and the German Bureau, see Chapter 5.
2. Cuénoud, *Section Alliés, Rapport général d'activité*, 20 August 1945. BAr E 27/14852.
3. Cuénoud, *Section Alliés, Rapport général d'activité*.
4. Cuénoud, *Section Alliés, Rapport général d'activité*.
5. See Chapter 5.
6. Cuénoud, *Section Alliés, Rapport général d'activité*. BAr E 27/14852.
7. Cuénoud, *Section Alliés, Rapport général d'activité*.
8. The system of questioning people arriving in Switzerland and the controversies surrounding this practice will be discussed in Chapter 5.
9. See Cuénoud to Masson, 28 December 1942. *Rapport d'activité du Bureau France/Section Alliés du 1.9.41 au 31.8.42*. BAr E 27/14852.
10. The outpost in Ajoie was in service until January 11, 1945; it maintained radio contact with Poland, southern Germany, Belgium, eastern France, and Alsace. See Cuénoud, *Section Alliés, Rapport général d'activité*. BAr E 27/14852.
11. During the peak of its activities, the outpost in Lausanne for example had 59 agents, 16 of whom were on permanent assignment and 19 on temporary assignment; 24 agents were listed as "volunteers."
12. Cuénoud, *Section Alliés, Rapport d'activité* (1 September 1942 to 31 December 1943), 8 April 1944. BAr E 27/14852.

13. Cuénoud, *Rapport d'activité du Bureau France pendant l'année 1941*, 30 December 1941. BAr E 27/14852.

14. Cf. Anthony Cave Brown, *The Secret War Report of the OSS* (New York, 1976), 25: "The trouble about the French resistance was that it was indiscreet—and often dangerously and criminally so. As Ben Cowburn, an SOE agent who spent more time in France than almost any other agent, reported afterwards, 'Security in France was nil, and 95 percent of the people arrested were caught simply because their friends had been incapable of keeping their mouths shut'."

15. Cuénoud, *Rapport d'activité du Bureau France* (1 September 1939 to 31 August 1940), 30 October 1940. BAr E 27/14852.

16. Cuénoud, *Rapport d'activité du Bureau France* (1 September 1939 to 31 August 1940).

17. Cf. Cuénoud's statement: "The need to constantly recruit new people [was] detrimental to the service due to the fact that the briefing and training of agents was a long and tedious process." *Rapport d'activité du Bureau France pendant l'année 1941*. BAr E 27/14852.

18. Cuénoud, *Rapport d'activité du Bureau France* (1 September 1939 to 31 August 1940). BAr E 27/14852.

19. Cuénoud, *Section Alliés, Rapport général d'activité*. BAr E 27/14852.

20. One year later, Schellenberg told Masson that he had the same suspicion. After the war, Hans Bernd Gisevius, who had worked for the German *Abwehr* during the war, explained that the documents that had been found at *La Charité-sur-Loire* were "one of the reasons why it was assumed that Swiss Intelligence forwarded all its material to the Allies." Interrogation of Gisevius by Major Fürst, special magistrate of divisional court 6, 14 May 1947. (Document in this author's possession.)

21. Cuénoud, *Rapport d'activité du Bureau France pendant l'année 1941*. BAr E 27/14852.

22. Cf. Cuénoud's statement: "Just to give an example, it is difficult to obtain forged French papers or to forge them on our own. It is virtually impossible to obtain authentic food cards for the agents who go to France; we have to resort to using forged cards. The agents have great difficulties finding transport to get around. It is difficult to find lodgings for our personnel; they do not always have the papers that are needed for a certain region, so they cannot stay at hotels nor eat at the restaurant because the police check everyone. It is very difficult to pay the agents in French francs (foreign currency transactions are forbidden), etc." *Rapport d'activité du Bureau France pendant l'année 1941*. BAr E 27/14852.

23. Cuénoud, *Rapport d'activité du Bureau France pendant l'année 1941*.

24. See Cuénoud to Masson, 28 December 1942, *Rapport d'activité du Bureau France/Section Alliés du 1.9.41 au 31.8.42*. BAr E 27/14852.

25. Cuénoud, *Section Alliés, Rapport général d'activité*. After it had gradually increased to 200,000 francs, on September 22, 1942, Federal Councillor Kobelt hiked the annual budget for Army Intelligence by 100,000 francs to 300,000 francs. Cf. Masson to Chief of the General Staff Huber, 20 August 1942: "As it has become more and more difficult to procure intelligence (due in part to

strict surveillance, in part to curbed traffic, etc.), expenses have once again increased during the current year." BAr E 27/9507.

26. Cf. Masson to Commander-in-Chief, 27 July 1942: "In your letter No. 10793 of July 3, 1942, to the Chief of the General Staff, you asked Group Id to do some investigating in order to obtain detailed information about the fortification projects that the Germans have undertaken in Belgium and France. It is my honor to inform you that we were able to put together a special 'team' for this delicate mission. . . . The fortification zones and the areas where earthwork is being done are meticulously guarded by troops or special guards, and our agents have had to take some risks; some of them had to advance all the way to the Channel. Our investigation is still in progress . . ." (BAr E 5795/327).

27. Cuénoud, *Section Alliés, Rapport général d'activité*. BAr E 27/14852.

28. See Cuénoud to Masson, 28 December 1942, *Rapport d'activité du Bureau France/Section Alliés du 1.9.41 au 31.8.42*. BAr E 27/14852.

29. Cuénoud, *Section Alliés, Rapport d'activité* (1 September 1942 to 31 December 1943). BAr E 27/14852.

30. Cuénoud, *Section Alliés, Rapport général d'activité*. Cf. Heinz Abosch, "Krieger im Schatten: Wahrheit und Legende der Résistance," in *Neue Zürcher Zeitung*, 18–19 June 1988, no. 140: "There were traitors and denunciators—could it have been otherwise? Many resistance fighters could no longer bear the systematic torture to which they were subjected after being arrested. . . . It was impressive how many of them quietly made sacrifices; in that 'undercover war' there was no room for vociferous heroism. It was the time of anonymous deeds that only a few knew about and that did not leave any traces. Obviously the active resistance was only a minority, but more and more people viewed them with sympathy. Once the war had been decided, of course, the 'silent majority' talked about its own heroism even though it had not been heroic. This is a trivial event that has been observed time and again in history." On this issue, see, among others, Henri Michel, *Histoire de la Résistance en France* (Paris, 1972); Henri Noguères, *Histoire de la Résistance en France* (Paris, 1967).

31. The agent was Alfred Carnet, who was sentenced to death. However, on March 22, 1945, by 126 yea to 80 nay, parliament converted his death sentence to life in prison.

32. Cuénoud, *Section Alliés, Rapport général d'activité*. BAr E 27/14852.

33. Cuénoud, *Section Alliés, Rapport général d'activité*.

34. Cuénoud, *Section Alliés, Rapport général d'activité*.

35. Cuénoud, *Section Alliés, Rapport d'activité* (1 September 1942 to 31 December 1943). BAr E 27/14852.

36. Cuénoud, *Section Alliés, Rapport général d'activité*. BAr E 27/14852.

37. Cuénoud, *Section Alliés, Rapport général d'activité*.

38. Cuénoud, *Section Alliés, Rapport général d'activité*.

39. Cuénoud, *Section Alliés, Rapport général d'activité*.

Chapter 5: The German Bureau—Axis Section

1. On August 30, 1939, in a letter to the General Staff Unit, Minger stated, "If possible, the position in question on Army Intelligence should be filled with an

officer who has a law degree because some legal background is required for dealing with a number of issues, such as counterintelligence, censorship, etc." BAr E 27/9521.

2. Minutes of Federal Council meeting, 25 September 1939. BAr E 1004.1 1.

3. Ernst, *Tätigkeitsbericht Bureau D*, 15 October 1940. BAr J.I.140/4, vol. 2.

4. Ernst, *Tätigkeitsbericht Bureau D*, 15 October 1940.

5. On Hausamann's "double role," on September 30, 1940, Military Attorney General Trüssel wrote to the Commander-in-Chief: "On one hand, he serves as a body of the Intelligence Section by supplying reports on the situation abroad and information about movements of troops; on the other hand, he is a propaganda body of the army toward the press and the political parties. He *should* report to the Intelligence Section on all these activities." Trüssel considered it "dangerous if [Hausamann acted] as a body of the Intelligence Section at one moment and as an informant for political parties and propaganda bodies the next, [adding] one does not really know to whom he reports and who supervises his activities." BAr E 5795/448, vol. 1.

6. On September 26, 1940, Army Intelligence wrote to the Commander-in-Chief: "On one hand, as an officer who is assigned to the Army Staff he has to be considered a member of the military; on the other hand, he works for a civilian intelligence organization that was set up during a time of peace and has continued operating since wartime duty began." BAr E 5795/448, vol. 1.

7. Cf. Masson's statement to Chief of the General Staff Huber, March 30, 1945: "Hausamann was the one with whom I established our network abroad before the war, at the time the Swiss Deuxième Bureau consisted of a head of section and his secretary. This network was set up before 1939, has not been modified very much since then, and deals with general issues. The other bureaus do military and topographic research in a more narrow sense and use a larger number of agents. Hausamann is still able to correspond via undercover radio stations while the other bureaus have to use numerous frontier runners and different kinds of agents (one single 'chain' often consists of 12 to 15 agents working for one connection)." BAr E 27/9507. In a letter to Chief of the General Staff de Montmollin, Masson wrote about Hausamann's attitude: "Overall, Hausamann showed a sympathetic, sometimes even a friendly, attitude toward his superior. . . . Hausamann had a lot of respect for me and was very devoted to me." Masson recalled "Hausamann's tendency to 'surround' his superior with advice (there is only a three-year age difference between the two of us) and with certain 'initiatives' that were supposed to be useful to me, but about which I did not know at the time they were taken." Masson to Chief of the General Staff, to the attention of the Military Department, July 12, 1947 (classified as secret; testimony in the case of Hausamann vs. Kummer/Schmid). BAr E 27/9846.

8. Hausamann to Commander-in-Chief, April 10, 1944. Archives of H.R. Kurz.

9. Hausamann, *Bericht über die Informationsreise vom 26.V.38 bis 31.V.38*, 1 June 1938. BAr E 27/9848.

10. A lot of nonsense has been written about Roessler's sources. According to one account, General Jodl, Hitler's personal chief of staff, of all people, supplied information to Roessler! It is established, however, that Roessler was connected to the Führer's headquarters, the German Armed Forces High Command

(OKW) as well as the German Army High Command (OKH), top authorities of the German Air Force and Navy, the Replacement Army, and the War Economy and Armament Office. (Documentation by Hausamann at the archives of H.R. Kurz.)

11. After the war, Hausamann told Werner Rings about his informants: "I was . . . mostly looking for contacts with foreign diplomats. They included, among others, Minister Masaryk, the Czech Envoy in London, with whom I ended up getting along very well and who informed me about everything he knew. There were other diplomats in several capitals. However, I was mostly interested in *contacts with foreign intelligence services*, with which I established radio contact." Werner Rings, interview with Hausamann, 6 to 14 May 1968. AfZ files of Werner Rings.

12. Hausamann to Alphons Matt, 5 May 1966. Archives of H.R. Kurz.

13. Hausamann had two radio stations for contacting foreign countries. In addition, Hausamann explained, "Another radio network had been set up inside Switzerland; it consisted of 20 small transmitters the size of a cigar box that were connected with Teufen, the headquarters. This network [inside Switzerland] had orders to maintain radio contact with the Army Command in the *Reduit* in the event that Switzerland was occupied." The transmitters were manned by retired telegraph operators and other carefully selected people. Hausamann explained, "The transmitters were put into service only once for a test run, then they had to be silent in order not to give themselves away." Rings, interview with Hausamann, 6 to 14 May 1968.

14. Rings, interview with Hausamann, 6 to 14 May 1968.

15. Cf. Commander-in-Chief's comment to Chief of the General Staff, 10 April 1943: "Reports by . . . Major Hausamann are not all of the same interest, and some of them are full of remarks that are supposed to influence the command." BAr E 5795/327.

16. For instance, on August 29, 1939 at 13.33 hours, Hausamann telegraphed from Teufen to Bern that the Germans would launch their attack on Poland on September 1. As a result of the close cooperation between Bureau Ha and Procurement Office 1 in Lucerne, shortly after the beginning of the war Bureau Ha was transferred from Teufen to Kastanienbaum, a small village less than 10 miles outside Lucerne, and later to Kriens, a suburb of Lucerne. (See Intelligence Section to Commander-in-Chief, 26 September 1940. Archives of H.R. Kurz.)

17. Hausamann to Masson, 24 August 1942. BAr E 27/9837, vol. 5.

18. Assistant Chief of Staff for the Front to Masson, 29 September 1939. BAr E 5795/327.

19. Lieutenant General Hans Frick (was chief instructor of the Swiss Army from 1944 to 1953) to Erwin Tschudi, 7 November 1969. Concerning Hausamann, he stated, "I was his chief Masson's immediate superior, and I did not trust him at all. During the short period of time from August to December 1939, the time I was transferred from my post as Assistant Chief of Staff, Hausamann alerted us at least on three occasions about an imminent German attack or an amassing of German troops at the border; these alerts turned out to be completely false." (However, Hausamann denied these allegations shortly before he

died; in January 1973 he told Professor Marcel Beck, "I do not know anything about [these false alerts]. On the contrary, in Alphons Matt's book (page 41) you can read the text of one of my reports, which I wrote at the request of the General Staff, in which I *refuted* information according to which a large number of troops were stationed in southern Germany." Files of Tschudi.) In his letter, Frick continued, "I consequently told Masson to dismiss Hausamann from Army Intelligence, but Masson implored me to let Hausamann stay on because he was a very valuable staff member. Unfortunately I gave in to Masson's request. . . . It may be inappropriate for you [Tschudi] to describe Hausamann as 'a hooligan, a man craving for sensation, and a skilled windbag'; it would have been sufficient to talk about his 'boundless need for recognition'." (Document in this author's possession.)

20. On January 18, 1941, Werner Müller, the Deputy Chief of Intelligence, wrote to Hausamann, "I am asking you to stop constantly criticizing the measures ordered by the Army Command. . . . This is none of Intelligence's business. . . . The same applies to your criticizing the fact that internees have been deported." BAr E 27/9508, vol. 7. However, Colonel Müller had his own ideas about criticism; when Waibel protested against transferring Wilhelm Lützelschwab from Counterintelligence back to the troops, Müller was indignant, replying: "It is unbelievable that transferring a corporal gives rise to so many discussions. This is apparently due to the fact that civilians believe that every measure has to be justified." BAr E 27/9508, vol. 10. Annoyed subordinates used to call Colonel Müller a "Quadratschädel" (literal translation "square skull," i.e., "blockhead"), a term that referred to both his sometimes authoritarian attitude and the shape of his head. (During conversations with this author between 1985 and 1988, Meyer-Schwertenbach's widow constantly referred to Colonel Müller by that provocative name.)

21. After resigning as director of the Hausamann firm in early 1942, during the time he worked for Group Id he was paid the salary of a top consultant of the General Staff Unit. In a letter dated March 28, 1942, Hausamann thanked Masson for this arrangement, adding, "I told you several times before that it is very important to me not to become an *official* of the federal administration." BAr E 27/9838.

22. On May 28, 1940, Hausamann wrote to Masson, "[Schafroth asked] me once again why I was acting this way. I told him verbatim, 'Because it is my duty as a citizen'." Then Schafroth harshly asked Hausamann what he thought he was doing, adding, "Are you an officer or not? If not, what exactly are you?" Hausamann stood up and reported absent. Schafroth reacted vehemently, exclaiming, "Outrageous! You should be locked up immediately." BAr E 27/9840.

23. Waibel to Intelligence Section, 7 August 1947 (testimony in the case Hausamann vs. Kummer). BAr J.I.137 1974/64, vol. 9.

24. Historians have to discount some of Hausamann's most dramatic statements. His eloquent style made many things sound more extraordinary than they actually were. That does not diminish Hausamann's merits but puts the network of connections of *Bureau Ha* in perspective.

25. Cover name for *Bureau Ha*.

26. During the war, *Bureau Ha* received between 12,000 and 13,000 francs monthly from Army Intelligence for its services, amounting to about 150,000 francs
annually. By way of comparison, in 1942 Procurement Office 1 and its outposts
spent a total of just over 79,000 francs, in 1943 approximately the same
amount as *Bureau Ha*, and in 1944 280,000 francs, twice as much as *Bureau
Ha*. (Documents in the author's possession.)
27. Waibel to Masson, 31 May 1940. BAr E 27/9840.
28. On April 1, 1940, Masson wrote to the Assistant Chief of Staff for the Front:
"This officer has been part of the army's General Staff for many years. Captain
Hausamann accomplishes the missions with which he is entrusted with absolute
devotion, great zeal, conscientiousness, precision, and talent as an organizer. He
is loyal and open; I fully trust him." BAr E 27/9508, vol. 4.
29. On January 7, 1941, Masson wrote to the Commander-in-Chief, "After many
years of observation (. . . he has been working for our section for ten years), we
know that Captain Hausamann always keeps to the straight and narrow without being concerned about whether the political right or left likes it." BAr E
27/9508, vol. 7.
30. Fuhrer, "Die Schweiz im Nachrichtendienst," 409–410.
31. Hans Frick, Commander of 7th Division, to Masson, 15 November 1942. BAr
E 27/9843.
32. Masson to Lieutenant General Hans Frick, 15 December 1966. Files of
Tschudi.
33. On July 28, 1947, Allen Dulles wrote to Hausamann, "I always appreciated
your staunch and forthright position during the war, and your clear vision of
what the Nazi menace meant to the type of civilization which Switzerland and
America represent." Princeton University Library, Allen W. Dulles Papers, Box
30.
34. Chief of the General Staff to Commander-in-Chief, 1 January 1941 (handwritten). BAr E 5795/86. Some of Hausamann's unpleasant traits of character have
to be weighed against his total commitment to the Officers' Conspiracy of summer 1940 and, following its uncovering, his major contribution to the creation
of its successor organization, the *Action for National Resistance*, a body that
played a valuable role in fighting against defeatist tendencies and a tendency to
accommodate Germany. In retrospect, to outsiders his merits in connection
with keeping Switzerland independent seem to far outweigh the negative
aspects of his character.
35. Masson to Chief of the General Staff, 22 May 1944. BAr E 27/14340. Masson
referred to Major Peter Burckhardt of the General Staff, who had replaced
Colonel Hans von Werdt in May 1943.
36. In a letter to Masson dated October 25, 1939, Waibel explained:
    Even though he had been advised not to leave his post, *two days*
    before the Germans mobilized their entire armed forces, our mili-
    tary attaché, who was ignorant about the situation, traveled to
    Switzerland to take care of some personal business. He returned to
    Berlin on the fourth day of mobilization; there he surprised me by
    asking me whether the Germans had really called up the armed
    forces. If I had not decided, out of my own initiative, to stay in

Berlin after mid-August due to the threatening situation instead of going on vacation, we would not have had one single military reporter in Berlin *during the entire time that the Germans mobilized their troops and deployed them to their first positions.* It would be hard to imagine a more blatant case of someone making a false assessment of the situation. (BAr J.I.140/4, vol. 1.)

On the way in which the German mobilization, which was ordered on August 25, 1939, was *camouflaged* and the way in which the troops were deployed to the borders, see Burkhart Mueller-Hillebrand, *Die Blitzfeldzüge 1939–1941: Das Heer im Kriege bis zum Beginn des Feldzuges gegen die Sowjetunion im Juni 1941* (Frankfurt a.M., 1956), 15 ff.

37. Waibel to Masson, 25 October 1939.

38. From fall 1938 to the outbreak of the war, Max Waibel attended the War Academy in Berlin, the training facility for the General Staff of the German Army. See Military Department, detailing order, 15 July 1938. BAr E 27/12054. Even though he was a Swiss citizen, Waibel was fully accepted by his 26 classmates. Waibel commented: "There was hardly any secret that I did not know. . . . For that reason, I dare say that there were probably not many foreigners in Germany who were able to observe the military-political events from a better angle than I was at the War Academy." Waibel, Bericht, 26 February 1963. BAr J.I.137 1974/64, vol. 13.

39. Ernst, *Tätigkeitsbericht Bureau D*, 15 October 1940. BAr J.I. 140/4, vol. 2.

40. Ernst wrote: "Overall the border guards have been doing a good job. However, some negative effects have been noticeable because they lack systematic training." Ernst, *Tätigkeitsbericht Bureau D*, 15 October 1940.

41. Major Combe, notes used for a meeting on 3 May 1924 between Major General Roost and Arnold Gassmann, director of the federal customs authorities, 28 April 1923. BAr E 27/9492. For his meeting with Gassmann, Chief of the General Staff Roost used the first assessment that Combe had made one year earlier, two months after the border brigades had begun their intelligence activities.

42. Eidgenössische Oberzolldirektion, "Instruktion betreffend die Mitwirkung der Zollorgane beim militärischen Nachrichtendienst," 21 June 1923. BAr E 27/9492. The instructions were addressed exclusively to the heads of the border patrols; they were "to be communicated in a suitable manner to the concerned heads of section, heads of checkpoints, and border patrols." (Federal Customs Inspector Häusermann to the regional customs authorities, 21 June 1923. BAr E 27/9492.)

43. On 5 and 7 March 1923.

44. In order to maintain the necessary secrecy, "as few people as possible" were involved in the intelligence activities. Oberzolldirektion, "Instruktion," 21 June 1923.

45. Major Combe, notes used for meeting on 3 May 1924. BAr E 27/9492.

46. As an exception, the Chief of the General Staff and the Chief of Intelligence were authorized to communicate verbally with customs officials during official visits. However, these visits, for which the two officers received special visitor passes from the federal customs authorities, served only to exchange informa-

tion. The two men were not allowed to issue orders or instructions directly to border patrols.

47. Federal customs authorities to regional customs authorities in Basel, Schaffhausen, and Chur, 4 April 1939. BAr E 27/9492.
48. Federal customs authorities to regional customs authorities, 4 April 1939.
49. Federal customs authorities to regional customs authorities, 4 April 1939.
50. The good relations were maintained beyond World War II. See Chief of Intelligence Daniel to federal customs authorities, 11 October 1950. BAr E 27/9492.
51. In an order dated September 15, 1939, Masson stated, "Captain Waibel shall be assigned to the 'German Bureau' as Captain Ernst's deputy." BAr E 5795/327.
52. Waibel, *Bericht*, 26 February 1963. On several occasions, Ernst voiced a similar opinion about Waibel.
53. Ernst, *Tätigkeitsbericht Bureau D*, 15 October 1940. BAr J.I. 140/4, vol.2.
54. Masson, "Befehl für die Organisation des Bureau Deutschland," 21 October 1939. BAr E 27/9476.
55. After Ernst left Army Intelligence in mid-1943, Waibel was temporarily put in charge of both procurement and evaluation for the Axis Section. See Masson to Chief of the General Staff, 21 October 1943. BAr E 27/9508, vol. 14.
56. On January 22, 1971, Emil Häberli, the head of the procurement sub-office in Basel, wrote in the *National-Zeitung* (No. 34):
    > Waibel was well-educated. However, he was not only a humanist but also human. As a chief and comrade he was generous, understanding, and he spoke in a human manner, even with this subordinates; he was averse to raising his voice in a commanding fashion. . . . In unpleasant and difficult situations, Waibel never lost his composure nor the humor that is typical of people from Basel. He had a way of laughing from the bottom of his heart that made other people who had already begun to despair laugh and regain confidence. Max Waibel was a kind person who became a real friend for many staff members, regardless of their rank.
57. Gerold Walser to this author, 9 August 1988.
58. Ernst in *Basler Nachrichten*, No. 33, 23–24 January 1971.
59. Waibel, *Bericht*, 26 February 1963.
60. Eberhard, *Tätigkeitsbericht der Sektion Achse*, 25 July 1945. BAr E 27/14851.
61. Eberhard, *Tätigkeitsbericht der Sektion Achse*, 25 July 1945.
62. Ernst, *Tätigkeitsbericht Bureau D*, 15 October 1940.
63. "N.S.1" was the official abbreviation for "Nachrichtensammelstelle 1" (Procurement Office 1). N.S.3 to N.S.9 reported to the head of the French Bureau, Bernard Cuénoud, as indicated in an order dated October 10, 1940, issued by Masson's deputy, Werner Müller (BAr E 5795/327). Apparently N.S.2 was supposed to be the official abbreviation for *Bureau Ha*; however, only N.S.1 ended up being commonly used, to identify Waibel's office.
64. On November 12, 1940, Waibel wrote to Colonel-Divisional-Commander Dollfus, the Adjutant General of the Army, "We have frequently had the experience that certain personalities consider that their statements would not reach

the 'right person' if they were not directly addressed to the Commander-in-Chief or an army unit commander." BAr E 27/14334.

65. Waibel, *Tätigkeitsbericht der N.S.1 vom 1. September 1939–31. August 1940.* BAr E 27/14850.

66. Waibel, *Bericht über die Tätigkeit der N.S.1 während des Aktivdienstes 1939/45,* 20 July 1945. BAr E 27/14850. In these instances, true signals still had to be distinguished from inverted signals. Germany deliberately led Swiss citizens whom it was expelling through regions with massive movements of troops. Ernst later explained: "I remember a number of cases where Swiss were channeled to us who were supposed to tell us that they had witnessed a deployment of troops. They did see a deployment, but partly in the opposite direction; that was intentional." Rings, "Interview mit Alfred Ernst," 29 August 1972. AfZ files of Werner Rings.

67. Ernst von Schenck was a co-founder of the *Action for National Resistance*, which was created on September 7, 1940 at the initiative of Hans Hausamann as the civilian "successor organization" of the disbanded Officers' Conspiracy. Other founding members included Walter Allgöwer, Karl Barth, August R. Lindt, and Hans Oprecht. Ernst von Schenck wrote the *Information der Woche*, a weekly overview of major foreign political facts which could not be published in the regular Swiss press due to the censorship that was in place and was therefore mailed to every member of the new organization in a closed envelope. Among the members who joined the *Action for National Resistance* by making an oath and signing a document were Albert Oeri, Karl Meyer, William Rappard, and the three future Federal Councillors Feldmann, Weber, and Spühler. (Information and documents supplied by Alfred Braunschweig, a Protestant minister who had joined the secret organization at the instigation of his friend Karl Barth.)

68. Abteilung Nachrichten- und Sicherheitsdienst, *VII. Quartalsbericht* (1.7.41–30.9.41), 3 November 1941. BAr E 27/14849.

69. Masson, *Ergänzender geheimer Bericht.* BAr E 27/14849.

70. The Bureau was created on October 6, 1942 on orders of the Assistant Chief of Staff Id; the Commander-in-Chief had a keen interest in it. See order by Masson, 6 October 1942, and Commander-in-Chief to Chief of the General Staff, 7 October 1942. Both documents are at BAr E 27/9480.

71. Masson, *Ergänzender geheimer Bericht.* BAr E 27/14849.

72. Statement made by Waibel in his *Bericht 1939/45,* 20 July 1945. BAr E 27/14850.

73. In an effort not to miss any opportunity for procuring intelligence, Army Intelligence was also interested in *systematically recording railway traffic across the border.* Every train that was arriving from abroad or departing for a foreign country was to be checked by qualified personnel, and the travelers and staff on the train were to be interviewed briefly about their destination, observations abroad, the situation along the route, and the mood among the population. In fall 1939, shortly after the army was mobilized, this monitoring activity and the daily reporting to Army Intelligence "was satisfactory at practically all train stations along the border" (Chief of Intelligence to command of 2nd Army Corps, 26 January 1940. BAr E 27/9482, vol. 4). In Basel, however, the situation was

somewhat complicated. Unfortunately Army Intelligence showed little psychological skill; Schafroth lectured the involved parties, accusing them of lacking goodwill. His offensive tone, accusations, and insinuations did not help to promote cooperation, resulting in an extended unpleasant dispute between Army Intelligence and the command of the city of Basel, its police officers, the command of the 2nd Army Corps, and other involved parties. This dispute was clearly caused by Army Intelligence. The issue of stepping up the efforts to procure intelligence in Basel was finally discussed at a conference in Basel (on February 12, 1940; for its results, see Captain Hausherr of the General Staff [command of 2nd Army Corps] to Army Intelligence, 14 February 1940. BAr E 27/9482, vol. 4).

74. Waibel, *Tätigkeitsbericht der N.S.1 vom 1. September 1939–31. August 1940.* BAr E 27/14850. An official at the Department of Foreign Affairs wrote:
    During the first months after the beginning of the war, the interviews by bodies of Army Intelligence were conducted right after the trains had arrived at the border station. The concerned persons were brought into a special room. Of course the other travelers and the foreign authorities quickly found out what these interviews were all about. Numerous travelers complained, and the Intelligence Service realized that this system was not expedient. As a consequence, a different method was introduced for questioning travelers. (Federal Department of Foreign Affairs, note for file by an unknown person, 18 November 1941. BAr E 2001 (D) 3, vol. 3.)
    Around February 16, 1940, after a field trip to the border station of St. Margrethen, canton of St. Gallen, a Counterintelligence inspector reported:
    The so-called "intelligence people" at the train station are a much greater evil than the German officials; they should be done away with. As you probably know, in St. Margrethen and at other train stations the army has established so-called Intelligence Bureaus. The team that is assigned to this bureau is supposed to interrogate travelers returning from Germany or arriving for a vacation in Switzerland about the situation in Germany and the things that they experienced there. When they find a case that interests them, with their typewriter in their lap they accompany the traveler all the way to St. Gallen, questioning him on every detail without paying any attention to who else listens in on the conversation in the train compartment. I believe that it would be safer for our country to drop these interviews at the border and have them conducted at a later time by professionals. The travelers arriving in the country should only be recorded, and the concerned persons should then receive a written note at their place of stay. . . . In order to convince you about this idea, I would like to mention just one incident that I experienced on the 8th. A Swiss living abroad who had arrived on the noon train was all agitated when he stepped onto the platform, asking several travelers where he could get his passport back. Another traveler explained to him in pol-

ished High German that he did not need to worry; the passport would be returned to him at the bureau once he had been questioned about the situation in Germany. Somebody else stood behind the speaker; this person was Gestapo official Trummer, who certainly did not like what he had just heard. . . . Not enough caution is used regarding these interviews. (BAr E 27/9914.) The Counterintelligence inspector pointed his finger at a sore spot. Initially the Intelligence staff was indeed somewhat careless and overzealous, which was detrimental to the success of the interviews. By introducing the immigration form, most travelers could be questioned discreetly at their homes. An official from Army Intelligence usually contacted travelers by telephone, telling them, "John Doe from the Army Command speaking. I would like to speak with you on behalf of the Army Command. I prefer not to mention the subject of our interview over the phone. I will inform you verbally about it and show you proof of my identity when we meet." Whenever a traveler wanted to find out more about the subject of the interview, the official specified that it was about his trip abroad. Explanation by Werner Müller to Minister Bonna, the head of the Foreign Service at the Department of Foreign Affairs, 30 August 1941. BAr E 27/9508, vol. 9.

75. Both Swiss citizens and foreign nationals filled out an immigration form (see "Rigi" to Schafroth, 24 February 1940. BAr E 27/9914). However, on March 1, 1940, Army Intelligence informed the Police Section of the Justice and Police Department that it did not take long to realize "that foreigners [did] not take [the] recording procedure seriously at all; they [did] not hesitate to supply a wrong address." BAr E 27/9508, vol. 3.

76. Cf. Masson's statement: "Hence, the Attorney General's Office is able to keep track of foreigners' movements in Switzerland, follow the tracks of suspects (especially in the area of political espionage, which falls under its authority), and handle certain specific cases effectively and quickly together with the cantonal police authorities." Masson, "Relations entre le Département politique fédéral et le Service des renseignements," 24 October 1941. BAr E 27/9483, vol. 1.

77. The head of the respective Bureau ("Rigi," German, French, or Italian Bureau) had to issue orders to conduct any interview.

78. Nachrichtensektion, *I. Quartalsbericht über den Aktivdienst (1. Januar 1940–31. März 1940)*, 30 April 1940. BAr E 27/14849.

79. Gruppe Id, *I. Halbjahresbericht über den Aktivdienst (1. Januar 1942–30. Juni 1942)*, 12 August 1942. BAr E 27/14849.

80. See Waibel, *Bericht 1939/45*. BAr E 27/14850.

81. Waibel, *Bericht 1939/45*.

82. Gruppe Id, *II. Halbjahresbericht (1. Juli-31.Dezember 1942)*, 29 January 1943. BAr E 27/14849.

83. Nachrichtensektion, *II. Quartalsbericht über den Aktivdienst (1. April 1940–30. Juni 1940)*, 11 July 1940. BAr E 27/14849.

84. Gruppe Id, *II. Halbjahresbericht*. Cf. also Cuénoud's statement, "In this context, we would like to mention the nearly total silence that the English and American pilots have been keeping who were forced to land in our country."

Cuénoud, *Rapport d'activité, Section Alliés*, (1 September 1942 to 31 December 1943), 8 April 1944. BAr E 27/14852.

85. Waibel, *Bericht 1939/45*. BAr E 27/14850.

86. Waibel, *Bericht 1939/45*.

87. Waibel, *Bericht 1939/45*.

88. See Waibel, *Bericht 1939/45*.

89. The Federal Police were initially against introducing the form in all of Switzerland, causing a lot of valuable material to be lost.

90. Interviews with Swiss returning home and instructions for Swiss traveling abroad were organized according to the following principle: the responsible head of bureau was free to conduct an interview, or issue instructions, on his own or entrust one of his staff with that task, regardless of the concerned person's place of residence. (Important political missions abroad had to be approved by Masson or his deputy, Müller. See minutes of meeting on 13 October 1941. BAr E 27/9483, vol. 1.) Hence, Cuénoud was allowed to issue instructions to someone from St. Gallen who was traveling to France, and Ernst or Waibel were allowed to visit friends in French-speaking Switzerland who were traveling to Germany. Or the responsible head of bureau could have the closest outpost conduct the interview or issue the instructions; e.g., he could ask the *Speer* outpost to interview a traveler from St. Gallen who had returned from France. In this case, the responsible head of bureau was allowed to enclose a questionnaire or written instructions with the form. Depending on the result of the interview, of course, he was authorized to conduct a second interview or have a second interview conducted by the outpost. Even though this principle was considered to be appropriate, due to the *lack of personnel* it could not always be applied. Masson consequently supported any request for additional staff when it appeared to be justified.

91. Waibel, *Tätigkeitsbericht der N.S.1 vom 1. September 1939–31. August 1940.* BAr E 27/14850.

92. Häberli found out only after the fact about his being on the Gestapo's wanted list since 1938; toward the end of the war, he was warned through the Viking channel that he should watch out and remember the *Jacob* case, i.e., that he risked being kidnapped by the Germans. Häberli added: "After that the Army Command gave me a Doberman to protect me. However, initially I was more afraid of the dog than of German measures." Werner Rings, interview with Häberli, 23 June 1969. AfZ files of Werner Rings. The allusion to the *Jacob* case was a hint that Häberli understood very well; he had been in charge of the investigation in the kidnapping case of Jacob and got the Gestapo official Wesemann to confess. On this case, see Jost Nikolaus Willi, *Der Fall Jacob-Wesemann (1935/1936): Ein Beitrag zur Geschichte der Schweiz in der Zwischenkriegszeit*, (Bern/Frankfurt a.M., 1972).

93. Häberli, *Tätigkeitsbericht Pfalz vom Kriegsbeginn bis 31. August 1940*, 30 October 1940. BAr E 27/14850.

94. Häberli, *Tätigkeitsbericht Pfalz (1. September 1942–31. Dezember 1943)*, 22 January 1944. BAr E 27/14850.

95. Häberli, *Tätigkeitsbericht Pfalz*, 22 January 1944.

96. The *L* connection was a French channel. Häberli explained, "French

Intelligence officers with whom I was friends informed me about the positions of German troops in France." These officers worked for French Army Intelligence in Vichy, which opposed the collaboration policy with Germany. Häberli commented, "They may have informed Vichy about their findings, but they definitely informed us—out of friendship." Werner Rings, interview with Häberli, 23 June 1969.

97. Häberli, *Tätigkeitsbericht Pfalz*, 22 January 1944. BAr E 27/14850.

98. On August 9, 1988, Gerold Walser told this author, "I received orders exclusively from Hy (Dr. James Haefely) and reported exclusively to him."

99. However, the working conditions were anything but ideal. On November 21, 1942, the head of the Axis Section informed Masson that Häberli and his entire staff had resigned because they had not been able to find a satisfactory solution concerning their employment situation. Alfred Ernst said that the staff had taken back their letters of resignation for the time being, but he warned that if no acceptable solution could be found, one had to expect the entire *Pfalz* sub-office to resign, adding, "I do not think that I need to point out what consequences this would have for the procurement of intelligence, which is poor to begin with." BAr J.I.140/4, vol. 4.

100. See Häberli, *Tätigkeitsbericht Pfalz*, 22 January 1944. BAr E 27/14850.

101. Gerold Walser to this author, 9 August 1988.

102. Gerold Walser to this author, 9 August 1988.

103. Waibel, *Tätigkeitsbericht der N.S.1 vom 1. September 1939–31. August 1940*. BAr E 27/14850.

104. Captain Brandt, M.S.S. office, Schaffhausen, *Tätigkeitsbericht "Salm," 1. September 1942–31. Dezember 1943*. BAr E 27/14850.

105. Waibel, *Tätigkeitsbericht der N.S.1 vom 1. September 1939–31. August 1940*.

106. Waibel, *Tätigkeitsbericht der N.S.1 vom 1. September 1939–31. August 1940*.

107. Captain Gyr, *Tätigkeitsbericht M.S.Z. (1. September 1942–31. Dezember 1943)*, 19 January 1944. BAr E 27/14850.

108. Lienert, *Tätigkeitsbericht M.S.G. (1. September 1942–31. Dezember 1943)*, 18 January 1944. BAr E 27/14850.

109. Lienert, *Tätigkeitsbericht M.S.G.*, 18 January 1944.

110. Lienert, *Tätigkeitsbericht M.S.G.*, 18 January 1944.

111. In a letter to the Assistant Chief of Staff for the Front, on December 3, 1940, Masson explained that 1st Lieutenant Bustelli should be called up in order to set up an intelligence office in Ticino. Masson argued: "Especially since Border Brigade 9 has been called off duty, it has become necessary for bodies of Army Intelligence to permanently monitor the border area in southern Ticino. This monitoring activity will replace the inadequate reconnaissance activities for which the Ticino police have been responsible until now together with the Intelligence Service of the border troops that were on duty." BAr E 27/9508, vol. 7.

112. Cf. 1st Lieutenant Luy's explanation: "This officer cannot receive any guarantee from our I[ntelligence] S[ervice] that upon his return to Switzerland after finishing his mission in Milan, in his civilian life he will have a position that is at least equivalent to the one he would have had to give up if he had stayed on in

our service." 1st Lieutenant Luy, *Rapport d'activité du bureau "Italie"* (1 September 1940–31 August 1941), 30 December 1941. BAr E 27/14851.

113. Luy, Rapport d'activité du bureau "Italie," 30 December 1941.

114. Cf. Masson's statement: "The reports from Lugano . . . must be compared with those of the other research centers because some of the information is wrong; they must all be carefully double-checked." Masson to Lieutenant General Constam, commander of the 3rd Army Corps, 20 May 1944. BAr E 27/9502.

115. Masson stated: "The reports by Bustelli contain detailed information, several pieces of which have not been verified. They are verified either in Lucerne (N.S.1) or at the 'Italian Bureau' (Intelligence Service, General Staff), where a synopsis of the political-military situation in Italy is made in cooperation with the 'German Bureau'." Masson to Chief of the General Staff, 17 March 1944. BAr E 27/9502.

116. See Bustelli to Waibel, 20 August 1945. BAr E 27/9983, vol. 8.

117. Ernst, *Tätigkeitsbericht Bureau D*, 15 October 1940. BAr J.I. 140/4, vol. 2.

118. Eberhard, *Tätigkeitsbericht der Sektion Achse*, 25 July 1945. BAr E 27/14851.

119. Masson remarked, "The future Chancellor Konrad *Adenauer*, who was more or less aware that he was an informant for our Service through his friend, the Swiss Consul in Cologne [von Weiss], was of great help to us." Masson, *Tribune de Lausanne*, 6 February 1966.

120. Eberhard, *Tätigkeitsbericht der Sektion Achse*, 25 July 1945. BAr E 27/14851.

121. Eberhard, *Tätigkeitsbericht der Sektion Achse*, 25 July 1945.

122. There was a risk that information would merely repeat, instead of confirming, what Army Intelligence had already found out through other channels. As Ernst explained, this was a result of the system of the information market. He remarked, "Of course several intelligence services had to communicate with each other according to the principle, '*do ut des*'; if you wanted to have something, you had to give something in return. As a consequence, this information kept being exchanged." Rings, interview with Alfred Ernst, 29 August 1972. AfZ files of Werner Rings.

123. Cuénoud, *Section Alliés, Rapport général d'activité*, 20 August 1945. BAr E 27/14852.

124. Cuénoud, *Section Alliés, Rapport général d'activité*, 20 August 1945.

125. Nachrichten- und Sicherheitsdienst, *VI. Quartalsbericht (1. April 1941–30. Juni 1941)*, 26 July 1941. BAr E 27/14849.

126. Masson, *Bericht über den Aktivdienst 1939–1945 der Abteilung Nachrichtendienst im Armeestab*. BAr E 27/14849. (The report was compiled by Colonel Schafroth on orders of Masson.)

127. Masson came to the same conclusion in his supplementary secret report on wartime duty, which he wrote to the attention of the Chief of the General Staff.

128. Masson's judgment at the end of wartime duty sounded considerably more positive than the one he had made during the first half of the war (on this issue, see also Masson's opinion about the Department of Foreign Affairs in connection with the case of Ernst Mörgeli, in Chapter 8).

129. Masson, *Ergänzender geheimer Bericht*. BAr E 27/14849.

130. That information is included in the same supplementary secret report by Masson.

131. Cuénoud, *Section Alliés, Rapport général d'activité*, 20 August 1945. BAr E 27/14852.
132. Cuénoud, *Section Alliés, Rapport général d'activité*, 20 August 1945.
133. Waibel, *Bericht 1939/45*. BAr E 27/14850.
134. Waibel, *Bericht 1939/45*.
135. Waibel, *Bericht 1939/45*.
136. At that time army headquarters was located in Worb.
137. Waibel, *Bericht 1939/45*. However, in order to do justice to other staff on Army Intelligence when assessing their performance, it must be pointed out that, unlike the other staff members, Waibel personally knew his excellent informants and their cover names, so that he was in a better position to trust them. Still, good information is not of much use if it does not reach its recipient. Surprisingly, the information within Army Intelligence was routed so poorly that the Chief of the General Staff annotated the "Latest Nightly News" of 9–10 May 1940 (Intelligence Section no. 225) by writing, "The Intel[ligence] Service *did not do its job correctly*. I found out [about the German Air Force activities along our border] through the radio, and I had to inquire several times with the Intel[ligence] Service before receiving any information" (see opposite page). BAr E 27/9915. Following that incident, the duty service was improved.
138. Waibel, *Bericht 1939/45*. BAr E 27/14850.
139. Rolf Eberhard, *Tätigkeitsbericht der Sektion Achse (7. August 1944–31. Dezember 1944)*, 29 January 1945. BAr E 27/14851.
140. In 1938, Army Intelligence actually spent Sfr. 47,942.05; in 1939, Sfr. 189,987; in 1940 an additional 100,000 francs, i.e. Sfr. 286,448.50; in 1941, as much as Sfr. 299,724. In 1943, expenditures increased to Sfr. 588,630, and in 1944 to Sfr. 748,381.90, the maximum level of spending during the war. In 1945, the final year of the war, they dropped to Sfr. 400,000 following politically understandable but short-sighted spending cuts that resulted in the Intelligence Service being virtually abolished. (Bracher to Kobelt, 29 November 1945. BAr E 27/9507).
141. Eberhard, *Tätigkeitsbericht der Sektion Achse*, 25 July 1945. BAr E 27/14851.
142. Eberhard, *Tätigkeitsbericht der Sektion Achse (7. August 1944–31. Dezember 1944)*. BAr E 27/14851.
143. Eberhard commented, "There is something offensive about this attitude. Moreover, it does not contribute at all to clearing up the 'cases'." Eberhard, *Tätigkeitsbericht der Sektion Achse (7. August 1944–31. Dezember 1944)*.
144. Eberhard, *Tätigkeitsbericht der Sektion Achse*, 25 July 1945. BAr E 27/14851.
145. Eberhard, *Tätigkeitsbericht der Sektion Achse (7. August 1944–31. Dezember 1944)*. BAr E 27/14851.
146. Eberhard, *Tätigkeitsbericht der Sektion Achse (7. August 1944–31. Dezember 1944)*.
147. Waibel, *Bericht 1939/45*. BAr E 27/14850.
148. Waibel, *Bericht 1939/45*.
149. In order not to jeopardize their future careers, the top staff members on Army Intelligence were frequently forced to serve in regular units or teach General Staff courses if they had the status of an instructor. When Masson refused to take over the command of a regiment, arguing that he was indispensable on the

L e t z t e   N a c h r i c h t e n

der Nacht vom 9. / 10. 5. 40.   *erhalten zu 0800*

Spez. Dienst: Deutsche Luftwaffe im gesamten Raum W. der Weser seit 9.5.

    1800 in höchster Alarmbereitschaft.
    10.5. 0700 soll ziviler Luftschutz, Ordnungspolizei usw. Bereitschaft melden.

Gz. Br. 3 : Am 10.5.40. 0520 haben Fliegerbomben das Bahngeleise bei Delémont unterbrochen.

Fl. & Flab.Trp.: Kantonspolizei meldet bisher unbestätigt die Unterbrechung des Bahngeleises bei Courrendlin durch Bombenabwurf.
Diese Nacht Grossfliegerangriff von Bodenseegegend her längs der Rheingrenze nach Frankreich hinein, es wurden u.A. überflogen Schaffhausen, Basel, Pruntrzipfel.

4. A.K. 0300 Häufige Ueberfliegungen durch deutsche Fls. bis nach Weinfelden.
       0600 <u>Grenzsperre an Nordgrenze.</u> (von Grenzwachtkdo. Schaffhausen bestätigt).

DNB. Die Reichsregierung hat an die belgische und niederländische Regierung ein Memorandum gerichtet, in welchem die Reichsregierung feststellt, dass sie Unterlagen und Berichte in Händen hat, die einwandfrei den Beweis erbringen, dass der englischfranzösische Angriff gegen Deutschland unmittelbar bevorsteht und dass dieser Vorstoss an die Ruhr über Belgien und die Niederlande erfolgen wird. Die Reichsregierung hat deshalb den deutschen Truppen den Befehl erteilt , die Neutralität dieser Länder mit allen militärischen Machtmitteln der Reichs sicherzustellen. Ein anderes Memorandum hat die deutsche Regierung an die luxemburgische Regierung gerichtet.

                         Der Pikettoffizier:

                         sig. Oberstlt. Schafroth.

[handwritten note]

Switzerland's Chief of the General Staff, Jakob Huber, found out about the beginning of Germany's western campaign through the radio (BAr E 27/9915). *See* page 318, endnote 137.

Intelligence Service, he was harshly criticized by his superiors (including
Labhart). This absurd policy was a serious handicap for Army Intelligence,
resulting in some grotesque situations. In 1942, for example, the Head of the
French Bureau was absent for 67 days, the Head of procurement from the
entire area of the Axis powers was absent for 54 days, the head of the Studies
Bureau was absent for 130 days, and the head of the German Bureau, who was
mainly responsible for evaluating the procured intelligence, was absent for as
many as 157 days! On May 8, 1944, Masson explained to the Chief of the
General Staff, "One of the basic requirements for providing timely and thorough information is *continuity* in the work of the Intelligence Service." (BAr E
27/9508, vol. 15.) Hausamann had criticized this situation at a much earlier
point in time, stating:

> Someone who is not permanently up to date concerning the course
> of events will never be able to accurately decide whether a piece of
> information is important or irrelevant. He will put 'minor' pieces
> of information away because they do not mean anything to him.
> However, for someone who has a full picture of the context, a
> seemingly insignificant detail might be the missing clue. In other
> words, one has to work *full-time* on the Intelligence Service or not
> work there at all. Everything else is unserious and amateurish, but
> an intelligence service cannot accept any unserious approach nor
> any amateurism. (Hausamann to Masson, 13 August 1941. BAr E
> 27/9838.)

Considering this repeated criticism, the frequent absences of key staff members
can hardly be justified. This author agrees with Masson, who told the
Commander-in-Chief, on May 20, 1942, "I consider that during wartime duty
and under the current circumstances, the General Staff should have priority
over training courses when it comes to assigning officers." (BAr E 27/9519.)
The individual officers should not be blamed for their frequent absences; the
unfortunate situation was due to the fact that the rules concerning the promotion of officers could not be formulated in a way that took into account the
special requirements of a unit such as the Intelligence Service.

150. Cf. Alfred Ernst's statement: "I am also concerned about the personnel-related
difficulties at the Pfalz office (unpleasant situation for the staff members, who
are of outstanding merit). The structure that we have been building up with a
lot of difficulties since 1939 risks falling to pieces." Ernst, *Tätigkeitsbericht
Bureau D,* 28 December 1942. BAr J.I.140/4, vol. 4.

151. Ernst, *Tätigkeitsbericht Bureau D,* 15 October 1940. BAr J.I. 140/4, vol. 2.

152. Waibel, *Bericht,* 26 February 1963. BAr J.I. 137 1974/64, vol. 13.

153. *Tätigkeitsbericht Bureau D, 1 September 1940–31 August 1941.* BAr J.I.140/4,
vol. 3.

154. Ernst to Masson, 15 October 1940. BAr J.I.140/4, vol. 2.

155. "Everything depends on personal connections, which can be created only after
months or years of work and cannot be easily transferred [to someone else]."
Tätigkeitsbericht Bureau D, 1 September 1940–31 August 1941. BAr J.I. 140/4,
vol. 3.

156. Members of the French 45th Army Corps under General Daille, which was

forced to flee to Switzerland during France's collapse and was interned there. See minutes of Federal Council meeting of 18 June 1940. BAr E 1004.1 1.

157. Ernst, *Tätigkeitsbericht Bureau D*, 15 October 1940. BAr J.I. 140/4, vol. 2.

158. Interrogation of Bernhard Mayr von Baldegg, 8 June 1945. BAr E 5330 1982/1, vol. 205. Mayr acted as chief of staff of N.S.1 and was Waibel's deputy.

159. Masson stated: "All of them are officers who continue making themselves available in spite of the dangers. When they travel by car, their information is much more useful to us because they drive on the roads that we have instructed them to take in areas that are of utmost importance for an opponent's deployment activity at our border. . . . It should also be pointed out that the large majority of our permanent or temporary agents have not accepted one single penny for their work even though their expenses have been anything but minimal." Masson to Chief of the General Staff, 30 September 1940. BAr E 27/9508, vol. 6.

160. Ernst, *Tätigkeitsbericht Bureau D*, 15 October 1940. BAr J.I. 140/4, vol. 2.

161. Waibel, *Bericht*, 26 February 1963. BAr J.I. 137 1974/64, vol. 13.

162. Waibel had encountered the same experience with the Legation's attitude as early as the time that he was detailed to the War Academy in Berlin.

163. Waibel, *Bericht*, 26 February 1963. BAr J.I. 137 1974/64, vol. 13.

164. Ernst to Masson, October 15, 1940 (BAr J.I.140/4, vol. 2), quoting from a letter by Frölicher.

165. As a potential deployment area and an area where German troops could be stationed before they attacked Switzerland. (It was not until 1942 that Ernst managed, with great difficulty, to set up his own network there.)

166. Ernst, *Tätigkeitsbericht Bureau D*, 15 October 1940. BAr J.I. 140/4, vol. 2.

167. Ernst, *Tätigkeitsbericht Bureau D*, 15 October 1940. Due to their status, consuls were relatively free to move around.

168. Counselor Karl Stucki was Head of Switzerland's Consular Service. He later played a part during the meeting between Pilet-Golaz and Schellenberg's emissary, SS Major Eggen.

169. Statement quoted by Waibel, *Bericht*, 26 February 1963. BAr J.I. 137 1974/64, vol. 13.

170. Ernst to Masson, 27 November 1941. BAr J.I.140/4, vol. 3.

171. On the case of Ernst Mörgeli, see page 173.

172. "They should handle administrative issues, defend the interests of certain Swiss citizens, and take advantage of their official travels to make an assessment of the level of occupation by German troops in certain zones." Masson, *Activité politique de la section de renseignements*, 9 August 1940. BAr E 5795/327.

173. See Ernst, *Tätigkeitsbericht Bureau D*, 15 October 1940. BAr J.I. 140/4, vol. 2.

174. These consulates were called "reinforced consulates."

175. Ernst to Masson, early 1942 (documentation for answering Pilet-Golaz' letter of 27 December 1941). BAr J.I.140/4, vol. 4.

176. Ernst to Masson, 15 October 1940. BAr J.I.140/4, vol. 2.

177. Urs Schwarz commented: "The Military Attaché, Colonel Hans von Werdt, was a weathercock. The son of a Swiss who had served in the Austro-Hungarian Empire took part in World War I as a member of the Austrian Army, but then he became an instructor in the Swiss Army. Nevertheless, he sided with the

German brother-in-arms." (Urs Schwarz, "Schicksalstage in Berlin," *Neue Zürcher Zeitung*, 8 August 1986, no. 181.) This fact did not remain hidden to the Allies; in late 1940, the aide of the U.S. Military Attaché in Berlin reported to Washington, DC:

> November 12 [1940]—Conversation with the Swiss Military Attaché. . . . The only hope for peace in Europe is a German victory. If Germany wins she will be the only strong power capable of straightening out the European mess. . . . If England wins the war we may expect another Versailles Treaty more unjust than the last one and another great European war within a quarter of a century. If, by the United States' help, England is able to continue the war to a stalemate, Russia will win because she will be able to launch her world revolution on a weakened Europe. . . . American help can only mean misery to Europe and it may even mean disaster. (Lt. Colonel G.S.C. W.D. Hohenthal, Military Attaché Report Germany no. 17,789, "General estimate of the situation as of December 9, 1940." National Archives, Washington, DC, RG 165, Military Intelligence Division 2656–320/12.)

178. Ernst, *Tätigkeitsbericht Bureau D*, 15 October 1940. BAr J.I.140/4, vol. 2.
179. Commander-in-Chief to Pilet-Golaz, 13 August 1940. BAr E 27/9483, vol. 1. (The meeting had taken place on August 3, 1940, whereupon Guisan asked Masson to give his opinion, which he forwarded to the Head of the Department of Foreign Affairs together with his own letter.)
180. Masson to Commander-in-Chief, 9 August 1940. BAr E 27/9483, vol. 1.
181. On July 19, 1940, the day Hitler made a last "appeal for peace" to Great Britain at the Reich parliament (which Great Britain rejected on 22 July), Regamey discussed the international situation with Masson. Regamey was depressed about Masson being worried (see Regamey to Masson, 9 August 1940. BAr E 5795/327). The following day, when he noticed that his partner at the law firm, Colonel Victor Perrier of the General Staff, was also very concerned about the international situation, Regamey came up with the idea of using Dr. Monfrini as an intermediary, explaining, "[In September 1939,] Dr. Monfrini had told me about his personal relations with Mussolini, from which Switzerland might benefit whenever the opportunity presented itself." (Regamey to Masson, 9 August 1940.)
182. Masson to Commander-in-Chief, 9 August 1940. (BAr E 27/9483, vol. 1.) Regamey confirmed, "You replied that the potential mission by Dr. Monfrini fell under the authority of the Department of Foreign Affairs." (Regamey to Masson, 9 August 1940. BAr E 5795/327.)
183. On July 22, 1940, Monfrini told Regamey that Pilet-Golaz had just talked to him for a long time over the phone regarding a mission to Mussolini. (See Regamey to Masson, 9 August 1940.)
184. Explanation by Regamey on the conversation that he was going to have with Monfrini a few days later. (Regamey to Masson, 9 August 1940.)
185. Regamey to Masson, 9 August 1940.
186. See Divisional Court 5, session of 26/28 June 1947 in Lucerne, sentence against Hans Wilhelm Otto Eberhard/Hans Schorer (documents in this author's

possession). This *Eberhard* was of course not Captain Rolf Eberhard, the head of the Axis Section.

187. Hans Eberhard; regarding the circumstances, see endnote 188 below.

188. Ketterer arrived in Stuttgart during the first half of November 1939. The consulate told him about a certain Hans Eberhard, who was supposedly working for Swiss Intelligence. Ketterer contacted him, and the two men soon began to work fairly closely together. On December 26, 1939, they met with the Head of the German Bureau, Alfred Ernst, in Bern to discuss the information that they had and talk about the setup for a comprehensive intelligence network in southern Germany. However, Hans Eberhard did not only work for the German Bureau but was at the same time agent no. 636 at the German Military Intelligence regional headquarters in Stuttgart, department III/F (which was in charge of counterespionage against foreign intelligence services, most of all abroad). The Head of the regional headquarters in Stuttgart, Major Ehringer, alias Ackermann, had set Eberhard on to Ketterer in order to obtain regular information about the Swiss 1st lieutenant's activities.

Hans Eberhard had grown up in Zürich; in 1934 he co-founded and then temporarily headed the local "National Front" organization in Aarau. In November 1938, the Attorney General's Office opened a preliminary investigation against him and had his home searched because of his right-wing extremist activities. His employer subsequently dismissed him without notice, and the military suspended him based on article 51 of the military law. At the end of 1938, he emigrated to Germany. Around the time that the war began, Eberhard, who had not been in touch with any Swiss living in Germany, nor with the Swiss Consulate in Stuttgart until then, contacted Consul Suter, allegedly in order to take the necessary steps for being readmitted to the Swiss Army. A short time later, in October 1939, Eberhard traveled to Switzerland and presented the same request to Major General Eugen Bircher, the commander of the 5th Division. At the same time, he offered to procure information from southern Germany. Eberhard tried in vain to also establish a connection with Hausamann in Teufen. Bircher knew Eberhard; in fall 1935, he had admonished him to be more moderate in his extremist writings. Eberhard promised to heed his warning and henceforth signed his articles by using a pseudonym. Due to Bircher's mediation, in fall 1939 Eberhard was recruited by Swiss Army Intelligence in order to procure information in Stuttgart.

The Ketterer affair was a flop for the Germans insofar as the 1st lieutenant had become mistrustful, so that they could not prove anything against him when they arrested him. Nevertheless, because of his "merits" in connection with disbanding the Ketterer circle, as a sign of recognition Eberhard was introduced to Admiral Canaris. Eberhard's importance to German Intelligence was due to the position for which he was slated once the war was won and which was prepared for him in October 1940. At that time, he was ordered to move to Paris and open a reputable business with the financial support of the German Military Intelligence regional headquarters. (For that purpose, the regional Intelligence headquarters set up a pharmaceutical laboratory for him.) Once the German occupation was over, he was supposed to continue working for German Counterintelligence, camouflaging his activity by pretending to be a successful Swiss businessman.

In 1947, Switzerland's Divisional Court 5 considered that Eberhard had acted with cool deliberation, taking advantage of the fact that *Swiss Intelligence was in a state of improvisation* at the time. At the end of June 1947, it sentenced him to 12 years in prison. Eberhard got away with this relatively mild sentence because a number of his crimes had fallen outside the statute of limitations. (Documents in the author's possession.)

189. However, his fellow Swiss staff members from Stuttgart who were also arrested (some 12 to 18 men) were interned at concentration camps for up to five months and then expelled from Germany. Some of them were exchanged with German nationals who had been detained in Switzerland. Several of Ketterer's informants suffered permanent physical disabilities because they had worked for Swiss Intelligence. (Documents in the author's possession.)

190. Masson to Commander-in-Chief, 9 August 1940. BAr E 27/9483, vol. 1.

191. Chief of the General Staff Huber to Pilet-Golaz, 28 May 1940. BAr E 5795/327.

192. Huber to Pilet-Golaz, 28 May 1940.

193. Huber to Pilet-Golaz, 28 May 1940.

194. Huber to Pilet-Golaz, 28 May 1940.

195. It is known today that these were inverted signals and the German troop movements were part of a cunning ploy; this does not speak against the reconnaissance mission with which Ritter was entrusted.

196. Cf. the letter by the Chief of Intelligence to the Foreign Service at the Department of Foreign Affairs dated 16 March 1940 (written by Schafroth):

> We are perfectly aware of the risks involved in procuring intelligence. . . . We do not think that reports by a diplomatic representative can easily replace information supplied by interested individuals who have been trained by the military, know the country, know various groups of people, and have a variety of sources of information available. On the other hand, this is not espionage per se but reporting on issues of rather general interest that we and our informants, who have received specific instructions for a particular mission, assess in a completely different manner than an official representative. During the current difficult times, it seems advisable to us to utilize every available source of information. . . . It is a real pleasure for us to see how much patriotism and *understanding the Swiss living abroad* have been showing for the needs of the *Intelligence Service*. An unexpectedly large number of them have *volunteered to offer their services* to us. We consider that these gentlemen, who act out of patriotism and are certainly aware of the implications of their actions, should not be *prevented by the Swiss government representatives* in the host country from carrying out their endeavor, which is absolutely commendable from the military's perspective. . . . It seemed very awkward, for example, that a Swiss Consul General (Milan) *right-out forbade* a volunteer of our Service, who is liable to serve in the army, *to work for us.* . . .

Unfortunately we are *not* able to consider this Consul's motives . . . as a sign of the kind *understanding* that your Department usually shows *for the importance of Swiss Army Intelligence.* (BAr E 27/9483, vol. 1.)

197. Minister Paul Ruegger, who was Switzerland's Envoy in Rome and London during the war, confirmed to this author that he had been able to assist the Intelligence Service *only behind Pilet's back.* (Verbal communication, September 1987.)

198. Minister Paul Ruegger to Pilet-Golaz, 29 September 1941. (Quoted in Masson's report of 24 October 1941. BAr E 27/9483, vol. 1.) Ruegger had a very positive attitude toward the efforts of Army Intelligence; in his letter of September 29, 1941 to Minister Bonna, he wrote:

> [This claim is] all the more surprising as my entire staff strictly abides by the instructions that I have been giving it all along, i.e. to take a very prudent and objective approach and limit itself to the tasks of the Swiss legation in Italy. The information on which the circular in question is based undoubtedly comes from Bern. . . . In addition, I would like to reiterate that I have *boundless confidence in the actions of our military attaché*, Colonel von Wattenwyl; his services are extremely valuable for the Legation, and at the same time he fulfills in an exemplary manner the task of representing our army. Of course one could say that other states actually do what *our country is insultingly accused of doing.* (BAr E 5795/327.)

199. Ruegger to Pilet-Golaz, 29 September 1941. BAr E 5795/327.

200. In his extensive report of October 24, 1941, Masson pointed out that, after a careful analysis, Minister Ruegger's letter to Pilet-Golaz (who had triggered the new controversy) had turned out to be "absolutely gratuitous." In a letter dated October 17, 1941, Colonel von Wattenwyl had reported, "Minister Ruegger is perfectly reassured following the explanations that we have given him about our bodies' activities at the consulates." (Letter quoted in Masson's report of Oct. 24, 1941. BAr E 27/9483, vol. 1.)

201. Cf. Pilet-Golaz' statement: "Let me state once again—my sense of responsibility forces me to insist until I obtain satisfaction—that the procedures that have been applied until now have to be urgently modified, our representation abroad has to be exonerated, and the interests of the Swiss abroad have to be taken care of." Pilet-Golaz to Kobelt, 5 and 17 October 1941. BAr E 27/9483, vol. 1.

202. Commander-in-Chief to Kobelt, 25 October 1941. BAr E 27/9483, vol. 1.

203. Masson, "Relations entre le Département politique fédéral et le Service des renseignements," 24 October 1941. BAr E 27/9483, vol. 1.

204. Alfred Ernst, minutes of briefing on 13 Oct. 1941 in Interlaken, 13 October 1941. BAr E 27/9483, vol. 1.

205. Colonel Karl von Wattenwyl of the General Staff (born 1884, died 1965) was military attaché in Rome as of 1938. His father, Joh. Ludwig Eduard von Wattenwyl, had served in the British Navy. The military attaché's brother-in-law, Minister Paravicini, had been Switzerland's envoy to England for many years. Colonel von Wattenwyl usually went to see him when he was on visit in

Bern. Of course the Italian Envoy in Bern, Attilio Tamaro, did not fail to notice that fact.

206. Ernst, minutes of briefing, 13 October 1941. BAr E 27/9483, vol. 1.
207. Ernst, minutes of briefing, 13 October 1941.
208. Ernst, minutes of briefing, 13 October 1941.
209. Ernst, minutes of briefing, 13 October 1941.
210. Masson, "Relations," 24 October 1941. BAr E 27/9483, vol. 1.
211. Cf. Major General Peter Burckhardt's statement: "What was essential was . . . that National Socialism was a revolutionary, new attitude that wanted to force its opinion on other countries. . . . From the perspective of intelligence, this meant that *strictly military aspects could not be the only decisive criteria* for assessing and evaluating information [because] from a strictly military point of view . . . after the campaign in France, Switzerland [was] not under any military threat anymore. . . . Logically speaking, it was obvious that if Germany had been victorious and as a consequence the so-called Third Reich had ruled over Europe, throwing Switzerland back on its own resources, our country would have had to adapt in one way or another." Burckhardt, note to the attention of this author, 2 March 1988.
212. Masson, "Relations," 24 October 1941. BAr E 27/9483, vol. 1.
213. Allusion to Arthur Fonjallaz, a former training officer who was a member of Masson's personal information network but turned out to be a double agent. (See page 263ff.)
214. On October 14, 1941, N.S.1 had received a document mentioning increased surveillance activities to which Swiss were subject in Germany. The document stated, among other things:

> The responsible German authorities have not failed to notice that many Swiss living in Germany who used to be loyal toward Germany have changed their attitude toward the Reich. The Secret State Police has noticed that Swiss who used to be considered reliable now openly express their anti-German, and especially their anti-regime, attitude; some of them actually express this attitude with unsurpassed vehemence. The authorities of the German Reich know exactly what the daily reports that are sent to Switzerland say about the mood in the Reich, the economic difficulties (shortages and lack of supplies), the war economy, the situation concerning raw materials, the political situation, etc. *Moreover, the authorities of the German Reich also know exactly what is written in the reports by the Swiss diplomatic representation in Germany, which are sent to Switzerland.* The responsible authorities in Berlin have ordered the Swiss diplomatic representations as well as their entire personnel in Germany and in the occupied countries to be kept under strict surveillance! (Document attached to Pilet's letter to Kobelt, 17 October 1941. BAr E 27/9483, vol. 1.)

Because this document dealt primarily with *political* issues, Masson decided to forward it to the Department of Foreign Affairs. For that purpose, he sent Lieutenant Colonel Schafroth to Peter Anton Feldscher, a head of section at the Foreign Service. Three days later—in the process, committing an injustice against the Intelligence Service—Pilet-Golaz expressly based his new complaint about Army Intelligence on that document (see Pilet-Golaz to Kobelt, 17 October 1941).

215. Cf. General Guisan's statement to Kobelt, 25 October 1941: "It seems to me that [Masson's] conclusions speak for themselves. I do not need to add anything to them." Masson remarked: "It is Intelligence's task to alert the [Army] Command early enough so that the steps that need to be taken in order to get the army ready for action can be taken in time and the army is ready to stand the decisive test with all its means. It is the Commander-in-Chief's responsibility to alert the Federal Council so that this can be accomplished. Hence, the Commander-in-Chief of the Army can only fulfill this responsibility if he is given the essential means that allow him to be vigilant." (BAr E 27/9483, vol. 1.)

216. However, it is not difficult to find evidence showing that the opposite was true. See for instance Commander-in-Chief to Federal President Pilet-Golaz, 21 May 1940, in which General Guisan refutes Pilet's criticism of Masson. BAr E 27/9502.

217. Pilet-Golaz was very proud of that for the rest of his life. Information supplied by Jacques Pilet to this author, 9 March 1988.

218. Pilet-Golaz to Kobelt, 27 December 1941. BAr E 27/9483, vol. 1.

219. On January 18, 1942, Werner Müller wrote to Masson:

> The officers whom Federal Councillor Pilet-Golaz called "elements" did not interfere in any foreign or domestic policy issue. [The investigation files show] that the Army Command had absolutely no reason to remove Majors Waibel and Ernst and Captain Hausamann from the Army Staff. The officers' meeting in Lucerne was above all a reaction to the unfortunate radio address that Federal Councillor Pilet-Golaz had made on June 25, 1940, an address that *all Swiss* were appalled to hear. The three suspected officers should be credited in large part for the fact that the domestic political consequences that were beginning to become apparent for some time [as a result of this speech] did not take on larger proportions. Together with other people, these officers instilled new confidence in the population, taking great pains outside their work hours to convince it that Switzerland would resolutely be defended in the event of an attack. Its confidence had been shaken in an alarming manner because of Federal Councillor Pilet-Golaz' speech. I may say without exaggerating that the effects of this speech can still be felt today.

Müller explained that other incidents such as Pilet receiving representatives of the National Movement of Switzerland, a right-wing extremist front group, caused the population to mistrust Pilet as a politician, adding:

> I would like to point out that the people know what Federal Councillor Pilet-Golaz told the wife of a U.S. diplomat about democracy. . . . It is not surprising that officers of the army were deliberating how the spirit of defeatism that had been sowed in 1940 could be opposed. In any event, I take exception to officers

of our unit who have shown right-out excellent performances being subject to comments such as the ones that Federal Councillor Pilet-Golaz likes to make about them. These officers deserve to be treated differently by a member of the Federal Council, even if they made some formal mistakes and were subject to disciplinary sanctions because of that. What matters most is that the officers who have been called "elements" are certainly at least as good Swiss as Mr. Pilet-Golaz. (BAr E 27/9483, vol. 1.)

220. Pilet-Golaz stated, "The most serious difficulties have been created in connection with the famous bureau in Lucerne." Pilet-Golaz to Kobelt, 17 October 1941. BAr E 27/9483, vol. 1.

221. Werner Müller to Masson, 18 January 1942. BAr E 27/9483, vol. 1.

222. A more recent example where this happened was the war over the Falkland Islands in 1982; cf. Lawrence Freedman's statement: "Many of the problems reflect not only long-standing institutional problems—*Foreign Office versus military intelligence* and inter-service rivalry . . ." Lawrence Freedman, "Intelligence Operations in the Falklands," *Intelligence and National Security* 1, no. 3 (September 1986), 310.

223. As a typical example, in mid-November 1943, in connection with the so-called Pétain Crisis, lack of coordination resulted in a bothersome overlapping of activities. (The Germans thwarted Pétain's attempt to proclaim, on November 13, 1943, Vichy France's return to a parliamentary system. Pétain consequently threatened to resign. Germany reacted by stepping up its occupation policy and giving up its efforts to make it look as if France had some sovereignty left. On this matter, see Nerin E. Gun, *Les secrets des archives américaines: Pétain, Laval, De Gaulle* [Paris, 1979], 188ff.) On January 14, 1944, Minister Stucki, the Swiss Envoy in Vichy, wrote to the Commander-in-Chief:

On 24 November, Colonel de Blonay [the Military Attaché] informed me that the General Staff had ordered him to supply additional information on the "Pétain Crisis." He consequently asked me to tell him about the confidential information that I had received through top authorities. Since the Department of Foreign Affairs had already been informed in detail about this purely political issue, to me this new request seemed to be unwarranted and unnecessary. Nevertheless, I granted [Colonel de Blonay's] request. However, I believed that if the occasion arose I should inform the Head of the Department of Foreign Affairs . . . that I had been under the impression at other occasions that the General Staff was asking its representative in France to report on issues that I considered to be my business rather than theirs. However, since I know that the army intends to work exclusively in the country's interest, just as we do, I have never attached too much importance to the issue and have worked together smoothly with Colonel de Blonay for almost six years. (BAr E 27/14132.)

After Stucki had informed Pilet-Golaz about his impression, the Department of Foreign Affairs and Army Intelligence were at odds for some time. Such incidents could have been avoided if the two parties had held regular meetings to discuss common issues.

224. Hermann Böschenstein, for example, remembers Pilet's "tendency to show off in front of [parliament] committees by making unnecessary, bold forecasts about the end of the war. Even when speaking with foreign diplomats he acted as if he was very well informed, and toward Swiss heads of mission who were on home leave he bragged how knowledgeable he was." Hermann Böschenstein, *Vor unsern Augen. Aufzeichnungen über das Jahrzehnt 1935–1945* (Bern, 1978), 259.

225. Cf. Masson's statement: "We acknowledge that Federal Councillor Pilet-Golaz as well as his predecessor accepted the principle of this cooperation; however, unfortunately we noticed later on that *in reality* attempts were made to invalidate this principle by neutralizing our investigations, especially in connection with the couriers and the attachés at the consulates." Masson, "Relations," 29 January 1942. BAr E 27/9483, vol. 1.

226. Bureau D, *Jahresbericht 1942*. BAr J.I. 140/4, vol. 4.

227. Commander-in-Chief to Kobelt, 6 May 1943. BAr E 27/9483, vol. 1.

228. Bracher noted, "Major Daniel sets great store in reassuring Federal Councillor Pilet that the consular agents will under no circumstances have to enter in contact with any agents. Their activity will consist exclusively of driving along some routes on which the Intelligence Service would like to have some information, the way it used to be done until recently." Bracher, note, 19 May 1943. BAr E 27/9483, vol. 1.

229. Kobelt to Pilet-Golaz, 20 May 1943. (Personal and secret. Via messenger.) BAr E 27/9483, vol. 1.

230. Pilet-Golaz to Kobelt, 15 June 1943. BAr E 27/9483, vol. 1.

231. Kobelt to Pilet-Golaz, 22 September 1943. The letter was identical to a draft by Major Daniel dated 21 September 1943. BAr E 27/9483, vol. 1.

232. Chief of the General Staff to Commander-in-Chief, 8 October 1943. BAr E 27/9483, vol. 1.

233. The secretary of the Military Department annotated the letter by scribbling, "The Dept. of For[eign Affairs] is silent!" (14 October 1943.)

234. Kobelt to Pilet-Golaz, 19 October 1943. BAr E 27/9483, vol. 1.

235. Bracher, note for Kobelt, 12 November 1943. BAr E 27/9483, vol. 1.

236. Kobelt, note for Secretary of the Department Burgunder [12 November 1943, handwritten]. BAr E 27/9483, vol. 1.

237. Kobelt to Commander-in-Chief, 23 November 1943. BAr E 27/9483, vol. 1.

238. At the end of the war, Chief of the General Staff Huber painted a vivid picture of the lack of cooperation between the various authorities, stating:
    [It is regrettable] that it was impossible to establish a normal working relationship between the Intelligence Service and the bodies of the Department of Foreign Affairs, the police dealing with foreign nationals, and the Attorney General's office, which should all have been pulling in the same direction. Masson blamed the others for that shortcoming. In my opinion, both sides are to blame because they were both over-ambitious, touchy, and self-opinionated. Each side wanted to be the only savior of the country. It is not easy to

get adults to stop being vain and craving for recognition; many
people actually turn that way when they get older. However, I
noticed that these traits of character were more predominant in the
Intelligence Service than in any other branch of the military. The
situation reminded me of English detective stories in which the
Scotland Yard officer, the private detective, and the newspaper
reporter try to beat each other to the clue that resolves the case
and, much to the criminal's delight, unintentionally put a number
of obstacles in each other's way. That is about the way things were
between the bodies of the army and the Departments, and that was
the way things were between several officers within the Intelligence
Service. (Huber to Commander-in-Chief, 26 July 1945. [Personal
and secret.] BAr E 5330 1982/1, vol. 205.)

239. Waibel, *Bericht 1939/45*. BAr E 27/14850.

240. Waibel, *Bericht 1939/45*.

241. In connection with the disbanding of Alexander Rado's network, in 1944 Mayr
von Baldegg was arrested and detained for 9 days by the Federal Police because
of his official contacts with Rudolf Roessler. Not least objectionable was the fact
that Werner Müller had personally given the Federal Police the go-ahead to
arrest Mayr. Later on, Mayr was granted a compensation because his imprison-
ment had obviously been unwarranted.

242. Once again, however, there were some absurd exceptions. Jakob Leonhard,
whom Swiss Intelligence had infiltrated into the Gestapo as a double agent,
recalls: "There was a strange catch about my trips to [my German contact person in] Basel; concerning my work for Swiss Intelligence, I had to report to the
Zürich police, who did not want to miss the chance of making a big killing. As
a consequence, the police in Basel were not informed about my mission!
Hence, I had to be on my guard not only against the German spies but also
against our own police." Jakob Leonhard, *Als Gestapo-Agent im Dienste der
schweizerischen Gegenspionage* (Zürich/New York, 1945), 20–21.

243. Waibel, *Bericht 1939/45*. BAr E 27/14850.

244. Assistant Head of the Police Section at the Federal Justice and Police
Department.

245. Waibel, *Bericht 1939/45*. BAr E 27/14850.

246. Waibel, *Bericht 1939/45*.

247. As of January 1, 1944, Group Id was renamed Group Ib. See page 41ff.

248. Ernst, *Jahresbericht 1942* (1 September 1941–31 August 1942), 28 December
1942. BAr E 27/14851.

249. Ernst, *Jahresbericht 1942*.

250. In a personal letter to Kobelt, Hausamann complained about the difficult
atmosphere within the Intelligence Service, writing:
> You have to know about the situation in Group Id. . . . For the last
> two years, Colonel Müller has kept the morale up among the
> Group, being accessible and available for anyone at any time. He
> has managed to keep the Group together. The first year of the war
> was terrible for anyone whom Messrs. Cuénoud, Schafroth, and
> Daniel did not like. Instead of being happy about a good perform-

ance, one did everything to disparage it. Work was made unbelievably difficult. The following example, which concerned me personally, will show you what the situation was like back then. For
almost one year, Lieutenant Colonel Schafroth, who acted as an
intermediary between yours truly and the Chief of Intelligence at
the beginning of the war, swept my reports under the carpet
because they did not fit into his political concept. In August 1940,
this was discovered through a coincidence, and it was Colonel
Müller who took drastic action by sidelining Lieutenant Colonel
Schafroth through official channels. (Hausamann to Kobelt, 6
November 1942. BAr E 5800/1, vol. 1. See the letter on page 332.)

251. Cf. Müller's statement: "Differences between . . . Lieutenant Colonel Cuénoud
of the General Staff and . . . Major Waibel of the General Staff . . . have never
been really set aside since March of this year." Müller considered that this situation was due to the touchiness and over-eagerness of individual staff members
of Army Intelligence. Werner Müller to Masson, 29 July 1942. BAr E 27/9519.

252. Ernst, *Jahresbericht 1942*. BAr E 27/14851.

253. Investigating Magistrate Otto Müller to Military Attorney General, attn.
Commander-in-Chief, 8 August 1945. BAr E 5330 1982/1, vol. 205.

254. See Alfred Ernst, "Der Schweizerische Nachrichtendienst im Zweiten
Weltkrieg," *Allgemeine Schweizerische Militärzeitschrift*, no. 12 (1972).

255. Investigating Magistrate Otto Müller to Military Attorney General, 8 August
1945. BAr E 5330 1982/1, vol. 205.

256. The following section is based mainly on the vivid description of R. Harris
Smith, *OSS: The Secret History of America's First Central Intelligence Agency*
(Berkeley, Los Angeles, London: University of California Press, 1972).

257. David K. E. Bruce, "The National Intelligence Authority," *Virginia Quarterly
Review* (Summer 1946), 355–369, cited on 363.

258. Calvin Hoover, *Memoirs of Capitalism, Communism, and Nazism* (Durham:
Duke University Press, 1965), 197.

259. Bruce, "The National Intelligence Authority," 358.

260. Fred Israel, ed. *The War Diary of Breckinridge Long* (Lincoln: University of
Nebraska Press, 1966), 234.

261. William Leahy, *I Was There* (New York: McGraw-Hill, 1950), 71.

262. "The single appointment to which State did not object was that of a charming
editor of *Vogue* as 'fashion attaché' at the American embassy in Stockholm. She
admirably promoted American clothing design in Sweden while secretly working with the Danish resistance on behalf of the OSS. Far less dainty spies and
saboteurs reached neutral capitals as 'cultural attachés' and were greeted with
something less than joy by the American ambassadors." Smith, *OSS: The Secret
History of America's First Central Intelligence Agency*, 24. See also Katherine
Breaks, "Ladies of the OSS: The Apron Strings of Intelligence in World War
II." *American Intelligence Journal*, vol. 13, no. 3 (Summer 1992), 91–96.

263. Donald McLachlan, *Room 39* (London: Weidenfeld and Nicolson, 1968), 233.

264. From a 1941 Donovan memorandum to the President, in the Goodfellow
Papers, Stanford. Cited in R. Harris Smith, *OSS: The Secret History of America's
First Central Intelligence Agency*, 35.

ARMÉE SUISSE   SCHWEIZERISCHE ARMEE   ESERCITO SVIZZERO

COMMANDEMENT DE L'ARMÉE   **ARMEEKOMMANDO**   COMANDO DELL'ESERCITO

No. 1820
In der Antwort vermerken — A indiquer dans la réponse
Da indicare nella risposta

11.5.42 W/me

Herrn Oberst i/Gst. Müller,
Stellvertretender Chef der Gruppe Id
<u>Armeekommando.</u>

Herr Oberst,

Ich habe die beiliegenden Fichen überprüft. Auf Grund
unserer internen Postkontrolle konnten wir feststellen,
dass uns die Fichen im beiliegenden Couvert vom Grenzwachtposten Boncourt am 5.5.42 zugestellt worden sind.

Wir schicken dann die Fichen wie üblich dem Bureau France
zur Einvernahme bezw. Kontrolle, da diese Leute in dessen
Tätigkeitsbereich fallen. Anscheinend hat aus diesem Um-
stande das Bureau France irrtümlicherweise geschlossen,
wir hätten die Einvernahmen durchgeführt.

Gerade aus der Tatsache, dass die Fichen, die uns irr-
tümlich zugingen, an das Bureau France weiter geleitet werden,
sollte dieses doch den Schluss ziehen, dass wir ihm diese
Leute zuhalten und nicht eine eigene Organisation auf-
gezogen haben. Ich bedaure dieses andauernde Misstrauen
und die Ueberempfindlichkeit, die man uns seitens des
Bureau France dauernd entgegen bringt und verstehe nicht,
warum der Leiter des Bureau France, wenn er glaubt, Grund
zu Reklamationen zu haben, sich nicht an mich wendet,
sondern immer andere Instanzen damit belästigt.

Ich bin in den letzten Tagen nun zwei Mal ohne jeglichen
Grund durch das Bureau France der Kompetenzüberschreitung
bezichtigt worden, gedenke aber nicht, mich ad in finitum
attackieren zu lassen.

In vorliegendem Falle muss der Grenzwachtposten Boncourt,
mit welchem wir keinerlei Verbindung haben, vom Bureau
France angewiesen werden, wohin er seine Fichen zu schicken
hat.

N.S. 1/Ter.Kdo. 8

Major i/Gst.Waibel.

The work atmosphere at Army Intelligence was soured by constant feuds among the various bureaus. In this letter, Major Max Waibel, the head of Procurement Office 1, tells the Deputy Chief of Intelligence, Colonel Werner Müller, that he is tired of being accused by the French Bureau of overstepping his authority by receiving immigration forms from the border checkpoint in Boncourt. He explains that these forms were sent to him by mistake, so he forwarded them to the French Bureau, as should be expected. Waibel complains that the head of the French Bureau did not discuss the issue directly with him but rather "bothered" others about it (BAr E 27/9519). *See* pages 330 (note 250) and 331 (note 251).

Chapter 6: The Initiator of the Connection

1. Meyer liked his wife and close friends to call him "Wolf," short for Wolfgang, which in German had a ring to it similar to "Jack" for John.
2. For example, the bill for the now famous meeting of March 1943 at the "Bären" inn in Biglen between General Guisan and SS General Schellenberg was made out to *Dr. Ritsburg* (sic). BAr J.I.121/67. The fake name had an aristocratic flavor to it.
3. ID for army members wearing civilian clothes, No. 61577, issued on October 28, 1941 by the head of the Security Service at the army command, Colonel Werner Müller of the General Staff. BAr J.I.121/5. To Swiss ears, the alias "Hans Kunz" followed by "from Grafenried" subconsciously created the impression that would be created by someone in the U.S. named "Joe Smith, from Smallville"—of someone honest, almost common, and probably not overly bright, Grafenried being a small and unremarkable farming village on the outskirts of Bern.
4. See Kurt Emmenegger, *Q.N. wusste Bescheid* (Zürich, 1965), and Kurz, *Nachrichtenzentrum*, 72 and 121, note 84.
5. On May 28, 1945, Meyer told the investigating judge, Colonel Otto Müller: "Until 1934 I worked as a lawyer, then I became a writer of detective stories. Until the war, my only other activity besides writing consisted of looking after my estate, which includes about 23 acres of nursery, fields, and meadows." BAr E 5330 1982/1, vol. 205.
6. They included *D.K.D.R. im Gotthardexpress* (D.K.D.R. is an abbreviation for "Der Kreis der Rächer"—the Circle of Avengers), and *Mord um Malow*. On the occasion of Meyer's 70th birthday, on August 4, 1964 (morning edition), the *St. Galler Tagblatt* wrote, "Für den Kenner der heimischen Literatur gilt Schwertenbach zusammen mit dem älteren Friedrich Glauser als Schöpfer des Kriminalromans schweizerischer Observanz"—experts in Swiss literature consider Schwertenbach and Friedrich Glauser, who is older, as the creators of the Swiss-style detective story.
7. Between 1930 and 1940, the *Neue Zürcher Zeitung* published his stories *Meinand Resich* (anagram for "Mein andres Ich"—My Other Self; nos. 1871–2112, 1931), Nerven (history of the story in no. 1574, 1932, actual story in nos. 1574–1614, 1932), *Der 'kriminelle' Schuhputzer* (no. 244, 1936), *Wie man's macht, ist's falsch* (no. 623, 1936), *Die Grossbank* (no. 1749, 1936), *Kümmerli vor dem Polizeirichter* (no. 2206, 1936), *Nächtlicher Spuk auf Schloss X* (no. 911, 1937), *Der seelsorgerische Briefträger* (no. 1447, 1937), *Die englischen Sechs* (no. 1600, 1939), *Indizien* (nos. 2104 and 2112, 1939), and *Der Blinde mit den verbundenen Augen*, a crime novella (no. 522 and 528, 1940); it reviewed *D.K.D.R. im Gotthardexpress* (no. 804, 1931), *Die weissen Waden* (no. 1174, 1934), *Kümmerli, der Kleinbürger* (no. 2040, 1937), and *Die Frau, die es nicht war* (no. 2276, 1938).
8. Hans Rudolf Schmid had been press officer at the 1939 Swiss National Fair. Due to his position at army headquarters, he was in close contact with Army Intelligence.
9. Hans Rudolf Schmid at the funeral service for Paul Meyer, alias Wolf

Schwertenbach, 19 September 1966. BAr J.I.121/40. In a series of articles in
the *Tages-Anzeiger* (October 19–26, 1945), Schmid had commented on the
Masson affair in a way that exonerated Masson; however, Hans Hausamann felt
attacked by the articles because, without mentioning his name, Schmid accused
him of having started the campaign against Masson. The result was a long-
standing legal battle over the question whether Schmid had libeled Hausamann
(see BAr E 27/9846).

10. Schmid at Meyer's funeral service, 19 September 1966. (Speech in this author's
possession.)

11. Excerpt from the settlement document. BAr J.I.121/37. During the war,
Masson allowed Meyer to go on a special leave every week from Saturday morning to Monday night because Meyer had argued:

> I own an estate with a commercial nursery, which, in addition to
> some writing activities, helps me make a living. Since I am not
> married, I have to rely *exclusively* on hired labor (50% of my staff
> are currently also on duty), and I have to look after things myself if
> I want to avoid gradually losing my livelihood. I will be able to put
> my special skills at the disposal of the army command and the
> Intelligence Service only if the requested leave is granted to me.
> After August 28, 1939, while serving on the border unit, I was able
> to look after things and make the necessary arrangements any time
> because my duty station was only 3 kilometers from my home.
> (Meyer to Lieutenant Colonel Werner Müller, attn. Masson, 9
> November 1939. BAr E 27/9528.)

12. After the war, the guest book was used several times as evidence in court; for
example, see the decree by the Zürich cantonal jury, 17 September 1947.

13. On this issue, see for instance Hausamann to Lützelschwab, 31 January 1948.
BAr J.I.137 1974/64, vol. 12. In his book *Zwischen allen Fronten* (p. 189),
Alphons Matt took over the rumor, stating, "[This is] strange if you consider
that at the beginning of the war, Dr. Meyer had absolutely no material posses-
sions."

14. In an official report dated March 22, 1969, the notary's office and land registry
of Ermatingen stated that the terms of the mortgage had not changed since the
date of the purchase. See Erwin Tschudi to Alphons Matt, 20 April 1969. BAr
J.I.121/33. Nevertheless, the unkind rumor persists to this day. On 22–23
March 1997 the feature editor of *Der Bund* reiterated the allegations and
refused to print an erratum, although his attention was drawn to the obvious
misstatement of facts. (Documents in this author's possession.)

15. Meyer's second wife, who was born in Burgdorf, canton Bern, also used several
names. Her official name was Johanna Friederike Verena Meier-Ruef; her pseudonym was Patrizia Verena Schwertenbach-Meyer. She remarried after Paul
Meyer's death and was henceforth known as Mrs. Frey-Meyer, alias Dr. Patrizia
Verena Frey-Schwertenbach. In documents she is often called "Pat." Her highly
attractive physical appearance and her captivating charm as a hostess had some
influence on the close relationship her husband Captain Meyer established first
with Schellenberg's aide Eggen and later on with Schellenberg himself. When
the German spy chief fell ill (which happened several times while he was in

Switzerland), she acted as his nurse, thereby getting a glimpse of Schellenberg which contrasted with his merciless actions at the Reich Security Central Office. (Conversations with this author, 1984–1988.)

16. Statement by Captain Meyer, minutes of hearing by investigating judge of divisional court 6, 2 August 1945 (BAr E 5330 1982/1, vol. 205) and verbal communications by Patrizia Schwertenbach to this author, 1984–1988.

17. His unit had the official abbreviation "Gz Füs Kp I 275."

18. Assistant Chief of Staff for the Front to Adjutant General's office, 31 October 1939. BAr E 5795/327. Effective the end of 1940, Meyer was promoted to captain; Masson wrote to Meyer, "[Regarding] your nomination to the rank of captain, which I consider above all as a deserved reward for your work . . . I would like to use this opportunity to tell you once again how much I appreciate the devotion with which you have been working with us and the useful and delicate job you have been doing." BAr J.I.121/20. Alfred Ernst ridiculed Meyer's promotion, calling it a promotion *honoris causa* (Ernst to Werner Müller, 19 December 1942. BAr J.I.140/4, vol. 4).

19. Zürich's police inspector Wiesendanger had recommended Meyer-Schwertenbach to the head of the Security Service (minutes of hearing by investigating judge of divisional court 6, 3 August 1945. BAr E 5330 1982/1, vol. 205). Wiesendanger often accompanied Meyer to his meetings with Eggen or Schellenberg. The police inspector of the city of Zürich and Meyer had been friends since going to school together.

20. On October 14, 1939, the Intelligence Section wrote to the Assistant Chief of Staff for the Front, "Lieutenant Colonel Müller of the General Staff, who is in charge of dealing with special issues for the Intelligence Section, and occasionally also for the Assistant Chief of Staff for the Front and the Chief of the General Staff, and who acts as a liaison body with counter-intelligence, absolutely needs an officer as his aide and deputy; if possible, that officer should have a law degree. We request that you detail First Lieutenant Meier Paul to that position" (BAr E 27/9508, vol. 1). The letter was written by Müller.

21. Because of his function on army security, in Zürich Meyer-Schwertenbach was given the nickname "Spezialmeyer." See note for file by Hausamann, 30 September 1943. Archives of H.R. Kurz.

22. BAr J.I.121/42.

23. Counterintelligence, as well as the police section and the military police, were sub-sections of the Security Service (see page 57ff.).

24. Meyer expressed his own conviction in his "Gedanken eines Offiziers zum politischen Umbruch unserer Zeit" (An Officer's Thoughts on the Current Political Upheaval), in which he stated, among other things:
     The army must no longer "stand with ordered arms" before the domestic political events. . . . If we recognize that a foreign country sponsors a Swiss revival movement, the country is about to be threatened. We must no longer wait but act immediately. Such foreign interference must be nipped in the bud. . . . In order to work against the defeatist ideas among the population and young people's indifference towards the state and politics, the idea of the

Swiss state and defense must be brought into the army, the schools,
and the population. Swiss Independence Day is a special opportunity for the army to do so. (Undated, possibly written for the occasion of Independence Day on August 1, 1940. BAr J.I.121/46)

25. Among other things, Meyer-Schwertenbach participated in the surveillance of
the "National Movement of Switzerland" (Nationale Bewegung der Schweiz,
NBS), which the Federal Council outlawed on November 19, 1940 based on
the evidence that Meyer and others had gathered. On December 10, 1940,
Federal Councillor Baumann, the head of the Justice and Police Department,
wrote to Minger that the Attorney General's office had been in permanent
contact with the Special Service of Army Intelligence concerning the NBS,
adding, "On orders of Colonel Müller of the General Staff, 1st Lt. Meyer, who
dealt exclusively with the NBS, regularly went to see the head of the federal
police to discuss and evaluate the available information. . . . Today the head of
the federal police explicitly refers to this cooperation, which was welcomed by
both sides and has resulted in their sharing the same opinion" (BAr E
27/11198). See also Meyer to Federal Councillor von Steiger, 14 November
1944. BAr J.I.121/31. The NBS had been founded in June 1940 by a small
group of people but became very popular within a short time, probably in part
due to the devastating impact of the collapse of France. In the propaganda
material that it distributed in public, the NBS indicated that it aimed to take
over power in Switzerland and reshape the country as an autocracy. On
September 10, 1940, Federal President Pilet-Golaz received two leaders of the
movement, Ernst Hofmann and Max Leo Keller, together with Jakob
Schaffner, a prominent Swiss Nazi Party member in Germany (the event subsequently became known in Swiss history as "the reception of the Front movement"). Bbl 1946 I 59. A report by Germany's Envoy Köcher to the German
Ministry of Foreign Affairs dated November 27, 1940 indicates that the
Federal Council may have had additional reasons to outlaw the NBS; Köcher
wrote, "I have been told by someone absolutely reliable that the Federal
President [Pilet-Golaz] explained to a third party that the Federal Council had
outlawed the NBS because the Social Democrats in parliament had declared
that they would not refrain from demanding the two vacant Cabinet seats at
the upcoming Federal Council elections if the NBS was not outlawed."
National Archives, Washington, DC, T-120/1906, German Legation Bern,
784/4; see Daniel Bourgeois, "L'image allemande de Pilet-Golaz, 1940–1944,"
Studien und Quellen 4 (Bern, 1978): 88–89.

26. For example, General Guisan ordered Meyer-Schwertenbach to look into the
supposed machinations of Colonel Däniker (see page 355, endnote 154). See
Meyer's notes on his meeting with the Commander-in-Chief, 27 March 1942.
BAr J.I.121/1.

27. The contacts resulted, among other things, in a *special report* dated January 16,
1941 on the German Intelligence Service's opinion about General Guisan and
on the British Intelligence Service that was allegedly very busy in Switzerland,
and a *special report* dated January 6, 1942 concerning the ultimate supremacy
of the NSDAP over the Wehrmacht ("[it is said that] as long as Hitler,
Himmler, and the military's Chief of the General Staff Jodl are in charge of

Germany, a revolution can be ruled out"). Both documents are at BAr
J.I.121/20.

28. BAr J.I.121/58.

29. In this matter, the driving force was the Commander-in-Chief's wife, who
trusted Meyer-Schwertenbach, "of whose intelligent devotion and loyalty my
husband can be sure" (Mrs. Mary Guisan to Meyer, 27 August 1941. BAr
J.I.121/5).

30. Meyer-Schwertenbach, diary entry on his discussion on January 27, 1943 with
the Commander-in-Chief concerning his transfer from Interlaken to Zürich.
Meyer later added, "From that moment on, I reported only to Masson +
Commander-in-Chief." BAr J.I.121/1. Waibel did not agree with Meyer on
that issue and in fall 1943 a conflict erupted between the two.

31. Meyer, interrogation by investigating judge of divisional court 6, 3 August
1945. BAr J.I.121/54. However, Meyer continued to liaise with police and military authorities. The police inspector's office of the city of Zürich actually sent
Meyer another 1,495 reports, which he forwarded to the federal police.

32. See Werner Müller to Chief of the General Staff, 4 July 1941. BAr E 27/9508,
vol. 9.

33. Werner Müller to Masson, 16 January 1943. BAr E 27/9528.

34. Müller to Masson, 16 January 1943.

35. Werner Müller to Masson, 16 January 1943 (personal). BAr E 27/9528.

36. Müller to Masson, 16 January 1943 (personal).

37. In the original text, this phrase is underlined.

38. Müller to Masson, 16 January 1943 (personal). BAr E 27/9528.

39. Meyer-Schwertenbach to Commander-in-Chief, 7 November 1942. General
Guisan annotated the letter in handwriting, stating, "received in person." BAr E
5795/451 and J.I.121/15.

40. Barbey to Masson, 13 November 1942. BAr E 5795/451. Barbey annotated the
copy of the letter in handwriting, stating, "[phone call] of Nov. 13, 1942 by
Col. Brig. Masson; [he said,] 'the order has been carried out.' B." BAr E
5795/327.

41. Note by Meyer-Schwertenbach, 18 November 1941, "Colonel [Werner] Müller
confirms that [information] to me. [He says that] he told the Commander-in-
Chief about it, [adding that] Hausamann first reported it and Jaquillard is now
dealing with the issue. [He explains that] Pilet-Golaz also monitors the Federal
Councillors" (BAr J.I.121/1).

42. Minutes of meeting regarding the tapped telephone conversations in Interlaken,
27 November 1942. Secret. BAr E 5795/451.

43. The tapping agents, Leo Steinmann and Mathilde Schaad on the daytime shift,
Andreas Glarner and Karl Immer on the nighttime and Sunday shift, were not
officials of the postal and telephone service but private individuals in a position
of absolute trust. Their supervisor, Colonel Paul Wittmer of the Press and
Radio Section, had made background checks before hiring them. It seems that
the tapping agents never abused the confidence that was placed in them.

44. Cf. Lieutenant General Huber's statement, "I made an effort and looked
through the transcripts of the tapped telephone conversations. They do not
include many interesting things; most of them concern black marketeering and

infringements of rationing regulations." Minutes of meeting, 27 November 1942. BAr E 5795/451.

45. General Guisan made some extensive handwritten annotations to the minutes concerning the issues that he intended to raise in a "discussion with Huber." He stated, "One should not use the term 'cowards'! There was no denunciation." Moreover, the Commander-in-Chief did not like the Chief of the General Staff's biting final remarks, explaining, "If he considered that there were *cowards*, why did he not bring the issue up dir[ectly] with me rather than expressing it in the unacceptable conclusions of these minutes." In the minutes, Huber also remarked, "[It is unpleasant to see] that there are denouncers who, before addressing the issue with the responsible chief, circumvent the official channels to intervene in instructions issued or approved by the Chief of the General Staff." General Guisan countered this argument by commenting, "I did not know that he had issued these instructions; he for his part had actually forgotten about them. . . . My task as Commander-in-Chief obviously allows me to collect a lot of information in the entire army.—Collecting it does not mean adopting it! I have to check on these things." Guisan argued that the affair of the tapped telephone conversations showed that it was necessary for him to keep an eye on everything. In addition, the Commander-in-Chief once again criticized Masson, stating, "*Masson not well enough informed about what goes on.*" Nevertheless, it was important to him to be in close contact with Group Id, explaining, "This must not create any mistrust nor any disagreements" (BAr E 5795/451). In a letter to the Chief of the General Staff dated December 5, 1942, the Commander-in-Chief put an end to the matter, stating, "I would like to point out that from a legal viewpoint, there is no objection to monitoring telephone conversations; . . . hence, I authorize [Counterintelligence] to resume its monitoring activities, as proposed by the Assistant Chief Id" (BAr E 5795/327). Henceforth, a number of telephones that were available to a well-defined group of people were no longer tapped.

46. Masson to Waibel, 20 January 1943. BAr E 5330 1982/1, vol. 205.

47. This was an *administrative* measure. Information by Colonel Werner Müller, the deputy of the Assistant Chief of Staff Id, to Waibel, 14 May 1943. BAr E 5330 1982/1, vol. 205.

48. BAr J.I.121/42. To his surprise, through these terms of reference Meyer realized that, contrary to Masson's instructions of January 20, 1943, Waibel had named Captain Eugen Gyr as head of the *Uto* sub-office instead of him. Meyer protested, but in vain; Masson wanted to see how well Waibel's structure worked before considering any changes. For the time being, the Assistant Chief of Staff Id also rejected Meyer's suggestion to make him Masson's direct subordinate, plausibly arguing that for management reasons he tried to keep the number of direct subordinates as small as possible. See Meyer to Masson, undated handwritten draft letter in response to Masson's letter to Meyer, 17 December 1943. BAr J.I.121/20.

49. The cantonal and municipal police authorities had their own units to counter subversive activities and espionage. These special units dealing with a wide range of subversive activities had different names in different cantons and towns, such as "*Intelligence Service*" or "*Political Section.*"

50. Meyer to Masson, undated draft letter, probably around 20 December 1943. BAr J.I.121/20.
51. On this issue, see Chapter 5.
52. Waibel, *Organisation des Bureaus Uto*, 16 July 1943. BAr J.I.121/42.
53. For his new assignment, Meyer-Schwertenbach was able to rely on well-established relations; cf. his statement to Police Inspector Albert Wiesendanger on 4 November 1941:

> After two years of activity as head of the Intelligence and Security section's Special Service, I would like to thank you and the gentlemen at your political bureau very much for your valuable cooperation with, and support of, our service in the army. I guess I may use this opportunity to let you know that *in terms of politics the city of Zürich is by far the "most interesting" place in Switzerland*. It is in large part due to you and your political aides at the office of [Hüni/Frei] that we have been able to inform the Commander-in-Chief and the army's Security Service extensively and promptly about our domestic political situation. (BAr J.I.121/20.)

The letter was apparently expected to be put on file, as Meyer used the formal pronoun "Sie" to address Wiesendanger; as former classmates and long-term friends, in private Meyer and Wiesendanger were likely to use the informal pronoun "du" to address each other.
54. Waibel, *Organisation des Bureaus Uto*, 16 July 1943. BAr J.I. 121/42.
55. Travel expenses, meals, and similar expenses.
56. Captain Gyr, *Reglement betreffend Organisation des Bureau Uto*, 30 June 1943. BAr J.I.121/42.
57. Masson to Meyer, 17 December 1943. BAr J.I.121/1 (quoted in connection with Hausamann's claims about Meyer-Schwertenbach in his lawsuit against *Freies Volk*).
58. Masson to Meyer, 17 December 1943. BAr J.I.121/1.
59. However, that did not hamper the good relations between Gyr and Meyer (see Gyr to Masson, 1 December 1943. BAr J.I.121/1). Waibel later told a court why he had not named Meyer, explaining, "I could not, nor did I want to, use Meyer as head of the intelligence bureau in Zürich because I knew that he was *not trustworthy*." Waibel, statement as a witness, Territorial Court 3A, 22 November 1945. BAr E 5330 1982/1, vol. 205. Waibel expressly instructed Captains Häne and Gyr to keep important information secret from Meyer-Schwertenbach. For that purpose, the two officers used a safe to which Meyer had no key.
60. Meyer, handwritten note for the file, undated [probably November 1943]. BAr J.I.121/1. Concerning the spelling and style, see page 446.
61. Unlike Meyer-Schwertenbach, who never found out, we were able to establish *who* had informed the Commander-in-Chief: It was Lützelschwab who wrote to the General, "Moreover, I would like to ask you once again to summon Major Waibel to your office in order for him to be able to inform you about Captain Meyer." Lützelschwab to Commander-in-Chief, 13 August 1943. BAr J.I.137 1974/64, vol. 4.

62. Meyer, handwritten note for the file, undated [probably November 1943]. BAr J.I.121/1.
63. On November 30, 1943, Meyer wrote to Masson of ". . . the information that you *have received from Schellenberg in Berlin*, according to which you should watch out for your subordinate Major W. because he asked a German for information concerning [my and my aide Captain Holzach's] machinations in connection with our German connection because he needed some additional information to complete his file." BAr J.I.121/20.
64. "hermetisches Schweigen": Meyer to Waibel, 29 November 1943. BAr J.I.121/1.
65. On August 25, 1943, General Guisan wrote to Lützelschwab, "I will summon Major Waibel to my office in order to receive information from him about Captain M[eyer]" (BAr J.I.137 1974/64, vol. 4.). On November 9, 1943, the Commander-in-Chief informed Basel's state attorney, "I have spoken with Major Waibel about Captain M[eyer]. I will look into the matter." BAr J.I.137 1974/64, vol. 4.
66. Meyer, handwritten note for the file, undated [probably November 1943]. BAr J.I.121/1.
67. A number of letters show that initially the two officers were on good terms. In early January 1941, Waibel congratulated the head of the Special Service, Meyer, on his promotion to the rank of captain, stating, "I also feel a need to thank you very much for your understanding at the Special Service, and I hope that this year we will once again manage to pull off many *deals*. Cheers! Yours truly, your comrade Waibel" (document in this author's possession).
68. Meyer commented, "Obviously I refuse to inform W[aibel] about my activity. . . . I am at the Colonel-Brigadier's disposal. Officially 3 days on duty per week—I am working on the relation with E[ggen]." Meyer, handwritten note for the file, undated [probably November 1943].
69. See Chapter 1.
70. On this issue, see Chapter 10, particularly page 237ff.
71. In a note for the file dated January 27, 1943 on a meeting with the Commander-in-Chief, Meyer wrote, "[The Commander-in-Chief said] that he had made some inquiries among the officers, and no one said that he mistrusted me; on the contrary, he explained that everyone had a favorable opinion about me, adding that *I was too sensitive* and too pessimistic because I was probably overworked. He advised me to take a vacation and no longer pay any attention to the matter, assuring me that *after all he trusted me*." BAr J.I.121/1.
72. Waibel explained, "Back then Captain Meyer was assigned to me as intelligence of[ficer] for the city of Zürich *after he had been removed from headquarters*." Statement by Waibel as a witness during the hearing of evidence by the investigating judge of territorial court 3A, Captain H. Studer, for the courtmartial proceedings against Meyer-Schwertenbach, 22 November 1945. The proceedings were later abandoned.
73. However, objectively speaking there was an urgent need to increase the staff at *Uto*. On February 20, 1942, in a letter to the attention of Masson, Alfred Ernst complained to Werner Müller, "We keep getting less and less information from Zürich, *the most important center*." In the 1942 annual report of the German

Bureau dated December 28, 1942, he insisted, "The *Uto* group should urgently be rebuilt." Both documents are at BAr J.I.140/4, vol. 4.

74. (Meyer, handwritten note for the file, undated [probably November 1943]. BAr J.I.121/1).

75. Mayr von Baldegg to Investigating Judge Otto Müller, 8 June 1945. BAr E 5330 1982/1, vol. 205.

76. The head of the *Uto* sub-office had unsuccessfully objected to granting Meyer's request, stating, "I would extremely regret if you granted this request . . . because the close relations that [Meyer] has with the local police authorities would be lost." Gyr to Masson, 1 December 1943. BAr J.I.121/1.

77. On July 16, 1945, Military Attorney General Eugster wrote to General Guisan, "[In connection with the characteristics and methods of Intelligence's executive bodies,] not only the *creation* of, but also the *choice of staff* for, the *rather fictitious office in Zürich*, which was to deal with Colonel-Brigadier Masson's personal channel to Himmler's SS headquarters, leaves an extremely unpleasant impression." BAr E 5330 1982/1, vol. 205.

78. Concerning his refusal to appoint Meyer-Schwertenbach as head of Army Intelligence's sub-office in Zürich, on June 12, 1945, Waibel explained to Investigating Judge Otto Müller:

> However, after a short time it became apparent that he could not be used. I was instructed to keep an eye on Captain Meyer, so I gave him *terms of reference* in the form of an order, by which he did not abide. Hence, I demanded that he be punished, which never happened. I never received any information from Captain Meyer. [In fact, Meyer intentionally left out his name and sent his information directly to Schafroth and Masson; Waibel did not know about that.] At my request, he was taken off the list of staff that reported to me. BAr E 5330 1982/1, vol. 205.

On June 20, 1945, during the interrogation by Investigating Judge Otto Müller, Masson for his part stated:

> I had Captain Meyer report directly to me because there were differences between him and Major Waibel. Colonel [Werner] Müller no longer wanted to keep Captain Meyer under him; he considered that Captain Meyer should be discharged. After that Major Waibel also told me that he no longer wanted to keep Meyer in his service. I was occasionally told by Colonel [Werner] Müller and Major Waibel that Meyer had a bad reputation; however, these allegations could not be substantiated. BAr E 5330 1982/1, vol. 205.

79. Paul Meyer's military record booklet. BAr J.I.121/35. During wartime duty, Captain Meyer served a total of more than 1,200 days (excluding leaves).

Chapter 7: Early Stages of the Masson-Schellenberg Connection

1. They soon became close friends; Henry Guisan was Meyer's best man at his wedding in 1941 and introduced him to his father, the Commander-in-Chief. Guisan Sr. was not unhappy about his son being friends with Meyer; Guisan

Jr.'s business partner Ernest-Otto Knecht explained, "General Guisan apparently wanted Meyer to keep an eye on his son." (Ernest-Otto Knecht, industrialist, to Samuel Haas, director of the *Schweizer Mittelpresse* [news agency], shorthand notes, 16 October 1945. BAr E 27/10033). The Commander-in-Chief's wife made a similar comment about Meyer-Schwertenbach.

2. Fuhrer, *Spionage*, 79.

3. Fuhrer, *Spionage*, 79.

4. After the war, Eggen claimed that he did not remember whether the transaction had been concluded before or during the war (see Eggen to investigating judge of 2nd division, 14 July 1945. BAr E 5330 1982/1, vol. 205). The date given in this study is supported by evidence from Hans Hausamann and the Ordnance Section.

5. The number of submachine guns varies from one reference to another: Ilsemann, Eggen, Lützelschwab, and Hausamann mentioned 120, 263, 290, and 300 pieces, respectively.

6. The Bergmann type (7.36 Mauser caliber) submachine guns were made by the *Schweizerische Industriegesellschaft (SIG)* in Neuhausen. After the war, Germany's Major General von Ilsemann explained, "Apparently *these submachine guns were later found during the rebellion by the Iron Guard in Romania*" (Major General von Ilsemann to Military Attorney General Eugster, 11 January 1946. BAr E 5795/335).

7. Supposition by Chief of the General Staff Huber, see Huber to Commerce Section at the Swiss Federal Department of Economic Affairs, 16 January 1941. BAr E 27/19357.

8. Chief of the General Staff Huber to Commerce Section, 16 January 1941. BAr E 27/19357.

9. Muntwyler was serving there at that time.

10. The letter by Reich Ministry of Economic Affairs Berlin to Eggen, 4 November 1940 (reference V Ld [D] 137 215/40), signed by Tüngeler, stated, "I confirm that I will approve the supply of gasoline for delivery to Luchsinger & Co., Zürich, Switzerland, in exchange for the 290 submachine guns, accessories, and spare parts purchased from the *Schweiz. Industrie-Gesellschaft*, Neuhausen, via the Luchsinger company" (copy at BAr E 27/19357).

11. Huber to Commerce Section, 16 January 1941. BAr E 27/19357.

12. Huber to Commerce Section, 16 January 1941.

13. On January 11, 1946, Major General von Ilsemann told Military Attorney General Eugster, "Later on I began to have doubts whether this transaction was all right, so [I] reported it to Berlin." (General Guisan annotated the document by hand, writing, "2/21/46, copy made of file v[on] Ilsemann that Bracher lent to me.") BAr E 5795/335.

14. Huber to Commerce Section, 16 January 1941. BAr E 27/19357.

15. Eggen presented a blank currency certificate worth 60,000 Reichsmarks as a down payment; in exchange, as early as the next day, on November 9, 1940, he received the guns. Kriegstechnische Abteilung (Ordnance Section), note for file, 3 September 1941. BAr J.I.137 1974/64, vol. 4.

16. Minister Jean Hotz, the director of the Commerce Section at the Swiss Federal

Department of Economic Affairs, called it a "*very shady* business." Hotz to army command, 10 January 1941. BAr E 27/19357.

17. See Fuhrer, *Spionage*, 129, note 275; Eggen, interrogation, 1 May 1945. BAr E 27/10032; Hausamann, indictment in the case against *Die Tat*/Dr. Kummer, 7 July 1947. BAr E 27/9846. Knecht claimed, "At that time, negotiations were also undertaken with Germany concerning the delivery of gasoline; Guisan [Jr.] was a party to the negotiations and Meyer acted as an advisor." Knecht, conversation with Samuel Haas, 16 October 1945. BAr E 27/10033.

18. When the gasoline was not delivered, the Ordnance Section complained to Luchsinger & Co., the company that had arranged the gun transaction. Luchsinger & Co. informed the Ordnance Section that, contrary to the agreement, the gasoline would not be delivered free of shipping charges to the Swiss border but would have to be picked up in Romania with cisterns from Switzerland, adding, "On the 7th of this month, our informant in Berlin informed us that the . . . gasoline would be made available free on board Giurgiu (harbor on the Danube south of Bucharest)." (Luchsinger & Co., Zürich, to Ordnance Section, 10 December 1940. BAr E 27/19357.) In a letter to the army command dated January 10, 1941, the director of the Commerce Section at the Swiss Federal Department of Economic Affairs stated, "Due to the fact that the free gasoline will not be delivered directly from Germany to the Swiss border free of shipping charges but has to be picked up with Swiss cisterns, the transaction in exchange for the export of guns is *absolutely worthless*. Probably everyone knows that Switzerland could purchase enough gasoline in Romania but lacks shipping capacity to import a sufficient amount of it." BAr E 27/19357. On September 3, 1943, Major von Steiger, head of Imports and Exports at the Ordnance Section, told Lützelschwab, "Hence, the whole compensation with gasoline became an illusion, and we could not help but think that from the onset this had been a *carefully planned bluff* in order to get hold of the guns." BAr J.I.137 1974/64, vol. 4.

19. Meyer, note for file, 14 November 1941. BAr J.I.121/1. An intelligence officer of the Zürich cantonal police "had received orders to check with the G[erman] Ministry of Economic Affairs and the German Armed Forces High Command what the deal with the gasoline was all about." He concluded "that they did not know anything about the deal and that the guns had been allotted to the SS, not the Wehrmacht." Information by Zürich Intelligence Service, 22 November 1941 (archives of H.R. Kurz). "Apparently Major [von] Steiger from the Ordnance Section and the Swiss Commerce Section declared that they would see to it that Eggen could not return to Switzerland." Zürich Intelligence Service, 1 July 1942. Archives of H.R. Kurz.

20. BAr J.I.121/1.

21. Meyer, statement to investigating judge of territorial court 3A, 3 December 1945. BAr E 27/10027, vol. 1. (The charges were later dropped.)

22. Masson was promoted to Colonel-Brigadier effective March 1, 1942.

23. That information is based on Meyer's statement to investigating judge H. Studer, territorial court 3A, 3 December 1945. BAr E 5330 1982/1, vol. 205. Neither Werner Müller nor Masson contested having been consulted by Meyer.

24. That is, the immigration ban on Eggen.

25. Reference to the gasoline that Switzerland was supposed to receive in fall 1940 in exchange for the sale of submachine guns.

26. The Commerce Section, to be precise (now called State Secretariat for Economic Affairs).

27. On August 13, 1943, Lützelschwab wrote to the Commander-in-Chief: "In the meantime I spoke with the Head of Imports and Exports at the Ordnance Section about E. It is true that the Ordnance Section had said that it did not want Mr. E. to enter Switzerland anymore. Even today Major von Steiger believes that *E. is a terrible black marketeer ('übler Schieber') whom you cannot trust at all.*" BAr J.I.137 1974/64, vol. 4.

28. Iwan von Ilsemann, the military attaché at the German Legation in Bern, did not sympathize with the Nazis. See page 370, endnote 70.

29. "I clarified that and was informed by Berlin that E. would like to come to Switzerland so that he could prove that he was not responsible for the fact that the deal had (not) worked out because Switzerland had turned down lead-free gasoline. He would also be able to get jobs for Switzerland. So I decided to try to change the Department of Trade and Commerce's mind but to no avail. And it was then that I realized that the German legation had been backing Major von Steiger (from the Technical Department of Warfare) as Ilsemann and E[ggen] are enemies due to the fact that he [Eggen] is a member of the SS." Meyer, note for file, 14 November 1941.

30. Meyer, note for file, 14 November 1941. BAr J.I. 121/1.

31. For Swiss Intelligence.

32. Meyer, note for file, 14 November 1941. BAr J.I. 121/1.

33. Meyer, note for file, 14 November 1941.

34. In the note for the file of 14 November 1941, Meyer indicated that he introduced himself by his pen-name *Schwertenbach*. The version presented in this study is consistent with Meyer's statement before divisional court 6 (2 August 1945. BAr J.I.121/54), which seems more plausible because Meyer introduced himself as Henry Guisan Jr.'s legal advisor. Eggen later also remembered hearing the name *Ritzburg* (Eggen, "Abhörungsprotokoll der Schweizerischen Bundesanwaltschaft," 1 May 1945. BAr E 5330 1982/1, vol. 205, and E 27/10032). The contradiction might be due to the fact that Meyer made no secret of his pen-name *Schwertenbach*. Perhaps in passing Meyer and Guisan Jr. talked about Meyer's activity as a writer, mentioning his nom de plume in that connection.

35. Meyer, note for file, 14 November 1941. BAr J.I. 121/1.

36. Meyer, note for file, 14 November 1941.

37. Concerning the gasoline that the Swiss were supposed to receive in exchange for the submachine guns.

38. Meyer, note for file, 14 November 1941. BAr J.I. 121/1.

39. However, when he first mentioned Eggen to Meyer, Henry Guisan Jr. had explicitly referred to the intelligence aspect; see Meyer, note for file, 14 November 1941. BAr J.I. 121/1.

40. Head of Security Service to Assistant Chief of Staff Id, 16 January 1943. BAr E 27/9528.

41. Head of Security Service to Assistant Chief of Staff Id, 16 January 1943.

42. Head of Security Service to Assistant Chief of Staff Id, 16 January 1943.
43. At the National Archives in Washington, DC, this author came across a telling statement that Eggen made on March 18, 1948 during his second interrogation in Nuremberg in connection with the *Wilhelmstrasse* trial. Eggen remarked: "I own an export and import business. *I am first of all a merchant. . . . Personally I have nothing to gain or lose.*" National Archives, Washington, DC, RG 238 M 1019 R 15.
44. Meyer used to make his castle available free of charge for stylish meetings during which the guests and their entourage were often served copious meals for several days.
45. The available reference material does not provide any conclusive evidence about the intended use of the barracks. In 1945, Masson ("La ligne Eggen-Schellenberg," 14 June 1945. BAr E 5330 1982/1, vol. 205) stated that they were slated for the German troops at the front in the East. However, strictly speaking there was no front in the East before June 22, 1941. It is therefore up to each reader to make his or her own conjectures about their intended use. In any event, this author finds the shipping instructions from Berlin (H. Weidenmann to Swiss Wood Syndicate, 23 March 1942. BAr J.I.121/74) informative: the first 200 barracks were to be shipped to Francesco Parisi in *Oranienburg* near Berlin, and the remaining barracks to the same recipient in *Dachau* near Munich. On June 2, 1942, Weidenmann informed Meyer that "about 200 barracks [had] been built near Berlin." BAr J.I.121/74.
46. In the framework of the Swiss Confederation's wartime setup of the national economy, the Swiss Wood Syndicate, which had been founded in 1939, had a monopoly on exports of barracks and cut pine-wood timber. On this issue, see *Die Schweizerische Kriegswirtschaft 1939/1948: Bericht des Eidgenössischen Volkswirtschaftsdepartementes* (Bern, 1950), 793 ff.
47. Hausamann stated, "However, the German Armed Forces High Command . . . was displaced in this role by the SS, which wanted to do business on its own whenever a deal promised to be profitable." (Hausamann, indictment in case against *Die Tat*/Dr. Kummer, 7 July 1947.) In several transcripts of tapped telephone conversations between October 1941 and January 1942, there is evidence for the fact that the Wehrmacht's interest was flagging and the SS's role was increasing. BAr J.I.121/45.
48. Eggen to the special investigating judge of the 2nd Division, 14 July 1945. BAr E 5330 1982/1, vol. 205.
49. Eggen, "Abhörungsprotokoll der Schweizerischen Bundesanwaltschaft," 1 May 1945.
50. Lützelschwab, "Bericht in Sachen Eggen," 5 June 1945. BAr E 5330 1982/1, vol. 205. Hausamann made a similar statement, arguing, "In order to cover up his spying activities, conduct the profitable business transactions that higher-ranking SS officials liked conducting, and, towards the end of the war, smuggle looted funds out of Germany and avoid paying taxes, SS Major Eggen was manager of the *Warenvertriebs GmbH* in Berlin." (Hausamann, indictment in case against *Die Tat*/Dr. Kummer, 7 July 1947.) However, in specialized German and U.S. publications this author did not find any reference to that firm. In Nuremberg, Eggen stated on that issue: "Do you mean the

Warenvertriebs G.m.b.H.? That was the import company handling the transaction with the barracks. After all, the SS and the Wehrmacht could not act as German partners. The *Warenvertriebs G.m.b.H.* had been founded by me; it already existed when the wood [barracks] transaction began." When Norbert G. Barr asked him, "Who were the partners at the company?," Eggen replied, "One other man, [Max] Baumann, who was president. He and I founded the company together." Interrogation of Eggen, Justice Palace Nuremberg, 16 March 1948. National Archives, Washington, DC, RG 238 M 1019 R 15.

51. Eggen, "Abhörungsprotokoll der Schweizerischen Bundesanwaltschaft," 1 May 1945. BAr E 5330 1982/1, vol. 205.

52. Lützelschwab, "Bericht in Sachen Eggen," 5 June 1945. BAr E 5330 1982/1, vol. 205. Concerning Weidenmann, see also page 149.

53. The Haengers had been in contact with Eggen as early as January 1941 concerning a business deal relating to skis. See Major von Steiger (Ordnance Section) to Lützelschwab, 3 September 1943. BAr J.I.137 1974/64, vol. 4.

54. Ernest-Otto Knecht. See page 341, endnote 1, and page 343, endnote 17.

55. Lützelschwab, "Bericht in Sachen Eggen," 5 June 1945. BAr E 5330 1982/1, vol. 205.

56. Lützelschwab, the head of the Political Section at the Basel-Stadt police department, had become aware of these relations in early 1943 in connection with another investigation; the statements made in this study are based on the material that he gathered for that investigation on behalf of Federal Councillor Kobelt. BAr E 27/14131.

57. On that issue, see Lützelschwab to Kobelt, 24 February 1943. BAr E 27/14131.

58. Lützelschwab to Kobelt, 24 February 1943. BAr E 27/14131.

59. The police report attested that both Haenger Sr. and Haenger Jr. were extremely capable and enterprising, adding: "However, the various telephone conversations that we had the opportunity to record also revealed that the Haengers are rather unscrupulous and will get involved in anything that promises to be profitable to them; they personally said so on several occasions. Hence, skilled as they are, they find an easy way around the regulations concerning the war economy, do business on a large scale on the black market, and fail to declare their war-related profits, some of which must be quite significant" (BAr E 27/14131). It is therefore not surprising that the two businessmen were included on the *Black List* established by the United States. An excerpt of that list dated July 15, 1943 was appended to Army Intelligence's internal information bulletin of August 2, 1943 (copy to the attention of the Commander-in-Chief. BAr E 5795/333).

60. Henry Guisan explained: "[During a first meeting at the restaurant at the train station in Lausanne,] Mr. Haenger Sr. asked me to help him with a transaction that he suggested setting up. Its objective was to supply Swiss workshops with work by overhauling Swiss cars and trucks that the army was no longer using." Colonel [Henry] Guisan to General Guisan, 12 March 1943. BAr E 27/14131.

61. Henry Guisan Jr. remarked, "I made some inquiries, which were not unfavorable, and told the *Special Service* at Army Intelligence and Security about the case." Colonel [Henry] Guisan to General Guisan, 12 March 1943. BAr E 27/14131.

62. Guisan Jr. had known Knecht for a long time; he was a member of the board of directors at the *Pergametal S.A.* company, where Knecht was vice president. (The *Pergametal S.A.* was a subsidiary of the *Poudres de Métaux S.A.* company, where Knecht was president.) Henry Guisan explained, "Je voulais éviter d'être entièrement minorisé par des gens que je ne connaissais pas." ("I wanted to avoid being in the minority against people whom I did not know.") Colonel [Henry] Guisan to General Guisan, 12 March 1943. BAr E 27/14131.

63. Weidenmann advanced the share capital of Sfr. 50,000 (Lützelschwab, note for file, 21 July 1943. BAr J.I.137 1974/64, vol. 4). The *Extroc S.A.* had its business address at the offices of the *Poudres de Métaux S.A.,* and the two firms shared the same staff (information on the Extroc S.A., January 1942. BAr J.I.121/74).

64. That is what State Attorney Lützelschwab suspected. See Lützelschwab to Kobelt, 14 February 1943. BAr E 27/14131.

65. Cf. transcript of a tapped telephone conversation of February 23, 1942, in which dubious businesspeople were debating whom they could invite to join the board of directors of their company as a camouflage. They also discussed inviting Guisan Jr. Captain Meyer of the Special Service, who processed the transcript by the Press and Radio Section on behalf of Army Intelligence, annotated the document by writing, "Because of his father's position, *dubious* characters try to get Guisan to join their shareholding companies for *decorating purposes.* 1. *Mineral- & Metall-A.G.*, 2. *Extroc . . .*" (BAr J.I.121/45). Meyer had apparently made a correct analysis of the milieu but considered that taking the risk of entering into contact with these businesspeople was defendable because the contacts could be interesting for the Intelligence Service.

66. Knecht, conversation with Samuel Haas, 16 October 1945. Ba E 27/10033.

67. Guisan Jr. believed that *he* had asked Knecht to join the *Extroc S.A.* (see endnote 62 above). However, the written evidence indicates that it was the other way around. Lützelschwab later testified in court that he considered Guisan Jr. "a very nice but rather *rash* charmer." (Lützelschwab, testimony, Zürich district court, 2 May 1947. BAr J.I.121/63)

68. Cf. Meyer, note for file, 5 June 1942; Guisan Jr., Captain Meyer, and the president of the Swiss Wood Syndicate, Jules Paillard, went to see the Commander-in-Chief in Lausanne. Paillard complained that the Chief Engineer of the Army had not given him any indication how many wooden barracks the army needed. He said that since the wood supply was limited, the Wood Syndicate could not accept any orders from abroad; on the other hand, however, 800 carpentry shops were looking for work. General Guisan promised to find a solution to the problem; in the future all orders would be handled by the Wood Syndicate. BAr J.I.121/1.

69. Knecht, conversation with Samuel Haas, 16 October 1945. BAr E 27/10033.

70. Knecht, conversation with Samuel Haas, 16 October 1945.

71. Colonel [Henry] Guisan to General Guisan, 12 March 1943. BAr E 27/14131.

72. Colonel [Henry] Guisan to General Guisan, 12 March 1943. Toward the Commander-in-Chief, Guisan Jr. used altruistic arguments to justify his action, arguing, "A breaking off of the ongoing negotiations would have been harmful for Switzerland." Colonel Guisan to General Guisan, 12 March 1943.

73. Meyer, statement to investigating judge H. Studer, territorial court 3A, 3 December 1945. BAr E 5330 1982/1, vol. 205.

74. Meyer, statement to investigating judge H. Studer, 3 December 1945. On November 24, 1941, Meyer wrote to Eggen, "What matters most is for me to have authorization to introduce you directly to the Wood Syndicate as a client placing an order." BAr J.I.121/74.

75. Due to Meyer, Eggen also had direct access to Federal Councillor Walter Stampfli, the head of the Federal Department of Economic Affairs. Cf. note for file of meeting by Stampfli with Eggen and Knecht (Meyer was unable to attend the meeting because he was on duty), 18 December 1941:

> Federal Councillor Stampfli for his part pointed out that he was glad that the transaction had been concluded directly with the Wood Syndicate, without any intermediary. He explained that Switzerland had considered as unpleasant the fact that the previous transaction concerning 2,400 barracks that had been concluded with the *Wehrmacht* had included a 4.5 percent commission at the expense of the Swiss manufacturer. Federal Councillor Dr. Stampfli also emphasized that this commission had had to be added at Germany's explicit official request.

Stampfli was also glad that the Swiss Wood Syndicate and a representative of the Commerce Section at the Department of Economic Affairs had been invited to a meeting in Berlin with the Reich representative for wood construction: "He hoped that this meeting would set things straight once and for all between the Swiss wood processing industry and the German authorities." BAr J.I.121/74.

76. Apparently the initiative for these negotiations was taken by Germany, which was interested to know what Switzerland's production and export capacities were; see letter by authorized representative for wood construction, Berlin, to Commander in Chief of SS and Police [Heinrich Himmler] (SS Central Office), attn. Captain Eggen, 29 December 1941. BAr J.I.121/74.

77. Agreement between Swiss Wood Syndicate and *Warenvertriebs G.m.b.H.*, 22 January 1942, concerning the construction and delivery of barracks for the *Waffen SS* Office Berlin. BAr J.I.121/74.

78. On February 12, 1942, the Swiss Legation in Germany (1st Secretary Ochsenbein) wrote to Chief of Labor Künzel, Reich Labor Service, that the 400 barracks for the Wehrmacht that were already under construction should be delivered first, adding, "However, the German Army High Command has canceled the first and second amended contracts calling for the delivery of an additional 400 + 960 barracks. Instead, for the time being, Switzerland will deliver 500 'Cron' type barracks from its own wood supplies to the SS." BAr J.I.121/74.

79. The Swiss Federal Railways made empty coal wagons available for transporting the barracks. Meyer, note for file on SHS meeting, 28 February 1942. BAr J.I.121/74.

80. These were type J.C.B.VI wooden barracks that could easily be dismounted. They were named after the engineer who designed them, Jean Cron from Basel. The barracks were 6 meters wide and 24 meters long. (Assembly instructions, 6

March 1942. BAr J.I.121/74.) In Nuremberg, Eggen explained to the U.S. investigating judge: "They were rather small and had a double floor and double beams. They lent themselves particularly well for storing heavy items. Normal barracks have only one-directional beams; they can be used only temporarily but not for storing purposes. . . . They were intended for the storage needs of the Operations Department of the SS Central Office." Interrogation of Eggen, Nuremberg, 16 March 1948. National Archives, Washington DC, RG 238 M 1019 R 15.

81. On March 27, 1942, the Swiss Wood Syndicate wrote to Meyer, "Today the last of the 500 barracks [of the first delivery] crossed the Swiss border." BAr J.I.121/74.

82. Agreement between *Warenvertriebs G.m.b.H.* and SHS, 15 April 1942. BAr J.I.121/44.

83. The agreement was dated November 19, 1942. The Swiss Federal Department of Economic Affairs approved it by telegram on December 17, 1942. However, since the trade agreement between Germany and Switzerland expired in January 1943, foreign currencies were temporarily unavailable for purchasing barracks, so the agreement could not be executed as planned. See Jules Paillard, SHS president, "Bericht vom 4. März 1943." BAr J.I.121/74. However, there were some additional reasons for the business not to materialize; see endnote 84, below.

84. The difficulty consisted in obtaining the wood that was required to build the barracks. Even though Germany had assured that it would supply the materials as agreed on January 22, 1942, the wood was not delivered. As a consequence, the second set of barracks was also made with wood from Switzerland. However, a third set of 1,000 barracks could not be manufactured because of a shortage of imported wood. Moreover, difficulties arose from the conditions that Switzerland had imposed on Germany for the delivery of 100 tons of iron; see minutes of SHS meeting, 16 June 1942. BAr J.I.121/74.

85. The agreement is at BAr J.I.121/74.

86. These were large twin barracks containing two two-bedroom apartments and several adjoining rooms.

87. Jules Paillard to investigating judge Captain Egli, 11 July 1945. BAr E 5330 1982/1, vol. 205.

88. Meyer, statement to Captain H. Studer, investigating judge of territorial court 3A, 3 December 1945. His statement is corroborated by other documents, e.g. a letter by the SHS to the *Warenvertriebs G.m.b.H*, 28 January 1942. BAr J.I.121/74.

89. In fact, as an authorized recipient and confirmation agent for the *Warenvertriebs G.m.b.H.*, Meyer received about 12,000 francs, an amount that does not seem to be excessive in view of the Sfr. 12 million transaction. (In his investigation report, Supreme Court Justice Couchepin came to the same conclusion. BAr E 27/10027, vol. 1.) Henry Guisan Jr. for his part received a similar amount, Sfr. 13,407.00, as a commission. The payments that Meyer and Guisan received were definitely reasonable when compared with payments made during a previous purchase of wooden barracks. The audit report by the Swiss Federal Auditing Office dated September 14, 1945 revealed, among other things, that

the honorable carpenter Gustav Bohny from Basel (one of the co-founders of the *Labor Penny*, a social program for relieving unemployment in Basel in the 1930s) had received a total of Sfr. 808,576 in commissions plus Sfr. 150 per barrack for arranging three deals with the Wehrmacht; hence, he earned a total of Sfr. 1,066,421 in connection with the deal, which generated a turnover of Sfr. 21 million. The criminal investigation that Federal Councillor Stampfli ordered on January 9, 1946 as a result of the audit report was abandoned on September 27, 1946, concluding that neither the SHS nor any of the involved persons could be accused of any wrongdoing in connection with the SS barracks deal. On the contrary, in his final report, Otto Gloor, the head of the criminal investigation service at the Department of Economic Affairs, described all of these persons as *serious* and *conscientious*. BAr J.I.121/74.

90. See Hausamann, indictment against *Die Tat*/Dr. Kummer, 7 July 1947; and Lützelschwab, "Bericht in Sachen Eggen," 5 June 1945. However, documents show that for his activity as authorized recipient of the *Warenvertriebs G.m.b.H.*, Meyer received *payments from the Swiss Wood Syndicate* (receipts at BAr J.I.121/74); see also Eggen, "Abhörungsprotokoll der Schweizerischen Bundesanwaltschaft," 1 May 1945.

91. Meyer, statement before territorial court 3A, 3 December 1945. BAr E 5330 1982/1, vol. 205.

92. Meyer, statement before territorial court 3A, 3 December 1945.

93. Meyer, statement before territorial court 3A, 3 December 1945. (See page 366, endnote 18.)

94. Letters of 26 January and 2 February 1943. BAr J.I.121/74.

95. Letters of 3 July 1942, 26 January 1943, and 30 December 1943. BAr J.I.121/74.

96. Meyer to Otto Gloor, head of the criminal investigation service at the Swiss Federal Department of Economic Affairs, 7 February 1946. BAr J.I.121/74.

97. Hans Martin Zeidler (born January 4, 1911 in Wilhelmsburg, near Hamburg) was a lawyer who also had a master's degree in political science. On September 1, 1939, he was appointed inspector at the security police and the Security Service in Düsseldorf; in 1940 he was put in charge of the Cologne sector of the Security Service; in 1942 he was named economic officer at the Kiel sector of the Security Service. Between summer 1942 and the end of April 1944, he headed the economic branch at Office VI of the Reich Security Central Office.

98. "Abhörungsprotokoll Zeidler," Schweizerische Bundesanwaltschaft, 5 February 1946. BAr E 27/10027, vol. 1.

99. "Abhörprotokoll Zeidler," Schweizerische Bundesanwaltschaft, 5 February 1946.

100. "Abhörprotokoll Zeidler," Schweizerische Bundesanwaltschaft, 5 February 1946.

101. After the war, the "ignominiously famous businessmen" (expression used by Kobelt) incited the Head of Switzerland's Military Department to intervene with the Ordnance Section because he had found out that Haenger Jr. had a license for arms trading. On September 10, 1948, Kobelt wrote to the Ordnance Section, "We would like to point out to you that [Walter Rudolf Haenger] is a businessman who does not exactly have a good reputation; on several occasions he has come into conflict with the law." René von Wattenwyl, the head of the Ordnance Section, consequently looked into the matter. A short

time later, when looking at the files of the Attorney General's office, he discovered that a criminal investigation had been opened against Haenger in November 1948 by the authorities of the canton of Basel-Stadt on suspicion of document forgery and attempted fraud. On January 10, 1949, von Wattenwyl reported to Kobelt that the documents that were seized at Haenger's concerning his activity as an arms broker clearly indicated "that Haenger tried to arrange the sale of war matériel that was officially intended to go to Venezuela but was going to be rerouted somewhere else, probably to the Middle East." In a decree dated January 14, 1949, Kobelt subsequently revoked R.W. Haenger's trading license (see Director of Federal Military Administration to Ordnance Section, 18 January 1949). All documents referred to in this endnote are at BAr E 27/19394, vol. 4.

102. Lützelschwab to Kobelt, 24 February 1943. BAr E 27/14131. One week earlier, the Head of the Military Department had received the Basel State Attorney at the latter's request; on that occasion, Lützelschwab gave him detailed information about the *Extroc S.A.* See Kobelt, "Tagebuch," entry of 16 February 1943. BAr E 5800/1, vol. 1.
103. The officer who later accompanied Schellenberg to Biglen.
104. Lützelschwab, note for file, 21 November 1942. BAr J.I.137 1974/64, vol. 2.
105. Lützelschwab, note for file, 21 November 1942.
106. Telex of 21 November 1942, AHQ Security Service to Basel-Stadt. BAr J.I.137 1974/64, vol. 2.
107. Lützelschwab to Colonel Werner Müller, 22 November 1942. BAr J.I.137 1974/64, vol. 2, and E 27/10019.
108. Lützelschwab, telephone conversation with Sergeant Bleiker, Zürich city police, 24 November 1942. Recorded by Bitterli. BAr J.I.137 1974/64, vol. 2.
109. Documents at BAr J.I.137 1974/64, vol. 2; Müller, note for file on telephone conversation with Lützelschwab, 24 November 1942, 2:45 p.m. BAr E 27/10019.
110. Müller, note for file on telephone conversation with Lützelschwab, 24 Nov. 1942.
111. In the same telephone conversation with Lützelschwab, Müller explained: "You know about the IPA, the newspaper that it used to publish, and whom it used to keep attacking. Through that channel I was able to put an immediate end to these attacks." However, Masson also took credit for getting the smear campaign against General Guisan to end; see the section "Meyer Puts Masson in Contact With Eggen" later in this chapter.
112. However, in fall 1942 Lützelschwab did not know anything yet about the Masson-Schellenberg connection.
113. Written evidence at BAr E 27/14131.
114. At least that was the official reason that was given. However, the federal government also hesitated to promote Henry Guisan Jr. because he was acquainted with a woman named *Irma Loebel*, who had a bad reputation. On December 29, 1942, Kobelt wrote in his diary that at the Cabinet meeting Federal Councillor Pilet-Golaz had voiced reservations about Guisan's promotion, presenting information that he had received from Jaquillard, the commander of the Vaud cantonal police and head of Army Counterintelligence. This informa-

tion was new to Kobelt; he had never heard of the woman. In spite of Pilet's reservations, he was in favor of promoting Guisan because there were no military arguments against it. Following the Cabinet meeting, the Federal Council held its New Year's Eve banquet, which General Guisan also attended. Out of politeness, on that occasion Kobelt did not mention the discussion concerning Guisan Jr. to the Commander-in-Chief, which General Guisan later held against him (BAr E 5800/1, vol. 1). In a note dated February 1, 1947, Bracher noted about the matter concerning Irma Loebel: "In September 1942, it became known that Colonel Guisan had relations with Ms. Irma Loebel, a former Czech national. Because Loebel was said to enjoy a certain protection by Germany and the Vaud cantonal police pronounced itself against extending Loebel's residence permit, in September 1942 the Vaud Justice and Police Department decided to have her expelled." BAr E 5800/1, vol. 1.

115. Because Henry Guisan's promotion was postponed, General Guisan and the Federal Council were at odds for some time. See file BAr E 27/14131. Guisan Jr. ended up being promoted effective December 31, 1942.

116. Regarding the situation at that time, see page 186ff.

117. Kobelt to Commander-in-Chief, 5 January 1943. BAr E 27/14131. The letter was drafted by Major Bracher at Kobelt's request but was never sent to the addressee.

118. On April 5, 1943, Kobelt wrote to Lützelschwab, "The Commander-in-Chief of the army has informed me that all ties between Colonel Guisan and *Extroc* have been severed and that Colonel Guisan was officially taken off the list of board members as of March 31, 1943." BAr E 27/14131.

119. In view of the dubious characters who were involved in the business, that was entirely possible.

120. American Legation, Bern, memorandum to State Department, Washington, DC, 13 December 1944. National Archives, Washington, DC, RG 59, Department of State Decimal File 854.24/12-1344.

121. However, the Extroc company was not involved in the transaction. The Americans had stipulated that "due care be taken that no *proclaimed listed* firms or individuals be permitted to participate in the barrack transaction." Minutes of negotiations, 12 December 1944. National Archives, Washington, DC, RG 59, Department of State Decimal File 854.24/12-1244.

122. Huddle to Secretary of State, 30 December 1944. National Archives, Washington, DC, RG 59, Department of State Decimal File 811.20 Defense (M) Switzerland/12-3044.

123. See page 138.

124. Investigating judge Colonel Otto Müller described Eggen as "intelligent, skillful, hyperactive, [someone who] has a winning manner and an impressive appearance; in addition, he is probably shrewd; in short, [he is] a very suitable personality for Germany's foreign service" (final report on the gathering of evidence concerning Masson, 9 July 1945. BAr E 5330 1982/1, vol. 205). In addition to German, Eggen spoke French, English, and some Spanish. Eggen to investigating judge Müller, 26 May 1945. BAr E 5330 1982/1, vol. 205.

125. Meyer, note for file, 14 November 1941. BAr J.I. 121/1. Cf. also Heinrich Rothmund (head of the federal police section at the Justice and Police

Department) to Masson, 15 November 1943: "So far the police dealing with foreign nationals have allowed Mr. Eggen to enter the country whenever you needed him to be present. Since you asserted that you might need that foreigner on short notice, every three months our legation in Berlin was authorized to issue a visa to Mr. Eggen right away and inform us about it after the fact." BAr E 5795/455.

126. Meyer, note for file, 14 November 1941. BAr J.I. 121/1.

127. See page 136ff.

128. The Intelligence Service of the Zürich cantonal police discovered that Weidenmann used large amounts of money to bribe people. It was unclear where those funds came from (information by Intelligence Service Zürich, 1 July 1942. BAr J.I.137 1974/64, vol. 2). Six months earlier, in a note for the file, the Zürich Intelligence Service had stated: "The different pieces of information unquestionably show that Weidenmann must be involved in *industrial espionage* on behalf of Germany; on the side, he is a black marketeer and arms dealer. What is actually sad rather than funny about this matter is the fact that he runs his business with the authorization of the police dealing with foreign nationals" (23 December 1941). BAr J.I.137 1974/64, vol. 2.

129. Intelligence Service of the Zürich cantonal police, 1 July 1942. Archives of H.R. Kurz.

130. BAr J.I.121/1. Weidenmann's first request for a work permit and residence permit for Switzerland had been submitted to the cantonal police dealing with foreign nationals on January 14, 1935 by Dr. W. Chiodera, for whose law firm Meyer had started working in 1923.

131. Cf. Zürich Intelligence Service, note for file, 29 June 1942, "Eggen is the *guy with the special aircraft*." BAr J.I.137 1974/64, vol. 2.

132. Cf. Meyer, note for file, 14–16 November 1941, "[Eggen] says he wants to purchase estates along Lake Geneva." BAr J.I.121/1.

133. Lützelschwab to Kobelt, 24 February 1943. BAr E 27/14131.

134. From November 14 to 16, 1941.

135. BAr J.I.121/1.

136. The following information is based on "Abhörprotokoll der Bundesanwaltschaft," 1 May 1945. BAr E 5330 1982/1, vol. 205. The statements that Eggen made on that occasion match the information included in his SS personnel file, which is kept at the Document Center Berlin. See Fuhrer, *Spionage*, 128, note 270.

137. In Nuremberg, Eggen stated: "Because I was very interested in these things, during the lectures I put some designs on paper. I created the design for a liquid gauge. It was suggested to me that I have the thing patented. I received a patent and a registered design. This liquid gauge was purchased by the Reich Food Estate" (interrogation of Eggen, Justice Palace Nuremberg, 16 March 1948). National Archives, Washington DC, RG 238 M 1019 R 15. The Reich Food Estate (*Reichsnährstand*) had been established through a law of September 13, 1933, by the German Minister for Food and Agriculture, Walter Darré, one of the few Nazi party leaders who was an expert in his field, although he subscribed to most of the Nazi myths. The Reich Food Estate was a huge organization with authority over every conceivable branch of agricultural production,

marketing, and processing. In his capacity as Reich Peasant Leader, Darré personally headed the organization. The fact that Eggen's invention seemed to interest Darré's organization was in itself a rather remarkable feat.

138. After the war, Eggen claimed that membership to both bodies was a precondition for studying at any German university (which was of course *not* true).

139. Reinhard Heydrich headed the Reich Security Central Office (RSHA). After his assassination in 1942, he was replaced by Ernst Kaltenbrunner, who was later executed as a war criminal in Nuremberg.

140. Eggen to the Swiss Attorney General's office, 1 May 1945. BAr E 5330 1982/1, vol. 205.

141. See page 348, endnote 76.

142. Eggen to Swiss Attorney General's office, 1 May 1945. BAr E 5330 1982/1, vol. 205. However, according to Eggen, the Reich Security Central Office and the Reich Economic Ministry never actually worked together to procure intelligence, saying that the SS Procurement Office never sent any report to the RSHA.

143. Eggen, 2nd interrogation, Justice Palace Nuremberg, 18 March 1948. National Archives, Washington DC, RG 238 M 1019 R 15.

144. "Daten-Memorial," entry under the dates of 14–16 November 1941. BAr J.I.121/58.

145. *Wilhelmstrasse* trial against Ernst von Weizsäcker and Co. Interrogation of Eggen, Justice Palace Nuremberg, 16 March 1948. National Archives, Washington DC, RG 238 M 1019 R 15.

146. See page 345, endnote 45.

147. The following statement made by an informant returning from Berlin demonstrates that this compliment was not simply an empty phrase. Two weeks before Eggen made that comment, Masson had received a letter from J. Bührer, the director of the *Eisen- und Stahlwerke A.G.* in Schaffhausen (also known by the abbreviation G+F), in which he stated:

> In my explanations concerning the general impressions that I was able to receive during my stay in Berlin from October 6 to 10, 1941, I may not have put enough emphasis on a pleasant incident. During my conversations with them, several individuals in the army and the ministries (e.g. General von Leeb, the chief of his staff, Lieutenant Colonel Löhr of the army's General Staff, Major Schaede of Todt's ministry) expressed their *special respect for the reliability, thoroughness, and accuracy with which the Intelligence Service of our army was working under your command.* I would like to congratulate you on this statement." Bührer to Masson, 31 October 1941. BAr E 5795/327.

Masson used witness accounts such as this one as a valuable means to support his point of view in the conflicts with Pilet-Golaz.

148. Meyer, notes, 14–16 November 1941. BAr J.I.121/1.

149. See Christopher Chant, *The Encyclopedia of Codenames of World War II* (London, 1986), and, more recently, the excellent compilation by Silvia Rosser, *Eine Auswahl wichtiger Codenamen aus dem Zweiten Weltkrieg*, 2 volumes (Bern, 1990).

150. Eggen talked about the "very sudden occupation" without using the cover name for the operation. The plan was supposed to be carried out in part on September 8, 1943 under the codeword Achse. See, among others, Hans-Adolf Jacobsen, *Der Zweite Weltkrieg* (Frankfurt a.M., 1965), 249–250.

151. In his notes, Meyer only used commas and hyphens, so the statements by the two men are not clearly distinguished; on the editing aspect, see page 446.

152. Meyer alluded to the failed Operation *Wartegau*. In order to take revenge for the Swiss Air Force's shooting down German fighter planes, during the night of June 13–14, 1940 Göring infiltrated 10 saboteurs into Switzerland. They had orders to demolish major airport installations in Spreitenbach, Biel-Bözingen, Payerne, and Lausanne. However, the secret command operation was poorly organized and was almost immediately uncovered. Nine saboteurs, including two Swiss, were arrested; on November 16, 1940, territorial court 2 sentenced them to life in prison. The tenth saboteur entered the country on his own and was expelled right away. (Meyer therefore mentioned only *nine* saboteurs.) The German saboteurs were pardoned at the end of 1950 or beginning of 1951 and expelled; the two Swiss were released from prison in mid-June 1955. On this matter, see Investigating Judge Otto Gloor, territorial court 2, to Air Force and Anti-Aircraft Defense, 24 June 1940; Major General Hans Bandi, Air Force and Anti-Aircraft Defense Commander, to Otto Gloor, 26 June 1940. Both documents are at BAr E 27/10101. The most recent report on the incident is by Ernst Wetter, *Duell der Flieger und der Diplomaten: Die Fliegerzwischenfälle Deutschland–Schweiz im Mai/Juni 1940 und ihre diplomatischen Folgen* (Frauenfeld, 1987), 150 ff. See also: "Bundesblatt I" 1946 119; Huber, *Bericht des Generalstabschefs*, 493; Barbey, *P.C. du Général*, 19; Raymond Gafner, *General Guisan: Gespräche* (Bern, 1953), 71 (photographs); Bonjour, *Neutralität* IV, 104–108; Janusz Piekalkiewicz, *Schweiz 39–45: Krieg in einem neutralen Land* (Stuttgart, 1978), 231–33; Fuhrer, *Spionage*, 28 and 107, note 154.

153. Eggen's entry in the guest book supports this argument. He wrote, "Wenn Deutschland siegt, ist es eine hohe Ehre für Wolfsberg. Wenn es unterliegen sollte, eine Verpflichtung." ("If Germany wins, it would be a great honor for Wolfsberg. Should Germany lose, it would be a commitment.")

154. On May 15, 1941, Colonel Gustav Däniker of the General Staff, the commander of the Walenstadt training facility, had written a memorandum on his observations and impressions during a stay in Germany. In this memorandum, he put the entire blame for the tense relations with Germany on Switzerland. Däniker had considerable influence among officers, and numerous copies of his memorandum were circulated. General Guisan entrusted Meyer-Schwertenbach with special missions to look into Däniker's activities (see page 436, endnote 17, and page 126).

155. Between 1939 and 1940, General Maurice Gamelin was Commander-in-Chief of the French Armies. With this question, Eggen may have referred to the "La Charité" affair. Meyer was informed about that affair at an early stage. Information from Patrizia Meyer-Schwertenbach to this author, 18 December 1984.

156. The word "him" refers to General Guisan.

157. However, this assessment does not correspond to the official German view. In an (undated) assessment of the Swiss Army, Military Attaché von Ilsemann wrote about General Guisan, "Excellent image, strong personality, very solid bulwark against the NSDAP's efforts in Switzerland." BAr E 27/14334 (see Fuhrer, *Spionage*, 136, note 19).

158. See page 360, endnote 203.

159. Eggen probably exaggerated about, rather than downplayed, his role and influence among Himmler's staff. His apparent expertise with concluding major deals as well as his self-confident, spirited manner reinforced the Swiss' impression that they were dealing with an important personality of the National Socialist regime.

160. Masson made sure that no one interfered with him in this matter; cf. his letter to the Commander-in-Chief dated March 15, 1945, in which he firmly stated: "My special network of informants is exclusively my concern; it falls under my own responsibility . . . in principle, I do not have to account for it to anyone." BAr E 27/10019.

161. Dr. Max Husmann, director of the Montana Institute on Zugerberg. He had contact with Italy's Baron Luigi Parilli, among others. See Masson to Werner Müller, 8 June 1945. BAr E 5330 1982/1, vol. 205.

162. Along with Waibel, Husmann and Parilli played an important role in the negotiations between Allen Dulles and SS General Wolff that resulted in the German troops' capitulation in northern Italy. On that issue, see Georg Kreis, "Das Kriegsende in Norditalien 1945," *Schweizer Monatshefte* 6 (1985).

163. Masson to Eugster, 14 June 1945. BAr E 5330 1982/1, vol. 205. Some of the informants were Swiss, including Carl J. Burckhardt. Reports by Burckhardt are at BAr E 27/9708.

164. Michael I. Handel, "Intelligence and Problem of Strategic Surprise," *Journal of Strategic Studies* (June 1984), 239.

165. See Handel, "Problem of Strategic Surprise," 240.

166. Cf. Handel, "Problem of Strategic Surprise," 250: "Generally speaking, perceptual errors are the result of projecting either one's own culture, ideological beliefs, military doctrine, or expectations on the adversary (i.e. seeing him as a mirror image of oneself) or of wishful thinking, that is, molding the facts to conform to one's hopes." In recent scholarly works and publications, the trendy term "empathy" has been coined to describe what Masson tried to do, i.e. look at the situation from the opponent's perspective. Basically that term merely describes a quality that makes a successful lawyer or diplomat and that is required for dealing with other individuals in everyday life: the ability to put oneself in someone else's position and to see an issue from that other person's perspective. Mirror thinking is insidious precisely because we erroneously assume that the opposing party sees things the way we see them. For example, Switzerland's concept of dissuasion requires foreign countries to consider as real Switzerland's ability and determination to defend itself. It would be dangerous for Switzerland to take into account only the fact *that* it is able to accomplish its task without also verifying *whether* foreign countries actually consider that Switzerland's readiness has the effect of a deterrent, or, to put it in Roberta

Wohlstetter's words, whether the opposite side interprets the emitted signals "correctly."

167. See Handel, "Problem of Strategic Surprise," 241.
168. Handel, "Problem of Strategic Surprise," 241.
169. Oscar Reile, *Macht und Ohnmacht der Geheimdienste* (Munich, 1968), 29 ff. As early as 1934, due to differences of opinion with NSDAP representatives, Reile quit as head of the criminal investigation department in Danzig, whereupon he became a captain on Germany's intelligence and counterintelligence. Between 1941 and 1944, Reile held a key position with military counterintelligence in Germany's occupied territories in the West.
170. Reile, *Macht und Ohnmacht*, 29 ff. Reile makes a remarkable statement (p. 85) about Canaris' ability "to find, at least in some areas, *common* interests with every one of his reference persons and thereby get some *cooperation* going that was *to both parties' advantage*." Masson could have made the same statement about his own network, at least about the connection with Schellenberg.
171. In the case of his connection with Schellenberg, Masson set great store in pointing out that he "did not *look for* this contact; it was the result of a *coincidence*." Masson to Military Attorney General Eugster, 14 June 1945. BAr E 5330 1982/1, vol. 205.
172. Masson, "La ligne Eggen-Schellenberg," report to the attention of the Military Attorney General, 14 June 1945. BAr E 5330 1982/1, vol. 205.
173. Masson, "La ligne Eggen-Schellenberg." However, see page 368, endnote 55, for a different assessment of the situation by Switzerland's Intelligence Service.
174. Masson, "La ligne Eggen-Schellenberg." BAr E 5330 1982/1, vol. 205.
175. Masson, "La ligne Eggen-Schellenberg."
176. Masson, "La ligne Eggen-Schellenberg."
177. Masson, "La ligne Eggen-Schellenberg."
178. See Masson to Eugster, 14 June 1945. BAr E 5330 1982/1, vol. 205.
179. Masson, "La ligne Eggen-Schellenberg." BAr E 5330 1982/1, vol. 205. Masson remembered after the fact that it was Meyer-Schwertenbach who had first talked to him about Eggen.
180. See page 150ff.
181. In view of the fact that Masson pretended to be someone else, it appears strange, if not altogether careless, that he chose to meet Eggen at the *Schweizerhof* hotel. First of all, another customer could have recognized him and addressed him by his real name; moreover, this made it easy for German intelligence to place an observer at the bar in order to see to whom Eggen was introduced. Six months later, in the same carefree manner, which appeared to border on negligence, Switzerland's Chief of Intelligence chose an inn for the secret meeting between General Guisan and Schellenberg (see Chapter 9, especially pages 192 and 194.
182. See Meyer to Masson, 26 April 1962 (BAr J.I.121/20); Masson to Eugster, 14 June 1945 (BAr E 5330 1982/1, vol. 205); Eggen during his interrogation by the Swiss Attorney General's office, 1 May 1945 (BAr E 27/10032). Regarding Masson's attitude in the controversy about the press, see page 3ff. As early as October 1, 1938 (September crisis and Munich Conference), the Chief of the General Staff Section, Lieutenant General Labhart, noted in his diary,

"Lieutenant Colonel Masson . . . once again points out the irresponsible comments by our press on Germany." (BAr J.I.49 1, vol. 2.) On this issue, General Guisan sided with Masson. In spring 1941, upon returning from a surgeons' convention in Germany, Major General Eugen Bircher reported to General Guisan that Weizsäcker was irritated about the Swiss press. Interestingly, the Commander-in-Chief annotated the letter by stating: "Switzerland's situation more dangerous than in 1940 . . . The *case of Switzerland* is being discussed. . . . We do not want to fall flat on our face because of the press." Bircher to Commander-in-Chief, 12 April 1941. BAr E 5795/436. On this issue, see also Heller, *Eugen Bircher*, 184 ff.

183. Meyer, several notes, 1941. BAr J.I.121/1.
184. Masson, "La ligne Eggen-Schellenberg." BAr E 5330 1982/1, vol. 205. However, Eggen might merely have flattered his Swiss hosts in order to emphasize his positive attitude toward Switzerland. When looking at the reference material, this author sometimes had the impression that the Swiss attached a bit too much importance to such statements.
185. Masson told the Military Attorney General, "It was not my primary intention to use Eggen for obtaining information on military matters; I simply wanted to set the record straight concerning some incidents or a certain attitude of which the Germans unfairly accused us." Masson to Eugster, 14 June 1945. BAr E 5330 1982/1, vol. 205.
186. Masson to Eugster, 14 June 1945 (see page 356, endnote 159).
187. On October 23, 1941, Barbey stated in his diary: "In a duplicated lampoon, a certain IPA in Budapest attacks the Commander-in-Chief, declaring that he has sold himself 'to Jewish-Pluto-Masonic influences,' is a 'lackey of the Anglo-Saxon policy,' 'a champion of the *Bunker* strategy,' etc. It is quite clear who is behind this lampoon; one feels that some Swiss abroad who work against their own country have a hand in it." Barbey, *P.C. du Général*, 96. IPA pamphlets are at BAr J.I.140/4, vol. 9.
188. On March 20, 1942, the head of the Foreign Service at the Department of Foreign Affairs wrote to Frölicher, "On February 9 of this year, a German Gestapo official named Trummer, who worked at the passport office at the border to the canton of St. Gallen, was arrested in Switzerland. In the course of the investigation he made confessions from which it became clear that he was the intermediary who transmitted Burri's pamphlets. On March 3, [1942], he committed suicide in prison." BAr E 2001 (D) 3, vol. 3. (Concerning Trummer, see page 313, endnote 74.)
189. "Bericht des Bundesrates an die Bundesversammlung über die antidemokratische Tätigkeit von Schweizern und Ausländern im Zusammenhang mit dem Kriegsgeschehen 1939–1945 (*Motion Boerlin*)," Bbl 1946 I 63.
190. See page 437, endnote 30.
191. "Bericht des Bundesrates zur Motion Boerlin," Bbl 1948 III 1039. In that report, the Federal Council stated, "Burri has been incriminated on more accounts than any other National Socialist who had to be sentenced by the Federal Penal Court" (p. 1043).
192. It was the Chief of Intelligence in person who took the initiative in that matter;

cf. Masson to Commander-in-Chief, through official channels, 10 December 1941:

> When the pamphlet entitled "General Guisan—eine schwere Belastung für die Schweiz" [General Guisan—a heavy burden for Switzerland] was published by Burri, the head of the international press agency IPA, I had the honor of proposing that several steps be taken, either by our military attaché in Berlin or through other channels, in order to get this Swiss abroad to stop showing such a scandalous attitude. The Commander-in-Chief told me not to do anything for the time being, explaining that the Federal Council would take care of the matter via the Federal Department of Foreign Affairs. I am sorry to notice . . . that this affair continues being discussed in Berlin and that Franz Burri . . . continues publishing his propaganda, which is detrimental to our country's higher interests (BAr E 27/9508, vol. 9).

193. Interrogation of Eggen, 1 May 1945. BAr E 27/10032.
194. During the interrogation by the Americans in connection with the Nuremberg trials for war criminals against Ernst von Weizsäcker and Co., Eggen stated, "So Masson asked me to obtain, through my position at the Operations Department of the SS Central Office, a ban on this newspaper." The investigating judge asked him, "Was the Operations Department of the SS Central Office the suitable authority [to enforce the ban]?" Eggen replied: "No. The newspaper was published by Berger's entourage. . . . Juettner spoke with Berger, and then the newspaper was banned." When he was asked why the paper was banned, Eggen responded: "At that time, Juettner desperately needed the barracks as well as some machinery for his repair shops. I told him that this group [Masson, Meyer-Schwertenbach, Guisan Jr.] would help us get these things. I said, 'If you help them, they will help you in return to get the things'." (Interrogation of Eggen, Justice Palace Nuremberg, 16 March 1948. National Archives, Washington DC, RG 238 M 1019 R 15.) This explanation appears more plausible than the one he gave immediately after the war in his "Bericht" (see endnote 196 below), where he said that Burri's articles could jeopardize the recruitment of Swiss volunteers for the *Waffen SS*.
195. Office group B of the Operations Department of the SS Central Office. One of that group's tasks consisted of recruiting new members for the *Waffen SS*. See the organizational chart in Fuhrer, *Spionage*, 164–165.
196. Eggen, "Zusammenfassung meiner Ausführungen vom 13.11.1945 und 15.11.1945." BAr E 27/10026. The document is listed under the name "Protokoll Eggen" [minutes concerning Eggen], which is not accurate; cf. Kobelt's statement to Hausamann: "You mention 'minutes concerning Eggen.' Because that name creates the impression that these are official minutes of a hearing, which is not proven, I am calling the document in question 'Bericht Eggen [report by Eggen]' rather than 'minutes'." Kobelt to Hausamann, 28 October 1946. BAr E 27/10034.
197. Interrogation of Eggen, 1 May 1945. BAr E 27/10032.
198. Interrogation of Eggen, 1 May 1945. However, Eggen's and Schellenberg's statements are the only ones that exist on that matter.

199. Eggen, "Zusammenfassung meiner Ausführungen." BAr E 27/10026.
200. Barbey, *P.C. du Général*, 100. This was the first time Barbey mentioned the connection between Masson and Schellenberg.
201. Barbey, *P.C. du Général*, 100. For instance, Eggen had predicted that the German offensive in Russia would come to a standstill.
202. Barbey, *P.C. du Général*, 100.
203. In a manuscript dated around March 1948, Lützelschwab mentioned the "*direct telephone line from Meyer-Schwertenbach's Wolfsberg Castle to Himmler's staff in Berlin*, which (according to Lieutenant Colonel Barbey) Colonel-Brigadier Masson rejected, considering it as too bold." Lützelschwab remarked:

> Even the most harmless, good-natured shepherd boy would not believe that the Germans, who in their desperate war urgently depended on every single functioning telephone line, would have reserved a direct line for the communication between Ermatingen and Berlin that would have served someone else's interests rather than their own. After all, they hardly had enough lines available to maintain contact with the heavy war industry in southern Germany when their network was still in working order, let alone when the Allied bombers started tearing it to pieces. (BAr J.I.137 1974/64, vol. 12.)

Chapter 8: Extending the Connection

1. He requested that Ernst Mörgeli, a staff member of Swiss Intelligence who had been arrested in Germany, be released from prison.
2. Masson, "Attestation," 10 May 1948. BAr E 27/10039.
3. By this phrase, Masson meant to say, "without creating a stir." (However, the following sentence in the main text shows that Masson definitely planned to attend the meeting in his capacity as Switzerland's Chief of Intelligence.)
4. Masson, "Attestation," 10 May 1948. BAr E 27/10039.
5. Cf. Masson's statement: "I do not know why Sch[ellenberg] did not want to come to Switzerland. Maybe a question of prestige?" (Masson, "Rapport." BAr E 27/10027, vol. 1.) Schellenberg claimed that Hitler had warned him not to travel to Switzerland (see page 369, endnote 58).
6. Masson, "Rapport." BAr E 27/10027, vol. 1; Masson, "Attestation." BAr E 27/10039; Masson, "Le récit de l'affaire Schellenberg," *Tribune de Genève*, no. 297, 19 December 1961.
7. Masson, "Rapport." BAr E 27/10027, vol. 1.
8. One year later, though, Masson had changed his opinion on that matter (see page 207ff.).
9. To the United States goes the honor of setting up the first effective police force concerned solely with combatting crime when, in 1789, President George Washington appointed 13 U.S. Marshals and so created the nation's oldest federal law enforcement agency. It was not until the early 19th century that Europe became police-minded in any modern sense (in 18th-century Europe, France, Germany, Austria, and Russia had their own state police, but these were chiefly instruments of tyranny, and political repression and had little to do with

the prevention of criminal activity.) In 1817 the Parisian Sûreté was set up, and in 1829 London's Metropolitan Police, called "Bobbies" after their initiator Sir Robert Peel. Soon almost every other country or major city in the world followed suit: in 1844, e.g., the New York City Police was formed with its distinctive eight-point copper badge (ever afterward earning American policemen the nickname "cops" or "coppers"). But then a few outstanding police officers and lawyers suddenly began to realize that in the last decade and a half of the 19th century crime had gone international. Criminals could therefore no longer be treated on a purely national basis. It became imperative to coordinate the world's police forces in their battle against this increasingly mobile new enemy. The man who stepped forth to undertake this task was perhaps the most unlikely candidate of all: the ruler of one of the world's smallest states, Prince Albert I of Monaco. In April 1914 Albert invited leading jurists, police officers and lawyers from all over the world to attend the grandiosely named "First International Criminal Police Congress" in Monaco. One hundred eighty-eight delegates (including three women) from 24 countries attended. Switzerland was among them, but the United States and Great Britain showed little interest, the United States being represented by a solitary judge from Dayton, Ohio, and Britain by a magistrate from Hove on the Sussex coast and a barrister and two solicitors from London. Yet, the Congress was undoubtedly a great success. It founded a single organization to centralize certain types of information that could be used by the police in all countries. But, at Sarajevo some three months later, an assassin killed Archduke Franz Ferdinand of Austria-Hungary, and, amid the horror of World War I, the Monaco project was shelved.

Five years after the Great War's end, the project was taken up again, this time by Dr. Johann Schober, the Austrian chief of police and also police chief of Vienna and twice Chancellor of the new Republic (1921–1922 and 1929–1930; from December 1930 to February 1932, he was Vice Chancellor and Foreign Secretary of Austria). His call was well received, and on September 3, 1923, delegates from 20 states, including Switzerland, the United States, but not Great Britain, assembled in Vienna. The Congress proved an indisputable triumph. After only five days of earnest debate, it ended with the formation of a brand-new phenomenon in world policing: the *International Criminal Police Commission* (ICPC) with a permanent International Bureau in Vienna and annual General Assemblies to be held in various European capitals.

From its inception the ICPC was not an operational police entity, having neither a working police force nor international agents who work across other countries' borders. Instead, it is still an organization whose purpose is to facilitate, co-ordinate and encourage police co-operation as a means of combatting international crime. This is accomplished through a worldwide network that links the police forces of the 176 countries that are members of Interpol today. It was not until the 1940s that it got the popular name of "Interpol," and in 1956 its full title was changed to *International Criminal Police Organization—Interpol*. At first, it was essentially an Austrian operation. Schober was elected President and his assistant, Dr. Oskar Dressler, was appointed Secretary General. At the 1928 General Assembly in Antwerp the member states decided they should contribute one Swiss franc for every ten thousand of their inhabitants to provide a budget for the organization.

There is a lack of agreement at present as to which states joined the organization in 1923 and which came in later. The special issue of Interpol's *International Crime Police Review* prepared for the inauguration of the new headquarters at Lyons in November 1989 by the French President, François Mitterrand, claims that France joined in 1923. In fact, individual senior French police officers attended the Congress, but France did not officially join until December 1928. Again, the 1989 review says that the United States joined in 1923. This is even a more basic error. New York police chief Richard E. Enright's pioneering enthusiasm was not followed up. J. Edgar Hoover, in charge of the FBI for 48 years from 1924 until his death in 1972, took a very long time to make up his mind whether or not to join. In the words of an unpublished FBI internal report, "Interpol and its Association with the FBI": "From 1925, when the Bureau of Investigation [the word 'Federal' was not added to the Bureau's title until 1935] first recorded information relative to the ICPC's creation of various bureaus to aid in the apprehension of international criminals, until 1938, a 'wait and see' approach prevailed regarding any US commitment to the ICPC." It took 15 years before the FBI joined Interpol in 1938—but by then a lot had happened to the organization. For its part, Great Britain joined in 1928 but did not bother to set up its own National Central Bureau (NCB, as it is still called in Interpol jargon) until 21 years later.

10. See Rothmund to Federal Councillor von Steiger, 5 May 1944. BAr E 27/10024.
11. See Werner Müller to Military Attorney General Eugster, 15 March 1946. BAr E 27/10036.
12. Once Hitler and his Nazis assumed power in Germany in January 1933, the pressure for union between Germany and Austria increased. The country's independence was doomed and German annexation was only a question of time. It was in this context that the International Criminal Police Commission's General Assembly, held in Vienna in September 1934, voted for a resolution that, for a trial period of five years, the President should automatically be the serving police chief of Vienna. Many senior police officers, not to mention their governments, had been less than happy about the thought that, with the looming unification of Austria and Germany, control of the world's only international police organization would pass into German hands. At least, now they could relax to some extent; after all, it was laid down in the Commission's own rulebook that its senior office-holders had to remain Austrian. And, of course, the real head of the Commission was still the Austrian Secretary General, Oskar Dressler. Even so, within a month he showed he was not exactly unsympathetic to the Nazi cause. Despite the Commission's alleged non-involvement in political crimes, in October 1934 Dressler allowed the organization's official channels to be used by the French police to warn their German colleagues about—of all things—a plot against Adolf Hitler's life.

What Winston Churchill called "the gathering storm," which culminated in World War II, could now be scented in the business of the Commission. "While hitherto the Germans had sent as delegates to the Commission's

General Assemblies men who were professional police officers of high standing, they now began to send up-and-coming young Nazi thugs." (Sir Ronald Howe from Scotland Yard in his memoirs.) Such a man was Karl Daluege, who was executed after the war in Prague for war crimes he committed as Hitler's last "Protector of Bohemia and Moravia." Two other Hitler nominees to Interpol's General Assemblies were the professional policemen Arthur Nebe, the head of the German CID (later garrotted for his part in the July 1944 plot), and Karl Zindel, police assistant to the German Interior Ministry.

In June 1937, Great Britain had at last been persuaded to play host to a General Assembly in London. The delegates confirmed the trial requirement laid down by the 1934 General Assembly that the Viennese police chief had to automatically be the Commission's president for another five years. But this did not pay off as the delegates had expected. Oskar Dressler, Secretary General of the International Police Commission since its inception, was only too happy to co-operate with his new masters when on March 12, 1938 Hitler annexed Austria to the Reich. Reinhard Heydrich, Himmler's second-in-command, immediately wanted to appoint himself the Commission's new president, and he had an argument of spurious legality. "Since the adoption of a resolution in 1934," Sir Ronald Howe quotes him as saying, "The Head of the Vienna Police has been the President of the ICPC. Austria is now an integral part of Germany, and the resolution should therefore apply to the Director of the Security Police of the Third Reich, namely myself." Applying the same logic, he also wanted the Commission's headquarters to be moved to Berlin at once. But Dressler counselled caution. He made the point that the next General Assembly was due in Bucharest in only two months' time. There was no need to frighten off the other powerful members at this early stage, especially since the USA was almost on the brink of joining, and he was sure that (as indeed happened) Great Britain and France would be content to accept the position, so long as the new regime was not too strident. Heydrich, who was after all only 34, was persuaded to play a waiting game for the post he coveted. A cynical stopgap appointment was agreed to: Otto Steinhäusel, a former high-ranking Austrian police officer and notorious Nazi, had recently been released from prison after years of incarceration for offenses against the Austrian state. That he was Austrian and not German would placate other members of the Commission; that he was a Nazi hero would make the new regime's supporters equally happy. The supreme masterstroke, however, was that Steinhäusel was known to have contracted tuberculosis during his years in jail and was not expected to keep the ambitious Heydrich waiting too long. And so, on 15 April 1938, an avowed Austrian Nazi and ex-convict was appointed President of Interpol.

There was still one more hurdle to overcome: At the 1938 General Assembly at Bucharest, a French delegate proposed that the organization's headquarters should be moved from Vienna to Geneva, the Swiss city that also housed the League of Nations, in a neutral country known for its independence and not likely to succumb to Nazi pressures. At the end of a tense debate, however, the resolution was defeated. (Had it been otherwise, Captain Meyer-Schwertenbach probably never would have met Schellenberg, and the whole story to be told in this book might never have happened.) The delegates agreed to meet again at the next year's General Assembly in September 1939—in Berlin. But of course that never took place. By then, Germany had invaded Poland and World War II had broken out.

The official view has always been that Interpol "ceased to function," as a Metropolitan Police Detective Training School hand-out said boldly in 1971. François Mitterrand, in his speech at the ceremonial inauguration of Interpol's new headquarters at Lyons in November 1989, referred to this period, stating, "As was only to be expected, the Nazi invasion [of Austria] led to the institution being used for unacceptable ends, against the wishes of its founders and most of its members."

But this is what happened: On June 20, 1940, two days before the Fall of France, the ailing stopgap Interpol President, Steinhäusel, died, and at once Reinhard Heydrich staked his bid for the post that two years earlier Dressler had advised caution in claiming. Now there was no need for such delicacy. For not only was Germany triumphant, so also was Heydrich within the Nazi police hierarchy. Second only to Heinrich Himmler, the supreme German police chief, he was the most powerful and most feared man in the Nazi apparatus of horror. He was no longer merely, as before, head of the *Sicherheitspolizei*, the German Security Police, and also of the *Sicherheitsdienst*, the SD, the small but elite intelligence unit of the secret police. He had been upgraded to Director of the newly created and massive RSHA (*Reichssicherheitshauptamt*), the Reich Security Central Office into which was merged the Security Police, the SD, the *Kripo* (the ordinary CID under Arthur Nebe)—and the dreaded *Gestapo* itself. In this key post, Heydrich controlled, under Himmler, all branches of the German police, the concentration camps and the extermination squads. He was one of the most brutal and ruthless of all the Nazi leaders.

Now Heydrich demanded not only the presidency of Interpol but also that its headquarters, the International Bureau, should be transferred from Vienna to Berlin. He wrote to all Interpol members asking if they agreed to both proposals and—in the middle of a major war—gave them just three weeks' time to reply. He also said that no reply would be treated as a vote in favor. Switzerland was among the 15 member states accepting; J. Edgar Hoover discreetly chose not to reply. So, in August 1940 Heydrich became President of Interpol, and the headquarters was transferred to Berlin, where it became part of the Fifth Bureau of the RSHA (the Gestapo being the Fourth Bureau). Interpol was now a sister organization of the Gestapo. Heydrich confiscated a wealthy Jewish merchant's luxurious suburban villa which offered social amenities of the highest quality in furnishing and equipment. The actual address was Am Kleinen Wannsee 16, as Captain Meyer-Schwertenbach soon was to learn. (This was also the address that was on the invitations to the notorious conference at Wannsee; the actual venue of the conference was, however, changed afterward, and the participants met on January 20, 1942 in the guest and conference house of the SS—a three-story stucco villa, now used as a Holocaust memorial and education center—at Am Grossen Wannsee 56/58. It was at this address that Meyer-Schwertenbach was actually staying. A street map of Berlin will confirm that they are two different roads, or rather one long road on either side of an intersection. On one side of the road it is called "Am Grossen Wannsee" and "Am Kleinen Wannsee" on the other.)

There was perhaps one unexpected consequence of the move to Am Kleinen Wannsee 16—it lost Interpol the support of J. Edgar Hoover's FBI. The United States did not officially become Hitler's enemy until December 11, 1941 when, four days after Pearl Harbor, Germany and Italy declared war. Throughout 1940 and early 1941, the FBI had continued to cooperate on a routine basis with the ICPC, putting Wanted Notices in the organization's magazine and on occasion requesting from the International Bureau back-up material on international criminals in whom the Bureau was interested. It was only when one such request came back from Dressler, in a letter dated September 23, 1941 on printed notepaper giving the organization's new address, that a Hoover aide realized that something important had happened. In an internal memorandum dated November 22, 1941, he queried whether the Bureau should remain in contact with the Commission "in view of the fact that by so doing the Bureau might be said to tacitly recognize that Germany had taken over the Commission." Hoover reacted swiftly, deciding, "It is desired that in future no communication be addressed to the International Criminal Police Commission, whose present address is Berlin, Germany."

The Swiss, meanwhile, continued, as did the Swedes, to share information with the Commission, as can be seen in the *Internationale Kriminalpolizei* for June 30, 1943, which carried two items from Switzerland, one of them about forged currency (although not on the scale of Operation Bernhard).

When Heydrich was assassinated in May 1942, Himmler did not immediately name a successor. Arthur Nebe carried on as the Commission's Acting President, and for a while Himmler himself took over the running of the RSHA. Then, in January 1943, he appointed the 40-year-old Austrian police chief and longtime Nazi Ernst Kaltenbrunner as head of the Security Police and director of the RSHA, and, thus, automatically President of the Commission. He was hanged in Nuremberg in 1946 as a major war criminal.

Interpol was revived after World War II in 1946, largely due to the efforts of five high-ranking police officers, one each from Switzerland, Great Britain, Sweden, Belgium, and France. The Swiss delegate was the same Colonel Werner Müller in whose name Captain Meyer-Schwertenbach had gone to Berlin in July 1942; as head of the *Sicherheits- und Kriminalpolizei* of Bern, he was immediately re-elected to the administrative board. Over the following years, Interpol expanded and, as of the year 2000, counted 178 member states.

Endnotes 9 and 12 are based mainly on notes to this author by Rolf Spring of Interpol Bern ("Interpol and Switzerland," July 11, 2001) and Dr. Suzanne Braunschweig ("Wannsee" file, 29 July 2003), as well as on Fenton Bresler, *Interpol* (London, 1992); Sir Ronald Howe, *The Pursuit of Crime* (London, 1961); Michael Fooner, *Interpol: Issues in World Crime and International Criminal Justice* (New York/London, 1989); John Parker, "What Lies Behind the Modesty of Interpol?," *Eastern Journal of International Law*, vol. 3, no. 3 (October 1971), 239–242; William R. Slomanson, "Civil Actions Against Interpol: A Field Compass," *Temple Law Quarterly*, vol. 57, no. 3 (1984), 553–599.

13. Armand Mergen, *Die BKA Story* (Munich/Berlin, 1987), 59–60. Armand Mergen was professor of criminology at the University of Mainz.

14. Mergen, *Die BKA Story,* 59–60.

15. According to a circular dated December 8, 1941, "Under the new German leadership [the ICPC was supposed] to be expanded and turned into a world-wide criminal police department." Mergen, *Die BKA Story*, 60.

16. Masson explained, "We could not force him to go because this was a strictly civilian matter." *Gazette de Lausanne*, April 22, 1962.

17. Masson in *Gazette de Lausanne*, April 22, 1962.

18. Masson supported Meyer's request for a leave of absence by arguing, "This officer has very valuable relations in Germany and will probably have the opportunity to meet some of his correspondents." Masson to Chief of the General Staff, July 3, 1942. BAr E 27/9528.

19. Meyer, notes on 1st trip to Berlin, July 7–9, 1942. BAr J.I.121/1. Meyer also wrote: "Colonel Müller of the General Staff explained that if my mission failed, I would have to accept the responsibility for it and could under no circumstances implicate the Intelligence Service. He said that he and Masson would deny being informed about it, whereupon Masson told me in Müller's presence, 'Meyer, of course I would back you'." (Meyer, notes on 1st trip to Berlin.) The Chief of Intelligence was known for his great sense of responsibility toward his staff members and his readiness to lay himself open to attack on their behalf if necessary. In a private letter dated December 3, 1942, Hausamann commented, "Masson is an incredibly decent person. . . . What is tragic about Masson is the fact that sooner or later he will stumble and fall precisely because of his decency—a virtue that is very hard to find these days—because he remains loyal to his friends even when they are struck by a misfortune. By the way, even though his 'case' is hopeless, his decency is what keeps inspiring me to make corrections for him and intervene in his favor whenever I can" (BAr E 5800/1, vol. 1). Lieutenant General Robert Frick, who was Switzerland's Chief of Intelligence between 1946 and 1949 and Chief Instructor of the Army from 1958 to 1965, later recalled that Masson's loyalty toward his staff resulted "In a really special work atmosphere under this great chief. . . . This was of course also true for the influence that he had on the numerous personalities at Army Intelligence, who all basically felt that they were his friends; they worked there primarily because they were devoted to their boss." (Werner Rings, interview with Lieutenant General Robert Frick, July 1, 1969. AfZ files of Werner Rings.)

20. The barracks deal and Meyer's job as a reception agent for the *Warenvertriebs G.m.b.H.* served as a welcome cover-up for his trip to Berlin (even though by then the Germans knew in what capacity Meyer served at the Swiss Intelligence and Security Service). In agreement with Masson, the head of the Special Service used business-related arguments to justify his request for a five-day leave to travel abroad, stating:

> I am the legal advisor and representative of a major trading firm in Berlin with regard to its activities in Switzerland. They have asked me to travel to Germany for urgent business talks. Since these talks are also in the interest of the Swiss economy and have been approved by the Swiss Wood Syndicate, I consider that I should

not forgo this trip. I would therefore like to ask you to grant me a leave from July 6 to 11, 1942 and recommend that the Chief of the General Staff and the Adjutant General approve of this leave for traveling abroad. (Meyer to Masson, July 1, 1942. BAr E 27/9528.)

21. See report by intelligence service Zürich, December 18, 1942. BAr J.I.137 1974/64, vol. 2.

22. Meyer noted, "My trip and my permanent visa are evidence of the *power* that these authorities have." Meyer, notes on 1st trip to Berlin. BAr J.I. 121/1.

23. "The house was built in 1915 by a man who made toothpaste, then sold to a white-collar criminal who, while in prison, sold it to a Nazi foundation which used its leafy and tranquil setting as a retreat for senior officers of Hitler's intelligence service." Fenton Bresler, *Interpol*, 62.

24. In the 1980s, scholars discovered that this term was not accurate; instead, one should speak of the affair of *Dampierre* or *Dijon*. Lieutenant General Hans Senn (an accomplished historian himself) did some research on the cooperation talks between France and Switzerland and discovered that the Germans had found the bulk of the documents concerning these talks at the *Dampierre* barracks in *Dijon*, not at the train station in *La Charité-sur-Loire*. The staff of French Army Group 3 had left the intervention plans for Switzerland there when it withdrew from the area. (See Hans Senn, "Der Stand neuester Erkenntnisse: Militärische Eventualabmachungen der Schweiz mit Frankreich 1939/40," *Neue Zürcher Zeitung*, no. 204, September 2, 1988.) However, since history books have associated *La Charité* with the cooperation talks between France and Switzerland ever since the discovery of the documents was publicized during the war, this author will continue to use *La Charité* in that context. Similarly, *Operation Tannenbaum*, the cover name for the draft of a German plan to invade Switzerland, was made into the collective term for all pigeonholed draft plans by the Third Reich's General Staff against Switzerland.

25. Masson in *Gazette de Lausanne*, April 22, 1962.

26. File at BAr J.I.121/1.

27. Cf. Urs Schwarz' statement, "My colleague Albert Müller, who is the main expert on everything relating to Germany . . ." Urs Schwarz, *Schicksalstage in Berlin* (Lenzburg, 1986), 11.

28. Albert Müller for his part had well-informed sources as well, including a "rather young but very experienced and influential diplomat who had been working in Germany for five years, until November 1941; he [knew] key party and military circles" there and stayed in touch with them as well as with individuals with whom Hitler had been socializing for many years. Müller added, "As far as I am concerned, based on numerous examples and experiences in the last few months, the quality of this diplomat's information and his ability to judge are beyond doubt." Notes by Albert Müller, December 1, 1942. BA E 27/14334.

29. On this extended strategy, see page 36ff.

30. Albert Müller to Federal Council, December 1942. (The full text of the 20-page memorandum is filed at Bretscher's personal archives. Excerpts are included in Bonjour, *Neutralität*, vol. VII, 232–235; moreover, in an extended endnote Bonjour explains the circumstances surrounding the writing of the docu-

368 NOTES TO PAGES 167–171

ment.) The memorandum was circulated among the members of the Federal Council.

31. Albert Müller to Federal Council, December 1942.
32. Albert Müller to Federal Council, December 1942. These favors or services included granting visas without creating any red tape.
33. Albert Müller to Federal Council, December 1942.
34. Albert Müller to Federal Council, December 1942.
35. Meyer, notes on 1st trip to Berlin. BAr J.I. 121/1.
36. Meyer, notes on 1st trip to Berlin.
37. Meyer, notes on 1st trip to Berlin.
38. Meyer, notes on 1st trip to Berlin.
39. Meyer, notes on 1st trip to Berlin. De facto, Bibra was the national NSDAP leader in Switzerland; he replaced Wilhelm Gustloff, who had been assassinated in Davos in 1936. Cf. Pierre Th. Braunschweig, *Ein politischer Mord: Das Attentat von Davos und seine Beurteilung durch schweizerische Zeitungen* (Bern, 1980).
40. Meyer, notes on 1st trip to Berlin. BAr J.I. 121/1.
41. Meyer, notes on 1st trip to Berlin.
42. See page 160ff.
43. Meyer, notes on 1st trip to Berlin. BAr J.I. 121/1.
44. Meyer, notes on 1st trip to Berlin.
45. This statement recalls Albert Müller's warning that when they initiate a direct contact, one should expect "the German mediators [to] try even harder to . . . show their honest intentions and well-meaning attitude." (See page 167ff.)
46. Meyer, notes on 1st trip to Berlin. BAr J.I. 121/1.
47. Meyer, notes on 1st trip to Berlin.
48. Meyer, notes on Waldshut. BAr J.I.121/1.
49. Meyer, notes on Waldshut.
50. Fuhrer, *Spionage*, 78–79.
51. On that issue, see Fuhrer, *Spionage*, 79.
52. Meyer, notes on Waldshut. BAr J.I. 121/1.
53. Meyer, notes on Waldshut.
54. Meyer, notes on Waldshut. From today's perspective, that seemed to be a blatant case of luring Masson into seeing Schellenberg. It is surprising that Masson, who had been so astute on other occasions, took the bait.
55. Masson did not let Eggen know that he had diverging assessments of the situation. As early as 10 weeks after Hitler's surprise attack on the Soviet Union, Swiss Intelligence predicted that Germany would be defeated in the East. On August 26, 1941, Masson's deputy Werner Müller had sent the Chief of the General Staff a "Report on the current situation in the war," in which he stated: "Today it is *safe* to assume that the German Armies will *not succeed* in crushing the Russian Armies. Every available piece of information allows us to predict that the German plan to destroy the Russian Armed Forces *will fail miserably. The German Army Command will not achieve its strategic objective!*" (Werner Müller, "Report on the war—political situation of the time." BAr E 27/9911, vol. 2; italics in the original text). Moreover, one year later, a few days before meeting Eggen, Masson received an analysis from the Head of *Bureau Ha* that

confirmed the earlier assessment. On August 16, 1942, Hausamann wrote to Masson that in view of the fact that the Russians had *strategic reserve troops* on the order of more than 90 well-equipped and well-trained motorized divisions, he concluded: "*The situation is hopeless for the leadership of the German Reich!* It can only win itself to death. If a 'second front' is established in the West in the upcoming weeks it will collapse sooner, if no 'second front' is created in the West, it will do so later" (archives of H.R. Kurz). Even though Werner Müller and Hausamann turned out to be correct, there was one element of uncertainty. On April 1, 1942, in an assessment of the situation, Alfred Ernst had been self-critical, admitting that it was "almost impossible to assess the prospects of the two parties in the East according to objective criteria. We do not know how many troops the Russians have available, nor do we know exactly what means the Germans have been able to mobilize for the decisive battle" (BAr J.I.140/4, vol. 4). In addition, Switzerland *could* have been affected by the conflict in spite of Germany's looming defeat. Hence, regardless of the good long-term prospect it was not illogical for Masson to continue his efforts at keeping the war away from Switzerland. In his assessment of the situation of August 26, 1941, Werner Müller had remarked: "We have drafted . . . this report in order to force ourselves to look at the war as a *global issue* with all its repercussions and possibilities. Certain repercussions are bound to materialize; we are one of the 'possibilities.' It is up to us to recognize that in time." BAr E 27/9911, vol. 2 (emphasis in original).

56. Meyer, notes on Waldshut. BAr J.I. 121/1.
57. Meyer, notes on Waldshut.
58. Schellenberg insisted on meeting Masson in *Germany*. Masson explained, "I found out later that Schellenberg was afraid of being ambushed, of *being kidnapped* in Switzerland and handed over to the British, just like Rudolf Hess!!" (Masson, "Attestation," May 10, 1948. BAr E 27/10039.) Schellenberg claimed that Hitler had dissuaded him from traveling to Switzerland because he was bound to bring a *hornets' nest* down about his ears. However, Schellenberg hid the fact that, by allowing the meeting to be held in Germany, Masson offered the SS officer a *tactical advantage*. Masson may not have realized that, or he accepted it as an advance concession.
59. See page 155ff.
60. Barbey, *P.C. du Général*, 130.
61. Cf. Barbey's statement in an interview with Werner Rings, July 15–17, 1968/3 November 1969: "[Masson] talked to me about his plan. He basically told me two things; first, that the first objective of his plan was to convince Schellenberg that Switzerland was determined to defend itself against any aggressor, no matter where it came from. That was one thing. Second, he considered that this channel could contribute to restricting the German spying activities in Switzerland." AfZ files of Werner Rings.
62. Barbey, diary entry of September 3, 1942.
63. Barbey, *P.C. du Général*, 130–131.
64. Barbey, *P.C. du Général*, 131.
65. Barbey, *P.C. du Général*, 131.
66. Masson to Eugster, June 14, 1945. BAr E 5330 1982/1, vol. 205.

67. However, Masson entered into direct contact with Canaris only *after* his meeting with Schellenberg in Waldshut. In fall 1942, Switzerland's Chief of Intelligence had sent a *signal* to that effect. The contact was established through Canaris' aide Hans Bernd *Gisevius*, whom Masson first met in early 1943. The meeting was once again held at the *Schweizerhof* hotel in Bern. On that issue, see, among other things, the case file on v.d.Heydt/Steegmann/Gisevius (in the files of divisional court 6), BAr E 5800/1, vol. 1, as well as Masson's statement as a witness in the Gisevius case, May 14, 1947, and the interrogation of Gisevius May 14, 1947. Both documents are at BAr E 27/10064.

68. Cf. Masson's statement: "One will agree that for a chief who is responsible for his men, it was a fundamental duty to take care of those who risked their lives outside our country. Our concern for them was all the more justified as many of them had accepted to go on their delicate mission out of patriotism, without expecting any material gain from it." Masson, "Notre dossier allemand," *Tribune de Lausanne* January 16, 1966. (On this issue, see also page 366, endnote 19.)

69. Masson, "Blick zurück in dunkle Tage," *Luzerner Neueste Nachrichten*, March 27, 1962.

70. Masson in *Tribune de Lausanne*, February 6, 1966. After the war, when Brigadier General Iwan von Ilsemann tried to obtain a residence permit in Switzerland, in a letter to the Swiss Federal Immigration Police dated September 6, 1945, Colonel Werner Müller supported the German's request, stating:

> It is established beyond question that v. Ilsemann remained a true friend of our country even when defending us in Germany meant *taking personal risks*. Due to his "indoctrination by Swiss ideas," as the German Armed Forces High Command and particularly the Party used to call it, [in July 1944] he was removed from his post as military attaché in the most unscrupulous manner and was replaced by v. Horn, a man of the Party. By the way, Mr. von Ilsemann has the confidence of top personalities, and rightly so. I know that Federal Councillor Kobelt, Lieutenant General Frick, Major General Flückiger, and many others hold von Ilsemann in high esteem. . . . Allied military circles also have a . . . high opinion of him; the English Military Attaché for instance told me, "We know that v. Ilsemann is a decent fellow; we do not have anything against him, and we also know that he is a good friend of Switzerland." . . . In conclusion, I would like to emphasize that among the numerous citizens of the German Reich with whom I was in contact either through the service or in private, v. Ilsemann is the only one whose cause I support in my capacity as deputy to the Assistant Chief of Staff Ib and head of the Security Service. I am convinced that an injustice would be done if v. Ilsemann had to leave our country. (BAr E 27/9508, vol. 17.)

Lieutenant General Hans Frick, who was the author of the well-known *Brevier der Taktik* (*Guide on Tactical Matters*, 1943) and served as the Swiss Army's

Chief Instructor from 1944 to 1953, also used his influence with Kobelt on
behalf of Ilsemann. He commented:

> [The German General] never had the attitude of a conqueror that
> made so many Germans very disagreeable, especially during the
> war; moreover, I have every reason to believe that he was never a
> "Nazi." General v. Ilsemann was a very close friend of General
> [Werner] von Fritsch's, who, as we all know, was kicked out by
> Hitler as early as before the war and was driven to his death
> because he had warned against the war [the so-called Blomberg-
> Fritsch affair]. . . . By the way, the National Socialists had pushed
> [Ilsemann] out of his civilian position, and it was only due to his
> friendship with General v. Fritsch, who was still Commander-in-
> Chief [of the Army] at the time, that he was readmitted to the
> army and subsequently appointed military attaché. (Hans Frick to
> Kobelt, January 15, 1946. BAr E 27/10109.)

71. Masson, "L'affaire Schellenberg," *Tribune de Lausanne*, February 6, 1966.
72. Liaison officer between Army Intelligence and the Attorney General's office; see
    page 126.
73. In a handwritten annotation, Alfred Ernst claimed that this was the *case of Emil
    Knüttel*. However, the Head of the German Bureau was wrong; Knüttel, who
    had worked against Switzerland with a whole group of agents, subsequently
    renounced his extraterritoriality privileges because he feared that he might be
    punished in Germany. On May 19, 1943, Switzerland's territorial court 2A sen-
    tenced him to 15 years in prison.
74. Ernst to Masson, April 19, 1942. Strictly confidential. BAr J.I.140/4, vol. 4. In
    that letter, Alfred Ernst added:

> Next week Dr. Frölicher is coming to Bern. Since it is to be expect-
> ed that as usual he will defend the German point of view instead of
> the Swiss one, I recommend that you insist and point out to the
> Department of Foreign Affairs that for the time being the Germans
> have only made allegations against Dr. Mörgeli that are probably
> unfounded. Otherwise we fear that the Department of Foreign
> Affairs will also adopt the German point of view and claim that it
> was Dr. Mörgeli's own fault that he was arrested. So we would have
> to leave him to cope with his destiny all by himself.

75. Ernst to Masson, "Bericht betreffend Fall Dr. Mörgeli," April 10, 1942. BAr E
    27/9508, vol. 10.
76. See page 99 and 323, endnote 188.
77. Ernst, "Bericht Mörgeli." BAr E 27/9508, vol. 10. Ernst explained: "Mörgeli
    accomplished his task in Stuttgart with a lot of tact and skill. I never had the
    slightest reason to complain about anything he did. I also know that Consul
    Suter was very satisfied with his performance. Dr. Mörgeli always worked with
    great enthusiasm at the Consulate, and I have been told that his work was
    impeccable in every respect." By making these remarks, Ernst wanted to pre-
    vent the Department of Foreign Affairs from complaining that Mörgeli might
    have been meeting with agents and had been caught in the clutches of German
    Counterintelligence through his own fault.

78. Ernst underlined these words in his report.
79. Ernst, "Bericht Mörgeli," April 10, 1942. BAr E 27/9508, vol. 10.
80. Ernst, "Bericht Mörgeli."
81. The explanation in Lüönd, *Spionage und Landesverrat in der Schweiz*, vol. 2, 73 has to be corrected accordingly.
82. Rings, interview with Mörgeli, May 30, 1968. AfZ Bestand Werner Rings.
83. Located halfway between Stuttgart and Nuremberg.
84. Ernst, "Bericht Mörgeli." BAr E 27/9508, vol. 10. The Head of the German Bureau categorically denied giving Mörgeli any instructions to collect that type of information, arguing, "The information that he is accused of having received from that Swiss concerns issues in which we have never been interested; we would not have accepted the risk of getting hold of it." (Ernst, "Bericht Mörgeli.")
85. Ernst, "Bericht Mörgeli." Experts at the Intelligence Service discovered that the design contained only "useless information that had been known for a long time." Werner Müller and Alfred Ernst subsequently warned Mörgeli against accepting any other similar reports.
86. Ernst was undoubtedly right not to attach much importance to the fact the Swiss who had denounced Mörgeli during the interrogation by the Gestapo had also been arrested. He explained, "In the Ketterer case, as a matter of form the Germans had also arrested the Swiss who had acted as an agent provocateur." Ernst to Masson, April 10, 1942. BAr E 27/9528.
87. Cf. Ernst's statement: "Compared with the activity of the German consular agents in Switzerland, who do not restrict themselves to receiving reports but actively organize the intelligence service and contribute to procuring intelligence, passively receiving a document certainly appears to be a perfectly harmless act." Ernst, "Bericht Mörgeli," April 10, 1942. Bar E 27/9508, vol. 10.
88. On this issue, see page 184.
89. Rings, interview with Mörgeli, May 30, 1968. AfZ Bestand Werner Rings.
90. Even though the efforts undertaken by the Department of Foreign Affairs in the Mörgeli case did not yield any results (which explains why Alfred Ernst wrote several sharply-worded letters), by analyzing the available reference material this author discovered that the government had not been sitting around doing nothing. However, due to the unproductive relations between the Department of Foreign Affairs and Army Intelligence (see page 97ff.), Army Intelligence had a blurred vision concerning the Department of Foreign Affairs' efforts to resolve the case. On June 17, 1942, Pilet-Golaz addressed the Head of the Justice and Police Department, Federal Councillor von Steiger, writing: "[Mörgeli's] prolonged detention is affecting him physically and mentally. You certainly know that he was about to get married. . . . [I promised Colonel-Brigadier Masson] to do everything I could and could not do to have Dr. Mörgeli freed. . . . [I am convinced] that protecting our citizens abroad is of greater interest to us than relentlessly hitting the foreigners who commit an offense in Switzerland." Pilet-Golaz consequently asked von Steiger to arrange an exchange of prisoners, adding, "Let me state this once again: the case of Dr. Mörgeli deserves to receive our kind attention" (BAr E 27/9528). Two days later Pierre Bonna, the Head of the Foreign Service at the Department of

Foreign Affairs, addressed Masson to explain to him why, after more than three months, Mörgeli continued being kept in custody and why it had not been possible yet to have him freed; he stated: "There are two reasons why our efforts have not yet been successful; first, the accusations raised against Mr. Mörgeli, about which I have to admit we do not have any precise information, are supposedly not limited to transmitting information on spying activities against our country; and second, an exchange [of prisoners] is encountering some difficulties for which we are not to blame. Nevertheless, let me assure you that we will do everything we can to have the prisoner released." Bonna to Masson, 19 June 1942. BAr E 27/9528.

91. On this issue, see Chapter 5.
92. German Bureau, 1942 annual report (1 September 1941–31 August 1942). BAr J.I.140/4, vol. 4.
93. German Bureau, 1942 annual report.
94. Masson in *Luzerner Neueste Nachrichten*, 27 March 1962.
95. Masson, "Notre dossier allemand," *Tribune de Lausanne*, 16 January 1966.
96. Masson, "Blick zurück in dunkle Tage," *Luzerner Neueste Nachrichten*, 27 March 1962.
97. Masson to Military Attorney General, 14 June 1945. BAr E 5795/448, vol. 3. By making this statement, Masson alluded particularly to the fact that due to negotiations with Eggen and Schellenberg, he had on several occasions managed to have numerous prisoners freed from German concentration camps. Eduard von Steiger criticized Masson for saving many lives, describing his actions as "inadmissible acts of encroachment" (von Steiger to Eugster, 27 April 1945. BAr E 27/10024). Lützelschwab objected to Federal Councillor von Steiger's attitude, stating, "In reality, as usual he played the unprincipled old fox. My files contain ample evidence of that." Lützelschwab to Hausamann, 26 October 1947. BAr J.I.137 1974/64, vol. 11. Looking back, Allen Dulles evidently did not have Federal Councilor von Steiger in mind when he stated: "In any discussion of Swiss neutrality in World War II, it would be seriously remiss to omit the humanitarian role of Switzerland. It was a refuge and an island of humane and charitable undertakings for the persecuted, the homeless and the displaced." Allen Dulles, *The Secret Surrender* (New York, 1966), 30.
98. During the maneuvers of the 6th Division.
99. As Chief of the General Staff Section, Labhart worked in the same capacity as General Krejcí.
100. Labhart to Military Department, "Besuch der tschechoslowakischen Manöver vom 31. August bis 3. September 1937," June 7, 1937. BAr E 27/12521, vol. 1; Minger to General Staff Section, "Abkommandierung von Labhart und Dubois," June 10, 1937. BAr E 27/12521, vol. 1; Labhart, "Rapport sur les Manoeuvres de l'Armée Tchécoslovaque." BAr E 27/12521, vol. 2. (The fact that the report was written in French indicates that Dubois was its author.)
101. Fuhrer, *Spionage*, 80. (However, contrary to what Fuhrer implies by his way of stating the facts, Labhart visited Czechoslovakia in 1937, not in 1936.)
102. Bonjour, *Neutralität*, vol. V, 71–72.
103. See page 367, endnote 24.
104. On that issue, see Chapter 9.

105. Fuhrer, *Spionage*, 80.
106. See page 170ff.
107. Cf. Masson's statement: "I could just as well have worn my uniform . . . but it was useless for the *Swiss* authorities (customs, etc.) to see a Swiss officer cross the border in a uniform." Masson, "Rapport." BAr E 5795/448, vol. 3.
108. The customs officials had been instructed not to check the two gentlemen's identity.
109. A 40-meter-long bridge across the Rhine connects Laufenburg, Switzerland, and Laufenburg, Germany. Almost exactly three years later, on that same bridge General Guisan met General Koenig, the Commander-in-Chief of the French Armed Forces in Germany (de Lattre de Tassigny's successor); see Barbey, *P.C. du Général*, 278.
110. Peter Burckhardt, a future major general who had driven Masson and Meyer to the border, was able to intervene in time to prevent the sergeant from raising the alarm and thereby creating a stir (verbal communication by Burckhardt to this author, February 10, 1988 and reiterated during conversations from 1992 to 1999).
111. See page 355, endnote 152.
112. See page 376, endnote 119.
113. Masson, "Le récit de l'affaire Schellenberg," *Tribune de Genève*, 19 December 1961.
114. Masson, "Blick zurück in dunkle Tage," *Luzerner Neueste Nachrichten*, 26 March 1962.
115. Accoce & Quet, *Moskau wusste alles*, 17.
116. Nor *Bureau Ha* nor its "informant" Roessler, alias Lucy.
117. Once Accoce and Quet's story had been publicized in Switzerland by means of a preprint in the Swiss weekly *Weltwoche*, on February 27, 1966 Meyer sent an extended letter to his former superior Masson to complain about once again being harshly criticized because of the connection with Schellenberg. Even if he wrote the letter in sarcastic language, he had trouble hiding his bitterness about the renewed attack, which was all the more provocative to the involved persons because the story that the two French journalists had written was simplistic and unrealistic. Meyer wrote to Masson:

> In spite of the editors' favorable foreword on your behalf, it is obvious that H[ans] H[ausamann] was involved in the series of articles entitled, "Der Krieg wurde in der Schweiz gewonnen" [The War Was Won in Switzerland]. One did not hear much about him anymore because his indirect (through Kimche) and direct smear campaigns and self-adulation did not trigger any response in Eastern Switzerland nor among the military; so he recently supplied some material to Mrs. [Alice] Meyer for her book [*Anpassung oder Widerstand* (Frauenfeld, 1966)]. Mrs. Meyer for her part does not have any reference other than the fact that she is the widow of Prof. Carl Meyer, who Wiesendanger had placed in custody for two days on your orders at the time! . . . The positive aspect about the latest *Weltwoche* article is the fact that one does not dare to mess with you anymore because—just like General Guisan—you

have rallied the Swiss behind you. Your excellent series of articles in
the *Tribune [de Lausanne]* has undoubtedly contributed to that.
However, the amateurish, sensational way in which the "case of
Waldshut" [*sic*] has been reported is detrimental. I do not think
that you could be responsible for the article—following your interview [with the two journalists; see page 455ff.]. No one will believe
that Switzerland's Chief of Intelligence recklessly walked into
"enemy territory" all by himself to meet an unknown gentleman
gangster whom he was supposed to recognize based on a photograph that Lucy had given him *in Lucerne*. (This is how you can
tell that H.H. contributed to that story; he claims that he became
involved in our connection even though he did not know that it
existed; he wants to have his share in the Schellenberg connection
and link it with the Viking connection!) There is a lot of primitive,
non-military affected behavior and talking in that article!—Only
some *dumb cluck* would think that this is what Switzerland's intelligence service is all about. What is worse, however, is the fact that
this scribble in the *Weltwoche* was presented to the readers as a
"documentary report," thereby creating the impression that you
had actually said these things to the journalists during the interview. Those who have read your well-written series of articles in
the *Tribune*, which were written with a lot of wit and humor, will
be able to judge for themselves—but who in German-speaking
Switzerland reads the *Tribune de Lausanne*? As your "adjutant," I
recommend that you carefully read the manuscript (blueprint) of
the upcoming book and refuse permission to print it until the article on Waldshut tells the truth and reflects your position (especially
the artless interview) and Schellenberg is no longer represented as a
gangster. Otherwise, as head of the Special Service and *the
Commander-in-Chief's unofficial intelligence officer* I would have to
consider using my own *documentation* and taking up my pen in
order to erect a "memorial" to you, Guisan, and Schellenberg. The
NZZ would definitely preprint my version of the story because I
can produce written evidence for everything; that would make history. I would insist on that right in response to your and my being
denigrated. But let us talk about that at our next meeting. It is too
bad that one begins to feel one's age. I wish you a speedy recovery.
Forever yours truly, W[olf] Sch[wertenbach]. (BAr J.I.121/20;
emphasis in original.)

However, the publication of an account from Meyer's and Masson's point of
view remained only an intention; Meyer died six and a half months after writing that letter, and Masson did not recover from his illness either, dying just a
year after his companion of "Waldshut."

118. Masson, "L'affaire Schellenberg," *Tribune de Lausanne*, 6 February 1966.
(However, the available reference material tends to indicate that Schellenberg
skillfully created that impression with his Swiss counterpart.) The conversation
was held during a *walk in the woods*. Meyer noted, "Masson and Schellenberg

walked in front, Eggen and I followed them. I do not know what Masson and Schellenberg discussed." Meyer, notes on Waldshut. BAr J.I. 121/1.

119. From the very beginning, Schellenberg cleverly pushed Masson into the role of the one who was inferior. Surprisingly Masson, who was shrewd on many other occasions, fell for this game. After all, according to Meyer (see page 170ff.) the meeting had been suggested by the *Germans*. Was Masson intimidated because of the long wait at the German customs office? Could Schellenberg's "accident" have been cleverly staged as part of a war of nerves? There are no conclusive answers to these questions. Once again, however, these circumstances show the problematic nature of the entire endeavor.

120. Masson, "Was geschah damals?" *Tages-Anzeiger*, March, 26, 1962.

121. Masson, "Le récit de l'affaire Schellenberg," *Tribune de Genève*, 19 December 1961.

122. Masson, "L'affaire Schellenberg," *Tribune de Lausanne*, February 6, 1966.

123. General Banwell R. Legge

124. Quoted from Accoce & Quet, *Moskau wusste alles*, 18.

125. Masson, "Le récit de l'affaire Schellenberg," *Tribune de Genève*, December 19, 1961.

126. Masson, "Le récit de l'affaire Schellenberg."

127. Accoce & Quet, *Moskau wusste alles*, 18–19. This interpretation does not seem to be far-fetched considering that a female German agent was working as a cook for Allen Dulles, the Head of the Office of Strategic Services in Bern. (When Gisevius informed him about that fact, Dulles rid himself of the spy by leaking a discreet message to the Swiss Federal Police.)

128. Masson, "Le récit de l'affaire Schellenberg," *Tribune de Genève*, December 19, 1961.

129. Masson, "Rapport." BAr E 27/10027, vol. 1.

130. Masson, "Blick zurück in dunkle Tage," *Luzerner Neueste Nachrichten March*, 27, 1962.

131. Masson, "Attestation." BAr E 27/10039.

132. Masson, "Attestation."

133. Masson, "Attestation."

134. Masson, "Attestation."

135. Masson, "Le récit de l'affaire Schellenberg," *Tribune de Genève*, December 19, 1961.

136. Paulus capitulated less than five months later, on February 2, 1943. On this issue, see also Barbey, *P.C. du Général*, 128, 132 (entries dated August 8, 1942 and September 9, 1942). Masson's assessment of the situation was remarkable, especially when considering the time at which he made it; on August 19, 1942, Paulus had ordered the attack on Stalingrad; six days later the Soviet High Command declared the city under siege. However, the full-scale Soviet counteroffensive did not begin until November 19, 1942; three days later the German 6th Army was encircled. Masson's assessment speaks for his analytical skills; he realized at a fairly early stage that the Wehrmacht had once and for all lost control of events on the German-Soviet front.

137. Masson, "Rapport." BAr E 27/10027, vol. 1.

138. Masson, "Le récit de l'affaire Schellenberg," *Tribune de Genève*, December 19, 1961.
139. Barbey, *P.C. du Général*, 132.
140. Reference to Meyer's efforts as a mediator.
141. Meyer, notes on Waldshut. BAr J.I. 121/1.
142. Barbey, *P.C. du Général*, 133 (entry dated September 29, 1942).
143. Barbey, *P.C. du Général*, 134.
144. Barbey, *P.C. du Général*, 134.
145. Barbey, *P.C. du Général*, 134.
146. Masson, "Rapport." BAr E 27/10027, vol. 1.
147. Masson, "Rapport."
148. Barbey, *P.C. du Général*, 134.
149. See page 171ff.
150. Barbey, *P.C. du Général*, 134.
151. Following a number of attempts by Masson and Meyer to put pressure on Eggen. For both Switzerland's Chief of Intelligence and Captain Meyer, a successful conclusion of this matter had become a criterion for testing how valuable the entire connection was; if Mörgeli had not been released, it would have been discredited. As for Schellenberg's and Eggen's motivation, General Guisan's supposition may have been correct; in a handwritten note dated January 11, 1943, he wrote, "[Schellenberg h]as had Mörgeli freed after ten months of detention, . . . *without asking for anything in exchange.* [He did it] simply out of *prestige* and in order to prove that he keeps his promises" (BAr E 5795/333). For a different possible explanation, see page 184.
152. Mörgeli was left in the dark about his fate until the very last moment; he later explained:
> In the evening of December 23, [1942], the warden came to see me and said, "Pack your belongings, tomorrow you will be taken away from here!" I feared the worst. The next day I was driven to Stuttgart, where I was kept at the Gestapo quarters and had a relatively good lunch with a Gestapo official. He was the one who told me, "You can go back home to Switzerland now." Then I was brought to the airport in Stuttgart, was put on a plane and was given a paper according to which my name was *Brinkmann.* I do not know why. In the afternoon of December 24, [1942,] I arrived in Dübendorf. (Rings, Interview with Mörgeli, May 30, 1968. AfZ Bestand Werner Rings.)

Mörgeli did not find out until fall 1945, in connection with the National Council's debate on the Masson affair (see Chapter 1), that he owed his liberation to the Masson-Schellenberg connection.
153. Once Mörgeli was back home safely, it was easier to discuss the case. On June 2, 1942, Ernst had implored Masson's deputy Werner Müller "not to leave [Mörgeli] in the lurch any longer in Germany but to *free him at all cost.*" (Italics underlined in the original.) BAr E 27/9528.
154. Ernst to Masson, December 27, 1942. BAr J.I.140/4, vol. 4.
155. Especially through the fact that Mörgeli's successful liberation strengthened

Masson's confidence in the connection and made him grateful toward his German partners.

156. Rings, Interview with Mörgeli, May 30, 1968. AfZ Bestand Werner Rings.

Chapter 9: General Guisan's Involvement in the Connection

1. In a note for the file regarding a meeting with the Commander-in-Chief on March 27, 1942, Meyer reported General Guisan as asking him whether he considered the political situation in Switzerland to be safe. The head of the Special Service replied:

> Yes, I do. There is no need to be concerned about the domestic political situation, and I will be able to inform you in detail about *Germany's plans* shortly; as you know, I am in *direct contact with top German authorities* that are well-disposed toward us. It is due to them that the IPA had to cease treating you with hostility, General. *Colonel Masson informed you about that.* This is my connection; I am the one fostering it. The gentlemen [with that expression Meyer apparently referred to Eggen and other persons involved in the wooden barracks deal; Schellenberg did not travel to Switzerland until half a year later] are going to come to Switzerland in a few days; afterward I will have more information. [I] know the gentlemen through the Sp[ecial Service]; *it was your son who introduced me to them.*

Meyer reported the Commander-in-Chief as reacting with surprise to this last piece of information. BAr J.I.121/1.

2. *Der Bund*, no. 483, 16 October 1945.
3. *Der Bund*, 16 October 1945.
4. "Amtliche Mitteilung zum Fall Masson," 8 March 1946. BAr J.I.121/63.
5. Barbey, *P.C. du Général*, 154 (entry of 5 March 1943).
6. Kreis, *La Charité*, 152.
7. Bonjour, *Neutralität*, vol. V, 68.
8. Meyer reported Eggen as adding: "However, the fact that the Commander-in-Chief is dismissing [pro-German Lieutenant General Ulrich] Wille [as Chief Instructor of the Armed Forces] effective December 31, 1942 is a *faux pas* and further weakens [General Guisan's] position. It is due to [Meyer's] and Masson's intervention that he is still . . . tolerable." (Meyer, diary notes, Christmas Day 1942. BAr J.I.121/1.) On Christmas Eve, Eggen had accompanied Swiss intelligence officer Mörgeli back to Switzerland, whereupon Meyer invited him to spend the Christmas holiday at his castle.
9. On September 8, 1942; see page 170ff.
10. Lothar Gruchmann, *Der Zweite Weltkrieg* (Munich, 7th ed., 1982), 229.
11. Operation *Attila*.
12. Jean Rudolf von Salis, *Eine Chronik des Zweiten Weltkrieges: Radiokommentare 1939–1945* (Zürich, 1981), 258. On February 8, 1940, Federal President Pilet-Golaz had asked J.R. von Salis, a history professor at the Swiss Federal Technical Institute in Zürich, to write a weekly situation report for Swiss national public radio entitled "Weltchronik." Beginning in November 1940,

the reports were aired every Friday evening, meeting with an extremely wide response. Because the show was rebroadcast via short-wave radio, it could be heard overseas as well. In his memoirs, von Salis stated, "It was an intellectual adventure for a historian to publicly comment on history in the making. . . . Reporting accurately on military operations and political developments was the most reliable way of ascertaining the truth." J.R. von Salis, *Grenzüberschreitungen* (Zürich, 1978), vol. 2, 80, 83. Interestingly, von Salis did not have any contact with Swiss Army Intelligence, nor did he personally know any top officer in the army. He based his assessments of military developments on *open sources*, including Hans Delbrück's *Geschichte der Kriegskunst im Rahmen der politischen Geschichte* (1920–1923) for issues relating to land warfare, Charles de Gaulle's 1934 work on tank warfare, and U.S. Admiral Alfred Mahan's *The Influence of Sea Power upon History* (1890). He also used Colonel Oskar Frey's situation reports published in the daily *Basler Nachrichten* and shrewd commentaries by Franz Carl Endres, a former Bavarian officer, published in the Swiss weekly *Weltwoche*. In addition, he systematically listened to short-wave programs of all warring parties. Much to his surprise, he noticed that both the BBC and Radio Moscow were quoting him. (Oral and written communications by v. Salis to this author in 1982–1988.) The Swiss historian's impartial assessments of the situation met with an unexpectedly wide response. A short time after the war, when he was on a mission in Czechoslovakia for the public Swiss aid organization *Schweizer Spende*, Hans Hausamann benefited from the fact that people in many countries had been listening to the "Weltchronik," reporting:

> The trailer of the Department of Foreign Affairs was marked with the Swiss flag. When I stopped somewhere along the road in Czechoslovakia, a huge Czech suddenly approached me, shouting, "Nemec!" Of course I immediately replied, "no, Svycar!," i.e., "no, Swiss!" He refused to believe me, so we kept going back and forth until I suddenly had the idea to pretend that I was von Salis. I shouted, "von Salis!" He instantly opened his arms wide open and wanted to give me a hug, exclaiming, "Oh, von Salis! Oh, von Salis!" (Werner Rings, interview with Hausamann, 6 to 14 May 1968.) AfZ files of Werner Rings.

13. Barbey, *P.C. du Général*, 138.
14. Von Salis, *Chronik*, 258 (commentary of 13 November 1942).
15. Sir Winston Churchill, *Great War Speeches* (London, 6th ed., 1965), 173–174. Selection of *The War Speeches of the Rt. Hon. Winston S. Churchill*, compiled by Charles Eade (3 vols.).
16. Cf. Masson's statement: "This fortress, which has a rather pompous name, stretches along a resistance line across Holland, Belgium, eastern France, the Maritime Alps, the Apennines south of Switzerland, then along the Danube toward Bucharest and Odessa, and up across Poland in the form of a rampart in the east. Switzerland is geographically included in this European defense system." Masson, *Tribune de Lausanne*, 28 November 1965.
17. Guisan, report on wartime duty, 49. Cf. the secret report by the Axis Section (Alfred Ernst) dated December 19, 1942 "concerning the importance of the

railway connections between Germany and Italy." The report stated that in the
framework of the Anglo-American troops' strategic operations following
Germany's occupation of Vichy France, the railroads linking the two Axis powers, which indirectly included the transalpine tunnels on Swiss territory, became
extremely important. Masson summed up the report that he had asked the Axis
Section to undertake by remarking, "It is *possible, if not probable*, that the
Germans will be tempted to lay their hands on our railroads as a *preventive* step
in order to have enough time to put them back in working order before the
operations of spring 1943." Masson to Commander-in-Chief, December 23,
1942 (the report and Masson's cover letter are filed at BAr E 5795/329).

18. Cf. the secret report dated October 1940 concerning "talks that an officer of
the Reich War Ministry held with several gentlemen whom we know to be reliable. Our informants unanimously call the officer in question a reliable and
important man who is absolutely patriotic but rejects the party and has a lot of
sympathy for Switzerland." The report states, among other things, "According
to some German military and economic circles, *Switzerland underestimates its
importance within Europe. The Gotthard and Simplon railroad tunnels and the
Swiss franc are political and economic assets*; Switzerland is not sufficiently aware
of their significance." The report is filed among the unregistered secret documents of Federal Councillors Minger and Kobelt, 1939–1944; it was part of
the background information that was used to draft the Federal Council's report
concerning General Guisan's report on wartime duty. BAr E 27/15067.

19. Guisan, report on wartime duty, 50.

20. On November 7, 1942, Alfred Ernst warned Masson, "It is crucial not to let us
be maneuvered under any circumstances, not even by a possible Allied attack
against us nor any German promises, which are worthless anyway, into one single front with the *German Reich, which is heading for disaster*." BAr J.I.140/4,
vol. 4.

21. Eggen had asked for the meeting primarily to complain to Wiesendanger and
Meyer-Schwertenbach that Colonel Werner Müller, the head of the security
service, had him spied on (see page 382, endnote 36). Apparently the Swiss
agent was so clumsy that it did not take Eggen long to notice that he was kept
under surveillance. Cf. Meyer's note dated February 25, 1943, in which he
wrote, "[Eggen says] that he has done a lot for Switzerland and has come to
improve our lot if po[ssible], but he had to realize that he is mistrusted. The
three of us discuss the situation at Wiesendanger's office." (BAr J.I.121/1.)
Eggen knew, and correctly so, that his position was already strong enough to
protest loudly against the surveillance to which he was subject in Switzerland,
even though it was much more discreet than the surveillance which foreigners
were expected to put up with in Germany. Moreover, he was able to count on
the sympathy of intelligence officer Meyer-Schwertenbach, who was outraged
about Müller's "impertinence." See the figure on page 458.

22. Albert Wiesendanger, born June 29, 1893, died October 9, 1970, Ph.D. in law,
police inspector and civil protection inspector of the city of Zürich. He studied
law in Zürich and Berlin; in 1917 he started working for the district court in
Zürich while preparing for the bar exam. In the 1928 local elections, the Social
Democrats won the majority of seats in the city parliament, making Police

Inspector Otto Heusser, a Liberal Democrat, unacceptable. He was consequently transferred to become head of the cantonal penitentiary in Regensdorf. Mayor Emil Klöti nominated his fellow partisan Albert Wiesendanger as Heusser's successor; effective September 1, 1928, the city council appointed him to the position of police inspector. Because on several occasions some fellow partisans had been trying to make Wiesendanger accommodating toward them, shortly after starting in his new position he left the Social Democratic party in order to be politically independent. In 1937 the Independents presented him as a candidate for the Zürich cantonal government, but he was not elected. Wiesendanger reorganized the city police; his merits included creating a forensics unit. Moreover, he co-founded the Swiss Police Institute in Neuchâtel. In 1958 he retired after serving as police inspector for 30 years. During his spare time he enjoyed writing, a hobby that he shared with his former schoolmate Meyer-Schwertenbach. After his death, the *Neue Zürcher Zeitung* (no. 480, October 15, 1970, noon edition) called him a "man who was always in a good mood and to whom humans meant a lot." His published works include, among others, *Das Bild des Menschen* (Zürich, 1963), *Ein Polizeibrevier* (Zürich, 2nd ed., 1960), *Wortkristalle* (Zürich, 1960; a collection of sayings and proverbs, including, "It is often better to be cautious than brave").

23. Meyer, note for file, February 25, 1943 (BAr J.I.121/1). The alleged serious threat that Eggen mentioned probably served primarily to convince his Swiss counterparts of the need to establish close relations with Schellenberg. This author did not find any reference to specific plans by Hitler against Switzerland during that time. However, based on the strategic situation at the time, ideas such as the one reported by Meyer suggested themselves to the Germans. Such discussions contributed to a sense of apprehension that culminated in the alert of March 1943 (see Chapter 10).

24. Meyer, note for file, February 25, 1943. Schellenberg expressed the same idea to General Guisan (see page 193). Bonjour (*Neutralität*, vol. V, 70), who bases his account on Major Hans Bracher's notes (March 12, 1943, BAr E 27/10022), comes to the same conclusion (even though not all the details that Bracher reported were accurate).

25. Guisan, report on wartime duty, 52.

26. Head of Axis Section to Masson, January 27, 1943. BAr J.I.140/4, vol. 5.

27. On that day, General Guisan issued "Instructions on how reservists shall react in case of a surprise attack," stating, among other things, "Should information be disseminated through the radio, flyers, or other means that questions the Federal Council's and the army command's determination to put up resistance, it shall be considered as an invention of enemy propaganda. *Our country shall defend itself to the utmost, with all means, against any aggressor.*" The instructions were signed jointly by Federal President Pilet-Golaz and General Guisan. (The entire German text of the instructions is published in Hans Rudolf Kurz, *Dokumente des Aktivdienstes* [Frauenfeld, 1965], 56.)

28. Head of Axis Section to Masson, January 27, 1943. BAr J.I. 140/4, vol. 5.

29. Masson to Kurz, February 2, 1962. Archives of H.R. Kurz.

30. Masson to Federal President Paul Chaudet, January 25, 1962 (draft letter, was not mailed). Archives of H.R. Kurz.

31. Masson to Meyer, April 18, 1962. BAr J.I.121/20.
32. Masson's very pointed statements concerning the affair of *La Charité* should not mislead one about the fact that he was generally *reluctant* to talk about the matter. In summer 1962, when Federal Councillor Friedrich Wahlen asked Masson to comment on Kimche's book, the former Chief of Intelligence turned to Hans Rudolf Kurz for advice, writing:
   Do you think that for the sake of "historical truth" I should mention the serious incident [of *La Charité*] in my report? On one hand, I do not want to cast any shadow on General Guisan's memory; on the other hand, it would of course allow me to explain and justify my contacts with Schellenberg, because I continue to insist—I believe that I have convinced you of that—that Biglen *wiped out "La Charité"* by reestablishing the Germans' confidence in our army. (Masson to Kurz, July 26, 1962. Archives of H.R. Kurz.)
33. Meyer, note for file, January 27, 1943. BAr J.I.121/1.
34. Guisan, report on wartime duty, 52.
35. See Meyer, note for file, January 27, 1943.
36. Eggen was in Switzerland from February 15 to 16 and February 25 to 26, 1943. The police inspector of the city of Zürich, Albert Wiesendanger, was in charge of Schellenberg's security during the Germans' visit. In a note for the file dated February 16, 1943, Meyer remarked that the head of the Security Service, Colonel Werner Müller of the General Staff, was "trying, behind everyone's back, through the Zürich cantonal police, to keep Peter under surveillance in order to find out what Masson, Peter, and [Meyer] were up to because [Meyer] no longer [kept Müller] informed." (BAr J.I.121/1; on that issue, see page 126ff.) "Peter" was the confidential first name that Meyer used for Eggen. Eggen's first name was in fact Hans and his middle name Wilhelm, but his family used to call him Peter. (See endnote 39 below.)
37. Cf. Meyer's statement, "The head of the customs authorities has received orders from Schaffhausen to let the car cross the border without stopping it, but he tries to find out from me and Wie[sendanger] who the gentlemen are, etc." Meyer, notes, March 2, 1943. BAr J.I. 121/1.
38. Hans Rudolf Fuhrer, interview with Sergeant Bleiker, the detective at the Zürich city police who was Schellenberg's driver during the latter's visits to Switzerland. (Professor Hans Rudolf Fuhrer kindly made the tape recording of the 1978 interview available to this author.)
39. Soon after meeting him, Masson and Meyer started calling Schellenberg exclusively by that nickname—another indication of the rather dangerous degree of confidentiality with which the two Swiss officers approached the German Chief of Intelligence. Neither Masson nor Meyer knew that in German files they for their part were identified as "Senner I" and "Senner II" (see page 16). "Senner" is the German word for an Alpine herdsman and dairyman; the term may allow one to draw certain conclusions about Schellenberg's opinion of Masson and Meyer.
40. Cf. Alfred Ernst's statement:
   Obviously Switzerland will not be left out of [the New Europe] as

the only European country. First it will be "fit" into the Axis bloc
by being subject to economic and political pressure. I suspect that
this pressure will be sufficient to make us obedient. There is no
doubt that more than ever before Germany is using its influence
on key Swiss economic circles and has already been tremendously
successful with that strategy. Numerous economic leaders are
induced to accept Germany's requests because they hope to make a
good profit in the Axis-led "New Europe." Everything suggests that
our economy is gradually but surely becoming entangled [in the
Axis powers' economy] without noticing it and will hardly be able
to free itself from its grip anymore. Once we are economically
dependent, we will be just steps away from being politically subju-
gated. (Ernst to Masson, assessment of the situation [for the
Chief's personal information], November 27, 1941. BAr J.I.140/4,
vol. 3.)

41. Meyer meant to say "in Germany's interest."
42. Meyer, notes, March 2, 1943. (The unintentionally compromising statement
    adds credibility to Meyer's testimony (see page 436, endnote 22).
43. Schellenberg had put that idea in Meyer's head during their meeting at
    Wannsee (see page 169). Paul Meyer-Schwertenbach was interested in politics
    but was not a member of any party. He had a bourgeois background, and his
    ideas came close to those expressed by the Radical Democratic party.
    (Information by Patrizia Schwertenbach to this author, December 1986).
44. That was the reason why Meyer was outraged when he found out that the
    head of the Security Service had Eggen spied on; he feared that the trusting
    relationship that he and Masson had been building up with the Germans
    could be jeopardized through the surveillance activity, which was an *expression
    of mistrust.*
45. His trying hard to do so makes it look as if he had to convince not only his var-
    ious contacts but also himself that what he had become involved in was correct.
46. Telephone conversations between Rothmund and Meyer-Schwertenbach, which
    the head of the Special Service secretly recorded, confirm that impression.
    Meyer did use some of the expressions that Rothmund quoted in his letter.
    (Telephone conversations between Meyer and Rothmund, April 15, 1942
    [recorded on gramophone records]. BAr J.I.121/50 and 50a at HA Z-k/38 and
    HA Z-k/39.)
47. Rothmund to Federal Councillor von Steiger, May 5, 1944. BAr E 27/10024.
48. See page 170ff.
49. Since the meeting between Guisan and Schellenberg was to be kept secret and
    Captain Meyer knew that the telephones at the Schweizerhof hotel in Zürich
    were tapped, he had Lieutenant Colonel B. Rüfenacht, the Assistant Chief of
    Security, make the reservations from Bern. (Meyer, note for file re: telephone
    conversation with Masson, March 1, 1943. BAr J.I.121/1.)
50. Masson, "La vérité sur la 'conspiration' de Biglen," *Tribune de Lausanne,*
    February 13, 1966.
51. That was probably the reason why he had chosen the same hotel as the venue
    for his first meeting with Eggen. This author's reservations concerning the

incompatibility between the intention to keep a low profile and the choice of the meeting place also applies to Schellenberg's visit; see page 357, endnote 181.

52. Cf. Barbey's statement: "I remark that one could have chosen a more discreet 'pub' and hotel. Masson does not deny that." Barbey, *P.C. du Général*, 155.

53. Cf. Meyer's statement: "18:15, pick up Ma[sson] at hotel, is dressed in uniform; [Masson takes off in his own car;] then to the Bellevue [to pick up Schellenberg and Eggen]; drive to Biglen together in two cars; [we] *speed, get lost*, but arrive on time after all." (Meyer, notes, March 3, 1943. BAr J.I. 121/1.) The minor incident once again shows that an Intelligence Service constantly has to expect even the most meticulously planned undertaking to fail; even though Sergeant Bleiker of the Zürich city police had grown up in Bern and knew his way around the area, he got lost on the way to the meeting. Because the night had already fallen and it was pitch-dark as a result of the blackout, Bleiker drove too far, and after turning around he happened to come across a small road that led to Biglen. (H.R. Fuhrer, interview with Bleiker, 1978. Tape recording in this author's possession.) It is unlikely that General Guisan would have waited a long time for Masson's German guests. If the meeting with the Commander-in-Chief had been called off, the Swiss' poor navigation skills would have left a rather pitiful impression on Schellenberg; moreover, the incident might have jeopardized the entire connection because the SS officer would probably have felt fooled.

Allen Dulles relates a similar experience while he was engaged in his secret negotiations for the surrender of German troops in northern Italy: "Gaevernitz and I motored back to Bern in the early hours of March 12th [1945]. It was bleak and cold; the roads were covered with snow and we were depressed. To add to our troubles we became hopelessly lost. Swiss road signs had been taken down early in the war against the threat of German invasion. We could manage in daylight because we knew the landmarks on the way, but now we had to steer by the stars. At one small village we vainly pounded on door after door, hoping we could rouse some native who could give us directions. But the Swiss farmer is a sound sleeper and we got no response at all. Eventually—I am not sure how we managed it—we got back to Bern just before dawn." Allen Dulles, *The Secret Surrender* (New York, 1966), 101.

54. Meyer, notes re: "Biglen," March 3, 1943. BAr J.I.121/1.

55. Masson, "La vérité sur la 'conspiration' de Biglen," *Tribune de Lausanne*, 13 February 1966. Based on Masson's account, Roberto Bernhard described the relaxed atmosphere by writing, "Due to the bonhomie that is typical of the farmers from the canton of Vaud, General Guisan [managed . . .] to put Schellenberg, who had come from the agonizing atmosphere in the Reich, into a mood that resembled that of a delighted vacationer." *Neue Berner Zeitung*, no. 205, 2–3 September 1967.

56. Masson, "La vérité sur la 'conspiration' de Biglen," *Tribune de Lausanne*, 13 February 1966.

57. Masson, "La vérité sur la conspiration de Biglen."

58. An interesting statement by Schellenberg; the issue that he addressed will be dealt with in Chapter 10.

59. Masson, "La vérité sur la 'conspiration' de Biglen," *Tribune de Lausanne*, 13 February 1966.

60. "A simple business card or any document carrying his signature." (Masson, "La vérité sur la 'conspiration' de Biglen.")

61. Masson, "La vérité sur la 'conspiration' de Biglen," *Tribune de Lausanne*, 13 February 1966.

62. On April 12, 1943, General Guisan and Captain Meyer were both invited to the *Sechseläuten* festivities in Zürich. During their trip back to Interlaken, they once again discussed the meeting in Biglen. Meyer noted, "[The General says that] Schelli asked him whether Germany could really count on Switzerland's absolute determination to defend itself; he replied that if [Schellenberg] was not his guest he would feel insulted. When Schelli said that Berlin was concerned about his safety in Switzerland, the General replied that if he was the least bit worried, he would personally accompany him to the border." Meyer, diary, April 12, 1943. BAr J.I. 121/1.

63. Masson stated, "I did not reveal any secret to him by telling him about these things because the foreign military attachés in Bern knew about them. However, this was an interesting 'special connection' for us." Masson, "La vérité sur la 'conspiration' de Biglen," *Tribune de Lausanne*, February 13, 1966.

64. Masson to Federal President Chaudet, January 25, 1962. Archives of H.R. Kurz.

65. After the fact, the Commander-in-Chief also seemed to have second thoughts about the guest book entry, calling up Captain Meyer about it later that night. Meyer, notes on March 3, 1943. Ba J.I. 121/1.

66. Wiesendanger's executor thinks that he remembers the police inspector saying that *he* had removed the page from the guest book and then destroyed it. Either Wiesendanger was deluding himself or the executor just could barely recall what had happened. Patrizia Meyer-Schwertenbach was even shown on Swiss television, holding up the page that her husband had cut out of the book. The page remained in Captain Meyer's possession until 1966. Masson once tried in the 1960s to get it for his own archives by reasoning that Meyer had been his subordinate after all. Captain Meyer had been planning to write his memoirs in the mid-sixties so he loaned the page along with other documents from his archives to an editor of *Stern*—a German news magazine that was going to publish the book. However, Meyer-Schwertenbach died rather unexpectedly in 1966, and the book project remained unrealized. The materials that had been loaned sank into oblivion at the publisher's office in Hamburg. When Meyer's widow finally remembered about the page and asked for it back, it was missing along with other original documents. (Information conveyed to this author by Patrizia Schwertenbach, February/March 1985.) Willi Gautschi was the first person to get hold of an old photocopy of the page while he was working on his monumental biography of Guisan. The document is reproduced in Willi Gautschi's *General Henri Guisan* (New York: Front Street Press, 2003), 471.

67. The document was signed by "General Guisan." A signed copy of the text is at BAr E 27/10022. (Emphasis added.)

68. Guisan replaced the phrase "several great statesmen" with the phrase "the great statesman and Reich Chancellor Bismarck."

69. On February 3, 1943.
70. See Masson to Commander-in-Chief, 29 January 1943 (information regarding Ms. Ljungström and suggestions on what Guisan should reply in the interview). BAr E 27/9508, vol. 13; and General Guisan to Przybyszewski Westrup, Swedish Minister, March 11, 1943. BAr E 5795/334.
71. Masson had already warned about that at a preliminary meeting; Meyer noted, "Too dangerous—too many familiar faces, sports event; will not be able to keep [meeting] secret. [Masson says that] he wants to leave decision up to the Commander-in-Chief." (Meyer, notes, February 26,1943. BAr J.I.121/1.)
72. According to Meyer-Schwertenbach, Schellenberg talked mostly about trivial details of Hitler's personality, such as, "does not smoke, vegetarian . . . loves dogs, is very polite with women." Meyer, diary, March 6, 1943. BAr J.I.121/1.
73. Meyer, note, March 6, 1943. BAr J.I.121/1.
74. Meyer, diary, March 7,1943.
75. Barbey, *P.C. du Général*, 155.
76. Even though by rights Schellenberg should have been called *Colonel* at that time, he was addressed as General from the start in Switzerland. It is unclear whether Eggen called him that in Meyer-Schwertenbach's presence to stress Schellenberg's position. What is known, however, is that Masson was under the impression right from the beginning that his German counterpart had the same rank as he did. (The Swiss rank of Colonel Brigadier is equivalent to a one-star General.) In many documents dating back to as early as 1942 Schellenberg was referred to as *Brigadeführer* or *General*. It even appears that the Germans themselves were not quite sure about Schellenberg's rank; cf. documents by German Foreign Minister Ribbentrop dated October 1 and 7, 1943, respectively, in which Ribbentrop calls Schellenberg a *Brigadeführer*, hence a *General*. However, Schellenberg was promoted from *Standartenführer* (colonel) to *Brigadeführer* (brigadier general) effective June 21, 1944. (Document Center Berlin, personnel file of Walter Friedrich Schellenberg.) The title of *SS-General* is a colloquialism. The correct title was "SS-Brigadeführer and General der Polizei."
77. That was a diplomatic way of stating the facts. Five weeks earlier, on May 13, 1943, the remainder of the German-Italian Army Group in Africa had capitulated, putting an end to the fighting in North Africa. It was just a matter of time until the Allies would set foot on the European mainland; two weeks after Ribbentrop wrote that note, on July 10, 1943, British and U.S. armed forces landed in Sicily. Hence, chasing "the English and Americans from the Mediterranean area" was no longer an issue.
78. Ribbentrop, note to the Führer, June 22, 1943. National Archives, Washington, DC, files of the German Ministry of Foreign Affairs (Auswärtiges Amt), domestic affairs (Inland) II g, secret matter of the Reich (Geheime Reichssache), XII, 1943, T-120/715.
79. Barbey, *P.C. du Général*, 155–156 (entry of March 10, 1943). In 1968, Werner Rings asked him, "And what about your opinion twenty-five years after the fact?" Barbey responded, "My current opinion is closer to my gut reaction." Rings, interviews with Barbey, 16–17 July 1968, November 3, 1969. AfZ files of Werner Rings.

80. Alfred Ernst, "Nachrichtendienst," *ASZM*, no. 12 (1972).

81. See Kobelt, diary, March 11, 1943 (typewritten by Kobelt based on his short-hand notes). BAr E 27/10022. Incidentally, that same night some members of the Biglen village council were having a drink at the *Bären*, talking about the secret atmosphere surrounding the dinner. The owner of the mill in Biglen knew Bracher through the military and told him about the dinner. Bracher subsequently inquired with Barbey, the innkeeper in Biglen, and the police in Bern, whose suspicion had already been aroused through the incident concerning the missing page from the guest book.

82. Kobelt, diary, meeting with Commander-in-Chief, March 12, 1943 in Interlaken. BAr E 27/10022.

83. Kobelt, diary, March 12, 1943.

84. Kobelt, diary, March 12, 1943. Fuhrer (*Spionage*, 129, note 294) interprets the General's *attempt at covering up the facts* as an indication "that Guisan had been playing a more active role in the relations between Schellenberg and Masson" than he admitted. However, that behavior might simply be a reflection of the anything but perfect relationship between Federal Councillor Kobelt and the Commander-in-Chief. It is unlikely that Guisan would have tried to wiggle his way out of telling the truth if Kobelt's predecessor Minger had still been in office. That interpretation is supported by the fact that Kobelt for his part played Guisan false by failing to tell him that he knew about Schellenberg's visit. Both Guisan and Kobelt were not straightforward with each other concerning that issue.

85. Kobelt, diary, March 12, 1943. BAr E 27/10022.

86. Kobelt, diary, March 12, 1943. As a matter of fact, General Guisan did not have precise information on Schellenberg's role at the Reich Security Central Office; cf. Masson's statement in a letter to Guisan:

> You recently asked me to give you *details about "Mr. Biglen's" function*. He reports directly to Himmler and is in charge of general (political, economic, strategic) information on behalf of the *party*. He is in indirect contact with General Canaris, the army's Chief of Intelligence. He often has the opportunity to see Hitler and brief him about the situation, especially in Central Europe. He is ranked "general" but has never been a commander. His exact title is "Standartenführer" [= SS colonel]. (Masson to Commander-in-Chief, June 26, 1943. BAr E 5795/455.)

Actually, Masson too did not know what Schellenberg's exact tasks were; cf. his letter to General Guisan dated March 15, 1945, in which he stated: "At the time I met Schellenberg (in 1941), he was not in charge of Office VI [which was not true!] but took care only of the general issue of political-military information by addressing synopses to the Führer. I do not think that he was personally in charge of setting up the German spying network; at that time, it was mostly General [his correct title was Admiral] Canaris, the Wehrmacht's chief of intelligence, who took care of that." (BAr E 27/10019.)

87. Kobelt, diary, March 12, 1943. BAr E 27/10022.

88. Kobelt, diary, March 12,1943.

89. Commander-in-Chief to Kobelt, March 15, 1943 (handwritten). BAr E 27/10022.
90. See Kobelt to Commander-in-Chief, March 22,1943. BAr E 5795/334.
91. The word is underlined twice in the original text.
92. Commander-in-Chief to Masson, March 22, 1943. BAr E 5795/334 (italics by Guisan). 29
93. Kobelt to Commander-in-Chief, March 29, 1943. BAr E 5795/334.
94. Werner Rings, interview with former Federal Councillor Enrico Celio, 30 June 1969. AfZ files of Werner Rings.
95. Rings, interview with Celio.
96. Ibid.
97. Ibid.
98. Ibid.
99. Former Federal Councillor Enrico Celio later remarked, "Il generale Guisan era stato furbo astuto con me per essere venuto la sera prima a raccontarmi il fatto del suo colloquio con il generale Schellenberg ed io non mi sono mai pentito di essergli stato buono, evitando che egli potesse avere delle noie con lo stesso Consiglio Federale 30 per questo colloquio con il generale tedesco." ("Coming to see me the night before [the Cabinet meeting] to talk to me about his meeting with General Schellenberg was a clever and cunning move by General Guisan, and I did not regret being kind to him, preventing him from getting into trouble with the Federal Council because of that meeting with the German general.") Rings, interview with Celio, June 30, 1969. AfZ files of Werner Rings.
100. The minutes of the Federal Council meeting of April 5, 1943 (BAr E 1004.1 1) stated: "The Head of the Military Department reports on the Commander-in-Chief's meeting with a foreign high-ranking officer that had been arranged by Colonel Masson. He presents the draft of a letter by the Military Department to the Commander-in-Chief. Following a thorough discussion and after deleting one item, the letter is approved. . . . The Head of the Department of Foreign Affairs, *Federal Councillor Pilet-Golaz, did not participate in the discussion.*"
101. Kobelt to Commander-in-Chief, April 6, 1943. BAr E 5795/334.
102. Guisan annotated Kobelt's letter, writing by hand, "*Dulles* has been informed by me." (Regarding Allen Dulles, see page 202ff.)
103. Guisan annotated that passage, writing, "Jealousy!"
104. Guisan annotated that phrase, writing, "Did not deal with that but the *military*, the army's attitude!"
105. Commander-in-Chief to Kobelt, April 7, 1943. BAr E 5795/334.
106. The fact that the Commander-in-Chief responded as early as the day after Kobelt had written the letter on behalf of the Cabinet seems to be an indication that he wanted to settle the matter once and for all.
107. On that matter, see page 11.
108. Hausamann, note for file, October 26,1943. BAr J.I.137 1974/64, vol. 4. Hausamann remarked concerning the document, "So much about today's intermezzo, recounted from memory but undoubtedly close to a verbatim account."

109. On October 1, 1943, Ribbentrop wrote to Köcher (to the Envoy's personal attention):

> General Guisan's talks with SS Brigadier General [*sic*] Schellenberg that have been mentioned by Federal Councillor Pilet-Golaz were the result of the relations between [our] security service and Switzerland's secret service; they were held on 3 March of this year in Biglen near Bern and on 6 March in Arosa. During these talks, General Guisan declared that Switzerland would defend its southern front in the Alps under any circumstances, against any attack, to the last drop of blood. He said that he gave the Führer his word of honor as an officer that Switzerland had no contact with the Allies that was in violation of its strict neutrality; instead, the country was absolutely determined to defend the southern front. General Guisan said that if Switzerland had reason to hope that it would not be subject to any German preventive attack, against which it would of course defend itself, he would even consider the possibility of sending a large number of Swiss troops off duty in order to make them available for the economy, thereby indirectly contributing to increasing Germany's war potential while maintaining Switzerland's neutrality.

(Meyer-Schwertenbach had used a similar argument in a meeting with Schellenberg; see page 190. It is uncertain whether General Guisan actually used that argument or if Schellenberg falsely attributed it to him. If he did say something to that effect, it was no more than a *tactical* argument because there is clear evidence indicating that in fact General Guisan was in favor of *increasing* the number of troops on duty rather than reducing it.) Then Ribbentrop quoted the declaration that Switzerland's Commander-in-Chief had transmitted to Schellenberg in Arosa, adding:

> In the course of the conversation, General Guisan finally assured [Schellenberg] that, contrary to how we kept reproaching him, he had not entered into any agreement with the French at the time, and that he had no contact whatsoever with the Allies. *Brigadier General Schellenberg is supposed to verbally give General Guisan an affirmative answer to his declaration whenever the opportunity presents itself, but that has not been done yet.* . . . A number of French military documents that fell into our hands in fall 1940 reveal that the [Swiss Army's] general staff had held talks anticipating this war, e.g., with the French. Afterward, during the entire winter of 1939–1940, General Guisan was in secret contact with the French Supreme Command. Back then [the Swiss] took preventive steps that were similar to those taken during Mr. Schellenberg's visit; they discussed extensively with Lieutenant Colonel Garteiser what assistance the French Armed Forces could offer Switzerland in case Germany violated Switzerland's neutrality. One of these documents states verbatim, 'Hence, Switzerland's airspace will be defended almost exclusively by the Allied air force.' General Guisan's claim that he had not entered into any agreement whatsoever with the

French at the time is therefore wrong. . . . I would like you to comment on the issues again; in particular, please tell us whether you believe that in view of the attitude of Switzerland's general staff, which has proven to be insincere as evidenced through the talks with the French, the Swiss are serious about defending themselves against an attack by the English and Americans. . . . So far the Swiss' assertions that they will defend their country against any attack have appeared to be credible. However, because General Guisan held talks with the French that the Swiss Federal Council tolerated but failed to admit to us, any Swiss statement must be questioned, even when it is made by people of official stature. (National Archives, Washington, DC, files of German Ministry of Foreign Affairs [Auswärtiges Amt], domestic affairs [Inland] II g, secret matter of the Reich [Geheime Reichssache], XII, 1943, T-120/715.)

110. On October 7, 1943, Köcher replied to Ribbentrop:
General [Guisan's] written declaration to SS Brigadier General Schellenberg dated March 6, [1943] that I have received does not contain any statement that contradicts Switzerland's official policy. I have reason to believe that by now the General, who is not well inclined towards us, has learned a few lessons as well. . . . The Military Attaché [von Ilsemann] told me that even those Swiss officers who oppose General Guisan do not believe that he is capable of breaking his own word. The Military Attaché's information is all the more significant as General Guisan did not only give SS Brigadier General Schellenberg his word of honor as an officer but also made a written declaration, a fact that the above-mentioned officers ignore. . . . To sum it up, it is my duty to inform you that I believe that the Swiss are serious about defending themselves with utmost determination and by using all available military means against an attack by the English and Americans. (National Archives, Washington, DC, files of German Ministry of Foreign Affairs [Auswärtiges Amt], domestic affairs [Inland] II g, secret matter of the Reich [Geheime Reichssache], XII, 1943, T-120/715.)

111. Hausamann, note for file, October 26,1943. BAr J.I.137 1974/64, vol. 4. The U.S. diplomat asked Hausamann whether he knew Köcher. The Swiss intelligence officer wrote, "I said that I did, adding that Köcher had grown up in Switzerland and was therefore familiar with our way of thinking. . . . I replied that as far as I knew *Köcher* had always been *extraordinarily correct* and *very polite*." (Hausamann, note for file, Oct. 26, 1943. BAr J.I.137 1974/64, vol. 4.) According to Dulles, Köcher was indignant about the German Ministry of Foreign Affair's request, arguing that if Berlin thought that it was necessary to obtain information through someone like Schellenberg, there was no point in the Envoy reporting to Berlin. In this connection, it is interesting to note that Detective Bleiker of the Zürich police noticed that during his stays in Switzerland, Schellenberg was constantly apprehensive about running into

someone from the German legation, which was intentionally left in the dark about his visits. (H.R. Fuhrer, tape-recorded interview with Bleiker, 1978.) Daniel Bourgeois (*Le Troisième Reich*, 228–229) considers that it was "highly unlikely" that Ribbentrop was not informed about Schellenberg's trip to Switzerland. In fact, he suggests that Ribbentrop could have been a driving force behind Schellenberg's idea to meet General Guisan because Germany's Foreign Minister was very much interested in knowing what stance the Swiss Army would take in the event of an Allied invasion of Italy.

Based on what is known today, Hausamann's very positive opinion about Köcher needs to be modified. On August 8, 1942, Erich Lemberger of the Reich Railway Central Office in Zürich, the head of the German colony and the local NSDAP group in Zürich, and his secretary Buob were arrested by the police on charges of espionage on behalf of Germany. On August 11, 1942, Köcher sent a telegram to the German Ministry of Foreign Affairs, stating, "Because no release from prison so far, suggest retaliating immediately by arresting Swiss citizens who are in similar positions; thank you for informing me by wire about steps that have been taken." (Document no. NG-5024, Office of Chief Counsel for War Crimes. BAr E 27/10109.) Georg Kreis (*La Charité*, 116) calls Köcher a "*supposed* friend of Switzerland," and Daniel Bourgeois ("L'image allemande de Pilet-Golaz, 1940–1944," *Studien und Quellen* 4 (1978), 124–125) ironically asks:

> [Was] Köcher a friend of Switzerland who consequently wanted to help it by showing how receptive Pilet-Golaz was to the new Europe? The postwar Federal Council and G. de Reynold, in his memoirs, believed that Köcher exercised a moderating influence. The texts that are available to us today show that after summer and fall 1940 he did try to moderate the Nazi subversive program in Switzerland and that after the turn of events in 1942–1943 he vehemently pleaded the cause of Switzerland's neutrality. However, in 1940 it was Köcher who suggested that Germany and Italy jointly protest against the Commander-in-Chief's speech at the Rütli, and he was the one who suggested that Rudolf Hess receive Max Leo Keller. . . . As one can see, in summer 1940 Köcher had no scruples about helping the Swiss Nazis. Moreover, in his famous suggestions of fall 1942 on how to stabilize German-Swiss relations, he wanted to obtain nothing less than General Guisan's resignation by publishing the papers of *La Charité* concerning Switzerland! In short, his expressions of friendship were not very convincing.

112. Wilhelm Lützelschwab to Kobelt, November 10, 1943. BAr J.I.137 1974/64, vol. 4.

113. Dulles: "My real tasks . . . were to gather information about the Nazi and Fascist enemy and quietly to render such support and encouragement as I could to the resistance forces working against the Nazis and Fascists in the areas adjacent to Switzerland which were under the rule of Hitler or Mussolini." Allen Dulles, *The Secret Surrender* (New York, 1966), 15.

114. In a memorandum to the Director of the OSS, Washington, DC, dated August

23, 1945, Chief of Mission/Switzerland Robert P. Joyce wrote that on July 6, 1945 Dulles had handed over the direction of the OSS office in Bern to him before leaving Switzerland for Wiesbaden, Germany, the following day. (National Archives, Washington, DC, RG 226, E.T.O. Switzerland, July 1945, Washington History Office OP-23, entry 99, folder 31, box 8.)

115. Dulles succeeded General Walter Bedell Smith, who had been appointed Under Secretary to Secretary of State John Foster Dulles, Allen's brother.

116. In spring 1942 General Donovan, Head of the American office of Strategic Services, decided to establish a new center in neutral Switzerland. The State Department gave its consent that the OSS representative could work covered as a diplomatic employee of the American embassy. "Donovan hired an experienced facilitator from the NBC shortwave news desk, Gerald Mayer, to go to Switzerland in May as advance man." (Peter Grose, *Gentleman Spy: The Life of Allen Dulles* [Boston/New York, 1994], 149.) When Allen Dulles, who had been working for the OSS office in New York, heard about that, he applied for the position as Head of this OSS branch and got it. "At first, Donovan wanted me to go to London to work with him and David Bruce there in cementing our relations with the British Intelligence Services. I finally persuaded him, however, to let me go to a less glamorous post, but one where I felt my past experience would serve me in good stead; namely, to Switzerland." (Allen Dulles, *The Secret Surrender*, 14.) As Peter Grose rightly said, the subsequent two and a half years Dulles was to spend in Switzerland had a decisive influence on his later life: "Bern established Allen's standing as a spymaster." (Grose, 162.) Already at the initial briefings Dulles was warned that he might not be able to take over his new duties at all. There was no direct flight connection between New York and Switzerland. "The United States was already at war with Germany, and I had, of course, to avoid crossing territory under Nazi control. The only way for an American to reach Switzerland at that time was by flying to Lisbon and then crossing Spain and Vichy France to Geneva. But when I left New York I knew that Operation Torch, the secret American-British landing in North Africa, was planned for the early days of November. We estimated in Washington that as soon as the landing took place the Nazis would move immediately to occupy all of Vichy France. The military necessity for them to control the French ports on the Mediterranean would be urgent. Toulon could not be left to the French Navy. Unfortunately, because of bad weather, my plane for Lisbon was held up a couple of days in the Azores. I had lost valuable time. The landing, I knew, was imminent. From Lisbon I flew to Barcelona. The rest of the journey across Spain and Vichy France was to be by train. It was already November 8th when I took the train from Barcelona." (Allen Dulles, *The Secret Surrender*, 15–16.) Even before Dulles crossed the border over to Vichy France, he bumped into a Swiss diplomatic courier who told him that the Allies had begun to land in North Africa. Dulles did not want to turn back even though he realized that the trip would from then on be a dangerous undertaking. The Germans would presumably "occupy the lines of communication across France and would stop and search the trains. I knew that my trip would be through an area close to where plenty of German troops were stationed. If I was picked up by the Nazis in Vichy France, the best I could hope for would be internment for the dura-

tion of the war. My diplomatic passport would be of little use to me. It was a tough decision, but I decided to go ahead." (Allen Dulles, *Secret Surrender*, 16.) After driving straight through France by night, Dulles arrived at the town of Annemasse, "the last stop in France where all passengers for Switzerland had to alight to have their passports examined. . . . I had been told in Washington that there would probably be a Gestapo agent at this frontier. I was the only one among the passengers who failed to pass muster. The Gestapo man carefully put down in his notebook the particulars of my passport, and a few minutes later a French gendarme explained to me that an order had just been received from Vichy to detain all Americans and British presenting themselves at the frontier and to report all such cases to Marshal Pétain directly. I took the gendarme aside and made to him the most impassioned and, I believe, most eloquent speech that I had ever made in French. [Cf. Mary Bancroft: "He understood French and German and thought he spoke them quite well, but it may perhaps be kinder to draw a veil over that latter assumption! No matter how much progress he made in languages, his accent remained atrocious. I do not speak Italian myself, so I can't evaluate his skill in that language. However, he had many dealings with Italians." Mary Bancroft, *Autobiography of a Spy* (New York, 1983), 141.] Evoking the shades of Lafayette and Pershing, I impressed upon him the importance of letting me pass. I had a valid passport and visa and there was no justification for holding me up. I assured him Marshal Pétain had many other things to worry about on that particular day besides my case. I also let him glimpse the contents of my wallet. Neither patriotic speeches nor the implied offer of a small fortune seemed to move him. He went off to make his telephone call, leaving me to pace the platform. I began to case the area in the hope of carrying out my plan of slipping away on foot to avoid being trapped there. It wouldn't have been easy. Finally around noon, when it was about time for the train to leave for Geneva, the gendarme came up to me, hurriedly motioned for me to get on the train, and whispered to me, *'Allez, passez. Vous voyez que notre collaboration n'est que symbolique.'* (Go ahead. You see our cooperation [with the Germans] is only symbolic.) The Gestapo man was nowhere to be seen. Later I learned that every day, promptly at noon, he went down the street to the nearest pub and had his drink of beer and his lunch. Nothing, including landings in Africa, could interfere with his fixed Germanic habits. The French authorities had gone through the motions of phoning Vichy, as they had been ordered to do. But once the Gestapo man had left his post for his noon siesta, they were free to act on their own, and they did. Within a matter of minutes I had crossed the French border into Switzerland legally. I was one of the last Americans to do so until after the liberation of France. I was ready to go to work." (Allen Dulles, *The Secret Surrender*, 16–17.)

117. See Dulles' statement in his notes for a presentation on "National requirements for intelligence and the tools for fulfilling them," Air War College, Maxwell Field, Alabama December 9, 1946. Under item 2 of his presentation he talked about "The Intelligence from Switzerland," pointing his finger at the United States' lack of preparations; he noted, "Lack of established lines—Failure to

build up *key centers—such as Berne.*" (Princeton University Library, Allen W. Dulles Papers, box 26.)

118. Allen Dulles knew his way around Bern. "I found an apartment in the Herrengasse, in the delightfully picturesque and ancient section of the Swiss capital near its cathedral. This arcaded and cobblestoned street ran along the ridge above the river Aare. It was near where I had lived and worked twenty-four years before in the last months of World War I. Then, as a young diplomat, I had received my first training in the work of intelligence in neutral Switzerland, during a world war. Between my apartment and the river below grew vineyards which afforded an ideal covered approach for visitors who did not wish to be seen entering my front door on the Herrengasse. From the terrace above I had an inspiring view of the whole strech of the Bernese Alps." (Allen Dulles, *The Secret Surrender*, 17–18.) The ground-floor apartment at 23 Herrengasse was to become very sought after. Cf. Mary Bancroft, relating her first visit there, "I made some comment about how very attractive the apartment was and how lucky I thought he was to have found it. *'It suits my needs perfectly,'* he said." (Mary Bancroft, *Autobiography of a Spy*, 133.) Dulles would later report to Washington, "These quarters are unique as to location and adaptability for our use and comprise adequate living quarters for 2 or 3 persons plus substantial office space." The United States was renting the premises from a former Belgian envoy to Switzerland. (Dulles to OSS Washington, DC, May 11, 1945. National Archives, Washington, DC, RG 226, entry 134, box 232, Wash-Sect-R&C-4, folder "Berne April '45 to May '45.")

119. Gerry Mayer, who General Donovan had sent ahead to build up the new OSS office, had scouted the small community of American residents for talents that could be useful. "Dulles eventually approached every American citizen living in Switzerland. Some were former officials of the League of Nations at Geneva, others permanent expatriates with business interests or family in Europe. *Most agreed to help.*" (R. Harris Smith, *OSS*, 211.) One of Dulles' employees from the very beginning was Mary Bancroft, a writer and journalist who belonged to Carl Gustav Jung's inner circle. "Mary was an immediate asset, with her literary style and curiosity, her ease in French and German, and her natural sophistication in a man's world. Mayer put her to work analyzing the German press, even bringing her Jungian insights to the speeches of Hitler, Göring, and Goebbels." (Grose, *Gentleman Spy*, 163.) Barely a month after Allen Dulles' arrival in Bern, at the beginning of December 1942 when she had already been working for Gerry Mayer for several months, he arranged a meeting between Mary Bancroft and Allen Dulles in Zürich. "That evening when I [Mary Bancroft] told Jean [Rüfenacht, her Swiss husband] that I had met the newly arrived special assistant to the American minister, he sighed in mock despair. 'Oh, you Americans! Everyone knows Dulles is the head of your Intelligence Service here—except, of course, you Americans! I assume you will be working for him. That's all right with me. But please be discreet, will you? Remember, the Swiss will know everything you do." (Mary Bancroft, *Autobiography of a Spy*, 129.) In the process a close working relationship and a close personal friendship developed quickly. Shortly after they started working together, Dulles remarked, "We can let the work cover the romance—and the romance cover the work!" All the

same, their relationship remained a well-kept secret. (Mary Bancroft, *Autobiography of a Spy*, 137.) The work part developed into a strict routine. Every morning precisely at 9:20, Dulles in Bern would telephone Mary Bancroft in Zürich to say what memos and reports he wanted from her that day, whom she should go to, or whom she ought to see to extract whatever information might be of use. Once a week, Mrs. Bancroft would travel by train to Bern, check in at the Schweizerhof hotel across from the main railway station, and then go over to Herrengasse 23 to get debriefed by Dulles. Then the two would sit together in his study and prepare for "his nightly phone call to the States, which went out over a line that was listened in on by the Swiss and presumably also by the Germans. No hard intelligence gathered by the American agents could be given for fear of revealing their whereabouts or activities. However, anything published in the European press could be used along with items attributable to 'a well-informed source'." (Mary Bancroft, *Autobiography of a Spy*, 145.) After only a very short period of time, Dulles had built up a vast network of contacts and connections that could be used for OSS interests. Cf. Bancroft: "*Useful* was a word that was constantly on his lips. He judged everyone and everything by the yardstick of its usefulness in the war effort, even going so far as to wonder why one of the men at the legation was getting married—he didn't consider the girl he was marrying 'useful'." (Mary Bancroft, *Autobiography of a Spy*, 134.) From the start Dulles had considered it important that his address was not kept secret so that it became a place to turn to.

120. Cf. President Truman's statement: "Mr. Dulles, within a year, effectively built up an intelligence network employing hundreds of informants and operatives, reaching into Germany, Yugoslavia, Czechoslovakia, Bulgaria, Hungary, Spain, Portugal, and North Africa, and completely covering France, Italy, and Austria. He assisted in the formation of various Maquis groups in France and supported the Italian partisan groups both financially and by pinpointing airdrops for supplies. The exceptional worth of his reports on bombing targets and troop movements both by land and sea was recognized by diplomatic, military, and naval agencies of the United States government. Particularly notable achievements by Mr. Dulles were first reports as early as August 1943 of the existence of a German experimental laboratory at Peenemünde for the testing of a rocket bomb, his report on the flooding of the Belgian and Dutch coastal areas long before similar information came in from other sources, his report on rocket-bomb installations in the Pas de Calais, and his reports on damage inflicted by the Allied Air Forces as a result of raids on Berlin and other German, Italian, and Balkan cities, which were forwarded within two or three days of the operations. Mr. Dulles, by his superior diplomacy and efficiency, built up for the U.S. government enormous prestige among leading figures of occupied nations taking refuge in Switzerland. He carried out his assignments in extremely hazardous conditions, and, despite the constant observation of enemy agents, was able to fulfill his duties in a manner reflecting the utmost credit on himself and his country. After the German collapse, Mr. Dulles headed the Office of Strategic Services mission in Germany, which supplied highly important and essential intelligence to American Military Government, occupation, and diplo-

matic offices during the difficult postwar period. His courage, rare initiative, exceptional ability, and wisdom provided an inspiration for those who worked with him and materially furthered the war effort of the United Nations." (Harry S Truman, Citation to accompany the award of the Medal for Merit to Allen W. Dulles, July 18, 1946. Princeton University Library, Allen W. Dulles Papers, box 19.)

121. On September 17, 1965, Allen Dulles wrote to John Toland, "I always denied that I was Roosevelt's Special Representative, but the Swiss press carried this rather consistently, and my denials were quite useless." (Princeton University Library, Allen W. Dulles Papers, box 146.) In his own description entitled *The Secret Surrender* (p. 18) Allen Dulles noted: "This flattering designation, in all its vagueness, was widely circulated, and even if I had wished to do something about it there was little I could do. A public denial would merely have advertised the report. Of course, it had the result of bringing to my door purveyors of information, volunteers, and adventurers of every sort, professional and amateur spies, good and bad. Donovan's operating principle was not to have his senior representatives try to go deep underground, on the very reasonable premise that it was futile and that it was better to let people know you were in the business of intelligence and tell them where they could find you. The unsolicited Swiss newspaper publicity put this principle into practice in short order, though not exactly in the terms I would have chosen for myself."

122. In his notes for an NBC television program on "Japanese Surrender Negotiations" dated March 26, 1965, Dulles wrote, "My official job was as a member of the American legation at Berne, but I was working with General William J. Donovan, head of the OSS. The rumor had spread about that I had been sent to Switzerland by President Franklin D. Roosevelt as his special representative. While this was not strictly true, *many of my reports did reach the White House and came to the attention first of President Roosevelt and then, after his death, President Truman.*" (Princeton University Library, Allen W. Dulles Papers, box 239.) At the presidential archives of the Franklin D. Roosevelt Library, Hyde Park, NY, this author indeed found numerous reports by Dulles that the President had apparently personally read.

123. Werner Müller, assistant chief of Group Id, to head of Foreign Office at the Federal Department of Foreign Affairs, December 26, 1942. Müller based his information on a "Political Report" by Hausamann dated December 24, 1942. Both documents are at BAr E 27/9980. Allen Dulles appraised the situation as follows: "The Swiss position in regard to my mission observed the proper decorum of neutrality, but it was a *benevolent neutrality*. The Swiss had to be assured, of course, of my discretion and good sense, and my full understanding of their position. For example, the Swiss desired to forestall any action on our part which, if it came to the attention of the Germans, could be thrown up to the Swiss as an instance of favoring one belligerent over the other. There was fear that any blatant breach of neutrality would be taken by the Germans as an excuse for reprisals. I cooperated to the utmost, by making it clear to the Swiss that I had no interest in spying on any Swiss measures of defense. The stronger they were in their preparations against a German attack, the better we liked it. The Germans, on the other hand, had agents and saboteurs in Switzerland spy-

ing out Swiss defense secrets. Scores of German agents were arrested, and a few were shot. We realized, of course, that the Swiss Intelligence Service, in the normal course of business, had contact with both German and Allied intelligence. Since the Swiss were neutral, they could maintain such connections with each group of belligerents, and in their own defense interest they were wholly justified in doing so. Misunderstandings were minimized by the fact that one set of Swiss intelligence officers worked chiefly with the Germans, and another with the Allies. Colonel Roger Masson, of the Swiss General Staff, had contact with Walter Schellenberg, the head of Himmler's Intelligence Service, and Max Waibel and his close associates consulted with us." (Allen Dulles, *The Secret Surrender*, 29.)

124. Cf. General Donovan's statement: "Switzerland is now, as it was in the last war, the *one most advantageous place for the obtaining of information concerning the European Axis powers*. Analysis of the telegrams reaching the State Department from various posts in Europe in which we still have representatives shows that the *information from Switzerland is far more important than from any other post*." (General William J. Donovan, memorandum for the President, May 27, 1942. Franklin D. Roosevelt Library, President's Secretary's File, box 166, folder 11, "OSS: Donovan Reports.")

125. However, Dulles soon realized that the unwanted publicity worked very much to his advantage, with members of all warring parties, including the neutrals, trying to establish contact with him precisely because of his intelligence-related task.

126. See Walter Laqueur and Richard Breitman, *Breaking the Silence* (New York, 1986), 191 (footnote).

127. Cf. Trevor-Roper's statement, "Like so many Germans, [Schellenberg] was an admirer, a despairing admirer, of the British Intelligence Service—an organisation of which he indeed knew very little, but of which he had evidently read much in those amazing novelettes which filled the reference library of the Gestapo." Hugh R. Trevor-Roper, *The Last Days of Hitler* (London: Macmillan & Co., 3rd ed., 1956), 30.

128. Military Attaché Berne, memorandum for the Director of Military Intelligence, December 9, 1920. National Archives, Washington, DC, RG 165, Military Intelligence Branch, 2610-R-5 (1).

129. Colonel H. Godson [U.S. Military Attaché in Bern] to Brigadier General M. Churchill, Chief Military Intelligence Branch, Washington, DC, September 16, 1918. National Archives, Washington, DC, RG 165, Military Intelligence Branch, 2243-17 (1918).

130. The excellent relations between Dulles and Swiss authorities were due not least to the fact that the head of OSS Switzerland showed a lot of understanding for the requirements of a credible neutrality policy; in his activities he made sure that he did not overstep the boundaries that the authorities had established. In reaction to a *Schweizer Illustrierte Zeitung* article (in no. 39 of September 21, 1953), Dulles wrote, "At no time did I have official Swiss clearance for clandestine wireless operations from any Swiss base. . . . There is no truth to this. . . . My regular wireless reports to Washington . . . were sent by the United States Legation in special code, as my book, 'Germany's Underground,' makes clear.

At no time, therefore, did I exploit my position in Switzerland for the operation of clandestine wireless." (Dulles, draft letter, no date [fall 1953]. Princeton University Library, Allen W. Dulles Papers, box 19.) Dulles knew that it was in his own interest not to try to outwit the Swiss. In summer 1944, he wrote to General Donovan, "Switzerland is [the] most incorruptible neutral nation in existence, and we must exercise the greatest tact in getting anything done here. The *Swiss counter-espionage is extremely wide awake*, and any mistake we made would eliminate the section of our organization which was involved—a serious matter with the absurdly small staff we possess." (Dulles to Director OSS, August 9, 1944. National Archives, Washington, DC, RG 226, entry 134, box 231, Wash-Sect-R&C-4, folder "Berne Incoming and Outgoing August 1944.")

131. Cf. the OSS's assessment of Switzerland in spring 1944, "Switzerland is the sole largely German speaking country of Europe which has not been engulfed by the Nazis and which has maintained those principles of freedom and democracy which must be inculcated in the new Germany if it is to become a peaceful state in Europe." OSS report, May 1, 1944 (transmitted from Bern to Washington, DC in plain language via radiophone). National Archives, Washington, DC, RG 226, entry 134, box 273, Wash-Sect-R&C-77, folder 3, "Berne-Radiophone-January 1944.

132. Cf. for instance Dulles' statement: "Recently I talked with General G[uisan] and made known to him that the situation in general was causing me some concern. He said that he would begin an investigation on his own. I think that his reason for requesting a talk with me was to try to gain some indication of whether or not it is probable that France will be invaded in the near future." (Dulles to OSS Director, Washington, DC, March 29, 1944. National Archives, Washington, DC, RG 226, entry 134, box 307, Wash-Sect-R&C-120, folder 2, "March 1944.")

133. Masson to Supreme Court Justice Couchepin, November 23,1945. BAr E 27/10027, vol. 1.

134. Józef Garlinski, *The Swiss Corridor: Espionage Networks in Switzerland during World War II* (London/Melbourne/Toronto, 1981), 121.

135. See pages 15 and 180.

136. See page 9 and 290, endnote 3.

137. Colonel Barnwell R. Legge to Assistant Chief of Staff, G-2, War Department, 22 October 1941, "Confidential Instructions on Obtaining Information." National Archives, Washington, DC, RG 319, Army Staff, ACSI, 1941–1945 Project Decimal Files, Switzerland.

138. Legge, "Confidential Instructions." It appears, however, that Masson exaggerated by exercising restraint toward the Allies; Chief of the General Staff Huber noted about a meeting with Masson, "American Military Attaché, Colonel *Legge*, is said to be *neglected* by Group Id. Change from earlier days." Huber underlined the word "neglected" seven times. (Lieutenant General Huber, notes on meeting with Masson, December 22, 1942. BAr E 27/14139.)

139. Cf. Allen Dulles' statement: "I did not see Hausamann while in Switzerland this time, but hope to do so on a subsequent visit if he would like to see me. If you happen to see him, you might mention this to him and see how he feels about

it." (Dulles to Walther Hofer, July 22, 1965. Princeton University Library, Allen W. Dulles Papers, box 142.)

140. Cf. B. Homer Hall's statement, "The OSS relationship with the Swiss, both from a military and political point of view, has proven mutually beneficial to the end that there have been many instances of complete cooperation in the gathering of intelligence." (B. Homer Hall, OSS Switzerland, to S.B.L. Penrose, April 23, 1945. National Archives, Washington, DC, RG 226, entry 99, box 99, Washington Historical Office-OP 23, envelope 660, "Budget material.")

141. Cf. the statement by OSS Bern:

> The Swiss, according to advices received by our source, possess drawings of rocket projectile catapults on the invasion coast. Source recommends that possibly we can arrange an exchange with them, since the Swiss would very much like to obtain the design of German radio equipment for beaming attacking airplanes. Our source says that the British captured the latter design in 1942 in a commando raid on Boulogne, and that he has this from a German inventor. (OSS Bern to OSS Washington, DC, April 6, 1944 (secret). National Archives, Washington, DC, RG 226, entry 134, box 307, Wash-Sect-R&C-120, folder 3, "Berne Incoming and Outgoing, April 1944.")

142. Cf. Garlinski's statement: "For his part Dulles was able to disclose those American plans of which the Swiss authorities needed to be appraised [*sic*]. They dealt with the country's neutrality and a number of minor concessions, mainly in favour of the Allied air units attacking targets in Germany and Italy." Garlinski, *The Swiss Corridor*, 121.

143. Lützelschwab stated that Hausamann wanted to protect the diplomat who had "proceeded in an absolutely undiplomatic manner, lodging his *protest by the back door*." (Lützelschwab to Kobelt, November 10, 1943. BAr J.I.137 1974/64, vol. 4.)

144. That was probably the main reason why Hausamann preferred to use Lützelschwab as an intermediary and remain in the background. One month before the meeting in Biglen, on February 5, 1943, Hausamann had written a controversial report according to which Pilet-Golaz had tried to convince U.S. Envoy Leland Harrison to conclude a separate peace treaty with Germany, arguing that "the Anglo-Saxons should let the Russians fight this war on their own." (Secret report, February 5, 1943. BAr E 5795/448, vol. 2.) Pilet-Golaz claimed that every word of that report was invented. Because Hausamann refused to reveal his informant's identity and was unable to substantiate his claim, on May 14, 1943 the Commander-in-Chief ordered the Chief of Intelligence to dismiss the head of Bureau Ha. At the same time, however, he recommended that Army Intelligence use Hausamann as a civilian agent (cf. Masson to Commander-in-Chief, 15 December 1943. BAr E 5795/448, vol. 2.) For about one year, Hausamann was not allowed to wear his uniform, which he considered to be a harsh and unfair punishment. After formally apologizing for his report, in 1944 he was readmitted to the military. (Documents at archives of H.R. Kurz.) If the allegations against Pilet-Golaz had been substantiated, the Foreign Minister might have become subject to a scandal resembling the affair surrounding Federal Councillor Arthur Hoffmann in 1917 (the Hoffmann-Grimm affair).

145. Lützelschwab explained, "I did not have any private relations with Hausamann. . . . As head of the political police, I was in contact with various authorities, including Army Intelligence, through which I came into contact with [Hausamann], among others." (Statement as a witness before the Zürich district court, May 2, 1947. BAr J.I.121/63.)

146. On November 9, 1943, Lützelschwab personally gave Kobelt a paraphrase of Hausamann's note for the file of October 26, 1943 (BAr J.I.137 1974/64, vol. 4); the following day he supplied the Head of the Military Department with additional information, which he had requested from Hausamann after the meeting with Kobelt.

147. Lützelschwab to Kobelt, November 10,1943. BAr r J.I. 137 1974/64, vol. 4.

148. See Masson to Supreme Court Justice Couchepin, November 6, 1945. BAr E 27/10027, vol. 1.

149. Masson to Couchepin, 6 Nov. 1945. Could Masson really expect Köcher or Ilsemann to confirm Allen Dulles' report?

150. Masson to Couchepin, Nov. 6, 1945. BAr E 27/10027, vol. 1.

151. Masson to Couchepin, Nov. 6, 1945: "Il m'apparaissait utile, pour ne pas *finassieren* plus longtemps, que Schellenberg fût informé de ce que pensaient certains Alliés et Suisses sur son 'honorabilité'. " BAr E 27/10027, vol. 1 (emphasis in original).

152. Annotation in a different handwriting, "No visa, therefore 2nd trip for H[olzach]." Due to the Federal Council's mistrust of the Masson-Schellenberg connection, following the meeting in Biglen, Eggen had difficulty in obtaining a visa to enter Switzerland; from late summer 1943 on, Masson and Rothmund were constantly at odds because of that.

153. Schellenberg to Masson, December 19, 1943. BAr E 27/10027, vol. 1. The German officer closed the letter with the words "Yours truly, your old sincere friend Walter Schellenberg."

154. Based on the papers of Allen Dulles that this author has studied, that seems unlikely.

155. In any event, such a document would be in contradiction with Schellenberg's report to Foreign Minister Ribbentrop (see page 196ff.).

156. For background information on Eggen's visit and its original purpose, see page 236 and 414, endnote 108.

157. Meyer, notes of April 14, 1943 re: meeting between Masson, Meyer, and Eggen in Muri near Bern. BAr J.I.121/1. On that occasion, Eggen said that Berlin knew that Meyer-Schwertenbach had resigned from his post at the Special Service of the security service. He explained that authorities at the Federal Palace in Bern had been told about Meyer being used elsewhere within Army Intelligence, adding, "[Werner] Müller is throwing spanners in the works. If he continues doing that, Schelli will not be able to maintain [the connection] any longer." (Meyer, notes of April 14, 1943. BAr J.I. 121/1.)

158. See Meyer, notes of April 13, 1943 re: meeting between Masson, Meyer, and Eggen in Muri near Bern. BAr J.I.121/1. Similar false reports and rumors had been circulating on earlier occasions. On September 24, 1940, the intelligence unit of the 4th Army Corps reported to Army Intelligence, "Through interrogations of Swiss who have returned from Italy, it has become clear that civilian

as well as military circles in Italy are perfectly convinced that the RAF has air force bases in our country from which the English bombers launch their raids on Italy. This causes a disturbing degree of ill humor toward our country." On September 27, 1940, Werner Müller, the deputy Chief of Intelligence, forwarded the report to the Commander-in-Chief, remarking, "We consider that steps should be taken through diplomatic channels to protest against these absurd rumors in Berlin and Rome and to tell the people that this information is false." (BAr E 27/9508, vol. 6, and E 27/9973.)

159. Meyer, notes, April 14,1943. BAr J.I. 121/1.

160. Meyer, notes, April 13,1943.

161. See Commander-in-Chief to Federal Councillor von Steiger (Kobelt's substitute), 17 July 1943. BAr E 27/9528. (The letter is erroneously dated June 17 instead of July 17.) Guisan's restraint was obviously due to his being reprimanded by the Federal Council because of the meeting in Biglen.

162. Pilet-Golaz, "Conférence avec le Colonel brigadier Masson," note for file, June 24, 1943. BAr E 2809/1.

163. Pilet-Golaz, note for file, June 24, 1943: "Le contact a été assez rapide, et, d'après Masson, complet: *atomes crochus*." BAr E 2809, vol 1. Pilet-Golaz' detailed records of his conversations reveal not only that he had an excellent memory but also that he was a remarkable stylist—a fact he tended to be rather conceited about. (Coversations between this author and Pilet-Golaz Jr., 1986–1988.)

164. From October 16 to 18, 1942, at Meyer-Schwertenbach's invitation Schellenberg stayed incognito at Wolfsberg Castle. He wrote in the guest book, "10/16–18/1942. Thank you very much for the kind hospitality. I hope to see you again soon at the beautiful Wolfsberg! Walter Schellenberg." (Guest book made available to this author by Patrizia Schwertenbach.)

165. Masson could not know that the meeting in Biglen had caused Pilet and others to strongly oppose the connection as such, but through Kobelt's reaction of course he knew that the federal government was critical about General Guisan's contacts with Schellenberg.

166. Pilet-Golaz wrote: "According to what I have been told, Schellenberg allegedly reported that at the Brenner [Pass] a rather lively discussion was said to have taken place concerning Switzerland because someone allegedly showed, or referred to, a file establishing that aircraft frequently left from our airfields, particularly Belp, to clandestinely transport documents, merchandise, information, or individuals to England, and that one also transported French citizens the same way, etc." (Pilet-Golaz, note for file, 24 June 1943. BAr E 2809/1.) The language that Pilet used to relate the rumor indicates how skeptical he was about the things that Masson had told him.

167. Pilet-Golaz, note for file, June 24, 1943. BAr E 2809/1.

168. See page 106.

169. Pilet-Golaz, note for file, June 24, 1943. BAr E 2809/1.

170. National Councillor Hans Oprecht, president of the Social Democratic Party of Switzerland and brother of publisher Emil Oprecht, at whose house Allen Dulles and Hans Hausamann used to meet. See also page 291, endnote 16.

Hans Oprecht, along with Walther Bringolf, was one of the harshest critics of Pilet-Golaz' policy.

171. Pilet-Golaz, note for file, June 24,1943. BAr E 2809/1.

172. The minutes of the Federal Council meeting of June 25, 1943 indicate that both Kobelt and Pilet-Golaz opposed Masson's plan. (BAr E 2809/1 and E 1004.1 1.)

173. Kobelt to Commander-in-Chief, June 25, 1943. BAr E 5795/455.

174. Kobelt, "vertraulicher Zusatzbericht zum Fall Masson," February 22, 1946. BAr E 27/10027, vol. 1.

175. Pilet-Golaz to Kobelt, February 9, 1946. BAr E 27/10027, vol. 1.

176. At midnight on July 1, 1943 at the *Bellevue Palace* in Bern, Masson, Wiesendanger, Eggen, and Meyer were filled with consternation, discussing the situation. They decided that Masson should personally go to see Pilet-Golaz with Eggen in order to try one more time to convince the Foreign Minister to authorize Masson to travel to Germany. See Meyer, notes, July 1, 1943. BAr J.I.121/1.

177. Cf. Meyer's statement: "Pilet-Golaz promises Masson to receive Eggen at his private home—explains on a map where it is located. However, he says that he has to speak with [Kobelt's substitute] v. Steiger first." (Meyer, notes, July 3, 1943. BAr J.I.121.1.) The following day Masson followed up on the matter with Pilet. The Federal Councillor informed him that he had "asked Minister [Karl] Stucki to receive Eggen—and depending on [Stucki's] feedback by telephone he would be available to see [Eggen] afterward. Masson [went] to see Minister Bonna [the head of the Foreign Service at the Department of Foreign Affairs] who explain[ed] to him that Pilet-Golaz [could] *not* receive Eggen. Masson [lost] his patience, replying that he [was] being told fibs and that an officer [could] not cope with the *liars' mentality that prevail[ed] at the Federal Palace.*" (Meyer, notes, July 4, 1943. BAr J.I.121/1.)

178. Counselor Karl Stucki, note, July 5, 1943. BAr E 2809/1, vol. 4.

179. Stucki, note, July 5, 1943.

180. Ibid.

181. Ibid.

182. Ibid.

183. Pilet-Golaz to Kobelt, July 9, 1943. BAr E 2809/1, vol. 4.

184. Cf. Pilet-Golaz' statement in his letter to Kobelt, July 9, 1943:
      [Karl Stucki] had not been asked into that meeting in order to keep minutes; in his capacity as head of the political section, which maintains relations with the army and the Justice and Police Department, I wanted him to know right away what I had to tell Eggen and that I maintained a very clear position on that issue. I wanted him to hear it then and there rather than having to fill him in at a later date in order to prevent Eggen—one was used to that from the Germans—and Colonel Masson, who had become much too involved in that matter, from toning down the irreducibly negative parts of my statement after seeing me. . . . Mr. Stucki did not know what my intentions were; I had not talked to him about them, nor was I under any obligation to do so, even less so because

he was not one of my direct collaborators. (Pilet-Golaz to Federal
President Karl Kobelt, February 9, 1946. BAr E 2800 1967/60,
vol. 23.)

185. Eggen had voiced the same opinion to Minister Karl Stucki before.
186. Pilet-Golaz to Federal President Kobelt, "Mon entretien avec le Rittmeister
Eggen," February 9, 1946. BAr E 27/10027, vol. 1.
187. Pilet-Golaz used a diplomatic language to express his veto, telling Eggen:
"[The civilian authorities] do not want to put any obstacles whatsoever in the way of the relations between Masson and
Schellenberg; on the contrary, we would be pleased to see the good
relations last. Even though the civilian authorities have well-functioning *regular diplomatic channels* available for dealing in an official manner with issues relating to the relations between
Switzerland and Germany, it is perfectly all right with us if General
Schellenberg returns to Switzerland again on many occasions to
rest or do sports and talks to his friend Masson during that time."
[At the end of the conversation] Pilet said he hoped that Cavalry
Captain Eggen, who he said very skillfully defended Germany's
point of view but also had a lot of understanding for Switzerland,
would take it upon himself to defend with as much skill
Switzerland's point of view in Berlin, advocate understanding for
us, and see to it that no one was annoyed. (Minister Karl Stucki,
notes on meeting between Pilet-Golaz and Eggen, July 14, 1943.
BAr E 2809/1, vol. 4.)
Pilet read these notes at the Federal Council meeting of July 16, 1943.
188. Pilet-Golaz, "Mon entretien avec le Rittmeister Eggen." BAr E 27/10027, vol.
1.
189. The Head of the Federal Department of Economic Affairs, Federal Councillor
Walther Stampfli, had come up with the idea for the ban on foreign travels for
officers; cf. minutes of Federal Council meeting of July 16, 1943: "In order to
prevent similar incidents in the future, the Council should tell the
Commander-in-Chief that during the war it did not allow any high-ranking
officer to travel to Germany." (BAr E 2809/1, vol. 4, and E 1004.1 1.)
190. Federal Councillor von Steiger, deputy head of the Military Department, on
behalf of the entire Federal Council, to Commander-in-Chief, July 16, 1943.
BAr E 27/9528. Cf. von Steiger's statement:
I pointed out to the General that a case like Masson's could not
repeat itself; it is not acceptable for the General to tell the concerned high-ranking officer that he has no objections to his traveling abroad if the Federal Council approves of the trip and then
leaves it up to the officer to contact the Federal Council to obtain
its approval. I politely but firmly pointed out to the General that it
was his responsibility to come to an agreement with the Federal
Council before giving the concerned officer any response. The
General realized that that view was correct and assured me that he
would follow that procedure in the future. However, he insisted on
telling me that the Masson case had been the only case of that kind

and that no other higher-ranking officers had traveled abroad for any political purposes. (Von Steiger to Walther Stampfli, July 27, 1943. BAr E 2809/1, vol. 4.)

It should be pointed out, however, that Major General Eugen *Bircher's trips to Berlin* as well as the *medical missions to Germany's* Eastern front that he organized were of a highly political nature. On that issue, see the detailed account in Heller, *Eugen Bircher*, 196 ff.

191. Von Steiger to Commander-in-Chief, July 16, 1943. BAr E 27/10027, vol. 1.
192. See Meyer, note on lunch with General Guisan and Barbey, July 27, 1943. BAr J.I.121/1. In view of the Federal Council's position, the Commander-in-Chief took note of the upcoming trip only "unofficially" because Meyer-Schwertenbach once again used a private business trip as a cover-up. (Concerning the dates of the trip, see endnote 194 below.)
193. He had been on his first trip from July 7 to 9, 1942. Concerning the reasons for that trip, see page 166.
194. The trip took place from July 28 to 30, 1943. (In his note for the file, Meyer erroneously wrote *August* instead of *July*.)
195. Three days earlier, on July 25, 1943, two weeks after the Allied landing in Sicily, Mussolini had been ousted from power.
196. Meyer, notes on second trip to Berlin, July 28,1943. BAr J.I.121/1.
197. The report is dated August 3, 1943. (BAr E 5795/333.) General Guisan, Chief of the General Staff Huber, and Chief of Security Werner Müller received copies of it.
198. Masson, report, August 3, 1943. BAr E 5795/333.

Chapter 10: Test Case for the Connection: The Alert of March 1943

1. See Fuhrer, *Spionage*, 82.
2. Along with General von Buttlar, *Gisevius* was one of the main proponents of that interpretation; see Gisevius, statement to the investigating magistrate, Colonel Otto Müller, hearing of 25 June 1945. BAr E 5330 1982/1, vol. 205. Hans Bernd Gisevius, a Ph.D. in law, had started working in Zürich as an agent for German Intelligence on October 1, 1940, using the position of vice consul to camouflage his *Abwehr* activities. He belonged to Admiral Canaris' entourage. Even though he was an ambivalent character because his activities had also been directed against Switzerland, Waibel considered that in this instance he was a *trustworthy* witness; see Waibel to investigating magistrate Otto Müller, 27 June 1945. BAr E 5330 1982/1, vol. 205.
3. See Accoce & Quet, *Moskau wusste alles*, 208–230; Kimche, *General Guisans Zweifrontenkrieg*, 145–146; Matt, *Zwischen allen Fronten*, 194.
4. Hans Frölicher, *Meine Aufgabe in Berlin* (Bern, 1962), privately printed, 77. (His son Max Frölicher kindly offered a copy of the book to this author.)
5. Hans Rudolf Kurz, "Der März-Alarm 1943," *Der Fourier* no. 1 (1984).
6. Kurz, "Der März-Alarm 1943."
7. See page 23ff.
8. Concerning the international military-political situation, see page 187ff.
9. Secret report, 3 December 1942. On December 5, 1942, General Guisan trans-

mitted the report to Kobelt, to the attention of the entire Federal Council. BAr E 27/14334.

10. Secret report, 3 Dec. 1942.
11. Secret report, 3 Dec. 1942.
12. Secret report, 3 Dec. 1942.
13. Secret report, 3 Dec. 1942.
14. Secret report, 3 Dec. 1942.
15. On this matter, see, among others, Kurt Emmenegger, *Q.N. wusste Bescheid: Erstaunliche Informationen eines Schweizer Nachrichtenmannes aus den Kulissen des Hitlerkrieges* (Zürich, 1965). Like most other collaborators of Army Intelligence, Johann Conrad Meyer had to continue working in his civilian job to make a living; nevertheless, he regularly supplied N.S.1 with reports and summaries. In general, he typed a report of two to five pages a day, plus several special economic reports a week that dealt with the economic problems of the belligerent powers, particularly Germany and Italy. In addition, he interviewed international travelers on behalf of *Rigi* and evaluated the confidential reports by English and American press agencies. Writing the reports for N.S.1 was just the final phase of his work; before that he collected the information, got the flow of information going, and initiated new connections or re-established dormant ones. The personal contacts with his sources and informants were particularly time-consuming. *Sx* later recalled: "We often worked non-stop 24 hours a day. I don't know how we did it, but somehow we managed and survived. We were young, and we just knew that the quality and reliability of our work could be decisive." (Emmenegger, *Q.N. wusste Bescheid*, 67–68.) Like Meyer-Schwertenbach, Johann Conrad Meyer was temporarily assigned to the *Uto* sub-office.
16. Emmenegger, *Q.N. wusste Bescheid*, 118–119.
17. Special report no. 43, December 17, 1942. BAr E 5795/329. Concerning the source's capabilities, Max Waibel remarked, " In mid-March 1940, *Viking* supplied us with [Germany's] plan for the invasion of Scandinavia, on April 30, [1940,] it informed us about the beginning of the campaign in the West, and on May 1, 1941, about the campaign against Russia." (Special report no. 43, Dec. 17, 1942.)
18. Special report no. 43, Dec. 17, 1942. BAr E 5795/329.
19. *Rigi*, special report, December 18, 1942. BAr E 5795/329. (Even though the report was dated after report no. 43, it was numbered no. 42.)
20. In view of the circumstances at the Führer's headquarters at the time, Klaus Urner considers as quite absurd the idea that such a conference took place. (See Urner, "Im Visier der deutschen Spionage," *Tages-Anzeiger Magazin*, no. 13 [1982].) However, based on this author's research the information was accurate but was transmitted as an inverted signal (see page 229).
21. *Rigi*, special report, Dec. 18, 1942. BAr E 5795/333.
22. Forty to 45 miles per hour; even according to current standards, that is a high speed for moving troops.
23. *Rigi*, special report no. 42, Dec. 18, 1942. BAr E 5795/329.
24. Urner, "Im Visier der deutschen Spionage," 64.
25. Kurz, "Der März-Alarm 1943," *Der Fourier* no. 1 (1984).

26. Kurz, "Der März-Alarm 1943."
27. The day on which Operation Torch began; see page 187.
28. Commander-in-Chief to Kobelt, December 20, 1942. BAr E 27/14338. It is not clear what source supplied the information, nor when it was received. Based on Guisan's statement, it appears possible that this report also came from Viking.
29. *Kriegstagebuch des Oberkommandos der Wehrmacht (Wehrmachtführungsstab)*, vol. II, January 1, 1942–December 31, 1942, compiled and annotated by Andreas Hillgruber (Frankfurt a.M., 1963), 916 (entry by Helmuth Greiner). As far as this author can tell, Klaus Urner was first to notice the contradiction between the report by Swiss Intelligence and the OKW war journal (see Urner, "Im Visier der deutschen Spionage," which is a review of Hans Rudolf Fuhrer's 1982 Ph.D. thesis *Spionage*). Urner viewed the journal entry as written evidence for the fact that the alert of March 1943 was based on false information. This author would like to qualify that statement by adding that contradictions and pieces of information such as the one concerning November 8, 1942 that were obviously wrong indicate that Swiss Intelligence was *deceived*. However, a clear assessment of whether the alert of March 1943 was based on a real threat can be made only after analyzing all the documents that are referred to in this chapter.
30. The Führer's headquarters consisted of Hitler's immediate entourage as well as other staff that were not stationed at the same location. It included the command staff of the Wehrmacht and the Führer's escort battalion. From June 24, 1941 on, the Führer's headquarters was located at the *Wolfsschanze* camp in the Görlitz Forest, east of Rastenburg in East Prussia. The German Army High Command (OKH) and the Air Force Command had their field quarters in East Prussia as well, near Angerburg and Rominten, respectively; the German Navy High Command remained in Berlin. Between July 16 and November 1, 1942, the entire Führer's headquarters was stationed at the *Werwolf* camp, 15 kilometers northeast of Winniza in Ukraine. Hitler spent very little time at headquarters; in early 1942, the Führer, who was sometimes accompanied by his closest aides, spent several weeks at the Berghof in Berchtesgaden, where he stayed again in November 1942 for about 10 days. He also stayed in Berlin and Munich for short periods of time and paid a few short visits to the headquarters of the army groups in the East. The frequent absences from his staff created problems; see Andreas Hillgruber's introduction to the *Kriegstagebuch des Oberkommandos der Wehrmacht*, vol. II.
31. The only unit that remained at the Führer's headquarters was the field detachment of the Wehrmacht command staff, headed by the 1st general staff officer of the army at the Wehrmacht command staff, Colonel Baron Treusch von Buttlar-Brandenfels. (See *Kriegstagebuch des OKW*, entry by Greiner concerning 7 November 1942, 916.)
32. *Kriegstagebuch des OKW*, 922.
33. See Galeazzo Ciano, *Tagebücher 1939–1943* (Bern, 1946), 486 ff. (entries of 9–11 November 1942).
34. Hitler did not change his mind about France until November 9, 1942. On the evening of November 10 he decided to march into unoccupied southern France.

35. General Walter Warlimont, born 1894, died in 1976. In December 1940, together with Alfred Jodl, this loyal supporter of National Socialism had drafted the first plans for Operation *Barbarossa*, the invasion of the Soviet Union. On October 27, 1948, Warlimont was tried as a war criminal and sentenced to life in prison. His prison sentence was later reduced to 18 years, but he was released from the Landsberg penitentiary as early as 1957.

36. *Kriegstagebuch des OKW*, vol. II, explanations by General Warlimont re: Greiner's entry of November 9, 1942, 927.

37. See Emmenegger, *Q.N. wusste Bescheid*, 119.

38. Special report no. 44, January 16, 1943. BAr E 5795/329.

39. General Dietl spent most of the winter of 1942–1943 in Lapland, at the head-quarters in Rovaniemi. However, the war journal of the OKW shows that on January 15, 1943, of all days, the commander-in-chief of the German 20th Mountain Army arrived at the Führer's headquarters for talks (*Kriegstagebuch des OKW*, vol. II, 39 and 47, entries of 14 and 17 January 1943). Had the informant for Swiss Intelligence found out about Dietl's presence at the Führer's headquarters, wrongly concluding that Hitler had summoned him there to discuss an operation against Switzerland? Dietl actually went to the Führer's head-quarters to push ahead with preparations for blocking Russia's expected large-scale offensive in the northern sector of the front in the East.

40. Special report no. 44, January 16, 1943. On that issue, cf. the letter of March 23, 1943 by the Chief of Security (represented by Colonel Trachsel of the General Staff) to the command of *Groupe du Lac* (counterintelligence), which stated:

> A "Special Task Force for Switzerland" was created recently within the Gestapo that is stationed in France. . . . [It] works together with a second "Special Task Force for Switzerland" that is based in Stuttgart and is part of the Security Service of the SS. In close contact with German and Swiss informants, the mission of the two special task forces is to . . . prepare steps for the police to intervene in Switzerland in the event of a German occupation. The first step will be to *take* those individuals *out of action* who are to be eliminated in an interest to make the German operation run smoothly. These individuals allegedly include members of the federal government and some cantonal governments, top officers of the federal police, leading politicians, and certain editors. It is said that four lists are being prepared for Switzerland that will serve as the basis for the Gestapo's and the SS Security Service's intervention. List I is said to include those individuals who will have to be "secured" first in order to thwart reactions. List II supposedly includes those individuals whom one wants to call to account for the "hostility" that they have shown toward the Reich.

According to the report, the preparations of both special task forces inside Switzerland were supervised by von Bibra. (BAr E 27/14334)

41. Ernst Wilhelm Bohle, born 1903, died 1960, regional NSDAP leader and leader of the NSDAP foreign branches. At the *Wilhelmstrasse* trial in Nuremberg, Bohle was the only defendant who pleaded guilty. On April 14,

1949 he was sentenced to five years in prison; the time he had spent in custody was taken into account in the prison sentence. As early as December 1949, Bohle was released from prison after being pardoned by U.S. High Commissioner McCloy. He then worked as a merchant in Hamburg and died at the age of 57 in Düsseldorf.

42. See page 193.

43. Special report no. 44, Jan. 16, 1943. BAr E 5795/329.

44. Cf. Klaus Urner's ironic remark: "[That] scenario was probably meant to flatter the vain Swiss. It had little to do with the way Hitler actually made his decisions." Urner, "Im Visier der deutschen Spionage," 64.

45. Special report no. 45, January 26, 1943. BAr E 5795/329.

46. Commander-in-Chief to Kobelt, January 29,1943. BAr E 27/14334. The following day, Barbey noted in his diary, "Our intelligence service is producing a certain number of documents coming from the *Viking* source." (Barbey, *P.C. du Général*, 150.) Due to that diary entry, January 30, 1943 was erroneously believed to be the day when *Viking* had reported Germany's plans for an invasion. As far as this author can tell, Fuhrer (*Spionage*, 84) was the first scholar to point out, after analyzing the relevant reference material at the Swiss Federal Archives, that the first warnings had reached *Rigi* earlier than that.

47. According to a decision by the Federal Council dated February 10, 1942, the Advisory Board for Press-Related Matters consisted of twelve leading journalists who were named by the Federal Council and representatives of the Press and Radio Section. Its purpose was to liaise between the censorship authorities and the press. See Christoph Graf, *Zensurakten aus der Zeit des Zweiten Weltkriegs*, 126–127.

48. Kobelt, speech on the military-political situation, February 12, 1943. (Shorthand notes taken by Hans Neuenschwander.) BAr J.I.140/4, vol. 5.

49. A little less than two weeks earlier General Paulus had surrendered at Stalingrad with the remaining troops of the 6th Army.

50. Kobelt, speech on the military-political situation, February 12, 1943. BAr J.I. 140/4, vol. 5.

51. Kobelt, speech, February 12, 1943.

52. Masson, "La situation militaire internationale et la Suisse," February 16, 1943. BAr E 5795/448, vol. 2.

53. See Emmenegger, *Q.N. wusste Bescheid*, 119.

54. *Viking*, report, March 18, 1943. BAr E 27/14339.

55. *Viking*, report, March 18, 1943.

56. Nevertheless, the entry of March 19, 1943 in Army Intelligence's journal read, "Commotion among Group Id; 'Viking' announces that the OKW is about to make far-reaching decisions concerning Switzerland. First reinforcement measures and preparations." (BAr E 27/9509, vol. 5.) Also, Colonel Werner Müller requested that the Chief of the General Staff call up an additional three officers to serve on the Intelligence Service, arguing, "Last night we received reports that *make it look* as if it is *urgently required* to be more vigilant in the near future and for the Intelligence Service to be more active than usual." (Italics are underlined in the original text.) Werner Müller to Chief of the General Staff, March 19, 1943. BAr 27/9508, vol. 13.

57. Assistant Chief of Staff Id, potential scenario (secret), March 19, 1943. BAr E 27/14334.
58. On that issue, see, among others, Fuhrer, *Spionage*, 63 ff.
59. *Viking*, report no. 3277, March 19, 1943. BAr E 27/14339.
60. *Viking*, report no. 3280, March 20, 1943. BAr E 27/14339.
61. Erich von Manstein, born 1887, died 1973, was named field marshal on July 1, 1942 on the eve of his conquest of Sevastopol. He is considered to have been one of the most capable German commanders in World War II. He had drafted the plan of operations for the 1940 invasion of France that was characterized by an advance of massive tank forces through the wooded Ardennes and the conquest of crossing-points at the Meuse River. On November 27, 1942, von Manstein was put in command of the newly created Army Group *Don* that was supposed to rescue the encircled 6th Army. Even though it was too late for that, he successfully reorganized the retreating German armed forces. In February and March 1943 he managed to push the Russians back to the Donets and reconquer Kharkov (on March 14, 1943). General von Manstein was a military expert who was not interested at all in politics; he was indifferent toward the Nazis' goals, nor did he join the resistance movement against Hitler. After the war he was arrested by British troops and on December 19, 1949 a British courtmartial in Hamburg sentenced him to 18 years in prison. His sentence was later reduced to 12 years, but based on a medical certificate he was released as early as May 1953. Von Manstein subsequently worked as a military advisor for the West German government. He died in Irschenhausen near Munich at the age of 85.
62. *Viking*, report no. 3280, March 20, 1943. BAr E 27/14339.
63. See Barbey, *P.C. du Général*, 156 ff. (entry of March 20, 1943), and verbal statements by Major General Peter Burckhardt to this author, February–March 1988. Burckhardt accompanied Gonard to the meeting with the Commander-in-Chief. Several weeks later he was detailed to Berlin as military attaché.
64. Barbey, *P.C. du Général*, 156.
65. The Commander-in-Chief explained to the army unit commanders why he ordered the security measures, arguing:

> Our Intelligence Service, which was informed ahead of time about the beginning of the Allied offensive in Tunisia, has factual information according to which the events in the Central Mediterranean sector and the specific situation of our country are interdependent. . . . The belligerent parties are keeping a close eye on the issue of Switzerland's national defense and the army's degree of preparedness. *Even though the situation is definitely not alarming, it is serious enough* to justify taking some basic security measures now as well as some others that I may have to take in the course of the coming weeks if necessary. *The time has come to prove to foreign countries as well as our own country, through actions, that we adapt our preparations to the latest situation and to any contingency.*

(In the last sentence, General Guisan borrowed phrases from his Chief of Intelligence; see Masson's assessment of the situation on February 16, 1943 in the section "Warnings Received by Swiss Intelligence" earlier in this chapter.) Commander-in-Chief to commanders of 1st to 4th Army Corps, 1st to 9th Divisions, etc., March 23, 1943. BAr E 5795/327.

66. The actual number of troops on duty was calculated on the basis of the target number minus 20% of men on leave due to work in the agricultural sector.

67. "Massnahmen des Armeekommandos mit Rücksicht auf die gegenwärtige Lage, vom General in eigener Zuständigkeit erlassen," March 20, 1943. BAr E 27/14339.

68. Barbey, *P.C. du Général*, 157.

69. *Viking*, report no. 3285, March 22, 1943. BAr E 5795/334.

70. Masson to Commander-in-Chief, March 23, 1943. BAr E 5795/334.

71. Last German attempt at an offensive at the Eastern front.

72. According to unpublished notes by a participant at the conference, printed in Andreas Hillgruber, *Einführung [zum] Kriegstagebuch des Oberkommandos der Wehrmacht (Wehrmachtführungsstab)*, vol. II (Frankfurt a.M., 1963 [offprint]), 122.

73. At that time he was still a colonel on the General Staff.

74. Correspondence between Hans Rudolf Kurz and General von Buttlar-Brandenfels, 1954–1955. Archives of H.R. Kurz.

75. Because on September 24, 1942 Halder was replaced by General Zeitzler as chief of the general staff of the army (due to Halder's objection to Hitler's decision to take away troops from the rest of the front in order to conquer Stalingrad), and because there was a crisis of confidence between Hitler and Jodl, the chief of the Wehrmacht command staff. In October 1942, in the area of land warfare, the German Armed Forces High Command was split into two staffs that worked next to each other. Zeitzler was put in full charge of the Eastern front, whereas Jodl's Wehrmacht command staff remained responsible for the remaining theaters of war, which were henceforth called "OKW theaters of war."

76. General von Buttlar to H.R. Kurz, printed in Kurz, "Die militärischen Bedrohungen der Schweiz im Zweiten Weltkrieg," *Allgemeine Schweizerische Militärzeitschrift*, March 1955, 174–175.

77. Apparently *Viking's* contact person had found out about that discussion when he transmitted to N.S.1 the information about a conference of the top commanders of the German Army Police, the Security Service of the SS, and the Gestapo; see page 218ff.

78. On this issue, see, among others, Hans Rudolf Kurz, *Operationsplanung Schweiz: Die Rolle der Schweizer Armee in zwei Weltkriegen* (Thun, 1974), and Werner Roesch's Ph.D. thesis, *Bedrohte Schweiz: Die deutschen Operationsplanungen gegen die Schweiz im Sommer/Herbst 1940 und die Abwehrbereitschaft der Armee im Oktober 1940* (Frauenfeld, 1986).

79. On December 20, 1943, SS Colonel Boehme, a former Austrian chief of intelligence, presented a "Denkschrift über die Wehrlage der Schweiz unter besonderer Berücksichtigung einer erforderlich werdenden deutschen bewaffneten Intervention" (memorandum on Switzerland's military situation, with special consideration for a required future armed intervention by Germany). However, his plan contained so many false assumptions that it could not be further pur-

sued. See Hans Rudolf Kurz, "Im Blickfeld der fremden Generalstäbe," in *Die Schweiz im Zweiten Weltkrieg*, ed. H.R. Kurz (Thun, 1959), 63–64.

80. General von Buttlar to H.R. Kurz, printed in Kurz, "Die militärischen Bedrohungen," 174–175.

81. In spring 1943, Hitler removed Greiner as keeper of the war journal because of his anti-Nazi attitude.

82. The fact that in March 1943 the OKW war journal reported the Führer's head-quarters as discussing the fate of another neutral state shows that it would also have mentioned deliberations concerning Switzerland if such deliberations had been made. In connection with Russia's imminent large-scale offensive in the northern sector of the front in the East, *Sweden's* stance became very important. On March 10, 1943, the OKW war journal stated:

> In view of the inscrutable position of the Swedish government and the overt hostility of many Swedes, the Wehrmacht command staff suggested an order to Army Area Norway stating that it should think about steps that might have to be taken if Sweden intervened on the enemy's side. It has been suggested to order mobile warfare in order to prevent the landed enemy from combining forces with Sweden and shield the major harbors from the interior of the country. Moreover, every opportunity should be used to stage offensive operations across the border in order to nip possible Swedish attacks in the bud. In the event that Sweden remains neutral and defends itself on its own, our requests shall be presented to the Swedish government. The suggested order was not approved in that form. . . . The OKW is preparing an order informing army area Norway and the Commander-in-Chief of the 20th (Mountain) Army [General Dietl] about the Führer's order to army area Norway to establish, in cooperation with the high command of the 20th (Mountain) Army, a short study on the combat strategy for all of Scandinavia in the event that the military and political situation should change there. The following conditions shall be used as a basis . . . . The ordered preparations shall be handled by a very restricted circle and are exclusively a matter of the high command. The Navy High Command for Norway and Air Armada 5 may be involved in the study. At the Führer's order, this order is not issued. It will be communicated verbally to the Chief of the General Staff of the high command of (Mountain) Army 20 and the Ia of the Army High Command for Norway at the briefing of March 16[, 1943]. *(Kriegstagebuch des OKW (Wehrmachtführungsstab)*, vol. III, 1 January–December 31, 1943. Compiled and annotated by Walther Hubatsch (Frankfurt a.M., 1963), 199–200.)

83. Ret. Head of Section Helmuth Greiner to H.R. Kurz, printed in Kurz, "Die militärischen Bedrohungen," 175–176. It might be objected that Greiner's statement is no clear evidence for the argument that the alert of March 1943 was not based on any actual threat because Greiner did not know about the earlier German studies for an attack on Switzerland that have been discovered

since then. However, Kurz refutes that argument with the plausible explanation that the plans, about which every word is known today, were no plans of operation that were to be used right away; instead, they were drafts that had been established for possible future use and were put on file indefinitely. That was the reason why the keeper of the war journal was not informed about them. Kurz comments: "In reference to early 1943, that means that it is absolutely possible that in spring 1943 simple draft studies were made that were not reported to the [keeper of the] war journal; however, that is *highly unlikely* and would not fit in with the characteristics of the alert of March 1943. On the other hand, from Greiner's report it can be concluded that in early 1943 the German leadership definitely did not consider any immediate offensive action against Switzerland." (Kurz, "Die militärischen Bedrohungen," 176.)

84. The idea suggests itself that the issue of Switzerland was also raised in winter 1942–1943 when strategic matters were discussed. Opportunities for such discussions presented themselves at briefings concerning the situation per se, during conversations around Hitler's dinner table, or at officers' messes. The atmosphere at the Führer's headquarters, where some far-reaching decisions were made, is reflected in the personal notes of Major Gerhard Engel of the general staff, the army's personal adjutant at the Führer's HQ. On November 20, 1942 he wrote, "A typical assessment of the situation. Complete chaos because of the Romanians; everyone clings to Heim. Even Führer is totally uncertain about what to do. Opinions diverge, A[rmy] H[igh] C[ommand] does not make any specific suggestions either." And on 21 December he noted, "As before, no final decisions have been made." (Quoted by Andreas Hillgruber, *Einführung [zum] Kriegstagebuch des OKW*, 83 and 88.) On this and other occasions, every involved person expressed his requests, preferences, and opinions; since everyone, especially among the party, did not like Switzerland, some people certainly expressed harsh words and menaces against it and made demands. Because neither *Viking's* informants nor any of the other individuals who issued warnings were present at any major military and political discussions among the German leadership, generally receiving their information from third parties, it is not surprising that some information was distorted or made to sound more serious than it actually was. Moreover, the bodies of Swiss Army Intelligence that received warnings did not keep any of them back; whenever there was any doubt they preferred transmitting a warning rather than holding on to it, considering that the damage caused by a too pessimistic piece of information was smaller than that caused by underestimating a danger.

85. Minister Frölicher confirmed this information in his report on the critical times in the relations between Germany and Switzerland. He wrote: "In early 1943, when trade negotiations were held and we put up resistance to Germany's requests for additional credits, I also received a piece of information according to which Germany was once again discussing the issue of Switzerland. By that time the Anglo-Americans had purged Africa and were about to land in Sicily. Federal Councillor Pilet, who pointed out these rumors to me, agreed with me that this was trade policy-related scare tactics rather than any actual threat." (Frölicher to Federal Councillor Petitpierre, July 10, 1945. BAr E 2809/1, vol. 4.)

86. Max Petitpierre to Kobelt, October 2, 1945. BAr E 27/10028.

87. Cf. Cuénoud's statement: "In my opinion, 'March 1943' belongs to the category of 'unlikely' hypotheses." Cuénoud to Pierre Huser, October 7, 1966. Court files of Tschudi vs. Hausamann (made available to this author by Erwin Tschudi).

88. *"Den Schweizern ein bisschen Pfeffer in den Arsch streuen,"* see Emmenegger, *Q.N. wusste Bescheid*, 120.

89. Von Ilsemann, statement to Military Attorney General Eugster, January 11,1946. BAr E 5795/335.

90. Barbey, *P.C. du Général*, 158 (entry of 23 March 1943).

91. Meyer, notes re: alert of March 1943, March 19, 1943. BAr J.I.121/1.

92. Why should the Zürich Police Inspector have received such secret information? Probably Captain Meyer simply had an urge to share the threatening information with someone else.

93. Meyer, diary, March 19, 1943. BAr J.I. 121/1.

94. Concerning Weidenmann, see page 149.

95. "Dr. Berg" was Schellenberg's cover name in Switzerland. See interrogation of Eggen, Justice Palace Nuremberg, March 18, 1948. National Archives, Washington, DC, RG 238 M 1019 R 15.

96. Conversation between Meyer and Eggen, March 20, 1943. BAr J.I.121/69.

97. A method that was commonly used, particularly in letters and telephone conversations. The conversation was seemingly harmless, but the two men used cover sentences and clues that were known only to insiders. In his report on Army Counterintelligence's work during wartime duty, Chief of Counterintelligence Robert Jaquillard gave a particularly graphic example of that method. A seemingly trivial letter by an agent that had fallen into his hands read:

> I was able to also enlarge my collection of precious stones and crystals. I brought some splendid specimens with me. Some of the places where I found them were so strange that one might think that they had been placed there by human hands as unique monuments. In a relatively small area, I was also able to find some quite beautiful rocks with embedded crystals; some were small, others were large. I keep noticing that every scheme is new and interesting, even if nature adjusts to the existing conditions. Sometimes I receive some quite nice specimens from our friend Pet. Tollardo, who has some rare specimens once in a while and likes trading them. Maybe you could inquire with him if you are interested in anything particular.

Swiss Counterintelligence managed to filter the real meaning out of these harmless lines of text. The agent told the addressee:

> My observations in the mountains showed some good results. I brought some good sketches and drawings of bunkers with me. They are built in a way that makes you think that they have been fit into the landscape as monuments. In a relatively small area, I also saw some bunkers that are skillfully embedded in the rocks; some were small, others were large. I must say that they are well

adjusted to the conditions. Sometimes I receive information and plans from agent Tollardo, who has done some good work once in a while and likes selling these plans. You can approach him if you have anything in particular.

That example is quoted in Huber, *Bericht des Generalstabschefs* (appendix no. 2, 487–488).

98. Meyer, note, March 20, 1943. BAr J.I.121/1.
99. See page 383, endnote 49.
100. See page 30.
101. Meyer, diary, March 23, 1943. BAr J.I. 121/1.
102. Meyer, diary, March 23, 1943.
103. Meyer, diary, March 23, 1943.
104. The unsuspecting Swiss obviously did not realize what Eggen had the cheek to ask from them. Were they in all seriousness expected to thank the Germans for refraining from attacking Switzerland?
105. See page 207ff.
106. Meyer, diary, March 23, 1943. A few weeks later, the reasons for the planned visit with Himmler had changed; see page 207.
107. Meyer noted: "Then [Masson] calls Colonel v.Wattenwyl in Oberdiessbach, where the Commander-in-Chief is staying. He says, 'My information has been fully confirmed; the disaster would have hit us the day after tomorrow. You can go ahead and have your cup of coffee. I will tell you the details on Thursday.'" (Meyer, diary, 23 March 1943. BAr J.I. 121/1.) Eggen must have been a remarkable actor to be able to listen to that conversation without showing any reaction.
108. The letter read:
   Dear General:
      I feel a deep urge to thank you very much for everything that you have done so far, and especially for what you did recently, for our country and our bilateral relations. Mr. W. Eggen has informed me on your behalf. I would also like to thank you for the invitation to a meeting in Berlin at which our trust is to be deepened for the benefit of both states. This is the *only* way to once and for all remove any misunderstandings that may still exist. I look forward to seeing you again soon.
   Yours devoted ly,
   Masson. (Draft at BAr J.I.121/1.)
   The style in which the letter was written shows that Schwertenbach was its author; in addition, it clearly demonstrates what expectations Masson and Meyer had of their secret channel to Berlin.
109. Cf. Meyer's statement: "Afterwards we sit together until 12 at night, drinking a bottle of champagne; we are glad that we were spared that ordeal." (Meyer, diary, March 23, 1943. BAr J.I. 121/1.)
110. Meyer, diary, March 23, 1943.
111. Gottlob Berger, born 1896, was one of Himmler's key staff members. He was considered to be the driving force behind the efforts to build up the *Waffen SS* as an international army and use it as a tool to forge strong bonds among the

"ethnic German community" that was spread throughout Axis-controlled Europe. As head of the SS Central Office, Berger was a tough, unscrupulous organizer. After the war he was tried as an accessory to the Holocaust and on April 2, 1949 a U.S. tribunal in Nuremberg sentenced him to 25 years in prison. On January 31, 1951 the sentence was reduced to ten years, but Berger was released from prison the same year, after serving six and a half years. He died on January 5, 1975.

112. Franz Riedweg, a medical doctor, was born in 1907 in Lucerne. After finishing his studies, he became politically active as a member of the Swiss Federal Task Force against Communism that was headed by former Federal Councillor Musy. In 1938 he emigrated to Germany for ideological reasons. In summer 1938 he married a daughter of Werner von Blomberg, the Reich Minister of War and Commander-in-Chief of the Wehrmacht, whom Hitler had forced to resign in February 1938. On July 1, 1938, Riedweg joined the SS (SS no. 293,744). On Himmler's orders, in fall 1940 he was assigned to the Swiss Department of Branch VI at the Reich Security Central Office for six-months' training. During that time, Riedweg was able to network with other German authorities that also dealt with the "issue of Switzerland." In April 1941 he was transferred to the Regional Headquarters for Germanic Volunteers at the SS Central Office under Lieutenant General Berger, where he rose to the rank of SS lieutenant colonel. Himmler ordered Riedweg to set up a reception camp for illegal immigrants from Switzerland and Liechtenstein, verify their background, indoctrinate them, and then assign them to the armed SS or the German labor market. For that purpose, the SS Central Office purchased a large villa at Panoramastrasse 11 in Stuttgart. (Consular Agent Ernst Mörgeli, who was arrested by the Gestapo (see page 173ff, had found out about the existence of that center for agents through a coincidence; he did not have any special mission concerning the *Panoramaheim* but dealt with it only in the framework of his general task of defending the interests of Swiss citizens who lived in his consular district. Werner Rings, interview with Ernst Mörgeli, 30 May 1968. AfZ files of Werner Rings.) On October 19, 1944, Riedweg was stripped of his Swiss citizenship. (See Fuhrer, *Spionage*, 72; documents are at BAr E 27/10329 and 10468; his personnel file is at the Document Center Berlin.)

113. Riedweg in a private letter, October 20, 1987. (Document in this author's possession.)

114. Franz Riedweg was head of the "European Volunteer Center."

115. Gottlob Berger, Chief of SS Central Office, to Himmler, Reich Leader of the SS, April 19, 1943. (Photocopy of document in this author's possession.) On that issue, in a private letter dated October 24, 1987, Franz Riedweg commented:

> Berger's remark concerning Guisan certainly referred to Schellenberg's encounters with Masson and Guisan. Berger had close ties to Schellenberg. I knew Schellenberg well. He was a very cunning, ambitious guy, not a bad person. In 1947 he and I and another person were detained together at a castle in Denmark prior to Nuremberg. . . . I am convinced that his *claim* that he *prevented an attack against Switzerland* was simply a *calculated lie.* . . .

[Permanent Secretary] Weizsäcker kept telling me that Hitler never wanted to take an offensive stance toward Switzerland merely because of the complications that would be bound to occur with Mussolini. *Schellenberg wanted to extort favors from Masson.* Back then I did not know anything about the Schellenberg-Switzerland matter. That was why Berger remarked, 'Dr. Riedweg does not know that we have a promising connection to Switzerland.'" (Document in this author's possession.)

116. Cf. Captain Meyer's letter to General Guisan dated March 25, 1943, in which he wrote:

Dear General:

On this day, which will undoubtedly turn out to be a historic day in Switzerland's history on which God's providence has once again protected our dear country from danger and grief, the citizen and writer Wolf Schwertenbach, who knows all about the events, would like to thank you for what you have done in a mental combat for the well-being of the country. Since I also know that psychological elements ended up turning the scale in our favor, I did not fail to notice how much weight your word and the word of Colonel-Brigadier Masson carried. That is why I also know that it was not only rational reasoning but to the same extent your heart that saved us, for what do words mean when they are not heartfelt. [Your heart] created the necessary feeling of *trust* [underlined in the letter] when you declared that we would be merciless toward any intruder and fulfill our holy duty toward our home country in any situation. That was the only factor that decided our destiny this time. It was out of an instinct rather than with great foresight that I asked you several months ago, in the course of the quiet and systematic work that I have been doing from the ground up, whether you would be willing to confirm this declaration, which is perfectly matter-of-course for the Swiss but kept being questioned by the other side, to an influential foreign personality. Your willingness to do that, particularly your verbal statement and your warm-heartedness, ended up winning. Although I am aware that we are far from having escaped all dangers, this does not in the least diminish the success. (BAr E 5795/334.)

On March 26, 1943, the Commander-in-Chief thanked Meyer-Schwertenbach, replying, "Dear Captain: I have been touched by, and happy about, your short letter. We feel very satisfied that on that day our home country was spared from great looming dangers. I would like to take this opportunity to also express my heartfelt thanks to you for your cooperation on this difficult issue. I hope that our unambiguous declaration created the necessary confidence. . . . Yours truly, Your comrade, the General." (BAr E 5795/334.)

117. Meyer, diary, talks Masson-Meyer, April 8, 1943. BAr J.I. 121/1.
118. Meyer, diary, April 8,1943.
119. Meyer, diary, April 8, 1943.
120. Meyer, diary, April 8, 1943.

121. Colonel Werner Müller of the General Staff to Assistant Chief of Staff Id, April 2, 1943. BAr E 27/9528.
122. Cf. Werner Müller's statement: "If it is true that Captain Meyer is supposed to serve at AHQ again, I will oppose his transfer. There is no need for that officer to resume his intrigue at the army's command post." (Werner Müller to Masson, April 2, 1943.) By "intrigue" Müller referred to the affair of the tapped telephone conversations; see page 127ff.)
123. Waibel, statement as a witness before the jurors' court of the canton of Zürich, Washington, DC, September 15, 1947 (lawsuit of Hausamann vs. Kummer). BAr E 27/9846. At that time Waibel was working as military attaché at the Legation of Switzerland in Washington.
124. Masson to Supreme Court Justice Couchepin, hearing, November 2, 1945. BAr E 27/10027.
125. Masson to Couchepin, Nov. 2, 1945.
126. Because Waibel assumed that the talks at the Führer's headquarters about which *Viking* reported had actually taken place.
127. See page 196.
128. Waibel to Colonel Werner Müller of the General Staff, March 29, 1943. BAr E 27/14339. (Original in Waibel's personnel file.)
129. Waibel to Werner Müller, March 29, 1943.
130. Reference to the meetings in Biglen and Arosa.
131. Waibel to Werner Müller, March 29, 1943. BAr E 27/10027, vol. 1.
132. In March 1943, Meyer did not travel to Berlin to verify Viking's information; it was Eggen who traveled to Switzerland. The false information was probably based on a statement as a witness by Waibel that was not verified but was reported as such; subsequently Matt (*Zwischen allen Fronten*, 194), Kurz (*Nachrichtenzentrum Schweiz*, 69), and Fuhrer (*Spionage*, 85–86) incorporated Waibel's version. Perhaps Meyer's trip to Berlin in *July 1943*, which he undertook on orders of General Guisan and Masson, contributed to this erroneous information.
133. Waibel, statement as a witness, September 15, 1947. BAr E 27/9846.
134. Waibel, statement as a witness, September 15, 1947.
135. Masson to Meyer, April 20, 1962. BAr J.I.121/20.
136. Waibel to Werner Müller, March 29, 1943. BAr E 27/10027, vol. 1.
137. See Waibel to Colonel Otto Müller, June 12, 1945. BAr E 5330 1982/1, vol. 205.
138. Ernst to Masson, March 27, 1943. BAr J.I.140/4, vol. 5.
139. Masson to Alfred Ernst, June 14, 1943 (reply to Ernst's letter of March 27, 1943). BAr E 27/9521. Notice how long Masson waited before he replied to Ernst.
140. Masson to Alfred Ernst, June 14,1943. BAr E 27/9521.
141. Masson's written statement, which he later insisted was accurate, contrasts starkly with the facts, for which there is written evidence.
142. Masson referred to Eggen as "comrade." This is a revealing term in that Masson believed that he was able to deal with the German "as soldier to soldier" and considered that basis solid enough to build a trusting connection on it.
143. Masson to Alfred Ernst, June 14, 1943. BAr E 27/9521.

144. Alfred Ernst to Chief of the General Staff, June 25, 1943. BAr J.I.140/6.
145. Chief of the General Staff to Alfred Ernst, July 18, 1943 (handwritten). BAr J.I.140/6. Cf. Major General Hans Frick's statement to Alfred Ernst, in a letter dated August 11, 1943: "Ich freue mich für Sie, dass Sie vom ND weggekommen sind; es ist auf die Dauer ein ungesundes Klima und fördert sehr stark eine gewisse *déformation professionnelle.*" (I am happy to hear that you are no longer at the Intelligence Service; the atmosphere there is unhealthy in the long run and versatility is not encouraged whatsoever.) (BAr J.I.140/6.) Cf. General Donovan's psychological chief, Dr. Henry Murray of Harvard: "The whole nature of the functions of OSS were particularly inviting to *psychopathic* characters." (Dr. Murray made this remark during testimony as a defense witness in the 1950 trial of Alger Hiss, the former State Department official accused of being a Soviet spy.) R. Harris Smith, *OSS: The Secret History of America's First Central Intelligence Agency* (Berkeley, 1972), 7.
146. The head of *Bureau Ha* made some far-reaching suggestions in the letter in which, out of solidarity with Alfred Ernst, Max Waibel, and Emil Häberli, he threatened to resign from Army Intelligence if necessary. Hausamann wrote:

> I have been told that Colonel-Brigadier Masson seriously believes that it was due to his intervention that during the critical period of time about three weeks ago Reich Chancellor Hitler canceled an intervention against Switzerland that had already been decided. This change of mind has supposedly been achieved through his informants at the SS leadership, whom he allegedly contacted by telephone via Captain Meyer. The gentlemen at the SS must have had a good laugh when Switzerland's Chief of Intelligence and Security inquired over the telephone whether an attack was planned against Switzerland. . . . However, while this whole matter has something humorous about it, it also has some very serious aspects. After receiving information that comes from the German High Command, if Switzerland's Chief of Intelligence has his aide Meyer ask Himmler's adjutant SS General Sch[ellenberg] whether there really were any plans against Switzerland, in reality he tells Reichsführer of the SS Himmler that there is someone in the Führer's entourage who does not keep his lips tight. By doing that the Chief of Intelligence puts the people in jeopardy who were won over with great pain and by taking great risks, and on whose information we depend. *Switzerland's Chief of Intelligence takes care of the Gestapo's job, albeit unintentionally, and single-handedly deprives his service of its 'alarm bells'.* . . . Now that we know all that, it seems to be in Colonel-Brigadier Masson's and the country's best interest to put him in a different command post as soon as possible that corresponds to his rank. Federal Councillor, you said that he could for instance switch posts with Colonel-Brigadier Wacker [the commander of Mountain Brigade 12 and future commander of the 5th Division]. . . . To me that would be a proper and nice solution, exactly the way I like it. (Hausamann to Kobelt, 4 April 1943. BAr J.I.140/4, vol. 5.)

147. Folke Bernadotte, *Das Ende: Meine Verhandlungen in Deutschland im Frühjahr 1945 und ihre politischen Folgen* (Zürich/New York, 1945), 108. (If "Schellenberg's Report," which Bernadotte appended to the book, is accurate on this issue, Schellenberg made that statement to Himmler on April 13, 1945. The Reichsführer SS is said to have told his Chief of Intelligence, "'Schellenberg, I do not think that we will be able to work together with the Führer much longer; he is no longer up to his task. Do you think that de Crinis is right?'— 'Yes,' I replied. *'Of course I have not seen Hitler for two or three years,* but based on the way he has been acting lately I am convinced that it is high time for you [Himmler] to take action.'" This statement by Schellenberg was sent to *Bureau Ha* in the form of a supposedly anonymous note. On November 25, 1945 Hausamann transmitted it to Werner Müller or Supreme Court Justice Couchepin (it is no longer possible to clearly identify the recipient). BAr E 27/10027, vol. 1. Kobelt quoted Schellenberg's account in his confidential report of February 22, 1946 on the Masson case, concluding, "That means that Schellenberg was unlikely to be personally involved in averting the attack against Switzerland. Instead, *the decisive factor was the war economy.*" (BAr E 27/10027, vol. 1.)

148. See H.R. Trevor-Roper, *The Final Days of Hitler* (London: Macmillan & Co., 3rd ed., 1956), xvi.

149. As an ironic twist to history, Eggen made that confession exactly five years after *Viking* had issued the warning that triggered the alert of March 1943.

150. The written evidence indicates that the chronological order of events was actually reversed. Masson first met Gisevius in April 1943, *after* the alert of March 1943. On that occasion, Gisevius actually told Masson that "Case Switzerland" was not a top priority. Contrary to the channel to the Reich Security Central Office, Gisevius assured Switzerland's Chief of Intelligence that the entourage of Canaris and Oster that opposed the regime "had taken special precautions to notify Switzerland in time of a possible breach of its neutrality." (Gisevius, statement in connection with the criminal investigation against von Heydt, Steegmann, Gisevius, and Niederer, divisional court May 6, 1947. BAr E 5800/1, vol. 1.) Masson confirmed Gisevius' version of the facts.

151. Cf. the report by Sx of April 14, 1943 (see page 232ff.). Hitler not only opposed a military conflict with Switzerland but also, less than two weeks before the alleged alert of March 1943, he expressly decided that "the economic war against Switzerland [could] not be carried out as vehemently as planned." Apparently Hitler feared that his Italian allies might circumvent Germany's measures. Hitler made that telling remark on March 6, 1943 in a meeting with Albert Speer. See "Punkte aus der Besprechung beim Führer am 6. März 1943," Reich Ministry for Armament and War Production, note of March 11, 1943. German Federal Archives Koblenz, R 3/1507. (For background information on that issue, see Bourgeois, *Le Troisième Reich*, chapter IX, "Vers l'Anschluss économique?," 158–182, particularly 166; and Bourgeois, "Les relations germano-suisses pendant la seconde guerre mondiale: un bilan de 1944," *Schweizerische Zeitschrift für Geschichte* 32 (1982), 563 ff.

152. Eggen, third interrogation, Justice Palace Nuremberg, March 18, 1948. National Archives, Washington, DC, RG 238 M 1019 R 15.

153. Gerold Walser to this author, August 9, 1988.
154. Cf. Masson's statement of August 11, 1966 to Meyer and Hans Rudolf
Schmid: "Within our former Intelligence Service, two antagonistic groups . . .
were formed in German-speaking Switzerland, which was one of my greatest
disappointments." (BAr J.I.121/20.)

Chapter 11: Assessment of the Connection

1. Investigating magistrate, Captain H. Studer, to Colonel-Brigadier Eugster, 31
December 1945. BAr E 27/10027, vol. 1.
2. Masson, "La ligne Eggen-Schellenberg," 14 June 1945 (BAr E 27/10027, vol.
1), and Masson, "Attestation [pour] Walter Schellenberg," 10 May 1948 (BAr E
27/10039; document defending Schellenberg, who was standing trial in the
Wilhelmstrasse case in Nuremberg; was written against the expressed will of the
Federal Council).
3. Masson, "La ligne Eggen-Schellenberg."
4. See Bonjour, *Neutralität*, vol. V, 73, note 4.
5. It is all the more doubtful whether Schellenberg had anything to do with von
Bibra being replaced, since after the war he also claimed that it was due to him
that in spring 1943 the German delegate to the German-Swiss trade negotia-
tions had been replaced, thereby getting the stalled negotiations back on track.
(Schellenberg, statement, 13 December 1946, no. 403 b. Institute for
Contemporary History, Munich, Schellenberg files, 3, Z S 291.) However,
Daniel Bourgeois discovered that the German delegate, Johannes Hemmen, had
been unable to continue the talks due to an illness (see Hemmen/Köcher to
German Ministry of Foreign Affairs, telegram no. 1123, 25 May 1943. Political
Archives, Bonn, Ha. Pol. II a, Schweiz, Handel 13 A, vol. 2. Information kind-
ly supplied to this author by Bourgeois, 25 October 1988).
6. Gisevius stated: "In 1942, when in Switzerland's interest the head of the [Swiss
Federal] Police Section, Dr. Rothmund, was pressing ahead with his trip to
Berlin, I was the one who made some decisive moves that allowed him to
receive a visa after he had been waiting in vain for approximately six months.
Now Eggen takes credit for this achievement, and I think that even Dr.
Rothmund does not know that he owes his visa to Foreign Intelligence [at the
OKW]." (Gisevius, complaint to Swiss divisional court 6, 20 March 1947.
Archives of H.R. Kurz.)
7. Meyer, statement as a witness before the Zürich district court, 4 June 1947.
BAr J.I.121/1.
8. During that conversation, as well as during the subsequent conversation
between Masson and Meyer, once again a prearranged language was used (see
page 234); Rothmund was referred to as "Chamberlain." Masson asked Meyer,
"What did [Eggen] say out there [i.e. in Berlin]?" Meyer replied, "He just said
that everything was perfectly all right and that I should tell you so. He is very
glad, but of course I could not really speak with him openly. He only said to
tell you that the matter concerning *Chamberlain* was all right, was it not? . . .
He [Rothmund] will be informed about it by the people out there, through
normal [i.e. diplomatic] channels." Masson double-checked the information

with Meyer by asking him, "Who? The umbrella?" Meyer responded, "Yes, the umbrella will be told through normal channels." (Transcript of tapped telephone conversation by monitoring office Interlaken, telephone call by Captain Meyer to Colonel-Brigadier Masson, 10 September 1942. BAr J.I.121/45.)

9. The censorship authorities' transcript of Meyer's telephone conversation with Masson immediately following his conversation with Eggen shows that in an effort to make Rothmund realize how "prestigious" their secret channel to Berlin was, the two men discussed what would be a suitable way of letting Rothmund know that it was their connection that had succeeded in obtaining his visa. (Transcript of Meyer's telephone call to Masson.)

10. From fall 1943 on, Rothmund objected to Masson's connection with Schellenberg; cf. Masson's statement, "Rothmund . . . the person whom I must henceforth describe as a *saboteur* of Army Intelligence. . . . Dr. Rothmund is pretentious, jealously looks out for his own privileges, is hostile toward the Army, is the most perfect negative example of a federal official, and does everything he can to thwart the ceaseless efforts that I have been undertaking for years in the higher interest of our country so as to keep it neutral." (Masson to Commander-in-Chief, 21 November 1943. Document in this author's possession.)

11. Meyer, notes on meeting with Rothmund, November 1943. BAr J.I.121/1.

12. For that reason, Rothmund tried to prevent Eggen from entering Switzerland. Meyer complained to Rothmund about it. Meyer reported to his superior Masson about the conversation with the head of the Federal Police Section:

> [I told Rothmund that] in order for the Chief of Intelligence, who was responsible for calling up new troops and sending troops off duty, to be able to live up to the task that he had toward the Army Command, he needed to be able to continue to *summon the foreign informants* to Switzerland without any opposition by the civilian authorities. I argued that this was all the more justified as the Federal Council did not let you leave the country. [Rothmund] did not like these arguments, maybe because even the most primitive Swiss understands them. "Well, well, that is the track into which one wants to shunt the matter," he said furiously. I replied, "Whenever Masson summons his informants from abroad, he only has our country's military interest in mind." [Rothmund] subsequently remarked that he doubted whether the connection was that important because he had not achieved much with those people in G[ermany] even though they had been very nice to him. (Meyer to Masson, 23 November 1943 [strictly confidential]. BAr J.I.121/20.)

13. Eggen, "Zusammenfassung meiner Ausführungen vom 13.11.1945 und vom 15.11.1945," forwarded on 9 October 1946 by Colonel Werner Müller to the Military Attorney General. BAr E 27/10026.

14. For details on the Messerschmitt deal, see Ernst Wetter, *Geheimer Nachtjäger in der Schweiz* (Frauenfeld, 1989). (Major General Wetter kindly made the manuscript of his study available to this author before it was published.)

15. See Piekalkiewicz, *Schweiz 39–45: Krieg in einem neutralen Land* (Stuttgart/Zug,

1978), 297–313, particularly 305–306. (By the way, the crew of the Me-110 that had performed the emergency landing was interned at the *Bären* inn in Biglen and signed the same guest book in which General Guisan and Schellenberg had left their mark one year earlier.)

16. Interrogation of Skorzeny, First U.S. Army Interrogation Report, 1945 (reprinted in Piekalkiewicz, *Schweiz 39–45*, 305–306). Skorzeny was responsible for special tasks at Schellenberg's Office VI; in September 1943 he made a name for himself by freeing Mussolini from Gran Sasso and bringing him to Germany.

17. The former military attaché in Berlin was a close friend of General Legge, the U.S. military attaché in Bern.

18. Masson was particularly keen on having Giraud freed because the French general had been his instructor at the *Ecole supérieure de Guerre* in Paris. Allen Dulles, whom Masson had informed about Giraud's liberation, correctly argued, "Schellenberg is obviously attempting to buy immunity, as he has just delivered Gen. Giraud's family to Masson who repatriated them to France, and is apparently prepared to release further women and children." Telegram OSS Bern to OSS Washington, DC, London, Paris, and Caserta, 5 April 1945. National Archives, Washington, DC, RG 226, entry 134, box 162, file "Berne Caserta Oct 44–June 45."

19. Some of the contacts were maintained by former Federal Councillor Jean-Marie Musy. At the end of the war, Eggen told the investigating magistrate of divisional court 6, "It was also extremely difficult for Schellenberg to have to go through *former Federal Councillor Musy* for the repatriation campaigns because Schellenberg . . . knew about *his past* and his *opinion concerning financial matters.*" Eggen, statement as a witness before divisional court 6, 11 August 1945. BAr E 27/10109.

20. Reynaud was French Prime Minister in 1940.

21. Blum was French Prime Minister from 1936 to 1937, in 1938, and from 1946 to 1947.

22. Cf. the letter by the Wood Section at the War Industry and Labor Office of the Swiss Federal Department of Economic Affairs to Captain Meyer dated March 16, 1944, asking Meyer: "We would appreciate your continued assistance with procuring German transit visas for Swiss citizens. . . . You informed us that this time around unfortunately you could not make use of your German connections because the Swiss Federal Immigration Police failed to grant a visitor's visa to Mr. Wolfgang Schnurbusch, of German nationality, director of the *Warenvertriebs G.m.b.H.* in Berlin, who wanted to travel to Switzerland in order to discuss the delivery of Swiss barracks." The Wood Section asked Meyer to try once again to obtain the required visas "because they [were] very important for our country." It said that in exchange the War Industry and Labor Office had intervened with the Swiss Federal Immigration Police "in order to have all major points of view taken into account when Mr. Schnurbusch's request for a visitor's visa [was] examined." BAr J.I.121/74.

23. Cf. for instance Masson's statement to Meyer: "Please find the enclosed file for your information [file is missing]. I would appreciate your trying to see if you could *obtain the necessary visas through the 'E' channel.* The parents of Capt[ain]

Daniel have an absolutely clean record." Masson to Meyer, 6 October 1942. BAr J.I.121/20.

24. Cf. Masson's statement: "Within a very short period of time, Schellenberg arranged for our ski team, which was led by Captain Guisan, to transit through Germany on its way to Sweden. (Masson, "La ligne Eggen-Schellenberg." BAr E 27/10027, vol. 1.) It is doubtful whether this type of mediation is actually part of the tasks of an intelligence service.

25. Phrase that Masson used in a conversation with Gottfried Kummer, national news editor at *Die Tat*; see Kummer to Masson, 27 February 1948. BAr J.I.121/20.

26. Meyer, statement, 19 October 1945. BAr J.I.121/20.

27. Masson, "Rapport," 14 June 1945. BAr E 5330 98/39 v.1945. Masson later told Hans Rudolf Kurz that Schellenberg—who had a lot of children—had once asked him to buy rubber pants for his youngest child. Schellenberg's wife had not been able to buy them due to the shortage of rubber in Germany. (Information disclosed to this author, March 1985). Naturally, such small favors did foster better and stronger human relationships. Yet at the same time they underline the fact that Masson did not actually give anything in return for Schellenberg's "services."

28. Masson, "Rapport," 14 June 1945.

29. Masson, "Rapport," 14 June 1945.

30. Masson in *Luzerner Neueste Nachrichten*, 28 March 1962, no. 74.

31. The Unites States initially had an interest in a connection with Schellenberg as well; cf. OSS Bern's statement: "Our purpose is to contact persons who would be of real value to us at the present time. *Schellenberg*, [Karl] *Wolff* [lieutenant general of the SS and general of the *Waffen SS*; as of September 1943, he was the Wehrmacht's official commander in Italy], [Heinrich] *Mueller* [head of the Gestapo, Office VI of the Reich Security Central Office], all *Himmler men*, are in all probability the best choices. . . . The question is whether or not we can get any of them." OSS Bern to OSS Washington, 22 March 1944. National Archives, Washington, DC, RG 226, entry 134, box 191, file "IND-27 Berne, March-April 1944."

32. Dulles, telegram to OSS Washington, 4 February 1945. Princeton University Library, Allen W. Dulles Papers, box 22.

33. Dulles, telegram to OSS Washington, 4 February 1945. Dulles had already sent the following information to Washington on January 18, 1945: "I do not think Ecken [sic] is our man as *unfortunately he seems a bit too honest* but we may have another try at him." Dulles (OSS Bern) to Sasac and Saint, Washington, London, Paris, 18 January 1945 (Top Secret), National Archives, Washington, DC, RG 226, Entry 214, Box 7. The document was discovered by Dr. Neville Wylie from the University of Nottingham and kindly put at the author's disposal for an initial appraisal.

34. "Meeting of 493 with Hans Ecken [sic] of the SS," January 15, 1945. Top Secret. Supplement to Dulles' Report on the OSS-Report dated January 18, 1945. National Archives, Washington, DC, RG 226, Entry 214, Box 7. In this report the OSS agent 493 (U.S. Commercial Attaché in Zürich Frederick R. Loofbourow) described how the meeting had come about: "Last evening, Sunday,

at 6:30 Dr. Paul Meyer (Schwertenbach) rang the bell at my apartment, came in and told me that his SS contact was returning to Germany the following day, and that the three of us could have dinner at the Dolder [hotel]. He told me more about the man, which will appear below, and I accepted. They called for me in a taxi at 7:30. We had a pleasant dinner, returned to my place around midnight and talked till about 3:00 in the morning." The OSS staff member described Eggen's position in the following words: "Ecken [sic] is on the board of a large Berlin company with Dr. Westrick [sic]. He is also in the Ministry of Economics (Wirtschaftsministerium), The Ministry of War (Kriegsministerium), Department of War Weapons (Kriegswaffenamt), Schellenberg's SS office and Jüttner's office, who is head of the *Waffen SS*. He seemed to think that you [Dulles] had some connection with Jüttner and that he is on our white list for arranging the ransoming of the Manfred Weiss people. . . . He comes to Switzerland every couple of months." In an effort to stress Eggen's worthiness, Meyer-Schwertenbach steered the conversation he was having with the American to the plane incident that had occurred in Dübendorf: "In the course of the conversation at the Dolder Schwertenbach (hereinafter and on the telephone called 'Wolf') said, 'You know he brought us 12 Messerschmitts—that was a very generous thing to do for Switzerland.' I replied, 'Yes, but he had special reasons for that, as I know.' That shook them up and broke the ice, and they told me more of the story than I actually knew. It seems that when the secret night-fighter landed in Dübendorf by mistake last summer (see cable we sent on it based on Flute's inspection of it) it was Ecken [sic] who was sent to try to get it back at once. The Swiss refused. So Ecken [sic] asked that it be destroyed, offering 12 Messerschmitt 109Gs in return. The Swiss took the 12 planes and the Federal Council ruled that Switzerland could destroy interned property at the request of the owner. But the Federal Council also insisted that the Germans send a flier to inspect the plane before destruction to be sure it was still intact. A flier arrived, carrying his own explosives in a brief case, examined the plane and blew it up and burned it on Dübendorf field in the presence of Wolf and Ecken [sic] who say the fireworks were unforgettable, especially when the tracer amunition exploded. The delivery of the 12 planes and the payment of several million francs for them was a delicate matter and was all handled by Ecken [sic]." The extensive report is interesting especially because the OSS representative describes in great detail all the relevant information Eggen divulged to the American that evening (and which naturally also was passed on to Swiss Intelligence since Captain Meyer had been at the meeting the whole time). This description gives us a clear picture of what Eggen must have discussed with Meyer-Schwertenbach and Masson during their meetings, and why both Swiss men considered the contacts they had with Eggen to be productive. The report continues as follows, "Intelligence obtained from Ecken [sic]": "The Germans have definitely abandoned the idea of shooting V-1's from submarines at New York for political reasons. No really new V weapons are coming, only improvements, notably jet-propelled planes and Fledermaus planes. Fledermaus planes are the shape of a kite (or bat), are without armament, are rocket-propelled, have reinforced noses, and are designed to ram invading bombers. (The Wieser report that the British forgot to send on to us—dated roughly end of October—contained a lot on this subject). Both types of planes will be in use by May, will overcome our air superiority. However they will not be *kriegsentscheidend* [war-winning] just as our bomber superiority is not kriegsentscheidend. He says we get nowhere by bombing cities, and that *since eight weeks* [underlined in the original] Germany is invulnerable to strategic bombing. He harped on this, and repeated the eight-week period several times but did not explain it. I had the impression that he had in mind something like the putting into operation of several underground plants that would assure supplies of weapons. If so they must have included a synthetic oil plant or two because he said that the gasoline crisis of April [1944] had passed, and that his own ration which had then dropped to 80 litres per month is recently back up to 300 litres. In the meantime he had tried a brown coal generator on his car but had scrapped the thing as too inconvenient. He drives a small car between the various ministries he must visit—and the chauffeur he has had for the last five years was formerly the chauffeur of von Hindenburg. He never mentioned *Himmler* by name but referred to him always as der Reichsführer. He often said 'nicht der Führer sondern der Reichsführer.' Apparently Himmler has made the 'Führer' class, and due to the accent on the 'Reichs' his title sounded more imposing that Hitler's. However, I could get nothing out of him on the subject of who is running the country—he was very wary of the subject."

The OSS representative summarized under point 6 what Eggen told him with regard to counterespionage: "He [Eggen] was hipped on the subject of feeding our agents with misinformation, and I got the impression that this must be one of his main jobs. He claimed they knew the Allied agents in high positions in Berlin and made good use of them by feeding them. I gathered most of them were British agents, for it was only in this connection that he dragged the British into the conversation. He said once they had held a whole meeting of a production bureau just to give a man the impression that a plant had been opened at a certain place, and 10 days later the RAF bombed the place. When I dragged out my bête noire that our legation since the beginning of the war has reported 200 or 300 synthetic oil plants where only 20 to 25 exist, he said that just to show what he could do, he would send us 50 more within 10 days. I told him that would be very interesting and lots of fun, but he regretfully backed down a few minutes later when he realized that that would expose his channels for feeding us.

He said that our diplomatic and consular officers gossiped a lot and that he got voluminous reports of what they said. He also said he got 'blaue Papiere' from our offices. I asked him if he meant from Zürich and he said of course he couldn't say but from the look on his face I had the impression it was not Zürich—and the general tone of the conversation pointed more to the legation than to any consulate. I asked him what he meant by 'blaue Papiere,' did he mean carbon copies, and he dismissed the question with a 'no,' saying that he meant the kind of blaue Papiere you throw in waste baskets. I think he meant carbon paper, which is almost always blue in Germany."

Despite the fact that Eggen had initiated contact with the OSS, he hinted that he was a dedicated Nazi when the three men talked about the Germans' state of mind. "Ecken [*sic*] says morale reached its low just after July 20 [1944, Stauffenberg's failed assassination attempt at Hitler]. Has risen some since, is not high, but is going along on an even keel. He was emphatic and dogmatic in saying that measures had been taken making any repetition of July 20 absolutely out of the question. Another such 'Sauerei' can never happen." In the course of this lengthy discussion various political issues were touched on. Eggen openly admitted that he thought the war would last another two to three years and that there would be no winner at the end. "Europe would be Bolshevised clear to Gibraltar. America would lose millions of men and gain nothing. The American fleet would never get beyond its present position by the Philippines and Formosa (for some mysterious reason he refused to make clear—but which I suppose had to do with the Russians)." That was how Eggen switched the topic of conversation to the actual reason why he probably had called Meyer-Schwertenbach in to establish contact to the OSS: "He [Eggen] thinks that by June or July [1945] the Anglo-saxons will be ready to talk with the Germans about a more reasonable solution for the war." Hence the following remark made by OSS agent 493 under point 9: "Suggested meeting between you [Dulles] and Schellenberg." Eggen "says the Germans are already in contact with the Russians. He hopes the Anglosaxons will be willing to talk with the Germans *before* [in the original in capital letters] June or July. Schellenberg can bring you the proof that the Russians are not playing fair with us. Ecken [sic] began to speculate on you meeting Schellenberg in Konstanz. Wolf said it would be unreasonable to ask you to go to Germany, whereas Schellenberg would be safe in Switzerland. Ecken [*sic*] said it would be too conspicuous if Schellenberg left Germany. The two tossed the ball back and forth until I broke in with the statement that whether such a meeting should take place anywhere would require a lot of consideration, that it was well that we had made each other's aquaintance for any future eventuality and that that was sufficient for the present. Ecken [*sic*] asked me whether on this trip back to Germany he should ascertain from Schellenberg whether he would meet you. I said no, that we did not know your views. He suggested I get your views today and give them to him before he leaves tonight. I told him that there was no reason to rush things that way, that on his theory things would not be different until June or July, there was plenty of time for reflection. He let it go at that.

In our conversation I did not express any political opinion or any opinion about the course or the duration of the war or the nature of the postwar period. He was fairly voluble and did nearly all the talking. I was careful not to say anything that could not be quoted under any circumstances, and he did not ask questions nor press me for any opinion until the end of our conversation. . . . The meeting was very friendly throughout, served the purpose of getting aquainted and of *establishing a contact* . . . for any eventual future use."

35. OSS Bern to OSS Washington, London, Paris, and Caserta, 5 April 1945. National Archives, Washington, D.C., RG 226, entry 134, box 162, file "Berne Caserta Oct 44–June 45."

36. On that issue, see the subtle, precise analysis in Klaus Urner, *Der Schweizer Hitler-Attentäter* (Frauenfeld/Stuttgart, 1980), 14–60 (in passing), particularly 15–28.

37. Cf. David Kahn's statement:
> [Schellenberg] had a quiet way about him, quite different from the bullying pretentious hardness of most SS types. He spoke softly, almost shyly, in a clear tenor with exceptionally precise enunciation and with a boyish charm that was one of his greatest assets. . . . Not everyone liked him. Some of the older, street-brawler types of the SS despised him as effete; some officials regarded him as too pushy. . . . He was bright and perceptive: people meeting him often had the impression that he could form a clear picture of people and events on the basis of a few key facts. . . . In comparison with other members of the RSHA, Schellenberg seemed relatively sophisticated. He could lunch smoothly with foreigners and befriend young officials in the Foreign Office and the Propaganda ministry. He was credited with understanding foreign affairs.
> (David Kahn, *Hitler's Spies: German Military Intelligence in World War II* [New York, 1985], 260.)

However, Professor Trevor-Roper, who was asked by the British Intelligence Service to look into the circumstances of Hitler's death and therefore interviewed prisoners, including Schellenberg, put that statement in perspective, stating:
> Among the universally parochial minds of the SS, Schellenberg, its youngest general, enjoyed an *undeserved* reputation. He was credited with understanding foreign affairs. It is true that his notions were a little less extravagant than those of some of his rivals . . . . A North German, he was also exempt from the ideological gibberish of the Austrian and Bavarian Nazis. He believed not in force, nor in nonsense, but in subtlety; and he believed that he was subtle. This was perhaps his greatest mistake, for he was in fact a very trivial character. (Trevor-Roper, *The Last Days of Hitler*, 28.)

38. People who did not fall for Schellenberg's charm question even that quality. Anthony Cave Brown remarks:
> Nothing that Schellenberg had done, except Venlo [the malicious plot in which, in November 1939, Schellenberg kidnapped England's secret agents Stevens and Best to bring them to Germany], entitled him to the term so often accorded him by those whose job it was to study the young German spymaster, that of being "a genius." As Squadron Leader G.W. Harrison, the man who interrogated Schellenberg when he was captured, stated: "His demeanour at this camp has not produced any evidence of outstanding genius as appears to have been generally attributed to him. On the contrary, his incoherency and incapability of producing lucid verbal or written statements have rendered him a much more difficult subject to interrogate than other subjects of inferior education and of humbler status." (Anthony Cave Brown, *"C": The Secret Life of Sir Stewart Graham Menzies, Spy Master to Winston Churchill* [New York, 1987], 567.)

39. See page 249 for details concerning the 1944 incident at the Dübendorf air-field.
40. Gisevius, statement to investigating magistrate Otto Müller, 25 June 1945. BAr E 5330 1982/1, vol. 205.
41. On that issue, Eggen later stated in Nuremberg:
    Schellenberg offered to pay Masson an enormous amount of money should he underhandedly get Gisevius out of Switzerland. That was after July 20, 1944. [Gisevius had been one of the insti-gators of the failed assassination attempt on Hitler, but he man-aged to escape the Gestapo and went into hiding in Switzerland.] Schellenberg's main objective was not catching Gisevius but boost-ing his own image. There were two aspects to the issue for Schellenberg; on one hand he wanted to tie Masson down with money in a move against the Allies, and on the other hand he wanted to catch Gisevius in order to make a good impression on Himmler and other people. I know all the details about this because I was supposed to hold the negotiations. (Eggen, third interrogation, Justice Palace Nuremberg, 18 March 1948. National Archives, Washington, DC, RG 238 M 1019 R 15.)
42. Gisevius, statement to investigating magistrate Otto Müller, 25 June 1945. BAr E 5330 1982/1, vol. 205.
43. Peter Burckhardt to Supreme Court Justice Couchepin, 27 November 1945. BAr E 27/10027, vol. 1.
44. In a letter dated April 22, 1947, Trevor-Roper remarked to Folke Bernadotte, "Like you, I have had a great deal to do with Schellenberg. . . . As to Schellenberg's intelligence—I really feel that he speaks for himself. I have admitted that 'the fact that he began to work his passage home as early as 1942 separates him from the crasser intellects of the Party'." (National Archives, Washington, DC, RG 238 M 897 R 114.)
45. Cf. Folke Bernadotte's statement, "Schellenberg . . . of course was a Nazi." Bernadotte to Trevor-Roper, 17 April 1947. National Archives, Washington, DC, RG 238 M 897 R 114.
46. Peter Burckhardt to Couchepin, 27 November 1945. BAr E 27/10027, vol. 1. On that issue, cf. Trevor-Roper's statement:
    Schellenberg's motives, in thus saving life, were of course purely opportunist; for he was too "realistic" to indulge any humanitarian fancies. As he explained to a friend, the extermination of the Jews would have been unexceptionable if it could have been carried out completely; but since two-thirds of the Jews were out of reach, such a policy "was worse than a crime; it was folly." Schwerin von Krosigk's Diary, s.d. 15th April 1945. (Trevor-Roper, *The Last Days of Hitler*, 30, footnote 1.)
47. Investigating magistrate, Colonel Otto Müller, final report on the hearing of evidence against Masson, 9 July 1945. BAr E 5330 1982/1, vol. 205.
48. Colonel Otto Müller, final report.
49. Eggen, "Zusammenfassung meiner Ausführungen." In Nuremberg, when he was asked about that matter, Eggen told the U.S. investigating magistrate,

"Maybe Schellenberg believed that as part of his rivalry with the Ministry of Foreign Affairs he might play some political role via Switzerland. In order to fully understand that, you have to know how complicated the relations were between Ribbentrop and Schellenberg." The U.S. investigator interjected, "They were not that complicated; Schellenberg wanted to have Ribbentrop's post." Eggen responded, "Yes, he did. Through Switzerland (Masson) Schellenberg tried to play some political role and derive some advantage for himself." When the investigating magistrate remarked, "It seems to me that Schellenberg knew as little about politics as he did about intelligence," Eggen dryly replied, "Had he known more about it, I would not be sitting here today. . . . [Schellenberg does] not know anything at all about the international state of mind. He never got out of the country." Eggen, interrogation, Justice Palace Nuremberg, 16 March 1948. National Archives, Washington, DC, RG 238 M 1019 R 15.

50. Schellenberg, 2nd minutes, 13 November 1946 (quoted in the Federal Council's official report to the Zürich district court, 14 March 1947). BAr J.I.137 1974/64, vol. 8.
51. Schellenberg's Swedish contact person was Raoul Wallenberg, the diplomat who was later kidnapped by the Russians in Budapest. Written evidence on that subject is at the German Federal Archives in Koblenz.
52. Cf. Peter Burckhardt's statement: "It was striking that Schellenberg had an absolutely negative attitude toward Russia, which he kept describing as a threat to Europe." Peter Burckhardt to Couchepin, 27 Nov. 1945. BAr E 27/10027, vol. 1.
53. Schellenberg commented: "In retrospect, from the point of view of intelligence, the amount of information concerning the Western powers would have fit under the fingernails." (Schellenberg, statement, 2nd minutes, 13 November 1946; quoted in Federal Council's official report to the Zürich district court, 14 March 1947. On April 10, 1947, Hans Rudolf Schmid sent a copy of that statement to General Guisan, who in turn forwarded it to Masson on April 14, 1947 for his information. BAr J.I.140/1 and J.I.137 1974/64, vol. 8.)
54. Schellenberg, statement, 13 Nov. 1946. BAr J.I. 137 1974/64, vol. 8.
55. Schellenberg, statement, 13 Nov. 1946.
56. Fuhrer, *Spionage*, 75. Not all of Schellenberg's former aides who were questioned in Switzerland supported him, so they would have had no reason to reflect Schellenberg's position on that issue in a more positive light than it actually was.
57. See Bonjour, *Neutralität*, vol. V, 89.
58. However, Canaris had Gisevius personally explain to Masson that this ban did not mean much. In early 1943, during their first encounter at the *Schweizerhof* in Bern, Gisevius told Masson "on strictly confidential terms" that it was not possible to enforce the "gentlemen's agreement between officers" that Switzerland's Chief of Intelligence wanted to reach; he later explained:

I told Colonel-Brigadier Masson that if he and Admiral Canaris were to have an official meeting, Canaris would be forced to make whatever declaration he was asked to make; in particular, he would have to make assurances that the spying activities against

Switzerland would come to an end. However, [I said to Mr. Masson that] even if Canaris personally made such a declaration, Canaris was perfectly aware that it would offer no guarantee because in addition to his own organization, the Security Service was also involved in such spying activities; moreover, he could be asked to step down any day, and under the current circumstances in the Reich he would have no possibility of notifying Mr. Masson of any breach of the gentlemen's agreement that Mr. Masson had in mind. . . . [I told Mr. Masson that if he wanted to prevent Germany from continuing its spying activities] we could only advise him to rely exclusively on his own vigilance. I told Mr. Masson about the efforts that Canaris and, to a certain extent, yours truly had recently undertaken to put an end to the activities of the [German Security Service's] notorious center in Stuttgart and that basically the only thing that we achieved was to be systematically betrayed by the fanatics within our own organization. Also, a list compiled by Canaris showed that [Himmler's] Security Service was to be blamed for two out of every three death penalties that had been passed down until that time in Switzerland. Nevertheless, the Security Service could never be moved to give up its subversive activities. . . . [Mr. Masson] asked me to thank Admiral Canaris for his frankness and explained that his idea had been simply to put an end to Germany's ceaseless spying efforts. (Gisevius, statement before divisional court 6, May 1947. The statement is among Federal Councillor Kobelt's personal files. BAr E 5800/1, vol. 1.)

59. Masson to Commander-in-Chief, 15 April 1947. BAr E 5795/448, vol. 3.
60. In spite of the alert of March 1943, which from today's perspective has to be viewed as an exaggeration, one should keep in mind that on every other occasion *Viking* distinguished itself by supplying accurate information. It was precisely the fact that the tested and tried *Viking* line sounded the alarm that led Swiss Intelligence to take the warnings of winter 1942–1943 seriously.
61. Cf. the statement by Fritz Schwarz, editor-in-chief of the newspaper *Freies Volk*: "From the very beginning, the purpose of the preventive channel, which was set up with our Commander-in-Chief's knowledge and approval, was not to procure intelligence but to try to *influence the decisions of the German leadership*." (Fritz Schwarz in *Freies Volk*, 1 March 1946, no. 9. Schwarz' account of the "Masson case" angered Hausamann, who tried to bring Schwarz to court. In February 1948, in the presence of Federal President Celio and Federal Councillors Petitpierre and Rubattel, General Guisan addressed the Association of French-Speaking Swiss in Bern, reminiscing about wartime duty. The Commander-in-Chief stated, among other things: "A newspaper in Bern—I believe it was the *Freies Volk*—has already *vigorously* defended Masson, and *rightly so*. Please excuse me for having changed the subject for one moment." On February 19, 1948 [issue no. 49], the *Berner Tagblatt* commented, "In view of the entourage of Major Hausamann stirring up public opinion [against Masson], the General's statement should be particularly important." The news-

paper reported that the audience thanked Guisan for his statement by "applauding loudly.")

62. Hausamann to Kobelt, 28 November 1944. BAr E 27/9849.

63. Hausamann to Kobelt, 28 Nov. 1944.

64. Hausamann to Kobelt, 28 Nov. 1944.

65. Kobelt to Hausamann, 30 November 1944. BAr E 27/9849.

66. Kobelt to Hausamann, 30 Nov. 1944.

67. See Gottfried Kummer to Masson, 27 February 1948. BAr J.I.121/20.

68. See Hans Rudolf Schmid, "Klarheit über den 'Fall Masson'," a series of articles in *Tages-Anzeiger für Stadt und Kanton Zürich*, nos. 246, 247, 248 and 251, 19, 20, 22, and 25 October 1945.

69. Lützelschwab, manuscript, end of January 1948. BAr J.I.137/12.

70. Masson, interrogation, 20 June 1945. BAr E 5330 1982/1, vol. 205.

71. Masson to Chief of the General Staff, attn. Military Department, 12 July 1947. (Written statement as a witness in the lawsuit of Hausamann vs. Schmid/Kummer.) BAr E 27/9846.

72. Masson, interrogation, 20 June 1945. BAr E 5330 1982/1, vol. 205.

73. Cf. Masson's statement: "It is not our fault that Schellenberg was a member of the SS. Kimche would undoubtedly have wanted us to address a general at the Salvation Army. We would probably have had less trouble but it would not have been much use." Masson to Captain Paul Holzach, 24 March 1962. BAr J.I.121/20.

74. In Nuremberg, Eggen stated, "Schellenberg undoubtedly had some *suggestive power*." Eggen, 2nd interrogation, Justice Palace Nuremberg, 18 March 1948. National Archives, Washington, DC, RG 238 M 1019 R 15. Other people who had met Schellenberg made similar statements.

75. Barbey, *P.C. du Général*, 154 (entry of 5 March 1943).

76. Hausamann, note for file, 6 January 1944. Archives of H.R. Kurz. After the war, Schellenberg admitted that he had occasionally used Masson's and Meyer-Schwertenbach's names to add more weight to information that he had procured through other channels. However, there is written evidence showing that Masson did leak certain information to the Germans, the implications of which he was apparently unaware. Professor John W.M. Chapman of Sussex University kindly drew this author's attention to a German document that puts Masson's actions in a dubious light, even though in this particular case Masson had leaked the information to the *Wehrmacht's* Foreign and Counterintelligence Agency, the *Abwehr*, rather than to Schellenberg. Regardless of the addressee, the piece of information that Masson leaked to Germany was highly explosive. Moreover, from this incident one has to conclude that Dulles' remarks to Hausamann cannot simply be dismissed as an unfounded rumor. Professor Chapman writes:

> As the German side achieved little significant success after 1943 in resolving Anglo-American one-off pads and machine codes, they became more convinced than ever that the Allies could not possibly break their own ciphers, which were regarded as superior even to American systems. . . . Even when the *Swiss Intelligence Service provided eyewitness evidence that the Admiralty had been able to*

resolve the U-boat cipher during the Battle of the Atlantic, this was
dismissed as incredible.

Concerning the source of Swiss Intelligence's information, Professor Chapman
explains:

> The War Organization of the German Secret Military Intelligence
> Service in Switzerland obtained information from Colonel *Masson*
> via a contact of the Swiss Military Attaché in Washington in
> August 1943 that revealed various Allied technical developments
> for the prosecution of anti-submarine warfare. But the contact, a
> Swiss-American working in a senior secretarial position in the
> United States Navy Department who often went with U.S. naval
> missions to London, argued that "the real reason for the decline in
> shipping losses is as follows: . . . The English have in their
> 'Intelligence Naval Office' [*sic*] a quite outstanding aid in the
> struggle against U-boats. A special office since the outbreak of war
> has concerned itself exclusively with the decipherment of the
> German codes. For some months past, it has succeeded in reading
> all orders sent by the German Navy to the U-boat commanders,
> something that has tremendously simplified the hunt against the
> U-boats." OKW/Amt Ausl/Abw I M/T B. Nr. 1663/43 g.Kdos. of
> 18 August 1943 to Commander-in-Chief, Navy. The Chief of the
> Navy Signals Service reiterated the view expressed in the spring of
> 1943 that he "regards it out of the question that the enemy can
> make a current decipherment of our radio traffic." (John W.M.
> Chapman to this author, 10 November 1987.)

77. Hausamann, note for file, 6 January 1944. Hausamann must have used Dulles'
information as an opportunity to once again point out to his superior Masson
the risks that his doings involved but of which he was obviously unaware. In
any case, several days later Hausamann reported to Kobelt:

> I met with my chief yesterday. As usual, once again one could feel
> how human and decent he is. I am unable to tell whether he real-
> ized that he is at risk. I did not fail to give my warning the neces-
> sary urgency. M[asson] told me that he no longer systematically
> fostered the relations with E[ggen] but only saw him every few
> months or so whenever he ran into him. I have to assume that this
> is the case. However, it feels strange to me that now of all times the
> Washingtonians want to take up the subject as a "very serious"
> matter. I will do everything I can to prevent that from happening.
> However, we will be completely reassured only once the chief com-
> mands troops and has nothing more to do with the intelligence
> service. (Hausamann to Kobelt, handwritten letter, 11 January
> 1944. BAr E 5800/1, vol. 1.)

78. Mind you, that was not completely true. Because of the policy of neutrality
Major i Gst Hans Berli was commissioned to draft a military convention with
the German armed forces in February 1940. Hans Senn describes the situation
as follows in his excellent and exhaustive history of the Swiss General Staff during World War II: "Contact was not established with the German armed forces

as a precautionary measure. General Guisan believed that there was no reason to fear that the French would attack. He had the West case investigated more for internal reasons and did not consider it to be urgent. By the time operation orders West A and B were finally ready there was practically no danger from the West anymore. If Guisan had conducted preventive negotiations with the German armed forces due to the policy of neutrality all the same, he would have had to fear that Hitler would have misused them for his own purposes." Hans Senn, *Anfänge einer Dissuasionsstrategie während des Zweiten Weltkrieges,* Der Schweizerische Generalstab, vol. 7 (Basel, 1995), 139.

79. Masson to Paul Holzach, 24 March 1962. BA J.I. 121/20.
80. Masson to Meyer, 18 April 1962. A fortnight before Meyer's death, Masson put his argument in even clearer terms, noting, "the delicate affair of La Charité-sur-Loire, which *idiots really tend to forget and the devastating consequences of which justified to a great extent what we did.*" (Masson to Meyer, 1 September 1966. BAr J.I.121/20.
81. Colonel Arthur Fonjallaz, born 1875, died 1944. From 1896 to 1921, he worked as an instructor in the infantry, from 1923 to 1933 as an editor at the *Revue Militaire Suisse* and as a lecturer on the History of War at the Swiss Federal Technical Institute in Zürich. Because of his fascist convictions, at Minger's instigation he had to quit teaching (see minutes of Federal Council meeting of 20 October 1933. BAr E 1004.1 1). Fonjallaz last commanded infantry brigade 4.
82. "Rapport sur le Procès Arthur Fonjallaz (3 mars 1941)," 4 March 1941. BAr 2809/1, vol. 5.
83. "Rapport sur le Procès Fonjallaz."
84. Masson to Arthur Fonjallaz, 25 October 1939. (Document in this author's possession.)
85. Fonjallaz was lucky insofar as the Federal Criminal Court considered him as not entirely sane and the information that he supplied to the Germans as "not very valuable." On February 28, 1941 the colonel was sentenced to three years in prison; the eight months that he had spent in custody while awaiting trial counted toward the sentence. He died shortly after serving his sentence. If Fonjallaz had been arrested one year later, he could not have expected to receive such a mild sentence.
86. John W. McDonald, Jr. and Diane B. Bendahmane, eds., *Conflict Resolution: Track Two Diplomacy* (Washington DC: Foreign Service Institute, U.S. Department of State, 1987).
87. McDonald and Bendahmane, *Conflict Resolution,* 1.
88. Landrum Bolling, "Strengths and Weaknesses of Track Two," in Conflict Resolution, eds. McDonald and Bendahmane, 56.
89. Bolling, "Strengths and Weaknesses," 56.
90. Bolling, "Strengths and Weaknesses," 56.
91. In October 1962, John Scali was accredited as a correspondent at the U.S. State Department. He was a close friend of both Secretary of State Dean Rusk and President John F. Kennedy. The Soviets transmitted their suggestions on how to end the 1962 Cuban missile crisis through the KGB head in Washington, DC, Alexander Fomin, who in turn went to Scali. Acting as an

intermediary, Scali forwarded the information to the U.S. Government. McDonald and Bendahmane remark: "This is a case of a private citizen being used temporarily as a bearer of messages when the official channel was strained and overloaded because of a crisis." On that issue, see John Scali, "Backstage Mediation in the Cuban Missile Crisis," in *Conflict Resolution*, eds. McDonald and Bendahmane.

92. Bolling, "Strengths and Weaknesses," 56.

Chapter 12: Epilogue

1. Federal Councillor von Steiger blamed Masson for once again letting Eggen enter Switzerland, urging the Commander-in-Chief to investigate the matter.
2. Masson in *Tribune de Lausanne*, 3 February 1966.
3. Attorney General Stämpfli, "Internierungsverfügung," 3 May 1945. BAr E 5330 1982/1, vol. 205.
4. Cf. Cuénoud's statement:

   Masson asked me to accompany him and Cap[tain] Meyer on a quick visit to the *Kreuz* restaurant in Weier near Affoltern in order to provide some input concerning Mr. Eggen's possible transfer from Switzerland to Spain. . . . [Colonel-Brigadier Masson wanted me] to facilitate Mr. Eggen's transit through France by using my network of agents in that country. The entire discussion during our lunch revolved around that issue. Ultimately we came up against an insurmountable difficulty, i.e. how to ensure that Eggen could legally enter Spain. Since my network could not help Eggen cross the border between France and Spain under normal conditions, we simply had to give up that idea. (Cuénoud, head of Allied Section, to investigating magistrate Otto Müller, 18 June 1945. BAr E 27/9519.)
5. Hans Daufeldt had been a special representative of Schellenberg's Office VI, covering up his activities by officially acting as a German vice-consul in Lausanne. He had left Switzerland on March 14, 1945; as he enjoyed diplomatic immunity, no criminal proceedings were initiated against him. (See Bbl 1946 I 112. In official documents his name was sometimes spelled "Daufelt" or "Dauffelt.")
6. See Chapter 1.
7. Paul C. Blum, memorandum to Robert P. Joyce (Dulles' successor in Bern), 1 October 1945. The "X-2 Progress Report for September 1945" stated, among other things: "The most important case handled this month was that of Hans Wilhelm Eggen. He is a friend of Himmler's and an associate of Schellenberg's and a prominent member of the RSHA. He contacted us in Zürich and was *induced to accept our 'hospitality' in Milan*. He crossed at Chiasso October 1st and he is in the custody of X-2 Italy." National Archives, Washington, DC, RG 226, entry 99, box 8, folder 33, "ETO Switzerland-Sept 1945."
8. Masson, "Service Secret" [book review], *Revue militaire suisse* no. 6 (1994), 276–277.
9. Masson wrote an extensive declaration in Schellenberg's defense ("Attestation,"

10 May 1948), at the end of which General Guisan added in handwriting, "I confirm that this declaration is accurate, particularly the part concerning the services rendered to Switzerland by W. Schellenberg. Gen[eral] Guisan, Commander-in-Chief of the Army from 1939 to 1945." National Archives, Washington, DC, RG 238 M 897 R 114.

10. André Rochat in *H[eeres]P[olizei]-Bulletin*, no. 1 (1978).

11. Masson in *Luzerner Neueste Nachrichten*, no. 74, 28 March 1962.

Available Source Material

1. For the sake of clarity, abbreviations (mostly military ranks) that occur in source documents have been spelled out in this study; in addition, obvious mis-spellings and wrong sentence structures have been corrected. Some words or phrases have been italicized by this author to give them more emphasis, even within quotations. Whenever the emphasis appears in the original source, it has been specifically called out.

2. On December 15, 1954, in connection with a planned publication on the Intelligence Service, Masson wrote to Captain Meyer-Schwertenbach, "Unfortunately my own documentation is not very extensive nor voluminous, as we did not have any time to take notes concerning most of our 'actions'—at least that was the case for me." BAr J.I.121/20.

3. Ernst to Masson, 15 October 1940 (secret activity report on the *German Bureau* that he headed). BAr J.I.140/4, vol. 2.

4. Ernst to Masson, 15 October 1940. It is telling that Ernst addressed these fun-damental issues while he was being detained after taking part in the *Officers' Conspiracy*. During those 15 days of detention, for the first time since the beginning of the war he had some time to conceptualize his work as an intelli-gence officer and put his ideas in writing.

5. In the course of drafting his Ph.D. thesis on German military intelligence in World War II at Oxford University under H.R. Trevor-Roper.

6. In Switzerland, large quantities of documents were burned after World War II at the natural gas plant in Fribourg.

7. A major part of the reference material used for this study is filed under the heading "Schweizerische Landesverteidigung 1848–1950" (shelf-mark BAr E 27).

8. David Kahn, *Hitler's Spies: German Military Intelligence in World War II* (New York, 1985), ix.

9. The bibliography at the end of this book includes all unpublished papers and official files that have been consulted for this study.

10. Cf. Barbara W. Tuchman, *The Zimmermann Telegram* (New York, 1979), x, who states, "As we know from the many accounts of World War II espionage, *the truth often does not get into the record while the cover story does.*"

11. George F. Kennan, "Some Thoughts on Personal Papers in Public Libraries," *The Princeton University Library Chronicle,* Vol. 36 (Spring 1975), No. 3.

12. The Swiss Federal Archives in Bern and the Archives for Contemporary History at the Swiss Federal Institute of Technology in Zürich deserve to be mentioned in this connection.

13. For more information on Paul Meyer-Schwertenbach, see Chapter 6.
14. At the Swiss Federal Archives at shelf-mark J.I. 121.
15. Erwin Tschudi to Alphons Matt, 20 April 1969. BAr J.I.121/33. However, the companies officially kept diaries.
16. Cf. Tschudi to Leonhard Haas, director of the Swiss Federal Archives, 27 September 1966: "During wartime duty, for his own safety and in agreement with the General and Brigadier Masson, Captain Meyer made diary entries that were considered personal." BAr J.I.121/63.
17. The Commander-in-Chief entrusted Captain Meyer with such special tasks. As an example, Meyer drafted the General's order to the armed forces of October 1, 1941 concerning political activities in the army. BAr J.I.121/1.
18. As an example, the General complained that Jaquillard, the head of Counterespionage, a sub-section of Army Security, was *snooping* the officers at army headquarters in Interlaken. On October 28, 1942, Meyer noted in his diary after telling the General about tapped telephone conversations in Interlaken, "the General is visibly indignant. ... He says that J[aquillard's] methods are the same as *the Gestapo's*." BAr J.I.121/1.
19. When examining the documents, a few of her explanations turned out to be inaccurate, however. (Captain Meyer occasionally used the same abbreviation for several persons; for example, "E" was used for both a liaison officer at the Operations Department of the SS Central Office and one of Masson's agents in Geneva. The correct name can be identified only when looking at the context.)
20. See Boris Schneider, *Einführung in die neuere Geschichte* (Stuttgart/Berlin/ Köln/Mainz, 1974), 32.
21. See Chapter 6.
22. Strikingly, Meyer did not destroy the documents that could have shown him in an unfavorable light.
23. See Meyer's statement to Masson on 21 February 1948:
    > The article by Private First Class Lützelschwab in *Volk und Armee* that carries the erroneous title, "Reporting the Facts About the Masson Case," forces me to stop standing at attention for the first time after several years. Those who dutifully stand at attention too long because they wait for their superior to tell them, "at ease," will faint if they do not take things into their own hands. I was your subordinate, in the Schellenberg connection I worked directly with you and you trusted me, and when the military courts investigated you because you were accused of committing an indiscretion, I was automatically included in the investigation.

    He explained that Masson had been rehabilitated in public, adding:
    > But what about the officers that you used for the Schellenberg connection? You left them standing in the cold even if there was no evidence of any wrongdoing by them. I received a letter from the General in which he says that he asked you to publicly vouch for your subordinates "in one way or another." That was more than two years ago....So from now on I will have to go my own way in order to advance my own cause and the cause of the other officers who were involved in the Schellenberg connection....I hope that

my factual account will do justice to you. [It will be inevitable, however,] that *pieces of evidence have to be published that were not intended for the public.*

The original German text of the letter reflects how sick and tired Meyer-Schwertenbachs was of the attacks to which he had been subjected and how indignant he was about Masson failing to publicly support him. He wrote: "Der Artikel des Gefreiten Lützelschwab in *Volk und Armee* mit dem irrigen Titel ‹Tatsachenbericht im Fall Masson› zwingt mich, nach Jahren nun mein soldatisches Strammstehen aufzugeben. Wer allzu lange schweigsam in Achtungstellung verharrt, weil er in soldatischer Pflichterfülllung vergebens auf das erlösende Wort seines Vorgesetzten wartet, fällt zu Boden, wenn er sich nicht selbst hilft. Ich war Ihr Untergebener, in der Schellenberglinie Ihr unmittelbarer Mitarbeiter und Offizier Ihres Vertrauens und wurde, als man Ihnen Indiscretion [*sic*] vorwarf, automatisch miteinbezogen....Wo aber blieben wir Offiziere, die Sie in der Schellenberglinie eingesetzt hatten? Die liessen Sie auf der Strecke liegen, trotzdem auch ihnen nichts Uncorrectes [*sic*] vorgeworfen werden konnte. Ich habe einen Brief des Generals vor mir, worin er sagt, dass er Sie gebeten hätte, ‹sous une forme ou une autre› für uns Untergebene in der Öffentlichkeit einzustehen. Dies sind nun mehr als zwei Jahre her....So werde ich nun meine eigenen Wege gehen müssen, um mir und den anderen Offizieren der Schellenberglinie zu helfen....Möge mein Tatsachenbericht Ihrer Person gerecht werden. [Es werde sich allerdings nicht vermeiden lassen,] *dass Beweisstücke, die nicht an die Öffentlichkeit gehören, publiziert werden müssen.*" (BAr J.I.121/20.)

24. Lützelschwab testifying as a witness at the Zürich district court, 2 May 1947. BAr J.I.121/63.
25. Lützelschwab was the one who told Kobelt about Masson's contacts; as of February 1943, he acted as a regular informant for the Head of the Military Department. Cf. Lützelschwab to Colonel Otto Müller, the magistrate examining the case, 5 June 1945. BAr J.I.137 1974/64, vol. 6.
26. On November 9, 1943, the Commander-in-Chief wrote to Lützelschwab, "in the matter of E[ggen], I would like you to continue your inquiries." BAr J.I.137 1974/64, vol. 4.
27. Lützelschwab, *Zur Geschichte des "Offiziersbundes" von 1940* (report on the "Officers' Conspiracy," March 1963). BAr J.I.137 1974/64, vol. 13.
28. Gustav Adolf Wanner in *Basler Zeitung,* 18 May 1981.
29. After the war, at the request of the government of Basel-Stadt, Lützelschwab wrote a *Bericht des Regierungsrates über die Abwehr staatsfeindlicher Umtriebe in den Vorkriegs- und Kriegsjahren sowie die Säuberungsaktion nach Kriegsschluss* (Basel, 1946).
30. Based on a decision by the Federal Council on March 3, 1944, Major Ernst Leonhardt, "Nazi district leader of Basel" and founder of the "Swiss Society for Authoritarian Democracy," and Franz Burri were stripped of their Swiss citizenship. See, among other things, Bbl 1946 I 19 and BAr E 27/10212, as well as Fuhrer, *Spionage,* 81, 107, note 170, and 130, note 310.
31. Lützelschwab, questions and answers in preparation for testimony in the case of Hausamann vs. Kummer/Schmid, 2 May 1947. BAr J.I.137 1974/64, vol. 8.

32. At shelf-mark BAr J.I.137 1974/64.
33. As of fall 1943, Masson on several occasions used Holzach as a courier with Schellenberg after the Federal Justice and Police Department had started creating difficulties for Eggen in obtaining a visitor's visa for Switzerland.
34. Readers interested in consulting documents used herein are advised to check the NARA Internet database at *www.archives.gov* to verify which collections have in the meantime been transferred from Washington, DC and Suitland to the new Archives II complex at College Park, Maryland, which opened in January 1994.
35. This apt term was used by David L. Thomas, scientific assistant to Walter Laqueur at the Center for Strategic and International Studies at Georgetown University, Washington, DC. See "National Intelligence Study Center," *Foreign Intelligence Literary Scene Newsletter,* September/October 1986.
36. While doing research in summer 2003, this author noticed that individual documents had been rearranged, so it may be advisable to consult the library's online catalog at *www.princeton.edu/~mudd* if in doubt.
37. The papers of Allen W. Dulles were donated by Mrs. Clover Todd Dulles in 1973 and additional papers were supplied by Mrs. Joan Dulles-Buresch-Talley and Mrs. Clover Jebsen in 1974. The CIA removed some of these papers prior to their transfer to Princeton University, with the proviso that they would later be returned. Apparently, "later" was understood literally as, to this date, said papers are not available at the library.
38. Alfred Ernst, born December 13, 1904, died October 17, 1973, commander of the 2nd Field Army Corps from 1965 to 1969. After writing his postdoctoral thesis, *Die Ordnung des militärischen Oberbefehls im schweizerischen Bundesstaat,* in 1948, he taught military science and the history of war at the Universities of Basel and Bern. His unpublished papers are filed at BAr J.I. 140.
39. See Chapter 10.
40. As references for the information that follows in the main text, see *Periodische Berichte des Persönlichen Stabes* 1939–1944 (BAr E 5795/199), and *Weisungen und Befehle des Persönlichen Stabes* 1939–1945 (BAr E 5795/241).
41. In French, the staff was first called "Etat-major *particulier* du Général" (General's Special Staff); on March 17, 1944, its name was changed to "Etat-major *personnel* du Général" (General's Personal Staff). In a letter to Chief of the General Staff Labhart dated October 9, 1939, the Commander-in-Chief explained:

> I do not like the term "Bureau"; it sounds administrative, which is not at all its task. It is supposed to facilitate my tasks as a *commander.* I want to change its name. I am against the term "cabinet" because that makes it sound as if it was a ministry, which is more suitable for the bureau of a member of the government than for that of a Commander-in-Chief. I have decided to use the term "General's Personal Staff," which reflects both the military and the personal functions of the body that has to be at my disposal. (BAr J.I.49 1, vol. 1.)

42. In retrospect, Lieutenant General Huber wrote in a letter to Federal Councillor Kobelt dated January 31, 1947 that the Personal Staff "was *not totally harmless* as a working tool." In order to prove his point, he gave some examples of things

that he found out "by coincidence because letters were misdirected and got into [his] hands." Huber explained:

> Based on probability calculus, I do not think that I found out about all undercover actions and plots through these misdirected letters....To end this *unpleasant chapter* on a more pleasant note, here is an anecdote that sheds some light on the relationship between the Commander-in-Chief and his top aide, whom the Federal Council appointed upon his request. Shortly after starting my job as chief of the General Staff, the General gave me a sealed envelope and told me, "Open [it] only if a war breaks out." Of course I was curious; I thought that it was a will or something sim-ilar and put the envelope where I kept the most secret files in the event that a war broke out. Some time later, when I happened to be home (at that time we were still living in Bern), my wife asked me if it was true that the General would move to Mauensee castle if a war broke out. She said that she had heard this information at a tea party and wanted to know whether I would move there as well. I did not know the answer, so I asked the General about it at the next opportunity that presented itself. He was visibly astound-ed, and he ended the conversation by authorizing me to open the sealed envelope in question. It said that in the event a war broke out, the Commander-in-Chief would move his command post to Mauensee castle! The matter was so amusing that one could not be upset; instead, one brushed it aside, considering it as a boyish prank by the working instrument [i.e., the Personal Staff].
> *Nevertheless, the whole matter had a tormenting aspect.* (BAr E 5800/1, vol. 2.)

43. After the war, Barbey published interesting diary notes concerning the years that he served at the Commander-in-Chief's command post (*P.C. du Général* [Neuchâtel, 1948]). Quite a few officers were upset about his candid account because they felt exposed. On July 24, 1948, Roswell D. McClelland from the American legation in Bern reported to his close friend Allen W. Dulles, "The book had a great deal of success in French[-speaking] Switzerland, but rather upset some of the [Swiss German] army 'brass' of the *Kobelt school*" (Princeton University Library, Allen W. Dulles Papers, Box 37). In *Schweizer Monatshefte* (March 1948, No. 12), an unidentified author who used the pseudonym "Miles" acknowledged that Barbey had a keen sense of observation and had tal-ent describing scenes and characters in an extremely lively manner by using just a few expressions. Nevertheless, the reviewer concluded: "From a military view-point, the overall impression is negative; the book contains too many indiscre-tions that often degenerate into tactless statements." As a reference document for historians, however, Barbey's recordings are probably highly interesting, since "Miles" commented with surprise: "Barbey was present almost every-where. Moreover, when very important decisions were made he was basically designated to bring his opinion to bear, since he did not only edit many requests and orders but actually drafted them on his own; generally only minor

changes were made to them." (Maybe "Miles" was Colonel Fritz Rieter of the General Staff, the publisher of the *Schweizer Monatshefte* at the time.)

44. Shelf-mark BAr E 5795. The files were kept at the barracks in Lausanne at first, where the General had his office while he was writing his report on wartime duty. In 1947, the unclassified official files were transferred to the General Staff unit, which handed them over to the Federal Archives in 1966. The *secret* official files and the civilian files continued to be kept at the barracks in Lausanne until 1966, when Colonel Marguth and Lieutenant Colonel Barbey also handed them over to the Federal Archives. From 1969 to 1973, Eduard Tschabold filed the documents and wrote an informative introduction in the reference work for shelf-mark 5795.

45. General Guisan's private papers, which this author also consulted, are filed at BAr J.I.127.

46. See for example Meyer-Schwertenbach to Masson, 21 February 1948. BAr J.I.121/20 (see page 436, endnote 23).

47. See Colonel Otto Müller (magistrate examining the case) to Military Attorney General, 8 August 1945. BAr E 5330 1982/1, vol. 205. Theophil Sprecher von Bernegg reported that the same difficulties also existed during World War I. See *Bericht des Chefs des Generalstabes der Armee an den General über die Mobilmachung und den Verlauf des Aktivdienstes* (Bern, 2nd ed. 1923), 354–355.

48. During the years immediately following the war, Kurz' mediation on Masson's behalf was all the more welcome as Masson did not hide the fact that he was on bad terms with Federal Councillor Kobelt. For example, in a private, personal letter to Chief of the General Staff de Montmollin dated September 6, 1945, he remarked, "I *never got along* with Kobelt." Even in a letter to the Head of the Military Department dated October 2, 1945, he bluntly stated, "I know that you do not like me and that you have probably never been very interested in my fate." Both documents are at BAr E 27/9528.

49. At shelf-mark BAr J.I. 203.

50. Henri Guisan, *Bericht an die Bundesversammlung über den Aktivdienst 1939–1945* (Bern, [1946]), 52–53. (Referred to throughout this volume as "the General's report on wartime duty.")

51. Bernard Barbey, *P.C. du Général: Journal du chef de l'état-major particulier du général Guisan 1940–1945* (Neuchâtel, 1948). Cf. page 439, endnote 43.

52. On May 19, 1947, Kobelt issued instructions stating that the soldiers who used to serve on Army Intelligence had to keep silent about their former activities there in order not to give away the methods that had been used nor to expose the persons who had assisted Swiss intelligence. BAr J.I.137 1974/64, vol. 8.

53. Walter Schellenberg, *The Labyrinth* (London, 1956).

54. In his book, Kimche mainly presents the point of view of Waibel, Ernst, and Hausamann, who vehemently opposed Masson's connection with Schellenberg. Masson's reaction to the publication of Kimche's book was not free of anti-Semitic feelings. On April 18, 1962, he told Meyer-Schwertenbach, "As for the possibility of taking legal action against Kimche, …it would be humiliating for me and Switzerland if the Chief of Intelligence and Security was obliged to publicly account for his actions to a Jew who undoubtedly never served in our army." Two days later, in another letter to Meyer, Colonel-Brigadier Masson,

feeling denigrated, reiterated his thoughts, stating, "I hesitate to respond to Kimche's latest article because I do not want this 'guerilla' to continue in public, nor do I want the Jew to immediately react with an even nastier reply." The few facts that Kimche misstates have been corrected in this study based on evidence from source documents; nevertheless, his errors are counterbalanced by the surprising amount of sensitivity with which Kimche handled the subject. In fact, this author's interpretation of the events on many occasions matches that of Kimche, "this sinister Jew," as Masson described him in another letter to Meyer dated June 10, 1962. Masson's letters to Meyer quoted above are at BAr J.I.121/20.

55. *Tages-Anzeiger*, 24, 26, and 28 March 1962, nos. 71, 72, and 74.
56. Pierre Accoce/Pierre Quet, *La guerre a été gagnée en Suisse* (Paris, 1966). German translation: *Moskau wusste alles* (Zürich, 1966); English translation: *A Man Called Lucy* (New York, 1968). The three titles are an indication of the subject, Rudolf Roessler's "Werther" connection; its amazingly precise information was transmitted to Moscow, among other places, via Alexander Rado's network.
57. *Neue Zürcher Zeitung*, 3 April 1966, Sunday edition, no. 1465/1966. The article ended by commenting that in view of this latest distortion of the facts it was "strongly desirable that the Federal Council urge Prof. Bonjour to finish his report soon and prepare for its publication in a suitable format."
58. Masson to Kurz, 10 March 1966, "Unscrupulous people have taken advantage of my innocent trust; they wanted to write a bestseller at our expense." Archives of H.R. Kurz.
59. In his instructions of May 19, 1947, Federal Councillor Kobelt had ordered all soldiers who had served on Army Intelligence to keep silent (cf. page 440, endnote 52). In summer 1967, Masson's version of the story was published also in several Swiss German newspapers, including the *Neue Berner Zeitung* on 2–3 September 1967, no. 205.
60. The secret negotiations between Dulles and SS Lieutenant General Karl Wolff concerning the capitulation of the German troops stationed in northern Italy. The talks were held in Switzerland. Major Max Waibel of Switzerland's General Staff played an important part in the negotiations as a mediator (see page 281, endnote 67).
61. Allen Dulles to Pierre Quet, 8 February 1966. Princeton University Library, Allen W. Dulles Papers, Box 153.
62. Cf. page 283, endnote 80.
63. Lieutenant Colonel Erwin Tschudi, an aide of Masson who had also been a member of the General's Personal Staff for some time, ascribed Alphons Matt's publication to Hausamann's need for recognition and felt obligated to stand up for Meyer-Schwertenbach and Masson, who had both passed away by that time. Tschudi wrote some extensive "Remarks" dated April 20, 1969 that he submitted to the Military Attorney General, the Director of the Federal Archives, Leonhard Haas, the press officer at the Military Department, Hans Rudolf Kurz, and the editorial boards of *Weltwoche, Neue Zürcher Zeitung, Bund, Berner Tagblatt,* and *St. Galler Tagblatt.* Tschudi was supported by Lieutenant General Hans Frick, who had been Masson's superior for a short

time at the beginning of wartime duty when he was assistant chief of staff for the front, and Bernard Cuénoud, the head of the *Allied Section* of the Intelligence Service at the time, among other people. However, the "Remarks" resulted in Hausamann taking Tschudi to court. The lawsuit ended in Bern with an out-of-court settlement on February 20, 1970. Court files, Hausamann vs. Tschudi, 1969–1970 (Archives of Tschudi); letters by Tschudi to this author, 1986–1994. Before he died at the end of 1994, Erwin Tschudi offered this author numerous original documents, including, in particular, a large number of intelligence reports by "Bureau Ha."

64. Bonjour, *Neutralität*, vol. 5, chapter 3, 68–90.
65. Hans Rudolf Kurz, *Nachrichtenzentrum Schweiz* (Frauenfeld, 1972).
66. See Chapter 1.
67. Werner Rings, *Schweiz im Krieg* (Zürich, 1974), 377.
68. Daniel Bourgeois, *Le Troisième Reich et la Suisse 1933–1941* (Neuchâtel, 1974). Unfortunately his thorough study, which is based on a large number of previously unknown source documents, has not been translated.
69. In connection with the affair concerning the files of La Charité-sur-Loire (Bourgeois, *Le Troisième Reich*, 227–242).
70. Bourgeois, *Le Troisième Reich*, XIII.
71. Hans Rudolf Fuhrer, *Spionage gegen die Schweiz* (Frauenfeld, 1982).
72. However, there is an abundant amount of secondary literature on individual aspects of this study (see Bruno Lezzi, "Die Faszination der Nachrichtendienste," *Neue Zürcher Zeitung*, 7–8 September 1985, no. 205). A selection of the major works that have been consulted for this study are listed in the bibliography.
73. That does not mean that the connection fell into oblivion after 1982. Newspapers occasionally referred to it, such as the *Thurgauer Zeitung* in a series of articles, 13 April-8 May 1985, which was later published as a book (Albert Schoop, *Als der Krieg zu Ende ging* [Frauenfeld, 1985]), and the *Schweizerische Handelszeitung*, 20 June 1985, no. 25. More recently, Erwin Bucher wrote on the subject in the *Schweizerische Zeitschrift für Geschichte*, vol. 38, 1988, 276–302; however, his analysis does not go beyond the one made by this author in his 1985 study (Pierre Th. Braunschweig, *Die Nachrichtenlinie Masson-Schellenberg: Ein kontroverser Fall aus dem militärischen Nachrichtendienst der Schweiz im Zweiten Weltkrieg*, Bern, 1985), and the assessment that he makes of the alert of March 1943 is refuted in this study. In addition to radio reports and television documentaries surrounding this author's research, two works have been published since the publication of the first edition of *Geheimer Draht nach Berlin* (Zürich, 1989), that also look at the connection in some detail: Erwin Bucher, *Zwischen Bundesrat und General: Schweizer Politik und Armee im Zweiten Weltkrieg* (St. Gallen, 1991), and recently Willi Gautschi, *General Henri Guisan: Commander-in-Chief of the Swiss Army in World War II* (New York: Front Street Press, 2003)
74. Rings, *Schweiz im Krieg*, 377.

Available Source Material

THIS STUDY IS BASED primarily on previously unpublished source material from the Swiss Federal Archives and other Swiss and foreign archives.[1] However, intelligence is a field that is extremely secretive and is therefore not very well documented. Almost all official documents are classified as secret, and even private papers are very confidential.

No intelligence agency that has any sense of responsibility records for outsiders how it sets up its networks, who takes part in them, and who supplies what information. (The exception proves the rule.) Whenever possible it does not establish any files or it destroys them before they can get into the wrong hands. In addition, in the case under study, by being forced to keep up with the rapidly changing events of the war, intelligence had to focus on its most urgent tasks.[2] Systematically retrieving and evaluating organizational and tactical details had to be neglected in favor of keeping a close eye on the overall situation because it was "comparatively unimportant,"[3] or, as Alfred Ernst put it in fall 1940 for Army Intelligence as a whole, "*primum vivere, deinde philosophari*" (first we must live, then we can philosophize).[4]

For these reasons, some of the official documents do not yield much information. Nevertheless, as David Kahn has correctly stated:[5] "Although many records were destroyed, both accidentally and deliberately,[6] enormous quantities survive.[7] Repetition and corroboration within led me to believe that they accurately outline the whole topic, despite inevitable losses of detail."[8] Unpublished private papers frequently complement these official records, and in the case under study, the two most significant collections of private papers have been evaluated for the first time.[9] In fact, private source documents are indispensable for recovering some of the losses of detail that Kahn deplores, and they are sometimes decisive for being able to assess certain events. By comparing the official documents with the personal records of involved persons and supplementing or correcting the information provided therein,[10] one is offered a new perspective with subtle nuances of the connection that made Colonel-Brigadier Masson stumble and fall after the war.

In the United States, it is far more common than in Europe to hand over private records of public figures to easily accessible archives. While doing research, the American historian and diplomat George F. Kennan noted:

> [In Europe, private papers of persons who have played roles of distinction or of special interest in public life] are apt to remain either indefinitely or for very long periods in the hands of the family and subject to all the vicissitudes that such custody involves. . . . The heirs tend to be little interested, to leave the papers unordered and uncatalogued, to forget where they put them, and to bequeath them in turn to secondary heirs whose knowledge and interest is even smaller and who are often not even aware of their existence. In the end either there is a fire, or else some descendant cleans out the attic, discovers the papers, confronts them with total incomprehension and heaves them out. . . . There can be little doubt of the resulting loss to scholarship.[11]

Research that is based on source material is made significantly easier when such papers are kept at suitable archives, where they can be easily and rapidly consulted. In Switzerland, the credit for finding out in time about private document collections and for managing to preserve them for the public by using the necessary tact and diplomatic skills mostly goes to diligent archivists.[12] Scholars often obtain the most conclusive source material from people who remained largely unknown to the general public during their lifetime but who gained valuable insight into events through their position or contacts. This was the case for both Captain Meyer and State Attorney Lützelschwab.

The Unpublished Papers of Paul Meyer, aka Wolf Schwertenbach

Captain Paul Meyer was the man who acted in the background, pulling the strings between Masson and Schellenberg and taking an active part in the connection as Masson's close aide.[13]

Meyer-Schwertenbach's unpublished papers that are now at the Swiss Federal Archives[14] mainly include private written documents. In addition, there are a number of official documents from the time that Captain Meyer headed the *Special Service* of Army Intelligence and Security. The diary entries that he made between 1941 and 1945 are particularly valuable. They consist of a collection of minutes that he recorded from memory, notes, draft letters, and accounts of events; some are longer and more detailed than others.

When the troops were called up at the beginning of the war, the army forbade the soldiers to write diaries.[15] According to Lieutenant Colonel Erwin Tschudi of the General Staff service group, Captain Meyer made his entries in agreement with the Commander-in-Chief.[16] These entries served to keep a record of encounters, connections, and events. The notes include information not only about tensions among the officers' corps (the entourage of Wille and Däniker versus officers working closely with the General)[17] but also about the lack of trust among the officers of the Intelligence and Security service.[18] Moreover, the recordings indicate that the intelligence activities of Hans Hausamann and his *Bureau Ha* were criticized by other Intelligence staff.

Meyer's recordings about the meetings with Eggen and Schellenberg are of course particularly important for this study. The papers show how the Masson-Schellenberg connection was established, how it worked, what obstacles were put in its way, who took part in it, what ideas these people had, and what their (apparent) intentions were. This information has been a determining factor for making an assessment of the connection.

As a rule, the entries were written in pencil; some were annotated, mostly with explanations written in pen, at a later date by Captain Meyer, which could be an indication that these documents had to serve as evidence for third parties (in connection with a number of legal proceedings after the war). Notes are attached to some pages that were written later on by his widow Verena Meyer in which she gives explanations or makes comments.[19] Meyer's pocket-size agendas include the dates of meetings with General Schellenberg, his intermediary Eggen, Meyer's Swiss aide Holzach, and other persons. In addition, Captain Meyer used his agendas to write down his impressions about intelligence officers such as Masson and Hausamann.

Meyer's papers also include a large, apparently quite complete collection of newspaper clippings and publications on Switzerland's Intelligence Service, many of which he annotated by hand. After her husband's death in 1966, Verena Meyer supplemented the clippings with additional Argus news reports. The photo albums and books commemorating wartime duty are also interesting. The correspondence, which Eduard Tschabold meticulously arranged for easy reference, offers a glimpse of Captain Meyer's trusting personal relationships with General Guisan and Colonel-Brigadier Masson, among other things.

Quoting Meyer-Schwertenbach's recordings is difficult insofar as he some-times seemed to be in a great hurry to write down his observations and there-fore shortened numerous words, failing to use declinations, using dashes instead of periods and commas, and singular instead of plural endings. The quotes are therefore slightly modified from Meyer's jotted-down original text. The grammatical inconsistencies indicate that Captain Meyer took the diary-like notes for his own perusal without having any outside readers in mind. These unfiltered recordings make Meyer's papers all the more valuable as refer-ence material.

Meyer meets the basic requirements[20] that make him a reliable source of information. He obviously had the necessary intellectual capabilities, expertise, and writing skills[21] to report the truth. He was qualified to do so also because he was directly involved in the events; he was not simply an outsider observing them from a distance. It is more difficult to determine whether in addition to being capable of registering and reflecting the truth due to his social status, he was also willing to do so out of personal ambition or for other reasons. However, since Captain Meyer was convinced until the end of his life that his activity was important and valuable, he had no reason to falsify his private recordings, which were apparently supposed to serve as a memory aid for him-self. On the other hand, once fellow intelligence officers and the Federal Council began to make their opposition to the contacts with Schellenberg and Eggen felt, we cannot exclude that in some notes Meyer may have had an unconscious tendency to justify his own actions.

There is yet another reason for being cautious about Meyer's source mate-rial; not all of his recordings throughout the war were equally detailed. On one hand, this fact is one of the criteria that determines the selection of the focal points for this study, but on the other hand it raises the question of whether *all* notes have actually been preserved. However, Captain Meyer probably had no reason to destroy certain parts of his diary[22] because he was proud of the con-nection that he had initiated, considering it to have been very useful to Switzerland during times of great peril; he believed that his diary-like entries precisely proved his point.[23] Meyer's wife had no reason either to destroy parts of the diary. Moreover, one must not overlook the fact that, even though in this study Captain Meyer's critics are quoted extensively, in addition to General Guisan and Colonel-Brigadier Masson other people on the Intelligence and Security service supported Meyer. The dividing-line between the two camps was actually blurred.

What makes Captain Meyer's private papers and personal records valuable and at the same time shows their limits is precisely the fact that Meyer was a very directly involved witness of the things that he recorded on paper. By analyzing his unpublished papers, one gets an idea of how one of the principal involved persons experienced and assessed the events at the time. In instances where, objectively speaking, the perceived truth did not correspond to the facts, as appears to have been the case in the event of the alert of March 1943, one should keep in mind that action taken on the basis of wrong assumptions is not less decisive for the course of history than action taken on the basis of correct assumptions. Generally speaking, wrong assumptions do not necessarily lead to wrong results. This is an argument that some critics overlooked who accused Masson and Meyer of having been taken in by the Germans.

The Unpublished Papers of Wilhelm Lützelschwab

Wilhelm Lützelschwab played a special role among the critics of the Masson-Schellenberg connection. After the war, he explained, "I was the one who took the initiative. I did not plot against Masson, Meyer, Eggen, etc. but tried to curb their influence in what I think was a decent and honest manner."[24] In order to do so, he was in direct contact with Federal Councillor Kobelt[25] and General Guisan.[26]

Wilhelm Lützelschwab was born on January 30, 1905 in Riga, Latvia. His father was from Chénens, canton Fribourg, and his mother was Russian. He moved to Switzerland when he was 14 and studied law at the University of Basel, where he graduated with a Ph.D. in 1932. The same year he became a civil servant and in 1939 a state attorney. He got involved in public affairs already before the war, actively fighting the "Front" movement as of 1933 when he was a member of the Young Liberals. Lützelschwab stated: "There I was considered a 'Nazi-hater' and a man of the left. At the beginning of 1940, I became a member of the Basel-Stadt cantonal parliament, and during the entire ten years that I served there I was again considered as having a 'leftist' outlook, even though I was a member of the [conservative] Radical Democratic party."[27] As he believed that he had better chances of doing constructive work in the private sector than as a crime fighter,[28] Lützelschwab gave up his career as a civil servant to join the management of the "Pax" life insurance company, where he rose from the post of vice director to that of a member of the board of directors and general manager. He died in May 1981.

Between April 1941 and November 1943, Wilhelm Lützelschwab headed the political branch of Basel-Stadt's police department; this cantonal Intelligence Service was a large organization, with up to 100 employees. When he was appointed senior state attorney in August 1943, Lützelschwab became head of the entire state attorney's office of Basel-Stadt. Even though after October 1943 he was no longer directly involved in the work of the political police, he was considered an expert in matters relating to the political police and continued to be consulted on anti-subversive matters,[29] heading the investigation[30] and acting as prosecutor in the Leonhardt case in July and August 1944.[31]

Lützelschwab's unpublished papers that are filed at the Federal Archives in Bern[32] include mainly the correspondence, messages, and notes for the file that he received or wrote while he was in public office. The documents deal primarily with Colonel-Brigadier Masson's, Captain Meyer's, and Captain Holzach's[33] relations with Eggen and Schellenberg as well as with Colonel Guisan Jr.'s relations with the Extroc S.A. company, which indirectly played an important part in establishing the connection between the Swiss and German Intelligence Services. Most documents written after 1946 are part of Lützelschwab's correspondence with Hans Hausamann in connection with the latter's lawsuits against the *Die Tat* and *Freies Volk* newspapers. These legal battles in which Hausamann accused the newspapers of slandering him concerned events that had occurred in Switzerland's Intelligence Service, making the exchange of letters between Lützelschwab and Hausamann useful for this study. Considering Lützelschwab's importance between 1940 and 1945 as a staff member of Army Intelligence and Security, the collection of documents that he left to posterity appears to be incomplete. Nevertheless, it offers valuable information on how connections were organized and operated during wartime duty.

Research Material from Archives in the United States

In the United States, the National Archives in Washington, DC, the Princeton University Manuscript Library, and the Franklin D. Roosevelt Presidential Archives in Hyde Park, NY, contain a particularly rich amount of useful research material. The *National Archives in Washington, DC* and, since 1994, their extension, the huge Archives II complex in College Park, Maryland, are unimaginable treasure troves even for historians who have done extensive research in archives, boasting more than three billion written documents, two million maps and plans, five million photographs, nine million aerial photographs, 28,000 kilometers of film, and 122,000 video and audio recordings. This wealth of documents includes an unsurpassable amount of intelligence material documenting virtually every aspect of the United States' intelligence activities since World War I. The most significant group of intelligence-related documents from World War II consists of the collection of the Office of Strategic Services, the United States foreign intelligence branch. The documents are filed in Washington, DC or College Park, Maryland, according to Record Groups (RG).[34]

The most significant documents that are being used in this study are from the Office of Strategic Services (RG 226), the Military Intelligence Division of the War Department General Staff (RG 165), the Army Staff (RG 319), the Chief Counsel for War Crimes (RG 238), the U.S. State Department (RG 59), and United States missions abroad (RG 84), whose reports also include a sizable number of interesting intelligence-related details that had been put together by members of the diplomatic corps or that the State Department had received from other intelligence sources.

The OSS documents primarily include a massive amount of research and analysis (R&A) reports and materials from Secret Intelligence (SI) and Counterintelligence (X-2). Among the documents that the Central Intelligence Agency (CIA) declassified shortly before this study was undertaken and that are filed according to entries, this author focused in particular on the papers from the Office of Strategic Services in Bern; its telegrams for example are filed under entry number 134, which contains the wires from the foreign outposts of the OSS.

The files of the Nuremberg Tribunal were also very interesting for this study. In addition to numerous special reports on subjects such as the Reich Security Central Office in Berlin, counterintelligence activities in neutral countries, etc., the documents of the Chief Counsel for War Crimes include probably the most complete collection of the interrogation records of German officials, officers, and members of the Intelligence Services. Among these documents, this author came across the evidence that was used to defend SS Brigadier General Walter Schellenberg, including Masson's statement in favor of the German officer that is followed by a handwritten declaration by General Guisan, declarations by Meyer-Schwertenbach, former Federal Councillor Jean-Marie Musy, and French General Henri Giraud, as well as the interrogation records of SS Major Eggen.

This short list of some of the major records may be an indication for experts that the abundant source material that is available at the National Archives in Washington, DC is quite a challenge for scholars trying to dig up the *intelligence gold* [35] that is buried there. It is remarkable that in all instances that this author asked to see documents that were classified as secret or confidential, he immediately received permission to do so.

The personal papers of *Allen W. Dulles* are filed at *Princeton University's Seeley G. Mudd Manuscript Library in Princeton, New Jersey* and are part of the collection of 20th-century papers in public affairs, which included the unpublished records of close to 150 persons at the time this study was undertaken. The papers were meticulously filed by Nancy Bressler and Jean Holliday in a total of 310 filing boxes covering the period from 1845 to 1971. [36] The papers form part of the Department of Rare Books and Special Collections and comprise correspondence, speeches, writings, and photographs as well as audio tapes and phonograph records documenting the life of the lawyer, diplomat, businessman, and spy. A large number of them deal with Dulles' activity as a member of the U.S. delegation at the 1919 Versailles peace negotiations, his leading role at the Office of Strategic Services during World War II, his time at the CIA from 1950 to 1961, the last years of which he was its director, and his contribution, between 1963 and 1964, to the President's Commission to Investigate the Assassination of President John F. Kennedy that had been appointed by Lyndon B. Johnson. The Allen W. Dulles Papers collection is useful for understanding the role of both a private citizen and a public servant in shaping U.S. foreign policy, even if those seeking information about the time during his tenure at the helm of the CIA will be disappointed that CIA officials screened the collection before it was transferred to Princeton.[37]

Series 1, Correspondence, 1891–1969, documents Dulles' professional and personal activities from his early years at the State Department until his death in 1969. These generally handwritten letters are quite candid summaries of events in the countries where Dulles and people he knew were stationed. Although his activities at the OSS during World War II are not particularly well documented in his correspondence, Dulles' discussion of past activities with the contacts he established at the time provide some insight. Correspondence with Gero von Gaevernitz, William J. Donovan, Mary Bancroft, and others sheds light not only on their wartime activities but also on the sense of responsibility and kinship that Allen Dulles shared with these colleagues. Significant correspondents also include Hamilton Fish Armstrong, Thomas E. Dewey, Hugh Gibson, Joseph C. Grew, John C. Hughes, Hugh R. Wilson, and Karl Wolff.

Subseries 2, Books, 1902–1969, of Series 2, Writings, 1915–1969, includes drafts, galleys, articles, reviews, notes, and correspondence pertaining to Dulles' books and articles. Starting with his 1902 monograph on the Boer War, that subseries documents the composition and publication of *Germany's Underground, The Craft of Intelligence,* and *The Secret Surrender.*

Series 3, Speeches, 1926–1968, includes outlines, notes, clippings and some background material. Dulles used notes or outlines when speaking; consequently there are very few full copies of his addresses.

Series 5, Subject Files, 1915–1969, is arranged alphabetically by topic and comprises clippings, articles, reports, memoranda, interviews, correspondence, and speeches that Dulles compiled for reference purposes. The subjects range from *Abwehr* and the German Intelligence Service to visa regulations.

The *Franklin Delano Roosevelt Library* in Hide Park, NY, was the first of seven presidential libraries to collect and make available to researchers the private papers of a United States president and the official files of his administration. The well-arranged documents and manuscripts include 15 million pages. This author focused on the documents concerning Switzerland from the Official File and above all the President's Secretary's file, which includes the incoming and outgoing correspondence and memoranda that were considered as highly important and confidential at the time and that were therefore monitored by Roosevelt's personal secretary. The papers, which are filed alphabetically, are subdivided into five groups, the Safe Files, the Confidential Files, the Diplomatic Correspondence, the Departmental Correspondence, and the Subject File. The Subject File includes the OSS File comprising approximately 7,500 pages of documents, which consist primarily of reports that General William J. Donovan, Chief of the Office of Strategic Services, submitted to the White House once or several times daily to provide a synopsis of the information received by the field agents. The reports that landed on Roosevelt's desk through that channel frequently included reports from Bern by Allen Dulles. The files at the Franklin D. Roosevelt Library show, among other things, how important Bern was for U.S. intelligence during World War II.

Additional Source Material

Unpublished Papers of Alfred Ernst

Alfred Ernst,[38] a future lieutenant general, headed the *German Bureau* of Swiss Intelligence from September 1939, the time when the army was mobilized, to summer 1943, when he asked to be transferred to the operational section. As has been shown in this study, this transfer was due in large part to Masson's connection with Schellenberg.[39] Most documents of Ernst's "Intelligence" file are therefore from the period between October 1939 and summer 1943; above all, they include drafts and carbon copies of reports and letters submitted to, and received from, Masson. Some of the reports make an assessment of the military and political situation, analyze Germany's options for an attack on Switzerland, and make suggestions on how Switzerland should defend itself against a potential attack. The letters in which Ernst gives his political opinion about Nazi Germany and warns Masson about the connection with SS General Schellenberg are particularly interesting. Moreover, the Ernst files contain information about the structure and operations of the Intelligence Service; they demonstrate how the *procurement* of intelligence was organized and include information about the tensions between the Department of Foreign Affairs and Army Intelligence.

The General's Personal Staff

After his election as Commander-in-Chief, Guisan created a "General's Bureau," which consisted of four officers and one non-commissioned officer and was located at the Bellevue Palace hotel in Bern, immediately adjacent to the offices of the Department of Military Affairs.[40] As early as October 9, 1939, this "Bureau" was renamed "General's Personal Staff."[41] Guisan created the new body in order to have some influence on everything that had to do with preparations for a war (operations, training, materials, spirit of the troops, and contacts with civilians) as well as to circumvent the tensions that existed with the Chief of the General Staff at the time, Lieutenant General Jakob Labhart. Even though Labhart's successor, Jakob Huber, also repeatedly protested against the new body,[42] the General kept it in place. (He must have had an incentive to do so not least for practical reasons, as he could work much more effectively with this small staff than with the very large, bureaucratic structure of the army staff.)

The "General's Personal Staff" worked on all issues that had anything to do with the Army Command; they included four main areas of activities:

1. military command matters (preliminary work, suggestions and comments to the attention of the Federal Council, orders to the Chief of the General Staff and to individual troop commanders);
2. legal military matters (appeals for pardon and authorizations to have cases heard by civilian courts);
3. civilian matters (letters by soldiers, their families, or employers addressed directly to the Commander-in-Chief);
4. the Commander-in-Chief's external affairs (preparing inspection trips and representative obligations).

The structure of the Personal Staff was relatively simple; on average, it consisted of eight officers. Its first head was Samuel Gonard, a future corps commander, who was replaced by Major Bernard Barbey on June 11, 1940, when he took over the command of the operational section on the army staff.[43] The Chief of the Personal Staff supervised one or two General Staff officers, including Denys van Berchem, who were in charge of preparing requests and decisions on behalf of the military command. Two adjutants were in charge of the internal organization at the command post (sentries and chancellery). Two aides were available to the Commander-in-Chief and Barbey for special tasks. Mario Marguth was both the officer in charge of legal matters relating to the military and, as of fall 1942, General Guisan's 1st aide. These permanent staff members were joined by temporary heads of the secretariat and of chancellery as well as by a varying number of NCOs, soldiers, and members of the auxiliary service.

Due to the military situation, the General's Personal Staff moved its headquarters on several occasions. From Bern it was first transferred to Spiez, on October 18, 1939 to Gümligen castle, on April 1, 1941 to Interlaken, and on October 6, 1944 to Jegenstorf castle, where it remained stationed until the end of the war.

The files of the "General's Personal Staff"[44] include several ten thousand documents illustrating all of the General's activities during wartime duty. They comprise the originals of the letters, reports, requests, and memoranda that were addressed to the Commander-in-Chief, copies of the correspondence written at his command post, as well as the Commander-in-Chief's and his Personal Staff's personal working documents, drafts, minutes, and annotations. Many of these documents make it possible to backtrack how the supreme command made its decisions. Obviously the papers concern primarily military matters, such as issues relating to strategies, armament, supplies, and personnel, but they frequently also touch upon political aspects, thereby shedding light on how the Federal Council and the Commander-in-Chief mutually influenced each other's decisions and actions.

This study focuses mainly on the numerous files from the Intelligence and Security sector, in particular the documents dealing with Guisan's encounters and contacts with Schellenberg.[45]

Court Files

Even though the legal action that was undertaken was a very unpleasant experience at the time for the involved persons,[46] from a historian's perspective one must be grateful that a number of investigations, hearings of evidence, and trials were held by military and civilian courts after the war. During these proceedings, materials were filed that would not be documented otherwise. Incidentally, the disputes before the military courts show that intelligence faces a probably inevitable dilemma in a state governed by the rule of law: it cannot limit itself to methods that are perfectly legal and may therefore be used by anyone. However, by having to use, and becoming accustomed to using, means and methods that under certain circumstances are forbidden to other people, one's sense of justice may become blurred and one may gradually lose the ability to distinguish between what is *permitted* and what is *not permitted*. On the other hand, the civilian authorities must feel uneasy about Intelligence being allowed to use means that they are not permitted to use or that make it more difficult or impossible for them to do their job.[47] The touchy feelings that this dilemma created resulted in some grotesque situations during the war and seriously distracted from the success of some of the operations.

Private Archives of Hans Rudolf Kurz

The private archives of Professor Dr. Hans Rudolf Kurz include documents compiled during four decades of research in the field of military and neutrality history; they complement the documents available at the Federal Archives in Bern. The main material that this author consulted from these private archives were the "Masson/intelligence files" and the "Schellenberg" and "Hans Hausamann" files. Colonel-Brigadier Masson and H.R. Kurz were in frequent contact by mail; this was due not only to their friendship after the war but also to the influential position that Kurz held as a close aide and advisor to the Head of the Military Department; on some occasions, Masson may have hoped to indirectly reach the Federal Councillor through his friend.[48] For Kurz on the other hand, the contact with Masson was useful for his own research in the field of intelligence; a number of his files consequently include precise information concerning Masson that is not available in any other archives. Masson also regularly sent Kurz updates on his account of Army Intelligence during World War II.

Hans Hausamann usually sent Kurz carbon copies or photocopies of his extensive correspondence for his information and answered any questions that Kurz had during his research. The "Schellenberg" file included, among other documents, report *No. 52 to the Führer* dated January 1943, in which Schellenberg stated that Switzerland allegedly planned to call up its entire armed forces again.

Before he died in 1990, Prof. Kurz offered this author a number of documents from his archives. His sons handed over the remaining material to the Swiss Federal Archives, where it is now available to researchers in the form of personal unpublished papers.[49]

Studies on the Subject

Not much has been written about the Masson-Schellenberg connection so far, which is due in part to the fact that this is a complicated case and probably also to the fact that until recently the most conclusive documents were not available for research.

Apart from the polemics in the press following Masson's "interview," the first, albeit somewhat concealed, treatment of the subject was given in the

Commander-in-Chief's report on wartime duty.[50] In his diary, which was published in 1948, Barbey also made a few isolated allusions to the connection.[51] After 1948, everything was quiet for some time. Masson had to keep silent,[52] and in Schellenberg's memoirs, which were published posthumously in the 1950s,[53] Schellenberg contented himself with stating that through his relations with Masson he had tried to enter into contact with the Allies; he implied that for that reason he had successfully attempted to have Switzerland's neutrality respected.

It was not until the 1960s that three books were published that focused on Masson's contacts with the Reich Security Central Office. *Spying for Peace* by Jon Kimche, a dual British and Swiss national who was a foreign correspondent for the *Observer*, was published in 1961 in London; shortly afterward the German and French versions of the book were preprinted in the *Weltwoche* and the *Journal de Genève*, respectively, making the book very well known in Switzerland. Some former staff members of Army Intelligence as well as some experts massively criticized the successful but controversial book, accusing Kimche of reaching wrong conclusions by making conjectures and false assumptions. However, at least he deserves to be credited for bringing Masson out of his shell, so to speak. As he was indignant about what he considered to be Kimche's distorted interpretation of the events,[54] Masson finally agreed to present materials for an account of the matter from an entirely different perspective. This account was published in several Swiss French and Swiss German newspapers as a conversation that Hugo Faesi, a former press officer on the Army Command, had recorded with the former Chief of Intelligence.[55]

Five years later, Pierre Accoce and Pierre Quet, two French journalists, described Masson's encounter with Schellenberg in a fairly sensational and captivating, yet in many instances incorrect, fashion.[56] The *Neue Zürcher Zeitung* ironically described the authors as *the two James Bonds from Paris* and called their work "a lively mixture of bold allegations and established facts, [adding] in their 300-page book, the two authors jumbled so many things together and put so many inconsistencies on paper that it is actually surprising that they were able to at least spell Hitler's name correctly."[57] Based on a recommendation that the Swiss Embassy in Paris had issued to them, the two journalists had been received by Colonel-Brigadier Masson for an interview. However, the results that they presented in their book[58] forced the former Chief of Intelligence to once again break the silence that the Federal Council had imposed on him.[59]

Allen Dulles had been approached by the two French journalists as well. However, as he was working on his own account of "Operation Sunrise"[60] at that time, he only agreed to take a look at their manuscript. What he read reinforced him in his conviction that it was better not to get involved in their endeavor. He wrote to one of the authors, "I read with some amusement your Galley 36 describing the anonymous house in the Herrengasse, Zürich (this should have read Berne), and on my alleged methods of operation. On the whole, I found these observations more picturesque than accurate."[61]

In 1969, another journalist took a far more matter-of-fact approach on the same subject. In his account of *Bureau Ha* that was based on Hans Hausamann's extensive files, Alphons Matt briefly talked about the relations between Masson, Meyer-Schwertenbach, and Schellenberg.[62] Certain distortions in the book are explainable by the fact that Hausamann had been a resolute opponent of the connection.[63]

Edgar Bonjour looked at the Masson-Schellenberg connection in more detail than Matt. In volume 5 of his history of Switzerland's neutrality, he dedicated more than 20 pages to Guisan's meeting with Schellenberg.[64] His findings are based in part on a study by Hans Rudolf Kurz that was published in 1972. At the request of the Federal Council, Kurz had written a synopsis of Switzerland and World War II intelligence.[65] His account of the Masson-Schellenberg connection was based largely on the detailed government communiqué of 1946,[66] which he had helped to draft at the time. Two years later, in his look back at Switzerland during the war, Werner Rings explained that "some of the circumstances of the clandestine contacts and relations [had] yet to be cleared up."[67] Daniel Bourgeois, who wrote his Ph.D. thesis on the complex topic of the Third Reich's policy toward Switzerland[68] and made an extensive excursus[69] on Masson's connection with Schellenberg, came to the same conclusion as Rings, stating: "[Was this] childish loyalty to an old curiosity? No, it was more than that. This affair, or rather the inquiry about Switzerland's neutrality, made sense because it highlighted one of the fundamental aspects of the relations between the Reich and Switzerland ... that is, the dual policy of the Reich, which was interested, on the level of its global strategy, in Switzerland being neutral and at the same time, on the level of its ideology, in conquering the country."[70]

In 1982, in his systematic analysis of the German intelligence agencies that operated against Switzerland between 1939 and 1945,[71] Hans Rudolf Fuhrer presented some new findings. In his analysis, he also talked about Schellenberg's "special connection" with Meyer-Schwertenbach and Masson. Even though, for the Swiss side of the story, Fuhrer basically only examined the results of the investigation by Couchepin—making it possible to complement or correct some of his statements in this work—his study is valuable, as he included numerous diagrams representing the complicated structure of the German bodies that dealt with Switzerland on the intelligence level at the time.

Fuhrer thereby not only explained some confusing aspects of the context but also covered the *German* side of the subject of this study.

Those are the major publications dealing directly with the Masson-Schellenberg connection;[72] no real scholarly monograph was written on the topic prior to this study.[73] The source material that has been made available finally makes it possible to shed some light on the "circumstances [that] have yet to be cleared up"[74] about this connection.

Fg/Ck/   9329   15.4.43.

Betr. E g g e n   Hans-Wilhelm, geb.5.6.12, DRA., Kaufmann,
                             wft. in Berlin, Dahlmannstr.33.

       Wie aus den beiliegenden Einreisefichen hervorgeht, ist
der vorgt. Eggen seit Oktober 1941 via Dübendorf wiederholt in
die Schweiz eingereist mit der Begründung   zwecks Besprechungen
mit der Metallverwertung A.G. in Zürich und KIAA, Holzsyndikat,
in Bern. Eggen ist nun neuderdings am 13.4.43 in die Schweiz
eingereits und im Hotel "Schweizerhof" in Bern abgestiegen. Von
absolut zuverlässiger Seite konnte nun in Bezug auf die wieder-
holten Einreisen in Erfahrung gebracht werden, dass Eggen für
unseren ND arbeitet und jeweilen nach seinen Einreisen mit Persönlichkeiten dieses Dienstes Besprechungen pflegt. Ob und wieweit
Eggen aber seine Aufenthalte in der Schweiz nicht auch zu Gunsten
seines Heimatstaates oder des Auslandes überhaupt verwertet und
damit auch gegen die Schweiz Spionage treibt, konnte bisher nicht
festgestellt werden. Es dürfte jedenfalls angezeigt sein, Eggen
auch weiterhin in den Augen zu behalten.

Notiz: Eggen trägt auf beiden Schultern Wasser.
22.4.43.

The head of the Security Service, Colonel Werner Müller of the General Staff, put SS Major Eggen under surveillance (BAr E 27/10631). *See* pages 380 (note 21), 382 (note 36), and 383 (note 44).

Bibliography

IN SWITZERLAND, there are four official languages, and it is standard practice that even though everyone speaks and writes their own mother tongue, they can count on being understood by fellow countrymen who have a different mother tongue. Hence most of the documents of Swiss origin cited hereafter were written either in German, French, or Italian. For the original wording of those citations where only an English translation is given, readers are kindly advised to refer to my book *Geheimer Draht nach Berlin*.

Following is a selection of the main reference material used in this study; for a complete list of consulted materials, readers are referred to the endnotes.

UNPUBLISHED SOURCE DOCUMENTS

Swiss Federal Archives, Bern (BAr)

E 27	Landesverteidigung (National Defense), 1848 to 1950.
1082	Vol. 1: Dienstordnungen (Pflichtenhefte) der Generalstabsabteilung (service regulations [terms of reference] for the general staff section), 1930–1938; Vol. 2: Dienstordnungen der Generalstabsabteilung (service regulations for the general staff section), 1945–1947.
9467	Weisungen des Generalstabschefs vom 22. Februar 1938 betreffend Neuaufbau des Nachrichtendienstes (Chief of the General Staff's instructions of 22 February 1938 concerning the restructuring of the Intelligence Service).
9471	Vol. 1: Organisation des Sicherheitsdienstes der Armee nach dem Aktivdienst (organization of the Army's Security Service after wartime duty), 1946–1950; Vol. 2: Organization of the Army's Security Service after wartime duty, 1948–1949; Vol. 3: Entwurf zu einem Bundesratsbeschluss betreffend

Sicherheitsdienst der Armee und Verordnung über die Wahrung der Sicherheit des Landes (draft decree by the Federal Council concerning the Army's Security Service and ordinance on maintaining the country's security), 1950.

9475 Abteilung Nachrichten- und Sicherheitsdienst (Intelligence and Security Service, 2 vols.), including, among other documents: Organisatorisches (organizational matters); Einsetzung eines Verbindungsoffiziers der Gruppe Id des Armeestabes zum Eidgenössischen Militärdepartement, zum Politischen Department und zum Bundesrat (appointment of a liaison officer of Group Id of the Army Staff with the Swiss Federal Military Department, the Department of Foreign Affairs, and the Federal Council); Errichtung einer Zweigniederlassung der Nachrichtensektion in Burgdorf (establishment of a branch office of Army Intelligence in Burgdorf); Differenzen zwischen Bundesrat Kobelt und General Guisan weger der Verleihung des Titels "Oberstbrigadier" an Oberst Masson (differences between Federal Councillor Kobelt and General Guisan re: the bestowing of the rank of "colonel-brigadier" on Colonel Masson), 1942.

9476 Sektion Achse (Axis Section).

9482 Aussenbureaux, Nachrichtensammelstellen des Nachrichtendienstes (outposts, procurement offices of Army Intelligence); 13 vols.

9483 Differenzen zwischen der Nachrichtensektion und dem Eidgenössischen Politischen Departement betreffend die Informationstätigkeit der Militärattachés, die Nachrichtenbeschaffung mit Hilfe von Vertrauensleuten der Nachrichtensektion auf den schweizerischen Konsulaten, die Nachrichtenbeschaffung durch den Kurierdienst und durch die Grenzkontrolle der Einreisenden durch den Nachrichtendienst (differences between Army Intelligence and the Swiss Federal Department of Foreign Affairs re: military attachés' activities as informants, the procurement of intelligence by the courier service, and Army Intelligence's interrogating individuals entering the country).

9492   Mitwirkung der Grenzwächter, des Zollpersonals und der
        Postbeamten bei der Nachrichtenbeschaffung im
        Grenzgebiet; mit Instruktionen (involvement of border
        brigades, customs personnel, and mail carriers in the pro-
        curement of intelligence in the border area; including
        instructions), 1892–1950.

9494   Zusammenarbeit des Nachrichtendienstes mit kantonalen
        Polizeibehörden (Army Intelligence's cooperation with
        Cantonal police authorities).

9501   Dislokationen der Nachrichtensektion (moving of
        Intelligence Headquarters), 1939–1941.

9502   Dienstbetrieb der Nachrichtensektion im Aktivdienst (day-
        to-day operations of Army Intelligence during wartime
        duty).

9503   Dienstrapporte der Gruppe Id (official reports by Group
        Id), 1940–1942.

9507   Kredite für den Nachrichtendienst (credits granted to
        Army Intelligence), 1933–1947.

9508   Korrespondenzen der Nachrichtensektion (Army
        Intelligence's correspondence), 1939–1950 (27 vols.):
        vol. 1:   September 1939 - October 1939;
        vol. 2:   Novmber 1939 - December 1939;
        vol. 3:   2 January 1940 - 27 March 1940;
        vol. 4:   28 March - 20 May 1940;
        vol. 5:   21 May 1940 - 10 August 1940;
        vol. 6:   11 August 1940 - 31 October 1940;
        vol. 7:   1 November 1940 - 31 January 1941;
        vol. 8:   1 February 1941 - 30 June 1941;
        vol. 9:   1 July 1941 - 31 December 1941;
        vol. 10: 1 January 1942 - 31 May 1942;
        vol. 11: 1 June 1942 - 30 September 1942;
        vol. 12: 1 October 1942 - 30 December 1942;
        vol. 13: 31 December 1942 - 30 April 1943;
        vol. 14: 1 May 1943 - 31 December 1943;
        vol. 15: 1 January 1944 - 30 June 1944;
        vol. 16: 1 July 1944 - 31 December 1944;
        vol. 17: 1 January 1945 - 31 December 1945.

9509   Tagebücher der Nachrichtensektion (Army Intelligence's
        journals), 1939–1945:
        vol. 1: 31 October 1939 - 7 May 1940;

vol. 2: 1 May 1940 - 31 December 1940 (entries for 1st week of May almost identical with entries for 1st week of May in vol. 1);

vol. 3: 1941;

vol. 4: 1942;

vol. 5: 1943;

vol. 6: 1944;

vol. 7: 1945;

9510   Katalogisierung der Dokumentation des Nachrichtendienstes (cataloging of Army Intelligence's documentation), 1942–1947.

9516–9536   Personal der Abteilung für Nachrichten- und Sicherheitsdienst des Armeestabes und der Generalstabsabteilung (personnel of the Army Staff's and the General Staff section's Intelligence and Security Service); specifically:

9519   Unterdossier (sub-file on) Bernard Cuénoud, including Beschwerde von Oberstleutnant i Gst Cuénoud gegen die Majore i Gst Waibel und Ernst (Lieutenant Colonel Cuénoud's complaint against Majors Waibel and Ernst of the General Staff); Differenzen zwischen dem Chef des Chiffre-Bureau, Hauptmann Alder, und Cuénoud (differences between the head of the Cipher Bureau, Captain Alder, and Cuénoud), 1940–41;

9520   Unterdossier (sub-file on) Charles Daniel;

9521   sub-file on Rolf Eberhard;

            sub-file on Alfred Ernst;

9525   sub-file on Robert Jaquillard;

9528   sub-file on Roger Masson;

9536   sub-file on Max Waibel.

9538   Beilegung der Differenzen von Emil Häberli und Rolf Eberhard mit Bundesanwalt Stämpfli wegen des Strafverfahrens gegen Bernhard Mayr von Baldegg (settlement of differences between Emil Häberli/Rolf Eberhard and Attorney General Stämpfli in connection with the criminal proceedings against Bernhard Mayr von Baldegg), 1944, 1946.

9708   Korrespondenten der Nachrichtensektion. Darin Bewerbungen und Dienstangebote, Anfragen; Berichte, unter anderem von Carl J. Burckhardt (correspondents of the Intelligence Section, including applications and offers of services, inquiries, reports by Carl J. Burckhardt and others).

9750   Parlamentarische Debatte über die Schaffung von Militärattaché-Posten (debate in parliament re: creation of posts for military attachés).

9837   Bureau Hausamann in Teufen (5 vols.):
vol. 1: Organisation und Betrieb des Bureau Ha (setup and operations of Bureau Ha);
vol. 2: Dislokation des Bureau Ha im Winter 1940/41 (Bureau Ha's move in winter 1940–41);
vol. 3: Sende- und Empfangsanlage Hausamanns (Hausamann's transmitter and receiver);
vol. 4: Fernschreiber für das Bureau Ha (Bureau Ha's telegraph), 1943;
vol. 5: Verschiedenes (miscellaneous items), 1939–1945.

9838   Personaldossier (personnel file) Major Hausamann.

9839   Differenzen Hans Hausamanns mit Oberstleutnant Schafroth und Hauptmann Waibel wegen der Übermittlung der *Bureau Ha*-Berichte an die Nachrichtensammelstelle 1 (Differences between Hans Hausamann and Lieutenant Colonel Schafroth/Captain Waibel re: the transmission of *Bureau Ha's* reports to Procurement Office 1), 1940.

9842   Ehrverletzungsangelegenheit zwischen Hauptmann Hausamann und Hauptmann Zeugin wegen Indiskretionen Zeugin's gegenüber Oberst Gustav Däniker (Weitergabe von Äusserungen Hausamanns). Darin auch Anschuldigungen von Hauptmann Paul Schaufelberger und Hauptmann Zeugin gegen Hausamann betreffend seine Beziehungen zum britischen Geheimdienst; Aussagen Hausamanns über seine Beziehungen zu Oberst Däniker (Captain Hausamann's slander charges against Captain Zeugin as a result of Zeugin's indiscretions toward Colonel Däniker re: passing on information that Hausamann had told him, including accusations by Captains Paul Schaufelberger and Zeugin against Hausamann re: his relations with the British Intelligence Service; Hausamann's statements re: his relations with Colonel Däniker), 1941.

9843   Differenzen zwischen Hausamann und Oberstdivisionär Frick betreffend Äusserungen Fricks über die

Nachrichtendiensttätigkeit Hausamanns (differences between Hausamann and Major General Frick re: Frick's statements on Hausamann's intelligence activities), 1942.

9844   Untersuchung gegen Hausamann wegen seiner Meldung im Bericht Nr. 225 vom 5. Februar 1943 über einen angeblichen Sonderfriedensvorschlag von Bundesrat Pilet-Golaz zwischen den Angelsachsen und Deutschland; Entlassung und Wiedereinstellung Hausamanns als Nachrichtenoffizier; Differenzen zwischen General Guisan und Pilet-Golaz wegen der Erledigung der Angelegenheit (investigation of Hausamann re: his information in report no. 225 of February 5, 1943 concerning Federal Councillor Pilet-Golaz' alleged proposal for a separate peace agreement between the Anglo-Saxons and Germany; Hausamann's dismissal from, and readmission to, Army Intelligence; differences between General Guisan and Pilet-Golaz because of the way in which the matter was settled).
vol. 1: documents from 1943 to 1944
vol. 2: documents from 1943.

9845   Schlichtungsverfahren des Eidgenössischen Militärdepartementes in der Ehrverletzungsangelegenheit Major Hausamann/Hauptmann Haefely wegen Hausamanns Anschuldigungen gegen Haefely betreffend Verbindungen Haefelys zu Nazikreisen (mediation by the Swiss Federal Military Department in the matter of the slander charges of Captain Haefely against Major Hausamann because Hausamann had accused Haefely of having ties with Nazi circles), 1945–1946.

9846   Ehrverletzungsklage von Major Hausamann gegen Dr. Gottfried Kummer, Inlandredaktor der *Tat*, und gegen Dr. Hans Rudolf Schmid wegen Anschuldigungen in der Presse gegen Hausamanns Tätigkeit im Nachrichtendienst (Stellungnahmen von General Guisan, Bundesrat Pilet-Golaz, Oberstbrigadier Masson, Oberst Waibel, Bundesrat Kobelt; Aussagen und Darstellungen betreffend die Verbindung von Oberstbrigadier Masson und seinen Mitarbeitern zu Schellenberg und Eggen, März-Alarm 1943, Gefährdung der "Wiking"-Linie; "Protokoll Eggen" und Gegenbericht von Hausamann; Tätigkeit der Extroc S.A., Rolle von Oberst Henry Guisan; Warenvertriebs

G.m.b.H.) (Major Hausamann's slander charges against Dr. Gottfried Kummer, domestic affairs editor at *Die Tat,* and Dr. Hans Rudolf Schmid as a result of accusations in the press concerning Hausamann's activities for Army Intelligence [statements by General Guisan, Federal Councillor Pilet-Golaz, Colonel-Brigadier Masson, Colonel Waibel, Federal Councillor Kobelt; statements and opinions on the connection between Colonel-Brigadier Masson/his staff and Schellenberg/Eggen, the alert of March 1943, jeopardizing the *Viking* connection; Eggen's statements and counter-statement by Hausamann; activities of the Extroc SA, role of Colonel Henry Guisan; *Warenvertriebs GmbH*]).

9848 Nachrichtendiensttätigkeit von Hans Hausamann (Akten der Generalstabsabteilung). Darin unter anderem: Meldung über einen deutschen Angriffsplan aus dem Jahre 1943 gegen die Schweiz; angebliche Verbindungsleute für Hausamanns Nachrichtendienst in Österreich; Kontakte von Nationalrat Bringolf zu einem tschechoslowakischen sozialdemokratischen Flüchtling und Beziehungen Hausamanns zur schweizerischen Sozialdemokratie; Berichte Hausamanns über Waffenangebote an die schweizerische Armee; Versuch eines Österreichers, Nachrichtenmaterial dem schweizerischen Nachrichtendienst zu verkaufen; Berichte und Meldungen Hausamanns über die Lage, Stellungnahmen des Nachrichtendienstes dazu (1938–1950); Berichte Hausamanns über Reisen nach Österreich und in die Tschechoslowakei 1938 (intelligence-related activities of Hans Hausamann [files of the General Staff section], including, among other things, a report on Germany's 1943 plans for an attack against Switzerland; alleged contact persons of Hausamann's Intelligence Service in Austria; National Councillor Bringolf's contacts with a Czech Social Democratic refugee and Hausamann's relations with Switzerland's Social Democrats; Hausamann's reports on proposed arms sales to the Swiss Army; attempt by an Austrian national to sell intelligence material to Swiss Intelligence; Hausamann's situation reports and Army Intelligence's comments on them, 1938 to 1950;

Hausamann's reports on 1938 trips to Austria and Czechoslovakia).

9849   Nachrichtendiensttätigkeit von Major Hausamann (Akten der Direktion der eidgenössischen Militärverwaltung). Darin unter anderem: Berichte über die allgemeine militärische und politische Lage, die Situation in Rumänien und den Aufenthalt des rumänischen Ministers Gafencu in der Schweiz, das Verhältnis zwischen Wehrmacht und SS, das deutsche Reduit, Handelsbeziehungen mit der Tschechoslowakei, Technische Nothilfe des Schweizerischen Vaterländischen Verbandes; Aufenthalt von SS-Major Eggen in der Schweiz, Beziehungen zwischen Angelsachsen und Russen, Beziehungen von Nationalrat Hofstetter, Gais, zu Reichsführer-SS Himmler, Nachrichtenbeschaffung von Hausamann im Allgemeinen; Frage der Einrichtung einer direkten Verbindung in das Hauptquartier Eisenhowers (Major Hausamann's intelligence-related activities [files re: the direction of the Swiss Federal Military Administration], including, among other things, reports on the general military and political situation, the situation in Romania, and Romanian Minister Gafencu's stay in Switzerland, relations between the Wehrmacht and the SS, the German *Reduit*, trade relations with Czechoslovakia, emergency technical assistance by the Swiss Patriotic Federation; SS Major Eggen's stay in Switzerland, relations between the Anglo-Saxons and Russians, relations between National Councillor Hofstetter from Gais and Reich Leader of the SS Himmler, procurement of intelligence by Hausamann in general; issue of establishing a direct connection with Eisenhower's headquarters).

9911   Beurteilung der militärischen und politischen Lage der Schweiz und des Auslandes; Meldungen über deutsche und alliierte Angriffsabsichten gegen die Schweiz; Beurteilung der Angriffsmöglichkeiten gegen die Schweiz durch das Armeekommando (assessments of Switzerland's and foreign countries' military and political situation; reports on German and Allied intentions to attack Switzerland; Army Command's assessment of the possibilities for an attack against Switzerland); 2 vols.

9914   Nachrichtendienst im Grenzgebiet während des
        Aktivdienstes 1939–1945. Darin unter anderem:
        Organisation; Kontrolle der Einreise und Durchreise von
        Ausländern; Differenzen des Nachrichtendienstes mit dem
        Eidgenössischen Politischen Departement betreffend
        Befragung der Einreisenden (intelligence activities in the
        border area during 1939–1945 wartime duty, including,
        among other things, organizational aspects; the checking of
        foreigners arriving in, or transiting through, Switzerland;
        differences between Army Intelligence and the Swiss
        Federal Department of Foreign Affairs concerning the
        questioning of arriving travelers).

9915   Meldungen über die Lage im Grenzgebiet, unter anderem
        Bericht Massons vom 15. Mai 1940 über die Lage an der
        Nordfront (reports on the situation in the border area,
        including a report by Masson dated May 15, 1940 on the
        situation at the northern front).

9923   Bericht über Besprechung mit Helmut Maurer, ehemals
        persönlicher Mitarbeiter von Admiral Canaris (report on
        meeting with Helmut Maurer, former personal aide of
        Admiral Canaris).

9943   Meldungen und Berichte von Hauptmann Waibel aus
        Deutschland (information and reports from Germany by
        Captain Waibel), 1940.

9945   Fotos von Himmler an der Schweizergrenze im Juli 1940
        (photographs of Himmler's visit to the Swiss border, July
        1940).

9946   Einvernahme von Schweizern, die aus dem Ausland
        zurückkehren, 1940–1945. Darin unter anderem:
        Differenzen zwischen der Nachrichtensektion und dem
        Eidgenössischen Politischen Departement wegen der
        Befragung von Konsul Stucki aus Elbing durch Offiziere
        des Nachrichtendienstes (interrogation of Swiss nationals
        returning from abroad, 1940–1945, including, among
        other things, differences between Army Intelligence and
        the Swiss Federal Department of Foreign Affairs due to
        Consul Stucki's being questioned by officers of the
        Intelligence Service), 1942.

9953   Berichte über den deutschen Nachrichtendienst (reports on
        Germany's Intelligence Service)

9960   Tätigkeit der deutschen Spionageabwehr in der Schweiz (Aktennotiz und Abhörprotokoll der Schweizerischen Bundesanwaltschaft) (activities of German Counterintelligence in Switzerland [note for file and minutes of interrogation by Switzerland's Attorney General's Office], August to September 1946.

9968   Rapport sommaire sur l'évasion du general Giraud (summary report on General Giraud's escape), 1942

9973   Meldungen betreffend Gerüchte in Italien über die Errichtung britischer Fliegerstützpunkte in der Schweiz (reports on Italian rumors re: the establishment of British Air Force bases in Switzerland), 1940.

9980   Meldung des Armeestabes an das Eidgenössische Politische Departement betreffend die Anwesenheit von Allen W. Dulles in der Schweiz (information by the Army staff to the Swiss Federal Department of Foreign Affairs re: Allen W. Dulles' presence in Switzerland), 1942

9983   Korrespondenzen mit den Aussenbureaux. Darin unter anderem: Nachrichtenbeschaffung; Berichte und Meldungen, einzelne Tätigkeitsberichte über den Aktivdienst 1939–1945; Agenten; administrative und personelle Belange der Aussenstellen (correspondence with the outposts, including, among other things, the procurement of intelligence; reports and other information, a few activity reports on 1939–1945 wartime duty; agents; administrative and personnel matters relating to the outposts):
vol. 1: Bureau Pfalz (*Pfalz* outpost);
vol. 2: *Uto* outpost;
vol. 3: *Salm* outpost;
vol. 4: *Speer* outpost;
vol. 5: *Hörnli* outpost;
vol. 6: *Bernina* outpost;
vol. 7: *Simplon* outpost;
vol. 8: *Nell* outpost.

9984   Nachrichtenbulletins der Gruppe "Rigi" (information bulletins by the Rigi group):
vol. 1: nos. 1 to 108, 22 January to 31 December 1941
vol. 2: nos. 109 to 214, 1 January to 30 June 1942
vol. 3: nos. 215 to 358, 1 July to 31 December 1942
vol. 4: nos. 359 to 499, 1 January to 19 July 1943.

9989   Sammelberichte der Gruppe "Rigi"; Weisungen für Aufbau
               und Gestaltung der Berichte (reports compiled by the *Rigi*
               group; instructions on how to structure and lay out the
               reports), 1941.

10019–10040   Verbindung Oberstbrigadier Massons und Hauptmann
               Meyers mit Major Eggen und SS-General Schellenberg;
               darunter insbesondere (Colonel-Brigadier Masson's and
               Captain Meyer's connection with Major Eggen and SS
               General Schellenberg, including):

10021   Beziehungen von Holzach zu Eggen. Darin unter anderem:
               Meldungen von Lützelschwab über Eggens Reisen in die
               Schweiz, über die Beteiligung Meyer-Schwertenbachs und
               Holzachs an der Handelsfirma Intercommerz A.G.;
               Stellungnahmen General Guisans und Massons zur
               Zusammenarbeit des Nachrichtendienstes mit dem
               Eidgenössischen Justiz- und Polizeidepartement (Holzach's
               relations with Eggen, including Lützelschwab's reports on
               Eggen's travels to Switzerland, Meyer-Schwertenbach's and
               Holzach's involvement in the *Intercommerz AG* trading
               firm; statements by General Guisan and Masson on Army
               Intelligence's cooperation with the Swiss Federal
               Department of Justice and Police);

10022   Begegnungen von General Guisan mit Major Eggen und
               SS [Standartenführer] Schellenberg in Biglen und Arosa
               (General Guisan's meetings with Major Eggen and SS
               [Colonel] Schellenberg in Biglen and Arosa);

10024   Beweisaufnahme gegen Oberstbrigadier Masson und weit-
               ere Offiziere des Nachrichtendienstes wegen
               Kompetenzüberschreitungen des Nachrichtendienstes,
               Beziehungen zu Schellenberg und Eggen, Einsatz von
               Agenten (gathering of evidence against Colonel-Brigadier
               Masson and other officers of Army Intelligence suspected
               of overstepping the Intelligence Service's authority, relations
               with Schellenberg and Eggen, use of agents);

10026   Untersuchungen gegen Hauptmann Meyer-Schwertenbach
               und Hauptmann Holzach (investigations of Captain
               Meyer-Schwertenbach and Captain Holzach);

10027   Administrativuntersuchung gegen Oberstbrigadier Masson
               wegen seines Interviews mit den *Chicago Daily News* (darin
               Materialien betreffend Schweizerisches Holzsyndikat,

Baracken-Handel; Aussagen und Stellungnahmen von Major Hausamann zu Masson und der Verbindung mit Schellenberg; Aussagen von Major Waibel über die "Wiking"-Linie; Stellungnahme von Bundesrat Pilet-Golaz zur Affäre Masson; Bericht von Bundesrichter Couchepin) (administrative investigation of Brigadier General Masson due to his interview with the *Chicago Daily News*, including material on the Swiss Wood Syndicate, the barracks deal; statements and comments by Major Hausamann on Masson and the connection with Schellenberg; statements by Major Waibel on the *Viking* connection; statement by Federal Councillor Pilet-Golaz on the Masson affair; report by Supreme Court Justice Couchepin);

10028   Interpellation Nationalrat Dietschi-Basel vom 1. Oktober 1945 betreffend das Masson-Interview über die deutschen Invasionspläne im Frühjahr 1943 (interpellation by National Councillor Dietschi, Basel, dated October 1, 1945 re: Masson's interview on Germany's plan for an invasion in early 1943);

10029   Interpellation Nationalrat Bringolf vom 1. Oktober 1945 betreffend Aufschluss über die Angriffspläne Deutschlands gegen die Schweiz im März 1943, die Beziehungen Massons zu Schellenberg und über die deutsche Spionage gegen die Schweiz (interpellation by National Councillor Bringolf dated October 1, 1945 re: information on Germany's plans for an attack against Switzerland in March 1943, Masson's relations with Schellenberg, and Germany's espionage against Switzerland);

10032   Abhörungsprotokoll der Schweizerischen Bundesanwaltschaft vom 1. Mai 1945 betreffend Eggen (minutes of Attorney General's Office's interrogation of 1 May 1945 re: Eggen);

10033   Ausweisung von Major Eggen. Darin Aufzeichnungen über eine Besprechung von Direktor Samuel Haas (Schweizerische Mittelpresse) mit Direktor Ernest-Otto Knecht (Industrieller, Lausanne) über die Verbindung Masson-Schellenberg, die Rolle der Firma Extroc S.A. und des Oberst i Gst Henry Guisan (expelling of Major Eggen, including notes on a meeting between Samuel Haas, director of the *Schweizerische Mittelpresse* news agency, and

Ernest-Otto Knecht, industrialist from Lausanne, about the Masson-Schellenberg connection, the role of *Extroc SA* and of Colonel Henry Guisan of the General Staff);

10034   "Protokoll Eggen". Darin Eingabe von Hans-Bernd Gisevius an das Divisions-Gericht 6 betreffend die Beziehungen Massons zu Schellenberg und Eggen (statements by Eggen concerning his activities in Switzerland, including a statement by Hans-Bernd Gisevius on Masson's relations with Schellenberg and Eggen);

10035   Administrativuntersuchung gegen Justiz-Major Wüest wegen unerlaubter Abgabe von Militärakten aus der Untersuchung gegen Meyer-Schwertenbach und Holzach an die Partei Kummer im Prozess Hausamann gegen Kummer und Schmid (administrative investigation of Major Wüest of the military courts due to the unauthorized transmission of military files to Kummer, one of the defendants in the case of Hausamann vs. Kummer and Schmid, concerning the investigation of Meyer-Schwertenbach and Holzach);

10036   Anschuldigungen von Major Wüest gegen Oberst i Gst Werner Müller, Chef des Sicherheitsdienstes der Armee, 1946 (Kontakte Müllers mit SS-Obergruppenführer Heydrich, Beziehungen zu Eggen und Schellenberg) (Major Wüest's accusations against Colonel Werner Müller of the General Staff, chief of Army Security, 1946 re: Müller's contacts with SS Lieutenant General Heydrich, relations with Eggen and Schellenberg);

10039   Frage der Ermächtigung an Oberstbrigadier Masson zu Zeugenaussagen vor dem Internationalen Militär-Gerichtshof in Nürnberg 1948. Darin "Attestation" Massons betreffend Beziehungen zu Schellenberg (issue of whether Colonel-Brigadier Masson should be authorized to appear as a witness before the 1948 International War Crimes Tribunal in Nuremberg, including Masson's statement on the relations with Schellenberg);

10040   Auskunft über den Tod Walter Schellenbergs in Turin (Totenschein, Photos des Grabes) (information on Schellenberg's death in Turin, including death certificate, photographs of his tomb), 1952.

10056–10084   Einzelfälle betreffend Spionage, Sabotage, staatsgefährliche
              Umtriebe, Extremisten; darunter insbesondere (individual
              cases of espionage, sabotage, subversive and extremist activ-
              ities, including):
10064   Strafuntersuchung gegen Eduard von der Heydt,
              Steegmann, Gisevius, Niederer wegen Vorschubleistung zu
              militärischem Nachrichtendienst (criminal investigation of
              Eduard von Heydt, Steegmann, Gisevius, Niederer on sus-
              picion of encouraging military intelligence activities);
10065   Fall (case of) Dr. Max Husmann, Zugerberg.
10098   Vols. 1–12: Spionage- und Sabotageabwehr 1939–1945.
              Darin unter anderem: Instruktionen, Befehle;
              Bundesratsbeschluss vom 29. September 1939 und
              Instruktionen vom 5. Oktober 1939 über den
              Spionageabwehrdienst der Armee; Zusammenarbeit zwis-
              chen dem Spionageabwehrdienst der Armee, der
              Polizeisektion der Territorialabteilung, der Heerespolizei
              und den zivilen Polizeibehörden; deutsche Spionage in der
              Schweiz, Allgemeines, Studenten, Filmverleihfirmen, ver-
              schiedene Einzelfälle; Kontrolle der Ausländer;
              Überwachung der ausländischen Gesandtschaften und
              Konsulate; Verfahren bei der Behandlung der Spionagefälle,
              Entwurf zu einem Bundesratsbeschluss; Vorwürfe gegen die
              Generaladjutantur betreffend Nichtbeachtung der
              Warnung vor Major H. Pfister, 1944 (Counterintelligence
              and countersabotage, 1939 to 1945, including, among
              other things, instructions, orders; Federal Council's deci-
              sion of September 29, 1939 and instructions of October 5,
              1939 re: the Army's Counterintelligence Service; coopera-
              tion between Army Counterintelligence, the Police Branch
              of the Territorial Section, the Military Police, and the civil-
              ian police authorities; German spying activities in
              Switzerland, general information, students, film distribu-
              tion firms, several individual cases; monitoring of foreign
              nationals; surveillance of foreign legations and consulates;
              procedure to be followed in cases of espionage, draft deci-
              sion by the Federal Council; accusations against the
              Adjutant General's Office re: failure to heed warnings by
              Major H. Pfister, 1944).

10101   Auskunft des Kommandos der Fliegertruppen an die
               Militärjustiz über die Belegung und Bewachung der
               Flugplätze beim deutschen Sabotageversuch an schweiz-
               erischen Flugplätzen im Juni 1940 (information from the
               air force command to the military courts on the use and
               guarding of the air fields during Germany's June 1940
               attempt at sabotaging Swiss airfields).

10109   Untersuchung betreffend angebliche Spionagetätigkeit des
               ehemaligen deutschen Militärattachés General von
               Ilsemann in der Schweiz (investigation of alleged spying
               activity by Germany's former military attaché, General von
               Ilsemann, in Switzerland).

10212   Motion Boerlin vom 5. Juni 1945 betreffend
               Berichterstattung des Bundesrates an die
               Bundesversammlung über die Umtriebe ausländischer und
               vom Ausland abhängiger antidemokratischer
               Organisationen und Personen während des Aktivdienstes
               (motion by Boerlin dated June 5, 1945 asking the Federal
               Council for a report to parliament on subversion by for-
               eign and foreign-led antidemocratic organizations and indi-
               viduals during wartime duty).

10329   Spionageabwehr: Dossier Franz Riedweg
               (Counterintelligence: file re: Franz Riedweg)

10468   *Panoramaheim Stuttgart*

11198   Bekämpfung der staatsgefährlichen Propaganda in der
               Armee und Überwachung extremistischer
               Armeeangehöriger, unter anderem Referat von Oberst
               Maurer betreffend Kominform und schweizerische
               Linksextremisten (fight against anti-state propaganda in the
               Army and surveillance of extremists in the Army, includ-
               ing, among other things, presentation by Captain Maurer
               on Cominform and Swiss left-wing extremists), 1948.

12054   Abkommandierung von Hauptmann i Gst Max Waibel an
               die Kriegsakademie in Berlin (detailing of Captain Max
               Waibel of the General Staff to the War Academy in Berlin),
               1938–1940

12521   Vol. 1: Abkommandierung von Oberstkorpskommandant
               Labhart und Oberstleutnant Dubois zu den Manövern der
               tschechoslowakischen Armee in Böhmen (detailing of
               Lieutenant General Labhart and Lieutenant Colonel

	Dubois to the maneuvers of the Czech Army in Bohemia), August to September 1937; vol. 2: Rapport sur les Manoeuvres de l'Armée Tchecoslovaque (report on the maneuvers of the Czech Army), 29 August to 3 September 1937.
14131	Differenzen zwischen General und Bundesrat betreffend Beförderung von Oberstleutnant Henry Guisan (differences between Commander-in-Chief and Federal Council re: promotion of Lieutenant Colonel Henry Guisan)
14132	Differenzen zwischen General Guisan und dem Eidgenössischen Politischen Departement sowie Minister Walter Stucki (Vichy) (differences between General Guisan and the Swiss Federal Department of Foreign Affairs/Minister Walter Stucki [Vichy France], 1943–1944.
14299	Operationsbefehl Nr. 13 (order of operations no. 13).
14334–14348	Angriffspläne der Achsenmächte gegen die Schweiz; darunter insbesondere (Axis powers' plans for an attack against Switzerland, including):
14334	Verschiedene Meldungen betreffend die militärische Bedrohung der Schweiz durch Deutschland während des Krieges 1939–1945 (various pieces of information re: German military threats against Switzerland during the war of 1939 to 1945);
14335	Berichte über Besprechungen mit den Militärattachés von Deutschland und Frankreich (reports on meetings with the German and French Military Attachés);
14336	Berichte des schweizerischen Militärattachés in Berlin betreffend die deutschen Angriffspläne gegen die Schweiz 1940 (reports by the Swiss Military Attaché in Berlin on German plans for an attack against Switzerland in 1940);
14337	Mitteilung des schweizerischen Gesandten in Vichy an den Bundesrat betreffend Verhandlungen Admiral François Darlans mit den Deutschen zur Aufteilung der Schweiz (information by Switzerland's Envoy in Vichy to the Federal Council on Admiral François Darlan's negotiations with the Germans re: the splitting up of Switzerland), 15 July 1941;
14338	"Wiking"-Meldungen vom Dezember 1942 über deutsche Angriffsabsichten gegen die Schweiz (reports of December

1942 by *Viking* on Germany's intention to attack
Switzerland);

14339   "Wiking"-Meldungen vom März 1943 betreffend Gefahr
eines deutschen Angriffs auf die Schweiz; Massnahmen des
Armeekommandos (reports of March 1943 by *Viking* on
the threat of a German attack on Switzerland; steps decided by the Army Command);

14340   Meldungen der schweizerischen Gesandtschaft in Budapest
vom Mai 1944 betreffend Plan eines deutschen Angriffs
auf die Schweiz (reports of May 1944 by the Swiss
Legation in Budapest on German plans for an attack
against Switzerland);

14342   Gefährdung der Schweiz während des Krieges (Exposé der
Nachrichtensektion) (presentation by Army Intelligence on
the threats against Switzerland during the war), 8 August
1945;

14345   Mitteilungen des Grafen Soltikow vom Juni/Juli 1947 an
das schweizerische Konsulat München betreffend
Angriffspläne Hitlers gegen die Schweiz und Verhinderung
von deren Ausführung durch die Bewegung des "20. Juli"
(Canaris) (information of June–July 1947 by Count
Soltikov to the Swiss Consulate in Munich re: Hitler's
plans for an attack against Switzerland thwarted by the *July
20th* movement [Canaris]);

14346   Operationsplan "Schweiz" des SS-Waffenhauptamtes (plan
of operations for Switzerland by the Arms Department of
the SS Central Office).

14833   Aktivdienst-Berichte: Gruppe Ia Front (report on wartime
duty by Group Ia, front).

14847   Periodische Berichte der Kanzlei der Nachrichtensektion
(regular reports by Army Intelligence's chancellery), August
1939–August 1942.

14849   Berichte der Abteilung für Nachrichtendienst 1939–1945;
Quartals- und Halbjahresberichte (1939–1945 reports by
Army Intelligence; quarterly and semiannual reports).

14850   Berichte der Nachrichtensammelstelle 1 (reports by
Procurement Office 1).

14851   Berichte des *Bureau Deutschland* und der *Sektion Achse*;
periodische Berichte des *Bureau Italien* (reports by the

German Bureau and the Axis Section; regular reports by the Italian Bureau).

14852   Berichte des *Bureau France* und der *Section Alliés* (reports by the French Bureau and the Allied Section).

15067   Unterlagen zur Ausarbeitung des Berichtes des Bundesrates zum Generalsbericht; nicht registrierte Geheimakten von Bundesrat Minger und Bundesrat Kobelt (background information used for preparing the Federal Council's report on General Guisan's report on wartime duty; unregistered secret documents of Federal Councillors Minger and Kobelt).

19357   Waffenlieferungen nach Deutschland, insbesondere Ausfuhr von schweizerischen Maschinenpistolen nach Deutschland gegen rumänisches Benzin (arms shipments to Germany, in particular export of Swiss submachine guns to Germany in exchange for gasoline from Romania).

19394   *Vol. 4*: Walter Haenger, Waffenhandelsagent: Widerruf der Vermittlungsbewilligung 1948 durch Bundesrat Kobelt. Darin auch Chronologie betreffend Oberst Henry Guisan und Irma Loebel, Extroc S.A., Hauptmann Meyer (Walter Haenger, arms dealer: 1948 recall of his trading license by Federal Councillor Kobelt. Also included is the chronology of events concerning Colonel Herny Guisan and Irma Loebel, *Extroc SA*, Captain Meyer).

E 5795   **Persönlicher Stab des Generals (General Guisan's Personal Staff)**

86   Persönliche Korrespondenzen, Notizen und Protokolle des Generals, vorwiegend militärische Angelegenheiten (General Guisan's personal correspondence, notes, and minutes, primarily military matters), 1941

199   Periodische Berichte des Persönlichen Stabes (regular reports by the Personal Staff)

241   Weisungen und Befehle (instructions and orders)

325–347   Nachrichten- und Sicherheitsdienst, extremistische Bewegungen; darunter insbesondere (Intelligence and Security Service, extremist movements, including, in particular):

327   Nachrichtendienst. Darin unter anderem: Organisation, Personelles, Beziehungen zwischen Nachrichtensektion und

Eidgenössischem Politischem Departement; Fall Mörgeli; Probleme der Nachrichtenbeschaffung; Meldungen der "Wiking"-Linie über deutsche Invasionsabsichten; Berichte von Oberstbrigadier Masson über die internationale militär-politische Lage und deren Auswirkungen auf die Schweiz (Intelligence Service, including, among other things, its organization, personnel matters, relations between Army Intelligence and the Department of Foreign Affairs; Mörgeli case; problems with procuring intelligence; reports by *Viking* on Germany's intentions to stage an invasion; Colonel-Brigadier Masson's reports on the international military-political situation and its repercussions on Switzerland);

329   Nachrichten über die militärische, politische und wirtschaftliche Lage 1942: Meldungen, vor allem von "Wiking", über deutsche Angriffsabsichten gegen die Schweiz; Studie der Sektion Achse vom 19. Dezember 1942 über die Bedeutung der deutsch-italienischen Bahnverbindungen (information on the military, political, and economic situation in 1942: reports, above all by *Viking*, on Germany's intention to attack Switzerland; study of 19 December 1942 by the Axis Section on the significance of the railroads linking Germany and Italy);

330   Nachrichten über die militärische, politische und wirtschaftliche Lage 1943 (reports on the military, political, and economic situation in 1943), up to 30 April 1944;

333   Nachrichten aus privaten Quellen (reports from private sources), 1941–1945;

334   Zusammentreffen General Guisans mit SS-[Standartenführer] Schellenberg in Biglen (General Guisan's meeting with SS [Colonel] Schellenberg in Biglen);

335   Angelegenheit von "La Charité" (the matter of *La Charité*);

343   Sicherheitsdienst (Security Service), 1941–1945;

347   Nationalsozialistische Bewegung in der Schweiz und I.P.A.-Angelegenheit (Nazi movement in Switzerland and matter of the IPA).

433   Angebot Schellenbergs zur Lieferung von deutschem Flugzeugmaterial (Schellenberg's offer for the delivery of German aircraft supplies), 1944.

436   Persönliche Angelegenheiten von Oberstdivisionär Eugen
               Bircher: Kommando der 5. Division; publizistische
               Tätigkeit; Reisen nach Deutschland und Polen, unter
               anderem an den Kongress der deutschen Gesellschaft für
               Chirurgie in Berlin, 1940 und 1941; Begleitung der
               schweizerischen Ärzte-Missionen an die deutsch-russische
               Front, 1941–1943, mit Berichten (personal matters of
               Major General Eugen Bircher: command of the 5th
               Division; publishing activities; travels to Germany and
               Poland, including to the 1940 and 1941 congress of the
               German Surgeons Society in Berlin; missions to the
               German–Russian front in the company of Swiss medical
               teams, 1941 to 1943, including reports).
445   Differenzen zwischen Bundesrat und General wegen der
               Aufschiebung der Beförderung Oberstleutnant Henry
               Guisans (differences between the Federal Council and the
               General because of the postponement of Lieutenant
               Colonel Henry Guisan's promotion)
448   *Vols. 1–3*: Angelegenheiten von Major Hans Hausamann
               betreffend Nachrichtendienst und Bundesrat Pilet-Golaz;
               Prozess gegen H.R. Schmid (matters of Major Hans
               Hausamann re: Intelligence Service and Federal Councillor
               Pilet-Golaz; lawsuit against H.R. Schmid).
451   Persönliche Angelegenheiten von Oberst Robert Jaquillard,
               Chef der Spionageabwehr; Tätigkeit der Spab (personal
               matters of Colonel Robert Jaquillard, chief of
               Counterintelligence; activities of Counterintelligence).
455   Persönliche Angelegenheiten von Oberstbrigadier Masson
               und seine Tätigkeit im Nachrichtendienst (personal matters
               of Colonel-Brigadier Masson and his activities in the
               Intelligence Service).
546   Unterstellung der Abteilung Presse und Funkspruch unter
               den Bundesrat (subordinating the Press and Radio Section
               [PRS] under the Federal Council).

E 5330   **Militär-Justiz (military courts)**
1982/1   Vol. 205: Militärgerichtliche Untersuchungsakten betref-
               fend Verfahren gegen (military courts' investigation files re:
               procedures against):
               Major of the *Waffen-SS* Hans Wilhelm Eggen;

Colonel-Brigadier Masson;
Captain Meyer-Schwertenbach;
sowie weitere Offiziere des Nachrichtendienstes; mit
Zeugeneinvernahmen von (and other officers of the
Intelligence Service, including hearings of witnesses) Alfred
Ernst, Hans Hausamann, Wilhelm Lützelschwab, Max
Waibel, and others.

E 2809/1	**Handakten (personal files of) Federal Councillor Pilet-Golaz**
Vol. 4	Aperçu sur les dangers auxquels la Suisse fut exposée au cours de la guerre mondiale 1939–1945; Dossier "M. Grandi"; Dossier "M. Sokoline"; Dossier "Duc de Windsor" (overview of the threats to which Switzerland was subject in the course of World War II; files on "Mr. Grandi," "Mr. Sokoline," and "Duke of Windsor"; various sub-files, some of which Prof. Edgar Bonjour arranged according to subject matters.
Vol. 5	Korrespondenz Frölichers mit Pilet-Golaz sowie verschiedene Unterdossiers; darunter "Prise de congé du Baron de Bibra de la Légation d'Allemagne" 1943; Denkschrift von Oberstkorpskommandant Wille "Memorial zur Lage Juli 1941" (Frölicher's correspondence with Pilet-Golaz and various sub-files, including, "Baron von Bibra's resignation from the German Legation," 1943; Lieutenant General Wille's "Memorandum on the Situation, July 1941").
E 5800/1	**Handakten (personal files of) Federal Councillor Kobelt**
Vol. 1	*Militärisches.* Darin unter anderem: Tagebuch Bundesrat Kobelts von 1941–1948; Akten betreffend General Guisans Gespräche mit SS-[Standartenführer] Schellenberg in Biglen und Arosa, Korrespondenzen Kobelts darüber mit Pilet-Golaz, Frölicher und Hausamann, 1943–1950; Belange des schweizerischen Nachrichtendienstes; Briefe und Berichte Hausamanns an Kobelt, 1941–1945; personelle Angelegenheiten betreffend unter anderem General Guisan, Oberstkorpskommandant Labhart, Oberstdivisionär Bircher, Oberst Henry Guisan (military matters, including Federal Councillor Kobelt's diary,

1941–1948; documents on General Guisan's meetings with SS [Colonel] Schellenberg in Biglen and Arosa, Kobelt's correspondence on the issue with Pilet-Golaz, Frölicher, and Hausamann, 1943–1950; matters relating to Swiss intelligence; Hausamann's letters and reports to Kobelt, 1941–1945; personnel matters re:, among others, General Guisan, Colonel-Corps-Commander Labhart, Colonel-Divisional-Commander Bircher, Colonel Henry Guisan).

Vol. 2   Stellungnahmen zum Generalsbericht und Materialien zum bundesrätlichen Gegenbericht. Des weiteren (comments on General Guisan's report on wartime duty and materials for the Federal Council's counter-report. Also):
Innenpolitisches. Darin unter anderem: Akten zur Eingabe der "200" ("Aktion zur Wahrung der schweizerischen Neutralität"); Frage der Einführung der Vorzensur der Presse (1940/41); Angelegenheit Däniker (domestic policy issues, including files on the "Petition of the 200" [by the "Action for Keeping Switzerland Neutral"]; issue of whether to introduce pre-print censorship of the press, 1940–1941; matter concerning Däniker);
Aussenpolitisches. Wirtschaftsverhandlungen mit Deutschland und Italien, 1941; Verhandlungen mit der alliierten Kommission im Frühjahr 1945 (foreign policy matters; economic negotiations with Germany and Italy, 1941; negotiations with the Allied Commission, early 1945);
Nachkriegszeit. Anträge General Guisans zur Reorganisation und Umbesetzung der Armeeleitung für die Friedenszeit, Juni-August 1945; Neutralitätsfragen (time after the war; General Guisan's requests for restructuring, and changing the staff of the Army Command during times of peace, June to August 1945; neutrality issues).

J.I. 121   **Nachlass (unpublished papers of) Meyer, aka Schwertenbach**

1   Tagebuchaufzeichnungen und persönliche Notizen von Hauptmann Paul Meyer als Chef des Spezialdienstes im Sicherheitsdienst der Armee und als Offizier im Nachrichtendienst des Armeestabes (diary entries and personal notes by Captain Paul Meyer in his capacity as head

of the Special Service of the Army's Security Service and as intelligence officer of the Army Staff).

5   Album (scrapbook) 1942–1944, darin unter anderem (including): Zerstörung der Me-110 in Dübendorf 1944; Briefe an Hauptmann Meyer von General Guisan, Mme. Mary Guisan, Oberstbrigadier Masson, Bernard Barbey, Bundesrat Kobelt, Ernst Mörgeli; Rechnung des "Bären" Biglen vom 3. März 1943 (1944 demolition of a Me-110 in Dübendorf; letters to Captain Meyer by General Guisan, Mrs. Mary Guisan, Colonel-Brigadier Masson, Bernard Barbey, Federal Councillor Kobelt, Ernst Mörgeli; check of the *Bären* inn in Biglen for the dinner on 3 March 1943).

9 to 34   Korrespondenz-Akten; darunter insbesondere (correspondence, including, in particular):

9   Werner Balsiger, Chef der Bundespolizei (chief of the Federal Police);

10   Bernard Barbey, Chef des Persönlichen Stabes des Generals (chief of the General's Personal Staff);

12   Peter L. Burckhardt, Chef der Operationssektion der Generalstabsabteilung, 1943–1945 schweizerischer Militärattaché in Berlin (head of Operations in the General Staff section, Swiss military attaché in Berlin, 1943–1945);

13   Hans Wilhelm Eggen, Sturmbannführer und Major der Waffen-SS (major [of the SS] and major of the *Waffen*-SS);

15   General Guisan, including: Persönliches, Telephonüberwachung der Offiziere des Armeestabes in Interlaken durch die Spionageabwehr; Beziehungen zu Schellenberg und Eggen; März-Alarm 1943 (personal matters, Counterintelligence's monitoring of the telephone conversations of Army Staff officers in Interlaken; relations with Schellenberg and Eggen; alert of March 1943);

16   Madame Mary Guisan, Gattin des Oberbefehlshabers (the Commander-in-Chief's wife);

17   Oberst i Gst (Colonel) Henry Guisan (of the General Staff), Sohn des Generals (the Commander-in-Chief's son);

19   Oberst (Colonel) Mario Marguth, Kommandant des Generalsquartiers (commander of the Commander-in-Chief's quarters);

20   Oberstbrigadier (Colonel-Brigadier) Masson, including:
                     Persönliches; Beziehungen zu Eggen und Schellenberg;
                     Berichte über die militär-politische Lage; Stellung von
                     General Guisan gegenüber Deutschland;
                     Telephonüberwachung der Offiziere des Armeestabes durch
                     die Spionageabwehr; Organisation des Bureau Zürich,
                     Unterstellung von Hauptmann Meyer unter Major Waibel,
                     Differenzen mit Major Waibel; Agenten des schweiz-
                     erischen Nachrichtendienstes; Gefährdung der "Wiking"-
                     Linie durch die Linie Masson-Schellenberg (personal mat-
                     ters; relations with Eggen and Schellenberg; reports on the
                     military-political situation; General Guisan's position
                     toward Germany; Counterintelligence's monitoring of the
                     telephone conversations of Army Staff officers; setup of the
                     outpost in Zürich, Captain Meyer's subordination under
                     Major Waibel, differences between Meyer and Waibel;
                     agents of Swiss Intelligence; Masson-Schellenberg connec-
                     tion jeopardizing the *Viking* connection);

24   Oberst i Gst (Colonel) Werner Müller (of the General
                     Staff), Chef des Sicherheitsdienstes der Armee (head of the
                     Army's Security Service), darin unter anderem (including,
                     among other things): Persönliches; Vorschriften-Entwurf
                     betreffend Geheimhaltung (personal matters; draft instruc-
                     tions on secrecy);

25   Fritz Riediger, Verteidiger vor dem amerikanischen
                     Militärtribunal in Nürnberg ([Walter Schellenberg's]
                     defense attorney at the U.S. War Crimes Tribunal in
                     Nuremberg); betreffend Zeugenaussagen von Hauptmann
                     Meyer und Oberstbrigadier Masson zu Gunsten
                     Schellenbergs (re: statements as witnesses by Captain
                     Meyer and Colonel-Brigadier Masson in favor of
                     Schellenberg);

26   Heinrich Rothmund, Chef der eidgenössischen
                     Polizeiabteilung im EJPD (head of the Swiss Federal Police
                     Section at the Department of Justice and Police);

27   Oberstleutnant (Lieutenant Colonel) Paul Schaufelberger,
                     Leiter der militärtechnischen Auswertung im
                     Nachrichtendienst; über Differenzen zwischen den
                     Offizieren des Nachrichtendienstes (head of Evaluation of

technical military intelligence re: differences among Army Intelligence officers).

28   Walter Schellenberg, SS-Brigadeführer und General der Polizei; darin: Persönliches; Gesuch von Hauptmann Meyer um Freilassung französischer Persönlichkeiten aus deutscher Gefangenschaft (brigadier general of the SS and general of the police; material includes personal matters; request by Captain Meyer for the release of French personalities who were kept prisoner by the Germans).

30   Major Hans Rudolf Schmid, Chef des Pressebureau A.H.Q.; darin: Differenzen unter den Offizieren des Nachrichtendienstes, "Affäre Masson"; Prozessangelegenheiten (chief of the AHQ press office; material includes documents on differences among Army Intelligence officers, the "Masson affair," trials).

31   Federal Councillor Eduard von Steiger; betreffend Einreisen und Aufenthalte Eggens (re: Eggen entering and staying in Switzerland).

33   Lieutenant Colonel Erwin Tschudi, Stab der Gruppe für Generalstabsdienste; betreffend "Affäre Masson"; Differenzen unter den Offizieren des Nachrichtendienstes; Stellungnahme zum Buch von Alphons Matt, *Zwischen allen Fronten* (staff of the General Staff service group; material re: "Masson affair"; differences among the Army Intelligence officers; comments on Alphons Matt's book *Zwischen allen Fronten*).

34   Albert Wiesendanger, Polizeiinspektor von Zürich (Zürich Police Inspector)

35   Ausweisschriften von Hauptmann Meyer (Captain Meyer's identification papers)

37   Kaufbrief vom 23. März 1938 betreffend Erwerb des Schlosses Wolfsberg (settlement papers for the purchase of Wolfsberg castle on 23 March 1938).

40   Hinschied Hauptmann Meyers am 15. September 1966 und Herausgabe einer Gedenkschrift 1967 (Captain Meyer's death on September 15, 1966 and the 1967 publication of a commemorative booklet).

42 to 65   Chef des Spezialdienstes im Sicherheitsdienst der Armee und Offizier des Nachrichtendienstes im Armeestab; darunter insbesondere (head of the Special Service of the

	Army's Security Service and as intelligence officer of the Army Staff; material includes, in particular):
42	Pflichtenheft des Spezialdienstes; Pflichtenheft für Hauptmann Meyer; Organisation des Bureau *Uto*, Zürich (terms of reference of the Special Service; Captain Meyer's terms of reference; setup of the *Uto* outpost in Zürich);
43	Dienstleistungen, Sold (services, pay);
44	Rechnungen und Quittungen aus dienstlicher Beanspruchung (invoices and receipts for duty-related expenses);
45	Telephonabhör- und Telegrammzensur-Berichte des Armeestabes; unter anderem betreffend Gespräche Meyers mit Eggen in Berlin (reports on tapped telephone conversations and censored telegrams, including, among other things, reports on Meyer's conversations with Eggen in Berlin);
46	"Gedanken eines Offiziers zum politischen Umbruch unserer Zeit", verfasst von Hauptmann Meyer (Captain Meyer's "An Officer's Thoughts on the Current Radical Political Changes");
49	Entwurf von Hauptmann Meyer zu einem Armeebefehl betreffend die politische Betätigung von Wehrmännern (Captain Meyer's draft order to the armed forces re: soldiers' political activities);
50 and 50a	2 Schallplatten über die Aufzeichnung eines Gesprächs zwischen Hauptmann Meyer und Heinrich Rothmund (2 audio records containing a conversation between Captain Meyer and Heinrich Rothmund), 15 April 1942 (in HA Z-k/38 and 39);
51	Telephonüberwachung im Armeehauptquartier in Interlaken (tapping of telephone conversations at Army headquarters in Interlaken);
53	Auszug aus dem Gästebuch von Schloss Wolfsberg mit Daten von Besuchen, vor allem von General Guisan, Eggen und Schellenberg, in den Jahren 1941–1944 (excerpts of Wolfsberg castle's guest book, including dates of 1941 to 1944 visits, particularly by General Guisan, Eggen, and Schellenberg);
54	Einvernahmen von Hauptmann Meyer durch Justizhauptmann Wüest, Untersuchungsrichter des

Divisions-Gerichtes 6, wegen Verdachts auf verbotenen
Nachrichtendienst, Missbrauch der dienstlichen Stellung
und wegen der Beziehungen zu Eggen und Schellenberg
(interrogations of Captain Meyer by Captain Wüest, investigating magistrate of divisional court 6, on suspicion of
illegal intelligence activities and abuse of power, as well as
due to his relations with Eggen and Schellenberg);

55   Bericht betreffend Heimschaffung der Familie des franzö-
sischen Generals Henri Giraud und die Befreiung
amerikanischer Luftwaffen-Generäle dank der Beziehungen
Massons und Meyers zu Schellenberg und Eggen (report
on the repatriation of French General Henri Giraud's family and the liberation of U.S. Air Force generals due to
Masson's and Meyer's relations with Schellenberg and
Eggen);

57   Entwurf Hauptmann Meyers zu einer Erklärung von
Oberstbrigadier Masson zu Gunsten der Offiziere des
Nachrichtendienstes (Captain Meyer's draft declaration for
Colonel-Brigadier Masson in favor of Army Intelligence's
officers);

58   Daten über die Tätigkeit von Hauptmann Meyer, Chef des
Spezialdienstes im Nachrichten- und Sicherheitsdienst,
während des Aktivdienstes (time frame of the activities of
Captain Meyer, head of the Special Service of Army
Intelligence and Security, during wartime duty);

63   Prozess von Frau Patrizia Verena Meyer gegen Alphons
Matt wegen rufschädigender Behauptungen über
Hauptmann Meyer-Schwertenbach im Buch *Zwischen allen
Fronten* (lawsuit by Mrs. Patrizia Verena Meyer against
Alphons Matt on charges of defamation of Captain Meyer-
Schwertenbach in the book *Zwischen allen Fronten*).

66–73   Beziehungen zu SS-Sturmbannführer Eggen und SS-
Brigadeführer Schellenberg; darunter insbesondere (rela-
tions with SS Major Eggen and SS Brigadier General
Schellenberg, including, in particular):

66   Meldungen über Zusammentreffen von Oberstbrigadier
Masson mit SS-Brigadeführer Schellenberg und bezüglich
Einreisen von Major Eggen in die Schweiz (reports on
meetings between Colonel-Brigadier Masson and SS

Brigadier General Schellenberg as well as on Major Eggen entering Switzerland);

67   Spesenabrechnungen Hauptmann Meyers vom März 1943 betreffend die geheimen Zusammenkünfte von General Guisan mit SS-[Standartenführer] Schellenberg in Biglen und Arosa (Captain Meyer's March 1943 claims for reimbursement of expenses relating to General Guisan's secret meetings with SS [Colonel] Schellenberg in Biglen and Arosa);

68   Aufstellung Hauptmann Meyers über die bisherigen Ergebnisse seiner Beziehungen zu deutschen Stellen (zu Handen des Generals) (Captain Meyer's list of achievements as a result of his relations with German authorities, to the Commander-in-Chief's attention), 1943;

69   Entwurf Hauptmann Meyers [und Albert Wiesendangers] vom 4. März 1943 zu einem Schreiben General Guisans an SS-[Standartenführer] Schellenberg betreffend die Haltung der Schweiz gegenüber einem Angreifer (draft of General Guisan's letter of March 4, 1943 to SS [Colonel] Schellenberg concerning Switzerland's stance toward any aggressor, written by Captain Meyer [and Albert Wiesendanger]);

70   Entwurf Hauptmann Meyers zu einem Schreiben General Guisans an SS-Brigadeführer Schellenberg betreffend die Haltung der Schweiz und betreffend das Angebot Schellenbergs zur Nutzung von Patenten und Lizenzen der Luftwaffe durch die Schweiz (draft of General Guisan's letter to SS Brigadier General Schellenberg re: Switzerland's stance and Schellenberg's offer for Switzerland to use patents and licenses of the [German] Air Force, written by Captain Meyer) in 1944;

73   Aussagen Walter Schellenbergs über seine Beziehungen zu Masson, Meyer und Holzach (statements by Walter Schellenberg on his relations with Masson, Meyer, and Holzach).

74   Mitwirkung von Paul Meyer beim Baracken-Handel der Warenvertriebs G.m.b.H. Berlin mit dem Schweizerischen Holzsyndikat und der Extroc S.A. Lausanne; darin unter anderem: Beteiligung von Henry Guisan jun.; Kriegsgewinnsteuerpflicht von Paul Meyer (involvement of

Paul Meyer in the barracks deal between the *Warenvertriebs GmbH* and the Swiss Wood Syndicate/*Extroc SA* in Lausanne, including, among other things, Herny Guisan Jr.'s involvement; Paul Meyer's liability for paying a war profit tax).

J.I. 137 1974/64   Unpublished Papers of Wilhelm Lützelschwab
1   Korrespondenzen, Meldungen und Aktennotizen 1941. Darin unter anderem: Eggens Maschinenpistolen-Geschäft 1940; fremdenpolizeiliche Akten über Hermann Weidenmann; Vertrag zwischen Rudolf Haenger, Rudolf Walter Haenger, Henry Guisan und Ernest-Otto Knecht zwecks Gründung der Extroc S.A. (1941 correspondence, reports, and notes for the file, including, among other things, Eggen's 1940 deal for submachine guns; Swiss immigration police's files on Hermann Weidenmann; agreement between Rudolf Haenger, Rudolf Walter Haenger, Henry Guisan, and Ernest-Otto Knecht re: the founding of the *Extroc SA*).
2   Korrespondenzen, Meldungen und Aktennotizen 1942. Darin unter anderem: Eggen, Guisan jun., Extroc, Meyer-Schwertenbach; Bericht des Bureau Ha vom 16. August 1942 über strategische Reserven der Russen, mit der Voraussage, dass Deutschland den Krieg nicht mehr gewinnen könne (1942 correspondence, reports, and notes for the file, including, among other things, Eggen, Guisan Jr., *Extroc*, Meyer-Schwertenbach; report of 16 August 1942 by *Bureau Ha* on Russia's strategic reserves, including the prediction that Germany could no longer win the war).
4   Korrespondenzen, Meldungen und Aktennotizen Juni–Dezember 1943. Darin unter anderem: Lützelschwabs Orientierung von Bundesrat Kobelt über Henry Guisans Rolle beim Barackengeschäft mit der Waffen-SS, sowie über die vertrauliche Mitteilung Allen Dulles' an Hausamann wegen "Biglen" und des angeblichen negativen Berichtes, den Schellenberg in Berlin erstattete; daneben verschiedenen Fragen im Zusammenhang mit der Beziehung Oberstbrigadier Massons zu Eggen (correspondence, reports, and notes for the file, June to December 1943, including, among other things, Lützelschwab's infor-

mation to Federal Councillor Kobelt on Henry Guisan's part in the barracks deal with the *Waffen*-SS and on Allen Dulles' confidential information to Hausamann re: the meeting in Biglen and the negative report that Schellenberg allegedly submitted on that meeting in Berlin; also, various issues in connection with Colonel-Brigadier Masson's relations with Eggen).

6   Korrespondenzen, Meldungen, Aktennotizen 1945. Darin hauptsächlich: Beziehungen Oberstbrigadier Massons zu Schellenberg und Eggen, die "Affäre Masson"; Bericht Eggen vom 13./15. November 1945 und Gegendarstellung Hausamanns (1945 correspondence, reports, and notes for the file, including, above all, Colonel-Brigadier Masson's relations with Schellenberg and Eggen, the "Masson affair"; Eggen's report of November 13 and 15, 1945 and Hausamann's rebuttal).

8   Files of January–May 1947 on the Masson-Schellenberg connection (in connection with Hausamann's lawsuit against Kummer and Schmid and Lützelschwab's statement as a witness).

9   Korrespondenzen, Meldungen, Aktennotizen Juni–August 1947; hauptsächlich Briefwechsel zwischen Hausamann und Lützelschwab im Zusammenhang mit dem Prozess gegen Gottfried Kummer und Hans Rudolf Schmid (correspondence, reports, and notes for the file, June to August 1947, mainly the exchange of letters between Hausamann and Lützelschwab in connection with Hausamann's lawsuit against Gottfried Kummer and Hans Rudolf Schmid).

11   Files of October–December 1947, including: unveröffentlichtes Manuskript Hausamanns "Rund um den Nachrichtendienst und Sicherheitsdienst im Zweiten Weltkrieg, von einem Nachrichtenoffizier gesehen"; Auseinandersetzung über den Ehrverletzungsprozess Hausamann gegen Kummer/Schmid (Hausamann's unpublished manuscript "All Aspects of the Intelligence and Security Service During World War II from the Perspective of an Intelligence Officer"; dispute concerning Hausamann's lawsuit against Kummer and Schmid on charges of slander).

12	Files of 1948, including: Materialien zum Prozess Hausamann gegen *Freies Volk*, Bern; publizistische Unterstützung Hausamanns durch Lützelschwab in *Volk und Armee* (material on Hausamann's lawsuit against the *Freies Volk* newspaper, Bern; Lützelschwab's publicity support of Hausamann in the *Volk und Armee* magazine).
13	Files of 1962–1963, including: Max Waibels Bericht zum Buch von Kimche *Spying for Peace*, 26. Februar 1963; Darstellung Lützelschwabs betreffend den Baracken-Handel, 12. März 1963; Aufzeichnung Lützelschwabs betreffend den Offiziersbund von 1940 (Max Waibel's report on Kimche's book *Spying for Peace*, 26 February 1963; Lützelschwab's account of the barracks deal, 12 March 1963; Lützelschwab's notes on the 1940 Officers' Alliance).
15 to 16	Nachrichtendienst Bureau *Pfalz*, Basel (*Pfalz* outpost of Army Intelligence in Basel)

J.I. 140	**Unpublished Papers of Alfred Ernst**
1	Korrespondenzen 1945–1973 mit Peter Dürrenmatt, Generalstabschef Huber, Georg Kreis, Oberstbrigadier Masson und anderen. Ausserdem: Amtsbericht des Bundesrates an das Bezirksgericht Zürich über die Nachrichtenlinie Masson-Schellenberg, im Zusammenhang mit dem Prozess Hausamann gegen Kummer/Schmid, 14. März 1947 (correspondence between 1945 and 1973 with Peter Dürrenmatt, Chief of the General Staff Huber, Georg Kreis, Brigadier General Masson, and others. Also, Federal Council's official report to the Zürich district court on the Masson-Schellenberg connection in reference to Hausamann's lawsuit against Kummer and Schmid, 14 March 1947).
4	Vols. 1–9: Nachrichtendienst (Intelligence Service) 1939–1945, including, in particular: vol. 1: 1939. Beschwerde Waibels über die Unfähigkeit des schweizerischen Militärattachés in Berlin, von Werdt (Waibel's complaint about the incompetence of Switzerland's military attaché in Berlin, Colonel von Werdt), 25 October 1939; vol. 2: 1940. Verhältnis zwischen Nachrichtendienst und Politischem Departement; Zusammenfassungen mündlich-

er Berichte an Masson; Tätigkeitsbericht Bureau
Deutschland der Nachrichtensektion (relations between
Army Intelligence and the Department of Foreign Affairs;
summaries of verbal communications with Masson; activity
report of Army Intelligence's German Bureau);
vol. 3: 1941. Nachrichtendienstliche Meldungen und
Lagebeurteilungen (intelligence reports and assessments of
the situation).
vol. 4: 1942. Verhältnis zwischen Nachrichtendienst und
Politischem Departement; nachrichtendienstliche Berichte
und Lagebeurteilungen; Fall Mörgeli (relations between
Army Intelligence and the Department of Foreign Affairs;
intelligence reports and assessments of the situation;
Mörgeli case).
vol. 5: 1943. Darin unter anderem: Bemerkungen zum
Spezialbericht Nr. 45 "Rigi"; vertrauliche Rede Bundesrat
Kobelts vom 12. Februar 1943 über die militärisch-politis-
che Lage und deren Auswirkungen auf die Schweiz;
Analyse der Möglichkeiten eines strategischen Überfalls
durch die Achsenmächte und durch die Alliierten, von
Alfred Ernst, Frühjahr 1943; Reaktion auf Massons,
genauer Meyer-Schwertenbachs, Rückfrage bei
Schellenberg im Zusammenhang mit dem März-Alarm
1943 (including, among other things, remarks on special
report no. 45 by Rigi; Federal Councillor Kobelt's confidential address of February 12, 1943 on the military-political situation and its repercussions on Switzerland; analysis
of the possibilities of a strategic surprise attack by the Axis
powers or the Allies, by Alfred Ernst, early 1943; reaction
to Masson—or rather Meyer-Schwertenbach—verifying
with Schellenberg Viking's information, resulting in the
alert of March 1943);
vol. 9: Flugblätter der schweizerischen Nationalsozialisten
(I.P.A.-Korrespondenz mit Verleumdungen General
Guisans) (flyers by Swiss Nazis [IPA correspondence containing libels against General Guisan]).

6   Versetzung von Major Alfred Ernst von der Gruppe Id zur
Operationssektion (Major Alfred Ernst's transfer from
Group Id to the Operational Section).

J.I. 161   **Unpublished Papers of Walter Allgöwer**
1   Curriculum vitae
15, 17   Militär-politische Fragen (military-political issues)
18   Bundesrat Karl Kobelt. Darin unter anderem: Entwurf zu einem Presseartikel über einen Brief von Kobelt an Oberstleutnant Heinrich Frick aus dem Jahr 1941 betreffend Pressezensur (Federal Councillor Kobelt, including, among other things, draft article concerning Kobelt's 1941 letter to Lieutenant Colonel Heinrich Frick re: censorship of the press).
19   Artikel Allgöwers über allgemeine Militärfragen, Landesverteidigung und Kriegsgeschichte, 1938–1949 (articles written by Allgöwer between 1938 and 1949 on general military issues, the national defense, and the history of the war).
35   Aktion Nationaler Widerstand (Action for National Resistance)
47   *Volk und Armee:* Redaktionskommission, Liste von Sympathisanten (editorial committee, list of sympathizers).
49   Korrespondenz von Rolf Eberhard, dem Nachfolger Alfred Ernsts in der Sektion Achse (correspondence of Rolf Eberhard, Alfred Ernst's successor in the Axis Section).
62   Thoughts on Kimche's book *Spying for Peace* (no date, about 1962).
74   Korrespondenz über die Haltung von General und Bundesrat bezüglich der Frage "Anpassung oder Widerstand" (correspondence on General Guisan's and the Federal Council's stance about whether Switzerland should accommodate with Hitler's New Europe or resist any German pressure)

J.I. 127   **Unpublished Papers of General Henri Guisan**
4   Korrespondenz mit Hans Rudolf Kurz und Oberst Hans Bracher über deutsche Angriffspläne gegen die Schweiz während des Zweiten Weltkrieges (1951 correspondence with Hans Rudolf Kurz and Colonel Hans Bracher on Germany's plans for an attack on Switzerland during World War II).

30   Korrespondenz mit H.R. Schmid über die "Affäre Masson"
                         und den Hausamann-Prozess (correspondence with H.R.
                         Schmid on the "Masson affair" and Hausamann's lawsuit).

J.I. 49 1   **Unpublished Papers of Colonel-Corps-Commander Jakob**
                         Labhart

Vol. 1   Documents concerning his activity as chief of the General
                         Staff section, 1936–1939, as chief of the General Staff of
                         the Army, 1939, as commander of the 4th Army Corps,
                         1940–1947, and from the time of his retirement in
                         Merligen, 1947–1949.

Vol. 2   1936–1945 diaries, consisting of 9 booklets covering the
                         period from 25 May 1936 to 14 August 1945, with the
                         exception of the periods from 22 February to 14 August
                         1938 and from 2 October 1938 to 24 August 1939:
                         booklet I: 25 May 1936 to 21 February 1938;
                         booklet II: 11 September 1938 to 1 October 1938;
                         booklet III: 25 August 1939 to 31 December 1939;
                         booklet IV: 8 January 1940 to 1 January 1941;
                         booklet V: 2 January 1941 to 31 December 1941;
                         booklet VI: 2 January 1942 to 31 December 1942;
                         booklet VII: 4 January 1943 to 31 December 1943;
                         booklet VIII: 1 January 1944 to 31 December 1944;
                         booklet IX: 4 January 1945 to 14 August 1945.

Other reference material at the Swiss Federal Archives

J.I. 3   Unpublished papers of Federal Councillor Markus
                         Feldmann

J.I. 107   Unpublished papers of Hans Hausamann

J.I. 32   Unpublished papers of Max Waibel

E 1004.1 1   Minutes of Federal Council meetings

E 2001 (D) 2   Vol. 2: files of the Swiss Federal Department of Foreign
                         Affairs. (Militärische) Nachrichtenübermittlung der
                         Auslandschweizer an den Generalstab (transmission of
                         [military] information by Swiss living abroad to the
                         General Staff, 1940, 1942; file "Generalstabsabteilung"
                         [General Staff section]).

E 2001 (D) 3   Vol. 3: Files of the Swiss Federal Department of Foreign
                         Affairs. Nachrichtensektion der Generalstabsabteilung.
                         Darin unter anderem: Einvernahme von Einreisenden;

	Frage einer direkten Fühlungnahme des schweizerischen Nachrichtendienstes mit dem italienischen Nachrichtendienst; Spionageabwehr-Probleme mit Liechtenstein (Intelligence Branch of the General Staff section, including, among other things, interrogation of travelers entering the country; issue of whether Swiss Intelligence should enter into direct contact with Italian Intelligence; problems with Liechtenstein re: Counterintelligence).
E 2001 (E) 1	Vol. 8: Presse und Pressefreiheit (press and freedom of the press) in Switzerland.
E 2800 1967/60	Vol. 23: personal files of Federal Councillor Max Petitpierre, including: Briefe Pilets betreffend seine Kontakte mit Rittmeister Eggen und seine kritische Einstellung zur Nachrichtenlinie Masson-Schellenberg, sowie Unterlagen über die Auseinandersetzung wegen Hausamanns Meldung über angebliche Sonderfriedens-Bemühungen von Pilet-Golaz (letters by Pilet re: his contacts with Cavalry Captain Eggen and his critical stance concerning the Masson-Schellenberg connection; also, documents re: the dispute resulting from Hausamann's information that Pilet-Golaz allegedly tried to convince the U.S. to conclude a separate peace accord with Germany).

Private Archives of Hans Rudolf Kurz, Bern

Files re: Masson/Intelligence Service

1	Intelligence Service. Masson's own records.
2	"Masson case," 1945.
3	Masson/general information. Words of recognition; obituaries after Masson's death on 19 October 1967.
4	Roger Masson, "Fall Kimche" (Kimche case).
5	Roger Masson, "Fall Quet/Accoce" (Quet/Accoce case).

Files re: Schellenberg

1	Note for the file by Hausamann on the Masson-Schellenberg connection.
2	Schellenberg's "Report no. 52 to the Führer" of 6 January 1943 on Switzerland's alleged preparations for mobilizing its Armed Forces.

3   German translation of the "Statement made by
            Schellenberg" in London, 1945, during the interrogation
            by the British.
4   Press clippings on the last Nuremberg War Crimes Tribunal
            and Schellenberg's memoirs (with remarks by Federal
            Councillor Kobelt and H.R. Kurz).

Files re: Hausamann

1   Information, reports, and notes for the file by Hausamann,
            1939–1945.
2   Documents on Hausamann's lawsuits against
            Kummer/Schmid and Schwarz/Salzmann (*Freies Volk*,
            Bern), including minutes of interrogations, correspondence
            with the Attorney General's Office, the Military Attorney
            General, and Lieutenant Colonel René Keller, senior judge
            of divisional court 3A; evidence produced during the trials.
3   Mörgeli case.
4   1943 dispute between Hans Hausamann and Federal
            Councillor Pilet-Golaz.
5   Correspondence between Hausamann and Masson, 1966
            (Accoce/Quet case).
6   Hausamann's correspondence with former participants of
            the war, researchers, publicists, and other interested persons
            re: intelligence-related aspects of World War II.

Archives of Contemporary History (Archiv für Zeitgeschichte, AfZ), Swiss Federal Institute of Technology, Zürich

Files of Werner Rings
Transcripts of his interviews with:

Bernard Barbey	15 to 17 July 1968 and 3 November 1969
Edgar Bonjour	11 November 1969 and 27 October 1971
Willy Bretscher	17 May 1968
Enrico Celio	30 June 1969
Bernard Cuénoud	23 October 1969
Alfred Ernst	29 August 1972
Robert Frick	1 July 1969
Emil Häberli	23 June 1969
Hans Hausamann	6 to 14 May 1968
Hans Rudolf Kurz	21 October 1969 and 21 October 1971

Mayr von Baldegg 1	0 June 1969
Ernst Mörgeli	30 May 1968
Albert Wiesendanger	28 May 1969
Gerhart Schürch	11 June 1968

Private Archives of Rudolf J. Ritter, Rheineck

Documents on the Intelligence Service's structure (organizational charts, service regulations, legal framework), 1931 to 1948, and on signals-related matters during World War II.

Private Archives of Pierre Masson, Belmont

Documents and photographs concerning Colonel-Brigadier Roger Masson

Private Archives of Werner Rings, Ascona

Various pieces of factual information and his transcript of the television talk show *Tatsachen und Meinungen* of 22 May 1966 on the topic "La guerre a été gagné en Suisse" (The War Was Won in Switzerland); the talk show participants included host Alphons von Matt, Hans Hausamann, Xaver Schnieper, Rolf Bigler (of the *Weltwoche* newspaper), Otto Pünter, Marcel Beck, and Ritter von Schramm.

Private Archives of Erwin Tschudi, Bern

Various pieces of factual information and numerous documents on Hausamann's lawsuit against Tschudi and on the Intelligence Service, Hausamann's activities, the Masson-Schellenberg connection, Meyer-Schwertenbach (personality and activities).

Private Archives of Major General Ernst Wetter, Bern

Various pieces of factual information and various documents re: the Intelligence Service during World War II that Mr. Wetter generously offered to this author.

National Archives, Washington, DC

RG 59   General Records of the U.S. Department of State
               Department of State Decimal File 854.24 (Switzerland)
               Department of State Decimal File 811.20 Defense (M)
               Switzerland
RG 165   Records of the War Department, General and Special Staffs
               Military Intelligence Branch, 1918–1923
               Military Intelligence Division (MID), 1939–1943
RG 226   Records of the Office of Strategic Services (OSS)
Entry 99   OSS History Office Files (107 boxes)
               box 4 London Office Washington History-OP-23, folder 8
               box 7 E.T.O. Switzerland, June 1945; folder 30
               box 8 E.T.O. Switzerland, July to September 1945: folders
                   31–33
               box 18 folders 83 and 84
               box 99 Washington History Office-OP-23 envelope 586,
                   "OSS Organization and Functions," folder 1;
                   envelope 660, "Budget material borrowed by
                   Colonel Shallcross, returned by Security."
Entry 134   Washington Research and Analysis Branch; Radio and
               Cable (363 boxes), in particular:
               box 162 Folder "Berne-Caserta October 1944 to June
                   1945";
               box 165 Wash-Reg-R&C-56;
               box 191 File "IND-27 Berne, March to April 1944;
               box 231 Wash-Sect-R&C-4, folder "Berne Incoming and
                   Outgoing, August 1944";
               box 232 Wash-Sect-R&C-4, Berne April 1945 to May
                   1945;
               box 273 Wash-Sect-R&C-77, folder 3, "Berne-
                   Radiophone-January 1944";
               box 278 Wash-Sect-R&C-78, folder 19;
               box 307 Wash-Sect-R&C-120; folder 1, "Incoming, 2
                   January 1943 to 30 June 1943"; folder 2, "March
                   1944"; folder 3, "Berne Incoming and Outgoing,
                   April 1944."
RG 238   Records of the Chief Counsel for War Crimes: Collection
               of World War II War Crimes Records.

M 897	Records of the United States Nuremberg War Crimes Trials Interrogations, 1946–1949: Case XI, Ernst von Weizsäcker et al. ("Ministries case"), December 20, 1947–April 14, 1949.
Roll 114	Defense Exhibits of Walter Schellenberg, including "Attestation" (statement) by Colonel-Brigadier Masson with handwritten annotation by General Guisan; statements by Meyer-Schwertenbach, former Federal Councillor Musy, General Giraud, and others.
M 1019	Records of the U.S. Nuremberg War Crimes Trials Interrogations, 1946–1949:
Roll 15	Interrogation records of Hans Eggen.

Microfilms at the National Archives of files of the German Ministry of Foreign Affairs:

T-120/715	Abteilung Inland (domestic affairs) II g, Geheime Reichssache (top secret matter of the Reich), vol. XII, 1943.
T-120/1906	Deutsche Gesandtschaft (German Legation) Bern, 784/4: Die Nationalen Erneuerungsbewegungen in der Schweiz (national [pro-German] revival movements in Switzerland), 1939–1942.

Washington National Records Center, Suitland, VA (now National Archives, Washington, DC)

RG 319	Army Staff: Military Attaché Reports.
ACSI	Project Decimal Files, 1941–1945, Switzerland. Secret Message Files, Switzerland, Military Attaché 1943.

Franklin D. Roosevelt Presidential Library, Hyde Park, NY

PSF	The President's Secretary's File. Especially Box 166, Folder 11 "OSS: Donovan Reports"
OF	Official File

Princeton University Library, Seeley G. Mudd Manuscript Library, Princeton, NJ

Department of Rare Books and Special Collections, Public Policy Papers
Allen W. Dulles Papers

19	OSS 1943: Switzerland.

20   Selected Correspondence and Related Material: "Abwehr."
            Gisevius 1944.
22   Selected Correspondence and Related Material: Operation
            Sunrise 1945; OSS 1945.
26   Selected Correspondence and Related Material: file "OSS
            and 'successors'," 1946.
27   Selected Correspondence and Related Material: file
            "Switzerland." Correspondence with Pilet-Golaz and
            Eduard Waetjen.
30   Selected Correspondence and Related Material: concerning
            Gisevius and Hausamann.
32   Selected Correspondence and Related Material: file
            "Switzerland" (correspondence between Dulles and Pilet-
            Golaz).
            File "Waetjen" (Dulles supporting Waetjen).
37   Selected Correspondence and Related Material: file
            "Switzerland" concerning Barbey's publication *P.C. du
            Général.*
47   Selected Correspondence and Related Material: File
            "Waetjen" and file "Waibel."
142   Selected Correspondence and Related Material: Dulles' cor-
            respondence with Walther Hofer.
146   Selected Correspondence and Related Material: file
            "Toland, John."
153   Selected Correspondence and Related Material: File
            "Quet."
210   background material, including photographs, for *Secret
            Surrender.*
222   Speeches, statements, interviews, etc., 1950–1953: notes
            for presentation on "U.S. Government Intelligence
            Agencies," Army War College, Carlisle Barracks, PA, 15
            September 1953.
237   Speeches, statements, interviews, etc., 1964, including,
            among other things, roundtable discussion on "The
            Hidden Art of Intelligence," 29 March 1964.
238   Speeches, statements, interviews, etc., 1965: notes for NBC
            television program on "Japanese Surrender Negotiations,"
            26 March 1965.
246–247   Articles by others about or relating to Allen W. Dulles.
272   Photographs: Dulles during and after World War II.

Selected Papers of Philip Strong

5   The Intelligence Process, including, among other things, "Research and Intelligence." Lecture by Dr. W.L. Langer.

7   Remarks of Colonel Lawrence K. White, Deputy Director, CIA; C. Tracy Barnes (senior official, CIA), "Some Thoughts About Intelligence."

8   CIA, Office of Scientific Intelligence, Scientific Resources Division, "Depreciation of Intelligence with Time," 25 January 1954.

German Federal Archives, Koblenz

Hauptabteilung Deutsches Reich und Preussen (Main Section German Reich and Prussia)

R3/1507   Akten des Reichsministeriums für Rüstung und Kriegsproduktion (files of the Reich Ministry for Armament and War Production), 1940–1945, Führerbesprechungen (Führer's meetings)

Political Archives of the German Ministry of Foreign Affairs, Bonn

Handelspolitische Abteilung (Trade Policy Section) II a
            Switzerland, Commerce 13 A, Regierungsausschüsse (government committees).
            Vol. 2: files of 1942 and 1943.

PRINTED SOURCE DOCUMENTS

Amtliches Stenographisches Bulletin der Bundesversammlung. Nationalrat.
Bericht des Bundesrates an die Bundesversammlung über die antidemokratische
    Tätigkeit von Schweizern und Ausländern im Zusammenhang mit dem
    Kriegsgeschehen 1939–1945 (Motion Boerlin). Part 1 (28 December 1945):
    Bundesblatt 1946, vol. 1: 1–123. Part 2 (17 May 1946): Bundesblatt
    1946, vol. 1: 171–211. Part 3 (21 May 1946): Bundesblatt 1946, vol. II:
    212–271. Supplement (25 July 1946): Bundesblatt 1946, vol. II:
    1085–1187.

Bericht des Bundesrates an die Bundesversammlung über die Verfahren gegen nationalsozialistische Schweizer wegen Angriffs auf die Unabhängigkeit der Eidgenossenschaft. (30 November 1948.) Bundesblatt 1948, vol. III: 997–1073.

Bericht der Parlamentarischen Untersuchungskommission vom 22. November 1989 (PUK): Vorkommnisse im EJPD. [Bern, 1989.]

Ergänzungsbericht der Parlamentarischen Untersuchungskommission vom 29. Mai 1990: Vorkommnisse im EJPD. [Bern, 1990.]

Bericht des Regierungsrates über die Abwehr staatsfeindlicher Umtriebe in den Vorkriegs- und Kriegsjahren sowie die Säuberungsaktion nach Kriegsschluss. Dem Grossen Rate des Kantons Basel-Stadt vorgelegt am 4. Juli 1946. [Basel, 1946.]

Bonjour, Edgar. *Geschichte der schweizerischen Neutralität*, vols. VII-IX (documents). Basel/Stuttgart, 1974–1976.

Bretscher, Willy. *Im Sturm von Krise und Krieg: Neue Zürcher Zeitung 1933–1944 (siebzig Leitartikel).* Zürich, 1987.

Cave, Anthony Brown, ed. *The Secret War Report of the OSS.* New York, 1976.

Churchill, Winston S. *Great War Speeches.* 6th ed. London, 1965 (selection of The War Speeches of the Rt. Hon. Winston S. Churchill, compiled by Charles Eade (3 vols.).

Guisan, Henri. *Bericht an die Bundesversammlung über den Aktivdienst 1939–1945.* N.p., n.d. [Bern, 1946].

Frey, Oscar. "Die Lage der Schweiz 1941." *Kultur- und Staatswissenschaftliche Schriften 22* (1941).

Heiber, Helmut, ed. *Hitlers Lagebesprechungen: Protokollfragmente aus Hitlers militärischen Konferenzen 1942–1945.* Stuttgart, 1962.

Hofer, Walther. *Der Nationalsozialismus: Dokumente 1933–1945.* Frankfurt a.M.: Fischer-Bücherei (vol. 172), 1979.

Huber, Jakob. *Bericht des Chefs des Generalstabes der Armee an den Oberbefehlshaber der Armee über den Aktivdienst 1939–1945.* N.p., n.d. [Bern, 1946].

Schramm, Percy Ernst, ed. *Kriegstagebuch des Oberkommmandos der Wehrmacht (Wehrmachtführungsstab) 1940–1945.* (War journal kept by Helmuth Greiner and Percy Ernst Schramm.) Vol. II: 1942, compiled and annotated by Andreas Hillgruber. Frankfurt a.M., 1963. Vol. III: 1943, compiled and annotated by Walther Hubatsch. Frankfurt a.M., 1963.

Kurz, Hans Rudolf. *Dokumente des Aktivdienstes.* Frauenfeld, 1965.

Rapport de la Commission d'enquête parlementaire chargée de clarifier les faits d'une grande portée survenus au Département Militaire Fédéral, du 17 novembre 1990. [Bern, 1990.]

von Salis, Jean Rudolf. *Eine Chronik des Zweiten Weltkrieges: Radiokommentare 1939–1945.* Zürich, 1981.

Die schweizerische Kriegswirtschaft 1939/1948: Bericht des Eidgenössischen Volkswirtschaftsdepartementes. Bern, 1950.

von Sprecher, Theophil von Bernegg. *Bericht des Chefs des Generalstabes der Armee an den General über die Mobilmachung und den Verlauf des Aktivdienstes.* 2nd ed., Bern, 1923.

Memoirs, Diaries

Bancroft, Mary. *Autobiography of a Spy.* New York, 1983.

Barbey, Bernard. *Aller et retour: Mon journal pendant et après la "drôle de guerre" 1939–1940.* Neuchâtel, 1967.

Barbey, Bernard. *P.C. du Général: Journal du chef de l'état-major particulier du général Guisan 1940–1945.* Neuchâtel, 1948.

Bernadotte, Folke. *Das Ende.* Zürich/New York, 1945.

Böschenstein, Hermann. *Vor unseren Augen: Aufzeichnungen über das Jahrzehnt 1935–1945.* Bern, 1978.

Bringolf, Walther. *Mein Leben: Weg und Umweg eines Schweizer Sozialdemokraten.* Zürich, 1965.

Ciano, Galeazzo. *Tagebücher 1939–1943.* Bern, 1946.

Dexter, Robert. *Die langen Jahre 1939–1945.* Basel, 1979.

Dulles, Allen W. *The Craft of Intelligence.* New York, 1963.

Dulles, Allen W. *The Secret Surrender.* New York, 1966.

Eugster, Jakob. "Die Spionageabwehr im Aktivdienst." *Die Schweiz im Zweiten Weltkrieg: Das grosse Erinnerungswerk an die Aktivdienstzeit 1939–1945*, edited by Hans Rudolf Kurz. Thun, 1959.

Felfe, Heinz. *Im Dienst des Gegners: 10 Jahre Moskaus Mann im BND.* Hamburg/Zürich, 1986.

Frölicher, Hans. *Meine Aufgabe in Berlin.* Bern (printed privately), 1962.

Gilbert, G.M. *Nürnberger Tagebuch: Ehemaliger Gerichtspsychologe beim Nürnberger Prozess gegen die Hauptkriegsverbrecher.* Frankfurt a.M., 1962.

Gisevius, Hans-Bernd. *Bis zum bitteren Ende.* 2 vols. Zürich, 1946.

Guisan, Henri. *Entretiens accordés à Raymond Gafner à l'intention des auditeurs de Radio-Lausanne.* Lausanne, 1953. German version: *Gespräche.* Translated by Hans Rudolf Schmid and Gottfried Kummer. Bern, 1953.

[Hartmann, Willy]. *Hans Hausamann 1897–1974: Gedenkschrift zum 10. Todestag* (includes contributions by Gerhart Schürch, Georg Thürer et al.). St. Gallen, 1984.

Jaquillard, Robert. *La chasse aux espions en Suisse: Choses vécues, 1939–1945.* Lausanne, 1945.

Kempner, Robert M. W. *Ankläger einer Epoche: Lebenserinnerungen.* Frankfurt a.M./Berlin, 1986.

Lemmer, Ernst. *Manches war doch anders: Erinnnerungen eines deutschen Demokraten.* Frankfurt a.M., 1968.

Leonhard, Jakob. *Als Gestapo-Agent im Dienste der schweizerischen Gegenspionage.* Zürich/New York, 1945.

Marcionelli, Arturo. "Paul Ruegger à Rome." *A Paul Ruegger pour son 80e anniversaire, 14 août 1977* [compiled by Victor Umbricht]. Riehen/Basel, 1977.

Masson, Roger. "Unser Nachrichtendienst im Zweiten Weltkrieg." *Die Schweiz im Zweiten Weltkrieg: Das grosse Erinnerungswerk an die Aktivdienstzeit 1939–1945,* edited by Hans Rudolf Kurz. Thun, 1959.

Masson, Roger. "Le récit de l'affaire Schellenberg." *Tribune de Genève,* 19 December 1961.

Masson, Roger. "Was geschah damals?" *Tages-Anzeiger,* 24, 26, and 28 March 1962.

Masson, Roger. "Blick zurück in dunkle Tage: Erinnerungen Oberstbrigadier Massons, aufgezeichnet von Hugo Faesi." *Luzerner Neueste Nachrichten,* 26, 27, and 28 March 1962.

Masson, Roger. "Le paravent de la neutralité - ou bien de la protection divine?" *Tribune de Lausanne,* 12 December 1965. (This and the following six articles were published as part of the series "Personne n'a le droit d'oublier.")

Masson, Roger. "Lutte dans le brouillard." *Tribune de Lausanne,* 12 December 1965.

Masson, Roger. "En cours de route … quelques incidents." *Tribune de Lausanne,* 19 December 1965.

Masson, Roger. "Notre dossier allemand." *Tribune de Lausanne,* 16 January 1966.

Masson, Roger. "L'affaire Schellenberg." *Tribune de Lausanne,* 6 February 1966.

Masson, Roger. "La vérité sur la 'conspiration' de Biglen." *Tribune de Lausanne,* 13 February 1966.

Masson, Roger. "L'armée a rempli sa mission." *Tribune de Lausanne,* 6 March 1966.

Masson, Roger. "Mes contacts avec Schellenberg." *Gazette de Lausanne,* 22 April 1966.

Masson, Roger. "Schellenberg fidèle et dévoué." *Gazette de Lausannne,* 23 April 1966.

Masson, Roger."Nachrichtenchef Masson berichtet." *St. Galler Tagblatt,* 19, 21, and 22 August 1967.

Masson, Roger."Der schweizerische Nachrichtenchef berichtet." *Neue Berner Zeitung,* 2–3 September 1967.

Müller, Hans. *Bundesrat Karl Kobelt: Eine Gedenkschrift.* Bern, 1975.

Pünter, Otto. *Der Anschluss fand nicht statt: Geheimagent Pakbo erzählt. Erlebnisse, Tatsachen und Dokumente aus den Jahren 1930 bis 1945.* Zürich, 1967.

von Salis, Jean Rudolf. *Grenzüberschreitungen: Ein Lebensbericht* (2 vols.). Zürich, 1975/1978. Vol. 2: 1939–1978.

Schellenberg, Walter. *The Labyrinth.* London, 1956. [Original title: *Hitler's Secret Service: Memoirs,* New York, 1956; latest German edition: *Aufzeichnungen: Die Memoiren des letzten Geheimdienstchefs unter Hitler.* Edited by Gita Petersen. Wiesbaden/Munich, 1979.]

Schürch, Ernst. *Als die Freiheit in Frage stand: Erinnerungen aus der Sturmzeit der Schweizer Presse.* Bern, 1946.

Schwarz, Urs. *Schicksalstage in Berlin.* Lenzburg, 1986.

Surdez Denys. *La guerre secrète aux frontières du Jura.* Porrentruy, 1985.

[Umbricht, Victor]. *A Paul Ruegger pour son 80e anniversaire, 14 août 1977.* Riehen/Basel, 1977.

Secondary Sources

Accoce, Paul, and Pierre Quet. *A Man Called Lucy.* New York, 1968. [Original French version: *La guerre a été gagnée en Suisse.* Paris, 1966. German version: *Moskau wusste alles.* Zürich, 1966.]

Alem, Jean-Pierre. *L'espionnage à travers les âges.* Paris, 1977.

Amstein, André. "Verletzung militärischer Geheimnisse und militärischer Nachrichtendienst." *Schweizerische Juristenzeitung,* no. 8, 1945.

Andrew, Christopher. "American Presidents and Their Intelligence Communities." *Intelligence and National Security,* vol. 10, no. 4 (October 1995).

Andrew, Christopher M. "Christopher Andrew Questions Official Policy Toward the History of British Intelligence." *History Today,* 33 (January 1983).

Andrew, Christopher, and David Dilks, eds. *The Missing Dimension: Governments and Intelligence Communities in the Twentieth Century.* London, 1984.

Andrew, Christopher, and Jeremy Noakes, eds. *Intelligence and International Relations 1900–1945.* Exter, UK, 1987.

Bahnemann, Jörg. "Der Begriff der Strategie bei Clausewitz, Moltke und Liddell Hart." *Wehrwissenschaftliche Rundschau,* January 1968.

Baucom, Donald R. "Historical Framework for the Concept of Strategy." *Military Review,* March 1987.

Bindschedler, Rudolf L., Hans Rudolf Kurz, Wilhelm Carlgren, and Sten Carlsson, eds. *Schwedische und schweizerische Neutralität im Zweiten Weltkrieg.* Basel, 1985.

Birn, Ruth Bettina. *Die Höheren SS- und Polizeiführer: Himmlers Vertreter im Reich und in den besetzten Gebieten.* Düsseldorf, 1986.

Bolling, Landrum. "Strengths and Weaknesses of Track Two," in *Conflict Resolution: Track Two Diplomacy,* edited by John W. McDonald, Jr. and Diane B. Bendahmane. Washington, DC: Foreign Service Institute, U.S. Department of State, 1987.

Bonjour, Edgar. *Geschichte der schweizerischen Neutralität,* vols. IV and V. Basel/Stuttgart, 1970.

Böschenstein, Hermann. *Bedrohte Heimat: Die Schweiz im Zweiten Weltkrieg. Mit Beiträgen von Alfred Ernst und Ernst Bircher.* Bern, 1963.

Bourgeois, Daniel. *Le Troisième Reich et la Suisse, 1933–1941.* Neuchâtel, 1974.

Bourgeois, Daniel. "L'image allemande de Pilet-Golaz, 1940–1944." *Studien und Quellen [des Schweizerischen Bundesarchivs],* no. 4. Bern, 1978.

Bourgeois, Daniel. "Les relations économiques germano–suisses pendant la seconde guerre mondiale: un bilan de 1944." *Schweizerische Zeitschrift für Geschichte,* vol. 32 (1982).

Bozeman, Adda B. *Strategic Intelligence & Statecraft: Selected Essays.* Washington/New York/London, 1992.

Braunschweig, Pierre Th. *Die Nachrichtenlinie Masson–Schellenberg: Ein kontroverser Fall aus dem militärischen Nachrichtendienst der Schweiz im Zweiten Weltkrieg.* Bern, 1985.

Braunschweig, Pierre Th. *Ein politischer Mord: Das Attentat von Davos und seine Beurteilung durch schweizerische Zeitungen.* 3rd ed. Bern, 1980.

Braunschweig, Pierre Th. *Geheimer Draht nach Berlin: Die Nachrichtenlinie Masson–Schellenberg und der schweizerische Nachrichtendienst im Zweiten Weltkrieg.* 3rd ed. Zürich, 1990.

Braunschweig, Pierre Th. "In the Eye of the Hurricane—Switzerland in World War II." *Whittier Law Review*, Whittier, California. Volume 20, issue 3 (March 1999).

Braunschweig, Pierre Th. "Le Bureau France du Service de Renseignement suisse." *L'Année 1942: Le Tournant.* C.R.H.Q.—Université de Caen. Caen, 1993.

Breaks, Katherine. "Ladies of the OSS: The Apron Strings of Intelligence in World War II." *American Intelligence Journal* 13/3 (Summer 1992).

Brill, Heinz. "Der Strategiebegriff heute." *Europäische Wehrkunde,* no. 11, 1981.

Brunner, Dominique. "Was ist Strategie?" *Schweizer Soldat,* no. 2, 1976.

Bucher, Erwin. "Zur Linie Masson-Schellenberg." *Schweizerische Zeitschrift für Geschichte,* vol. 38, no. 3, 1988.

Buchheim, Hans. *Anatomie des SS-Staates.* 2 vols. Olten/Freiburg i.Br., 1965.

Buchheit, Gert. *Der deutsche Geheimdienst: Geschichte der militärischen Abwehr.* Munich, 1966.

Bullock, Alan. *Introduction to the Schellenberg Memoirs.* London, 1956.

Calder, James D. *Intelligence, Espionage and Related Topics: An Annotated Bibliography of Serial Journal and Magazine Scholarship, 1844–1998.* Westport, CT/London, 1999.

Campbell, Kenneth J. "Allen Dulles: An Appraisal." *Studies in Intelligence,* vol. 34, no. 1 (Spring 1990).

Campbell, Kenneth J. "John A. McCone: An Outsider Becomes DCI." *Studies in Intelligence,* vol. 32, no. 2 (Summer 1988).

Campbell, Kenneth J. "William J. Donovan: Leader and Strategist." *American Intelligence Journal,* vol. 11, no. 1 (Winter 1989–1990).

Cartier, Raymond. *Der Zweite Weltkrieg.* 2 vols. Munich, 1967.

Casey, William J. "The Clandestine War in Europe (1942–1945)." *Studies in Intelligence,* vol. 25, no. 1 (Spring 1981).

Casey, William J. "The American Intelligence Community." *Presidential Studies Quarterly,* vol. 12, no. 2 (Spring 1982).

Casey, William J. "The Threat and the Need for Intelligence." *Signal,* vol. 38 (October 1983).

Casey, William J. "OSS: Lessons for Today." *Studies in Intelligence,* vol. 30, no. 4 (Winter 1986).

Cave, Anthony Brown. *Bodyguard of Lies.* Toronto/New York/London, 1976.

Cave, Anthony Brown. *"C": The Secret Life of Sir Stewart Graham Menzies, Spy Master to Winston Churchill.* New York, 1987.

Chant, Christopher. *The Encyclopedia of Codenames of World War II.* London, 1986.

Churchill, Winston S. *The Second World War.* 6 vols. London, 1948–1954.

von Clausewitz, Carl. *Vom Kriege.* 16th ed. Bonn, 1952.

Constantinides, George C. "A Brief Review of OSS Literature." *Studies in Intelligence,* vol. 35, no. 4 (Winter 1991).

Constantinides, George C. *Intelligence and Espionage: An Analytical Bibliography.* Boulder, CO, 1983.

Crankshaw, Edward. *Die Gestapo.* Berlin, 1959.

Daniel, Donald C., and Katherine L. Herbig, eds. *Strategic Military Deception.* New York/Oxford, 1981.

Davis, Jack. *Improving CIA Analytic Performance: Strategic Warning.* The Sherman Kent Center for Intelligence Analysis, Occasional Papers, vol. 1, no. 1 (September 2002).

Davis, Jack. *Strategic Warning: If Surprise Is Inevitable, What Role for Analysis?* The Sherman Kent Center for Intelligence Analysis, Occasional Papers, vol. 2, no. 1 (January 2003).

DeCoster, Bryan D. "OSS Estimate of German Logistics on the Eastern Front, 1941–42." *Defense Intelligence Journal,* vol. 3, no. 1 (Spring 1994).

Deschamps-Adams, Helene. "An OSS Agent Behind Enemy Lines in France." *Prologue: Quarterly Journal of the National Archives,* vol. 24, no. 3 (1992).

Donovan, William J. "OSS-NKVD Liaison." *Studies in Intelligence,* vol. 7, no. 2 (Summer 1963).

Donovan, William J. "Sunrise Reports." *Studies in Intelligence,* vol. 7, no. 1 (Spring 1963).

Dethleffsen, E. "Die Aufgaben eines Auslandnachrichtendienstes." *Aussenpolitik,* no. 11, 1969.

Dulles, Allen W. "William J. Donovan and the National Security." *Studies in Intelligence,* vol. 3, no. 3 (Summer 1959).

Emmenegger, Kurt. *Q.N. wusste Bescheid.* Zürich, 1965.

Ernst, Alfred. "Die Armee im Aktivdienst 1939–1945." *Bedrohte Heimat: Die Schweiz im Zweiten Weltkrieg,* edited by Hermann Böschenstein. Bern, 1963.

Ernst, Alfred. "Der Schweizerische Nachrichtendienst im Zweiten Weltkrieg." *Allgemeine Schweizerische Militärzeitschrift,* no. 12, 1972.

Ernst, Alfred. *Neutrale Kleinstaaten im Zweiten Weltkrieg: Versuch einer vergleichenden Beurteilung der kriegsverhütenden Wirkung ihrer militärischen Bereitschaft.* Münsingen, 1973.

Farago, Ladislas. *Burn After Reading: The Espionage History of World War II.* New York, 1972.

Feldmann, Josef. "Eléments de stratégie suisse, IVe partie: La défense nationale militaire." *Revue militaire suisse,* nos. 7–8, 1984.

Feldmann, Josef. "Eléments de stratégie suisse, VIIe partie: Information, défense psychologique et protection de l'Etat." *Revue militaire suisse*, no. 1, 1985.

Fink, Jürg. *Die Schweiz aus der Sicht des Dritten Reiches, 1933–1945*. Zürich, 1985.

Freedman, Lawrence. "Intelligence Operations in the Falklands." *Intelligence and National Security*, vol. 1, no. 3 (September 1986).

Frick, Philibert. *Hans Frick: Années de formation et début de carrière d'un chef militaire (1888–1940)*. Mémoire de licence (M.A. thesis), Université de Genève, 1992.

Fuhrer, Hans Rudolf. *Spionage gegen die Schweiz: Die geheimen deutschen Nachrichtendienste gegen die Schweiz im Zweiten Weltkrieg 1939–1945*. Frauenfeld, 1982.

Fuhrer, Hans Rudolf. "Die Schweiz im Nachrichtendienst." *Schwedische und schweizerische Neutralität im Zweiten Weltkrieg*, edited by Rudolf L. Bindschedler, Hans Rudolf Kurz, Wilhelm Carlgren, and Sten Carlsson. Basel, 1985.

Fursenko, Aleksandr, and Timothy Naftali. "Using KGB Documents: The Scali-Feliksov Channel in the Cuban Missile Crisis." *Cold War International History Project*, vol. 5 (Spring 1995).

Garlinski, Józef. *The Swiss Corridor: Espionage Networks in Switzerland During World War II*. London/Melbourne/Toronto, 1981.

Gasser, Adolf. *Ausgewählte historische Schriften 1933–1983*. Basel/Frankfurt a.M., 1983.

Georg, Enno. "Die wirtschaftlichen Unternehmungen der SS." *Schriftenreihe der Vierteljahreshefte für Zeitgeschichte*, no. 7, Stuttgart, 1963.

Gerber, Urs. "Die 3. Division von 1938 bis 1951." *Die Berner Division 1875–1985*. Bern, 1985.

Graf, Christoph. *Zensurakten aus der Zeit des Zweiten Weltkrieges: Eine Analyse des Bestandes E 4450, Presse und Funkspruch 1939–1945*. [Reference guide of the Swiss Federal Archives.] Bern, 1979.

de Graumont, Sanche. *Der geheime Krieg: Die Geschichte der Spionage seit dem Zweiten Weltkrieg*. Munich, 1964.

Grier, Peter. "The Organization Spook: ... OSS ... Just Another Washington Bureaucracy." *Washington Monthly*, vol. 16, no. 11 (December 1984).

Gruchmann, Lothar. *Der Zweite Weltkrieg. Vol. 10 of dtv-Weltgeschichte des 20. Jahrhunderts*. 7th ed. Munich, 1982.

Gun, Nerin E. *Les secrets des archives américaines: Pétain, Laval, De Gaulle*. Paris, 1979.

Gunzenhäuser, Max. *Geschichte des geheimen Nachrichtendienstes: Literaturbericht und Bibliographie.* Frankfurt a.M., 1968.

Halter-Schmid, Ruth. *Schweizer Radio 1939–1945: Die Organisation des Radiokommunikators durch Bundesrat und Armee.* Bern, 1979.

Handel, Michael I. *The Diplomacy of Surprise.* Cambridge, MA, 1981.

Handel, Michael I. "Intelligence and the Problem of Strategic Surprise." *Journal of Strategic Studies,* June 1984.

Harris, William R. *Intelligence and National Security: A Bibliography with Selected Annotations.* Cambridge, MA, 1968.

Heideking, Jürgen. "Die 'Schweizer Strassen' des europäischen Widerstands." *Geheimdienste und Widerstandsbewegungen im Zweiten Weltkrieg, edited by Gerhard Schulz.* Göttingen, 1982.

Heller, Daniel. *Eugen Bircher: Arzt, Militär, Politiker.* Zürich, 1988.

Hillgruber, Andreas. *Der Zweite Weltkrieg 1939–1945: Kriegsziele und Strategie der grossen Mächte.* 4th ed. Stuttgart/Berlin/Cologne/Mainz, 1985.

Höhne, Heinz. *Canaris - Patriot im Zwielicht.* Munich, 1979.

Höhne, Heinz. *Der Orden unter dem Totenkopf.* Gütersloh, 1967.

Hofer, Viktor. *Die Bedeutung des Berichtes General Guisans über den Aktivdienst 1939–1945 für die Gestaltung des Schweizerischen Wehrwesens.* Basel/Stuttgart, 1970.

Hoffmann, Peter. *The History of the German Resistance 1933–1945.* 3rd English Edition. Montreal/Kingston/London/Buffalo, 1996.

Homberger, Heinrich. *Schweizerische Handelspolitik im Zweiten Weltkrieg.* Erlenbach/Stuttgart, 1970.

Jacobsen, Hans-Adolf. *1939–1945: Der Zweite Weltkrieg in Chronik und Dokumenten.* Darmstadt, 1959.

Jacobsen, Hans-Adolf. *Der Zweite Weltkrieg.* Frankfurt a.M., 1965.

Kahn, David. "The Significance of Codebreaking and Intelligence in Allied Strategy and Tactics." *Cryptologia,* vol. 1, no. 3 (July 1977).

Kahn, David. *Hitler's Spies: German Military Intelligence in World War II.* New York, 1985.

Kennan, George F. "Some Thoughts on Personal Papers in Public Libraries." *The Princeton University Library Chronicle,* vol. 36, no. 3 (Spring 1975).

Kent, Sherman. "Allen Welsh Dulles." *Studies in Intelligence,* vol. 13, no. 1 (Spring 1969).

Kent, Sherman. *Strategic Intelligence for American World Policy.* 2nd ed. Princeton, NJ, 1966.

Kimche, Jon. *Spying for Peace.* London, 1961. [German version: *General Guisans Zweifrontenkrieg.* Zürich, 1962.]

Knorr, Klaus. "Strategic Intelligence: Problems and Remedies." *Strategic Thought in the Nuclear Age,* edited by Laurence Martin. London, 1979.

Knorr, Klaus. "Strategic Surprise in Four European Wars," in Klaus Knorr and Patrick Morgan, eds. *Strategic Military Surprise: Incentives and Opportunities.* 2nd ed. New Brunswick/London, 1984.

Knorr, Klaus, and Patrick Morgan, eds. *Strategic Military Surprise: Incentives and Opportunities.* 2nd ed. New Brunswick/London, 1984.

Kreis, Georg. *Zensur und Selbstzensur: Die schweizerische Pressepolitik im Zweiten Weltkrieg.* Frauenfeld, 1973.

Kreis, Georg. *Auf den Spuren von La Charité: Die schweizerische Armeeführung im Spannungsfeld des deusch-französischen Gegensatzes 1936–1941.* Basel/Stuttgart, 1976.

Kreis, Georg. "Das Kriegsende in Norditalien 1945." *Schweizer Monatshefte,* no. 6, 1985.

Kurz, Hans Rudolf. "Die militärischen Bedrohungen der Schweiz im Zweiten Weltkrieg." *Allgemeine Schweizerische Militärzeitschrift,* no. 3, 1955.

Kurz, Hans Rudolf. *Die Schweiz in der Planung der kriegführenden Mächte während des Zweiten Weltkrieges.* Biel, 1957.

Kurz, Hans Rudolf, ed. *Die Schweiz im Zweiten Weltkrieg: Das grosse Erinnerungswerk an die Aktivdienstzeit 1939–1945.* Thun, 1959.

Kurz, Hans Rudolf. "Militärische Grundbegriffe: Der Nachrichtendienst." *Schweizer Soldat,* no. 5, 1972.

Kurz, Hans Rudolf. "Nachrichtendienst—Spionage." *Der Fourier,* no. 9, 1972.

Kurz, Hans Rudolf. *Nachrichtenzentrum Schweiz.* Frauenfeld, 1972.

Kurz, Hans Rudolf. "1939–1945: Le Général et les belligérants." *Le Général Guisan et la guerre mondiale 1939–1945.* Lausanne, 1974.

Kurz, Hans Rudolf. "Nachrichtendienst im neutralen Staat: Die Schweiz im Zweiten Weltkrieg." *Neue Zürcher Zeitung,* no. 56, 8 March 1975.

Kurz, Hans Rudolf. "Der März-Alarm 1943." *Der Fourier,* no. 1, 1984.

Kurz, Hans Rudolf. "Der Fall des deutschen Me 110 G." *Der Fourier,* no. 2, 1986.

Lagemann, John K. "Wild Bill Donovan." *Current History,* 52 (April 1941).

Laqueur, Walter. *A World of Secrets: The Uses and Limits of Intelligence.* New York, 1985.

Lüönd, Karl. *Spionage und Landesverrat in der Schweiz.* 2 vols. Zürich, 1977.

Luternau, Jürgen [alias Hermann Hagenbuch]. *Attachés, "Envoyés de marque" und Agenten: Vom Nachrichtenwesen der Armee.* Zürich, 1938.

MacPherson, B. Nelson. "Inspired Improvisation: William Casey and the Penetration of Germany." *Intelligence and National Security,* vol. 9, no. 4 (October 1994).

Martin, David C. *Wilderness of Mirrors.* New York, 1980.

Martin, Laurence, ed. *Strategic Thought in the Nuclear Age.* London, 1979.

Masson, Roger. "Service Secret 1940–1945." *Revue militaire suisse,* no. 6, 1964.

Matt, Alphons. *Zwischen allen Fronten: Der Zweite Weltkrieg aus der Sicht des Büros Ha.* Frauenfeld/Stuttgart, 1969.

May, Ernest R., ed. *Knowing One's Enemies: Intelligence Assessment Before the Two World Wars.* Princeton, NJ, 1986.

McChristian, Joseph A. *The Role of Military Intelligence 1965–1967.* Washington, DC: Vietnam Studies, Department of the Army, 1974.

MacDonald, Callum A. "The Venlo Affair." *European Studies Review,* vol. 8 (1978).

McDonald, John W., Jr., and Diane B. Bendahmane, eds. *Conflict Resolution: Track Two Diplomacy.* Washington, DC: Foreign Service Institute, U.S. Department of State, 1987.

MacDonald, Lawrence H. "The Office of Strategic Services: America's First National Intelligence Agency." *Prologue: Quarterly Journal of the National Archives,* vol. 23, no. 1 (Spring 1991).

Meier, Heinz K. "Intelligence Operations in Switzerland During the Second World War." *Swiss American Historical Newsletter* (February 1984).

Mergen, Armand. *Die BKA Story.* Munich/Berlin, 1987.

Meyer, Alice. *Anpassung oder Widerstand.* Frauenfeld, 1965.

Michel, Henri. *Histoire de la Résistance en France.* Paris, 1972.

Militärgeschichtliches Forschungsamt. *Das Deutsche Reich und der Zweite Weltkrieg.* Vols. 1–4, Stuttgart, 1979 ff.

Mosley, Leonard. *A Biography of Eleanor, Allen, and John Foster Dulles and Their Family Network.* New York, 1979.

Morawietz, Elisabeth. *Die politische und militärische Gefährdung der Schweiz durch das nationalsozialistische Deutschland.* Berlin, 1969.

Mosse, George L., ed. *Police Forces in History.* London/Beverly Hills, 1975.

Mowat, C. L., ed. *The Shifting Balance of World Forces, 1898–1945.* Vol. 12 of *The New Cambridge Modern History.* 2nd ed. Cambridge, 1968.

Näf, Beat. "Zur Entwicklung des schweizerischen strategischen Denkens." *Allgemeine Schweizerische Militärzeitschrift,* no. 11, 1982.

Noguères, Henri. *Histoire de la Résistance en France.* Paris, 1967.

Parker, John. "What Lies Behind the Modesty of Interpol?" *Eastern Journal of International Law,* vol. 3, no. 3 (October 1971).

Pettee, George S. *The Future of American Secret Intelligence.* Washington, DC, 1946.

Piekalkiewicz, Janusz. *Schweiz '39–'45: Krieg in einem neutralen Land.* Stuttgart, 1978.

Police de sûreté vaudoise, ed. *La police de sûreté vaudoise 1877–1977: Un siècle au service du Pays.* Lausanne, 1977.

Rapold, Hans. *Zeit der Bewährung? Die Epoche um den Ersten Weltkrieg 1907–1924.* Vol. V of *Der Schweizerische Generalstab.* Basel/Frankfurt a.M., 1988.

Reile, Oscar. *Macht und Ohnmacht der Geheimdienste.* Munich, 1968.

Reese, William. "Deception within a Communications Theory Framework." *Strategic Military Deception,* edited by Donald C. Daniel and Katherine L. Herbig. New York/Oxford, 1981.

Richelson, Jeffrey T. *Foreign Intelligence Organizations.* Cambridge, MA, 1988.

Rings, Werner. *Schweiz im Krieg 1939–1945: Ein Bericht.* Zürich, 1974.

Rings, Werner. *Europa im Krieg 1939–1945: Kollaboration und Widerstand.* Zürich, 1979.

Ritter, Rudolf J. *Die Entwicklung des Funkwesens bei den Schweizerischen Verkehrstruppen von 1905 bis 1979.* (Manuscript.) Bern, 1988.

Ritter, Rudolf J. *Die Funkertruppe: Beitrag zur Geschichte des Funkwesens bei den Übermittlungstruppen 1904 bis 1979.* Monographien zur Geschichte der Übermittlungstruppen, vol. 1. Bern, n.d.

Rochat, André. "Roger Masson." HP *[Heerespolizei]-Bulletin* no. 1–3, 1978.

Rosser, Silvia. *Eine Auswahl wichtiger Codenamen aus dem Zweiten Weltkrieg,* 2 vols. Bern, 1990.

Rowan, Richard Wilmer. *The Story of the Secret Service.* Garden City, NY, 1937.

Schneider, Boris. *Einführung in die neuere Geschichte.* Stuttgart/Berlin/Cologne/Mainz, 1974.

Schoch, Jürg. *Die Oberstenaffäre: Eine innenpolitische Krise (1915/1916).* Bern/Frankfurt a.M., 1972.

Schoop, Albert. *Als der Krieg zu Ende ging.* Frauenfeld, 1985.

von Schramm, *Wilhelm. Geheimdienst im Zweiten Weltkrieg: Organisationen - Methoden - Erfolge.* 4th ed. Munich/Vienna, 1983; 6th ed. revised and updated under the title *Geheimdienste im Zweiten Weltkrieg: Nach Öffnung der alliierten Geheimdienste fortgeführt, ergänzt und erweitert von Hans Büchler.* München, 2002.

Schulz, Gerhard, ed. *Geheimdienste und Widerstandsbewegungen im Zweiten Weltkrieg.* Göttingen, 1982.

Scott, Peter D. "How Allen Dulles and the SS Preserved Each Other." *Covert Action Bulletin,* 25 (Winter 1986).

Senn, Hans. "Der Stand neuester Erkenntnisse: Militärische Eventualabmachungen der Schweiz mit Frankreich 1939/40." *Neue Zürcher Zeitung,* no. 204, 2 September 1988.

Senn, Hans. *Anfänge einer Dissuasionsstrategie während des Zweiten Weltkriegs.* Vol. 7 of *Der Schweizerische Generalstab.* Basel, 1995.

Shirer, William L. *The Rise and Fall of the Third Reich: A History of Nazi Germany.* New York, 1963.

Slomanson, William R. "Civil Actions Against Interpol: A Field Compass." *Temple Law Quarterly,* vol. 57, no. 3 (1984).

Smith, R. Harris. OSS: *The Secret History of America's First Central Intelligence Agency.* Berkeley/Los Angeles/London, 1972.

Speiser, E. "Die schweizerisch-deutschen Handelsbeziehungen während des Krieges." *Schweizer Monatshefte,* no. 3, 1946.

Thomas, Martin. "The Discarded Leader: General Henri Giraud and the Foundation of the French Committee of National Liberation." *French History,* vol. 10, no. 1 (1996).

Thompkins, Peter. "The OSS and Italian Partisans in World War II: Intelligence and Operational Support for the Anti-Nazi Resistance." *Studies in Intelligence,* unclassified edition (Spring 1998).

Trevor-Roper, Hugh R. *The Last Days of Hitler.* 3rd ed. London, 1956.

Troy, Thomas F. "The 'Correct' Definition of Intelligence." *International Journal of Intelligence and Counterintelligence,* vol. 5, no. 4 (Winter 1991–1992).

Troy, Thomas F. "Knifing of the OSS." *International Journal of Intelligence and Counterintelligence,* vol. 1, no. 3 (Fall 1986).

Tuchmann, Barbara W. *The Zimmermann Telegram.* New York, 1979.

Urner, Klaus. "Die schweizerisch-deutschen Wirtschaftsbeziehungen während des Zweiten Weltkrieges." *Neue Zürcher Zeitung,* 28 November, 3 and 6 December 1968.

Urner, Klaus. *Der Schweizer Hitler-Attentäter: Drei Studien zum Widerstand und seinen Grenzbereichen.* Frauenfeld/Stuttgart, 1980.

Urner, Klaus. "Im Visier der deutschen Spionage." *Tages-Anzeiger Magazin,* no. 13, 1982.

Vetsch, Christian. *Aufmarsch gegen die Schweiz.* Olten, 1973.

Walker, David A. "OSS and Operation Torch." *Journal of Contemporary History,* vol. 22, no. 4 (October 1987).

Wanner, Philipp. *Oberst Oscar Frey und der schweizerische Widerstandswille.* 2nd ed. Münsingen, 1974.

Wark, Wesley K. "Fictions of History." *Intelligence and National Security,* vol. 5, no. 4 (October 1990).

Wark, Wesley K. "Great Investigations : The Public Debate on Intelligence in the U.S. after 1945." *Defense Analysis,* vol. 3, no. 2 (Fall 1987).

Wark, Wesley K. "In Never-Never Land?: The British Archives on Intelligence." *Historical Journal,* vol. 35, no. 1 (1992).

Wark, Wesley K. "Introduction: The Study of Espionage: Past, Present, Future?" *Intelligence and National Security,* vol. 8, no. 3 (July 1993).

Wark, Wesley K. "Three Military Attaches at Berlin in the 1930's: Soldier-Statesman and the Limits of Ambiguity." *International History Review,* vol. 9, no. 4 (November 1987).

Wark, Wesley K. "Beyond the Missing Dimensions: The New Study of Intelligence." *Canadian Journal of History,* vol. 24, no. 1 (April 1989).

de Weck, Hervé. "Sans renseignements pas de succès possible." *Revue militaire suisse,* no. 3, 1978.

West, Nigel [alias Rupert Allason]. *A Thread of Deceit: Espionage Myths of World War II.* New York, 1985.

Wetter, Ernst. *Duell der Flieger und der Diplomaten: Die Fliegerzwischenfälle Deutschland-Schweiz im Mai/Juni 1940 und ihre diplomatischen Folgen.* Frauenfeld, 1987.

Wetter, Ernst. *Geheimer Nachtjäger in der Schweiz.* Frauenfeld, 1989.

Whaley, Barton. *Codeword Barbarossa.* Cambridge, MA, 1973.

Willi, Jost Nikolaus. *Der Fall Jacob-Wesemann (1935/36): Ein Beitrag zur Geschichte der Schweiz in der Zwischenkriegszeit.* Bern/Frankfurt a.M., 1972.

Wistrich, Robert. *Wer war wer im Dritten Reich? Ein biographisches Lexikon: Anhänger, Mitläufer, Gegner aus Politik, Wirtschaft, Militär, Kunst und Wissenschaft.* Frankfurt a.M., 1987.

Wohlstetter, Roberta. *Pearl Harbor: Warning and Decision.* Stanford, 1962.

Wylie, Neville. "Keeping the Swiss Sweet: Intelligence as a Factor in British Policy towards Switzerland during the Second World War." *Intelligence and National Security,* vol. 11, no. 3 (July 1996).

Wylie, Neville. "Pilet-Golaz, David Kelly and British Policy towards Switzerland, 1940." *Diplomacy & Statecraft,* vol. 8, no. 1 (1997).

Wylie, Neville. "Pilet-Golaz and the Making of Swiss Foreign Policy: Some Remarks." *Schweizerische Zeitschrift für Geschicht,* vol. 47, no. 4 (1997).

Wylie, Neville. "Le rôle des transports ferroviaires en Suisse, 1939–1945 : Les aspects militaire, économique et politique." *Relations Internationales,* vol. 95 (1998).

Wylie, Neville (ed.). *European Neutrals and Non-Belligerents during the Second World War.* Cambridge, 2001.

Press

Allgemeine Schweizerische Militärzeitschrift (ASMZ)
Basler Arbeiterzeitung
Basler Nachrichten
Basler Zeitung
Der Bund
Chicago Daily News
Der Fourier
Freies Volk
Gazette de Lausanne
Journal de Genève
Luzerner Neueste Nachrichten (LNN)
Die Nation
National-Zeitung
Neue Berner Zeitung
Neue Zürcher Zeitung
Revue militaire suisse (RMS)
St. Galler Tagblatt
Schweizerische Handelszeitung
Schweizer Illustrierte
Schweizer Monatshefte
Schweizer Soldat
Tages-Anzeiger
Die Tat
Thurgauer Zeitung
Tribune de Genève
Tribune de Lausanne
Volk und Armee
Weltwoche

List of Abbreviations

Abw	Abwehr (German Army Intelligence and Counterintelligence)
AfZ	Archives for Contemporary History (Archiv für Zeitgeschichte), Swiss Federal Institute of Technology, Zürich
AG	Shareholding company (Aktiengesellschaft)
AHQ	Army headquarters
BAr	Swiss Federal Archives (Bundesarchiv), Bern
Capt.	Captain
cf.	compare
Col.	Colonel
CP	command post
Ed./ed.	Editor/edited by
ETO	European Theater of Operations
Fed.	Federal
f./ff.	and following page(s)
Gestapa	national HQ of the German Secret State Police (Geheimes Staatspolizeiamt)
Gestapo	German Secret State Police (Geheime Staatspolizei)
GmbH	limited liability company (Gesellschaft mit beschränkter Haftung)
HQ	Headquarters
ICPC	International Criminal Police Committee
IKPK	International Criminal Police Committee (Internationale Kriminalpolizeiliche Kommission (predecessor organization of Interpol)
IPA	International Press Agency

J.I.	Shelf-mark used at the Swiss Federal Archives for unpublished papers of private individuals
Lt.	Lieutenant
Lt. Col.	Lieutenant Colonel
Me	Messerschmitt aircraft
NBS	National Movement of Switzerland (Nationale Bewegung der Schweiz)
n.d.	no date
NDC	National Defense Committee
no.	Number
n.p.	no place
N.S.1	Procurement Office 1 (in Lucerne)
NSDAP	National Socialist German Workers Party
NZZ	*Neue Zürcher Zeitung*
OKH	German Army High Command (Oberkommando des Heeres)
OKW	German Armed Forces High Command (Oberkommando der Wehrmacht)
OSS	Office of Strategic Services (U.S. foreign intelligence service)
p.	page
pp.	pages
PRS	Press and Radio Section
RG	Record Group
RSHA	Reich Security Central Office (Reichssicherheitshauptamt)
SA	Shareholding company (société anonyme)
S.H.A.E.F.	Supreme Headquarters Allied Expeditionary Force
SHS	Swiss Wood Syndicate
SNCF	French National Railroad Company (Société Nationale des Chemins de fer Français)
S.O.E.	Special Operations Executive (British organization for secret operations)
SS	Schutzstaffel (Nazi party elite guard)
Waffen SS	armed SS, meant for military operations

Index